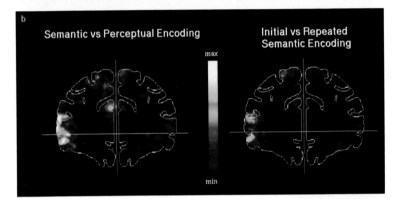

Functional activation maps. The left side of each image corresponds to the left side of the brain. In (a), greater activation is observed during semantic versus perceptual encoding (upper row) and during initial versus repeated semantic encoding (lower row). From "Functional Magnetic Resonance Imaging of Semantic Memory" by J.D.E. Gabrieli, et al, in *Psychological Science*, 7, 278-283, (1996).

In (b), the left image shows increased activation during semantic versus perceptual encoding in the left inferior prefrontal cortex and left cingulate cortex; the right image shows higher activation for initial versus repeated semantic encoding in the left inferior prefrontal cortex. From "Functional Magnetic Resonance Imaging of Semantic Memory" by J.D.E. Gabrieli, et al, in *Psychological Science*, 7, 278-283, (1996).

Brain regions activated in the analogy-literal comparison (white, higher activation; yellow, intermediate activation; red, lower activation). From "Toward Neuroanatomical Models of Analogy: A Positron Emission Tomography Study of Analogical Mapping" by Charles M. Wharton, et al, in *Cognitive Psychology*, 40, 173-197, (2000).

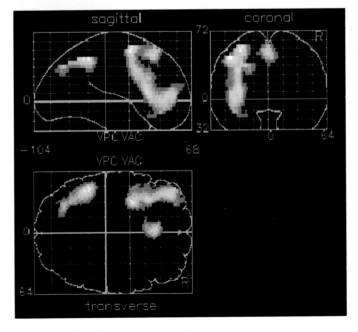

Cognition

Third Edition

MARK H. ASHCRAFT
Cleveland State University

PRENTICE HALL
Upper Saddle River, New Jersey 07458

Library of Congress Cataloging-in-Publication Data
Ashcraft, Mark H.
  Cognition / Mark H. Ashcraft.—3rd ed.
     p. cm.
  Rev. ed. of: Human memory and cognition. c1994.
  Includes bibliographical references and indexes.
  ISBN 0-13-030729-7
    1. Memory. 2. Cognition. I. Ashcraft, Mark H. Human memory and cognition. II.
  Title.

BF371 .A68 2002
153—dc21

2001021249

VP, Editorial Director: Laura Pearson
Executive Editor: Stephanie Johnson
Editorial Assistant: Carmen Garcia-Prieta
VP, Director of Production and Manufacturing: Barbara Kittle
Senior Managing Editor: Mary Rottino
Production Editor: Terry Routley
Project Liaison: Randy Pettit
Prepress and Manufacturing Manager: Nick Sklitsis
Prepress and Manufacturing Buyer: Tricia Kenny
Director of Marketing: Beth Gillett Mejia

Senior Marketing Manager: Sharon Cosgrove
Creative Design Director: Leslie Osher
Art Director: Anne Bonanno Nieglos
Cover and Interior Designer: Circa 86, Inc.
Cover Art: Cooper/Stock Illustration Source, Inc.
Director, Image Resources: Melinda Lee Reo
Image Specialist: Beth Boyd-Benzel
Photo Researchers: Julie Tesser, Zina Arabia
Manager, Rights and Permissions: Kay Dellosa

This book was set in 10/12 Garamond by Carlisle Communications, Ltd.
and printed and bound by R. R. Donnelley & Sons Company.
The cover was printed by Phoenix Color Corp.

© 2002 by Prentice-Hall Inc.
A Division of Pearson Education
Upper Saddle River, New Jersey 07458

Earlier edition © 1994 by HarperCollins College Publishers.

Printed in the United States of America

10 9 8 7 6 5 4 3 2 1

ISBN 0-13-030729-7

Prentice Hall International (UK) Limited, *London*
Prentice Hall of Australia Pty. Limited, *Sydney*
Prentice Hall Canada Inc., *Toronto*
Prentice Hall Hispanoamericana, S.A., *Mexico*
Prentice Hall of India Private Limited, *New Delhi*
Prentice Hall of Japan, Inc., *Tokyo*
Pearson Education Asia Pte. Ltd., *Singapore*
Editora Prentice Hall do Brasil, Ltda., *Rio de Janeiro*

To the wife of my life

Mary Helen Homerin Ashcraft

Brief Contents

Contents

CHAPTER **9**   **Language   347**

Preface

To the Student

The psychology of human memory and cognition is fascinating, dealing with questions and ideas that are inherently interesting; how we think, reason, remember, and use language, to name just a few. When cognitive psychologists talk research at conventions, they are agitated, intense, and full of energy. In contrast to this enthusiasm, however, undergraduate texts often portray the field as dull, too concerned with the minutiae of experimental method and technical jargon and not concerned enough with the interesting issues.

Without slighting the empirical foundation of the field, I have tried to capture some of the excitement of the area. All professors want their students to understand the material, of course, but I also want you to appreciate cognitive psychology as one of the most interesting and memorable topics of your student career. Several features of the book are designed to accomplish this.

- To engage your interest and understanding, examples of the main points are sprinkled throughout the text. Most of the chapters have a box that asks you to Prove It; it gives you a demonstration project that can be done quickly to illustrate the points being made in that chapter. Furthermore, several demonstrations per chapter are available on the book's Web site at http://www.prenhall.com/ashcraft. You can conduct most of these miniature experiments with only moderate effort and little or no equipment. These are some of the best ways to see memory and cognition in action.

- Mastering the terminology of a new field can be difficult. To help you with the jargon, critical terms are boldfaced in the text and defined immediately in italicized print. Each chapter's terms are listed at the end of the chapter, and the entire collection of terms and definitions appears in the Glossary at the end of the book. Try studying for exams by playing a Jeopardy-like game with the glossary; one person reads a definition, the other names the defined term.

- Each major section of a chapter ends with a brief Section Summary. This along with the listing of glossary terms at the end of each chapter should help you check your understanding and memory as you study. Note that some people find it helpful to read the Section Summaries first as a preview of the section's content.

- The Web site also has Suggested Readings, articles and books that can help you pursue a particular topic. These are updated periodically, so check back occasionally to see what's new.

- I have intentionally used a more colloquial style than is customary in the field (or in texts in general), using the first person, posing direct questions to the reader, inserting parenthetical commentary, and so on. My students have told me that these features make the book more enjoyable to read; one said "it's interesting—not like a textbook," which I took as a compliment. Some professors may expect a more formal, detached style, of course. I would rather have you read and remember the material than have you cope with a book selected because of a carefully pedantic style. Besides, you will have plenty of time to deal with boring books in graduate school.

To the Instructor

Like the first two editions, this edition is directed primarily toward undergraduates at the junior and senior level, who are probably taking their first basic course in memory and cognition. It has also been used successfully in introductory graduate surveys, especially when first-year students need a more thorough background in memory and cognition.

There is much continuity between the second edition of *Human Memory and Cognition* and this edition, now titled simply *Cognition:* The foundation areas in cognition are still covered thoroughly, as you'll see in the Table of Contents. But this revision has several new features that you'll want to note.

- Since the second edition of this book was published in 1994, there has been a tremendous increase in the study of memory and cognition with the technologies and perspectives of cognitive neuroscience, or neurocognition, as I often call it. To reflect the centrality of those approaches to the topic, the book no longer segregates the neurocognitive evidence in a separate chapter. Instead, this edition integrates that material throughout the book. A major section of Chapter 2 provides background information on neurons and the brain, so even students without formal coursework on the biological basis of cognition will be prepared for the neurocognitive evidence they'll encounter throughout the book.

- There has been a thorough updating of the book, adding important new topics and developments that are central to the field, such as false memory research, the rapidly expanding research on working memory's influences, new research on the varieties of attention, and new strides in online investigations of comprehension and reading. There has also been some careful pruning of topics and streamlining of presentation.

- As in the first two editions, I have tried to strike a balance between basic, core material and cutting-edge topics. As cognitive psychology continues to evolve, it is important to maintain some continuity with older topics and evidence. Students need to understand how we got here, and instructors cannot be expected to start from scratch each time they teach the course. But revising the book continues to be a very revealing exercise in how cognitive psychology has changed in the past few years.

- In a variety of ways, this edition uses Web-based resources for professors and students alike. Each chapter includes Web-based activities, denoted by the CW symbol in the margins. Students will find demonstrations and exercises on the book's Web page (http://www.prenhall.com/ashcraft), along with Suggested Readings. Where possible, I note which readings are appropriate for undergraduates and which are too difficult for students at that level. The *Instructor's Manual* is also heavily Web-based; the Web pages include graphs and illustrations from the book that can be downloaded or printed onto transparencies. A test item file also is available via the Web; make sure your Prentice Hall sales representative gives you the necessary information to take advantage of these e-resources.

I hope that the balance between classic research and current topics, the style I have adopted, and the standard organization I have used will make the text easy to teach from and easy for students to read and remember. More important, I hope that you will find my portrayal of the field of cognitive psychology useful. As always, I am delighted to receive the comments and suggestions of those who use this book, instructors and students alike. Write in care of the Psychology Department, Cleveland State University, Cleveland, OH 44115. My e-mail address is m.ashcraft@csuohio.edu.

Acknowledgments

The list of students, colleagues, and publishing professionals who have helped shape this project continues to grow. For editorial support and assistance, I thank Jane Sudbrink, Denise Workman, Rebecca Strehlow, Jean Dal Porto, Catherine Woods, Marcus Boggs, Heide Chavez, Eric Stano, and Jayme Heffler. Professional colleagues who have assisted across the years include R. Reed Hunt, John Jonides, Michael Masson, James S. Nairne, Marjorie Reed, Gregory B. Simpson, Richard Griggs, Richard Jackson Harris, Donald Homa, Paul Whitney, Tom Carr, Frances Friedrich, Dave Geary, Mike McCloskey, Morton Gernsbacher, Art Graesser, Keith Holyoak, George Kellas, Mark Marschark, and Fred Smith. In addition to many of my undergraduate classes, I'd like to thank a few special students who have helped in a variety of ways, from reading and critiquing to duplicating and checking references: Mike Faust, David Fleck, Elizabeth Kirk, David Copeland, and Don Seyler. I'm very grateful to all.

Mark H. Ashcraft

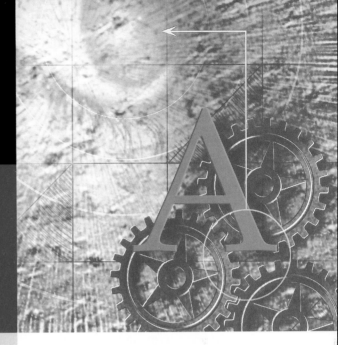

CHAPTER 1

Cognitive Psychology: An Introduction

> *What a piece of work is man. How noble in reason! How infinite in faculty! In form and moving how express and admirable! In action how like an angel! In apprehension, how like a god! (Act 2, scene 2, of Shakespeare's Hamlet)[1]*
>
> *One difficulty in the psychological sciences lies in the familiarity of the phenomena with which they deal. A certain intellectual effort is required to see how such phenomena can pose serious problems or call for intricate explanatory theories. One is inclined to take them for granted as necessary or somehow "natural." (Chomsky, 1968, p. 24)*

This book is about human memory and cognition, and specifically about the scientific study of human memory and cognition. Let's start with a quick definition of terms and return later for the more formal definitions. For the moment, consider memory and cognition to be *the mental events and knowledge we use when we recognize an object, remember a name, have an idea, understand a sentence, or solve a problem.* In this book, we consider a very broad range of subjects, from basic perception through complex decision making, from seemingly simple mental acts such as recognizing a letter of the alphabet to very complicated acts such as participating in a conversation. We will ask questions such as How do we read for meaning? How do we memorize facts? What does it mean to forget something? How do we know that we *don't* know something? The unifying theme behind all this is one of the most fascinating and important questions of all time: How do people think?

Note right away that we are interested in an empirical, scientific approach to human memory and thought. This places us in the branch of modern psychology usually called cognitive psychology. What drives the field is research, the results of experiments and the explanations of models and theories. We will deal with many of these experiments, explaining why they were done, what sorts of questions they answer, what directions they suggest for future studies, and so on. By contrast, this book does not deal in any serious way with nonempirical or philosophical approaches to the human mind. Of course, we do not deny the profound influence philosophy has had on psychology; indeed, psychology began as an offshoot of philosophy. And it is obviously true that we all—cognitive psychologists included—have been shaped and influenced by our culture and intellectual history in countless ways. Nonetheless, the discipline of psychology has largely accepted the empirical, scientific approach to the study of mind and behavior; purely philosophical approaches are viewed skeptically, at least until tested in empirical research. Thus one of the central features of modern

---

[1]Unlike Shakespeare, modern writers have been sensitized to the sexist bias implied by the use of *man, he,* and so on in a generic sense. I have attempted to avoid such usage whenever possible. Where such usage could not be avoided or when I simply grew tired of the plural or collective terms, I have tried to alternate between *he* and *she* on a section-by-section basis. I also occasionally use the term *subjects* instead of *individuals* or *participants* to refer to the human participants in research.

cognitive psychology is its allegiance to objective, empirical methods of investigation; this is one of the shiniest badges we wear. We are experimentalists, and this is the approach you will read about in this book.

After reading the previous paragraph, a few of you may be thinking, "Well, that's the bad news. Now, where's the good news?" Here it is. Within the boundaries of objective scientific methods, cognitive psychology is asking an enormous range of fascinating questions. Since the beginnings of modern cognitive psychology nearly 50 years ago, there has been a true explosion of interest in cognition and in the cognitive approach to human behavior and thought. Questions that were on the back burner for too long— such as "How do we read?" or "How do we use language?"—are now active areas of research. The pent-up interest in these questions, unleashed during the cognitive revolution of the late 1950s, has yielded tremendous progress. Furthermore, we now acknowledge, seek, and sometimes participate in the important contributions of disciplines such as linguistics, computer science, and the neurosciences. This interdisciplinary approach, this joining of diverse forces, is called **cognitive science**, *the scientific study of thought, language, the brain —in short, the scientific study of the mind.*

The most basic purpose of this book is to tell you what has been discovered about human memory and cognitive processes and to share cognitive psychology's conclusions and insights about the particularly human activity called thought. The most highly sophisticated, flexible, and efficient computer available today is your memory, with its collection of mental processes. How does it work? As amazing as electronic computers are, their capabilities are primitive compared with what you do routinely in even a single minute's worth of thinking. The need to understand ourselves is basic, and this includes an understanding of how our mental apparatus operates.

Another purpose of this book is to describe how cognitive psychology has made these discoveries. Your appreciation of the information in this book will increase if you also understand how cognitive research is done, how new knowledge is acquired in the scientific pursuit of cognition. Few of you will become cognitive scientists yourselves, but presumably most of you who are reading this book have decided to major in psychology or a cognate field. Because the cognitive approach has come to influence many areas in modern psychology, your mastery of psychology as a whole will be enhanced by an understanding of cognitive psychology.

A final purpose of this book is to illustrate the pervasiveness of cognitive psychology and its potential impact on other fields outside psychology proper. As you read a moment ago, cognitive science is already a multidisciplinary field. This fusion of disciplines represents the conviction that researchers in linguistics, artificial intelligence, the neurosciences, and even anthropology can contribute important ideas to psychology and vice versa. Psychology has a long tradition of influencing educational practice, and the potential for cognitive psychology to continue these contributions is both obvious and important. Even such diverse fields as medicine, law, and business are incorporating some of cognitive psychology's findings. But it should not be surprising that cognitive psychology is relevant to so many other fields. After all, what human endeavor doesn't involve thought?

Table 1-1 SUMMARY OF THE INTUITIVE COGNITIVE ANALYSIS

Processes	Topic and Chapter
Sensory and perceptual	
Focus eyes on print	Visual perception, sensory memory: Chapter 3
Encode and recognize printed material	Pattern recognition, reading: Chapters 3 and 10
Memory and retrieval	
Look up and identify words in memory	Memory retrieval: Chapters 5–8
Retrieve word meanings	
Comprehension	
Combine word meanings to yield sentence meaning	Semantic retrieval, comprehension: Chapter 7–10
Evaluate sentence meaning, consider alternative meanings	Comprehension: Chapters 9 and 10
Judgment and decision	
Retrieve answer to the question	Semantic retrieval: Chapters 8 and 9
Determine reasonableness of question	Comprehension, conversation: Chapters 9 and 10
Judge speaker's intent and knowledge	Decision making and reasoning: Chapter 11
Computational (Question 2)	
Retrieve fact knowledge	Semantic retrieval: Chapter 7
Retrieve knowledge of how to divide and execute procedure	Procedural knowledge: Chapters 6, 11, and 12

Thinking About Thinking

Let's begin to develop an intuitive feel for our topic by considering some examples, coming back later to improve our quick definitions of the terms *memory* and *cognition*. For all three examples that follow, you should read the question and come up with the answer, but more importantly you should try to be as aware as possible of the thoughts that pass through your head as you consider the question. The first question is easy:

1. How many hands did Aristotle have?

For such a ridiculously easy question, of course we are not particularly interested in the correct answer, "two." We are most interested, however, in the thoughts you had as you considered the question. Most students report a train of thoughts something like this: "Dumb question, of course he had two hands. Wait a minute—why would a professor ask such an obvious question? Maybe Aristotle had only one hand. Nah, I would have heard of it if he had had only one hand—he must have had two."

A bit of informal cognitive analysis will uncover some of the different activities you engaged in while arriving at your answer. Keep track of the analysis with the list in Table 1-1; as you read the later questions, refer to Table 1-1 to see which processes and steps apply to all the questions and what new ones should be added. Bear in mind that Table 1-1 merely illustrates the intuitive analysis; it is no substitute for the full description of these processes and steps found later in the book.

First, although you were no doubt unaware of it, a large group of perceptual processes were brought into play to deal with the written words of the question. Highly overlearned visual processes focused your eyes on the printed line, then moved your focus across the line bit by bit, registering the printed material into some kind of memory system. Smoothly and rapidly, another set of processes looked up the encoded material in memory and identified the letters and words. Of course, few if any readers of a college text pay conscious attention to the nuts and bolts of perceiving and identifying words unless the vocabulary is unfamiliar or the printing is faint. Yet your lack of awareness of these stages does not mean they didn't happen; ask a first-grade teacher about the difficulties children have in learning to identify letters and their sounds and putting these components together into words.

We have encountered two important lessons of cognitive psychology already. First, mental processes can occur with very little conscious awareness. This is especially (or maybe only) true of processes that have received a great deal of practice, such as reading skills. Second, even though these processes can operate very quickly, they are quite complex, involving difficult motor, perceptual, and mental acts. Their complexity makes it even more amazing how efficient, rapid, and seemingly automatic they are.

As you identified the individual words in the first question, you were also accessing or looking up the meanings of those words and then fitting those meanings together to understand the question. Surely you were not consciously aware of looking up the meaning of the word *hands* in a mental dictionary. Just as surely, however, you did search for and find that entry in memory, stored with all your other general knowledge about the human body. A few students often insist that they wondered whether the question might be referring to a different Aristotle—maybe Aristotle Onassis—because a question about the philosopher Aristotle's hands seems so odd.

Now we are getting to the meat of the process. With little effort, we retrieve the information from memory that the word *Aristotle* refers to a human being, a historical figure from the distant past. Many people know little about Aristotle beyond the fact that he was a Greek philosopher. Yet this seems to be enough, combined with what we know to be true of people in general, to determine that he was probably just like everyone else: He had two hands. Those who consider Aristotle Onassis seem to reach the same stage as well. Even though they may know a few facts about this more contemporary person (Greek shipping magnate, married Jacqueline Kennedy), they probably find no specific information in memory about the number of hands he had, so they make the default assumption that it was two. Think of how differently you would have understood the question if it had been "How many hands does Aristotle have?" Tipped off by the present tense, would you have searched your memory for a still-living person named Aristotle? Would you have explicitly asked yourself whether Aristotle Onassis was dead, or would you have tried to find some unusual, maybe metaphorical way of interpreting the question?

At a final (for now) stage, people report a set of thoughts and judgments that involve the reasonableness of the question, similar in many respects to the interpretations of remarks in a conversation. In general, people do not ask obvious questions, at least not of other adults. If they do ask an obvious question, it is often for another reason such as a trick question or sarcasm. Consequently, students report that for a time they decided that maybe the question wasn't so obvious after all. In other words, there

IN DEPTH

Interpreting Graphs

If you're good at interpreting data presented in graphs, do not bother with the rest of this box; just study the figures. But students often struggle with graphed material, not understanding what is being shown nearly as well as their professors think. Because you will encounter a lot of graphed data in this book, you need to understand what you are looking at and what it means. Take a moment to go through these simple graphs to see how they are put together and what to pay attention to when you interpret the data.

The figure in this box is a fairly simple graph of **reaction time** data, the time it takes to react to a stimulus by making a particular response. We almost always abbreviate *reaction time* as *RT,* and it is usually measured in milliseconds (msec or ms), thousandths of a second. In the figure, the label on the *y*-axis says "Vocal RT"; in other words, these subjects were making vocal responses, and the researchers measured the time between the onset of a simple multiplication problem and the participant's vocal response. The numbers on the *y*-axis show you the range of RTs that were observed. The dependent variable is always the measure of performance we collect in the experiment—here it is vocal RT—and it always goes on the *y*-axis.

The *x*-axis in the left panel is labeled "Multiplication problems," and I've plot-

ted just two problems, 2×3 and 6×9. It is more customary to show a more general variable that this on the *x*-axis, as shown in the right panel. There you see a point for a whole set of small multiplication problems, from 2×3 up to 4×5, a set of medium size problems such as 2×7 and 8×3, and a set of large problems , such as 6×8 and 9×7. So the *x*-axis label in the right panel says "Size of problem." A general rule for the proportions of a graph is that the length of the *x*-axis is slightly shorter than the height of the *y*-axis; a 3 to 4 (or maybe a 4 to 5) ratio is about right, so that if the height of the *y*-axis is 4 inches, the *x*-axis should be about 3 inches. Notice that the *y*-axis is now in whole seconds, to save some space and preserve the graph's proportions.

Now the data. The points we plot in the graph are almost always the mean or average of the dependent variable, RT in this case. Both panels of the graphs show two curves or lines each, one for college students, the other for fourth-grade students; Campbell and Graham (1985) tested fourth-graders and college students on the simple multiplication problems. Notice first that the curves for fourth-graders are much higher. If you read the values from the *y*-axis in the left panel, the average fourth-grader took, 1,940 milliseconds to answer "6" to the problem 2×3, compared to 737 milliseconds for

was a return to memory to see whether there was some special knowledge about Aristotle that pertains to his hands. The next step is truly fascinating. The majority of students claim to have thought to themselves, "No, I would have known about it if he had had only one hand," and they decide that indeed it was an obvious question after all.

This lack-of-knowledge reasoning process is a fascinating topic because so much of our everyday reasoning is done without benefit of complete knowledge. In the average college student. In the right panel, the average fourth-grader took about 2,400 milliseconds to respond to small problems, 4,100 to medium, and 4,550 to large. Compare this much greater increase in RT as the problems get larger with the pattern for college students: There was still an increase, but only from 730 milliseconds to almost 900 milliseconds.

Why did Campbell and Graham find slower performance for fourth-graders? No doubt because college students have had far more practice in doing simple multiplication problems than fourth-graders. In other words, college students know multiplication better, have the facts stored more strongly in long-term memory, and so can access and retrieve the facts more rapidly. It is a perfectly sensible, cognitive effect that the strength of information in memory influences the speed of your retrieval. And it is easily grasped by looking at and understanding the graphed results. (You will read about this experiment again in Chapter 2, including a variety of interpretations for the other major result in the figures, that RT was longer for the larger problems.)

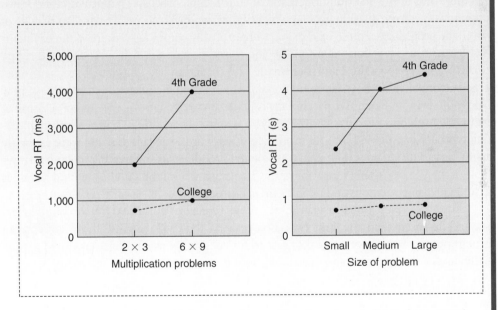

Vocal reaction times (RTs) to multiplication problems. (Data from Campbell & Graham, 1985.)

an interesting variation, I have asked students, "How many hands did Beethoven have?" Knowing of Beethoven's musical fame typically leads to the following inference: "Because he was a musician, he probably played the piano, and he could not possibly have been very successful at it with only one hand; therefore he must have had two." An occasional student goes even further with the intriguing answer, "Two, but he did go deaf before he died."

Now *that's* interesting! Someone found a connection between the disability implied by the question "How many hands?" and a related shred of evidence in memory, Beethoven's deafness. Such an answer shows how people can also consider implications, inferences, and other unstated connections as they reason and make decisions: it shows what a great deal of knowledge can be considered even for a simple question. The answer also illustrates the role of prior knowledge in such reasoning, where the richer body of information about Beethoven can lead to a more specific inference than was possible for the Aristotle question.

Although this informal analysis does not exhaust the discussion of cognitive processes in reading, memory retrieval, or comprehension, it does orient you to some of the important features of cognitive psychology and its subject matter. Let's continue with the other questions to see what else is in store for you in this book.

2. What is 723 divided by 6?

This question clearly relies on a different kind of knowledge than the Aristotle question: the knowledge of arithmetic that you learned in grade school. Just as was true as you read the words in the first question, many of your mental processes happened more or less automatically for the division problem: identifying the digits, accessing your knowledge of arithmetic procedures, and so on. Yet you were probably consciously aware of the problem-solving steps in doing long division: Divide 6 into 7, subtract 6 from 7 to get the first remainder, bring down the 2 and then divide 12 by 6, and so on. These steps are mentioned at the bottom of Table 1-1, "Computational," which would include your knowledge of how to do long division. Cognitive psychology is no less interested in your mental processing of arithmetic problems or in the knowledge you acquired in school than in the informal reasoning processes you used for Question 1. In other words, the fact that you were explicitly taught how to divide does not make your mental processes less interesting to study. If anything, it may make them more interesting because we might be able to find parallels between teaching methods and people's mental processes.

The third question is in many ways more typical of cognitive psychology's interests and research than the first two. For reasons that will become more convincing throughout the book, a great deal of research in cognitive psychology has timed people as they make simple yes-or-no decisions about questions such as the following:

3. Does a robin have wings?

Most adults find themselves unable to say much of anything about the train of thoughts they considered when answering this question. Indeed, many people insist, "I just knew the answer was yes." (In honesty, many people also question the sanity of an investigator who asks such trivial questions.) One purpose of the informal analysis for Question 1 was to illustrate just how much of our cognitive processing can occur below the level of awareness, or automatically. As you probably realize by now, cognitive psychology does not find the notion that "I just knew it" to be particularly useful, however certain you are that no other thoughts occurred to you. Clearly, you had to read the words, find their meanings in memory, check the relevant facts, and make your decision in a similar fashion to the previous examples. Each of these steps (and there are many more steps involved here) is a bona fide mental act, the very substance of cognitive psychology. Furthermore, each step takes some amount of time to be completed. A question such as Question 3 takes adults about 1.3 seconds to answer; the question "Does a robin have feet?" takes a little longer, around 1.5 seconds. Even such small time differences can give us a wealth of information about mental processing and human memory.

What seems strikingly different for Question 3 is that almost none of the mental processes required much awareness or conscious activity; the question seems to have been processed automatically. Because such automatic processes are so pervasive in mental activity, cognitive psychologists are particularly interested in understanding them.

■ Section Summary

- Cognitive psychology is the scientific study of human memory and mental processes, including such activities as perceiving, remembering, using language, reasoning, and solving problems.
- Intuitive analysis of examples such as "How many hands did Aristotle have?" and "Does a robin have wings?" indicates that many important mental processes can occur automatically, that is, very rapidly and below the level of conscious awareness; experimental evidence presented later in the book supports these intuitive conclusions.

Memory and Cognition Defined

Now that you have an idea of the topics we are concerned with in cognitive psychology, we need to state more formal definitions of the terms *memory* and *cognition*. It will also be useful to spend a moment discussing the topics you will and will not find covered in this text. Most of us have a reasonably good idea of what the term *memory* means, something like "being able to remember or recall some information." As defined in *Webster's New World Dictionary* (1980), memory consists of "the power, act, or process of recalling to mind facts previously learned or past experiences." Note that both of these definitions are hopelessly circular; memory is "being able to remember" or "the process of recalling to mind." Although this circularity is unfortunate, the definitions to point to several critical ideas (note that the circularity is almost built in to the words, all of which came from related Indo-European bases meaning "to think" and "to remember").

First, the event or information being recalled from memory is one from the past. In other words, we remember things from the past but experience things in the present. Quite literally, any past event that is currently recalled is evidence of memory; it could be a childhood memory from years ago or something that only happened moments ago. Second, the term *memory* usually refers to a process, a mental act in which stored information is recovered for some current use. This recovery or retrieval of what has been placed in memory specifies the process of interest, a "getting out" of what was previously "put in." Note that the term **retrieval** here includes both varieties of remembering: the conscious, intentional recalling to mind implied in Webster's definition and the more automatic (or even unaware) kind of retrieval discussed in the examples earlier.

Finally, the term *memory* also refers to a place, a location where all the events, information, and knowledge of a lifetime are stored. This sense of the word is especially evident in the models and theories of cognition that rely on divisions such as short-term and long-term memory. Although it is obviously true that there is some physical location in your brain where facts and processes are stored, this "location" sense of the word often is taken somewhat metaphorically; regardless of where it happens, there is some memory system that holds information for later retrieval. But especially with the advent of modern imaging devices such as positron emission tomography (PET) scans and magnetic resonance imaging (MRI), the neurosciences are making remarkable progress in exploring functions and processes as they occur—or occasionally are disrupted—in the brain, and identifying regions and areas responsible for those functions and processes. Chapter 2 introduces you to some of this new methodology and orientation, preparing you to read about recent advances in our knowledge of brain–cognition relationships throughout this book.

A formal definition of the term *memory* captures the essential ingredients of the preceding discussion. Consider **memory** to mean *the mental processes of acquiring and retaining information for later retrieval and the mental storage system that enables these processes.* Operationally, memory is demonstrated when the processes of retention and retrieval influence your behavior or performance in some way, even if you are unaware of the influence. Furthermore, we understand this definition to include not just retention across hours, weeks, or years but even across very brief spans of time, in any situation in which the original stimulus event is no longer present. Note also that *memory* refers to three different kinds of mental activities in this definition: initial acquisition of information (usually called learning or encoding), subsequent retention of the information, and then retrieval of the information (Melton, 1963). Because all three activities are logically necessary to demonstrate that remembering has taken place, we include them in our broader definition of the term *memory* as well.

The term *cognition* is much richer in its connotations and indeed is almost an umbrella term for all higher mental processes. One dictionary defines it as "the mental process or faculty of knowing, including aspects such as awareness, perception, reasoning, and judgment" (*The American Heritage College Dictionary*, 1997). *Cognitive Psychology*, Neisser's (1967) landmark book, claimed that *cognition* "refers to all the processes by which the sensory input is transformed, reduced, elaborated, stored, recovered, and used . . . [including] such terms as *sensation, perception, imagery, retention, recall, problem solving*, and *thinking*" (p. 4). For the present, we will use a definition that is somewhat easier to remember, but just as broad: **cognition** is *the collection of mental processes and activities used in perceiving, remembering, thinking, and understanding, as well as the act of using those processes.*

Whereas our definition of the term *memory* is fairly specific, note that the definition of *cognition* is still somewhat slippery. A term such as *thinking* in a scientific definition begs for clarification, or at least a catalog of examples. You might decide that dreaming is a perfectly valid act of cognition, according to the definition. You would then be puzzled that cognitive psychology generally ignores dreaming (but see G. Mandler, 1984, and Antrobus, 1991, for example). Why do we include some topics but ignore others?

One purpose of the examples in the previous section is to suggest that cognitive psychology is largely, though not exclusively, interested in what might be considered everyday, ordinary mental processes. The processes by which we read and understand, for instance, are entirely commonplace—not simple by any means, but certainly routine. On the other hand, we should not amend the definition to include only "normal" mental activities. It is true that cognitive psychology generally does not deal with the psychologically "abnormal," such as the varieties of thought disturbance associated with schizophrenia (but a cognitive approach to these problems is certainly possible). The problem with excluding the "nonnormal" processes is that the unusual or rare may also be tossed out, impoverishing our science in the process. Rather than change the definition, we will merely assume that *cognition* usually refers to the customary, commonplace mental activities that most people engage in as they interact with the world around them. As you will see, this still casts a rather broad net as we fish for topics to investigate and interpretations to explain our results.

Nonetheless, there are still omissions, sometimes glaring and sometimes not. To the distress of some (e.g., Neisser, 1976), most of our research deals with the sense modalities of vision and hearing rather than other sensory ways of knowing the world, and focuses very heavily on language; as Keil (1991, p. 287) quipped, "Minds talk a lot . . . they see a little, but they don't feel much else." More disturbing, possibly, is our reliance on seemingly sterile experimental techniques and methods (this is Neisser's more substantive criticism), techniques that ask simple questions and may therefore yield overly simple views about the operation of cognitive systems. In Neisser's term, much of our cognitive research lacks **ecological validity,** meaning that it is not representative of the real-world situations in which people think and act. As a simple example, imagine how different your reading and comprehension processes might be if you were shown this paragraph one word at a time, each word for only a fraction of a second. The method would prevent you from slowing down when your comprehension lagged, from returning your gaze to a previous word or sentence you may have misinterpreted, and so on. And yet this method has been used to investigate reading and comprehension.

Although Neisser's criticism was sensible, it was possibly premature. We find great complexity in cognitive processing, even when artificially simple tasks are performed. At our current level of sophistication, we might be overwhelmed if our tasks were also permitted to be more complex or if we tried to investigate the full range of a behavior in all its detail and nuance. In other words, in the early stage of investigation it is reasonable for scientists to take a **reductionistic** approach, *attempting to understand complex events by breaking them down into their components.* After all, an artificially simple situation can sometimes reveal rather than obscure a process, and sometimes we gain insight by preventing a process from occurring in its regular fashion (see Mook, 1983, for a fine discussion of the entire issue of ecological validity). Of course, it is also reasonable to expect that scientists eventually will put the pieces back together again and deal with the larger event as a whole. In fact, recent developments seem to hold just that sort of promise.

■ Section Summary

• Memory is the mental processes of retaining information for later use and retrieving such information, and the mental storage system that allows this retention and retrieval.
• Cognition is the collection of mental processes and activities used in perceiving, remembering, and thinking, and the act of using those processes.

An Introductory History of Cognitive Psychology

You have now encountered cognitive psychology by example and by definition, so now we turn to its history and development. This treatment should give you a better appreciation of what cognitive psychology is and how it became so (more thorough presentations of this material are listed in the Suggested Readings on the book's Web page, including two sources I have relied on heavily: Leahey, 2000, and Lachman, Lachman, & Butterfield, 1979). Figure 1-1 summarizes the main patterns of influence that produced cognitive psychology and then cognitive science, with approximate dates shown along the side. As you read, study the figure to decide which pathways indicate positive influences, where ideas and questions from an earlier movement continued to inspire the approach that followed. Think also about the pathways that indicate negative influences, where the later approach specifically rejected elements of its predecessor.

To a remarkable extent, the scientific study of human memory and cognition is quite new. Although elements of our explanations, and certainly many of our experimental tasks, appeared even in the earliest years of psychology, the relevant body of work and theorizing has been created since the 1950s. And yet, as is true of most topics in psychology, interest in human memory and cognitive processes is as old as recorded history. Aristotle, born in 384 B.C., considered the basic principles of human memory and proposed a theory of memory in his treatise *De Memoria (Concerning Memory;* Hothersall, 1984). Even a casual reading of ancient works such as Homer's *The Iliad* or *The Odyssey* reveals that people have always wondered about how the mind works and how to improve its functioning (as told in Plato's *Phaedrus,* Socrates fretted that the invention of written language would weaken reliance on memory and understanding, just as modern parents worry that calculators will weaken children's mastery of math). Philosophers of every age have considered the nature of thought and memory. Descartes even decided that the ultimate proof of human existence is our awareness of our own thought: *Cogito ergo sum,* "I think therefore I am" (Descartes, 1637, p. 52, in Hothersall, 1984, p. 28). Given this preoccupation with thought and mind in Western culture, it is no wonder that Ebbinghaus's (1908, p. 1) comment, "Psychology has a long past but only a short history," is so widely repeated in histories of psychology.

The critical events at the beginning of psychology's "short history" occurred in the mid- to late 1800s. It was as if the important intellectual and cultural influences of the day converged most strongly on one man, Wilhelm Wundt, and on one place, Leipzig, Germany. In 1879, Wilhelm Wundt established the first laboratory for psychological

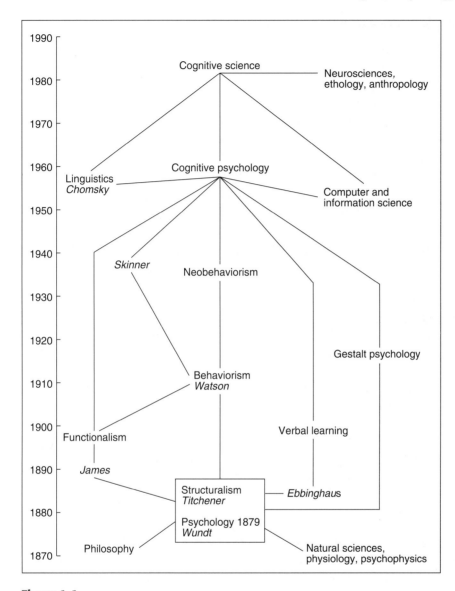

Figure 1-1

experiments, at the University of Leipzig. Of course, several notable individuals had already begun what was later seen as research on psychological topics: Weber and Fechner's work in psychophysics, Helmholtz's discoveries about the speed of neural impulses, and Broca's and Wernicke's identification of brain regions devoted to language processes (Banich, 1997), for instance. There was even a laboratory established by American psychologist William James in 1875, although apparently it was used largely for classroom demonstrations rather than experimental studies. Despite these developments, there is a consensus that 1879 marks the beginning of the formal academic, empirical discipline of psychology, a separate discipline from either philosophy or physiology. Wundt built his work on the advances that came before him, developments that gave rise to psychology and psychological research. It is these developments we turn to now.

Anticipations of Psychology

We begin with Aristotle, who for two reasons is the historical first we typically point to in psychology. Aristotle generally is viewed as the first philosopher to have advocated an empirically based natural science approach to understanding. Although he was certainly not the only great thinker to have insisted on observation as the basis for all science, he was the first to express this fundamentally important idea. Second, Aristotle's inquiry into the nature of thought and mind by his own natural science method led him to a reasonably objective explanation of how learning and memory take place. This explanation could not be considered a theory of memory by modern standards, nor should we expect it to be. On the other hand, the basic principle Aristotle identified, that of *associations*, has figured prominently in most psychological theories of the past century.

Equally important to psychology as a whole was *Aristotle's insistence that the mind is a* "blank slate" at birth, a **tabula rasa,** or clean sheet of paper (Watson, 1968; this term often is translated as the "blank wax tablet"). This notion claims that the experiences of the individual are of paramount importance because experience, rather than inborn factors, "writes" a record onto the blank paper. It is possible that no other issue has so preoccupied philosophers of all ages, an issue we call the nature versus nurture or heredity versus environment debate. In cognitive psychology, we encounter the controversy in several places, most notably when we discuss theories of language (see Chapters 2 and 9).

Most other anticipations of psychology date from the Renaissance and later periods and consist largely of developments in scientific methods and approaches. By the mid-1800s, positions such as Descartes's rational approach had been discarded by scientists in favor of observational or empirical methods. By the time psychology appeared, the general procedures of scientific inquiry had been developed and, for the most part, were accepted by all scientific disciplines and areas. There was widespread agreement on the need for science to be based on objective procedures and methods such as careful quantification and definition and empirical observation. Given the notable progress made in scientific fields such as physics, biology, and medicine by the mid-1800s, it is not surprising that the early psychologists thought the time was ripe for a true science of the mind.

Early Psychology

Four early psychologists are of particular interest in our study of cognitive psychology. They are Wilhelm Wundt, Edward Titchener, Hermann von Ebbinghaus, and William James.

Wilhelm Wundt To a large extent, the early psychologists were students of Wilhelm Wundt (1832–1920); this was especially true of the early American psychologists (Benjamin, Durkin, Link, Vestal, & Acord, 1992). Beginning in 1875, when he moved

Wilhelm Wundt.

to the University of Leipzig, he directed more than 200 doctoral theses on psychological topics (Leahey, 2000). Such important psychologists as William James, Hugo Munsterberg, Charles Spearman, James McKeen Cattell, and Edward Titchener studied with Wundt, investigating primarily the topics Wundt felt were appropriate to the new science of the mind. Wundt continually updated his book *Principles of Physiological Psychology*, reporting new results obtained in his laboratory, and also founded the first journal devoted to psychological research, *Philosophical Studies* (neither of these titles seems to match modern connotations of the terms). His influence was far reaching because his was the first truly psychological system. In fact, Leahey (1992b) credited Wundt with starting the only true scientific revolution in psychology.

Unfortunately, Wundt's interests in the last 20 years of his career went largely unrecognized until quite recently. His work on language, according to Leahey (2000), foreshadowed some modern insights to a remarkable degree but was largely ignored even in his own time. And his work on child psychology and other applied topics (his term was *Volkerpsychologie*, or psychology of the people) was rejected; the influential Titchener, for instance, believed that these topics simply did not belong in psychology. American psychologists, never enthusiastic about contributions from Europe, may have even found an additional excuse for their narrow and biased attitudes; Wundt was an enthusiastic German nationalist during World War I (Benjamin et al., 1992).

Wundt believed strongly that the proper topic for psychology to study was "conscious processes and immediate experience"; today, we would place these topics somewhere near the areas of sensation, perception, and attention. To study such processes in a scientific manner, an approach to which Wundt was thoroughly dedicated, he devised the method of *selbst-beobachtung*. Translated literally as "self-observation," this method of investigation generally is known in English as **introspection,** *a method in which one looks carefully inward,* *reporting on inner sensations and experiences.* By all accounts, Wundt intended this to be a careful, reliable, and, above all else, scientific method. For instance, Hothersall (1984, pp. 88–89) noted, "Wundt's introspection was a rigidly controlled, arduous, experimental procedure. . . . To yield valid introspections Wundt insisted that certain rules be enforced: the observer had to be 'master of the situation,' that is, in a state of 'strained attention'. . . . All observations were to be repeated many times; and finally, experimental conditions were to be varied systematically to allow a general description of mental contents." The observers in these experiments needed a great deal of training in the method, so that they would report only the elements of experience that were immediate and conscious. Reports in which memory intruded—Wundt's term was *mediate experience*—were excluded.

Edward Titchener For American psychology in Wundt's tradition, the most important figure was Edward Titchener, an Englishman who came to Cornell University in 1892 to direct its psychology laboratory. Titchener's work with Wundt had convinced him that psychology's knowledge was obtainable only with the introspective method. As his career at Cornell progressed, Titchener became even more firm in this conviction and even more narrow in his definition of psychology. Concerns with mental illness, educational applications, social psychology, and other areas (including Wundt's broader interests) were "impure" because they could not be studied with introspective methods. Like Wundt, Titchener insisted on careful control and rigorous training for his introspectors, who were required to avoid what he called "the stimulus error" of describing the physical stimulus rather than the mental experience of that stimulus. Moreover, "certain introspections were defined as correct, and certain others as in error, with the final authority being Titchener himself" (Hothersall, 1984, p. 105). By these means, Titchener studied *the structure of the conscious mind, the sensations, images, and feelings that were the very elements of the mind's structure.* He called this **structuralism,** the first major movement or school of psychological thought (see Figure 1-1).

As you might expect, such an exclusive system of psychology, relying as it did on the ultimate authority of Titchener to validate its observations, was destined for difficulties. As other researchers applied the introspective methods in their own laboratories, differences and contradictory results began to crop up. For instance, a controversy developed over "imageless thought" (see Leahey, 2000, for example). Researchers of the Würzburg School found evidence of imageless thought in their studies. When Titchener found no such evidence in his own studies, he claimed that the Würzburg researchers' findings were wrong, merely the product of sloppy methods and poorly trained observers. (In a similar dispute, over sensory and motor reaction times, Titchener's methodological criticism was that the subjects had been untrained observers. He would surely have disapproved of modern insistence on naive volunteers from Intro Psych.) These disputes, along with other developments, hastened the decline of Titchener's once-powerful structuralism.

Hermann von Ebbinghaus In contrast to the doomed structuralism of Wundt and Titchener was the theoretically modest but eventually more influential work of

Hermann von Ebbinghaus.

Hermann von Ebbinghaus (see Chapter 6). Ebbinghaus was a contemporary of Wundt in Germany, although he never studied with Wundt in person. In fact, Ebbinghaus's achievements in studying human memory and forgetting are all the more impressive largely because he worked outside the establishment of the time. Watson (1968) noted that Ebbinghaus was familiar with Wundt's writings but, if anything, viewed Wundt's pessimism about studying higher mental processes as a challenge rather than a deterrent to pursuing that work. Historical accounts suggest that Ebbinghaus read Wundt's book, decided instead that a study of the mind by objective methods *was* possible, and set about the task of figuring out how to do it.

Lacking a formal laboratory and serving in a nonpsychological academic position with no similar-minded colleagues, Ebbinghaus was forced to rely on his own resources to study memory, even to the extent that he alone served as a subject in his research. Ebbinghaus's goal was to study the mind's process of association formation, using thoroughly objective methods. He reasoned that for this goal to be accomplished, he needed to use materials that had no preexisting associations. Thus the first step in his method involved constructing stimulus lists of *nonsense syllables*, consonant–vowel–consonant (CVC) triads that seemingly by definition were of uniform meaningfulness: To wit, they had no meaning whatsoever. Ebbinghaus would learn a list (e.g., of 16 items) to an arbitrary criterion of mastery (e.g., two perfect recitations), then set the list aside. On some later occasion, he would relearn the same list, noting how many fewer trials he needed for relearning to the same criterion. The measure of learning in these studies was the "savings score," the number (or proportion) of trials that had been saved in memory between the first and second sessions. By this method, Ebbinghaus examined forgetting as a function of time that intervened between the two learning sessions, degree of learning or overlearning, and even the effect of nonsense versus meaningful material (he compared forgetting curves for nonsense syllables and meaningful poetry).

Ebbinghaus's methods and results, described in his 1885 book, were acclaimed widely as the very model of scientific inquiry into the processes of memory; for instance, Titchener praised Ebbinghaus's work as the most significant progress in studying associations since Aristotle (1919; cited in Hall, 1971). Indeed, it is difficult to point to another psychologist of his day, aside from Freud, whose specific contributions or methods continue to be used. It is certainly true that the field of verbal learning, throughout the 20th century, owed a great deal to Ebbinghaus; after all, he was the first to invent a reasonably scientific, enduring method to study memory and mental processes. The Ebbinghaus tradition, depicted in Figure 1-1, is one of the strongest of all the influences on cognitive psychology. Perhaps no other influence in the figure is as positive as this century-old tradition begun by Ebbinghaus.

William James American philosopher and psychologist William James, a contemporary of Wundt, Titchener, and Ebbinghaus, provided at Harvard an alternative to Titchener's rigid system. His approach to psychology was a kind of **functionalism** in which *the functions of consciousness, rather than its structure, were of interest.* Thus James asked questions such as "How does the mind function?" and "How does it adapt to new circumstances?"

James's informal analyses led to some strikingly useful observations on a variety of topics in psychology. To note one of interest to us, he proposed that memory consists of two parts: an immediately available memory of which we are currently aware and a larger memory, usually hidden or passive, that is the repository for past experience. The notion of a memory system divided into several parts, based on their different functions, is widely

William James.

popular today. Indeed, the first serious models of human information processing, in the 1950s and 1960s, included exactly the two kinds of memories James discussed in 1890.

Probably because of his personal distaste for experimentation and his far-reaching interests beyond the topic of memory, James seems not to have espoused the Ebbinghaus methods of studying memory, although he apparently had high regard for Ebbinghaus's work. Titchener dismissed James as a "half hearted" researcher (Boring, 1950), interested in topics Titchener found inappropriate. Ultimately, however, James's far-reaching thoughts and proposals were far more influential to the whole of psychology than any of Titchener's work (see Miller's introduction to the 1983 edition of James's 1890 book).

Given other developments at the time, however, James's influence on the psychology of human memory and cognition was delayed. For it was John B. Watson, in 1913, who stridently solidified the new direction American psychology was taking, a direction that specifically rejected both the structuralist and functionalist approaches as well as many of their concerns. This new direction was behaviorism.

Behaviorism and Neobehaviorism

It is a mistake to suggest that all American psychology from 1910 through the 1950s was completely and thoroughly behaviorist in its viewpoint. During this period, the fields of clinical, educational, and social psychology, to name just a few, continued in their own development, pursuing their own agendas. In a sense, these other branches of psychology developed in parallel to behaviorism; they were contemporary fields with little contact or mutual influence. Furthermore, Leahey (2000) noted that there were significant changes within behaviorism itself, changes that eventually smoothed the transition to cognitive psychology; Leahy called it "mediated neobehaviorism," meaning that there were some unobservable, mediating variables included in neobehaviorism's theorizing. Nonetheless, experimental psychology traditionally has been the discipline of researchers concerned with learning, memory, perception, thought, and related topics. These psychologists, mostly in academic settings, were responsible for the birth and rearing of behaviorism and for its eventual dominance in American experimental psychology.

Everyone who has taken introductory psychology knows of John B. Watson, the early behaviorist who offered, "Give me a dozen healthy infants, well-formed, and my own specified world to bring them up in and I'll guarantee to take any one at random and train him to become any type of specialist I might select—doctor, lawyer, artist, merchant, chief and, yes, even beggarman and thief, regardless of the talents, penchants, tendencies, abilities, vocations, and race of his ancestors" (Watson, 1924, p. 104). Although Watson admitted in his very next sentence that he was exaggerating, he made it clear that he viewed experience as the primary factor in determining even the largest aspects of one's behavior. Rarely in the history of science has anyone taken so extreme a position on the nature versus nurture issue as Watson did (histories of psychology note that this extreme position of "environmentalism" was not typical of his early, scholarly works but only of his later writings).

Watson's firm belief, stated unequivocally in his 1913 "manifesto," was that observable, quantifiable behavior was the proper topic of psychology, not the fuzzy and unscientific concepts of thought, mind, and consciousness. He viewed attempts to understand the "unobservables" of mind and thought as inherently and hopelessly unscientific and pointed to the unresolved debates in structuralism as evidence. Thus psychology was redefined as *the scientific study of behavior,* the program of **behaviorism.** There was no room here for hidden or internal mental processes because behavioral laws were supposed to relate observable behavior to objective, observable stimulus conditions within the environment. To Watson, being a doctor was merely a matter of learning appropriate "doctor behaviors." No appeal to the mind, to innate abilities, or to mental activities was necessary, and no important limitations on the learning process were acknowledged.

Why did such a radical redefinition of psychology's interests have such broad appeal, gain so many adherents, and become so dominant? There is no doubt that part of the enthusiasm for a psychology of behavior, and the belief that a science of behavior was a reasonable goal, was the work that Pavlov and others were doing on learning. Here was a definite, scientific approach that was going somewhere, in contrast to the seemingly endless debates in structuralism. (Strangely, Watson seems to have been unaware of Ebbinghaus's careful, empirical studies of learning and memory, work that even the dogmatic Titchener saw as valuable.) Furthermore, the measurement and quantification that accompanied behaviorism seemed to be a hallmark of the already successful sciences such as physics. By modeling psychology on their methods and quantification, psychology might gain acceptance as a true science as well (Leahey, 2000, calls this mentality "physics envy").

Beginning in the late 1890s (Leahey, 2000), the new behaviorism attracted many practitioners and adherents. In a very real sense, Watson's 1913 article was not a rallying cry but a final statement of behaviorist triumph. Not all psychologists were eager to climb on this bandwagon, however. Naturally enough, some took an early wait-and-see attitude. For instance, Titchener's loyal student Edwin G. Boring, whose definitive book *A History of Experimental Psychology* appeared in 1929, condescended in his preface that behaviorism was "as yet undignified by the least trace of antiquity." In his 1950 edition, however, Boring admitted that "for a while in the 1920s it seemed as if all America had gone behaviorist" (p. 645, although this admission is contained in a chapter somewhat pejoratively called "Behavioristics"). And other research traditions, especially the *verbal learning* tradition begun by Ebbinghaus, continued their work. But these traditions became "second-class citizens" as behaviorism's emphasis on observable stimuli and responses came to dominate American experimental psychology.

From the standpoint of cognitive psychology, this period of behaviorism and then neobehaviorism was one of inactivity because of the influence of Watson and the other leading behaviorists. For instance, the word most commonly used to describe Watson is *antimentalistic.* Any concept or idea that smacked of mentalism, such as *consciousness, memory,* and *mind,* was to be excluded from psychology, according to Watson's view. This restriction in the scope of psychology, in hindsight, seems almost a willful blindness to the existence of obviously important phenomena. And it certainly produced some curious and convoluted explanations. For instance, because of the need to explain such ostensibly mental activities as thought and language in nonmentalistic terms, Watson developed the notion of implicit behavior. Implicit or covert behavior was a reduced, inner version of the normally observable behavior that psychology investigated. Thus "thought" to Watson was "nothing more than subvocal talking or muscular habits learned in overt speech which become inaudible as we grow up" (R. I. Watson, 1968, p. 427).

Although a few psychologists continued to pursue cognitive topics—Bartlett of Great Britain is a notable example—the most visible part of American experimental psychology focused instead on observable, learned behaviors, especially those of animals (but see Dewsbury, 2000, for the history of research on animal cognition during the behaviorist period). Even the decidedly cognitive approach of Tolman, whose article "Cognitive Maps in Rats and Men" (1948) is still worth reading, included much of the behaviorist tradition: concern with the learning of new behaviors, animal studies, and interpretation based closely on the observable stimuli in an experimental situation. Gestalt psychology, which emigrated to the United States in the 1930s (Mandler & Mandler, 1969), always maintained an interest in human perception, thought, and problem solving but never captured the loyalties of many American experimentalists (although we look back now at some of their research with greater respect).

Thus the behaviorist viewpoint continued to dominate American experimental psychology until the 1940s, when B. F. Skinner emerged as one of its most vocal, even extreme advocates. Much in keeping with Watson's earlier sentiments, Skinner also argued that mental events such as thought have no place in the science of psychology— not that they are not real, necessarily, but that they are unobservable and hence unnecessary to a scientific explanation of behavior.

Dissatisfaction with Behaviorism: The Winds of Change

As we saw earlier, it is difficult, if not impossible, to determine precisely when historical change takes place, when a movement or trend gains sufficient recognition to be proclaimed a *fait accompli*. We agree that 1879 saw the founding of academic, empirical psychology, yet we point to important research, and even to books with "psychology" in their titles, that predate 1879. Watson's 1913 article has been viewed as the manifesto that instituted behaviorism, yet it is more properly viewed as the culmination of two decades of gradually shifting allegiances.

It is even more difficult to pinpoint historical change when it is recent and somewhat controversial. Many current psychologists look kindly on the idea that there was a cognitive revolution in the mid- to late 1950s, an abrupt change in research activities, interests, and scientific beliefs on the part of experimentalists, a definitive break from the previously dominant behaviorism. (To be sure, several current psychologists do not look kindly on the idea of a cognitive revolution; see Leahey, 1992a, p. 458, who suspected that such talk was largely a kind of "radical chic" appropriate to the 1960s.) And it is indisputably true that the experimental psychology of today is radically different from that of the 1940s and 1950s. Psychology seemed to "lose its head" during behaviorism's day in the sense that memory, thought, and other mental activities were largely ignored. Conversely, our psychology of today has "come back to its senses" and to its memory and mental activities as well.

Because of the nature and scope of these changes, many psychologists regard the current cognitive approach as a revolution, a revolution in which behaviorism was rejected because of its lack of progress on—or even interest in—important questions. It was replaced with cognitive psychology and the information-processing approach. Lachman, Lachman, and Butterfield (1979) provided an especially compelling account of the cognitive revolution from the standpoint of Kuhn's (1962) classic work on the history of science. However, some historians, claim that the cognitive revolution was not a true scientific revolution at all but merely "rapid, evolutionary change" (see Leahey, 1992b, for this lively counterargument). In either case, the years from 1945 through 1960 were a period of crisis for American neobehaviorism and of rapid reform in the thinking and research of experimental psychologists. The serious challenges to neobehaviorism came both from within its own ranks and from outside, prodding psychologists toward the new direction to be taken.

Challenges and Changes: The 1940s and 1950s To neobehaviorism, the ultimate importance of learning—the acquisition of new behaviors by means of conditioning—was an absolute article of faith. This *was* psychology. Although some behaviorists paid lip service to the notion of instincts, species-specific behaviors, and other nonlearned sorts of behavior, none of the important theories of learning gave serious consideration to these ideas. Speaking anthropomorphically, the animal subjects often thumbed their noses at such theoretical purity and behaved according to their own laws. Researchers began finding significant instances in which conditioned behaviors, supposedly under the control of reinforced learning, began to change in the direction of instinctive behavior. For instance, "the Brelands found instances in which animals did not perform as they should. In 1961, they reported their difficulties in a paper whose title, 'The Misbehavior of Organisms,' puns on Skinner's first book, *The Behavior of Organisms*. For example, they tried to teach pigs to carry wooden coins and deposit them in a piggy bank. Although they could teach behaviors, the Brelands found that the behavior degenerated in pig after pig. The animals would eventually pick up the coin, drop it on the ground and root it . . . [as if] 'trapped by strong instinctive behaviors' that overwhelm learned behaviors" (Leahey, 2000, p. 501). Garcia's work (Garcia, McGowan, & Green, 1972) on conditioned nausea led to similar conclusions. Rather than associating the current environment with beginning to feel sick, rats correctly associated the nausea with the fluid they'd drunk an hour earlier, a sensible instinctive outcome that defied behaviorism's laws.

For the theoretical system of behaviorism, committed to the *tabula rasa* position that exalts learned behaviors, these were serious difficulties. No ready explanation was available to account for instinctive drift by means of the principles of reinforced learning, or the fact that the immediately present stimulus was less important than the fluid that actually induced nausea. And incorporating instincts into the theories would have been a blunt admission that the laws of conditioning and learning were not general, that

they were modified by other overpowering, central factors. To make matters worse, Skinner asserted that a theory of behavior was not even necessary, finding theory building to be a distraction from the main business of gathering data. Such a position seemed to undermine the intense efforts that had been exerted in developing and testing theoretical positions such as Hull's (1943) and Tolman's (1948). What an unpleasant time to have been a behaviorist, beset by significant nonlearned behaviors, unresolvable theoretical disputes, and a position that asserted that theorizing was a waste of time!

World War II Lachman et al. (1979) made an additional point about this growing dissatisfaction within the ranks of the neobehaviorists. They noted that many academic psychologists were involved with the U.S. war effort during World War II, in one capacity or another. Psychologists accustomed to studying animal learning in the laboratory were "put to work on the practical problems of making war . . . trying to understand problems of perception, judgment, thinking, and decision making" (p. 56). Many of these problems arose because of soldiers' difficulties with sophisticated technical devices: skilled pilots who crashed their aircraft, radar and sonar operators who failed to detect or misidentified enemy blips, and so on.

Lachman et al. (1979) were very direct in their description of this situation: "Where could psychologists turn for concepts and methods to help them solve such problems? Certainly not to the academic laboratories of the day. The behavior of animals in mazes and Skinner boxes shed little light on the performance of airplane pilots and sonar operators. The kind of learning studied with nonsense syllables contributed

THE FAR SIDE   By GARY LARSON

"Stimulus, response! Stimulus, response!
Don't you ever *think*?"

little to psychologists trying to teach people how to operate complex machines accurately. In fact, learning was not the central problem during the war. Most problems arose after the tasks had already been learned, when normally skillful performance broke down. The focus was on performance rather than learning; and this left academic psychologists poorly prepared" (pp. 56–57). As Bruner, Goodnow, and Austin (1956) put it, the "impeccable peripheralism" of stimulus–response (S–R) behaviorism became painfully obvious in the face of such practical concerns.

To deal with these practical concerns, wartime psychologists were forced to conceive of human behavior in a different fashion. The concepts of attention and vigilance, for instance, were important to an understanding of sonar operators' performance; experiments on the practical and then theoretical aspects of vigilance began (see especially Broadbent, 1958, Chapter 6, and Wickens, 1984, on the emergence of human factors as a distinct area of psychology). Decision making was a necessary part of this performance, too, and from these considerations came such developments as signal detection theory. These wartime psychologists also rubbed shoulders with professionals from different fields—those in communications engineering, for instance, from whom new outlooks and perspectives on human behavior were gained. They had seen firsthand how empty the behaviorist toolbox was and how other approaches held promise for their own work. Thus these psychologists returned to their laboratories after the war determined to broaden their own research interests and those of psychology as well.

Verbal Learning   **Verbal learning** was the *branch of experimental psychology that dealt with human subjects as they learned verbal material, items or stimuli composed of letters or sometimes words.* Earlier, the ground-breaking research of Hermann von Ebbinghaus was mentioned, in which desirably objective methods for studying human memory were invented and used. This work started the verbal learning tradition within experimental psychology (see Chapter 6), defined rather atheoretically as the learning of verbal materials. Even casual examination of published articles during the 1920s and 1930s reveals a fairly large body of verbal learning research, with reasonably well-established methods and procedures. Tasks such as serial learning, paired-associate learning, and to an extent free recall were the accepted methods of investigation, using Ebbinghaus-inspired nonsense syllables.

Verbal learning held many beliefs that were similar to those of the behaviorists. For example, those in verbal learning agreed on the need to use objective methods; although an occasional allusion to subjects' introspections was made, this was usually in the sense that they "confirmed" the conclusions drawn from more objective measures. There was widespread acceptance of the central role of learning as well, conceived as a process of forming new associations. And yet, much like their forefather Ebbinghaus, the verbal learners were curiously atheoretical, interested more in pursuing "fruitful" avenues of research than building theoretical edifices. They were "behavior*alists*," in Leahey's (1992b) description, committed to the methods of observing behavior but not bound to the "empty organism" view of radical behaviorism or any other theoretical movement: They were theoretical agnostics, as it were.

Lachman et al. argued that this atheoretical viewpoint in verbal learning circles made it easy for psychologists to accept the new cognitive psychology of the 1950s and 1960s: If you are not committed to a theory, you do not mind switching to another when the time comes. It clearly also made them more open-minded. There were many indications in their results that an adequate psychology of human learning and memory needed more than just observable behaviors. For instance, the presence of meaningfulness in almost any "nonsense" syllable had been acknowledged early on; Glaze (1928) titled his paper "The Association Value of Nonsense Syllables" (and apparently did so with a straight face). At first, such troublesome associations were merely controlled in the experiments, to avoid contamination of the results. Later, it became apparent that the memory processes that yielded those associations were more interesting to study than to control. Hall (1971) called this the "new look" in verbal learning, with its greater emphasis on memory rather than learning processes.

In this tradition, Bousfield (1953; Bousfield & Sedgewick, 1944) reported that, under free recall instructions, words that were associated with one another (e.g., *car* and *truck*) tended to cluster together in recall, even though they had been arranged randomly in the stimulus list. In this research, there was clearly the implication that existing memory associations led to the reorganization of the words during recall. Such obvious evidence of processes occurring between the stimulus and the response—in other words, mental processes—slowly led verbal learning to propose a variety of mental operations such as rehearsal, organization, storage, and retrieval. The lack of theoretical commitment to the behaviorist canon of antimentalism facilitated this change.

We can point to one outstanding achievement of the verbal learning tradition, however theoretically undeveloped the work was. To a very large extent, the researchers in the verbal learning area devised and refined laboratory tasks of learning and memory that remain useful today. In their acceptance of the need for objective procedures and methods, the verbal learners borrowed from Ebbinghaus's example of careful attention to rigorous methodology. From this they developed tasks that, we still agree, seem to measure the outcomes of mental processes in valid and useful ways. Some of these tasks naturally were more closely associated with behaviorism than others, such as the paired-associate learning task. Because these tasks lent themselves to tests of S-R associations in seemingly direct ways, they became somewhat overused. (Some have noted the popularity of the paired-associate task and the verbal learners' tendency to study performance on the task rather than the principles of human memory revealed by the task. A professor of mine likened this situation to "an archaeologist who studies his shovel.") Nonetheless, verbal learning gave cognitive psychology an objective, reliable methodology for studying mental processes, research that was built upon later (e.g., Stroop, 1935), and a set of inferred processes such as storage and retrieval to begin investigating. Therefore, the influence of verbal learning on cognitive psychology, as shown in Figure 1-1, was almost entirely positive.

Linguistics The changes in verbal learning from its early work to its emergence as cognitive psychology around 1960 seem to have been quite evolutionary, a gradual shifting of interests and interpretations that blended almost seamlessly into cognitive psychology. In sharp contrast, 1959 saw the publication of an explicit, defiant challenge to behaviorism. Watson's 1913 article has been called a behaviorist manifesto, crystallizing the view against introspective methods and those who practiced them. To an equal degree, Noam Chomsky's 1959 article was a cognitive manifesto, an utter rejection of purely behaviorist explanation of the most human of all behaviors: language.

A bit of background is needed to appreciate the significance of Chomsky's article (see Leahey's Chapter 14, titled "Years of Turmoil," for an amplified version of this story). In 1957, B. F. Skinner published a book titled *Verbal Behavior*, a treatment of human language from the radical behaviorist standpoint of reinforcement, stimulus–response associations, extinction, and so on. His central point in this book was that the psychology of learning, that is, the conditioning of new behavior by means of reinforcement, provided a useful and scientific account of human language use. In oversimplified terms, Skinner's basic notion was that human language use, "verbal behavior,"

Noam Chomsky.

followed the same laws of learning that had been discovered in the animal learning laboratory: A reinforced response is expected to increase in frequency, a nonreinforced response should extinguish, a response conditioned to a certain stimulus should be emitted to the same stimulus in the future, and so on. In principle then, human language, obviously a learned behavior, could be explained by the same sort of mechanism as any other learned behavior, with knowledge of the current reinforcement contingencies and past reinforcement history of the individual.

Noam Chomsky, a linguist at the Massachusetts Institute of Technology, reviewed Skinner's book in the journal *Language* in 1959. The very first sentence of his review notes that many linguists and philosophers of language "expressed the hope that their studies might ultimately be embedded in a framework provided by behaviorist psychology" and therefore were interested in Skinner's formulation. Chomsky alluded to Skinner's optimism that the problem of verbal behavior would yield to behavioral analysis because the reinforcement principles discovered in the animal laboratory "are now fairly well understood . . . [and] can be extended to human behavior without serious modification" (Skinner, 1957, cited in Chomsky, 1959, p. 26).

But by the third page of his review, Chomsky stated that "the insights that have been achieved in the laboratories of the reinforcement theorist, though quite genuine, can be applied to complex human behavior only in the most gross and superficial way. . . . The magnitude of the failure of [Skinner's] attempt to account for verbal behavior serves as a kind of measure of the importance of the factors *omitted* from consideration" (p. 28, emphasis added). The fighting words continued. Chomsky asserted that if the critical terms *stimulus, response, reinforcement,* and so on are used in their technical, animal laboratory sense, then "the book covers almost no aspect of linguistic behavior" (p. 31) of interest. His central theme was that Skinner's account used the technical terms in a nontechnical, metaphorical way, which "creates the illusion of a rigorous scientific theory

[but] is no more scientific than the traditional approaches to this subject matter, and rarely as clear and careful" (pp. 30–31).

To illustrate his criticism, Chomsky noted the careful operational definitions that Skinner provided in the animal learning laboratory, such as for the term *reinforcement*. But unlike the distinct and observable pellet of food in the Skinner box, Skinner claimed that reinforcement for human verbal behavior can be administered by the person exhibiting the behavior, that is, self-reinforcement. In some cases, Skinner continued, reinforcement could be delayed for indefinite periods, or never be delivered at all, as in the case of a writer who anticipates that her work may gain her fame for centuries to come. When an explicit and immediate reinforcer in the laboratory, along with its effect on behavior, is generalized to include nonexplicit and nonimmediate (and even nonexistent) reinforcers in the real world, it truly does seem, as Chomsky argued, that Skinner had brought along the vocabulary of a scientific explanation but left the substance behind. As Chomsky bluntly put it, "A mere terminological revision, in which a term borrowed from the laboratory is used with the full vagueness of the ordinary vocabulary, is of no conceivable interest" (p. 38). The explanation was merely dogmatic, not at all scientific.

Chomsky's own position on language, emphasizing the novelty of human language and the internal rules for language use, is discussed in Chapter 9; there, the strong influence of linguistics on cognitive psychology (Figure 1-1) is described in some detail. For now, the essential message involves the impact of Chomsky's review on experimental psychology (not to mention the impact on linguistics itself; see Wasow, 1989). As Lachman et al. (1979) pointed out, this dispute could not easily be dismissed by psychologists as irrelevant. Language *was* an important behavior—and a learned one at that—to be understood by psychology. A dominant approach that offered no help in understanding such an important behavior was useless, not to mention embarrassing.

To a significant number of people, Chomsky's arguments summarized the dissatisfactions with behaviorism that had become so apparent. For these people, the irrelevance of behaviorism to the study of language, and by extension to the study of any significant human behavior, was now painfully obvious. In combination with the other developments, the wartime fling with mental processes, the expansion of the catalog of such processes by verbal learning, and the disarray within behaviorism itself, it was clear that the new direction for psychology, growing in influence throughout the 1950s, would take hold.

■ Section Summary

- The modern history of cognitive psychology began in 1879 with Wundt and his use of introspection. The behaviorist movement rejected the use of introspections and substituted the study of observable behavior as the true goal of psychology.
- Modern cognitive psychology, which dates from approximately 1960, rejected much of the behaviorist position but accepted many viewpoints, assumptions, and methods from fields such as verbal learning, linguistics, and computer science. Depending on your definition, this was at least a rapid, evolutionary change in interests, if not a true scientific revolution.

Cognitive Psychology and Information Processing: The New Direction

If we had to pick a date that marks the beginning of cognitive psychology, one that indicates as accurately as possible when cognitive psychology started, we might pick 1960. This is not to say that significant developments in the study of cognition were not present before this date, for they were. This is also not to say that most experimental psychologists who studied humans became cognitive psychologists that year, for they did not. As with any major change, it takes a while for the new approach to catch on, for people to learn the new rules, to feel free to speak the new language, and, indeed, to decide that the new direction is worth following (some decided it was not worth following; see Skinner, 1984, 1990, for example). Several significant events clustered around the year 1960, however, events we look back on from our short period of hindsight as having been significant departures from the mainstream that came before. Just as 1879 is considered the formal beginning of psychology and 1913 the beginning of behaviorism, so 1960 seems to approximate the beginning of cognitive psychology in its modern form.[2]

Let's pick up the threads of what came before this date, to see what the new cognitive psychology and information processing approaches were all about. One of the most significant threads was Chomsky's 1959 review; such a forceful argument against a purely behaviorist position could not be—and was not—ignored. Chomsky argued that the truly interesting part of human language, indeed the very key to understanding it, was exactly what Skinner had omitted from his book: mental processes and cognitive structures. Chomsky also argued that language users follow rules when they generate language, rules that are stored in memory, cognitive structures operated on by mental processes. The so-called empty organism psychology of stimulus–response connections was empty in the sense that behaviorists did not deal with properties of the organism that come between the physical stimulus and the behavioral response. In Chomsky's view, it was exactly there, *in* the organism, where the key to understanding language would be found.

To a large extent, researchers in verbal learning and other fields were making the same claim. As noted, Bousfield (1953) found that subjects cluster or group words together on the basis of associations among the words. Memory and a tendency to reorganize on the part of the subject clearly were involved in this performance. Where were these associations? Where was this memory? And where was this tendency to reorganize? They were in the subject, of course, in human memory and mental processes. A particularly clear statement of the involvement of a subject's mental processes appeared in

---

[2]Gardner (1985, p. 28) stated, "There has been nearly unanimous agreement among the surviving principals that cognitive science was officially recognized around 1956. The psychologist George A. Miller . . . has even fixed the date, 11 September 1956." Miller recalled a conference from September 10 to 12, 1956, at MIT, attended by leading researchers in communication and psychology. On the second day of the conference, there were papers by Newell and Simon on the "Logic Theory Machine," by Chomsky on his theory of grammar and linguistic transformations and by Miller himself on the capacity limitations of short-term memory. Others that Gardner cited suggest that, at a minimum, the 5-year period 1955 to 1960 was the critical time during which cognitive psychology emerged as a distinct and new approach. By analogy to psychology's selection of 1879 as the starting date for the whole discipline, 1960 is special in Gardner's analysis: In that year, Jerome Bruner and George Miller founded the Center for Cognitive Studies at Harvard University.

Tulving's 1962 article, "Subjective Organization in Free Recall of 'Unrelated' Words'." Even when the words to be learned were unrelated, subjects still reorganized them, a strategy for recall that was clearly coming from within the organism.

During the 1950s, there were reports on human attention, first from English researchers such as Cherry and Broadbent, that were thematically related to the wartime concern with attention and vigilance. Again, fascinating attentional and perceptual processes were being isolated and investigated, processes whose unseen, mental nature could not be denied and yet whose existence could not be denied either. A classic paper in this area, Sperling's monograph on visual sensory memory, appeared in 1960. (MacLeod, 1992, noted that there was a marked increase around 1960 in citations to the rediscovered Stroop [1935] task.)

Possibly the single most startling development of this period, certainly in terms of its impact on society, was the invention of the computer. Initial work had begun in the 1930s and 1940s on what we now call computer science, although philosophers had conceived of such a machine in general terms long before the technology existed to build one (e.g., Haugeland, 1985). At some point during the 1950s, a few psychologists realized the possible relevance of computing machinery to issues in psychology. It dawned on psychology, in a sense, that in some interesting and possibly useful ways, computers behave much like people (not surprising, according to Norman, 1986, p. 534, because "the architecture of the modern digital computer . . . was heavily influenced by people's naive view of how the mind operated"). They take in information, do something with it internally, then eventually produce some observable product. The product gives clues to what went on during the internal phase. The various operations performed by the computer were not unknowable merely because they occurred internally, of course. They were under the direct control of the computer program, the instructions given to the machine to tell it what operations to perform.

The realization that human mental activity might be understood by analogy to the seemingly intelligent (or at least intelligent-acting) machine was a significant breakthrough. Especially important to the analogy was the notion of symbols and their internal manipulation. That is, the computer is a symbol-manipulating machine; its operation involves interpreting the symbols fed to it in the computer program, then performing the operations that those symbols specify. The insight that the human mind might also be fruitfully considered as a symbol-manipulating machine or system usually is attributed to Allen Newell and Herbert Simon. According to Lachman et al. (1979), their conference in 1958 had a tremendous impact on those who attended, for at this conference Newell and Simon presented an explicit analogy between information processing in the computer and information processing in humans. This important work, probably as much as anything he did in the field of economics, was the basis for the Nobel prize awarded to Simon in 1978.

Among the many indirect results of this conference was the 1960 publication of a book by Miller, Galanter, and Pribram called *Plans and the Structure of Behavior*. The book suggested that human problem solving could be understood as a kind of planning in which mental strategies or plans guide behavior toward its eventual goal. Why was this book viewed as a scientific contribution, involving as it did such mentalistic ideas as plans, goals, and strategies? Because the mentalistic plans, goals, and strategies were not just unobservable, hypothetical ideas. Instead, they were ideas that in principle could be exactly specified, in a program running on a lawful, physical device: the computer. (We will have much more to say about computers and computer models of cognition throughout the book.)

The Assumptions of Cognitive Psychology

We turn finally to three assumptions that pervade the field of cognitive psychology: that mental processes exist, that they can be studied scientifically, and that people are active information processors.

Mental Processes Exist Surely by now you have figured out the single most defining feature of the new cognitive psychology: a scientific interest in human mental activity and processes. Whereas the behaviorists intentionally avoided any theorizing about the higher mental processes, these processes are exactly what cognitive psychology investigates. Our most basic assumption in cognitive psychology is that human mental processes exist, that they are absolutely key to a complete, useful psychology.

Mental Processes Can Be Studied Scientifically Not only do mental processes exist, but their very reality means that they are an appropriate topic for scientific inquiry. That is, we believe that an objective, scientific study of mental processes can be accomplished and is exactly the province of the science of psychology. In science, saying that a phenomenon or effect exists basically is the same as saying that it can be studied by the objective, quantifiable methods of scientific practice. By saying that mental processes exist, we are also claiming that they are lawful, systematic events and that they can be studied.

We are very mindful of the checkered history of investigations into the higher mental processes. We fault the structuralists, such as Wundt and Titchener, not for their interests but for their methods. Note that our biggest lesson from the behaviorist period, and also from the example set by verbal learning, was the lesson about scientific methods and procedures. Unlike the structuralists, we in cognitive psychology rely on measures of behavior that are as objective and reliable as possible. That is, we attempt to unravel the complex questions of mental activity with tasks and measures of behavior that are quantifiable, open to scientific scrutiny, easily replicated by other investigators, and faithful to the scientific empirical tradition. As best we can, we avoid measures that are colored by subjective bias or influence, as the old introspectionism was.

Active Information Processors A third basic assumption, implied by the first two, is the notion that humans are active participants in the act of cognition. Miller (cited in Pylyshyn, 1984) called us *informavores*, beings that actively obtain and process information (in fact, Miller was referring to all information-processing systems by that term, even the kind built with silicon chips). The behaviorist, in contrast, viewed the subject as a largely passive creature, one who waited around for a stimulus to occur, then responded to it in ways determined by previous conditioning and current stimulus conditions.

Cognitive psychology specifically rejects this behaviorist outlook as it applies to humans. We firmly believe that humans actively process the environmental stimuli around them, selecting some parts of that environment for further processing, relating those selected parts to information already stored in memory, and then doing something as a result of processing. And if no external stimulation is present, we occupy ourselves with internal, mental stimulation. (To prove the point, try this. Stop reading for a moment, and try to keep your mind completely inactive and blank for a full minute—no thoughts, recollections, or even daydreams.)

We believe that people do not passively respond on the basis of simple conditioning or reinforcement. Instead, people respond actively on the basis of their mental processing of events and information. And, as you saw in the examples at the beginning of the chapter, an enormous amount of mental activity can underlie even very simple question answering. All this mental processing is evidence of the active nature of people and their cognitive processes.

These three features form the core of cognitive psychology: our assumptions that human mental activities exist, that those activities can be studied scientifically, and that the person doing the relevant mental activities is an active information processor. These ideas have a *metatheoretical* status in cognitive psychology. That is, they are above and beyond any particular theory of cognitive processes; they are so central to our discipline that they are assumed to be true. It is the various implications drawn from them that are tested in our experiments.

■ Section Summary

- The three most basic assumptions of cognitive psychology are that mental processes exist, they can be studied scientifically, and humans are active information processors.

Key Terms

behaviorism (p. 20)	introspection (p. 15)	retrieval (p. 9)
cognition (p. 10)	memory (p. 10)	structuralism (p. 16)
cognitive science (p. 3)	reaction time (p. 6)	*tabula rasa* (p. 14)
ecological validity (p. 11)	reductionism (p. 11)	verbal learning (p. 25)
functionalism (p. 18)		

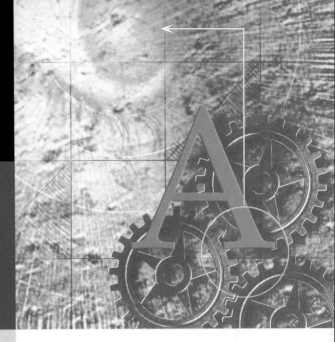

CHAPTER 2

The Cognitive Science Approach

The basic reason for studying cognitive processes has become as clear as the reason for studying anything else: because they are there. . . . Cognitive processes surely exist, so it can hardly be unscientific to study them. (Neisser, 1967, p. 5)

The human operates as an information processing system [IPS] . . . a system consisting of a memory containing symbol structures, a processor, effectors, and receptors. . . . There is no evidence that the human LTM [long-term memory] is fillable in a lifetime, or that there is a limit on the number of distinguishable symbols it can store. Hence, we assume that the IPS has a potentially infinite vocabulary of symbols, and an essentially infinite capacity for symbol structures. (Newell & Simon, 1972, pp. 19–20, 792)

A basic tenet of cognitive psychology was the computer analogy for the mind: the mind is to the brain as software is to hardware in a computer. . . . The problem with the computer analogy is that hardware and software are independent only for very special types of computational systems . . . systems that have been engineered . . . to make [them] independent . . . . The brain was "designed" by very different pressures. . . . As cognitive psychologists finally began to learn about neuropsychology, it became apparent that cognitive functions break down in characteristic and highly informative ways after brain damage. (Feinberg & Farah, 1997, p. 15)

This chapter, like the first, is largely introductory. In Chapter 1, you got a general idea of what cognitive psychology is all about, and you read a bit of its history. The purpose of that material was to make cognitive psychology a living, breathing *thing* for you—not some obscure, academic quest that only Ph.D.s can be interested in, but a dynamic and vibrant approach to questions of human memory and thought. I tried to give you some of the flavor of the field and a sense of the excitement cognitive psychologists feel for their topic by describing some of the shouting matches that gave birth to cognitive psychology. A student 40 years ago, fired with curiosity about how memory works, would have been sent off to study retroactive interference, paired-associate learning, and serial position curves. The same student today is sent off to study human reasoning, paragraph comprehension, memory disruptions in stroke victims, and so forth. This is certainly a more rewarding set of questions to study; there has been progress (Simon, 1992).

Guiding Principles

Nonetheless, it is also true that these newer questions and interests often are difficult to pin down in a scientific fashion. The practitioners of a science need more than just the questions to decide what experiments ought to be done and how they ought to do them. In particular, scientists need a general framework to guide them, a set of assumptions that tells them where to start, what to look for, what to beware of. This general framework sometimes is called a **metatheory,** where *meta* means above or beyond. A metatheory is this *set of assumptions and guiding principles*, a kind of Michelin guide that helps us find our way through unknown territory.

To a large extent, cognitive psychology's Michelin guide or metatheory for many years was the **information-processing approach.** This broadly defined approach described cognition as *the coordinated operation of active mental processes within a multicomponent memory system.* The human information-processing system that was described was a general model of the human memory and cognitive systems, a model that went hand in hand with the broad approach known as information processing. Note that as it was originally used, the term *information processing* had a narrow connotation, one that emphasized a one-by-one sequence of mental operations in which one operation was assumed to end before another could begin. You will read about this strict information-processing approach and how it generated some important discoveries and ideas. You will also read about its drawbacks and limitations and how these led to the broader, less restrictive approaches of contemporary cognitive science. We'll talk a bit about the cognitive science approach and how some of the themes you will encounter in a moment fit into that approach.

A big part of that new cognitive science approach—the new look of cognitive science—is its multidisciplinary nature, the way it has opened up to ideas and discoveries from other research traditions. This is most dramatically illustrated by the influential role now played by the neurosciences, by investigations of the neural basis of cognition. Even as recently as 10 or 15 years ago, a cognitive psychologist could get along reasonably well—do important research, teach useful classes—with little or no knowledge of the human brain and its functioning. But now a wealth of new information is available to us about cognition and the brain—how cognitive processes are implemented in the brain, how brain damage in selected regions affects our mental processes, and how this evidence tells us a great deal about normal cognition. This evidence is especially dependent on several high-tech methods of brain imaging, methods originally developed for medical use. We will spend much time talking about the anatomy and functioning of the brain to prepare you to appreciate this important new evidence.

Themes

As we work through the various approaches, we will start to see themes that appear repeatedly across topics. Some of these themes have been important from the very beginning of modern cognitive psychology, or even the beginning of psychology in 1879; attention is an excellent example here. Others appeared later, augmenting and elaborating some of the early cognitive models you will study; the distinction between implicit and explicit memory is a good example. Finally, some have only recently been appreciated as relevant and useful and are still working their way through our research

Table 2-1 SEVEN THEMES OF COGNITION
Attention. This an all-important but poorly understood mental process. It is limited in quantity, essential to most processing, but only partially under our control. Is it a mechanism? A limited pool of mental resources?
Automatic versus conscious processing. Some mental processes occur automatically, whereas others are slow and deliberate, conscious, and demand lots of attention. Can *any* mental process become automatic?
Data-driven versus conceptually driven processing. Some processing relies heavily on the information we get from the environment (data-driven processing). Other processes rely heavily on our existing knowledge (conceptually driven processing). Conceptually driven processing can be so powerful that we often make errors, from mistakes in perception up through mistakes in reasoning.
Representation. How is information represented in memory? Can the variety of knowledge we have in memory all be formatted in the same mental code, or are there separate codes for the different types of knowledge?
Implicit versus explicit memory. We have direct and explicit awareness of certain types of memories; you remember the experience of buying this textbook, for example. But some memories or memory processes are implicit; they are there, but not necessarily with conscious awareness. This raises all sorts of interesting issues about the unconscious and its role in cognition; for instance, can an unconscious process affect your behavior and thinking?
Metacognition. This is awareness of our own cognitive systems and knowledge and insight into its workings. It is the awareness that prompts us to write reminders to ourselves to avoid forgetting something. But is this awareness and knowledge completely accurate? Does it sometimes mislead us?
Brain. Far more than the cognitive psychology of the 1960s and 1970s, brain–cognition relationships and questions concern us now. How and where a fact is stored *in the brain* is a very different question from how and where the fact is stored *in memory,* with radically different answers appropriate to each question. And yet the neurosciences and cognitive sciences are becoming more and more mutually relevant and influential.

methods and approaches; the neuroscience contributions are the best example. You won't find sections throughout this book labeled with the themes, however. Instead, the themes crop up across several areas of cognitive science, in several different contexts. If you can read a chapter and identify and discuss the themes that pertain to it, then you probably have a good understanding of the material. As a preview, see Table 2-1 for a list and brief description of seven particularly important themes that we'll encounter throughout the book.

Measuring Information Processes

Getting Started

Gernsbacher told of a thought-provoking illustration she encountered in a cognitive psychology course (which I in turn paraphrase here); call it the factory question. You are looking at a factory from a distant hill. You can't see into the factory, and you can't go inside either. Your task is to figure out what happens in the factory, what the factory does, and how it does it (Robertson & Gernsbacher, 1999).

One approach to the question is to watch what comes into the factory, to try to guess what happens inside; if wood is delivered, then the factory might make furniture but probably doesn't manufacture cars. Another is to watch what comes out; if it's boxes of cereal, you are in a better position to guess what happens in the factory than if the output is small metal things. Better than either of these methods is to watch both what comes in and what goes out, trying to make some kind of connection between the two.

More active, probing methods of answering the question might work too. For example, consider what might happen to the factory's output if you disrupted the arriving supplies in some way, say by slowing down their delivery. Would fewer outputs be produced in this situation? Would the factory's output be of lower quality? Or would the factory stop producing outputs altogether? What would happen if you doubled the inputs per unit of time? If the outputs didn't double too, then you might decide there was some internal limitation in the factory in terms of rate of production.

Cognitive psychology is faced with the same kind of problem you face in the factory example; indeed, this is the same problem we have always faced when wondering about how the mind works. Putting it simply, we want to know What happens in there? What happens in the mind—or in the brain, if you prefer—when we perceive, remember, reason, and solve problems? How can we peer into the mind to get a glimpse of the mental processes that operate so invisibly? What methods can we use, analogous to what you might do to answer the factory question, to obtain some scientific evidence on mental processes?

Time and Accuracy Measures

The question of how we peer into the mind to investigate mental processes boils down to a question of measurement: How do we measure mental processes in a scientifically acceptable way? Are there aspects of these otherwise unseen, unobservable mental events that *are* observable, that *can* be measured? You read in Chapter 1 about psychology's early, doomed method for studying cognitive processes, Wundt's method of introspection. What methods did the newly reborn cognitive psychology of the 1950s and 1960s use to overcome the problems Wundt and his followers encountered?

Of the four general types of measures used by cognitive science, two have been particularly common ways of obtaining the scientific evidence we seek: the *time* it takes to perform some task and the *accuracy* of that performance. Because these measures, both dating back to the 1800s, are so pervasive in our research, it is important to discuss them here at the outset. (The other two types, verbal reports and neuropsychological evidence, are discussed later in the chapter.)

Reaction Time Psychologists from different persuasions than cognitive psychology (and a few within cognitive psychology as well) bemoan our heavy reliance on measures such as **reaction time (RT),** *a measure of the time elapsed between some stimulus and the person's response to the stimulus* (RT is almost always measured in milliseconds [msec or ms] or thousandths of a second). Why is a time-based measure so important, especially when the actual time differences can be so small, say, on the order of 40 to 50 msec?

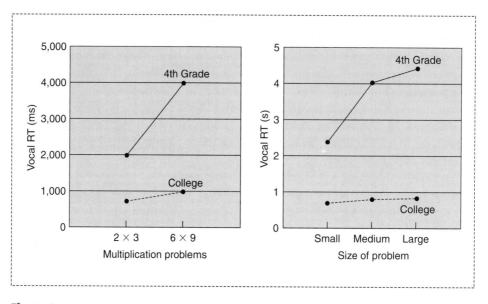

Figure 2-1

Vocal reaction times (RTs) to multiplication problems. Data from Campbell & Graham (1985).

Consider the following reasons. It has been known for a long time that individual differences among people often can be revealed by RT measures. In 1868, Dutch physiologist Donders (1868/1969) pointed out that the measure is potentially much more informative than this, in a proposal for studying the "Speed of Mental Processes" by means of RT. A moment's reflection should reveal why cognitive psychology uses reaction time measures so frequently: *Mental events take time.* Consequently, one way of "peering into the head" is to examine how long a certain set of mental processes takes to be completed. As Donders and many others have observed, careful comparisons of people's RTs to different stimuli can often give a strong clue to the mental processes going on internally.

Here's an example of the kind of reasoning that can flow from measuring RTs. A relatively recent area of research is known as mathematical cognition, investigating how we store mathematical knowledge in memory and how that knowledge is applied in various math tasks. Consider two simple arithmetic problems, such as $2 \times 3 = ?$ and $6 \times 9 = ?$ The left panel of Figure 2-1 shows the time it took a sample of fourth-graders and a sample of college adults to solve these problems (Campbell & Graham, 1985). The figure shows two important effects: an obvious age difference in which young children were slower than adults and an effect related to the problems, a longer RT for 6×9 than for 2×3. The right panel of the figure shows comparable functions for the entire range of multiplication problems, from small problems such as 2×3 to medium (e.g., 7×3) and large (e.g., 6×9) problems. For both age groups, the curves increase as the size of the problems increases, the problem size effect (e.g., Stazyk, Ashcraft, & Hamann, 1982).

Think of the basic assumption again: Mental processes take time. The implication here is that greater elapsed time is evidence that some process or subprocess took longer in one case than in the other. What could account for that? Most adults would agree that 6×9 is harder than 2×3, but that in itself is not a very useful observation; of course a harder decision will take longer to make. But why would 6×9 be harder? After all, we learned our multiplication facts in grade school. Haven't we had sufficient experience since then to equalize all the basic facts, to make them pretty much equal in difficulty? Apparently not, given the data in the figure.

So what might account for the increase in RT? It is unlikely that it takes longer to perceive the numbers in a larger problem, of course, and unlikely that it takes longer to start articulating the answer out loud once you have figured it out. On the other hand, a distinct possibility is that smaller problems have some kind of advantage in memory, perhaps something to do with knowing them better or being more certain about their answers. This might even result from an advantage dating back to grade school that somehow persisted into adulthood, such as the fact that arithmetic problems with smaller numbers (say from 2 to 4) are more common in grade school textbooks than large ones (Ashcraft & Christy, 1995; Clapp, 1924). Another possibility is that smaller problems are easier to figure out or compute in a variety of ways. Aside from simply remembering that 2×3 is 6, you could also count up by 2s or 3s easily and rapidly; counting up by 6s or 9s would take much longer and be much more error prone (LeFevre et al., 1996).

The point now is not to explain exactly why one kind of problem takes longer to solve than another (see Ashcraft, 1995, or Geary, 1994, if you want to track this down). Instead, the point is to illustrate how much more focused and interesting our questions about mental processing can be when we use time-based measures as our window on mental processes.

Accuracy   Not all of cognitive psychology's research is based solely on RT measures, of course. Often we are interested instead in some measure of the subject's accuracy, broadly defined. Sometimes we simply note which words a subject recalled correctly and which were omitted in recall. The earliest use of accuracy as a measure of mental processes was the seminal work by Ebbinghaus, published in 1885. As you will read in Chapter 6, Ebbinghaus compared correct recall of information in a second learning session with recall of the same material during original learning as a way of measuring how much material had been saved in memory.

Figure 2-2 shows a classic serial position curve, a graph showing the percentage of items correctly recalled from a list, plotted on the *x*-axis against each item's original position in the list. In this particular experiment (Glanzer & Cunitz, 1966), the items in the list were shown one at a time, and participants had to wait either 0, 10, or 30 s after seeing the list before they were allowed to recall the items. Making it even more difficult, the delay interval was filled with counting backwards by 3s (see Chapter 5 for details). In this situation, it is clear that the participants' memory of the items was influenced by an item's initial position in the list — recall was much higher for early items than for those buried in the middle of the list. And notice the big effect that delaying recall with backwards count-

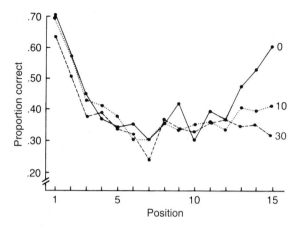

Figure 2-2

Serial position curves, showing the decrease in accuracy at the end of the list when 0, 10, or 30 s of backward counting is interpolated between study and recall.

ing had at the late positions in the list. Clearly, we cannot conclude that early list positions always had an advantage over late list positions–look how accurately the very last items were recalled when there was no delay interval. Instead, the bowed shape of the curve seems to be telling us something more complex and diagnostic about memory: Maybe recalling the items from the end of the list depends on a different kind of memory than recalling the early words, a kind of memory that can be disrupted by activity-filled delays.

More modern variations on simple list learning tasks look not only at percentage correct on a list but also at the incorrect responses, such as looking at any recalled words that were not on the studied list. Did the subject remember a related word such as *apple* rather than the exact word that was studied, *pear?* Was an item recalled because it resembles the target stimulus in some other way, such as remembering *G* instead of *D* when a string of letters was studied? Of course, this approach is similar to the Piagetian tradition of examining children's errors in reasoning, such as failure to conserve quantity or number, to examine their cognitive processes.

In more complex situations, the term *accuracy* takes on even richer connotations. For instance, if we ask participants to read and then paraphrase a paragraph, we do not score the paraphrase according to verbatim criteria (although the lack of verbatim memory of a paragraph is interesting in its own right). Instead, we score the paraphrase based on its meaning, on how well it preserves the ideas and relationships of the original. Preserving the gist, the overall idea, is something our memories do rather well according to most of the research findings (e.g., Neisser, 1981). Remembering exact, verbatim wording, on the other hand, is something we seldom do well at all. Although accuracy and inaccuracy in paraphrases can be a bit harder to pin down than simple recall of lists, they can be especially informative about memory processes (see Chapter 8).

Guiding Analogies

As you read in Chapter 1, a growing number of psychologists in the 1940s and 1950s became disenchanted with the behaviorist approach to psychology. It simply seemed too narrow and exclusionary to cope with complex human behavior and performance. During this period, the seemingly unrelated fields of communications engineering and computer science supplied psychology with some particularly intriguing ideas and useful analogies that were central to developing the human information-processing approach.

Channel Capacity To highlight just one, psychologists became fascinated with the issue of **channel capacity,** a concept borrowed from communications engineering. In the design of a telephone communication system, for instance, one of the built-in limitations is that *any channel—any physical device that transmits messages or information—has a limited capacity.* In simple terms, one telephone wire can carry just so many messages at the same time and loses information if the capacity is exceeded. Naturally, communications engineers tried to design equipment and techniques to get around these built-in limitations, thereby increasing the overall capacity of a channel.

At some point, psychologists noticed that in several important ways, humans could be thought of as limited-capacity channels too. After all, doesn't there seem to be a limit on how many things you can do, or think about, at a time? Maybe we are like transmitters of information, with a built-in limitation in the amount of information we can handle simultaneously. This insight lent a fresh perspective to human experimental psychology. Suddenly it made sense to ask questions such as How many sources of information can humans pay attention to at one time? What information is lost if we overload the human system? Where is the limitation, and how can we overcome it? We discuss some of this research and thinking in several chapters, especially those dealing with perception, attention, and short-term memory. For now, it's enough to say that this pollination of ideas from communications engineering helped the budding cognitive psychology determine its new approaches and directions.

The Computer Analogy Even more influential than the "message" that psychology received from communications engineering was the "input" from computer science. Although the limited-capacity channel idea is important, it is just one part of the general information-processing approach to human performance. Computer science, on the other hand, developed a machine that in many ways seemed to reflect the very essence of the human mental system. This machine, in its own way, seemed to do many of the things that humans do, things that cognitive psychologists very much wanted to understand. Because those things are unseen when both computers and humans do them, there was good reason for drawing *the computer analogy* to human cognition. Basically, this analogy said that human information processing may be similar to the sequence of steps and operations in a computer program, similar to the flow of information from input to output when a computer processes information. If this is true, then thinking about how a computer accomplishes various tasks might give us some useful insights into how humans process information.

There is at least one more reason for our reliance on computers and the computer analogy. Some of the most serious, ambitious theories in cognitive science are written as computer programs. Indeed, one important theorist with a computer-based model of cognition is so enthusiastic about the approach that the computer code of his basic theory is available on a Web site (for an introduction to this theoretical approach, go to http://act.psy.cmu.edu, or see Anderson & Lebiere, 1998). Researchers are encouraged to download the code and then modify and adapt it to their own particular research topics.

One important feature of computer-based theorizing involves explicitness. The formalities of computer programming force the theorist to be very precise and explicit in devising the pieces of a psychological theory; a vague concept might go unnoticed in a verbal theory, but vagueness just won't work in computer code. Interestingly, the enormous capacity of modern computers is also a factor in this approach; in fact, some theories require such a huge number of computations that they could not exist without high-speed computers to do the processing. A prime example of this is the connectionist modeling approach discussed at the end of this chapter.

■ Section Summary

- Information processing was the dominant metatheory, the dominant approach, in cognitive psychology until the mid-1970s. The approach claimed that mental processing could be understood as a sequence of independent stages of mental processing.
- Measuring information processes, the mental processes of cognition, has typically relied heavily on time and accuracy measures. Differences in reaction time (RT) can yield interpretations about the speed or difficulty of mental processes, leading to inferences about cognitive processes and events. Accuracy of performance, whether it measures correct recall of a list or accurate paraphrasing of text, also offers evidence about underlying mental processes.
- Although channel capacity was an early, useful analogy in studying information processing, a more influential analogy was later drawn between humans and computers, that human mental processing might be analogous to the sequence of steps and operations in a computer program. Computers still provide an important tool for theorizing about cognitive processes.

The Information-Processing Approach

Enough of computers for a while—it's time to explore the human information-processing system more carefully. We will examine both the original, narrowly defined strict information-processing approach and the current, broader approach that most cognitive psychologists adopt. We will present the standard theory of human information processing, a general description of the human information-processing system, the major outlines of which are still widely accepted. When we get to the section on process models, however, we will discuss the strict information-processing approach and how research was conducted within this framework. Process models were an important

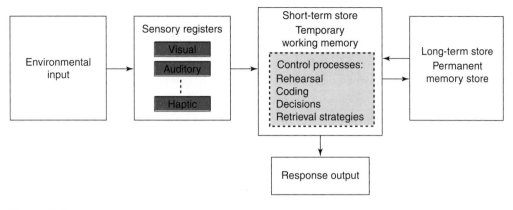

Figure 2-3

Information flow through the memory system in the Atkinson and Shiffrin (1968, 1971) model, the original standard theory in the information-processing approach.

adjunct to the standard theory but turned out to be too dependent on some assumptions that proved to be unwarranted. So, as the story unfolds, you will read about more recent developments, ideas that didn't fit into the strict approach very well, ideas that led to the current, broader cognitive approach.

The Standard Theory

Figure 2-3 illustrates the standard theory of human information processing as it existed in the early 1970s. It is adapted from one of the first such models to receive widespread acceptance, the Atkinson and Shiffrin (1968, 1971) model of human memory. Note first that the "hardware" of the system included three memory components: **sensory memory, short-term memory,** and **long-term memory.** At the input end of the model, environmental stimuli flow into the processing system, with each sense modality having its own sensory register or memory. Some of this encoded information is forwarded to short-term memory, a temporary working memory system with several control processes at its disposal. The short-term store could both transmit information to and retrieve information from long-term memory. It was also the component of the system responsible for response output, for communicating with the outside world in some observable fashion.

Let's use the multiplication example described earlier to trace the flow of processing through Figure 2-3. You read "2 × 3 = ?," and encode the visual stimulus into a visual sensory register; **encoding** is *the act of taking in information and converting it to a usable mental form.* Because you are paying attention to the task, the encoded stimulus is passed almost immediately to the short-term store, or short-term memory (STM). This STM is a working memory system where the information you are consciously aware of is held for further mental processing. For the multiplication example, the system determines that it needs to call on long-term memory (LTM) for the answer to the problem. One of the control processes in working memory initiates this search, while others maintain the problem until processing is completed. After the relevant memory search has occurred, LTM "sends" the answer, 6, to STM, where the final response can be prepared and sent to the appropriate device, say the speech mechanism.

At each step in this sequence, processing consumes some amount of time. By comparing these times and applying some basic reasoning, we can start getting an idea of the underlying mental processing. Thus, as you saw in Figure 2-1, a problem such as 2×3 takes college adults about 700 msec to answer, compared to slightly over 1,000 msec average for the problem 6×9 (values are taken from Campbell & Graham, 1985). The additional 300 msec might plausibly be due, as argued above, to the long-term memory retrieval stage, say because of differences in how easily the problems can be located in LTM.

A Process Model

Although the general Atkinson and Shiffrin model provided a useful summary function, investigators often needed something simpler and more focused as they developed explanations of their results. A common theoretical technique was to conceptualize performance in terms of a process model, a small-scale model that delineated the specific mental steps involved in a task and made testable predictions about the results. Formally, a **process model** is a *hypothesis about the specific mental processes that take place when a particular task is performed.*

A Process Model for the Lexical Decision Task Let's pick a task that is typical of research in cognitive psychology to explore the usefulness of process models and to see some of the limitations that paved the way for the more flexible, broadly defined information-processing approach. The task we are interested in here is the **lexical decision task,** or sometimes simply the "word/nonword task", *a timed task in which people decide whether letter strings are or are not English words* (see Meyer, Schvaneveldt, & Ruddy, 1975; this task and representative results are discussed further in Chapter 7). In this task, we show a series of stimuli, each a string of letters. On each trial, the participant must look at the letter string and decide whether the letters form a word; that is, "Is this letter string in your 'lexicon,' your mental dictionary?" On any given trial, the letter string might either be a true word, such as *MOTOR*, or it might be a nonword (usually called a pseudoword), such as *MANTY*. Participants are asked to respond rapidly but accurately, and the reaction time to each letter string is the main performance measure. (Note that the pseudowords are word-like in their appearance, spelling patterns, pronounceability, and so on, so that subjects won't judge all the stimuli on such tangential factors.)

Logically, what sequence of processes or events must happen in this task? In the process model shown in Figure 2-4, the first step or stage of processing involves *encoding* the stimulus, taking in the visually presented letter string and transferring it to the holding mechanism of short-term or working memory. Now that the stimulus resides in the mental system, working memory calls long-term memory, asking whether the stimulus is stored there. Some kind of *search* through long-term memory takes place, either

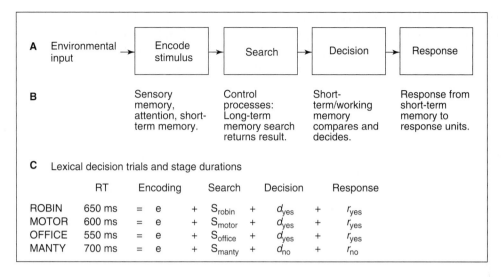

A Environmental input → Encode stimulus → Search → Decision → Response

B
| | Sensory memory, attention, short-term memory. | Control processes: Long-term memory search returns result. | Short-term/working memory compares and decides. | Response from short-term memory to response units. |

C Lexical decision trials and stage durations

	RT		Encoding		Search		Decision		Response
ROBIN	650 ms	=	e	+	S_{robin}	+	d_{yes}	+	r_{yes}
MOTOR	600 ms	=	e	+	S_{motor}	+	d_{yes}	+	r_{yes}
OFFICE	550 ms	=	e	+	S_{office}	+	d_{yes}	+	r_{yes}
MANTY	700 ms	=	e	+	S_{manty}	+	d_{no}	+	r_{no}

Figure 2-4

A A general process model, adapted from Sternberg (1969).
B A list of the memory components and processes that operate during the separate stages of the process model.
C A process analysis of the lexical decision task, where RT to each letter string is shown to be the sum of the durations of the separate stages. Note that for the three word trials, the only systematic difference arises from the search stage; encoding, decision, and response times should be the same for all three word trials, according to the logic of process models and the assumptions of sequential and independent stages of processing.

finding the letter string or not. In either event, the outcome of the search is returned to working memory and forms the basis for the subject's *decision*, either "yes" it's a word, or "no" it's not. If the decision is yes, then one set of motor *responses* is prepared and executed, say, pressing the button on the left; the alternative set of responses is prepared and executed for pressing the other button.

Lexical Decisions and the Word Frequency Effect Say that our results revealed a relationship between RT and the frequency or commonness of the words (this is not just a hypothetical result; word frequency is almost always an important influence on RT in the lexical decision task). For instance, we might have tested words at low, medium, and high levels of frequency in the language; *ROBIN* occurs quite infrequently, only twice per (approximately) million words, *MOTOR* is of moderate frequency, occurring 56 times per million, and *OFFICE* is of high frequency, occurring 255 times per million (all word frequencies from Kucera & Francis, 1967; for comparison purposes, the most frequent printed word in English is *THE*, occurring 69,971 times). It takes significantly longer to judge words of lower frequency than it does to judge high-frequency words (Allen & Madden, 1990; Whaley, 1978). This is the **word frequency effect.** Other variables are also known to affect the latencies or times, but the word frequency effect is enough here to develop our example of a process model and interpretation.

For the sake of argument, say that our low-frequency words such as *ROBIN* took an average of 650 msec, our medium-frequency words such as *MOTOR* took an average 600 msec, and our high-frequency words such as *OFFICE* averaged 550 msec. What does the process model in Figure 2-4 tell us about such a result? Logically, we would not expect that encoding the various words would be influenced by the frequency effect; otherwise we would have to make the improbable assumption that high-frequency words are more perceptible, easier to see. Because this is unlikely, we instead make the assumption that the encoding stage is unaffected by word frequency. The normal time needed for encoding, whatever that might be, should be the same for low-, medium-, and high-frequency words (and for pseudowords too). So encoding time for all trials should be a constant.

Likewise, all three of these trials will yield a successful search, so the same message is being sent to the decision stage in all three cases: "Yes, it's a word." Therefore, we would not expect any time differences in the decision stage for the low-, medium-, or high-frequency word trials, because they would all require the same decision (yes). And finally, "yes" responses should all take the same amount of time for the response stage; it should not take any longer to press the "yes" key for *ROBIN* or *MOTOR* than for *OFFICE* because all three words prompt the same response. Thus encoding, decision, and response stage times should all be constants, regardless of word frequency.

The only stage left is the search stage. And, on reflection, the search stage of processing seems very likely to be influenced by word frequency. For instance, it seems possible that the words in our language that are used more frequently are stored more strongly in memory, or maybe even stored repeatedly in memory (e.g., Logan, 1988); either possibility could yield shorter search times through memory. Alternatively, the more common words in our language might be encountered earlier, on the average, when we search through the mental lexicon. This would also produce shorter RTs to higher-frequency words. On these logical grounds, then, we might tentatively conclude that word frequency has an effect on the search stage of processing because word frequency is somehow embedded into people's long-term memory record for the words of their language. Any factor that affects the long-term memory search should influence the search stage of processing and should produce a time or accuracy difference because of the altered operation of that stage. Using the numbers supplied earlier, it seems that the search process takes an extra 50 msec for each change from high to medium to low word frequency.

The Strict Information Processing Approach

It is not appropriate now to develop a full-blown theory of long-term memory storage as a function of word frequency. Instead, you need to appreciate the nature of the process analysis or stage analysis that we just performed. Only when you understand this kind of analysis, and the assumptions embedded in this approach, will you be able to understand the important criticisms of the strict information-processing approach and see where the current approach has relaxed or discarded some of the strong assumptions in the typical process model.

The first assumption in such process models was the assumption of **sequential stages of processing.** It was generally assumed under this approach that there is *a sequence of stages or processes,* such as those depicted in Figure 2-4, *that occur on every trial, a set of stages that completely account for mental processing in the task.* Importantly, the order of the stages was considered to be fixed, on the grounds that each stage provides a result that is necessary for the operation of the next stage. More to the point, this assumption of sequential stages usually implied that one and only one stage or process can be performed at any one time. In other words, sequential processing not only means that the sequence of stages is fixed but also implies strict one-after-another operation.

The influence of the computer analogy is especially clear here. Modern computers have achieved extremely high speeds of operation, but most are still serial processors: They still perform operations one by one, in a sequential order. And yet there is no a priori reason to expect that humans are limited to one-by-one processing in all situations. Thus, this is where critics of the strict information-processing approach tended to cluster, at the assumption of sequential, one-at-a-time stages of processing.

The second assumption, really an extension of the first, was that the stages were **independent and nonoverlapping.** That is, *any single stage was assumed to finish its operation* completely *before the next stage in the sequence could begin, and the duration of any single stage had no bearing or influence on the other stages.* Thus, at the beginning of a trial, the encoding process starts, completes its operations entirely, and then passes its result along to the next stage in sequence, the search stage. Then and only then could the search stage begin, followed after its completion by the decision and then the response stages. With these assumptions, the total time for any trial could be interpreted as the sum of the durations for each independent stage; because mental processes take time and because each stage is a separate mental process, the total time for a trial could be viewed as the sum of the times for all the individual stages.

In our earlier example then, the 50 msec differences between *ROBIN, MOTOR,* and *OFFICE* would be attributed to the search stage. In other words, because encoding, decision, and response all take constant amounts of time, only the search stage is left to account for the time differences to the three levels of word frequency. The memory search for these words, then, is presumably slowed down when the words are of lower frequency.

Some Difficulties

What prompted cognitive psychology to move away from this strict information-processing approach and the simplicity of process models? We focus on just three of the difficulties that were encountered as a way of summarizing the field's maturation toward the updated, current cognitive approach.

Parallel Processing As research within the strict information-processing approach was done, new evidence accumulated that began to cast serious doubt on the assumptions of serial, nonoverlapping stages of processing. Instead of finding evidence that this or that mental process operated in a simple, one-by-one fashion, studies began documenting just the opposite: evidence that multiple mental processes can operate *simultaneously*, in **parallel.**

An excellent example (partly because it is intuitive, even if you are only moderately skilled at keyboarding) involves typing. Salthouse (1984) performed an in-depth examination of how skilled typists type and how performance changes across age. His data argued for a four-process model; the input stage encoded the to-be-typed material, a parsing stage broke large reading units (words) into separate characters, a translation stage transformed the characters into finger movements, and an execution stage triggered the keystrokes. Most significantly, all his evidence indicated that these multiple stages were operating simultaneously, in parallel; while one letter is being typed, another is being translated into a finger movement and the input stage is encoding upcoming letters, even as many as eight characters in advance of the one being typed. The point for now is that a strict process model explanation insists on sequential, serial processing and cannot easily account for performance resulting from parallel functioning of mental stages. Yet Salthouse's evidence was for parallel processing. Even the age effect he found argued for the importance of parallel processing; older typists counteracted the tendency toward slower finger movements by increasing their "look ahead" span at the upcoming letters. (The evidence of parallel processing has become even more convincing now that we are open to evidence from the neurosciences.)

Context Effects A second difficulty for simple process models and the strict information-processing approach arose when investigators took the effects of context into account. A simple example of this is the speed up in deciding that *MOTOR* is a word if you have already processed *MOTOR* recently; at a minimum, the process model would have to be expanded so that words presented on other test trials could influence performance on the current trial (see "repetition priming" in Chapter 6).

A more compelling demonstration of the effect of context comes from work on lexical ambiguity, the fact that many words have more than one meaning. As an example, Simpson (1981) had participants perform a modified lexical decision task, judging letter strings such as *DUKE* or *MONEY* after they had read a context sentence. When the letter string and sentence were related—for instance, "The vampire was disguised as a handsome count," followed by *DUKE*—the lexical decision on *DUKE* was faster than normal. The reason involved priming (again, see "priming" in Chapter 6), the notion that concepts and words in memory become activated in memory and hence easier to process. In this case, because the context sentence primed or activated the royalty sense of the word *count*, the lexical decision response to *DUKE* was speeded up.

Why was this kind of result a difficulty for the process model approach? This was a problem because there was no mechanism in simple process models to account for the priming effect, the speeding up of the lexical decision by context or some outside event (the sentence was "outside" of the timed trial). Look again at Figure 2-4; is there any component that allows a context sentence to influence the speed of the processes? No, you would need a meaning-based component that would hold recently activated meanings, a component that would speed up the search process when meanings matched but not when the meanings were unrelated. (A similar component would also have to be added to account for some of Salthouse's results on typing, such as the finding that familiar passages can be typed more rapidly than novel ones.)

Other Limitations   A final kind of limitation with the strict information-processing approach, with its emphasis on process models, involved other, often slower kinds of mental processing that cognitive psychology was interested in. As you probably noticed, process models were particularly applicable to RT results, to predicting RTs in different stimulus conditions (e.g., low-, medium-, and high-frequency words). Unfortunately, they tended to be less useful for accuracy-based investigations of cognitive processes; percentage correct on a list of words or the nature of one's errors in recall simply did not fit in with the sequential processing character of the process model approach.

In a similar vein, many of the cognitive processes we are interested in are slower and more complex than those investigated with process models. As you will learn in the last two chapters of this book, investigations of decision making and problem solving often involve processing that takes much longer than most RT tasks; for example, some cryptarithmetic problems (substitute digits for letters in the problem SEND + MORE; see Chapter 12) routinely take 15 to 20 minutes! Process models are virtually useless in such situations. Instead, a far more meaningful measurement of these mental processes would involve a verbal report or **verbal protocol** procedure, in which participants are asked to *verbalize their thoughts as they solve the problems.* In fact, this is the third type of measure in cognitive research that was mentioned earlier; it is less widely used than time and accuracy, but important nonetheless. Putting it simply, nothing in the process model approach could accommodate results from verbal protocol methods.

In short, the strict information-processing approach became too confining because of its embedded assumptions about sequential processing and because it tended to slight or even ignore certain kinds of data. Cognitive psychology needed a more broadly based approach to do justice to the range of mental processes that needed to be studied.

■ Section Summary

- The strict information-processing approach suggested that mental processing could be understood as a sequence of independent processing stages, such as the sensory, short-term, and long-term memory stages in the standard theory of Atkinson and Shiffrin.
- Process models, in particular, tended to be appropriate for fairly simple, rapid tasks that were usually measured by reaction times, such as the lexical decision task.

- Although the strict information-processing approach was responsible for many important developments and insights, evidence of parallel processing and context effects started to show some of its limitations; for example, research on skilled typing shows a high degree of parallel processing. Another difficulty was that slower, more complex mental processes, such as those in the study of decision making and problem solving, were not easily studied within the strict approach.

The Modern Cognitive Approach: Cognitive Science

The information-processing approach just described was a dominant way of doing business in cognitive psychology until the mid-1970s. Much of the research in cognitive psychology even today resembles research done under that approach–we still use RT measures, for instance. But the difficulties with that approach ultimately led to a broadened, less restrictive approach, now commonly called **cognitive science.** In general, cognitive science is the study of human thought, using all available scientific techniques and including all relevant scientific disciplines for exploring and investigating cognition. By expanding the range of methods and evidence we use, cognitive science takes a multidisciplinary approach to the study of cognition.

What follows is a two-part description of this approach. First, we focus briefly on some of the more traditional methods and techniques that still contribute to cognitive science and offer an update of the standard model you studied earlier. We then discuss at some length the background material you need to understand the biggest change in the field, material on the anatomy and functioning of the human brain. It is no longer possible to know cognitive psychology without knowing about the brain and about the evidence neuropsychology is contributing. To help you integrate this newer evidence into your understanding of cognition, this book presents important evidence from the neurosciences throughout rather than segregating it into its own separate chapter.

Updating the Standard Theory

Figure 2-5 shows a seemingly minor revision of the Atkinson and Shiffrin (1971) standard model, a revision in which the three memory components have been arranged in a triangle. Closer examination of the figure shows several other changes: The arrows between components are now bidirectional, each component can now affect each other component, and an attentional mechanism of some sort is shown as having an explicit influence throughout (the triangular, interactive scheme here was inspired by Neisser's 1976 notion of the "perceptual cycle").

Parallel Processing How do these changes fix what was wrong with the standard model of the late 1960s and early 1970s? Recall that the first difficulty with process models was the difficulty of parallel processing. Basically, in contrast to the rigidly serial, sequential nature of the standard model, evidence accumulated that different mental components could operate simultaneously, in parallel. Arranging the components in a

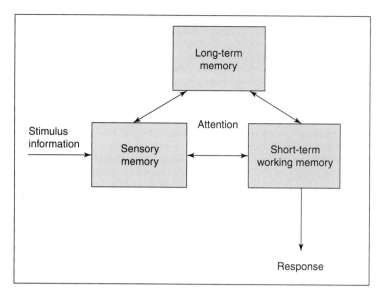

Figure 2-5

A revised information-processing model, showing how components can
continually interact with each other and how attention influences all three
components. Adapted from Neisser (1976).

triangle rather than in a horizontal row helps get away from the "first this, then the next
one" flavor of the standard model.

It also helps move us away from the simple computer analogy that formerly was so
central to the information-processing approach, the analogy that sold us on serial processing. Computers were —and for the most part still are—serial processors, but we now
believe that people definitely are not. Furthermore, the computer analogy told us that
one could understand the software of a system without having to worry about the hardware: You could study how the program worked, how it processed information, without
understanding the switches and wiring of the physical machine that did the computing.
The analogy therefore suggested that cognition could be understood with little or no
reference to the brain, to the physical organ in which cognition takes place.

An enormously important lesson we are continually learning from the neurosciences, however, is that this simple idea—that there is no real need to understand the
brain—is simply wrong. In compelling and clear ways, the brain shows countless ways
in which different cognitive components and processes—modules, if you like (Fodor,
1983)—are continually operating simultaneously, in parallel.

Context A second change, the bidirectional arrows, liberalizes the standard model even
more, helping to account for context and other effects. As you can see in the revised
model, information that is active in long-term memory, for example, can easily have an

effect *right now* on sensory memory, the input stage for external stimuli. Here is a simple example:

> As you read a sentence or paragraph, you begin to develop a feel for its meaning. Often you understand well enough that you can then skim through the rest of the material, possibly reading so rapidly that lower-level processes such as proofreading and noticing typograpical errors may not function as accurately as they usually do. Did you see the mistake?

What? Mistake? If you fell for it, you failed to notice the missing *h* in the word *typographical,* possibly because you were skimming but probably because the word *typographical* was expected, predictable based on meaning. You may have even "seen" the missing *h* in a sense. Why? Because your understanding of the passage, its meaningfulness to you, may have been strong enough that the missing *h* was supplied by your long-term memory.

We call such effects **top-down processing,** or **conceptually driven processing,** *when existing context or knowledge has an influence on earlier or simpler forms of mental processes.* It's one of the recurring themes in cognition (look again at Table 2-1). For another example, adapted from Reed (1992), read the following sentence:

> FINISHED FILES ARE THE RESULT OF YEARS OF SCIENTIFIC STUDY COMBINED WITH THE EXPERIENCE OF MANY YEARS.

Now, read it a second time, counting the number of times the letter *F* occurs.

If you counted fewer than six, try again—and again, if necessary. Why is this difficult?—Because you know that function words such as *of* carry very little meaning, your perceptual, input processes are prompted to pay attention only to the content words. Ignoring function words, and consequently failing to see the letter *F* in a word such as *OF,* is a clear-cut example of conceptually driven processing.

Fixing the Narrowness The final difficulty mentioned earlier concerned the narrowness of the strict information-processing approach, particularly its emphasis on RT measures of simple, fairly rapid mental processes. To a greater degree than was true before, cognitive science is now open to results based on a variety of research techniques, the verbal protocol technique prominently among them. To be sure, there are still detractors of the verbal protocol method, and studying the parameters of the method remains an important task (see Ericsson & Simon, 1993, for a recent update on how to do it). But the method is still useful, capable of revealing important observations about cognition. Furthermore, broadening cognitive psychology to include such techniques is very much in the spirit of other broadenings, in particular opening up to the evidence obtained from the neurosciences.

The early, strict information-processing approach and the research it generated were criticized soundly during the 1970s amid claims that the promise of cognitive psychology had been squandered, that there had really been no important progress (e.g., Neisser, 1976). A more temperate assessment, in my view, is that the early approach served its purpose. It gave us some important insights, helped illuminate some of its own shortcomings, and ultimately led us to discard some of the older approaches as we developed newer, more informative ways of doing science—sounds like the typical path of scientific progress, doesn't it?

■ Section Summary

- The strict information-processing approach to cognition was replaced with a broader, more inclusive approach now known as cognitive science. This approach describes cognition as the coordinated, often parallel operation of mental processes within a multicomponent memory system. The approach is deliberately multidisciplinary, accepting evidence from all the sciences interested in cognition.

Neurocognition: The Brain and Cognition Together

We start with a stunning story of cognitive disruption to motivate our current interest in neurocognition. Tulving (1989) described a patient known as K. C., a young man who sustained brain damage in a motorcycle accident. Some 9 years after the accident, he still showed pervasive disruption of long-term memory. The fascinating thing about his memory impairment was that it was selective: K. C. remains perfectly competent at language, his intelligence is normal, and he is able to converse on a number of topics. But when he is asked about an experience from his own past, he cannot remember; in Tulving's words, "he cannot remember, in the sense of bringing back to conscious awareness, a single thing that he has ever done or experienced in the past" (p. 362). For example, even though he remembers how to play chess, he does not remember ever having played it before. K. C.'s brain damage seemed to destroy his ability to access what we'll call episodic memory, his own autobiographical knowledge, while leaving his general knowledge system—his semantic memory—intact. This pattern is called a **dissociation,** *a disruption in one component of memory but no impairment of another.* Can these two forms of long-term memory, episodic and semantic memory, be the same given K. C.'s dissociation between the two? Probably not. So we now ask a more general question: How must the cognitive system be organized for disruptions such as these to take place?

The area of investigation we are introducing here is sometimes called *cognitive neuropsychology,* a "hybrid term . . . applied to the analysis of those handicaps in human cognitive function which result from brain injury" (McCarthy & Warrington, 1990, p. 1). As important as the evidence from brain damage is, we also need other kinds of evidence, such as information about the neurochemical and neurobiological activities that support normal learning and thought processes and changes in the brain that accompany aging. We are therefore interested in contributions from all the various neurosciences—neurochemistry, neurobiology, neuroanatomy, and so on—as they relate to human cognition. Because existing terms often have different or even controversial connotations, I have elected to call this field the study of *neurocognition,* the neuroscience of cognition.

IN DEPTH

Dissociations and Double Dissociations

The concept of **dissociation**—the opposite of association—is important, so we should spend a little more time on it.

Consider two mental processes that "go together" in some cognitive task, called process A and process B. By looking at these processes as they may be disrupted in brain damage, we can determine how separable the processes are.

Complete separability is a double dissociation. Evidence of a double dissociation requires at least two patients, with "opposite" or reciprocal deficits. For example,

- Patient X has a lesion in one region of the brain that has disrupted process A. His performance on tasks that use process B is intact, not disrupted at all.
- Patient Y has a lesion that has damaged process B, but tasks that use process A are normal, not disrupted by the damage.

Think of a double dissociation as illustrated in this simple Venn diagram and refer back to it later in the book as you read about processes that are dissociated. If these circles depicted actual brain regions, such as those used in language processes (Chapter 9), then damage to

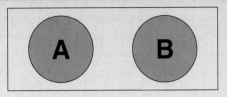

either of them could easily leave the other one unaffected.

- In a simple dissociation, process A could be damaged and process B intact, yet no other known patient has the reciprocal pattern. For example, semantic retrieval (retrieving the meaning of a concept) could be intact while lexical retrieval (finding the name for the concept) could be disrupted; this is called anomia. In this situation, lexical retrieval is dissociated from semantic retrieval, but it is probably impossible to observe the opposite pattern; how can you name a concept if you can't retrieve the concept in the first place?
- In a full or complete association (lack of dissociation), disruption of one of the processes always accompanies disruption in the other process. This pattern implies that processes A and B rely on the same region or brain mechanism, such as recognizing objects and recognizing pictures of those objects (see Chapter 3).

Understanding cognitive handicaps is an obvious goal; no one can dispute the importance of rehabilitation and retraining for patients with brain damage. But our interest in cognitive science goes a step further. We want to understand *normal* cognition from the standpoint of the human brain. That is, we want to learn about normal cognition through whatever means are available to us. Toward this goal, more and more investigators are beginning to examine the behavioral and cognitive effects of brain damage (e.g., McCloskey, 1992). As you will see throughout this book, sometimes the great misfortune of brain damage leads to a clearer understanding of normal processes.

Likewise, cognitive science is now putting to good use the new, high-tech brain imaging capabilities we have adopted from medicine. We can now use brain images based on positron emission tomagraphy (PET) scans and magnetic resonance imaging (MRI) to localize regions of activity during different kinds of cognitive processing, testing not just brain-damaged individuals but normal, intact ones as well (see Sarter, Berntson, & Cacioppo, 1996, for a thoughtful piece on interpreting such evidence).

We first cover a bit of neural functioning here, then look at some major anatomic features of the brain. We then conclude by talking about several methods of studying brain and cognition, including a computer-based modeling approach inspired by the neurosciences. Just as the cognitive influence on the neurosciences has been a rejuvenating one, in the opinions of several researchers (e.g., Moscovitch, 1979; Seron, 1982), the cross-fertilization for cognition has been crucial and will only become more so with time. Of course, we can focus only on a few highlights of the topic of neurocognition here; as Crick and Asanuma (1986, p. 333) said of their chapter, "It is clearly impossible to describe most of what is known, even though this represents [only] a tiny fraction of what one would like to know."

Basic Neurology

At birth, the human brain weighs approximately 400 g (about 14 oz). It grows to an average of 1,450 g in adults, slightly more than 3 lb, and is roughly the size of a ripe grapefruit. The basic building block of the brain, indeed of the entire nervous system, is the **neuron,** *the cell that is specialized for receiving and transmitting a neural impulse.* Neurons are the components that form nerve tracts throughout the body and in all brain structures. How many neurons are there in the brain? Unfortunately, the available estimates vary tremendously. Kolb and Whishaw (1996) suggest a grand total of 180 billion cells of all types in the brain, including not only neurons but nonneural cells too (e.g., connective and circulatory tissue). Some 80 billion of these cells, in Kolb and Whishaw's estimate, are "directly engaged in information processing" and cognition (p. 39). To put that figure in perspective, consider that the Milky Way galaxy has about 100 billion stars.

Neurons Figure 2-6A illustrates an idealized or prototypical **neuron.** The details of structure vary, but each neuron within the nervous system has the same general features. At one end of the neuron, many small branchlike fingers called *dendrites* gather a neural impulse into the neuron itself. In somewhat more familiar terms, the dendrites are the *input* structures of the neuron, taking in the message that is being passed along in a particular neural tract.

The central portion of each neuron is the cell body, or *soma*, where the biological activity of the cell is regulated. Extending from the cell body is a longish extension or tube, the *axon*, that ends in another set of branch-like structures called *axon terminals* or sometimes *terminal arborizations;* the latter term derives from the treelike form of these

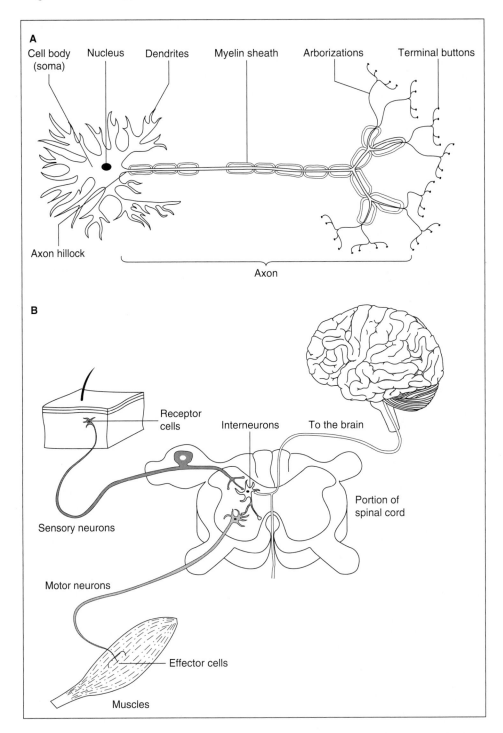

Figure 2-6

An illustration of the various structures of the neuron. Note that the lower diagram illustrates a sensory–motor reflex arc.

structures. The axon terminals are the *output* end of the neuron, the place where the neural impulse ends within the neuron itself. Obviously, this is the location where an influence on the next neuron in the pathway must take place.

Figure 2-6B is a schematic diagram of the basic elements of the nervous system that are activated during a simple reflex, such as jerking your arm away when you accidentally touch a hot stove. *Receptor cells* react to the physical stimulus and trigger a pattern of firing down a sequence of *sensory neurons.* The tracts of sensory neurons pass the message along into the spinal cord, which normally routes the message in two directions. For the simple reflex action, the message loops quickly through the spinal cord and then goes back out to the arm muscles through a tract of *motor neurons.* These terminate at the *effector cells,* which connect directly to the muscle fibers and cause the muscles to pull your arm away from the hot stove.

As the reflex triggers the quick return of a message out to the muscles, it simultaneously routes a message up the spinal cord and into the brain. Thus the second route involves only the central nervous system, the spinal cord and brain. There is only one kind of neuron in the central nervous system, called an *interneuron* or *association neuron.* Because we are concerned only with the brain here, we are interested only in the interneurons of the central nervous system. Thus, for the rest of the chapter, I simply refer to neurons rather than interneurons.

Synapses There may be relatively few or many axon terminals emanating from a single neuron. In either case, these terminals are adjacent to dendrites from other neurons. Thus an impulse within a neuron terminates at the axon terminals and is taken up by the dendrites of the next neurons in the pathway, the neurons whose dendrites are adjacent to the axon terminals. The *region where the axon terminals of one neuron and the dendrites of another come together* is the **synapse.** For the most part, the neurons do not actually touch one another (some regions of the brain contradict this rule). Instead, the synapses in the human nervous system are extremely small physical gaps or clefts between the neurons. Note also that the word *synapse* is used as a verb: A neuron is said to synapse on another, meaning that it passes its message on to that other neuron.

A general law of the nervous system, especially in the brain, is that any single neuron synapses on a large number of other neurons. The evidence for this *divergence* is that a typical neuron synapses on anywhere from 100 to as many as 15,000 other neurons (Kolb & Whishaw, 1996). Likewise, many different neurons can synapse on a single destination neuron, a principle known as *convergence.*

For the bulk of the nervous system, the bridge across the synaptic cleft involves chemical activity within the synaptic cleft itself. A neuron releases a chemical transmitter substance, or simply a *neurotransmitter,* from small *buttons* or *sacs* in the axon terminals. This chemical fits into specific receptor sites on the dendrites of the next neuron and thereby causes some effect on that next neuron. Two general effects are possible: excitation and inhibition. A *Type I* neuron contains a neurotransmitter that has an excitatory effect; it tends to activate or fire the neuron on which it synapses. *Type II* neurons, conversely, release a different kind of neurotransmitter, one that has an inhibitory effect;

it tends to prevent the firing of the neuron on which it synapses. As Crick and Asanuma (1986) pointed out, this "working assumption" about Type I and II neurons is important for several reasons, including the important observation that "no axon makes Type I synapses at some sites while making Type II at others" (p. 339). In other words, if neuron A makes an excitatory synapse on neuron B, then A will not also inhibit neuron C (but of course some other neuron could inhibit B or C).

Neurotransmitters Some 30 different neurotransmitters have been identified and studied (Iversen, 1979). Many seem to have rather ordinary functions, maintaining the physical integrity of the living organism, for instance. Others, especially acetylcholine and possibly norepinephrine, seem to have major influences on cognitive processes such as learning and memory (Drachman, 1978; Sitaran, Weingartner, Caine, & Gillin, 1978; Squire, 1987). Interestingly, decreased levels of acetylcholine have been found in the brains of people with Alzheimer's disease, with very low levels of acetylcholine associated with more severe dementia (Samuel, 1999). It is tempting to suggest this as part of the explanation for the learning and memory deficits observed among such patients, although it could be a side effect of the disease instead (e.g., Riley, 1989). In either case, the result suggests that acetylcholine plays some kind of essential role in normal learning and memory processes.

Before leaving the neuronal level of the nervous system, note that significant research is being done on various psychobiochemical properties of the neural system, such as the direct influence of different chemical agents on neurotransmitters and the resulting behavioral changes. As an example, Thompson (1986) described progress in identifying neuronal changes believed to underlie memory storage and retrieval. Just as various psychoactive drugs affect the functioning of the nervous system in a physical sense, current research is now identifying the effects of drugs and other treatments on the functioning of the nervous system in a psychological or cognitive sense (e.g., the effect of alcohol intoxication; Nelson, McSpadden, Fromme, & Marlatt, 1986).

Brain Anatomy

Ignoring many levels of intermediate neural functioning and complexity, we now take a tremendous leap from the level of single neurons to the level of the entire brain, the awesomely complex "biological computer." To account for all human behavior, including bodily functions that occur involuntarily (e.g., digestion), would entail an extensive discussion of both the central and the peripheral systems. But to explore neurocognition, we can limit ourselves to just the central nervous system, the brain and spinal cord. In fact, our discussion even omits much of the central nervous system, save for the neocortex (or cerebral cortex), which sits at the top of the human brain, and a few other nearby structures.

In Figure 2-7, the physically lower brain structures are collectively called the old brain or brain stem. This portion of the brain is older in terms of evolution, for the most part governing basic, primitive functions (e.g., digestion, heartbeat, and breathing). The old brain structures are present in all mammals.

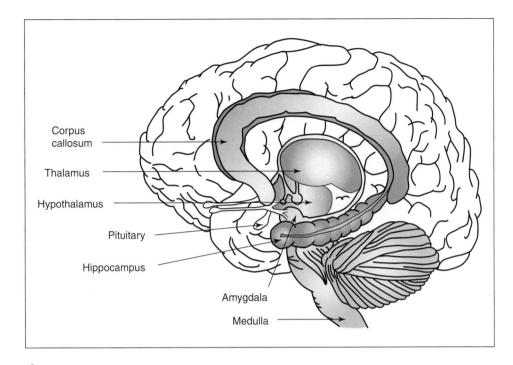

Corpus
callosum

Thalamus

Hypothalamus

Pituitary

Hippocampus

Amygdala

Medulla

Figure 2-7

Lower brain structures.

Figure 2-8 shows the **neocortex,** or **cerebral cortex,** *the top layer of the brain, respon-sible for higher-level mental processes.* The neocortex is a wrinkled, convoluted structure that nearly surrounds the old brain. Laid out flat, each of the two halves or hemispheres would cover about a square meter and be the thickness of the cover of a hardback book (from about 1.5 to 3 mm thick). The wrinkling is "nature's solution to the problem of confining the huge neocortical surface area within a skull that is still small enough to pass through the birth canal" (Kolb & Whishaw, 1996, p. 51). It is the most recent structure to have evolved in the human brain (*neo* means "new") and is much larger in humans than in other animals; com-pare the average weight in humans, 1,450 g, with that of the great apes, 400 g.

Because it is primarily responsible for higher mental processes such as language and thought, it is not surprising that the human neocortex is so large relative to the rest of the brain. About three fourths of the neurons in the human brain are in the neocor-tex. The number of neurons in the neocortex has been estimated at anywhere from 5 to 100 billion; from 10 to 20 billion is a safe, somewhat conservative figure.

The side or lateral view (*lateral* simply means "to the side") in Figure 2-8 reveals the four general regions or *lobes* of the neocortex; clockwise from the front, these are the *frontal lobe, parietal lobe, occipital lobe,* and *temporal lobe,* named after the skull bones on top of them (e.g., the temporal lobes lie beneath your temples). Note that these lobes are not separate from one another in the brain. Instead, each hemisphere of the neocortex

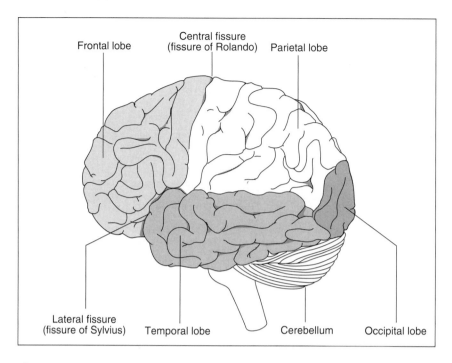

Frontal lobe

Central fissure
(fissure of Rolando)

Parietal lobe

Lateral fissure
(fissure of Sylvius)

Temporal lobe

Cerebellum

Occipital lobe

Figure 2-8

The four lobes of the neocortex.

is a single sheet of neural matter. The lobes are formed by the larger folds and convolutions of the cortex, with the names used as convenient reference terms for the regions. As an example, the central fissure, or fissure of Rolando, shown in the figure is merely one of the deeper folds in the brain, serving as a convenient landmark between the frontal and parietal lobes.

Three other subcortical (below the neocortex) structures are especially important to neurocognition. Deep inside the lower brain structures is the *thalamus,* meaning "inner room" or "chamber." It is often called the gateway to the cortex because almost all messages entering the cortex come through the thalamus (a portion of the sense of smell is one of the very few exceptions). In other words, the thalamus is the major relay station from the sensory systems of the body into the neocortex.

Just above the thalamus is a broad band of nerve fibers called the *corpus callosum.* As described later, the corpus callosum ("callous body") is the primary bridge across which messages pass between the left and right halves of the neocortex.

The third structure is the *hippocampus,* from the Latin word for "sea horse," referring to its curved shape. The hippocampus lies immediately interior to the temporal lobes, that is, underneath the temporal lobes but in the same horizontal plane. Research on the effects of hippocampal damage is described later in the book (especially in Chapter 6), including one of the best known case histories in neuropsychology, that of patient H. M.

Principles of Functioning

Two important principles of functioning in the neocortex are described here, necessary background knowledge for understanding the effects of brain damage on cognitive processes. These principles involve the ideas of contralaterality and hemispheric specialization.

Contralaterality When viewed from the top, the neocortex is seen to be divided into two mirror-image halves, the left and right cerebral hemispheres. This follows a general law of anatomy, that with the exception of internal organs such as the heart, the body is basically bilaterally symmetrical. What is somewhat surprising, however, is that *the receptive and control centers for one side of the body are in the opposite hemisphere of the brain.* This is **contralaterality** (*contra* means "against" or "opposite"). In other words, for evolutionary reasons that will probably remain obscure forever, the right hemisphere of the brain receives its input from the left side of the body and also controls the left side. Likewise, the left hemisphere receives input from and controls output to the right side of the body.

Hemispheric Specialization The second surprise concerning lateralization in the neocortex involves different specializations within the two cerebral hemispheres. Despite their mirror-image appearance, the two hemispheres do not mirror one another's abilities. Instead, each hemisphere tends to specialize in different abilities and tends to process different kinds of information. This is the full principle of **cerebral lateralization** and specialization: *different functions or actions within the brain tend to rely more heavily on one hemisphere or the other or tend to be performed differently in the two hemispheres.*

Table 2-2 SUMMARY OF DATA ON CEREBRAL LATERALIZATION

Function	Left Hemisphere	Right Hemisphere
Visual system	Letters, words	Complex geometric patterns Faces
Auditory system	Language-related sounds	Nonlanguage environmental sounds Music
Somatosensory system	?	Tactile recognition of complex patterns Braille
Movement	Complex voluntary movement	Movements in spatial patterns
Memory	Verbal memory	Nonverbal Memory
Language	Speech Reading Writing Arithmetic	Prosody Narrative Inference
Spatial processes		Geometry Sense of direction Mental rotation of shapes

Note. Functions of the respective hemispheres that are mediated predominantly by one hemisphere in right-handed people.

This is not to say that some process or function can happen *only* in one particular hemisphere. It merely says that there is often a tendency, sometimes strong, for one or the other hemisphere to be especially dominant in different processes or functions.

The most obvious evidence of lateralization in humans is the overwhelming incidence of right-handedness across all cultures and apparently throughout the known history of human evolution (Corballis, 1989). Accompanying this tendency toward right-handedness is a particularly strong left-hemispheric specialization in humans for language. That is, for the majority of people, language ability is especially lateralized in the left hemisphere of the neocortex; countless studies have demonstrated this general tendency (see Provins, 1997, for a review of the handedness–speech relationship).

In contrast, the right cerebral hemisphere seems to be somewhat more specialized than the left hemisphere for nonverbal, spatial, and more perceptual information processing (see Banich, 1997, and Moscovitch, 1979, for reviews of such left–right hemisphere characterizations). For instance, the evidence suggests that face recognition (Ellis, 1983) and mental rotation (Deutsch, Bourbon, Papanicolaou, & Eisenberg, 1988), both requiring spatial and perceptual processing, are especially dependent on the right cerebral hemisphere. Table 2-2 provides a summary of data on cerebral lateralization.

Most people have heard of these "left brain versus right brain" issues, often from the popular press. Such treatments are notorious for exaggerating and oversimplifying what is known about laterality and specialization. For instance, in these descriptions the left hemisphere ends up with the rational, logical, and symbolic abilities—the boring ones—whereas the right hemisphere gets the holistic, creative, and intuitive processes—the sexy ones. Corballis (1989, p. 501) noted that the right hemisphere achieves "a certain cult status" in some such treatments.

But even ignoring that oversimplification, it is far too easy to misunderstand the principle of hemispheric lateralization and specialization, too easy to say "process X happens in *this* hemisphere, process Y in *that* one." Even the simplest act of cognition, say naming a picture, involves multiple components, distributed widely across both hemispheres, and complex coordination of the components. Disruption of any one of those components could disrupt picture naming. Thus several different patients, each with dramatically different localized brain damage, could show an inability to name a picture, each for a different reason relating to different lateralized processes.

Nonetheless, there is a striking division of labor in the neocortex, in which the left cerebral hemisphere is specialized for language. This is almost always true; it characterizes up to 85% or 90% of the population. The percentages are this high, however, only if you are a right-handed male with no family history of left-handedness and if you write with your hand in a normal rather than inverted position (Friedman & Polson, 1981). If you are female, if you are left-handed, if you write with an inverted hand position, and so on, then the "left hemisphere language rule" is not quite as strong. In such groups, the majority have the customary pattern, but the percentages are not as high; for example, Bryden's (1982) review indicated that 79% of women have language lateralized to the left hemisphere. Thus directing language input to the left cerebral hemisphere is optimal and efficient for many people, but not for all. (For simplicity, however, we rely on the convenient fiction that language is processed in the left hemisphere for most people.)

Split Brain Research and Lateralization

Despite the exaggerated claims you often read, there has been a good deal of careful empirical work on the topic of lateralization and specialization of different regions in the two hemispheres. Among the best known is the research on split brain patients.

Before about 1960, evidence of hemispheric specialization was rather indirect; neurologists and researchers simply noted the location and kind of head injury that was sustained and the kind of behavioral or cognitive deficit that was observed after the injury. Sperry (e.g., 1964; Gazzaniga & Sperry, 1967), however, put the facts of anatomy together with a surgical procedure for severe epilepsy. In this operation, the corpus callosum is completely severed to restrict the epileptic seizure to just one of the cerebral hemispheres. For patients who needed this radical surgery, a remarkably informative test could be administered, one that could reveal the different abilities and actions of the two cerebral hemispheres. That is, from the standpoint of brain functioning, when a patient's corpus callosum is surgically cut, the two hemispheres cannot communicate internally with each other. Sperry's technique was to test such people by directing sensory information to one side or the other of the body (e.g., by placing a pencil in the left or right hand of such a patient or presenting a visual stimulus to the left or right visual field).

The effect of the surgery was to prevent the neural activation that arrived in one hemisphere from crossing over to the other hemisphere. Thus if a patient had a pencil placed in the left hand (the patients were prevented from seeing the objects and their hands, of course), the neural impulse was directed to the right hemisphere but then could not cross over into the left hemisphere. The patients usually were able to demonstrate the use for the object when the sensation was sent to the right hemisphere by making the appropriate hand movements, as if they were writing with the pencil. Nonetheless, they usually could not name the object unless it was placed in the right hand. This is exactly what would be expected from someone whose knowledge of language is localized in the left hemisphere but whose perceptual, nonverbal knowledge is localized in the right hemisphere. Similar effects were obtained with purely visual stimuli as well, that is, when the left half of a picture was projected to the right hemisphere and vice versa. (Incidentally, Sperry earned the Nobel prize for medicine in 1981 for his research; the award was made jointly to him and to Hubel and Wiesel, whose research on specialized feature detectors in the visual cortex is described in Chapter 3.)

Although the principle of laterality has been a mainstay of neurological research for a long period of time, recent evidence suggests that lateralization of skills usually is not as absolute as was previously believed (e.g., in the area of language and speech; see Chapter 9). For such reasons, current researchers usually subscribe to the less extreme version of this principle given earlier. For instance, we say that different functions tend to occur more or less efficiently in one hemisphere or the other, tend to occur somewhat differently in one side or the other (Friedman & Polson, 1981; Moscovitch, 1979), or that the two hemispheres contribute different components to an ability or process (see Gardner, 1985, and Gazzaniga, 1995, for useful discussions of this issue).

Methods of Investigation

The methods for investigating the structure and functioning of the brain fall into two broad categories, those involving medically based techniques and those based on behavioral assessments.

Lesions Needless to say, the investigation techniques used by Sperry, deliberate lesioning of the brain, are limited in their usefulness for revealing the secrets of cognitive processing. Only two kinds of subjects—laboratory animals and patients with medical conditions requiring brain surgery—can be used. A long-standing tradition, however, reports case studies of people or groups of people who by disease or accident have experienced damage or lesions, to the brain. Much of the evidence described throughout the book comes from victims of strokes, aneurysms, head injuries, and other accidental circumstances. In all cases, the site and extent of the brain lesion are important guides to the kind of disruption in behavior that is observed and vice versa (a clear description of the lesion method is found in Damasio & Damasio, 1997).

Direct Stimulation A variety of other techniques have also been used to study localization and specialization of function in the brain. In particular, consider the method of direct stimulation, pioneered by Penfield, the famous Canadian neurosurgeon. In Penfield's technique, the patient in brain surgery remains conscious during the surgery, with only a local anesthetic used to prevent pain in the scalp. The surgeon then applies

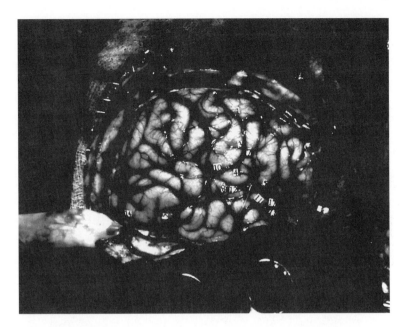

Figure 2-9

The exposed cortex of one of Penfield's patients. Numbers indicate the areas of the brain Penfield stimulated with the electric probe. When area 13 was stimulated, the patient recalled a circus scene. Stimulating other areas also evoked specific memories. From Penfield (1958).

minute electrical charges to the exposed brain, thus triggering very small regions. The patient is then asked to answer questions or report out loud the thoughts and memories that enter awareness. By comparing the patient's reports with the different regions that are stimulated, a kind of map of cerebral functioning can be developed (Figure 2-9).

Generally, the patients in Penfield's procedure reported ideas or episodes that had a dreamlike quality. Although they often reported seemingly distinct memories, it was seldom possible to check on the accuracy of these reports. Their dreamlike nature suggests that they were heavily influenced by reconstructive processes; that is, they may not have been genuine, recalled memories. On the other hand, by stimulating different regions of the exposed brain, a great deal has been discovered about the localization of different functions, kinds of knowledge, and so on, in different parts of the neocortex (e.g., Ojemann, 1982; Ojemann & Creutzfeldt, 1987; Penfield & Jasper, 1954; Penfield & Milner, 1958; for an update on such methods, see Gordon, Hart, Boatman, & Lesser, 1997).

Although such research often yields fascinating evidence, it has some clear difficulties. For one thing, it is necessarily restricted to clinical settings (i.e., patients needing brain surgery). Second, there is at least some evidence that the organization of a patient's brain function may differ substantially from the normal pattern (i.e., in epileptic patients; Kolb & Whishaw, 1996), thus limiting the generalizability of such results.

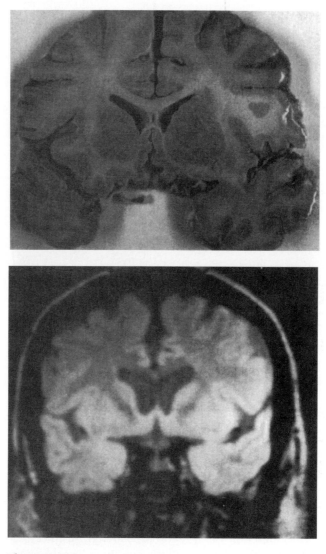

Figure 2-10

The clarity of a magnetic resonance imaging view (**B**) of the brain as compared with a photograph of a dissected brain (**A**). The position of the coronal section is shown in the line drawing.

Imaging Technology Much work is now being done with the recent developments in the medical technology of brain imaging (e.g., Toga & Mazziotta, 1996; see Posner, 1997, for a concise introduction). Imaging techniques such as the computed tomography (CT) scan and **magnetic resonance imaging (MRI)** can give surprisingly clear pictures of the structure of the brain, as shown in Figure 2-10. More exciting still are techniques that yield images of the *functioning* of the brain, such as the positron emission tomography

(PET) scan or functional MRI techniques (see the several color plates inside the cover of this book). In this technique, the image shows regions of the brain with heightened neural activity, with different colors reflecting high or low levels of blood flow, oxygen uptake, and the like. The logic here is very straightforward: If a region becomes active because of mental processing, the metabolic rate of that region increases, so increases in oxygenated blood flow are seen.

An obvious advantage to these techniques is that they show the brain in action rather than just showing the physical structures in the brain. Such scans are called *functional* because they show the brain as it is functioning, performing some mental task. A second advantage is that they can be applied with (apparently) minimal risk to normal subjects.

The set of color pictures from Tulving's (1989) article on the dissociation between episodic and semantic memory (color plate #3) relied on a similar procedure, computer-assisted detection of blood flow patterns in a patient injected with an irradiated substance that binds to oxygen in the blood. Note, however, that imaging techniques that measure blood flow have a time lag drawback; the increase in metabolic activity can lag anywhere from several hundred milliseconds to several seconds after the cognitive activity.

Electroencephalograms and Event-Related Potentials   Other techniques measure the brain's electrical activity online, immediately. Traditionally, brain wave patterns were studied rather crudely with electroencephalogram (EEG) recordings. In this technique, electrodes are attached to the subject's scalp, and the device records the patterns of brain waves. More recently, researchers have focused on **event-related potentials (ERPs),** the momentary changes in electrical activity of the brain when a particular stimulus is presented to the subject (e.g., Donchin, 1981; Rugg & Coles, 1995).

As an example, read the following sentence (adapted from Banich, 1997): "Running out the door, Patty grabbed her jacket, her baseball glove, her cap, a softball, and a skyscraper."

Of course you noticed that *skyscraper* does not fit the context of the sentence; it's called a semantic anomaly. What is fascinating is that the ERP recording of your brain wave activities would show a marked change about 400 msec after you read *skyscraper*, an electrically negative wave called N4 or N400. The N4 would be present, though smaller, if the last word in the sentence had been *lamp*, and at baseline if the last word were *bat*.

Osterhout and Holcomb (1992) found this N4 effect for semantic anomalies and also a similar effect when the grammar or syntax of the sentence violated normal language rules. They showed their participants control sentences along with sentences that contained grammatical or syntactic anomalies:

(Control) John told the man to leave.

(Anomalous) John hoped the man to leave.

With this manipulation of syntactic anomaly, Osterhout and Holcomb found a pronounced P6 or P600 effect, an electrically positive change in activity, roughly centered

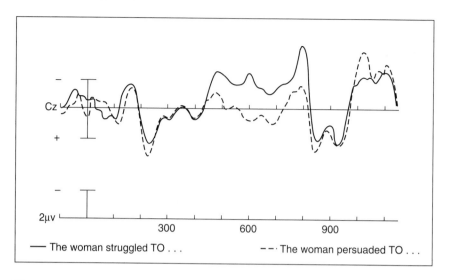

Figure 2-11

Mean ERPs to syntactically acceptable sentences (solid curve) and syntactically anomalous sentences (dotted curve). The P600 component, shown as a dip in the dotted curve, shows the effect of detecting the syntactic anomaly. Note that in this figure, positive changes go downward. Reprinted with permission from "Introduction and Overview" by E. D. Bigler, R. A. Yeo, and F. Turkheimer, in *Neuropsychological Function and Brain Imaging* (p. 10), edited by E. D. Bigler, R. A. Yeo, and E. Turkheimer, 1989, New York, Plenum Press.

on 600 msec after reading the word *to* (the word that signals the syntactic violation). Figure 2-11 shows their result. Clearly, our language comprehension system reacts differently—and very quickly—when we encounter unusual or incorrect sentences.

The ERP technology gives very little useful information about *where* such mental mechanisms are, although it can show in good detail *when* those mechanisms operate in an online task. By carefully controlling surrounding conditions and measuring the elapsed time since a stimulus was presented, we can begin to see how the electrical activity of the brain changes moment by moment when the subject is processing a stimulus.

■ Section Summary

- Aside from time and accuracy measures and more modern methods based on verbal reports, cognitive science specifically includes a variety of measures from the neurosciences, in particular brain imaging and ERP data.
- In addition to the basic functioning of neurons, a thorough understanding of modern cognitive science must include an understanding of brain anatomy and two important principles of brain function and architecture: the principle of contralaterality and the principle of hemispheric specialization. The latter refers to the fact that specific types

"NO GOOD. IT'S STILL NOT WORRYING ABOUT HOW IT'S DOING."

of processes (e.g., language) tend to be represented in and controlled by separate, lateralized regions of the brain.

- Older methods of investigating cognitive processes in the brain included studying the behavioral effects of brain lesions and direct stimulation of the brain during surgery. Modern imaging techniques such as PET and MRI scans, along with the important ERP technology, continue to yield important new evidence, and can be used on normal, intact participants.

Neural Net Models: Connectionism

We conclude the chapter with a very brief presentation on connectionism, an important computer-based approach to theories in cognitive science. Although you will encounter connectionism at several points throughout this book, it will be useful to learn a few general characteristics of this approach now, especially because of the strong similarities between this approach and that of neurocognition.

Connectionist models are often called **neural net models** or **parallel distributed processing (PDP) models;** the three terms are synonymous. They refer to *a computer-based technique for modeling complex systems*. A fundamental principle in connectionist models is that the simple nodes or units that make up the system are interconnected. Knowledge, all the way from the simplest to the most complex, is represented in these models as simple interconnected units. The connections between units can either be excitatory or inhibitory; that is, the connections can have positive or negative weights. The basic units receive positive and negative activation from other units, and depending on these patterns they in turn transmit activation to yet other units. Furthermore, the interconnectedness of these basic units usually is described as "massive" because there is no particular restriction on the number of interconnections any unit can have. That is, in principle, any bit of knowledge or information can be connected or related to an almost limitless number of other units.

Figure 2-12 illustrates an early connectionist model by McClelland and Rumelhart (1981), a model that dealt with word recognition. The bottom row of nodes or units represents simple features, simple patterns such as a horizontal line and a vertical line, each connected to letters at the next higher level, which in turn are connected to words at the top level. For simplicity, look at the feature on the far left, the horizontal line. The connection directly up from that to the capital letter *A* would be a positive, excitatory connection because the letter *A* has two horizontal lines. The connection from this feature up to the letter *N*, however, would be a negative, inhibitory one: If the feature detection system detects a horizontal line, that works against recognition of the letter *N*. In the same fashion, the capital *A* would have a positive connection up to the word *ABLE* because *A* is in the first position there, but it would have a negative, inhibitory connection to *TRAP* because *TRAP* does not begin with the letter *A*.

Referring to such models by the term *parallel distributed processing* highlights a different facet of the brain and the computer system. Mental processes operate in a thoroughly parallel fashion and are widely distributed across the brain; likewise, processing in a PDP model is thoroughly parallel and distributed across multiple levels of knowledge. As an example, even as the feature detectors at the bottom of the model are being matched to an incoming stimulus, word units at the top of the model may already be activated. Thus, activation from higher levels may influence processing at lower levels, even as the lower levels affect activation at higher levels.

Consider how the system would recognize the word *TRAP* in the sentence "After the bear attacked the visiting tourists, hunters went into the forest to set a trap." Even as the feature and letter detector units would be working on the *T*, then the *R*, and so forth, word units at the top would have already received activation based on the meaning and context of the sentence; with bears attacking tourists and hunters going into the forest, the word *TRAP* is highly predictable from the context, but *CART* would not be. Given this context, *TRAP* would be more easily recognized, perhaps because the features within the letters would have been activated by the context already. In this fashion, the comprehension and word recognition systems would be operating in parallel with the feature and letter detection systems, each making continuing, simultaneous contributions to each other and to overall mental processing.

The similarity of the connectionist scheme to the functioning of the brain is obvious and vitally important because it is widely believed that connectionist models

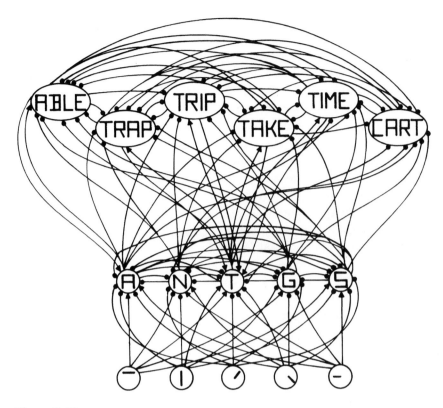

Figure 2-12

An illustration of part of McClelland and Rumelhart's (1981) PDP model of feature, letter, and word recognition. From "An Interactive Activation Model of Context Effects in Letter Perception: Part 1. An Account of Basic Findings" by J. L. McClelland and D. E. Rumelhart, 1981, *Psychological Review, 88,* p. 30. Copyright 1981 by the American Psychological Association. Reprinted by permission.

operate on the same—or at least very similar—basic principles as the brain (McClelland, Rumelhart, & Hinton, 1986). In other words, the connectionist framework may give us an excellent way of modeling and simulating cognitive processes as they function in the brain.

■ Section Summary

- The notion that human cognition is analogous to processing in a computer system has been abandoned at the detailed level, especially because of evidence of widespread parallel processing in humans. Connectionist (neural net, PDP) models can simulate such parallel processes, however, and therefore may be excellent ways of modeling human cognitive processes.

Key Terms

cerebral cortex (p. 59)
cerebral lateralization (p. 61)
channel capacity (p. 41)
cognitive science (p. 50)
conceptually driven
    processing (p. 52)
connectionist models (p. 69)
contralaterality (p. 61)
dissociation (p. 53)
encoding (p. 43)
event-related potentials
    (ERPs) (p. 67)
independent and
    nonoverlapping (p. 47)

information-processing
    approach (p. 35)
lexical decision task (p. 44)
long-term memory (p. 43)
metatheory (p. 35)
magnetic resonance
    imaging (MRI) (p. 66)
neocortex (p. 59)
neural net models (p. 69)
neuron (p. 55)
parallel distributed
    processing (PDP)
    models (p. 69

parallel processing (p. 48)
process model (p. 44)
reaction time (RT) (p. 37)
sequential stages of
    processing (p. 47)
sensory memory (p. 43)
short-term memory (p. 43)
synapse (p. 57)
top-down processing (p. 52)
verbal protocol (p. 49)
word frequency effect
    (p. 45)

CHAPTER **3**

Perception and Pattern Recognition

Even psychologists who ought to know better have acted as if they believed (1) that the subject's visual experience directly mirrors the stimulus pattern; (2) that his visual experience begins when the pattern is first exposed and terminates when it is turned off; (3) that his experience, itself a passive—if fractional—copy of the stimulus, is in turn mirrored by his verbal report. (Neisser, 1967, p. 16)

Where an object fails to be recognized by sight, it often happens that the patient will recognize and name it as soon as he touches it with his hand. This shows in an interesting way how numerous the associative paths are which all end by running out of the brain through the channel of speech. The hand-path is open, though the eye-path be closed. (James, 1890, p. 61)

It's a wonder we can see anything at all, or hear anything, for that matter. The structure of the eye is so implausible, even backward, and the ear so jury-rigged, so indirect, that our impressive sensory powers are all the more amazing. We can see the flame of a single candle, on a dark night, from a distance of 20 miles, and can hear a watch ticking 20 feet away in a large, quiet room (Galanter, 1962). And this sensitivity is far exceeded by the complexity of mental processing once perception begins. Because we "understand" what we have seen so quickly, with so little effort, "we can be deceived into thinking that vision should therefore be fairly simple to perform" (Hildreth & Ullman, 1989), and likewise for hearing too. As you will realize over and over in this chapter (and throughout this book), the mere fact that a process is rapid and happens out of your awareness does not mean it is simple, or simple to investigate. Indeed, if anything, just the opposite is probably true.

This chapter presents a basic study of perception and pattern recognition, in both the visual and auditory modalities. We focus especially on the mechanisms and properties of the visual and auditory sensory registers because they are at the intersection between the environment and the human cognitive system. Several theories of perception and pattern recognition are covered, including an elaboration of the connectionist model you studied in Chapter 2. And in the final section of the chapter, we consider brain-related disruptions in perception and pattern recognition, like those James was discussing in his quotation earlier. We will see what deficits in recognition tell us about the normal processes we take for granted.

Visual Perception

Figure 3-1 illustrates the basic sensory equipment involved in human vision. Light waves enter the eye, are focused and inverted by the lens, and are projected onto the **retina.** The retinal surface is composed of three basic layers of neurons: *rods and cones,*

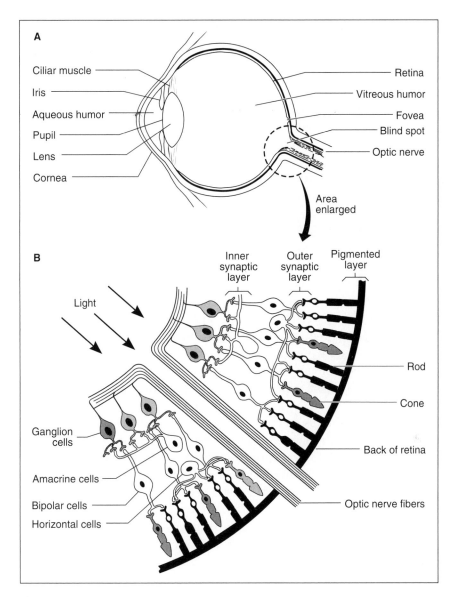

Figure 3-1

A. The structure of the human eye, foveal pit, the optic nerve, and other structures.
B. The retina, rods and cones, and ganglion cells. From Hothersall, 1985.

bipolar cells, and ganglion cells (see Figure 3-1B). The rods and cones form the back layer of neurons on the retina and are the first neurons stimulated by light. Thus these photosensitive neurons begin the process of vision. Patterns of neural firing from the rods and cones are forwarded to the second layer of neurons, the bipolar cells, which collect the messages and then pass them along to the third layer, the ganglion cells. The extended axons of the ganglion cells converge at the rear of the eye, forming a bundle known as the optic nerve. This nerve exits the eye and continues back through various structures in the optic system (e.g., the optic chiasm, the junction of the optic nerve from each eye), eventually projecting the neural message onto the visual cortex of the brain, in the lower rear portion of the skull.

A brief explanation is in order about how the eyes transmit visual information to the brain. The principle of contralaterality in vision is not as simple as "left eye to right hemisphere," as you might have expected. Instead, each eye transmits visual information to the occipital lobes of *both* hemispheres in the brain, to the region known as the visual cortex. In particular, each half of the retina picks up visual information from the contralateral visual field. As illustrated in Figure 3-2, if you focus straight ahead on a fixation point, the left half of each eye receives images from the right visual field (the house), and the right half of each receives images from the left visual field (the tree). All the information from the right visual field—the solid lines in the figure—is first registered by the left half of the retina and is then transmitted to the left hemisphere of the brain. Likewise, stimuli in the left visual field—the dotted lines—are projected to the contralateral (right) half of the retina, then sent to the right hemisphere. Thus, the contralaterality in vision is between the visual field and the initial hemisphere: left visual field to right hemisphere, right visual field to left hemisphere. (The split brain patients described in Chapter 2 were prevented from seeing their hands, because each eye transmits information to both hemispheres. The purpose of the tests was to see what each hemisphere could do by itself, which would have been thwarted if the patients had also seen the object.)

Of special interest in this quick physiology lesson is the idea of *compression*, a kind of transformation that both analyzes and summarizes the visual input. That is, the message that finally reaches the visual cortex represents an already processed and summarized record of the original stimulus. As Haber and Hershenson (1973) pointed out, only a fraction of the original light energy is registered on the retina; the rest is absorbed and scattered by the fluid and structures within the eye. Furthermore, the three-layered retina also loses information. There are approximately 120 million rods on each retina and about 7 million cones. Most of the cones lie in *the small area* known as the **fovea** (or foveal pit), *which provides us with our most accurate, precise vision.* At least some of the cones in the fovea seem to have their own "private" bipolar cells for relaying impulses: Only *one* cone connects with *one* bipolar cell instead of many cones funneling their information into one bipolar cell (technically, a cone *synapses* onto a bipolar cell). This is not the case in peripheral vision, however. About 20 degrees away from the fovea, tens or even hundreds of rods in the periphery converge on a single bipolar cell. Such many-to-one convergence clearly implies a loss of information because a bipolar cell cannot "know" which of its many rods triggered it.

Finally, only about 1 million ganglion cells combine to form the optic nerve. Here is still more compression and summarization of the neural impulses, now transmitted from the bipolar cells (again, there is evidence of the "private" pathway from some of the foveal cones and bipolar cells). Thus even the relatively "raw" messages reaching the

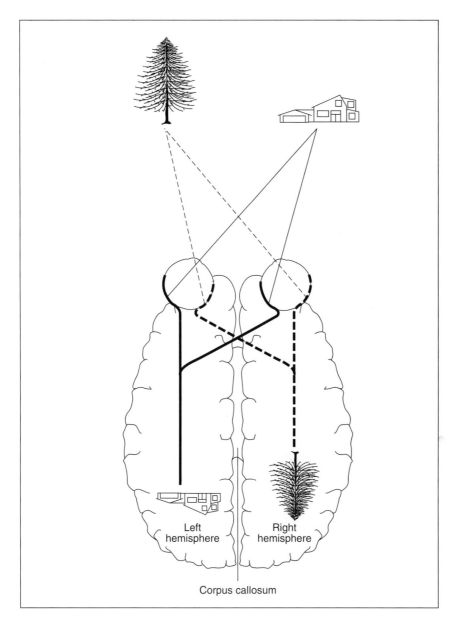

Figure 3-2

Binocular pathways of information flow from the eyes into the visual cortex of the brain. The patterns of stimulus-to-brain pathways demonstrate the contralaterality of the visual system.

brain, not yet processed by the cognitive system, have been reduced and summarized to a great degree.

Despite this summarizing, human vision is still amazingly sensitive and acute. Like all good summaries, the visual system preserves the most useful information, the edges, contours, and any kind of change, and omits the less useful, the unchanging, or steady-state information.

We have been talking about visual **sensation,** the *reception of stimulation from the environment and the initial encoding of that stimulation into the nervous system.* On the other hand, our primary interest concerns what happens next, what we *do* with this encoded information once the optic nerve has transmitted it to the visual cortex. In other words, we want to understand visual **perception,** *the process of interpreting and understanding sensory information.* In Levine and Shefner's (1981) words, "*Perception* refers to the way in which we *interpret* the information gathered (and processed) by the senses. In a word, we *sense* the presence of a stimulus, but we *perceive* what it is" (p. 1, emphasis added). Because doing something mentally with the raw sensory information is our primary focus, we need to explore the stages of visual perception and information processing. We begin by asking how the eye gathers information from the environment, then turn to the memory system that registers that information, visual sensory memory.

Gathering Visual Information

It is easy to believe, naively, that we take in visual information in a smooth and continuous fashion whenever our eyes are open. After all, our visual experience is of a connected, coherent visual scene that we can scan and examine at will. This is largely an illusion, however, one that you can easily disconfirm by a simple observation. Watch someone's eyes as he or she reads. You will see that your friend's eyes do not sweep smoothly across a line of print. Instead, they jerk across the line, bit by bit, with pauses between the successive movements.

Here are the facts. The *eye sweeps from one point to another in fast movements* called **saccades** (French for "jerk," pronounced "suh-KAHD"), movements that are interrupted by *pauses* called **fixations** (Figure 3-3). The saccade itself is quite rapid, taking anywhere from 25 msec to about 100 msec (Irwin & Carlson-Radvansky, 1996), depending on how far away the next fixation is. And it takes up to 200 msec to trigger the movement (Haber & Hershenson, 1973). During the saccade, there is suppression of the normal visual processes. Thus, for the most part, the eye takes in visual information only during stimulus fixation (and as explained later, probably only during the first brief moments of fixation). It is almost as if we are blind during the actual sweeping saccade movement (if the eye did encode information during the saccade, we'd see a blur).

Assume something in the range of 250–300 msec for an entire fixation–saccade cycle. At that rate, there is enough time for about three or four complete visual cycles per second. Each cycle registers a distinct and separate visual scene, although only a radical shift in gaze would make one cycle's input completely different from the previous one.

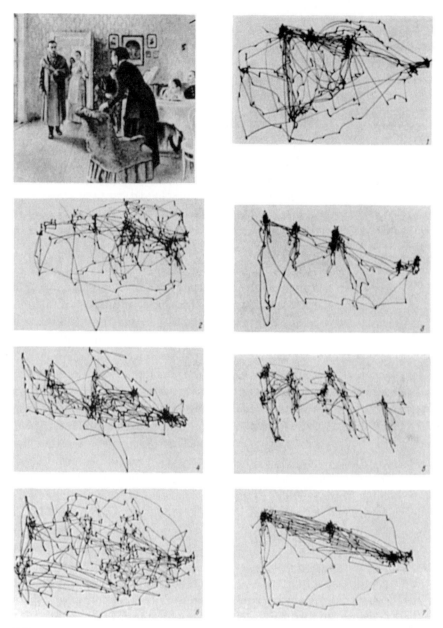

Figure 3-3

Saccade and fixation paths of a participant looking at the photograph in the upper left. The traces show fixations and paths when the participant merely viewed the photograph (Trace 1), had to estimate the economic status of the family in the photograph (Trace 2), judged the ages of the family members (Trace 3), guessed what the family had been doing before the visitor arrived (Trace 4), had to remember their clothing (Trace 5), had to remember the locations of the family members and objects (Trace 6), estimated how long the visitor had been away from the family (Trace 7).
From Yarbus (1967); adapted from Solso (1995).

PROVE IT

Yogi Berra supposedly once said something to the effect that "you can observe a lot just by watching." Very little of the evidence you're reading about in this chapter, however, can be observed easily without specialized apparatus; for instance, you need a tachistoscope to present visual stimuli in a highly controlled, precise fashion. But you can make some important and revealing observations just by watching someone's eyes (this also relates to material you will read about in Chapter 9).

Get very close to a friend's face and watch as he or she reads a passage of text silently and as he or she looks at a photo or drawing, maybe something as complex as the photo in Figure 3-3. At a minimum, what you'll see—the fast, jerky saccades of the eye movements—will disprove your intuitions that the eyes move smoothly and regularly across a line of print or systematically around a photograph or picture.

A final important detail concerns the triggering of saccades themselves, and more generally the engagement of visual attention. As Allport (1989) noted, there is a competitionlike situation in visual attention. On the one hand, attention must be interruptible. That is, we need to be prepared to react quickly to the unexpected, as when sudden movement alerts us to a possibly dangerous situation (a car running a red light as you drive through the intersection). While you are deliberately focusing your visual attention on one stimulus, the visual system must be able to react to other visual inputs, those outside the focus of visual attention to at least some degree (e.g., Theeuwes, Kramer, Hahn, & Irwin, 1998). As you will read later, much of this low-level processing appears to occur in parallel with other visual processing and involves detection of simple visual features (Treisman & Gelade, 1980).

On the other hand, visual attention should not be *too* interruptible. We cannot constantly be switching from one input to another—from the words in this sentence to your desk lamp to the scene outside your window to the color of the wall. If attention switched that frequently and erratically, visual (and mental) continuity would be destroyed. Balancing these competing tendencies is an ongoing process of monitoring; we evaluate the importance of current activity, of maintaining visual attention, and we judge that relative to the importance or urgency of stimuli outside the current attentional focus. The evidence suggests parallel processing here: simultaneous operation of deliberate eye movements, under the control of attention, and reflexive eye movements triggered by new, unexpected objects (Theeuwes et al., 1998).

Visual Sensory Memory

We turn now to visual sensory memory, the memory register that receives the visual input from the eyes. Because this memory system is so very brief, generally we have few useful intuitions about its operation. Unusual circumstances, however, can give us some clues. Thus we begin with such a circumstance.

Our perception of lightning is a mental event that reflects visual persistence.

Everyone has seen a flash of lightning during a thunderstorm. Think about that for a moment, then make a guess as to the duration of the light we see in an otherwise darkened backyard (or other visual scene) when a bolt of lightning strikes. Most people guess that the flash of light lasts a little more than a half second or so, maybe closer to a whole second sometimes. If your estimate was in this neighborhood, then it is reasonable, but not as an estimate of the physical duration of the lightning. The bolt of lightning is actually three or four separate bolts. Each bolt lasts about 1 msec, and there is a separation of about 50 msec between bolts. Thus the entire lightning strike lasts no more than about 2/10ths of a second, or 200 msec, and is composed of several individual flashes (Trigg & Lerner, 1981).

What was reasonable about your estimate? It was your *perception* of a flash of light extended in time. This phenomenon is called **visual persistence,** the *apparent persistence of a visual stimulus beyond its physical duration.* This phenomenon usually includes the subjective feeling that you can look around the scene and that the scene fades away rather than being "switched off." In Loftus and Irwin's (1998) words, "Two empirical facts are clear. . . . First, something that *looks like* the physical stimulus continues to be present for a brief time following stimulus offset. Second, *information can be acquired from the stimulus* for a brief period following stimulus offset in much the same way as it can be acquired while the stimulus is physically present" (p. 136).

In terms of the physiology of the visual system, the neural activity on the retina that is caused by the lightning flash does not outlast the flash itself. The eye itself does not continue to send "lightning" messages into the system after the flash is over (unless a retinal afterimage is involved). Nonetheless, your perception of the lightning is a mental event that reflects visual persistence: You perceive a lighted scene that then begins to

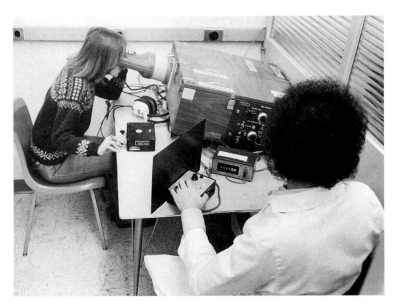

A tachistoscope in use.

fade away. Because any persistence of information beyond its physical duration defines the term *memory*, the processes of visual perception (as opposed to sensation) must begin with a visual memory system, some sort of *temporary visual buffer that holds visual information for brief periods of time.* This memory is called **visual sensory memory**; Neisser's (1967) term ***iconic memory*** is entirely equivalent.

Amount and Duration of Storage The classic cognitive research on the characteristics and processes of visual sensory memory was that reported by Sperling and his co-workers (1960; Averbach & Sperling, 1961). Sperling used a special apparatus for presenting visual stimuli, the ***tachistoscope,*** commonly known (and more easily pronounced) as a T-scope (*tachisto* is from Greek, meaning "very swift or rapid," as in *tachometer,* and *scope* refers to an instrument for seeing or observing). By using this apparatus, an investigator can present a visual stimulus for a carefully controlled period of time, usually on the order of milliseconds, and in a carefully controlled position, usually so that the stimulus is projected on the subject's fovea. The T-scope also permits the experimenter to control what is seen before and after the stimulus, the preexposure and postexposure fields. As investigators before him had, Sperling wondered about "the information available in brief visual presentations," the title of his important monograph in 1960.

A typical iconic memory experiment by Sperling presented arrays of letters and digits to subjects on a T-scope for very brief durations. In all cases, the subject's task was to report what he or she could remember from the display. For example, subjects were shown a series of trials, each with a 3 × 4 array of letters (three rows, four letters per row). The array was shown for 50 msec and was followed by a blank postexposure field. Finally, a sig-

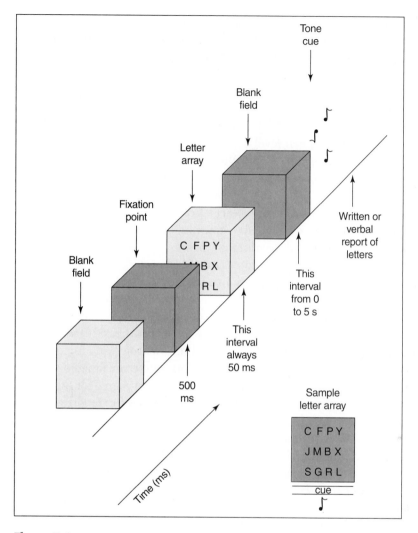

Figure 3-4

A schematic diagram of a typical trial in Sperling's (1960) experiments. After a fixation point appears for 500 msec, the letter array is displayed. The visual field after the display is blank. The tone cue can occur at the same time as the postfield, or it can be delayed up to 5 s. Data from Sperling, 1960.

nal was given to the subject to report the letters from the display. See Figure 3-4 for a schematic diagram of a typical trial.

Sperling found that subjects generally reported no more than four or five items correctly in this kind of test. When fewer than five items were shown, performance was essentially perfect, but when more than five were shown, subjects averaged about 4.5 letters correct; for a display of 12 letters, this is 37% accuracy. Furthermore, he found that this level of accuracy remained essentially the same for exposures as long as 500 msec, and even as short as 5 msec (Sperling, 1963). It appeared to Sperling that subjects' average of 4.5 items correct reflected a default strategy. That is, subjects said they could not possibly remember all 12 letters because the display seemed to fade from view too rapidly; even though they had seen the entire display, it disappeared too quickly. Consequently, they apparently decided before the trial began that they would focus or concentrate on just one or two of the rows, trying to maximize their performance on at least a part of the display. Their level of performance, about 4 or 5 items, was what would be expected based on the **span of apprehension,** *the number of individual items recallable after any short display* (also known as the *span of attention* or the *span of immediate memory*; see Chapters 4 and 5).

What distinguished Sperling's research from the many studies that preceded it was the ingenious condition he developed to contrast with these results. The condition just described, in which *subjects are to report any letters they can*, is called the **whole report condition** because the whole display was to be reported. The contrasting condition Sperling dreamed up is called the **partial report condition,** *in which only one of the rows was to be reported.* The logic behind this condition was absolutely elegant.

Sperling reasoned that *all* the letters of the display might be available initially but then might fade more rapidly than subjects could report them. If this is true, then subjects should be highly accurate on any one of the rows the experimenter might choose at random if they are told which row to report before too much fading has taken place. So in the partial report condition, he prearranged a special signal for the subjects: A high tone, sounded right after the display went off, was a cue for reporting the top row, a medium tone cued the middle row, and a low tone cued the bottom row. The crucial ingredient here is that the tone cues were presented after the display went off. Subjects had no way of knowing ahead of time which row they would be responsible for, so they had to be prepared to report any one of them.

Say that on a particular trial the low tone sounded right after the display went off. Given that the array should still be visible to the subject because of visual persistence, the subject should be able to focus mental attention on the bottom row and read out those letters accurately while they are still visible. This is exactly what happened. When the tone followed the display immediately, subjects' performance was 76% correct; that is, 76% of the cued row (about three of the four items) could be reported accurately. By logical extension, if performance was 76% on any randomly selected row, then the subjects' visual memory of the *entire* display must also be around 76%.[1]

This startling result suggested that immediately after a visual stimulus is displayed, a great deal of the stimulus information is available in visual sensory memory, much more than could be reported out loud. On the other hand, we would not expect this much of the display to remain visible and reportable for very long. After all, the whole report condition almost never exceeded four or five items, averaging 37% of the whole

---

[1]Professors use the same logic. I tell my class, "You are going to be tested on Chapters 1 through 3," then I only ask questions from Chapter 2. If you score 76% on this test, I infer that you also could have gotten about 76% on either of the other two chapters. Thus it seems that 76% of the total amount of information was available to you on the test.

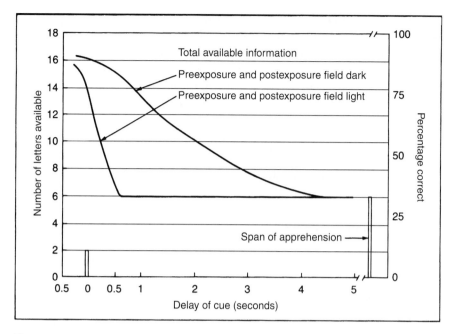

Figure 3-5

One subject's results on the number of letters available for report, as revealed by the partial report condition. The number of reportable letters drops sharply within 0.25 s when the postexposure field is light; the information persists much longer when the postexposure field is dark. The vertical bars on the *x*-axis show the number of letters reported under whole report. From Averbach & Sperling, 1961.

display. As expected, performance in the partial report group began to decline as the information in iconic memory began to fade. As the blank postfield interval got longer—more and more time passed until the tone—performance dwindled further. With a 1-s delay, partial report performance was 36%, almost exactly what the whole report condition achieved on the same materials (Sperling, 1960).

Similar results, from a study that showed 18 letters in the displays, are shown in Figure 3-5 in the curve for light prefields and postfields. In Sperling's words, "The explanation for these results is that the visual image of the stimulus persists for a short time after the stimulus has been turned off, and that the subjects can utilize this rapidly fading image. In fact, naive subjects typically believe that the physical stimulus fades out slowly" (1963, p. 22). This was our naive impression of the flash of lightning as well. As the fading continues, however, less and less of the original display is still visible in iconic memory, until by 1s the only reportable items are the few that were transferred into the more durable short-term memory store.

So, the results indicated that at least 17 of the 18 letters were available in the initial **icon** (the contents of iconic memory often are called the icon, *the visual image that resides in iconic memory*). This study (Averbach & Sperling, 1961) also varied the visual characteristics of the stimulus to demonstrate the particularly visual (as opposed to mental) nature of the icon and iconic memory storage. Dark preexposure and postexposure fields lengthened the useful readout period of iconic information when compared with light preexposure and postexposure fields (just as a lightning bolt is more visible in a nighttime storm than a daytime storm because of the contrast with the background illumination). More than 50% of the letters were still available after a 2-s cue delay when dark fields were used (see Figure 3-5). In contrast, accuracy dropped to 50% with light fields after only a quarter of a second. As would be expected of a visually based memory, the light and dark contrast of the stimulus display itself also affected the results, with better iconic visibility for sharper contrasts.

Finally, in all cases, the actual reporting of the letters was due to a "readout" or transfer process: The letters to be reported were transferred to the short-term memory system, which generated the written or spoken response (note that long-term memory is implicated here as well because the names of the letters have to be looked up in memory to be written or spoken). Just as we would expect from short-term memory, Sperling found that subjects' errors were often auditory rather than visual, such as substituting a letter or digit that sounded like the stimulus (*B* or *3* for *T*, for instance). Because the auditory nature of short-term memory was well known by this time (see Chapter 5), this was especially convincing evidence that iconic memories were shunted through short-term memory to be reported.

Erasure and Interference A related series of experiments by Sperling and others explored the loss of information from iconic memory more carefully. The original research suggested that forgetting was *a passive process like fading* or **decay**; that is, the mere passage of time degraded the icon, making it illegible after some short interval. This must certainly be true because care was taken to prevent subsequent stimuli from entering the visual store (the blank postexposure fields). But of course, in normal vision, no such blank field follows the visual input to our eyes: We look around continuously, shifting visual gaze from one stimulus to another all the time. What happens to iconic memory when a second stimulus is presented to the subject, when one visual scene is immediately followed by another? The answer, in short, was **interference,** *forgetting caused by the effects of intervening stimulation or mental processing.* This was the second reason for losing information from visual sensory memory.

A well-known study of this more elaborate situation was done by Averbach and Coriell (1961; reprinted in Coltheart, 1973). These investigators presented a display of two rows of letters, eight letters per row, for 50 msec. A blank white postexposure field, varying in duration, followed the display and was followed by a partial report cue. Unlike Sperling, however, Averbach and Coriell used a *visual* cue, either a vertical bar marker or a circle marker. The bar marker was positioned just above (or below) the position of the to-be-reported letter, and the circle marker was presented so as to surround the position where the to-be-reported letter had just disappeared. As in the Sperling procedures, subjects did not know ahead of time what letters would appear in the display or which letter they would have to report.

In their bar marker study, Averbach and Coriell found results that were very close to those obtained by Sperling, such as high performance with short delays of the cues, lower performance with longer delays, and an effective duration of about one quarter of a second. But the results from the circle marker study were somewhat different. When the circle marker cued the position to be reported, subjects were much less accurate than they were with the bar marker. In a second study, the circle marker was filled with grid lines and produced an even more dramatic decline in performance.

These results suggested strongly that the identical positioning of the circle had in some way erased the memory trace for the letter in that position. Note what an unusual event this is: *"A later visual stimulus can drastically affect the perception of an earlier one"* (Averbach & Coriell, cited in Coltheart, 1973, p. 16, emphasis added). This effect is called **backward masking.** The masking stimulus, if it occurs soon enough after the letter display, interferes with the perception of the earlier stimulus presented at the same position. In some backward masking studies, subjects claim that they saw *only* the mask, even though their other performance indicates that the sensory system did indeed register the first stimulus (data on this go back as far as Werner, 1935; see Kahneman, 1968, for a review). In general, *when the contents of visual sensory memory are degraded by subsequent visual stimuli*, the loss of the original information is called **erasure**, a specific kind of interference.

The Argument About Iconic Memory

The evidence collected by Sperling, Averbach and Coriell, and many others led cognitive psychology to propose that iconic memory was the initial step in visual information processing. The phenomenon of visual persistence, as revealed in the quarter-second duration of information presented by the T-scope, was replicated many times. This convinced cognitive psychology that iconic memory existed and that it was the important first phase in visual perception (Neisser, 1967). Theories of visual perception therefore included iconic storage as an integral part of visual perception.

An alternative view was expressed most strongly by Haber in his 1983 article "The Impending Demise of the Icon." Haber did not doubt the evidence on visual persistence, nor did he quibble with the term *icon* as a label for the mental image or "snapshot" preserved by visual persistence. What he claimed, however, was that this static icon is quite irrelevant to an understanding of normal visual perception. As he put it, only somewhat facetiously, "The notion of an icon as a brief storage of information persisting after stimulus termination cannot possibly be useful in any typical visual information-processing task except reading in a lightning storm" (1983, p. 1).

The logic behind Haber's conclusion was based in part on the concept of **ecological validity**, *that methodologies and tasks should resemble the real-world ecology of cognitive processing.* As Haber noted, no ordinary visual experience is even remotely similar to lab tasks using the T-scope. We do not normally see only brief flashes of visual stimuli in our environment, followed by a blank field. The only real-world circumstance that even comes close to resembling this is the brief illumination provided by a bolt of lightning.

Instead, the visual environment remains in view as long as we fixate our eyes on it. We have *continuous*, rather than momentary, exposure to visual scenes, and we can extract information from those scenes across as much time as we care to devote to them. In short, Haber argued that although iconic memory and visual persistence are real, they are irrelevant to the normal task of perceiving continuous visual information.

Haber's article was followed by a string of replies, some in favor of his conclusion, some opposed. Several (e.g., G. R. Loftus, 1983) attacked the philosophical basis of Haber's argument. Haber maintained that the visual stimulation provided by a T-scope is so artificial as to be ungeneralizable to real perceptual environments. Loftus, among others, criticized this view on the grounds that science has traditionally taken exactly this kind of reductionistic approach and has generally been well served by it. According to this counterargument, cognitive psychology's task is not to throw out the concept of iconic memory but instead to flesh it out and to determine how it contributes to normal visual perception.

A second criticism leveled by Haber involves the notion of the continuously available visual environment. Why would we build a theory of visual perception based on brief, discrete flashes of stimulation, he asked, when the normal visual environment is continuously present? As it happens, it may be unimportant for normal vision that the environment is continuously present, strangely enough—at least if we consider printed text to be a normal visual environment. Coltheart (1983), for example, pointed out that Sperling's original experiments included an examination of different durations of presentation; some trials presented the letter grid for only 5 msec, and some presented it for up to 500 msec. Interestingly, accuracy in these two extreme conditions was not appreciably different. In other words, subjects' reports were as accurate with only 5 msec of time to extract information from the display as they were with a full 500 msec.

The First 50 Milliseconds of Fixation A similar, very powerful demonstration was reported by Rayner, Inhoff, Morrison, Slowiaczek, and Bertera (1981), who examined performance during a text-reading task. After subjects had fixated a word for 50 msec, the word was replaced with a completely irrelevant stimulus, which remained in view for another 175 msec to fill up the rest of the fixation time. Surprisingly, replacing the word did not affect reading at all—participants usually did not notice that the word had changed. In Coltheart's (1983) words, "Continuous . . . sampling of the text throughout a fixation does not occur. Once the text has been fixated for 50 msec or so, its presence during the remainder of the fixation is *irrelevant* and makes *no* contribution to reading" (p. 18, emphasis added). Thus Haber's point about the environment—that we can continuously sample information from it—may be irrelevant to the way the eye actually extracts visual information. (For more information on reading, see Chapter 10.)

Finally, Haber noted that the static "snapshot" character of the icon seems irrelevant to the issues of how people perceive movement and how perception functions when our eyes, heads, and bodies move in relation to the visual environment. In response to such criticisms, several investigators have collected evidence on what might be called "dynamic icons," that is, iconic images that contain movement. For instance, Treisman,

Russel, and Green (1975) presented a brief (100-msec) display of six moving dots to their subjects and asked them to report the direction of movement. Partial report performance was superior to whole report performance, and accuracy under partial report declined across time. In short, the moving images of the dots were decaying just as the static letter grid had in Sperling's procedures (see also Finke & Freyd, 1985; Irwin, 1991, 1992; Loftus & Hanna, 1989).

In other words, visual perception is not a process of flipping through successive snapshots, with three or four snapshots per second. Instead, it may be more accurately described as a process of focusing on the visually attended elements of successive fixations, where each fixation encodes a dynamic segment of the visual environment. As Irwin (1991) put it, our "perceptual representation of the environment is built up via the integration of information across [several] saccadic eye movements" (p. 420).

In fact, integration across brief intervals of time can occur even *without* eye movements. The evidence presented by Loftus and Irwin (1998) shows that temporal integration—perceiving two separate events as if they had occurred at the same time—happens seamlessly when visual events occur within about 20 msec of each other. Equally interesting, it seems to happen without any conscious awareness that two separate events have occurred. Events separated by 40 msec or more, or separate events that themselves last for 40 msec or more, tend not to be integrated as completely. With these longer durations, in other words, people can more easily detect that two separate events happened rather than just one.

A Summary for Visual Sensory Memory

How do all these different results make sense: the wholesale input of visual stimulation, the persistence, decay, erasure, and integration of information, and the concept of visual attention?

Consider the following. Under normal viewing conditions, one moment's visual input replaces the previous visual input by means of erasure or "writing over." Under unusual circumstances, such as the single brief glimpse afforded by a T-scope, even the shortest stimulus displays will seem to last about 250 or 300 msec because of visual persistence, the duration of a normal iconic memory. With a blank postexposure field, which artificially prevents any subsequent stimulus, the perceptual fading of the icon is even visible.

The continuous stream of successive glimpses in normal vision, however, serves as an eraser under more normal viewing conditions. Under those normal circumstances, we are not aware of any fading. Note here that the rapid extraction of information during the first few milliseconds of exposure appears to be critical to the perception of continuous vision. Indeed, it may be that the first 50 msec or so are all we need to encode visual information. During the remaining time, we *attend* to the information—pay attention to it— and begin to replace that icon with new information from the next fixation.

The entire sequence of encoding visual information—selecting part of it for further processing, planning subsequent eye movements, and so on—is highly active and very rapid. The visual continuity we experience, our feeling that we see continuously, without breaks, pauses, or blank intervals, is due to the constant updating of visual sensory memory and to our focus on attended information. As we pay attention to a visual stimulus, we seem to be examining the readout from iconic memory. In the meantime, a new visual scene is being registered in sensory memory. Our mental processes then pick up the thread of visual information in the newly registered scene, providing a smooth transition from one attended display to the next.

Focal attention was Neisser's (1967) term for this *mental process of visual attention*, such as the mental redirection of attention when the partial report cue is presented. It seems that focal attention, or simply *visual attention*, might be the bridge between successive scenes registered by visual sensory memory. This bridging prevents us from sensing the blank space of time occupied by the eye's saccades by directing focal attention to elements of the icon. Although we *sense* a great deal of visual information, what we *perceive* is the part of a visual scene selected for focal, visual attention. To exaggerate a bit, what you are perceiving right now is not the printed page in front of you. Instead, you are perceiving the processed and attended portion of the displays that were registered in sensory memory, your iconic trace, as processed by visual attention.

■ Section Summary

- The eye sweeps across the visual field in short movements known as saccades, taking in information during brief fixations. The information encoded in these fixations is stored in visual sensory memory for no more than about 250 msec. This iconic image, which may include movement, fades rapidly or can be erased by subsequent visual stimulation. Much more information is stored in visual sensory memory than can be reported immediately. Information that is reported has been transferred to short-term memory by the process of focal attention.
- Some claim that an understanding of visual sensory memory, as it is usually studied in the lab, is of little use in understanding the real-world process of perception. More recent work suggests that we do not continuously extract information from the visual scene around us but instead extract most of the information we need within the first 50 msec of fixation.

Pattern Recognition: Written Language

We turn now to one of the most intriguing and debated topics in visual perception, the recognition or identification of visual patterns. The role of visual sensory memory in this process is to encode the visual information into the memory system. Yet we need to go more deeply into the memory system to understand how a visual stimulus is processed to a level at which it can be recognized as a familiar pattern. How does your cognitive system manage to input visual stimuli such as *G* or *tree* and end up recognizing them as familiar, meaningful symbols? How do we recognize patterns of handwriting, or different printed fonts, despite incredible variability?

The Template Approach

As Neisser (1967) pointed out, pattern recognition would be a simplified problem, though still thorny, if all the equivalent patterns we saw were identical. That is, if there were one and only one way for the capital letter *G* to appear, then the mental process that determines that it is a *G* would be easier to investigate. But obviously, the visual environment is not so conveniently organized. An enormous variety of visual patterns, in countless combinations of orientation and size, will all be categorized as the capital letter *G*, and likewise for all other letters, figures, shapes, and so on.

Perhaps this categorization is done by means of **templates,** *stored models of all categorizable patterns.* After all, when the computer at your bank reads your checking account number, it is performing a template matching process, trying to make physical identity matches between the numbers on your check and its stored templates for the digits 0 through 9. When the computer recognizes a pattern, it has matched it to one of its stored digit or letter templates.

Although the template approach has simplicity and economy on its side, it has very little else to recommend it. As an explanation of human pattern recognition, it is seriously flawed for a variety of reasons. We have already covered the primary reason, the enormous variability in the patterns that we can nonetheless recognize. Other reasons exist too; for example, how long would it take you to learn the infinite number of possible patterns that you can recognize or to search through them in memory? Would you have room left in memory for anything else?

Visual Feature Detection

A distinct improvement over the template approach is the notion of **feature analysis** or **feature detection**. A feature, in this approach, is a *very simple pattern, a fragment or component that can appear in combination with other features* across a wide variety of stimulus patterns. A good example of such a visual feature might be a single straight, horizontal line, a feature that appears in capital letters *A, G, H, L,* and so on; others would be vertical or diagonal lines, curves, and so forth. In Chapter 2 you read a brief introduction to a connectionist model of word recognition (refer back to Figure 2-12); the lowest level of representation in that model was exactly this, the feature level.

In general, feature theories claim that we recognize whole patterns by breaking them apart into the building-block features they contain. Rather than matching an entire templatelike pattern for capital *G*, then, maybe we simply break down the *G* into its features. When "circle opening right" and "horizontal straight" segments are detected, the features match with those stored in memory for capital *G*. Successful feature matches would be the necessary evidence of categorization, deciding that the pattern is indeed a *G*.

The feature approach has been popular enough that several investigators have proposed rather elaborate theories of feature-based pattern recognition and have carefully worked out the "catalog" of features in written or printed letters (e.g., Gibson, 1965). We'll discuss one such model in some detail because it is a particularly clear example of feature detection models and because it was described in a rather entertaining (for psychology) fashion. Understanding Pandemonium will also help you understand the reasons behind interactive, connectionist approaches.

Pandemonium Selfridge (1959), an early advocate of feature detection, described a model of pattern recognition he called **Pandemonium** (1959); an illustration of the model is shown in Figure 3-6. In Selfridge's imaginative description, Pandemonium reigns in the process of pattern recognition because of the mental mechanisms that process a visual stimulus. These mechanisms were *demons* in Selfridge's model, little mental demons who shout out loud as they attempt to identify patterns.

As the figure shows, a pattern is encoded by a set of *data demons*. Next, the *computational demons* begin to act. These computational demons are the feature analyzers in Selfridge's model; each one has a single, simple feature it is trying to match in the stimulus pattern. For instance, one demon might be trying to match a simple horizontal line, another would try to match a vertical line, another a curve opening to the right, and so on. When a computational demon matches a stimulus feature, it begins to shout excitedly.

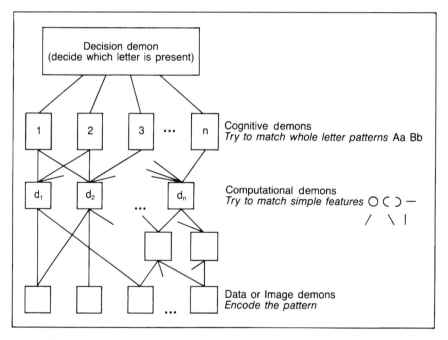

Figure 3-6

Selfridge's (1959) Pandemonium model. The image demons encode the visual pattern. The feature demons try to match the simple features present in the pattern. Cognitive demons represent the combination of features that are present in different letters of the alphabet; each tries to match the several computational demons that match the stimulus input. Finally, the decision demon identifies the pattern by selecting the loudest cognitive demon, the one whose features most nearly match the pattern being presented. Adapted from Selfridge, 1959.

At the next level up, listening to all this shouting is a set of *cognitive demons*. The cognitive demons represent the different letters of the alphabet, one for each letter. Each one is listening for a particular combination of demons to shout: For instance, the *G*-demon is listening for the "open curve" and the "horizontal bar" feature analyzers or demons to shout. Any evidence from the computational demons that suggests a match with the stimulus causes the cognitive demon to begin shouting as well: Based on the feature analysis evidence, it thinks that *it* is the matching pattern. Several of the cognitive demons will be shouting at once because several letters usually share some features (e.g., *C* and *G*). Thus the one who shouts the loudest is the one whose pattern is most nearly matched by the input stimulus. The loudest cognitive demon is finally heard by the *decision demon*, the highest-level demon in the model. This demon has the final say in recognizing and categorizing the pattern.

Aside from the vividness of the model's description of scores of shouting demons producing a noisy Pandemonium, Selfridge's model incorporated several ideas that are important to the entire issue of pattern recognition. First, at base, it was a feature detection model. The features that were detected and reported by the demons were elementary, simple features—components that in different combinations represent the letters of the alphabet being recognized (Selfridge's model was not limited to letters, but the process is more easily described using letters as examples).

There are now several related lines of evidence for feature detection in visual pattern recognition (e.g., Pritchard, 1961). Especially convincing are the neurophysiological studies showing that specialized visual cortex cells exist for various simple visual features and patterns. The most widely known evidence of this kind comes from research pioneered by Hubel and Wiesel (1962). Using sophisticated electrode implant procedures, these researchers found neurons in cats' brains that respond only to vertical lines, other neurons that respond only to diagonals, and so on. On the assumption that the human brain is not radically different from a cat's at the level of neuronal functioning, this suggests that feature detection may even have a physiological status in the nervous system (for similar evidence in monkeys, see Maunsell & Newsome, 1987). Furthermore, it means that psychological theories of pattern recognition must be compatible with this neurological evidence.

A second important notion in Selfridge's model was the idea of parallel processing; the computational demons all work at the same time, each one trying to match its own feature while all the others are doing the same thing. With this aspect of his model, Selfridge was pointing out that feature detection or analysis is probably a simultaneous or parallel process instead of a serial, "one after the other" process. This seems to be a very reasonable position, even if we use printed text as our only evidence. That is, the number of individual feature tests needed to recognize all the letters in a single line of print must be quite large. Given the speed with which adults can read a single line, we would have to assume an impossibly fast rate of feature detection if the process is occurring serially. Neisser, Novick, and Lazar (1963) found evidence consistent with the proposal of parallel processing of features when their subjects could scan for the presence of 10 different letters just as quickly as they could scan for 1.

Identifying a pattern with minimal cues.

Beyond Features: Conceptually Driven Pattern Recognition

Even Selfridge knew that the Pandemonium model was missing an important ingredient. Basically, Pandemonium was a completely bottom-up processing system, that is, a completely **data-driven processing system** in which *processing is driven by the stimulus pattern, the incoming data*. In Pandemonium, the patterns to be recognized came in to the image demons at the bottom, then were processed higher and higher until the top-level demon finally recognized the pattern.

And yet, Selfridge presented examples like those shown in Figure 3-7, illustrations of the way context can influence pattern recognition. How adequate is the bottom-up, feature detection approach as an explanation of visual pattern recognition? Did you "see" the words *THE* and *CAT* despite the unusual middle letters? Do you "see" the letter *B* and the number *13* in the bottom half of the figure, even though these two are identical? So what was the missing ingredient?

Context To pick up on the theme introduced in Chapter 2, the missing ingredient was context, a mechanism that would allow context and a person's expectations to influence the process of recognizing patterns. Such effects are called top-down processing, or **conceptually driven processing effects,** in which *context and higher-level knowledge*

TAE CAT

A

A,B,C,D,E,F
10,11,12,13,14

B

Figure 3-7

Top-down effects in pattern recognition. **A,** The effect of context on letter recognition (adapted from Selfridge, 1959). **B.** The effect of context on pattern recognition. The *B* and the *13* are identical. From Coren & Ward, 1989.

influence lower-level processes (remember "typograpical"?). In Figure 3-7, your knowledge of English words and spelling patterns leads you to perceive the middle letters as different, and looking at a line of numbers sets up an expectation for seeing *13* rather than *B*. Let's examine some experimental evidence that supports the feature theory approach but also makes the case for conceptually driven processing.

In Neisser's (1964) classic research on visual search, participants saw pages of characters, 50 lines of printed letters, with four to six letters per line. Their task was to scan the page as rapidly as possible to find the one occurrence of a prespecified letter (in other tasks, Neisser asked people to find the line *without* a certain character). As an illustration of the task, do the visual searches presented in Figure 3-8, timing yourself as you find the targets. Notice how hard it is to find a line *without* a specified letter and to find a letter that is physically similar to the distractor letters in the display.

Finding the *K* in the angular-letter column is difficult, as it was for Neisser's participants, because the features that define *K* are also sprinkled liberally throughout the angular letters. Likewise, finding the *Z* in the third column is much easier than finding it in the fourth. Because the third column contains mostly rounded-feature letters, most of the detectable features in the display can be ignored; the pattern recognition system can shut off the curve-detecting features when it is searching for the *Z* in this kind of display (see Duncan & Humphreys, 1989, for careful consideration of visual search when the similarity of targets and nontargets varies).

A. Search for *K*	B. Search for line without *Q*	C. Search for *Z*	D. Search for *Z*
EHYP	ZVMLBQ	ODUGQR	IVMXEW
SWIQ	HSQJMF	QCDUGO	EWVMIX
UFCJ	ZTJVQR	CQOGRD	EXWMVI
WBYH	RDQTFM	QUGCDR	IXEMWV
OGTX	TQVRSX	URDGQO	VXWEMI
GWVX	MSVRQX	GRUQDO	MXVEWI
TWLN	ZHQBTL	DUZGRO	XVWMEI
XJBU	ZJTQXL	UCGROD	MWXVIE
UDXI	LHQVXM	DQRCGU	VIMEXW
HSFP	FVQHMS	QDOCGU	EXVWIM
XSCQ	MTSDQL	CGUROQ	VWMIEX
SDJU	TZDFQB	OCDURQ	VMWIEX
PODC	QLHBMZ	UOCGQD	XVHMEI
ZVBP	QMXBJD	RGQCOU	WXVEMI
PEVZ	RVZHSQ	GRUDQO	XMEWIV
SLRA	STFMQZ	GODUCQ	MXIVEW
JCEN	RVXSQM	QCURDO	VEWMIX
ZLRD	MQBJFT	DUCOQG	EMVXWI
XBOD	MVZXLQ	CGRDQU	IVWMEX
PHMU	RTBXQH	UDRCOQ	IEVMWX
ZHFK	BLQSZX	GQCORU	WVZMXE
PNJW	QSVFDJ	GOQUCD	XEMIWV
CQXT	FLDVZT	GDQUOC	WXIMEV
GHNR	BQHMDX	URDCGO	EMWIVX
IXYD	BMFDQH	GODROC	IVEMXW
QSVB	QHLJZT		
GUCH	TQSHRL		
OWBN	BMQHZJ		
BVQN	RTBJZQ		
FOAS	FQDLXH		
ITZN	XJHSVQ		
VYLD	MZRJDQ		
LRYZ	XVQRMB		
IJXE	QMXLSD		
RBOE	DSZHQR		
DVUS	FJQSMV		
BIAJ	RSBMDQ		
ESGF	LBMQFX		
QGZI	FDMVQJ		
ZWNE	HQZTXB		
QBVC	VBQSRF		
VARP	QHSVDZ		
LRPA	HVQBFL		
SGHL	HSRQZV		
MVRJ	DQVXFB		
GADB	RXJQSM		
PCME	MQZFVD		
ZODW	ZJLRTQ		
HDBR	SHMVTQ		
BVDZ	QXFBRJ		

Figure 3-8

Neisser's (1964) search lists. In list A, the target is the letter *K;* in list B, the target is the line without the letter *Q;* in lists C and D, the target is the letter *Z.*

Without context.

There's the shortcoming: We have to "shut off" some feature detectors to explain fast search for *K* in the round-letter condition (analogously, in Duncan and Humphreys's [1989] approach, variations in the nontarget letters influenced the speed of search for targets). But where did the instruction to shut off those detectors come from? Not from the feature detectors themselves, of course. Feature detectors do only one thing—they detect visual features. Instead, this instruction came from some place "higher up," something like your realization that you could ignore all dissimilar letter shapes. This is the contribution of your existing knowledge to the lower-level process of feature detection—it's conceptually driven processing.

To be sure, pattern recognition starts by processing the incoming pattern, a bottom-up process; no one doubts that the cognitive system is triggered by the physical data or pattern and that it identifies patterns on the basis of stimulus features. Nonetheless, this bottom-up emphasis slights the contribution made by the cognitive system. It misses the effect of **context,** the influence of *surrounding information and your own knowledge.* We often identify a pattern that is *not* in original stimulus at all, such as the *the* in the last clause. You misread that sentence, didn't you? And now you know where the missing *the* came from: It came from you, from your knowledge of language. Top-level conceptual knowledge, already stored in memory, augments or assists lower-level processes such as pattern recognition.

We believe strongly that conceptually driven *and* data-driven processes are combined in most pattern recognition situations, not to mention more complex cognitive processes such as comprehension of language. And an excellent way to model this, to

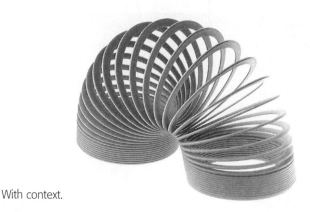

With context.

explore how this combination works, is within the connectionist model introduced in Chapter 2. Think of this model as Pandemonium Plus, a bottom-up model like Selfridge's with an added top-down processing effect.

Connectionism

Connectionism is a theoretical and computational approach to some of the most challenging issues in cognitive science. *Computational* refers to the ways in which the human cognitive system performs its mental operations. The term *compute* is used here in the verb sense of *process*; colloquially, *compute* means "figure out." Thus when you read and understand the sentence "The lightning snaked across the sky," you have computed the meaning of the sentence; you have determined, figured out what the sentence means. It is in this sense that we say that pattern recognition—or any other cognitive operation—involves the process of computation.

Furthermore, connectionist models involve a *massive* number of mathematical computations. A connectionist or parallel distributed processing model is always implemented as a computer model, with a set of formulae that perform computations on the model's basic units. Even if the number of units is fairly small, the number of separate computations in a single run of the model is staggeringly large because of the huge number of connections among the units. Thus we rely on high-speed computers to perform the calculations and to report the outcomes to us at the end of a run.

To flesh out the word recognition model (McClelland & Rumelhart, 1981; Rumelhart & McClelland, 1986) we'll use a model that recognizes four-letter words, such as *TREE*. We start with some of the basics of connectionism, including some of the special vocabulary you will encounter in this approach. Table 3-1 provides a list of basic terms and assumptions, with some explanations to help you understand the approach. Consult Table 3-1 and Figure 3-9 frequently as you read the next section.

Table 3-1 A PRIMER OF CONNECTIONIST TERMINOLOGY AND ASSUMPTIONS

Basic Statement of PDP Principles

Complex mental operations are the combined effects of the massively parallel processing that characterizes the network. The processing is distributed across all the levels of the network (hence the term *parallel distributed processing*).

The network is composed of (usually) three levels of units: the input level, hidden level, and output level. The internal "hidden" layer is invisible to an outsider. Units in each of these levels are interconnected (hence the term *connectionism*). The connections are either positively or negatively weighted.

Positive connection weights pass excitation, or excitatory activation, to the connected unit; negatively weighted connections pass inhibition, or inhibitory activation. A unit transmits its activation to connected units if it has received enough positive activation to reach threshold.

Connection weights are assigned as a function of training, in which feedback as to correctness or incorrectness leads to a mathematical adjustment of weights. When a network is given this procedure and the weights have stabilized, the network is said to have been trained up. Back propagation is the most commonly used training method, although others exist.

The obvious similarities between PDP models and the neurological structures and activities in the brain are usually quite intentional; connections sometimes are called synapses, excitation and inhibition are parallel to those processes in the neocortex, and the entire approach is commonly known as *neural net modeling*.

Lexicon of Other Connectionist Terms

Backpropagation	The most commonly used training procedure, in which the weight-adjusting phase proceeds from the output units back in to the other layers, each unit propagating a series of computations.
Delta Rule	The mathematical rule for adjusting weights during training, where delta (Δ) stands for "change."
Distributed representation	The representation for a letter, word, concept, and so on is said to be distributed because the knowledge is spread widely across the units and their weights.
Local minima	Occasionally in the training procedure, the system seems to have found the most stable baseline values for the weights, the global minimum; think of the global minimum as the deepest "valley." But the system may just be trapped in a local minimum or valley.
Massively parallel processing	Almost all units in the system have some role in each step of processing, and all units operate simultaneously.

Input Units Let's build the simple connectionist framework illustrated in Figure 3-9 piece by piece. In this structure there are three levels of units. First, at the bottom, are the *input units*. These are extremely basic, elementary "cells" in the structure, which receive the inputs from the environment. Our example is visual word recognition, so our input units are simple visual detectors. That is, we have a set of nine input units, each of which responds to the different basic visual features of the letters of the alphabet. To build on what you already understand, consider the input units to have exactly the same function as the data and computational demons in the Pandemonium model, shown in Figure 3-6. Our input units here encode and then respond to simple visual features in letters of the alphabet. Thus the input unit level in this illustration is the feature-detector level.

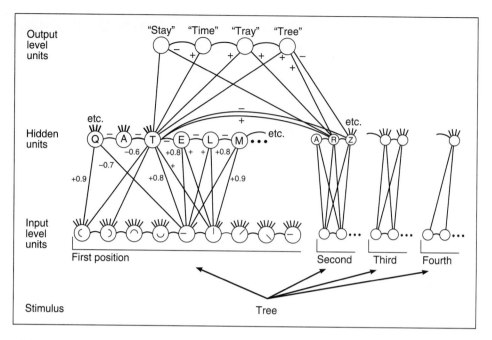

Figure 3-9

A portion of the PDP network for recognizing four-letter words. The bulk of the illustration involves identifying the first letter of the word.

Hidden Units How do these input units work? When a stimulus is presented to the input device, one or more of the input units matches the features in the stimulus. When this happens, each unit that matches activates a set of connected units in the middle level of the structure, the *hidden unit* level; *hidden* here simply means that this level is completely internal, always one step removed from either input or output. In our diagram, the hidden units correspond to the letter level. Note that the activation is sent across the pathways or connections that link the units together; *these* are the connections in connectionism.

The connections always have a weight attached to them, a weight that represents the relationship between the linked units. Some of the weights are positive, and some are negative. For example, in Figure 3-9, the horizontal straight bar feature has positive weights connecting it to the letters *T, E,* and *L* because those letters all contain that feature (to minimize confusion in looking at the figure, many of the connections have not been drawn fully, and only a few numerical weights are given). Conversely, the weights between the horizontal straight bar feature and the letters *C, O, Q,* and so on are negative. Likewise, all the curved features at the input level have positive weights to curved letters and negative weights to angular letters.

Hidden units that receive enough positive activation, called *excitation,* govern the outcome of processing (think of shouting demons). Units receiving negative activation, or *inhibition*, end up having little control over the outcome. Eventually, after all the weights have been factored into the computational formulae, activations at the output level come into play.

Output Units Where is this getting us? Imagine that you were trying to build a machine (program a computer) that could identify visually presented words, such as the four-letter words we are considering here. What you see in Figure 3-9 is primarily the connectionist network for the first position in the four-letter words. Three more sets of connections, shown in reduced form at the right of the figure, essentially duplicate the same connections again, once for each position in the four-letter word. Given these additional positions, we can now talk about the *output units*, the units that report the system's response to the question "What is this word?"

For simplicity, only a handful of four-letter words are shown at the level of output units in the figure. Note, however, that three of the word-level units are consistent with the letter detection performed on *T* in the first position; that is, three of the words begin with a *T*. Now think about the fuller representation of such a model, a model that identifies four-letter words. Each of the four input unit segments will perform as described earlier, forwarding both positive and negative activation to the hidden units, these in turn forwarding positive and negative activations to the output units. At the end of the run of the model, presumably one of the several output units will have received enough positive activation to exceed its threshold. When this happens, that unit responds by answering the question "What is this word?"

One more complexity is needed now, the one that gets top-down effects into the model. Reflect for a moment on how likely the spelling pattern *TZ* is at the beginning of English words. Not very likely, is it? On the other hand, *TA*, *TE*, *TI*, and similar consonant–vowel pairs are quite likely, as are a few consonant–consonant pairs such as *TH* and *TR*. These likelihoods are also represented in the network; to distinguish them visually from the other connections, they are shown with curve-shaped connections. The overall effect of these letter-to-letter weights is that the activations in the system can make up for missing features at the perceptual level.

Figure 3-10, taken from Rumelhart and McClelland's (1986) work, shows the final levels of activation for three possible words, given the partially obscured stimulus pattern shown at the bottom. The illustration shows an important feature of connectionist models: Enough knowledge is represented in the system, by means of the weights for letter-to-letter sequences, that the model identifies the word *work* even when the last letter could also be an *R*.

Why is this so important? It is important because it is a concrete illustration of the general theme of top-down or conceptually driven processing. If you saw the partially obscured pattern in Figure 3-10, you would identify the word as *work*, based on your knowledge that *worr* is not a word in English. Your higher-level knowledge of English words would be assisting your perceptual process here in service of identifying the word. This is *exactly* what's happening in the connectionist model; higher-level knowledge,

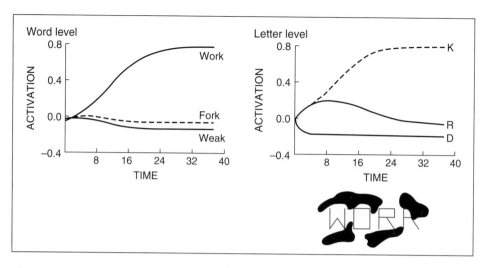

Figure 3-10

A possible display that might be presented to the connectionist model of word recognition and the resulting activations of selected letter and word units. The letter units are for the letters indicated in the fourth position of a four-letter display. Adapted from Rumelhart & McClelland, 1986.

coded as simple weighted connections in the massive network, is participating in the lower-level task of identifying letters.[2]

Such connectionist models satisfy the difficulty you read about earlier: the need for top-down processing in the Pandemonium model. In Figure 3-9 the top-down effect is especially prominent in the curved connections, which represent mutual excitation and inhibition of units. But the approach has far more important consequences than merely providing a way to repair Pandemonium. As you will read at several points in this book, connectionist accounts of a whole range of cognitive operations can provide new insights into ways of modeling and understanding human cognition.

■ Section Summary

• Recognition of visual patterns is certainly not a process of matching stored templates to a visual stimulus. Feature detection provides a much more convincing account of visual recognition, where the features being detected are elementary patterns that can be combined to form letters and other visual stimuli. A feature detection account of pattern recognition, such as Pandemonium, must be augmented by conceptually driven processes to account for the known effects of context in visual recognition. Current models of this sort include the powerful new connectionist approach.

[2]The handwritten census forms for the year 2000 U.S. Census were read by what is basically a connectionist system. The software identified letters and words both by analyzing features and by knowing what kinds of letter and spelling patterns were likely to be found on different questions. For instance, the system knew that "McN" is a likely spelling pattern in a person's last name but is unlikely as a spelling pattern in a person's job name or profession.

Object Recognition and Agnosia

How can these approaches to identifying letters and words be expanded to the real world, to recognizing a real tree, a real briefcase, or a human face? Some of the most significant work reported on the topic of object recognition involves a process very similar to the feature detection ideas you have been studying.

Recognition by Components

The basic idea proposed in Biederman's (1987, 1990) recognition by components (RBC) theory is that we recognize objects by breaking them down into their components, then looking up this combination of components in memory to see which object matches the combination. In this model, the human recognition system has a small number of *basic "primitives," simple three-dimensional geometric forms* like those shown in Figure 3-11. These forms are called **geons,** combined form of *geometric ions* (remember *ions* from chemistry?). Recognizing a briefcase, for example, involves analyzing the object into its two geons, the rectangular box (geon 2 in the figure) and the curved cylinder (geon 5). By itself, detecting the rectangular box geon would match the memory representation for "brick" or "box." When that component and the curved cylinder on top are detected, the combination would match what is stored in memory for "briefcase" or "suitcase."

Biederman (1987) argued that all three-dimensional objects in the world are composed of these simple geons, much as written language is composed of simple letters, combined and recombined in different fashions. Thus, when we recognize objects, we are breaking them down (*parsing* is the technical term) into their components and noting where the components join together. This pattern is then matched to information stored in memory to yield recognition.

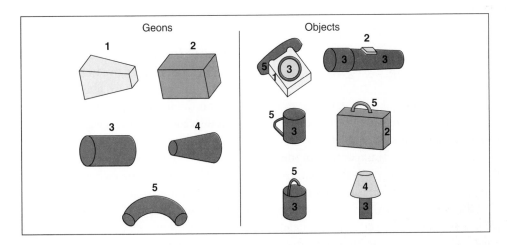

Figure 3-11

Geons (components) and the objects they make. From Biederman, 1990.

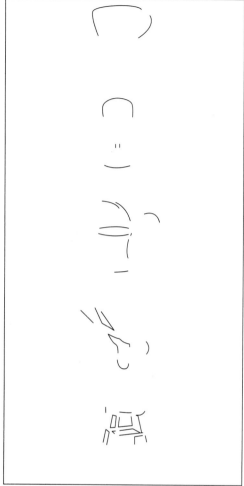

Figure 3-12

Nonrecoverable objects. From Biederman, 1987.

Two aspects of these patterns are particularly important. First, we find the edges of objects. This enables us to determine which edges maintain the same relationships to one another regardless of viewing orientation; however you look at a brick, the three long edges that are visible remain parallel to one another.

Second, we carefully scan regions of the pattern where the lines intersect, usually places where deep concave angles are formed. Look at the deep concave angles on the briefcase object in Figure 3-11, where the curved component joins the rectangle. Examining the edges and the areas of intersection enables us to determine which basic components are present in the pattern: rectangular solid joined on the upper surface by a curved segment. This description of the object is then compared with stored descriptions in memory, something like "Briefcase: rectangular solid joined on the upper surface by a curved segment." When we find a match between the identified components and the stored representation, we have recognized the pattern.

Evidence for RBC In his investigations of the RBC model, Biederman has discovered several important facts about the object recognition process. For one, the model's emphasis on the importance of intersections or junction points turns out to be critical. If a pattern is degraded, it matters a great deal *where* it was degraded. If segments of the smooth, continuous edges are missing, it is reasonably easy to fill in the missing parts from memory and so be able to recognize the pattern. On the other hand, if the parts that are missing are in important locations where components join together, recognition is much more difficult, or even impossible.

Figure 3-12 shows several "nonrecoverable" drawings, that is drawings for which people either cannot recover from the deletions or take much longer before recognizing the object. Look at these carefully now and try to figure out what the objects are. It is so difficult because the important intersection or junction locations have been deleted. Now look at Figure 3-13. Here you see recoverable versions of the drawings, in which parts of the continuous edges have been deleted but the intersections remain visible. It is no surprise here that it is relatively easy to identify the original objects (you *can* identify them, can't you?). In Biederman's data (Biederman & Blickle, 1985), participants never did worse than 30% errors in identifying recoverable patterns, even when 65% of the continuous line contours were deleted and the pattern was only shown for 100 msec. But when the same percentage of the junctions or inter-sections were deleted, as in Figure 3-12, participants made errors in the 100 msec condition almost 55% of the time.

As useful as it might be as a theory of object recognition, RBC still seems incomplete to some. For one, the model seems especially tied to bottom-up pro-cessing, even though there is ample evi-dence of context-facilitated recognition (e.g., Biederman, Glass, & Stacy, 1973; Palmer, 1975). Although mechanisms could be proposed to add top-down processes, of course, the thrust of the model is still the data-driven parsing and recognition of components. Second, the model suggests that perceiving compo-nents is the first major step in object recognition, suggesting that the whole is perceived by first identifying the compo-nents. There are data, however, that show people can perceive the overall shape and pattern of an object just as rapidly and

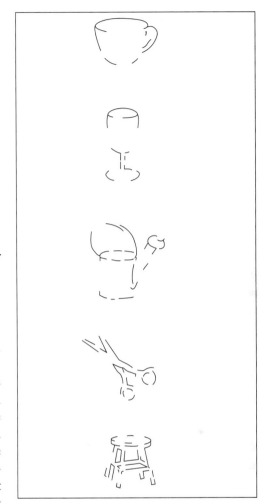

Figure 3-13

Recoverable objects. From Biederman, 1987.

accurately as they can perceive the components (e.g., Cave & Kosslyn, 1993). This of course contradicts the features-first aspect of the model.

We turn now to a third difficulty, neuropsychological evidence on object recogni-tion. In general, this evidence shows that object recognition probably is a joint effort between two mental processes and two different regions of the brain, one responsible for features and components—"bits and pieces," as it were—and another for overall shape and global patterns—the *gestalt*, or overall form. Interestingly, most of this neu-ropsychological evidence comes from studying people who, because of some kind of brain damage, have lost the fundamental ability we have been discussing here, the abil-ity to look at something and rapidly recognize what it is.

Agnosia

You've been reading about perception and pattern recognition, studying how mental mechanisms such as feature detection and top-down processing are responsible for our ability to recognize the stimuli around us. But we have not questioned *that* it happens, never thought that there might be problems in getting from a simple, ordinary stimulus to recognition of it. It is amazing to learn that a person can lose the ability to recognize objects, the ability to glance at something and immediately know what it is. There's an object, say a cup sitting on the kitchen counter or a briefcase sitting on the floor. We encode the stimulus, the set of features, into the visual system. It is then an automatic, seemingly instantaneous step from encoding to identification: You see the thing, and you immediately *know* that it's a cup—right?

Wrong. What you'll read about now is about a cognitive deficit, caused by brain damage, in which people can no longer perform the seemingly instantaneous mental steps of pattern recognition. There are certainly types of brain damage that can disrupt the recognition of printed language, letters and words, and you will read about some of this in Chapter 10, after the section on reading. But for now, we look at a different kind of disruption of recognition, when the recognition of objects—real-world *things*—is disrupted. We're talking about **agnosia,** defined as *a failure or deficit in recognizing objects*, either because the pattern of features cannot be synthesized into a whole or because the person cannot then connect the whole pattern to meaning (from the prefix *a*, meaning "not," and the Greek root *gnostic*, meaning "to know"; Freud is the one who first applied this name to this disorder). When this disruption affects a person's recognition of faces, sometimes while leaving object recognition intact, it is called **prosopagnosia,** a *disruption of face recognition*.

Bear in mind that when we talk about agnosia and agnosics (patients with agnosia), we are not talking about people whose basic sensory systems have been damaged. It is clear when a patient with agnosia is tested that the person can see, can detect visual stimuli; this is not a case of blindness. Instead, it is a cognitive, mental loss; the agnosic can input the basic visual stimulus but then cannot *do* anything with that encoded information.

Probably the most famous case of agnosia—and prosopagnosia too—is the title story in *The Man Who Mistook His Wife for a Hat* (Sacks, 1970), about an elderly music professor who had lost his ability to recognize objects and faces. At the end of a session with his doctor, he reached over and grasped his wife's head as if reaching to pick up his hat. In another meeting with the doctor, he was able to describe the components or elementary features of an object yet was unable to identify the object he was looking at.

> *"About six inches in length,"* he commented. *"A convoluted red form with a linear green attachment."*
>
> *"Yes,"* I said encouragingly, *"and what do you think it is, Dr. P.?"*
>
> *"Not easy to say."* . . .
>
> *"Smell it,"* I suggested.
>
> *"Beautiful!"* he exclaimed. *"An early rose. What a heavenly smell!"* (Sacks, 1970, pp. 13–14)

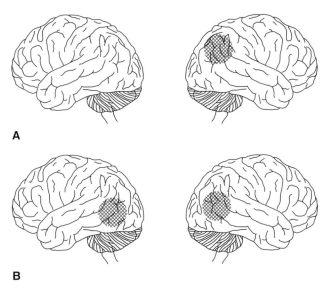

Figure 3-14

A, The left and right hemispheres of the brain, showing that apperceptive agnosia usually is limited to posterior (rear) regions of the right hemisphere parietal lobe (the cross-hatched region). **B,** both left and right hemispheres have cross-hatched regions at the junction of the temporal and occital lobes, the region usually damaged in associative agnosia. From Banich (1997).

He mistook the grandfather's clock in the hall for a person, and started with outstretched hand to greet it. Although he could describe the parts of an object (there were five "outpouchings," and so forth) he could not identify a glove that the doctor held in front of him. Dr. P., it seemed, had a serious and pervasive visual agnosia, a profound loss in the ability to recognize things through vision.

Although agnosia is not necessarily limited to vision—there can be auditory agnosias, for example—it is true that an agnosia is modality specific. That is, a person with visual agnosia has disrupted recognition of objects presented visually but no necessary involvement of hearing, touch, or other sensory systems (Dr. P. recognized the rose by smelling it). Likewise, there are subtypes of visual agnosia, each with a somewhat different type of deficit, each stemming from different regions of the brain.

The first form of visual agnosia is called **apperceptive agnosia,** *a basic disruption in perceiving patterns.* That is, although the ability to process rudimentary visual features, say color or brightness, is not disrupted, "the ability to coalesce this basic visual information into a percept, an entity, or a whole is lost" (Banich, 1997, p. 170). Figure 3-14 shows that the region most usually associated with apperceptive agnosia is in the right hemisphere, in the parietal lobe (the top right illustration). If the agnosia is severe, the person has almost no ability to discriminate between objects, for instance between a square and a rectangle, and is unable to copy or match simple shapes; such patients "seem to perceive only extremely small or local aspects of contour" (Banich, 1997, p. 171). In less severe cases, there can still be difficulties with patterns like those in Figure 3-13, the recoverable patterns that you probably had little or no difficulty identifying (Warrington & James, 1988). They somehow cannot fill in the missing contours to perceive the whole form or pattern.

In **associative agnosia**, the second major type of agnosia, the person seems able to construct a mental percept; he or she can combine the perceived features into a whole pattern. The disruption is that the person still *cannot associate the pattern with meaning*, still cannot link the perceived whole with stored knowledge about its identity. For example, a person tested by Ratcliff and Newcombe (1982) copied a drawing of a ship's anchor quite well and was able to give an accurate verbal definition of an anchor. The patient could not, however, identify the drawing he copied, nor could he draw an anchor from memory. In Gazzaniga, Ivry, and Mangun (1998, pp. 164–165), a patient with associative agnosia known as P.T. was shown a drawing of a combination lock. He perceived the overall round shape and the number markings around the edge but could only guess that the object was a telephone or a clock. Finally, with much prompting, he finally identified the lock, but only because he noticed that he had been twirling his fingers around, as if pantomiming how to open a combination lock.

Implications for Cognitive Science

What do these neurological disruptions mean for our understanding of normal perception and pattern recognition? How does evidence like this advance our understanding of cognition?

Start with the deficits known as apperceptive agnosia, where the *a* prefix to *perceptive* denotes some kind of perceptual failure. Here we have a serious disruption in a very early stage of perceptual processing, possibly even the first step after a stimulus is encoded into the visual system. It is a disorder of feature detection, a malfunction in the process of extracting features from visual stimuli. Biederman's (1990) geons, for instance, are not being identified, or at least not processed much beyond noticing small segments or junction points. Furthermore, it may be important that apperceptive agnosia seems to result from damage in the right hemisphere, in the parietal region; there is growing evidence that the right hemisphere is more involved in global processing, to include forming global patterns, and that the left hemisphere plays more of a role in local processing (i.e., processing small components and features). If so, then it seems reasonable to talk about a disrupted mechanism for forming a *gestalt* from the features, where this disrupted mechanism would correspond to the symptoms of apperceptive agnosia.

Associative agnosia is a deeper dysfunction: The *gestalt* or pattern has been formed but seems to have lost the associative pathway to the meaning and name of the object. As shown in Figure 3-14, the damaged regions in associative agnosia tend to be lower, more toward the temporal lobe, and in both hemispheres. This pathway, from the vision centers in the occipital lobe forward and down toward the temporal lobe, is commonly called the *"what" pathway*, the pathway that is activated when you look at something to decide *what* it is. The temporal lobes are particularly associated with areas related to language and word meaning. And connecting from a perceived pattern to the meaning and the name of that pattern is the impairment in associative agnosia.

In conclusion, the varieties of agnosia tell us at least three important things about the perception and identification of patterns and objects. First, detecting the features in a visual stimulus is a separate (and later) process from the sensory steps that encode a stimulus into the cognitive system. The basic features—whether horizontal lines in a capital *A*, geons, or something else—must be extracted from already encoded sensory information. Second, detecting the visual features is critical in constructing a perceived pattern, a percept. If the features cannot be extracted from the stimulus, then the person cannot "get" the *gestalt*, cannot form an overall pattern or percept. Finally, there is a separate step involved in hooking up the pattern with its meaning and name, involving the visual association from the pattern to the knowledge stored about it in memory. This is different from knowing the meaning and name of an object in verbal form. Indeed, given that P.T. only later realized what his pantomime meant, it seems likely that the visual association path can be isolated from all of the other ways of knowing about objects and patterns.

In short, simple, "immediate" recognition of objects—the cup, the briefcase—is neither simple nor immediate. The disruptions known as agnosia, whether caused by difficulties in feature detection or in associating patterns with meaning, provide additional evidence of the complexity of perception and pattern recognition.

■ Section Summary

- The Recognition by Components theory claims that we recognize objects by extracting or detecting three-dimensional components, geons, from encoded visual stimuli, then access memory to determine what real-world objects contain those components. The most informative parts of objects tend to be parts where the components join together; people have more difficulty recognizing objects when the intersections are degraded visually than when long, connecting segments are degraded.
- Studies of patients with visual agnosia demonstrate the complexity of perception and pattern recognition. Patients with apperceptive agnosia sometimes are unable to detect even elementary features from stimuli and therefore have difficulty in perceiving a whole pattern or gestalt. Those with associative agnosia can perceive the whole but still cannot associate the pattern with stored knowledge to identify the object.

Auditory Perception

Auditory stimuli consist of sound waves traveling through the air. The human auditory mechanism that responds to these stimuli is an amazingly awkward combination of components, a Rube Goldberg–type mechanism that translates the sound waves into a neural message. First, the sound waves are funneled into the ear, causing the tympanic membrane, or eardrum, to vibrate. This in turn causes the bones of the middle ear to

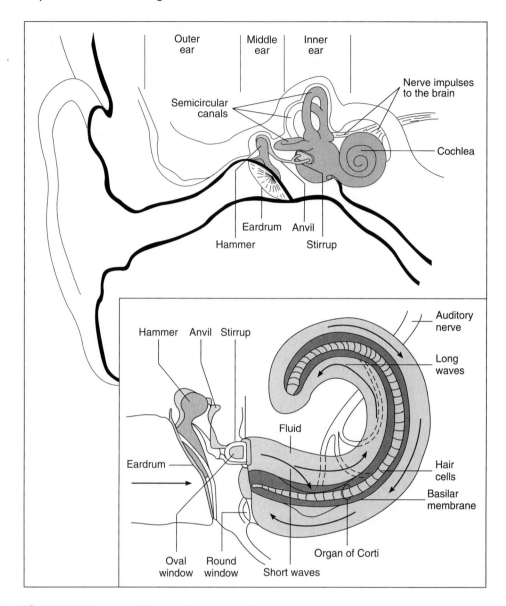

Figure 3-15

Gross structure of the human ear and a close-up of the middle and inner ear structures.
From Price, 1987.

move, which in turn sets in motion the fluid in the ear's inner cavity. The moving fluid then moves the tiny hair cells along the basilar membrane, generating the neural message, which is then sent along the auditory nerve into the cerebral cortex (e.g., Forgus & Melamed, 1976). Thus from the unpromising elements of funnels, moving bones, and the like (Figure 3-15) arises our *sense of hearing* or **audition**.

Interestingly, both ears project auditory sensations to both hemispheres of the brain, although the majority of the input obeys the principle of contralaterality. The primary auditory cortex, normally shown as a region in the superior (upper) medial (midway back) temporal lobe, actually extends somewhat further rearward in the brain, into the parietal lobe (Kolb & Whishaw, 1996; in Figure 2-8 in the last chapter, follow the Sylvian fissure to the rear of the temporal lobe to get an idea). Auditory input to the brain is sent to primarily to this auditory cortex, although at least four other nearby zones and several secondary areas are also affected.

The sensitivity of our sense of hearing is of particular interest because it defines the limits of our auditory world. A pure tone, such as that generated by a tuning fork, is a traveling sound wave with a regular frequency, a smooth pattern of up-and-down cycles per unit of time. Generally, humans are sensitive to patterns as low as 20 cps (cycles per second) and as high as 20,000 cps. Most of the sound patterns we are interested in, such as those generated by spoken speech, are of great complexity, combining dozens of different frequencies that vary widely in intensity or loudness. In terms of the sound wave patterns, these different frequencies are more or less superimposed and can be summarized in a spectrum (see examples under "Phonology" in Chapter 9).

In one sense, human hearing is not particularly impressive: Dogs, for instance, are sensitive to much higher frequencies than we are. In quite a different sense, our hearing is almost unbelievably complex. For instance, we can discriminate accurately between highly similar sounds even from birth: The slight difference between the sounds "pah" and "bah" is noticed by newborn infants (Eimas, 1975). And most impressive of all, we routinely convert the continuous stream of sounds known as speech into a comprehended message with little or no apparent effort at a rate of about two or three words per second. How does this auditory system work? How does it coordinate with our knowledge of language to yield recognition and comprehension so rapidly?

Auditory Sensory Memory

The term *auditory sensory memory* is used interchangeably with Neisser's (1967) term *echoic memory.* Both terms refer to a *brief memory system that receives auditory stimuli and preserves them for some amount of time.* Neisser's argument on the existence of echoic memory is still airtight: "Perhaps the most fundamental fact about hearing is that sound is an intrinsically temporal event. Auditory information is always spread out in time; no single millisecond contains enough information to be very useful. If information were discarded as soon as it arrived, hearing would be all but impossible. Therefore, we must assume that some 'buffer,' some medium for temporary storage, is available in the auditory cognitive system" (1967, pp. 199–200).

On the other side of the coin, it is equally clear that the memory system cannot (and should not) preserve the raw echoic memory trace forever. As was the case in iconic memory, only confusion would result if all auditory traces were held indefinitely. Thus the function of echoic memory is to encode the sensory stimulation into the memory system and hold it just long enough for the rest of the mental system to gain access to it.

Amount and Duration of Storage What is the effective duration of information stored in echoic memory? How long does encoded information reside there before it is lost? To answer these questions, we need a task that is the auditory analogue to Sperling's work. That is, we need a task that presents auditory stimuli briefly, in different auditory locations, and in such a way that we can cue selected parts of the auditory display for partial report.

Such a task was devised by Darwin, Turvey, and Crowder (1972; see also Moray, Bates, & Barnett, 1965). Darwin et al. devised what they called the three-eared man procedure, in which three different spoken messages came from three distinct locations. The subjects heard tape-recorded letters and digits through stereo headphones, with the tape engineered so that one message was played only into the left ear, one message was played only into the right ear, and the final message was played into both ears. Of course, the message played into both ears seemed to be localized in the middle of the subject's head, at the "third ear." Each of the messages contained three stimuli, say, *T 7 C* on the left ear, *4 B 9* on the right ear, and so on. Each sequence lasted 1 s on the tape recording, and all three sequences were presented simultaneously. Thus in the space of 1 s, three different sequences of letter and digit combinations were played, for a total of nine separate stimuli.

After the auditory messages were presented, subjects in the whole report condition had to report as many of the nine items as they could remember. Their performance averaged about four items correct, as shown in Figure 3-16. Subjects in the partial report condition were shown a visual cue, prompting recall of the left, right, or middle message. When the visual cue was presented immediately after the stimuli had been heard, performance on the cued ear was well above 50%, suggesting that nearly five items out of the original nine were still available. The advantage of partial report over whole report was maintained even with a 4-s delay in presenting the cue, although performance did decline during that waiting period (also shown in Figure 3-16). Thus the decline in accuracy suggested a decrease in the useful contents of auditory sensory memory, presumably because of a passive fading of information across longer delays.

Note two differences in these results compared with those for visual sensory memory. First, the estimated amount of information originally stored in auditory memory—estimated by partial report, of course—was not as impressive as the 75–90% values found for iconic memory. Darwin's subjects exceeded the level of about five items available out of the presented nine only on the third position items, those presented last in the sequences. Second, there is the distinct possibility that sensory traces reside in auditory memory for a longer time if they represent simpler information. In general, the 4-s duration found by Darwin et al. (1972) is longer than most estimates, probably because of the simplicity of the stimuli they used (most of the studies described later used coherent spoken language). In contrast, the 4-s estimate is much shorter than the 10-s storage found by Eriksen and Johnson (1964), but Eriksen and Johnson's subjects merely had to detect a simple tone while performing an attention-capturing task (they read novels for two hours; see also Watkins & Watkins, 1980).

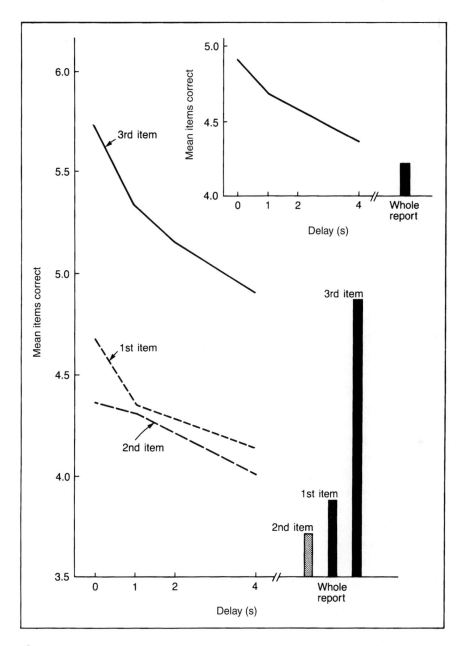

Figure 3-16

Partial report results in the "three-eared man" procedure. The average number of items recalled correctly is shown for the first, second, and third items in the three lists, across varying delay in the presentation of the partial report cue. The insert shows overall performance, along with the vertical bar that shows whole-report accuracy. From Darwin et al., 1972.

Persistence and Erasure of Auditory Information Without the process of redirected attention, the auditory trace in sensory memory simply vanishes with the passage of time, the auditory equivalent of passive fading in iconic memory. Recall, however, that there is also evidence of another kind of forgetting in iconic memory, due to erasure by subsequent stimuli. Is there any evidence of this kind of forgetting in auditory sensory memory, based on the interference of stimulus information encoded *after* the target information?

In a word, yes, although recent research indicates that a straightforward parallel with iconic persistence and erasure may be misleading, or even that a straightforward, purely auditory basis for what we have called auditory sensory memory may be somewhat inaccurate. We will consider the original evidence, then discuss the controversy over the current status and understanding of auditory sensory memory.

The best-known evidence on auditory persistence was presented by Crowder and Morton (1969; also Crowder, 1970, 1972). In their research, a list of nine digits was presented to all subjects in written form, at the fairly rapid rate of two items per second. In their Silent Vocalization condition, subjects merely saw the nine numbers and read them silently as they appeared. In the Active Vocalization condition, subjects not only saw the list but were also asked to name the digits out loud as they appeared on the screen. In the Passive Vocalization condition, subjects heard an accompanying tape recording that named the viewed digits for them. When Crowder and Morton examined subjects' recall performance, they found hardly any errors on the last item in the list when there was an auditory trace of that letter, that is, in the Active and Passive Vocalization groups. Errors here, as shown in Figure 3-16, were below 10%. These subjects had literally heard that last item, so presumably could perform simple readout on it from auditory sensory memory (in fact, the last three positions showed the auditory advantage). In other words, there appeared to be a lingering sensory trace for the last sounds that were heard. The Silent group, however, showed substantial errors on the last items, around 50%, because there was no auditory sensory memory trace for them. (Recall for the earlier positions presumably resulted from some combination of short- and long-term memory factors—rehearsal of some sort—and so is not of primary interest here.)

Thus Crowder suggested that the Vocalization conditions' recall for the last items was assisted by still-present traces in auditory sensory memory. This effect is generally known as the **modality effect**, *superior recall of the end of the list when the auditory mode is used instead of the visual mode of presentation.* Crowder (1972) argued that these results supported two distinct ideas, the existence of auditory sensory memory and the persistence of auditory traces in sensory memory across some short interval of time. Crowder's term for auditory sensory memory was *precategorical acoustic storage* (PAS). Because *categorization* implies recognition of the pattern, Crowder was claiming that this acoustic storage mechanism was *pre*categorical; that is, it occurred before categorization or pattern recognition.

Having established that auditory traces persist across time, even in an unrecognized form, Crowder went on to investigate another important point, auditory erasure. After

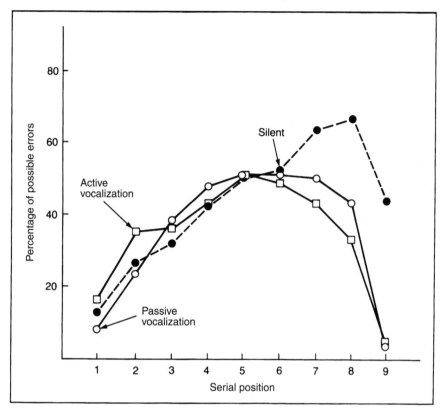

Figure 3-17

The number of errors in recall as a function of position in the list of items to be recalled. Note that the two vocalization groups show almost no errors on the last item, compared with the silent group, which had no auditory trace of the list.

they heard the items in the list, subjects in the *suffix* groups then heard one additional auditory stimulus: the word *zero* or a simple tone. Both groups were told that this final item was merely a cue to begin recalling the list. In reality, of course, the auditory *suffix* was intended to erase or interfere with the lingering auditory trace for the last items in the list.

As predicted, the zero–suffix group showed a high error rate on the last items, essentially the same error rate as the Silent group showed in the earlier study. The tone–suffix group, however, had very few errors on the last positions, just like the Vocalization groups mentioned earlier. It seemed as though the auditory suffix had indeed degraded or erased the auditory trace for the last digits in the list when the suffix was similar to the list. Figure 3-17 summarizes this program of research. The result is quite similar to the erasure effect in vision in that it varies depending on speech versus nonspeech suffixes, physical differences, and so on (see also Greene & Crowder, 1984, 1986).

In summary, auditory sensory memory is similar to the visual sensory memory system at a general level, but the details of storage duration and amounts are different. Both systems register sensory information and hold it for a brief period of time: 250–500 msec in vision but 2,000–4,000 msec in audition. This duration for auditory sensory memory, however, may vary with the complexity of stored information. Generally, more information is encoded in both systems than can be reported; however, capacity in auditory sensory memory, may be proportionately lower than visual sensory memory, although this issue is not an easy issue to pin down. The items held in both sensory systems are subject to loss over short periods of time, either by fading, when no other stimuli are encountered, or by erasure, when interfering auditory stimuli are processed. Finally, if attention is redirected during the critical interval, information can be sent to short-term memory, preventing it from being lost. Just as in vision, our normal auditory world usually is one of continuous auditory stimulation, not discrete bursts of sound followed by blank intervals.

Auditory Pattern Recognition

We will postpone most of our discussion of auditory pattern recognition until later. The reason for this is that much of the research on pattern recognition in hearing is more interesting in the context of two different topics: attention, which we cover in Chapter 4, and language, covered in Chapter 9. So here is a brief discussion of the topic, with just enough intriguing findings to propel you into Chapter 4 and a full treatment of the topic of attention.

Templates Attempts to understand how we recognize sounds, especially language sounds, have paralleled the work on visual pattern recognition. That is, there were some attempts at explaining auditory pattern recognition by templates, by claims that we identify incoming sounds by trying to match them to stored models or templates in memory.

These attempts were quickly abandoned, however, for an obvious reason: Not only do different people produce language sounds quite differently from one another, but even the same sound produced by the same speaker varies widely from time to time. Even more damaging to the template approach, the "same" sound varies from word to word, even when spoken by the same speaker.

In psycholinguistics this is called the **problem of invariance**; the problem is that *the sounds of speech are not invariant from one time to the next*. Instead, any particular sound changes physically depending on what sound preceded it in a word and what sounds are going to follow it.

Feature Detection Parallel to the work in vision, feature detection models of auditory pattern recognition were somewhat more successful than template models. But for the most part, research on feature detection leads to the same conclusion in audition as it did in vision: loads of evidence that *context* plays a decisive role, that is, conceptually driven processing.

Table 3-2 WARREN AND WARREN'S (1970) SENTENCES AND SUBJECTS' RESPONSES	
Subject Hears	**Subject Reports**
It was found that the *eel was on the axle.	wheel
It was found that the *eel was on the shoe.	heel
It was found that the *eel was on the orange.	peel
It was found that the *eel was on the table.	meal

Note The asterisks represent a deleted sound.

Conceptually Driven Processing   Let's just take two examples of research showing the effects of context, of conceptually driven processing effects. In the first, Pollack and Pickett (1964) tape recorded the idle conversations of volunteers who were waiting to be in a research project. The tapes were then played to other volunteers to see whether they could identify the words, which, of course, they could. But in the more interesting condition, individual words were spliced out of the tapes and presented in isolation. Here, only about half of all the presented words could be identified. Removing words from their normal context made it extremely difficult to recognize the patterns. By inference, then, context plays an important role in spoken word identification.

In the second example, Warren and Warren (1970) presented speech stimuli to their experimental subjects and asked them to report what they had heard. The tape recordings were carefully engineered so that one specific *language sound* (the technical term is **phoneme**) was removed from a single word. Participants heard the altered sentences shown in Table 3-2, where an asterisk indicates the sound that was removed. The word they recognized is shown at the right of each sentence. For instance, even though they heard "*eel," hearing the rest of the sentence, "on the axle," was sufficient for them to perceive the word *wheel*. In fact, most never even noticed anything strange at all about what they heard; it all sounded completely natural. It's a simple but powerful demonstration: Perception and identification of speech are heavily dependent on context, on top-down processing. It's also a nice reminder of the difference between sensation and perception, the physical, sensory nature of sensation, but the overwhelmingly cognitive nature of perception.

■ Section Summary

- Auditory stimulation is stored briefly in auditory sensory memory, for periods up to 4 s or so for language-based information. Although auditory sensory memory lasts longer than visual sensory memory, its capacity may not be as large as that of visual sensory memory. Generally, the last items in a list presented auditorially are recalled better than items presented visually, an effect known as the modality effect; furthermore, an auditory suffix added to the end of the list degrades performance on the last list items, demonstrating erasure from auditory sensory memory. Theories of auditory pattern recognition resemble those in vision; that is, they involve feature detection plus a substantial role for top-down processing.

Key Terms

agnosia (p. 106)

apperceptive agnosia (p. 107)

associative agnosia (p. 108)

audition (p. 110)

auditory sensory (echoic) memory (p. 111)

backward masking (p. 87)

conceptually driven processing effects (p. 94)

connectionism (p. 98)

context (p. 97)

data-driven processing system (p. 94)

decay (p. 86)

echoic memory (p. 111)

ecological validity (p. 87)

erasure (p. 87)

feature analysis (p. 91)

feature detection (p. 91)

fixation (p. 78)

focal attention (p. 90)

fovea (p. 76)

geons (p. 103)

icon (p. 85)

interference (p. 86)

modality effect (p. 114)

pandemonium (p. 92)

partial report condition (p. 84)

perception (p. 78)

phoneme (p. 116)

problem of invariance (p. 116)

prosopagnosia (p. 106)

retina (p. 74)

saccades (p. 78)

sensation (p. 78)

span of apprehension (p. 84)

tachistoscope (p. 82)

templates (p. 91)

visual persistence (p. 81)

visual sensory (iconic) memory (p. 82)

whole report condition (p. 84)

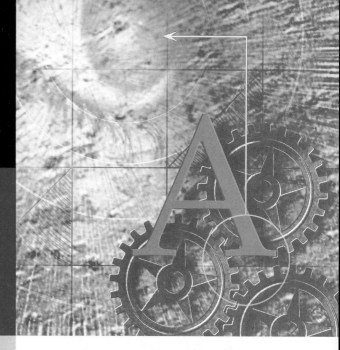

CHAPTER 4

Attention

Everyone knows what attention is. It is the taking possession by the mind, in clear and vivid form, of one out of what seem several simultaneously possible objects or trains of thought. Focalization, concentration, of consciousness are of its essence. It implies withdrawal from some things in order to deal effectively with others. (James, 1890, pp. 381–382)

As he did every morning after waking, Bill went into the bathroom to begin his morning ritual. After squeezing toothpaste onto his toothbrush, he looked into the mirror and began to brush his teeth. Although he brushed the teeth on the right side of his mouth quite vigorously, for the most part he ignored those on the left side. . . . He shaved all the stubble from the right side of his face impeccably but did a spotty job on the left side. . . . [After eating at a diner,] when Bill asked for the check, the waitress placed it on the left side of the table. After a few minutes, he waved the waitress over and complained, saying "I asked for my tab 5 minutes ago. What is taking so long?" (Banich, 1997, p. 235)

Attention, one of cognitive psychology's most important topics and one of our oldest puzzles in the study of the mind, in Neisser's (1976) description is "psychology's most elusive target." What does it mean to pay attention to something? To direct your attention to something? To be unable to pay attention because of boredom, lack of interest, or fatigue? What sorts of things, whether external stimuli or internal thoughts, grab or capture our attention? How much control do we have over our attention? Is it always a matter of concentration and determination when you pay attention to something? Or are some things easy to attend to, and if so, why? (Cognitive science says "attend to," meaning "pay attention," even though the dictionary claims that to be an archaic usage.) I have to work at paying attention to some things (most topics in a faculty meeting, for example). But for other topics, it seems effortless: A good spy novel rivets my attention, just as a great cognition lecture rivets yours (!).

Multiple Meanings of Attention

Attention is one of the most pervasive topics in cognitive psychology and one of the thorniest, possibly because we mean so many different things by the term. We apply the term *attention* to a huge range of phenomena, from the basic notion of arousal and alertness all the way up to consciousness and awareness. Some attentional processes are extremely rapid, so that we are aware only of their outcomes, and others are slow enough that we seem to be aware of them—and able to control them—throughout. In some cases, attention is very much like a reflex. Even when we are deliberately concentrating on something, that concentration can be disrupted and redirected by an unexpected,

Table 4-1 SIX MEANINGS OF ATTENTION

Input Attention	Controlled Attention
Alertness or arousal	Selective attention
Orienting reflex or response	Mental resources and conscious processing
Spotlight attention and search	Supervisory attentional system

attention-grabbing event, such as the sudden loud noise in the otherwise quiet library. In other cases, we are frustrated that our deliberate attempts to focus attention on some task are so easily disrupted by another train of thought; you try very hard to pay attention to a lecture, only to find yourself daydreaming about last weekend's party.

Table 4-1 presents a list of six different connotations of the term *attention*, different processes, phenomena, or ideas that in one way or another are involved in a study of attention. For organizational purposes, this chapter is structured around that list to impose some coherence on an otherwise confusing field, to help you see the forest and prevent your getting lost in the trees (the final type of attention in the table is nearly synonymous with short-term or working memory, so it is not discussed until the next chapter). Although other organizational schemes are possible, this approach should at least help you develop an understanding of the topic of attention and see how certain topics flow into others. The list will also help us avoid some of the confusion that arises when the general term *attention* is used for processes or mechanisms more precisely described by another term, such as arousal.

We'll rely on everyday examples and your intuitive understanding, but only so far as they help us understand the empirical concept of attention. And at every turn, we confront four interrelated ideas. *First*, we are constantly confronted with much more information than we can pay attention to. *Second*, there are serious limitations in how much we can attend to at any one time. *Third*, we can respond to some information and perform some tasks with little if any attention. And *fourth*, with sufficient practice and knowledge, some tasks become less and less demanding of our attentional processes.

Basics of Attention

Let's start by giving two rather general definitions for the concept of attention, both of which apply throughout the list in Table 4-1.

Attention as a Mental Process **Attention** can be thought of as *the mental process of concentrating effort on a stimulus or a mental event.* By this definition we mean that attention is an activity that occurs within the cognitive system, a process. This process focuses a mental commodity—effort—on either an external stimulus or an internal event. So when you examine a picture like that in Figure 4-1, you focus your mental energies on an external stimulus, the splotches and patches of black and white in a puzzling photograph. If you have never seen the photograph before, you struggle to identify it, to recognize the pattern in it; you are reduced to very heavy reliance on data-driven processing. As you puzzle

Figure 4-1

First identification of the pattern relies almost exclusively on data-driven processing, whereas later identification relies heavily on conceptually driven processing.

and wonder, searching for clues, you focus this mental effort in an attempt to identify the pattern; the effort you focused was attention. Attention is the mental process that focused your eyes on the figure and encoded the photograph into your visual system. Sustained attention then led, possibly after a long while, to identifying the dalmatian in the photo.

In principle, this focusing of your attention on a visual stimulus is no different than when you focus purely mental attention on a word, idea, or concept. For example, your professor says something unexpected (e.g., describing an idea as "green"), and you puzzle over the remark, trying to find a way of interpreting the remark that makes sense (can an idea that promotes conservation and ecology be described as "green"? See also Chapter 9). It is this concentration of attention we are illustrating here, attention focused on and driving the mental event of remembering, searching for information stored in your long-term memory, attempting to comprehend.

Attention as a Limited Mental Resource Now consider attention as a mental resource, a kind of mental fuel. In this sense, attention is *the limited mental energy or resource that powers the mental system*. It is a mental commodity, the stuff that gets focused when we pay attention. According to this definition, attention is the all-important mental resource necessary to run the cognitive system, to make it operate.

A fundamentally important idea here is the notion of limitations: Attention is limited, finite. We usually state this idea by talking about the limited capacity of the attentional system. Countless experiments, to say nothing of everyday experiences, show that there is a limitation in our attentional capacity, the capacity to attend to stimuli, to remember events that just happened, to remember things we are supposed to do. In short, there is a limit to how many different things we can attend to and do all at once.

It does not take very long to think of everyday situations that reveal these attentional limitations. I can easily drive down an uncrowded highway in daylight while I carry on a conversation with someone, maybe on a cell phone. I can easily listen to the news on the radio under normal driving conditions. In the middle of a heavy rainstorm, however, I can't talk to the person sitting in the passenger seat; in rush hour traffic, I can't (or shouldn't try to) do business on the cell phone. Under such demanding circumstances, the radio is an annoyance or an irritating distraction, and I have to turn down the volume.

Try a demonstration right now. First, count backwards by 3s out loud, starting from some arbitrary number such as 741. Get good at it, to the point that you can keep up a steady, challenging rhythm. Now, try counting backwards by 3s while you read a paragraph from this book. Neither of these tasks is too difficult by itself, another way of saying that neither task exceeds your attentional capacity. Doing them simultaneously, however, overtaxes the attentional system; you probably slowed down in your backwards counting or your reading or made some counting errors. Although you have sufficient attentional capacity to do either task alone, there is not enough to do them both together.

Basic Input Attentional Processes

We'll start with a section on the more basic types of attention listed in Table 4-1, those occurring early in the stream of mental processing. These are the processes that seem either reflexive or automatic, low-level in terms of informational content, and quite rapid. They are especially involved in *the basic processes of getting sensory information into the cognitive system*, so they can generally be called forms of **input attention.**

Alertness and Arousal

It almost seems axiomatic to say that part of what we mean by *attention* involves the basic capacity to respond to the environment. This most basic sense refers to alertness and arousal as a necessary state of the nervous system: The nervous system must be awake, responsive, and able to interact with the environment. At the physiological level, arousal is at least partly a function of the reticular activating system (RAS), a lower brain stem system in charge of, among other things, basic arousal and consciousness (Kolb & Whishaw, 1996). It seems clear, intuitively, that the nervous system must be aroused in order to pay attention. You cannot attend to stimuli while you are unconscious, of course, although certain stimuli can impinge on us and rouse us to a conscious state (e.g., alarm clocks, smoke detectors, or other loud noises).

Although nobody disputes that arousal and alertness are a necessary precondition for most cognitive processing, this view may overemphasize a kind of mental processing known as **explicit processing.** That is, explicit processes are those *involving conscious processing, conscious awareness that a task is being performed, and usually conscious awareness of* *the outcome of that performance.* The opposite is known as **implicit processing,** *processing with no necessary involvement of conscious awareness* (Schacter, 1989, 1996). As you will see later in the book, the distinction between implicit and explicit is often in terms of memory performance, especially long-term memory. When I ask you to learn a list of words and then name them back, that's an explicit memory task: You are consciously aware of being tested and aware that you are remembering words you just studied on the list. By contrast, you can also demonstrate memory for information *without* being aware of remembering it, a demonstration of implicit memory. For example, you can reread a passage of text more rapidly than you read it the first time, even if you have no recollection of ever reading the passage before (Masson, 1984).

Much evidence shows that some important mental processing can be accomplished with only minimal attentional involvement. Much of this is discussed later in the book, especially in sections on long-term memory. For now, consider just one study on alertness and arousal, conducted by Bonebakker et al. (1996). These investigators presented tape-recorded lists of words to surgery patients, one list just before and another during surgery, and then tested their memory for the words up to 24 hours later. Despite the fact that all the patients were given general anesthesia and were therefore unconscious during the surgery itself, they nonetheless demonstrated memory for words they heard during the surgery.

The powerful part of the demonstration was that performance was based on an implicit memory task, the *word stem completion task.* Patients were given word stems and told to complete them with the first word they thought of. To ensure that the task was measuring only implicit memory, patients were further asked to leave out or exclude any words they explicitly remembered hearing, such as the words they remembered hearing before receiving anesthesia. For example, say that they heard *BOARD* before surgery and *LIGHT* during surgery. When tested 24 hours after surgery, the patients completed the word stems (e.g., *LI_ _ _*) with words they had heard during surgery (*LIGHT*) significantly more frequently than they did with presurgery words (*BO_ _ _*) or with control words that had never been presented on the tapes. In other words, they remembered hearing *BOARD* and excluded it on the word stem task. Because they did not explicitly remember *LIGHT*, they finished *LI_ _ _* with *GHT*, presumably because their memory of *LIGHT* was implicit. The results demonstrated clearly that the patients had implicit memory of the word lists they had heard while they were under the anesthesia, a state very close to no alertness or arousal at all.

So you will understand this procedure better, and because we will encounter it several times in later chapters, here is a more focused, written version of the task. Imagine that you saw a list of words including *SCHOOL* and *SHELF.* Relying on explicit memory, you would probably complete the stem *SCH_ _ _* with *SCHOOL.* But if I asked you to exclude words you explicitly remembered, you would find another way of completing that stem, say *SCHEME;* likewise, you might exclude *SHELF* and write *SHELL.* By chance alone, you might complete the stem *CRA_ _ _* with *CRADLE* or *CRAYON,* neither of which you saw on the list. Here is the implicit part of the demonstration—if it works. Try it yourself. Complete the following word stems with the first word that comes to your mind: *PAP_ _*; *GRE_ _*. *PAPER* is a pretty common completion for the first one, but probably only because *paper* is a fairly common word (it has not appeared in this chapter yet). But if you completed the second one as *GREEN* without explicitly remembering that you read about "green ideas" earlier, then that probably was an implicit memory effect.

Reflexive Attention and the Orienting Response

Now consider another kind of attention, the kind caused by reflex responses in the nervous system. In a quiet room, an unexpected noise immediately grabs your attention away from what you were doing and often involves a reflexive turning of your head toward the source of the sound. In vision, of course, you turn your eyes and head toward the unexpected stimulus, the flash of light or sudden movement detected in your peripheral vision. This is the **orienting reflex** or **orienting response,** *the reflexive redirection of attention that orients you toward the unexpected stimulus.* This response is found at all levels of the animal kingdom and is present very early in life. Although a host of physiological changes accompany the orienting response, including changes in heart rate and respiration (Bridgeman, 1988), we focus on the more mental aspects of the response.

Current thinking suggests that the orienting reflex is a location-finding response of the nervous system. That is, an unexpected stimulus, a noise or a flash of light, triggers the reflex so that you can locate the stimulus, find where it is in space. This response enables you to protect yourself against danger, in the reflexive, survival sense; after all, what if the unexpected movement you detect is a rock thrown at you? Given that the response helps you locate the stimulus, it is not surprising that some of the neural pathways involved in this response correspond to the *"where" pathway* (a companion to the "what" pathway involved in object recognition). Briefly, the "where" pathway projects from the visual cortex to upper (superior) rearward (dorsal) regions of the parietal lobe in the brain; in fact, the "where" pathway is also called the dorsal pathway (and the "what" pathway is also called the ventral pathway).

Cowan (1995) noted that the kinds of stimuli that trigger the orienting reflex boil down to two basic categories: stimuli that are significant for the organism (the rock thrown toward your head) and stimuli that are novel. We orient toward a novel stimulus in an otherwise constant, unchanging, even monotonous background. We orient when something *different* occurs: the unexpected sound in the quiet library, the change in pitch in a professor's voice during a lecture, maybe the word *different* in italics in a textbook paragraph. Orienting focuses the organism so it can devote deliberate attention to the stimulus if warranted; Cowan (1995) called these voluntary attentive processes. In this sense, orienting is a preparatory response, one that prepares the system for further voluntary processing.

On the other hand, if the stimulus that triggered the orienting reflex then occurs over and over again, it is no longer novel or different; now it has become part of the normal, unchanging background. At this point the process of **habituation** begins to take over, *a gradual reduction of the orienting response back to baseline.* For example, if the unexpected noise in the quiet library is the ventilation fan coming on, you first notice it but then grow accustomed to it as it continues. You have oriented to the stimulus, and then that response has habituated, to the point that you will probably orient again when the fan *stops* running. When the constant noise stops, *that* is a change that triggers the orienting response.

Cowan (1995), among others, believes that a thorough understanding of this orienting reflex, along with habituation, can go a long way toward helping us understand attention in all its forms. For one thing, it is a kind of bridge, from the built-in reflexive process of attention to the voluntary, deliberate attentional system that we turn to next. Second, as you will see in a few moments, there are some important parallels between orienting and habituation on one hand and selective attention on the other.

Spotlight Attention and Visual Search

The last sense of *attention* to be considered among the input attentional processes is a kind of visual attention. It is closely related to perceptual space, that is, the spatial arrangement of stimuli in your visual field, and the way you search that space for information. But it is a different process than the orienting response to a visual stimulus that you just read about. In orienting, your attentional focus is captured by an unexpected stimulus, and your head and eyes move toward the stimulus. In spotlight attention, there is no movement of the eyes or head. Instead, there is a mental shift of attentional focus, as if a spotlight beam were focused on a region of visual space, enabling you to pick up information in that space more easily.

A large amount of work on this kind of visual attention has been reported, including several recent articles that have found distinct regions of the brain that seem to be involved in this focused, visual attention system. Here we concentrate especially on work by two investigators: Posner and his work on visual attentional focus and Treisman and her work on visual search.

The Spotlight of Visual Attention Consider Figure 4-2, which depicts three different kinds of displays in Posner's spatial cuing task (Posner, Nissen, & Ogden, 1978; Posner, Snyder, & Davidson, 1980). Subjects in this cued detection task are first asked to fixate the centered plus sign on the visual display, are then shown a directional cue, and finally see a simple target. The task merely asks subjects to press a button when they detect the target. For 80% of the cued trials, the arrow pointed to the direction where the target actually did appear 1 s later. On the remaining 20% of the cued trials, however, the cue was invalid: It pointed to the wrong side for the upcoming target. Neutral trials provided an uninformative cue, a two-headed arrow indicating that the target would appear equally often on the left or right. Throughout the task, subjects were required to maintain fixation on the plus sign. That is, they could shift only their *mental* attention to the space where they thought the target might appear but were not permitted to move their eyes in the direction of the cue.

The results, shown in Figure 4-3, were very clear. When subjects shifted attention to the correct area (the Valid 80% point in the figure), reaction time (RT) to detect the

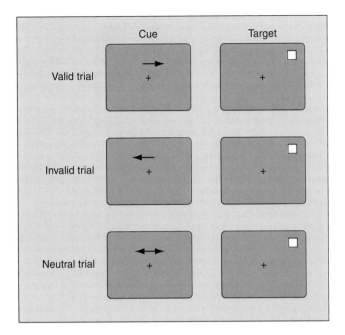

Figure 4-2

In Posner's spatial cuing task, the subject fixates on the plus sign in the center of the screen, then sees an arrow pointing left or right or a two-headed arrow. For the targets shown in the figure, with a target appearing on the right, the right-pointing arrow is a valid cue, the left-pointing arrow an invalid cue, and the two-headed arrow a neutral cue. In this experiment, one-headed arrow cues were valid on 80% of the trials.

target was significantly faster than the neutral, uncued condition. This speedup is known as a **benefit** or **facilitation,** a *faster-than-baseline response resulting from the useful advance information.* When the target appeared in the unexpected location, however, there was a significant **cost,** *a response slower than baseline because of the misleading cue.* Interestingly, further analysis suggested that the cost of having directed attention to the wrong place resulted from a three-part process, disengaging attention from its current focus, moving the attentional spotlight to the target's true location, then engaging attention at that new location.

Posner et al. (1980) concluded from this and related experiments that the attentional focus subjects were switching was a thoroughly cognitive phenomenon; it was not tied to eye movements or other overt behavior but to an internal focusing mechanism. They suggested that "attention can be likened to a spotlight that enhances the efficiency of detection of events within its beam" (p. 172). So **spotlight attention** is *the mental attention-focusing mechanism that prepares you to encode stimulus information.* Furthermore, Posner et al. suggested that this shift in attention is essentially the same as the redirection of attention in the orienting reflex, with one big difference: It is voluntary, under the subject's control.

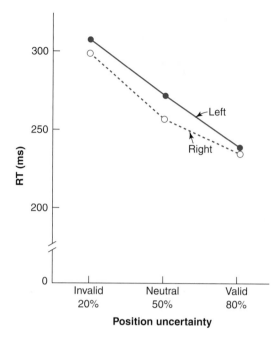

Figure 4-3

Consider the reaction time (RT) points in the neutral condition to be baseline performance on detecting targets. When a valid cue was presented, there was a reduction in RT for targets in both the left and right visual fields ("Valid 80%"). When the cue was invalid, there was a slow-down in detecting the target in both visual fields ("Invalid 20%"). From Posner, Snyder, & Davidson (1980).

Therefore, it can happen before a stimulus occurs and thus can be triggered by cognitive factors such as prior cuing and expectations. The orienting reflex is reactive in that the arrival of an unexpected stimulus causes the reaction. The mental spotlight type of attention, however, is cognitive; it results from a deliberate mental process.

As Cave and Bichot (1999) pointed out, countless studies of visual attention, many of them inspired by Posner's work, have adopted the spotlight metaphor in investigating visual attention, or as Johnston, McCann, and Remington (1995) called it, *input attention.* Much of that work has explored the characteristics and limits of visual attention, attempting to evaluate how useful the metaphor is. For instance, when a real spotlight shifts its beam from one location to another, it illuminates the locations between those two locations as it moves; the time it takes to change locations also depends on how far away the new location is. The evidence of visual attention, however, suggests that the mental spotlight does not sweep, enhancing the intermediate locations along the way, but instead that it jumps (much as the saccade does). On the other hand, there is also supportive evidence for the similarity between a real spotlight and spotlight atten-

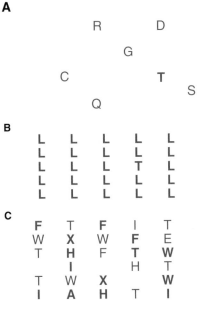

Figure 4-4

In the left panel, search either for a capital *T* or a boldfaced letter. In the other two panels, search for a bold-faced capital *T.*

tion. For example, there is evidence that the size of the spotlight beam can be altered, depending on circumstances, that a zoomlike process is part of the attentional spotlight, and that stimuli toward the center of the beam are facilitated more than stimuli on the fringes (see Cave & Bichot, 1999, for their extensive review of the literature).

Visual Search Look at Figure 4-4. In the first panel, search for either a letter *T* or a boldfaced letter; in the other two panels, search for a boldfaced *T.* As you performed these searches, you surely noticed that searching for *T* in the first panel was stunningly simple; it hardly seemed like a search, did it? Instead, didn't the T just "pop out" at you from the page? In contrast, searching for *T* in the middle panel probably was a slow process, and finding it in the last panel probably took even longer.

A distinguished series of studies by Treisman and her associates (Treisman, 1982, 1988, 1991; Treisman & Gelade, 1980) examined spotlight attention in terms of visual search and pattern recognition. Typically, participants in the experiments were told to search the visual display for either of two simple features (e.g., letter *S* or a blue letter) or a conjunction of two features (e.g., a green *T*). The search for a simple feature was called the disjunction condition: participants responded "yes" when they detected the presence of either of the specified features, either a letter *S* or a blue letter. In the conjunction condition, they had to search for the combination of two features, *T* and the color green. In the searches you conducted, the first panel search was a disjunction search, and the last panel illustrated a conjunction search (the target had to be both bold-faced and a *T*).

In the typical result (Treisman & Gelade, 1980, Experiment 1), subjects could search rapidly for either color or shape, and it made little or no difference whether they searched through a small or a large display; for instance, subjects were able to search through as few as 5 patterns or as many as 30 in about the same amount of time, approximately 500 msec. Because there was no increase in RT across the display sizes in the disjunction search condition, Treisman and Gelade concluded that visual search for a dimension such as shape or color occurs in parallel across the entire region of visual attention. Such a search, they suggested, must be largely automatic and must represent very early visual processing. In the results, shown in Figure 4-5, this is the flat, low function of the graph.

But when subjects had to search for a conjunction of features, such as a green *T*, they took much more time, up to 2,400 msec, as more and more distractor items filled the display (distractors for both conditions were brown *T*s and green *X*s). Such conjunction search, Treisman and Gelade reasoned, must be occurring in a more serial, one-by-one fashion and seemed to be a far more conscious, deliberate act. This is the steeply increasing function in Figure 4-5.

There is some debate about these interpretations, along with many follow-up studies. For example, Duncan and Humphreys (1989) showed that visual search rates depend critically on the kinds of distractor patterns through which subjects are searching and the similarity of those patterns to the targets (see also Duncan & Humphreys, 1992; Treisman, 1992). This is surely the case because finding the boldfaced *T* in the middle panel was difficult in part because all the letters were angular and boldfaced. And it was even harder in the last panel because of the many near misses, the large number of *T*s and boldfaced letters, all of which matched on one but not both of the target letter's features.

Contrasting Input and Controlled Attention

Aside from differences of opinion in interpreting the results from this area, however, one clearcut conclusion deserves special mention here. Treisman's two conditions provided clear evidence of both a very quick, automatic attentional process—essentially the capture of attention due to "pop-out"—and a much slower, more deliberate attention, the type used for the conjunction search. In line with Johnston et al.'s (1995) suggestion, we will stick with the term *input attention* for the fast, automatic process of attention, the type of process we have been talking about in this section. The slower one, in Johnston et al.'s terms, is *controlled attention*, to which we turn in a moment.

Consider the early, rapid stages of feature detection as relying on spotlight attention, a process operating very early in perception (Posner & Cohen, 1984). The spotlight is directed toward a visual display and "enhances the detection of events within its 'beam' " (Kanwisher & Driver, 1992). It provides the encoding route into the visual system. It is this attentional focus mechanism that provides early, extremely rapid feature

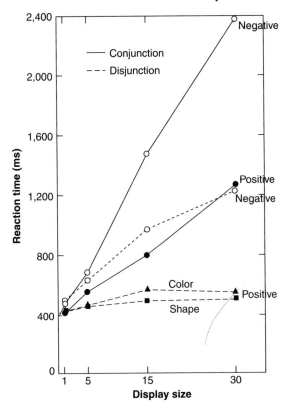

Figure 4-5

Search times when targets were of a specified color or shape. The dashed lines are for the disjunction search conditions (e.g., search for either a capital *T* or a bold-faced letter). The solid lines show search times for the conjunction condition (e.g., search for a boldfaced T). The important result is that disjunctive search times did not increase as the display size grew larger, but the conjunction search times did.

detection for the ensuing process of pattern recognition. It is especially visual; for instance, it has been called posterior attention because the earliest stages of visual perception occur in the posterior region of the brain, in the occipital lobe, as illustrated in Figure 4-6 (see also the inside front cover illustration of neural activity in the occipital lobe when a visual stimulus is presented).

The spotlight attention we are talking about—and we presume there is also an equivalent attention mechanism for audition—appears to be rapid, automatic, and perceptual. It is thereby distinguished from the slower, controlled or conscious attention process that matches the more ordinary connotation of the term *attention*. The "regular" kind is the

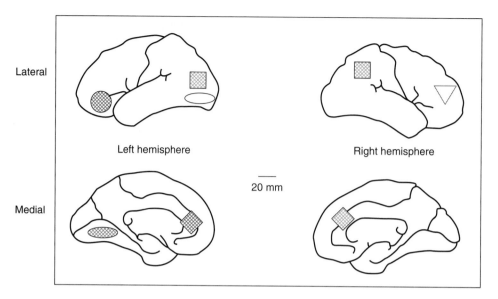

Figure 4-6

The top two drawings show lateral (side) views of the left and right hemispheres of the brain, and the bottom two show medial views, as if the hemispheres had been split down the center from front to back, showing inner portions of the cortex. The geometric shapes refer to different regions of the brain that are involved in attention; squares denote regions involved in the attentional network, the triangle denotes a region related to vigilance, and the diamond denotes a part of the anterior attentional network; the circle and oval denote word processing regions for semantic associates and visual word forms, respectively. Solso (1998).

conscious attention that we have loosely equated with awareness. Based on some neuro-physiological evidence, we might even call this frontal or anterior attention because activity in the frontal regions of the brain seems to accompany elements of conscious awareness, such as awareness of the meaning of a word (Posner et al., 1992).

Conscious or controlled attention prepares us to respond in a deliberate way to the environment. It is slower, operates in a more serial fashion, and is especially influenced by conceptually driven processes. Spotlight attention, however, is a basic, rapid attentional mechanism that seems to operate in parallel across the visual field, in a highly automatic fashion. It is especially data driven, funneling aspects of the environment into the cognitive system. Conscious attention then enables us to respond to that environment.

■ Section Summary

• Attention is a pervasive and complex topic, with meanings and connotations ranging from alertness and arousal up through the notions of automatic and conscious processing. A basic dichotomy is between attention as a mental process or mechanism and attention as a limited mental resource.

- Three basic senses of the term *attention* refer to alertness and arousal, the orienting reflex, and the spotlight of attention. These correspond to input attention, a fast process involved in encoding environmental stimuli into the mental system. Interestingly, in vision, the mental spotlight of attention can be shifted without any movement of the eyes, confirming the mental rather than perceptual nature of attention.

Controlled, Voluntary Attention

We turn now to several senses of the term *attention* that point to the controlled, voluntary nature of attentional processes. Input attention is what you have just studied, including the orienting response and spotlight attention. **Controlled attention,** in contrast, refers to forms of processing in which there is *a deliberate, voluntary allocation of mental effort or concentration. You* decide to pay attention to this stimulus and ignore others, and this paying attention may be effortful. The study of this later, controlled kind of attention begins with classic research done in the 1950s and 1960s on the process of selective attention.

Cognitive psychology has always been intrigued by the observation that at any moment, scores of different sensory messages are impinging on our senses. We can neither attend to all of them (we would be overwhelmed instantly), nor can we afford for our attention to be captured by one, then another, then another of the multiple sensory inputs (we would lose all coherence, all continuity). Therefore, it has always made sense to ask questions about **selective attention,** the *ability to attend to one source of information while ignoring or excluding other ongoing messages around us.* How do our mental processes

Dangerously divided attention.

In a classroom situation, students must constantly filter out the unimportant from the important details. This is an example of selective attention in auditory perception.

enable us to do this? How do you screen out the surrounding noises so you can hear just one? How can you listen covertly to the person on your right, who is gossiping about someone you know, while overtly pretending to listen to a conversational partner on your left? (And how did you notice in the first place that the person on your right was gossiping?) Somewhat the converse of selective attention is the topic of divided attention: How do we divide or share our attentional capacity across more than one source of information at a time, and how much information are we picking up from the several attended sources? When do we start reaching the limits of our attentional capacity?

Selective Attention and the Cocktail Party Effect

When you try to ignore the many stimuli or events around you so you can focus on just one, the ones you are trying to ignore are distractions that must be eliminated or excluded. *The mental process of eliminating those distractions, eliminating unwanted messages,* is called **filtering** or **selecting.** Some aspect of the attention mechanism seems to filter out the unwanted, extraneous sources of information so we can select the one message we want to pay attention to.

The process of filtering and selective attention seems to be straightforward in vision: You move your eyes, thereby selecting what you will pay attention to. As you just saw, however, attention is separate from eye movements: You can shift your mental attention even without eye movements. But in hearing, attention has no outward, behavioral component that is analogous to eye movements, so cognition has always realized that the selective attention process in hearing was thoroughly cognitive. This accounts for cognitive psychology's heavy investment in filter theories of auditory perception. If we cannot avoid hearing something, we then must select among the stimuli by some mental process, filtering out the unimportant and attending to the important. We turn now to investigations of selective attention in audition; in the process we bump into the need for more global theories of attention, memory, and cognition.

Dual Task or Dual Message Procedures   A general characteristic of many attention experiments, whether on vision or audition, involves the procedure of overload. In brief, we can overload the sensory system by presenting more information than it can handle at once and then test accuracy for some part of the information. In studies of auditory perception, this has usually involved a **dual task or dual message procedure.** *Two tasks or messages are presented such that one task or message captures the person's attention as completely as possible.* Because the person's attentional resources are so consumed by this primary task, there are few if any resources left over for conscious attention to the other information being presented. By varying the auditory characteristics or content of the messages, we can make the listener's job easier or harder. For instance, paying attention to a message spoken in one ear while trying to ignore the other ear's message is especially difficult when both messages are spoken by the same person. We can conclude from this that the initial encoding of the messages in auditory sensory memory included purely auditory features such as pitch and intonation.

Going one step further, when we examine performance to the attended task, we can ask about the accuracy with which the message is perceived and about the degree of interference caused by the second message. We can also look at the subject's accuracy for information that was not in the primary message, the unattended message in the other ear. If the subject shows any evidence of remembering the unattended message, or even some of its auditory features, we can discuss how unattended information is processed and registered in memory.

The Shadowing Experiments   Some of the earliest cognitive research on auditory pattern recognition and selective attention was performed by E. Colin Cherry (1953; Cherry & Taylor, 1954). Cherry was interested in the basic phenomena of speech recognition and attention. Cherry characterized his research procedures, and for that matter the question he was asking, as the cocktail party problem: How do we pay attention to and recognize what one person is saying when we are surrounded by other spoken messages? To simulate this real-world situation in the laboratory, Cherry (see also Broadbent, 1952) devised the workhorse task of auditory perception research, the **shadowing task.** In this task, Cherry recorded spoken messages of different sorts on tape, then played the tape to a subject who was wearing headphones. The subject's task was to "shadow" the message coming into the right ear, that is, to *repeat the message out loud as soon as it was heard.* In most of the experiments, subjects were also told to ignore the other message, the one coming to the left ear. (It makes no difference which ear is shadowed and which is ignored, of course. For simplicity, assume that the right ear always receives the to-be-shadowed attended message and the left ear receives the unattended message.)

Although this procedure sounds simple, it takes a surprising amount of attention and concentration to shadow a message accurately. On one hand, subjects were quite accurate in producing "shadows" and reported that the task was easy. Nonetheless, Cherry found that subjects' spoken shadows usually were produced in a monotone voice, with little intonational stress, and generally lagged behind the taped message by a second or so. Interestingly, subjects seem unaware of the strangeness of their spoken shadows and usually cannot remember much of the content of the shadowed message once the task is over.

Assured that the task consumed enough attention to leave little, if any, for other purposes, Cherry then began to vary the unattended message. In a typical session, the tape began with a continuous coherent message presented to the right (attended) ear and another coherent message to the left (unattended ear). Once the subject began to shadow, the message in the left ear was changed. At the end of some amount of time, subjects were interrupted and asked what, if anything, they could report about the unattended message.

Generally, subjects could report accurately on a variety of physical characteristics of the unattended message. For instance, they noticed if it changed from human speech to a tone. They usually detected a change from a male voice to a female voice. On the other hand, when the unattended message was changed to reversed speech, only a few subjects noticed "something queer about it." Changes from English to a different language generally went unnoticed, and, overall, the subjects were unable to identify words or phrases that had been on the unattended message. In a dramatic confirmation of this last result, Moray (1959) found that even a word presented 35 times in the unattended message was never recalled by the subjects (see also Wood & Cowan, 1995b).

Selection Models

It appears that almost any physical difference between the messages permits the subject to distinguish between them and eases the job of selectively attending to the target message (Johnston & Heinz, 1978). Eysenck (1982) called this Stage 1 selection; other investigators routinely call it early selection. Regardless of the name, this refers to the some of the earliest phases of perception, an acoustic analysis based on physical features of the message. The evidence is that people can select a message based on Stage 1 sensory information, based on loudness, location of the sound source, pitch, and so on (Egan, Carterette, & Thwing, 1954; Spieth, Curtis, & Webster, 1954; Wood & Cowan, 1995a).

Broadbent's Filter Theory This evidence, indicating that subjects could somehow tune their auditory mechanisms to one message and then ignore the other, prompted Donald Broadbent (1958) to propose a filter theory of auditory perception (actually, Broadbent's theory also covered memory, learning, and other more complex topics). In Broadbent's view, the auditory mechanism acts as a selective filter, as shown in Figure 4-7. Regardless of how many competing channels or messages are coming in, the filter can be tuned, or switched, to any one of the messages, based on characteristics such as loudness or pitch. Note that only one message can be passed through the filter at a time in Broadbent's the-

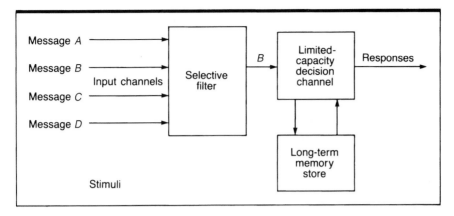

Figure 4-7

Broadbent's Filter theory of selective attention. Four messages are presented, yet only one is selected and passed to the limited-capacity decision mechanism. Adapted from Broadbent (1958).

ory. In other words, despite the many incoming signals, only one message can be sent along through the filter into the "limited-capacity decision channel," essentially the same as short-term memory. Only the information on the attended, "passed along" message can affect performance, in Broadbent's view, because only it gets past the filtering mechanism.

It was realized very quickly that Broadbent's filter approach had some serious shortcomings. For one, intuition tells us that we often notice information from a message we are not attending, as when you hear your name spoken in a crowded, noisy place. Moray (1959) found an exact laboratory parallel to this intuitive example: Although people did not recall a word presented 35 times to the unattended ear, fully a third of his sample heard their name spoken on the unattended channel (see Wood & Cowan, 1995b, for a modern replication of this effect). If Broadbent's theory were correct, then only the attended and passed-along information should be available for further cognitive processing, where attention is directed by physical cues. Yet clear evidence was available that unattended information could somehow slip past the filter.

Treisman's Attenuation Theory Treisman (1960, 1964) performed an important series of investigations to explore this slippage more closely. Treisman used the standard shadowing task but varied the nature of the unattended message across a much more subtle range of differences. She first replicated Cherry's findings that selective attention was easy when various physical differences existed between the messages. Then she turned to the situation in which physical differences were absent; both the attended and unattended messages were tape recorded by the same speaker. Because the same pitch, intonation, stress, and so on were on both messages, Stage 1 selection should not be possible. Yet she found that subjects could shadow quite accurately; they could attend selectively to one message while ignoring the other. The basis for the selection, however, was not any physical characteristic of the messages. Instead, subjects now performed their

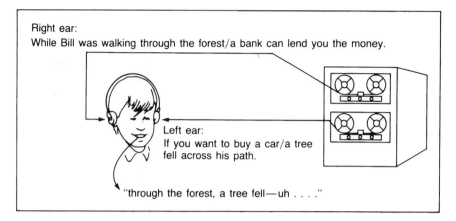

Figure 4-8

The shadowing task. Two messages are played simultaneously into different ears, then, at the slash, the ear-of-arrival is switched for the two messages. Adapted from Lindsay & Norman (1977).

selection on the basis of *message content*, what the message was *about* rather than what it sounded like. Eysenck (1982) called this *Stage 2* selection, in which the grammatical and semantic features are the basis for selection (*semantic* refers to meaning). A more conventional term for selection at this point is *middle selection*, certainly later in the stream of processing than early selection based on sensory features yet earlier than selection just at the moment of having to respond out loud with the shadowed speech.

To show the power of selection based on the content of the message, Treisman conducted a study now considered a classic (1960); the set-up for the experiment is depicted in Figure 4-8. Treisman arranged the tape recording so that the coherent message being shadowed by the subject was unexpectedly shifted to the unattended channel. Quite literally, the sentence the subject was saying switched from the right to the left ear. Despite a high degree of practice in shadowing the right ear and the high level of concentration needed, subjects routinely switched to the left ear message, the one that completed the meaning of the sentence they were shadowing. Although they did not continue to shadow the "wrong" ear for very long, when the meaningful sentence switched to the other ear, they also switched. Clearly, there must be some consideration of the unattended message, unlike the prediction from Broadbent's theory. Semantic elements of the unattended channel must be receiving some analysis, Treisman reasoned, or there would be no basis for preferring it when the sentences switched ears.

Based on such results, Treisman rejected the "early selection" notion embodied in Broadbent's theory, Eysenck's Stage 1 selection. Instead, she claimed that all incoming messages receive some amount of low-level analysis, including an analysis of the physical characteristics of the message. When the unattended messages yield no useful or important information, those messages are attenuated, in Treisman's terms; they are reduced not in their volume or physical characteristics but in their informational importance to ongoing processing. In the process of shadowing, we arrive at an identification of the words and phrases on the attended message.

Treisman (1965) felt that it was during this process of semantic analysis that we make our selection among messages—at Stage 2, selection at a "middle" stage. This scheme places selective attention well within the cognitive apparatus, of course, and permits attention to be affected by the semantic aspects of the message—that is, a top-down effect. The more extreme view, proposed by Deutsch and Deutsch (1963), claimed that selection takes place only after *all* messages have received full acoustic and semantic analysis (i.e., just before the response stage). This was a late selection theory, at Stage 3 in Eysenck's (1982) terminology, where the outcomes of all earlier analyses become conscious (for modern results against late selection, see Wood & Cowan, 1995a).

So the evidence is that much more information is getting into the cognitive system than strict selection or filtering would permit: the meaning of the words on the unattended channel, for example, in Treisman's study (1960; see also Lewis, 1970; Carr, McCauley, Sperber, & Parmelee, 1982, found comparable results for visually presented stimuli). Intrusion of the word *tree* into the subject's shadow, as shown in Figure 4-8, makes sense only if *tree* has been recognized as related to the forest theme of the shadowed message, an effect that implies some rapid process of accessing the meanings of words. How are such spoken patterns processed to the level of meaningfulness in the absence of explicit attention?

Norman's Pertinence Model Donald Norman (1968) proposed a useful modification to the Treisman scheme; his model, which specifically included a mechanism for top-down processing, is depicted in Figure 4-9. Despite the more complex illustration, the model is rather straightforward and very appealing. It claims that at any instant in time, attention to some piece of information, some message, is determined by two factors, sensory activation and pertinence.

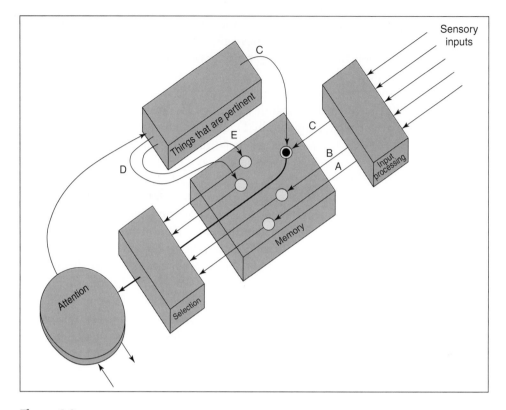

Figure 4-9

Norman's pertinence model. Adapted from Norman (1968).

Consider sensory activation first. If the message is loud, in a distinct voice, or otherwise salient from a sensory standpoint, its sensory activation will be high; that is the message you will pay attention to. In simple terms, if the stereo at the party is much louder than anything else, you will be unable to attend to anything but the music. The figure shows that messages A, B, and C have some degree of sensory activation, maybe the music and the two nearest conversations.

Now add pertinence to the mixture. At any moment in time, certain things—ideas, words, and so forth—are highly pertinent to you, and others are low in pertinence. Pertinence can be temporary, as in Treisman's results on message content; if you're listening to a message about a forest, words such as *tree* are high in pertinence. But pertinence can also be relatively permanent; your name probably stays at a high level of pertinence on a permanent basis, for instance. In either case, the higher an item is in pertinence, the closer that item is to its criterion or threshold for awareness. In the figure, items C, D, and E are highly pertinent. So **pertinence** is *the momentary importance of information, whether caused by permanent or transitory factors.*

Now all we have to do is add the pertinence and sensory activations together. In Norman's model, the items in memory that have the highest combination of sensory and

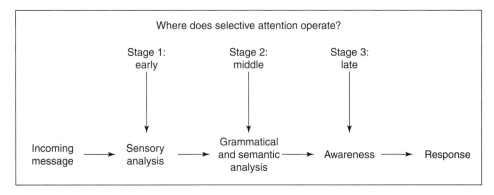

Figure 4-10

The sequence of processes in the shadowing task, with early, middle, and late operation of the selective attention mechanism. Adapted from Johnston & Heinz (1978).

pertinence scores are the ones that are selected for attention. Thus, selective attention in Norman's theory is a continuous process. On a moment-by-moment basis, the item with the highest combination score is selected for conscious, deliberate attention. In the figure, this is represented by the darkened item C; it is pertinent and has high sensory activation (maybe it's your name in one of those nearby conversations). To continue the shadowing example, hearing *forest* makes concepts such as *TREE* temporarily pertinent. That pertinence combines with the sensory input from the unattended channel ("a tree fell across his path"), so *tree* is selected and thus enters the attention component of the model.

Multimode Model of Attention   Where does this leave us, you ask? It leaves us knowing two things about selective attention. First, selective attention can occur very early in the processing sequence, based on very low-level, physical characteristics, as Broadbent proposed. It can also occur later, based on meaning or message content, as Treisman demonstrated. Second, it can be influenced by both permanent and temporary factors. Permanent factors include highly important information such as your name, and highly overlearned and personally important factors. Like you, I always hear my name, even when it is just a coincidence that a passerby says it. But I also always hear the word *psychology*, even when it's spoken on an unattended message. So names are not the only possible items that can be permanently boosted in their pertinence. Temporary pertinence factors include message content as well as momentary fluctuations in interests. In short, attention is flexible.

An important article, by Johnston and Heinz (1978), said just that, that attention is a highly flexible process that can operate in multiple modes. By *modes*, these authors meant the sort of factors described here as Stage 1, 2, or 3 models—operating in a physical mode, a meaning-based mode, and the like. This is illustrated in Figure 4-10. Johnston and Heinz's answer to the question "Where does selective attention operate?" is "Anywhere. Selective attention can operate in multiple modes: early, middle, or late."

There is an important limitation to this flexibility, however, which involves capacity. Johnston and Heinz pointed out that although selective attention can vary from

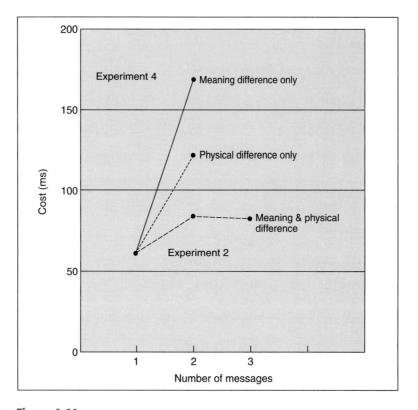

Figure 4-11

Results from Johnston & Heinz's research on the multimode model of attention. Data from Johnston & Heinz (1978).

quite early to quite late, the downside of this flexibility is that later selection uses more of our limited attentional capacity. Therefore, later selection tends to be slower or less accurate when it comes to remembering the information that was attended to.

Their data illustrated this tradeoff quite clearly. In their experiments, the subjects listened to multiple messages, some differing physically, some differing in terms of meaning, and some differing in both meaning and physical characteristics. They always had to remember information from one message, the target, and try to ignore any other messages that were also presented. While listening to the messages, they also had to monitor a light in front of them and press a button as soon as it came on. To make this challenging, the light came on at random, unpredictable intervals. The reasoning here was that detecting the light would be slower when participants listened to multiple messages because listening would use more attentional capacity. If selective attention is more difficult in some conditions because of similarities in the competing messages, this should slow down detection of the light.

This is exactly what happened, as illustrated in Figure 4-11. The figure shows the costs in performance—in other words how much slower the responses to the light were compared with baseline (higher costs on the graph mean worse performance than in the baseline condition). Having to listen to one message slowed down light detection by about 60 msec; this is the first point on the graph. It shows that burdening the attentional system with the extra task, listening to the target message, used some of the available attentional capacity, thus slowing down light detection.

Johnston and Heinz then went on to show how much more attentional capacity was drained when two or more messages were presented simultaneously, as in the shadowing research described earlier. In a second experiment, the target message was presented along with either one or two extra messages, the distractor messages (for a total number of messages of either two or three). But because the distractors differed both physically and in meaning from the target, this added only another 20 msec to the participants' time to detect the light; this is shown in the bottom curve in Figure 4-11. In other words, it took very little extra attention when given two types of cues, physical and meaning, to help them ignore the distractors. (It is not that difficult to ignore one or two nearby conversations if they are about different topics.)

But their fourth experiment examined the more taxing conditions for selective attention that you read about before (i.e., when the extra message differs only physically from the target or when it differs only in meaning). As the middle curve in the figure shows, the "physical difference only" task added 120 msec to participants' responses, showing a large drain on attentional capacity because of the difficulty of the listening task. This is rather like saying that Stage 1 selection, based on physical differences, costs the attentional system an extra 120 msec. And when only meaning differentiated the messages, the cost to light detection speed was a whopping 170 msec.

This is the crux of Johnston and Heinz's multimode model. Selective attention can operate early in the sequence of processing, or it can operate late. But as it operates later and later, extra capacity is consumed by the attentional mechanism. This slows down (and makes less accurate) any other ongoing process because it subtracts from the total pool of mental resources that are available for performance (see also Wood & Cowan, 1995a, 1995b).

In short, it boils down to the issue of capacity. We started with the notion of limited capacity, then worked through the models of selective attention. And now we run into the capacity issue again. Selective attention is flexible but consumes some of the limited capacity of the human processing system. The harder it is to attend selectively to just one of several competing messages, the more capacity the selective attention process uses.

■ Section Summary

- Controlled or conscious attention is a slower, more voluntary form of attentional process. Selective attention, the ability to focus on one incoming message while ignoring other incoming stimuli, is a complex ability, one investigated since the beginnings of modern cognitive science. The evidence shows that we can select one message and reject others, based on physical characteristics or on more semantic characteristics. The later the process of selection acts, the more demanding it is of the limited capacity of the attention mechanism.

Attention as a Mental Resource

An important and far-reaching meaning of the term *attention*—this one may be closer to our everyday meaning—treats attention as mental effort, as a mental resource that fuels cognitive activity. If we selectively attend to one particular message, we are deliberately focusing some mental energy on that message, concentrating on it to the exclusion of other messages (clearly what James had in mind in the quotation at the beginning of the chapter). This sense usually involves the notion that attention is a limited resource, that there is only so much of the critical mental fuel to be devoted here or there at any one time (Kahneman, 1973, also suggested that capacity might be somewhat elastic in that increasing the task load might also increase the subject's arousal, thus making additional resources available; see Eysenck, 1982, for a discussion of this point). As a group, approaches that emphasize this meaning of the term are called resource theories.

A corollary to this idea of limited capacity is that attention, loosely speaking, is the same thing as consciousness or awareness. After all, if you can be consciously aware of only one thing at a time, doesn't that illustrate the limited capacity of attention? And one more related idea, which you encountered in the previous section, is that this kind of attention is deliberate, willful, intended—*controlled attention. You* decide to pay attention to a signal, a stimulus coming into the mental system, or you decide *not* to pay attention to the signal. *You* decide to pay attention to the lecture instead of your memory of last night's date, and when you realize your attention has wandered, you willfully redirect it to the lecture, determined *not* to daydream about last night until class is over.

The James quotation at the beginning of this chapter is also interesting because of another insight he had about attention: the idea that probably only one process of conception can occur at a time but that we may seem to do more than one thing at a time if the other processes are habitual. When processes are less automatic, however, then attention must oscillate among them if they are done simultaneously, with no consequent gain of time. The key point, of course, involves the idea of automatic processes, that some mental events can happen automatically without draining the pool of mental resources we call attention. Putting it simply, the germ of James's idea, automaticity, has become central to cognitive psychology's views on attention, pattern recognition, and a host of other topics. And cognitive science has devoted a huge amount of effort to recasting James's ideas about automaticity and attention into more formal, quantifiable concepts.

Automatic and Conscious Processing Theories

In place of the former approach, the limited-capacity attentional mechanism and the need for filtering in selective attention, the current view is that a variety of perceptual and cognitive processes can be executed in an automatic fashion, *with little or no necessary involvement of a conscious, limited-attention mechanism.* Two such explicit theories of **automaticity** have been proposed, one by Posner and Snyder (1975) and one by Shiffrin and Schneider (1977; Schneider & Shiffrin, 1977). These theories differ in some of their

Table 4-2 DIAGNOSTIC CRITERIA FOR AUTOMATIC AN DCONSCIOUS PROCESSING

Automatic	Conscious
The process occurs without intention, without a conscious decision.	The process occurs only with intention, with a deliberate decision.
The mental process is not open to conscious awareness or introspection.	The process is open to awareness and introspection.
The process consumes few if any conscious resources; that is, it consumes little if any conscious attention.	The process uses conscious resources; that is, it drains the pool of conscious attentional capacity.
(Informal) The process operates very rapidly, usually within 1 s.	(Informal) The process is slow, taking more than a second or two for completion.

details but are similar in their overall message (see also Logan & Etherton, 1994; for discussions that oppose the idea of mental resources, see Navon, 1984, and Pashler, 1994).

Automatic Processing Posner and Snyder described three characteristics that are necessary for the "diagnosis" of an automatic process, listed for convenience in Table 4-2. First, an automatic process occurs without intention; in other words, an automatic process occurs whether you consciously want it to or not. A standard and compelling example of this is the result obtained in a Stroop task (named after the task described in Stroop, 1935). Words such as *RED GREEN BLUE YELLOW* were presented visually to subjects, written in mismatching colors of ink (e.g., *RED* printed in green ink). When subjects have to name the ink color, they must try to ignore the printed words themselves. This leads to tremendous interference, a dramatic slowing of the ink color naming, caused by the mismatching colors and the contradictory impulses to name the word and the ink color (this is an extremely easy demonstration to perform, by the way).

In Posner and Snyder's terms, accessing the meaning of the written symbol *RED* is automatic: It requires no intention, it happens whether you want it to or not. In the research that demonstrates automatic access to word meaning, the term we use is ***priming***. A word automatically *activates* or primes its meaning in memory and, as a consequence, primes or activates meanings closely associated with it. This priming then makes related meanings easier to access: Because of priming, they are boosted up, or given an extra advantage or head start (just as well water is pumped more easily when you prime the pump; see Dunbar & MacLeod, 1984, and MacLeod, 1991, for an explanation of Stroop interference based on priming). This is obviously the mechanism underneath Treisman's "tree–forest" result in the shadowing task, as well as the Lewis (1970) and Carr et al. (1982) results.

Second, an automatic process does not reveal itself to conscious awareness. You cannot describe the mental processes of looking up the word *RED* in memory. The lookup processes are automatic and are not available to conscious awareness. You are not aware of the operation of automatic processes, such as the perceptual mechanisms of looking at the visual pattern *T* and recognizing what it is. Contrast this with the awareness you had when you answered the Aristotle or division questions in Chapter 1.

PROVE IT

The Stroop Task

An almost fail-safe demonstration of automaticity, in particular the automatic nature of accessing word meaning, involves the Stroop task. With several different colors of marker pens, write a dozen or so color names on a sheet of paper, making sure to use a *different* color of ink than the word signifies (e.g., write "red" in green ink); alternatively, create a deck of 3 × 5 cards, with one word per card. Make a control list of noncolor words (e.g., "hammer, card, wall"), again in colored inks. Explain to your subject that the task is to name the *ink color* as rapidly as possible. Time the subject (the second hand/display on your watch is more than sufficient) on each kind of list. The standard result is that the color word list will require substantially longer for ink color

naming than the control list. Other useful control lists are simple blotches of color, to check on the speed of naming the colors, and pseudowords ("manty," "zoople," etc.) written in different ink colors.

Based on work by Besner and Stolz (1999) and Vecera, Behrmann, and McGoldrick (2000), you might be able to eliminate the Stroop effect by getting your subjects to focus on just *part* of the word, say the first letter position (this might be easier if you used the 3 × 5 card method). Their work, respectively, suggests that reading the whole word is a kind of "default" setting for visual attention, that might be changed depending on the task and instructions, and that our selective attention mechanism can select either whole objects (words) or their parts (letters) as the focus.

The third criterion of automaticity, according to Posner and Snyder, is that a fully automatic process consumes few if any conscious resources. Such a process should not interfere with other tasks, certainly not those that rely on conscious resources.[1] As an obvious example, walking is so automatic for adults that it simply does not interfere with other processes; you can walk and talk at the same time.

A fourth criterion is informal but nonetheless useful and is commonly noted as a characteristic of automaticity. Automatic processes tend to be very fast; as a rule, a response taking no more than 1 s is heavily automatic. (For evidence of very slow automatic processing, in a person with brain damage, see Wingfield, Goodglass, & Lindfield, 1997.)

Conscious Processing Let's contrast these diagnostic criteria for automaticity with those for conscious or controlled processing (see Table 4-2). First, conscious processes occur only with intention. They are optional, and can be deliberately performed or not performed by the subject. Second, conscious processes are open to awareness; we know

---

[1]Interference in the Stroop task occurs in part because the two automatic processes, reading the word and detecting the ink color, eventually compete with one another when it is time to make a response. That is, both processes are trying to output their results to the same speech mechanism, but the responses are incompatible ("red," "green"). When we say that an automatic process generally does not interfere with other processes, it is assumed that we are speaking of situations in which the two processes are not competing for the same response mechanism.

they are going on, and within limits we know what they consist of. Finally, and of greatest importance to the research, conscious processes use *attention*. They consume some of the limited attentional resources we have in the cognitive system.

A demanding conscious process should leave very few resources still available for use by a second task that also uses conscious processing. Driving during a hard rainstorm consumes too many resources for you to listen simultaneously to the news on the radio. Of course, if the second task can be processed fairly automatically, then both tasks may be able to proceed without interference; for example, you can walk while carrying on a serious conversation.

Integration with Conceptually Driven Processes We can go one step further now, integrating this explanation into the notion of conceptually driven processing. Attending to one of two incoming messages and then shadowing that message out loud demands conscious, deliberate attention. Such a process is under the subject's direct control, the subject is aware of performing the process, and the process consumes most of the available mental resources that can be allocated. Presumably, no other conscious process can be performed simultaneously with the shadowing task without affecting performance in one or the other task (or both). When the messages are acoustically similar, then the subject must rely on differences of content or meaning to keep them separate. But by tracking the meaning of a passage, the person's conceptually driven processes come into play in an obvious way. Just as subjects "restored" the missing sound in "the *eel was on the axle" (Warren & Warren, 1970), the shadowing subject "supplies" information about the message from long-term memory. Once you have begun to understand the content of the shadowed message, then your conceptually driven processes assist you by narrowing down the possible alternatives, by suggesting what might come next.

Saying that conceptually driven processes suggest what might come next is an informal way of referring to the important process of priming. You shadow "While Bill was walking through the forest." Your semantic analysis primes related information and thereby suggests the likely content of the next clause in the sentence; it is likely to be about trees, and it is unlikely to be about banks and cars. At this instant in time, your "forest" knowledge has been primed or activated in memory. It is ready (indeed, almost *eager*) to be perceived because it is so likely to be contained in the rest of the sentence. Then *tree* occurs on the unattended channel. Because we seem to access the meanings of words in an automatic fashion, the extra boost given to *tree* by the priming process pushes it over into the conscious attention mechanism. Suddenly, you're saying "a tree fell across" rather than sticking with the right-ear message. Automatic priming of long-term memory has exerted a top-down influence on the earliest of your cognitive processes, auditory pattern recognition and attention.

The Role of Practice and Memory If accessing word meaning is automatic, then you might be wondering about some of the shadowing research described earlier in which subjects were insensitive to the unshadowed message, failing to detect the word presented 35 times, the reversed speech, and so on. If word access is automatic, why didn't

The role of practice in automaticity.

these subjects recognize the words on the unattended channel? A very plausible explanation, in view of recent research, is practice. It now seems very likely that subjects' inability to detect or to be influenced by the unattended message was caused by their relative lack of practice on the shadowing task. As several studies have shown, with greater degrees of practice even a seemingly complex and attention-consuming task becomes easy, or less demanding of attention's full resources. In fact, Logan and Klapp (1991; see also Zbrodoff & Logan, 1986) suggested that the effect of practice is to store the relevant information in memory; that is, that the necessary precondition for automatic processing is memory.

One of the most compelling strengths of the Shiffrin and Schneider (1977) theory of automatic and conscious processing (actually, they use the term *controlled* instead of *conscious* processing) is the role they award to old-fashioned, repetitive practice. Their experiments asked subjects to detect one or more target stimuli in successively presented displays (e.g., hold targets *2* and *7* in memory, then search for either of them in successively presented displays of stimuli). For some subjects, the targets were consistent across hundreds of trials, always digits, for instance. This was called Consistent Mapping. For subjects in the Varied Mapping groups, the targets were varied across trials (e.g., *2* and *7* might be targets on one trial, *3* and *B* on another, *M* and *Z* on yet another).

The essential ingredient here is practice on the stimuli and task. Unlike the Varied Mapping groups, subjects who received Consistent Mapping had enormous amounts of practice in scanning for the same targets. Across many experiments, subjects in the Consistent Mapping conditions developed quick automatic detection processes for their unchanging targets, to the point that they could search for any of four targets in about 450 msec, even in the largest display size (four characters shown at once). Subjects in the Varied Mapping conditions, on the other hand, needed greater search times for larger displays. At the large display size, their four-target search time was 1,300 msec (Experiment 2, Schneider & Shiffrin, 1977). In the authors' interpretation, these subjects had not developed automatic detection processes because the stimuli they had to detect kept changing from trial to trial. In short, their search used conscious or controlled processing.

Rounding out their evidence on the effect of prolonged practice, Shiffrin and Schneider administered 2,100 detection trials to another group of subjects, consistently using one set of letters for the targets and a different set for the distractors. In the authors' words, "The subjects all reported extensive, attention-demanding rehearsal . . . during the first 600 trials of Experiment 1, but they gradually became unaware of rehearsal or other attention-demanding controlled processing after this point. . . . [They] gradually shifted to automatic detection" (1977, p. 133). After this lengthy procedure, Shiffrin and Schneider then reversed the target and distractor sets, forcing subjects to search for targets that were previously distractors and to ignore distractors that were previously targets. Shiffrin and Schneider suspected that "automatic detection would prove impossible and that the subject would be forced to revert to controlled search" (p. 133). This is exactly what happened. As shown in Figure 4-12, panel a, RTs after the reversal took 2,400 trials before they were as rapid as the search times became in the initial testing condition. And as panel B shows, accuracy quickly climbed above 80% in the initial testing condition, but it took 1,800 trials after the reversal of targets and distractors before accuracy reached near 80% again.

A Synthesis for Attention and Automaticity

Attention, in its usual, everyday sense, is essentially equivalent to conscious mental capacity or conscious mental resources. We can devote these attentional resources to only one demanding task at a time or to two somewhat less demanding tasks simultaneously, as long as the two together do not exceed the total capacity available. This devotion of resources means that few, if any, additional resources are available for other demanding tasks. Alternatively, if a second task is performed largely at the automatic level, then it can occur simultaneously with the first because it does not draw from the conscious resource pool (or, to change the metaphor, the automatic process has achieved a high level of skill; see Hirst & Kalmar, 1987). The more automatically a task can be performed, the more mental resources are available for other processes.

The route to automaticity, it appears, is practice and memory. With repetition and overlearning comes the ability to perform in an automatic fashion what formerly needed conscious processing. A particularly dramatic illustration of the power of practice is the Spelke, Hirst, and Neisser (1976) demonstration. With extensive practice, two subjects

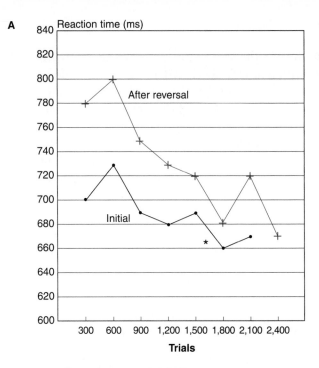

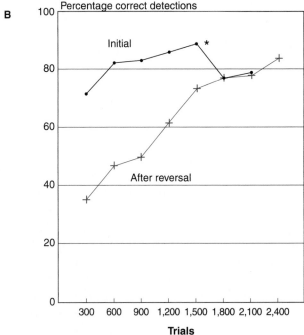

Figure 4-12

A, Reaction times from Shiffrin and Schneider's detection task for the initial 2,100 trials of detection and then for the 2,400 trials after the target and distractor sets were reversed. **B,** Percentage of correct detections of targets for the same initial and after-reversal conditions. In both, the asterisk denotes the point during the initial condition when the time for stimulus presentation was reduced from 200 msec to 120 msec.

The demands on attention and memory in flying a jet airplane are enormous. The pilot must simultaneously pay conscious attention to multiple sources of information while relying on highly practiced, automatic processes and overlearned actions to respond to others.

eventually were able to read stories at normal rates, and with high comprehension, while they simultaneously copied words at dictation or even categorized the dictated words according to meaning. The Shiffrin and Schneider results tracked the changes in performance across practice, showing a steady shift or migration from conscious to automatic. Significantly, once practice has yielded automatic performance, it seems especially difficult to undo the practice, to overcome what has now become an automatic and, in a sense, autonomous process (Zbrodoff & Logan, 1986).

Different degrees of practice, and therefore different degrees of automaticity, probably account for the varied results from the shadowing studies as well. As subjects gain more experience with the shadowing task, their shadowing presumably uses less and less conscious attention. This would release some of their conscious resources for other purposes. Among those other purposes is the conscious detection of related information, as Treisman found, or even detection of unattended channel information while shadowing (Moray himself, with presumably much practice at shadowing, outperformed less practiced subjects in reporting unattended channel information).

Disadvantages of Automaticity

We have been talking as if automaticity is a completely positive, desirable characteristic for mental processes, as if anything that reduces the drain on the limited available mental capacity is a good thing. This is not entirely true, however. There are several situations in which achieving automaticity can lead to difficulties (Reason, 1990).

You have encountered one of these already, in a sense. Schneider and Shiffrin's (1977) participants learned automatic detection processes in the Consistent Mapping condition: it took them no more time to search for four targets than for one after 2,100 trials. But when the target letters were switched, it took more than 2,100 additional trials for them to overcome the automaticity they achieved. It is hard to undo what has become automatic, in other words.

But does this have any practical application? Of course. We are often confronted with change, with situations that differ enough from what we have become accustomed to that some relearning has to take place. Your new car has some of its controls in a different location from where they were on the older one, so you have to overcome the habit of reaching to the left dashboard to turn on the lights (this is why some controls, e.g., accelerator and brake pedals, do not change position). If you switch to a new word processor after becoming fluent with a different system, it takes some relearning to overcome your accumulated practice with the old system.

More critically, sometimes we *should* be consciously aware of information or processes that have become too routine and automatic. Barshi and Healy (1993) provided an excellent example, using a proofreading procedure that mimics how we use checklists. All participants in their study scanned pages of simple multiplication problems. Five mistakes such as "$7 \times 8 = 63$" were embedded in the pages of problems. All participants saw the same sets of 10 problems over and over. But in the fixed order condition, the problems were in the same order each time; in the varied order condition, the problems were in a different order each time. Those tested in the fixed order condition missed significantly more of the embedded mistakes than those in the varied order condition; an average of 23% missed in fixed order but only 9% missed with varied orders. Figure 4-13 shows this result across the five embedded errors. Performance did improve in the fixed order condition as more and more of the mistakes were encountered. But the first multiplication error was detected only 55% of the time, compared with the 90% detection rate for the varied order group.

The fixed order of problems encouraged automatic proofreading, which disrupted accuracy at detecting errors. In fact, it took either an earlier error that *was* detected or a specific alerting signal (Experiment 3) to overcome the effects of routine, automatic proofreading.

The implications of this kind of result should be clear, as Barshi and Healy pointed out. Pilots are required to go through checklist procedures, say for landing an airplane, to ensure safety. Yet because the items on the checklist are in a fixed order, repeated use of the list probably leads to a degree of automaticity and probably a tendency to miss errors. This is exactly what happened in March 1983: A plane landed in Casper, Wyoming, without its landing gear down, even though the flight crew had gone through its standard checklist procedure and had "verified" that the wheels were down. In Barshi and Healy's words, this incident "reminded the crew and the rest of the aviation community that the countless repetition of the same procedure can lead to a dangerous automatization" (1993, p. 496).

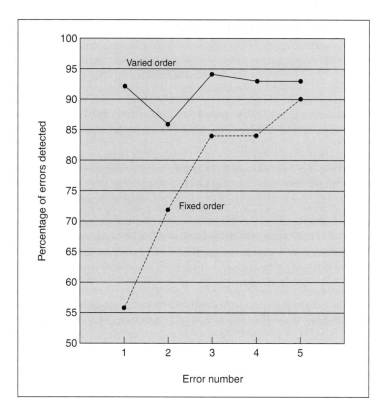

Figure 4-13

Results of Barshi and Healy's experiment showing the percentage of participants detecting the five embedded errors in proofreading multiplication problems. Problems were presented in fixed or varied order. Data from Barshi & Healy (1993).

■ Section Summary

- When attention is viewed as a limited mental resource, issues of task complexity become concerned with how automatic or controlled different mental processes are. Automatic processes are rapid, are not dependent on intent, are unavailable to conscious awareness, and place few if any demands on limited attentional resources; conscious or controlled processes are the opposite, rather slow, requiring intention, open to conscious awareness, and heavily demanding of attentional resources

- Mental processes become more automatic as a function of practice and overlearning. A disadvantage of automaticity is that it is difficult to reverse the effects of practice in an automated task, and automaticity can lead to errors of inattention.

A Disorder of Attention: Hemineglect

We turn now to the cognitive neuroscience of attention, an increasingly important adjunct to cognitive studies of attentional mechanisms. Some actively researched disorders of attention, including complex syndromes such as attention deficit, hyperactivity disorder (ADHD) are beyond the scope of this book (although some Suggested Readings are provided on the Web page). One in particular deserves consideration here because it bears on normal attention in several direct ways.

Go back to the beginning of the chapter and reread the quotation from Banich (1997) about Bill. Bill suffers from hemineglect, a syndrome that leads to such behavior as brushing only the teeth on his right, washing only his right arm, and shaving only the right side of his face. To most people, this phenomenon is almost too bizarre to believe, maybe because the processes of mental attention have always been so closely tied to perception and voluntary movement and so automatic that we think they are indivisible parts of the same process. Look at yourself in a mirror, then look at the left side of your face—no problem, you merely move your eyes, shift your direction of gaze, and look at it. If I ask you to stare straight ahead and then attend to something in your left field of vision, say the letter X on a computer screen, your normal response is to shift your eyes toward the left and focus on the target. You simply look at the X and pay attention to it. And as you read earlier, you can shift your mental attention to the left even without moving your eyes.

The syndrome known as **hemineglect,** or **hemi-inattention,** is a disruption in the ability to do just that, to refocus your attention to one side of your face or the other, to the X on the left of the computer screen. It is a *disruption or decreased ability to look at something in the (often) left field of vision and pay attention to it. Hemi* means "half," and *neglect* and *inattention* mean "to ignore" or "fail to perceive." Thus hemineglect is a disorder of attention in which one half of the perceptual world is neglected to some degree and cannot be attended to as completely or accurately as normal. Very often, the neglect is of the left visual field, for stimuli to the left of the current fixation, the current focus of attention. And because of the principle of contralaterality, it is not surprising that the brain damage leading to hemineglect is often in the right hemisphere, in particular certain regions of the right parietal lobe.

Here are the facts (see Banich, 1997, or Rafal, 1997, for complete treatments). A patient with hemineglect cannot voluntarily direct attention to half of the perceptual world, whether the to-be-perceived stimulus is visual, auditory, or any other type of sensation. In some cases, the neglect is nearly total, as if half of the perceptual world has simply vanished, is simply not there in any normal sense of the word. In other cases, the neglect is not total, so for such people it is more accurate to say that they are *less able* to redirect their controlled attention than are normal people. In either case, there is a disruption in the ability to control attention. Note that this is not a case of sensory damage like blindness or deafness. The patient with hemineglect receives input from both sides of the body and can make voluntary muscle movements on both sides. And in careful testing situations, they can also respond to stimuli in the neglected field. But somehow, the deliberate devotion of controlled attention to one side is deficient.

Bisiach and Luzatti (1978) presented a compelling description of patients with hemineglect. The afflicted individuals were from Milan, Italy, so before their brain damage they were quite familiar with the city, and in particular the main piazza in town, a broad open square with buildings and shops along the sides and a large cathedral at one end. These patients were asked to imagine themselves standing at one end of the piazza, facing toward the cathedral, and then were asked to describe what they could see. They uniformly described only the buildings and shops on the right side of the piazza. When asked to imagine themselves standing on the steps of the cathedral, facing back the opposite way, they once again described what was on their right side. From this second view, of course, what they described on their right was exactly what they had omitted from their earlier descriptions. Likewise, what they now omitted was what they had described earlier, the buildings and shops that now would be in their left visual field.

Critically important here is the observation that these reports, based on memory, were exactly the kind of reports patients with hemineglect give when actually viewing a scene; if these patients had been taken to the piazza, they probably would have seen and described it the same way in person as they did from memory. (For a similar account, see "Eyes Right!" in Sacks, 1970; the patient there eats the right half of everything on her dinner plate, then complains about not getting enough food.) Figure 4-14 shows some drawings made by patients with hemineglect. Here, patients were asked to copy drawings or to draw from memory, but the nature of their drawings was no different in either case. Even casual inspection of the drawings shows a dramatic neglect for the left-hand sides of the drawings: a flower with no petals on the left, a clock face with no numbers on the left. In the standard line bisection task ("draw a slash through the middle of a horizontal line"), hemineglect patients position the slash too far to the right, as if bisecting only the right half of the entire horizontal line. The illustrations in Figure 4-15 show a similarly revealing result. Here, the patient was asked to look at the top drawing in that panel and then draw the black part. Then the patient was asked to look at and draw the white part of the figure. In both cases, the patient was able to focus on whichever part was called for but could pay attention only to the right half of that part. Because the right half of the white part does not have a jagged edge, neither did the patient's drawing, and because the right half of the black part does have a jagged edge, the patient's drawing did as well.

A careful analysis of the range of disruptions seen in patients with hemineglect has recently been provided by Duncan et al. (1999) in the context of an umbrella theory called the Theory of Visual Attention (Bundesen, 1990). Duncan et al. noted that several important advances in our understanding of hemineglect have been made recently, especially when the patients are tested with some standardized cognitive tasks such as Posner's spatial cuing task, which you read about earlier. For example, it turns out that patients with hemineglect often can attend to stimuli in the neglected field but only if nothing else is displayed visually that might attract their attention. That is, they can detect a simple stimulus in the left visual field (or more properly, the field contralateral to their brain damage), even if that is the field they normally neglect. But this ability to detect the same stimulus is dramatically reduced if a stimulus in the right visual field (a stimulus in the ipsilateral or same-side field) is presented at

Model

Patients copy

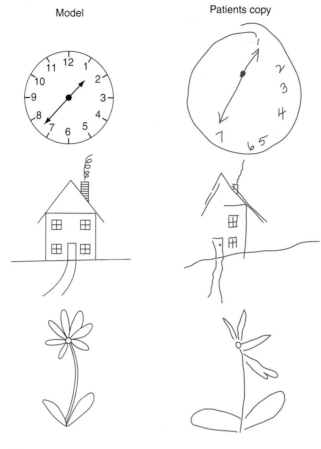

Figure 4-14

Drawings copied by a patient with contralateral neglect.
From F. E. Bloom and A. Lazerson. *Brain, Mind, and Behavior,*
2nd ed. New York: W. H. Freeman and Co., p. 300. Copyright
© 1988. Reprinted with permission of W. H. Freeman and Co.

the same time (see Danziger, Kingstone, & Rafal, 1998, for evidence of an orienting response in the neglected field).

This tendency to ignore the contralateral field when a competing stimulus is presented in the ipsilateral field is called extinction. It is apparently caused by something like attentional capture. When a right-side (ipsilateral) stimulus is presented, it captures the person's attention and prevents attention from being devoted to the left (contralateral). In a sense then, hemineglect patients may neglect one side only because there is usually something on the other side that captures their attention. In a very real sense, Bill might have been able to focus on shaving the left side of his face if he had not been able to see his right side.

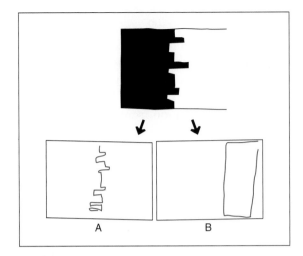

Figure 4-15

Object-based neglect is demonstrated by the copying performance of a patient with left hemispatial neglect. **A,** When asked to copy the black object, the patient did well because the jagged contour is on the right side of the black object. When asked to copy the white object, the patient was unable to copy the jagged contour because it is on the left side of the object being attended. From Marshall & Halligan (1994).

In a curious way, hemineglect seems to disrupt both the input and the controlled attention mechanisms. First, input attention is devoted largely or exclusively to a stimulus in the "good" or preserved field, the ipsilateral field (the term *ipsilesional* is also used, meaning "same side as the brain lesion"). The stimulus in this field captures the patient's input attention. But then, in terms Posner used to describe mental activity in the spatial cuing task, it appears that hemineglect patients cannot disengage attention from that ipsilateral stimulus. Because attention toward the right cannot be disengaged, they cannot shift their attention voluntarily to the left. Thus, capture of attention on one side has disrupted a shift of controlled attention toward the other side.

In their analysis, Duncan et al. (1999) noted that their patients with hemineglect showed standard deficits in attention to the contralateral side but also some rather strong bilateral deficits related to attentional capacity; in other words, there were accuracy deficits on the neglected side but capacity difficulties on both sides. Interestingly, there was little evidence that the conceptually driven aspects of their attention were affected. It may be some time before such results and their implications for the normal processes of attention are fully digested. But even now, it is clear that such fractionation of performance—some abilities preserved, some disrupted—will be important in our further understanding of attention.

■ **Section Summary**

• A specific disorder of attention, hemineglect, shows how the attentional system can be affected by brain damage, thus informing us about normal attention. In hemineglect, the patient is unable to direct attention voluntarily to one side of space, so he or she neglects stimuli presented in that side. The evidence suggests that this arises from an inability to disengage attention from a stimulus on the nonneglected side, hence disrupting the process of shifting attention to the opposite side.

Key Terms

attention (p. 121)
automaticity (p. 144)
benefit or facilitation
    (p. 127)
controlled attention (p. 133)
cost (p. 127)
dual task or dual message
    procedure (p. 135)

explicit processing (p. 123)
filtering (p. 134)
habituation (p. 125)
hemineglect or hemi-
    inattention (p. 154)
implicit processing
    (p. 124)
input attention (p. 123)

orienting reflex or
    response (p. 125)
pertinence (p. 140)
priming (p. 145)
selecting (p. 134)
selective attention (p. 133)
shadowing task (p. 134)
spotlight attention (p. 127)

CHAPTER 5

Short-Term Working Memory

Elementary memory makes us aware of . . . the just past. The objects we feel in this directly intuited past differ from properly recollected objects. An object which is recollected, in the proper sense of that term, is one which has been absent from consciousness altogether, and . . . is brought back . . . from a reservoir in which, with countless other objects, it lay buried and lost from view. But an object of primary memory is not thus brought back; it never was lost; its date was never cut off in consciousness from that of the immediately present moment. In fact it comes to us as belonging to the rearward portion of the present space of time, and not to the genuine past. (James, 1890, pp. 643–647)

The term capacity, as used in discussions of short-term memory, often conjures up images of a fixed number of items (e.g., 7 ± 2). However, my sense is that working memory capacity is NOT about a limitation in number of items in some limited set of metaphorical bins but about limitations in the ability to use controlled processing to maintain information in an active, quickly retrievable state. (Engle, 2000, in press)

Primary memory, elementary memory, immediate memory, short-term memory (STM), short-term store (STS), temporary memory, supervisory attention system (SAS), working memory (WM)—all these terms refer to the same memory component, the same aspect of the human information-processing system. It is this component where the "immediately present moment," in James's explanation, is held in consciousness. It is the location, so to speak, of the conscious attentional system discussed in Chapter 4. It is this component where active mental effort is expended, whether to remember a phone number from directory assistance or to help in memorizing your own new phone number. This is where comprehension takes place, the short-term, working memory system. What it is, what it does, and how it does it are the topics of this chapter.

Note that James's term *primary memory* suggests wrongly that it is the first memory stage. It's not, of course. A stimulus first encounters sensory memory and input attention components on its way into the information-processing system. But short-term memory is the first memory system we are conscious of, sufficiently aware of that we can offer intuitions and introspections about its functioning. Many but not all of those intuitions and introspections match what has been discovered empirically, not surprising given our metacognitive awareness of our own memories at work. On the other hand, some mental processes that occur in short-term, working memory are not revealed to consciousness: They are automatic. Naturally, these processes yield no useful introspections; indeed, people often naively feel that they do not exist. (This is why I have said that short-term memory is only roughly the same as consciousness. Although we are aware of the contents of short-term memory, we are not necessarily aware of the *processes* that occur in short-term memory.)

Modern cognitive research on short-term memory came hard on the heels of the selective attention studies of the mid-1950s.[1] George Miller's (1956) classic article, which we discuss shortly, is an excellent example of the upsurge in interest in short-term retention. A common observation, that we can remember only a small number of isolated items presented rapidly, began to take on new significance as psychology groped toward a new approach to the human memory system. Miller's insightful remarks were followed shortly by the surprising Brown (1958) and then Peterson and Peterson (1959) reports. An amazingly simple three-letter stimulus, such as *CHJ*, was forgotten almost completely within 15 s if the subject's attention was diverted by the distractor task of counting backward by threes. Such reports were convincing evidence that the limited capacity of the memory system was finally being pinned down and given an appropriate name: short-term memory.

As we proceed chronologically through the research, we will shift from the term *short-term memory* to *working memory*. Why do we need two terms for essentially the same system? Stated simply, the terms have historically different connotations. *Short-term memory* is the older of the two terms and conveys a somewhat simpler idea. It is the label we usually use when the focus is on the input and storage of new information. When a rapidly presented string of digits is tested for immediate recall, for example, we generally refer to short-term memory and imply a simple recycling kind of mental activity as an explanation of recall. Likewise, when we focus on the role of rehearsal we are examining how short-term memory assists in the memorization of new information, highlighting the "control processes" (Atkinson & Shiffrin, 1971; look back at Figure 2-4) that function in the short-term store. Operationally, short-term memory is observed whenever short retention is being tested—no more than 15 or 20 s—and when little, if any, transfer of new information to long-term memory is involved.

Working memory, on the other hand, is the newer term for this "short" component of the memory system and has been the subject of substantial research over the past 25 years or so. The term often has the connotation of a mental workbench, a place where conscious mental effort is applied (Baddeley, 1992a, 1992b; Baddeley & Hitch, 1974). The term usually refers to the mental workplace, the conscious attentional system where cognitive effort is expended. Thus, when word meanings are retrieved from long-term memory and put together to understand a sentence, working memory is where this putting together happens. It is the location of conscious, attention-consuming mental effort. Traditional immediate memory tasks may be a component of working memory research but usually are only a secondary task to the reasoning, comprehension, or retrieval task. Indeed, Baddeley proposed that the short-term memory responsible for digit span performance is but a single component of the more elaborate working memory system.

---

[1] There was also some research on short-term memory before the behaviorist period. For instance, Mary W. Calkins, the first woman to serve as president of the American Psychological Association, conducted such work in the 1890s and reported several important effects that were "discovered" in the 1950s and 1960s. See Madigan and O'Hara (1992) for an account of the "truly remarkable legacy" (p. 174) of this pioneering woman.

Finally, the terms themselves imply a somewhat different set of characteristics and inspired rather different kinds of research. Short-term memory is *short*–it doesn't last very long. The very term *short-term memory* embodies the notion of a limited-capacity system and situates that limitation in short-term memory. Why is short-term memory limited? It's too short! *Working memory*, on the other hand, includes the active verb *work*. This is an action-packed, busy place, a place where mental activity happens. Where is the limitation in this system? It's in how much work can be done at one time, how much working memory capacity there is to share among several simultaneous processes.

Short-Term Memory: A Limited-Capacity Bottleneck

If you hear a string of about 10 single digits, read at a constant and fairly rapid rate, and then are asked to reproduce the string in order, generally you cannot recall more than about 7 of the digits. The same result is obtained with unrelated words presented in a comparable fashion (see the Prove It projects for sample lists for immediate memory tests, and try testing a few willing volunteers). This is roughly the amount you can say out loud within about 2s (Baddeley, Thomson, & Buchanan, 1975) or the amount you can recall within about 4–6s (Dosher & Ma, 1998; see also Cowan et al., 1998). As Miller (1956) put it, "Everybody knows that there is a finite span of immediate memory and that for a lot of different kinds of test materials this span is about seven items in length" (p. 91). Indeed, this limit has been recognized for so long, it was included in the earliest intelligence tests (e.g., Binet's 1905 test; see Sattler, 1982). Small children and individuals of subnormal intelligence generally have a shorter span of apprehension, or memory span, so digit span is a reasonable diagnostic test in intelligence testing. In fact, in the field of intelligence testing, it is almost unthinkable to devise a test *without* a memory span assessment.

The Magical Number Seven, Plus or Minus Two

For our purposes, the importance of this limitation is that it reveals something absolutely fundamental about the human memory system. Our immediate memory cannot encode or input vast quantities of new information and hold that information accurately. Instead, there is a severe limit on how much can be encoded, held, and reported immediately. Miller stated that limit aptly in the title of his article: "The Magical Number Seven, Plus or Minus Two: Some Limits on Our Capacity for Processing Information." We can take large amounts of stimulation into the sensory memories, and we can hold truly vast quantities of information in the permanent long-term memory system. Yet the transfer of information between sensory and long-term memory is troublesome. Immediate memory is the narrow end of the funnel, the four-lane bridge between sensory and long-term memory with only one open tollgate; it is the bottleneck in our information-processing system. It imposes "severe limitations on the amount of information that we are able to receive, process, and remember" (Miller, 1956, p. 95).

Toll booths force a bottleneck in a highway's traffic flow.

Overcoming the Bottleneck And so the limitation remains unless the seven items we are trying to remember are richer, more complex items than seven single digits, or unless the items are grouped in some fashion, as in the 3–4 grouping of a telephone number or the 3–2–4 grouping of a social security number. In Miller's terms, *the richer, more complex item* is properly called a **chunk** of information, a unit that can hold something as impoverished as a single digit or letter, or as complex and elaborate as a word or phrase. By chunking individual items together into groups, we can overcome this limitation and "break (or at least stretch) this informational bottleneck" (Miller, 1956, p. 95).

What follows is a simple example of the power of chunking, of forming larger units:

BYGROUPINGITEMSINTOUNITSWEREMEMBERBETTER

No one can remember these 40 letters correctly if they are treated as 40 separate, unrelated letters in a string. But the effect of the chunking process is that grouping together the isolated items into a richer chunk enables us to retain more information. You can easily remember the eight words in this sentence because they are familiar words that combine grammatically to form a coherent thought. You can remember a social security number more easily by grouping the digits into the arbitrary 3–2–4 pattern. And you can remember a telephone number more easily if you further group the last four digits into 2 two-digit numbers.

Recoding Miller's central point, then, was that our short-term memories are inherently limited in the total amount of information that can be held at any one time. The limit seems to be seven units or chunks, plus or minus two. Any quantity greater than this, if it is to be retained successfully, must be grouped or chunked, again with a limit of about seven of these enriched chunks. The technical term for this process of *grouping items together, then remembering the newly formed groups* is **recoding**. By recoding, a novice begins to hear not the isolated dots and dashes of Morse code but whole letters, then words, and so on.

The principle behind recoding schemes is very straightforward: Recoding reduces the number of units to be held in short-term memory by increasing the richness, the information content, of each individual unit. Short-term memory therefore is not as heavily loaded with units after recoding, although the individual units are packed with more information than before. Forming these enriched units takes some difficult mental effort, however. Try recoding the longest digit list in the Prove It lists into two-digit numbers (28, 43, etc.), trying to remember these enriched units. This will illustrate the mental effort needed for this kind of recoding (in fact, Brooks & Watkins, 1990, suggested that there is already a subgrouping effect in the memory span, with the first half of the span enjoying an advantage over the second half).

Given the active, attention-consuming nature of recoding, you might feel that the *BYGROUPINGITEMS* example you saw earlier isn't quite fair. After all, the meaning and grammar make the sentence easily understood and eliminate the need for much of that hard mental work. Actually, the example clarifies the goal of any recoding scheme: to make the newly formed units as meaningful and as related to easily retrievable information as possible. A string of 40 digits, obviously longer than the capacity of short-term memory, can still be recalled accurately if your recoding scheme is powerful enough and if you can apply it flexibly and quickly. In fact, Miller described a person who could recall 40 binary digits (1s and 0s) without error by means of such a recoding scheme. He then noted that "if you think of this merely as a mnemonic trick for extending the memory span, you will miss the more important point that is implicit in nearly all such mnemonic devices. The point is that recoding is an extremely powerful weapon for increasing the amount of information that we can deal with. In one form or another we use recoding constantly in our daily behavior" (1956, p. 95).

Long-Term Memory Involvement in Recoding Two conditions seems especially important for recoding. First, we can recode if there is sufficient time to apply the recoding scheme or, perhaps more accurately, if there are sufficient mental resources available to do the recoding. Second, we can recode if the recoding scheme is a well-learned scheme or strategy, or even a highly overlearned one, as the Morse code or binary digit schemes become with practice. Here, a well-learned **mnemonic device,** *a rehearsal or recoding strategy,* is used as the basis for grouping the stimulus items to be recalled (e.g., Chase & Ericsson's [1982], subject could recall 82 digits in order by applying a highly practiced recoding scheme he invented for himself). Thus specialized long-term memory knowledge enabled recoding of the digits and in turn helped overcome the limitations of short-term memory. Note in general that two kinds of information are stored in long-term memory here: the specific facts as well as the overlearned recoding strategy. Thus the term *mnemonic* in the Miller quotation refers to any kind of remembering strategy, especially when long-term memory is involved.

One of Miller's soundest insights followed immediately from his remarks about mnemonic tricks: "In my opinion, the most customary kind of recoding that we do all the time is to translate into a verbal code. When there is a story or an argument or an idea that we want to remember, we usually try to rephrase it 'in our own words'" (1956, p. 95). As you have probably deduced by now, an adult's language comprehension skills are highly overlearned and have surely migrated toward automaticity. This makes rephrasing an excellent, flexible, and overlearned recoding scheme in the present context. Indeed, it is exactly this kind of recoding, based on your long-term memory and knowledge of the language, that helped you remember *BYGROUPINGITEMS*. (When I do this demonstration in class, students often recall something like "By grouping items together, we remember better," a clear demonstration of recoding by paraphrasing.)

But what about situations when no automatic recoding scheme is available, as in the less meaningful situation (for most of us) of remembering numbers instead of words? What is the fate of items in short-term memory when there is insufficient time or attention to apply a more conscious scheme? Can we merely hold the usual 7 ± 2 items?

The Brown–Peterson Task: Decay from Short-Term Memory

Under some circumstances, we cannot even hold *half* that many items in short-term memory. The research by Brown (1958) and Peterson and Peterson (1959) provided psychology with a compelling demonstration of this and is still viewed as trend-setting for the study of cognition. We will spend a few moments discussing the task and results because you will encounter the same kind of empirical hypotheses and tasks several more times in this book.

The central idea in the Brown and the Peterson and Peterson articles was that some forgetting might take place even during the course of learning new material and that this *forgetting might be caused simply by the passage of time before testing*—in other words, forgetting caused by **decay.** In the experiments, a simple three-letter stimulus was presented to the subjects, followed by a three-digit number. Subjects were instructed first to attend to the stimulus, then to begin counting backward by threes from the number they had been shown. The counting was to be done out loud, in rhythm with a metronome clicking twice per second. At the end of a variable-length period of counting, the subjects were asked to report the three-letter stimulus they had heard. The results of these studies apparently were so unexpected, and the number of researchers eager to replicate the study so large, that the task acquired a nickname that is still in use—the **Brown–Peterson task.**

The surprising result was that memory of the simple three-letter stimulus was only slightly better than 50% after 3 s of backward counting; accuracy dwindled to about 5% after 18 s of counting (Figure 5-1). The essential ingredient in this finding was the distractor task, the backward counting. The task clearly requires a great deal of attention (if you doubt this, try it yourself from any three-digit number, making sure to count backward twice per second). Furthermore, it surely prevents rehearsal of the three letters because rehearsal uses the same attention mechanism as the backward counting.

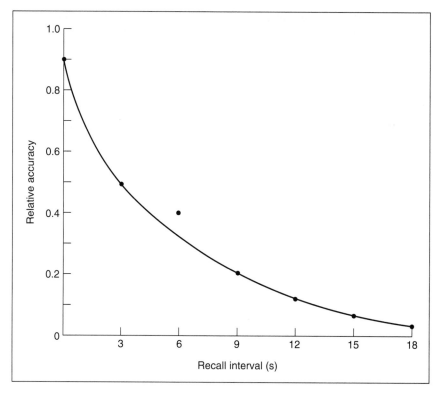

Figure 5-1

Relative accuracy of recall in the Brown–Peterson task across a delay interval from 0 to 18 s. Subjects had to perform backward counting by threes during the interval. From Peterson & Peterson (1959).

What was surprising was that the letters were forgotten so quickly even though short-term memory was not overloaded—a 50% loss after only 3 s (assuming recall would have been perfect with a zero-second delay). On the face of it, it seemed that the Petersons had presented evidence of a simple decay function in short-term memory: With an increasing period of time, less and less information remained in short-term memory.

Interference Versus Decay in Short-Term Memory

Later research, especially that presented by Waugh and Norman (1965) in their article "Primary Memory," questioned one of the assumptions made in the Peterson and Peterson report. The Petersons suggested that there should have been little, if any, interference from the distractor task to the memory test—from counting backward to recalling the three-letter stimulus—because letters and digits seemed so dissimilar. Therefore, the forgetting functions they observed were interpreted as evidence of simple decay of information from short-term memory. Waugh and Norman, however, felt that the distractor task might very well have been a source of interference. They noted that if the numbers spoken by the

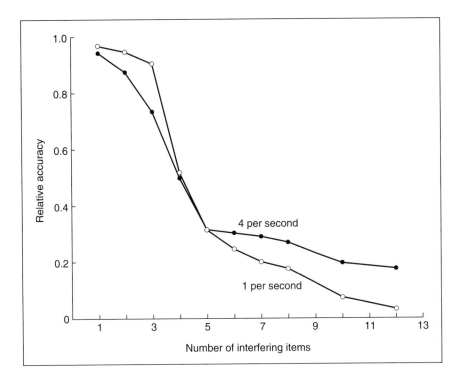

Figure 5-2

Relative accuracy in the Waugh and Norman (1965) probe digit experiment as a function of the number of interfering items spoken between the target item and the cue to recall; rate of presentation was either 1 or 4 digits per second.

subjects during backward counting had interfered with the short-term memory trace, then longer counting intervals would have provided more opportunity for interference because subjects would have produced more numbers during the longer interval.

Waugh and Norman's reanalysis of several short-term memory studies confirmed their suspicion. Especially convincing were the results from their own probe digit task. Subjects heard a list of 16 digits, read at a rate of either 1 or 4 digits per second. The final item in each list was a repeat of an earlier item, and it served as the subjects' probe or cue to write down the digit that had followed the probe in the original list. For instance, if the sequence *7 4 6 9* had been presented, then the probe digit *4* would have cued recall of the digit *6*.

For the issue of decay versus interference, the important part of their experiment was the time it took to present the 16 digits. Presenting the entire list took 16 s for one group but only 4 s for the other group. If forgetting were caused by decay from short-term memory, then the groups should have differed markedly in their recall because so much more time had elapsed in the 16 s group. Yet as Figure 5-2 shows, the two groups differed little in their recall accuracy.

The Waugh and Norman result suggested strongly that forgetting had been influenced by the number of intervening items between the critical digit and the recall test, not merely by the passage of time. In other words, forgetting in short-term memory was caused by interference, not simple decay. Thus the Peterson and Peterson distractor task had not only prevented rehearsal, as it was supposed to, but had also produced interference with the critical digit to be remembered, as it was *not* supposed to. The short-term memory trace had experienced interference from the events that followed it during the trial.

Note that it is almost impossible to test the simple decay theory adequately. To do so, we would have to present the stimulus material followed by a blank interval of time during which decay could take place, then the recall test. Yet, as the Petersons suspected, subjects will use a blank retention interval for rehearsal. And preventing rehearsal by introducing a distractor task yields interference. A straightforward test of decay theory seems to require an interval of time during which neither interference nor rehearsal takes place. Putting it bluntly, this goal can never be reached. On the other hand, the decay theory would have to predict the same amount of forgetting for the same interval of time, regardless of what kind of distractor task was being used; after all, the mere passage of time is *the* cause of forgetting according to decay theory.

A variety of experimental tests used this reasoning to examine the inadequacy of simple decay theory for short-term forgetting. In one study, Talland (1967) used the Brown–Peterson task with two different distractor activities. One group did subtraction during the retention interval, and the other group merely read the same numbers they would have spoken if doing subtraction. Not surprisingly, the group that actually had to do subtraction performed worse on recall than the reading group (see also Dillon & Reid, 1969), despite the same retention interval for both groups. Similarly, Peterson, Peterson, and Miller (1961) tested different kinds of stimulus materials, nonsense syllables versus words, while holding the retention interval constant. After 6 s of backward counting, word recall was significantly higher than recall of a three-letter nonsense syllable, again in disagreement with simple decay explanations. In short, different kinds of interference tasks and different kinds of stimuli produced different amounts of forgetting. Such results are almost impossible to explain by means of decay theory but are clearly sensible if forgetting from short-term memory is caused by interference.

Release from PI We will discuss one other famous line of research on this interference effect, a series of studies by Wickens (1972; also Wickens, Born, & Allen, 1963). Very shortly after the Peterson and Peterson report, Keppel and Underwood (1962) reported a startling effect that also challenged the Petersons' interpretation of decay. It seems that subjects forgot at the dramatic rate reported by the Petersons only after they had been tested on several trials in the short-term memory task. On the first trial, memory for the three-letter stimulus was almost perfect. Keppel and Underwood pointed out the straightforward reason for this result. As you experience more and more trials in the Brown–Peterson task, recalling the stimulus becomes more difficult because the *previous* trials are generating interference.

This form of interference is called **proactive interference (PI)**, *when older material interferes forward in time with your recollection of the current stimulus*. This is the

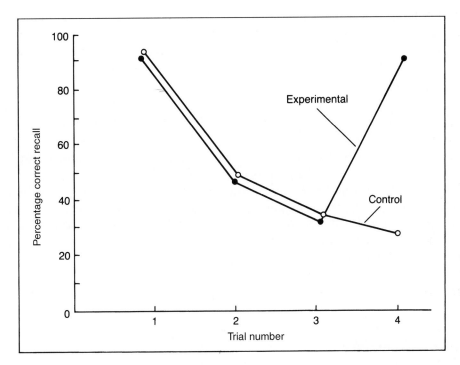

Figure 5-3

Recall accuracy in a release from PI experiment by Wickens, Born, and Allen (1963). Triads of letters are presented on the first three trials, and proactive interference begins to depress recall accuracy. On Trial 4, the control group gets another triad of letters; the experimental group gets a triad of digits and shows an increase in accuracy, known as release from PI.

opposite of **retroactive interference (RI),** in which *newer material interferes backward in time with your recollection of older items.* In other words, short-term memory loses information rapidly, say within 15 s, when similar material has already been presented and tested. The loss of information in the Brown–Peterson task, according to Keppel and Underwood, was caused by proactive interference.

The importance of Wickens's research was in his adaptation of the interference task, especially in the way he turned proactive interference to his advantage. Wickens presented three Brown–Peterson trials, using three words per trial as the stimulus. On the first trial, accuracy was near 90%, but it drifted down to about 40% on Trial 3. At this point, Wickens changed to a different kind of stimulus for Trial 4. Subjects who had heard three words per trial were given three numbers on the fourth trial and vice versa. The results were dramatic. When the nature of the stimulus was changed, performance on Trial 4 returned to the 90% level of accuracy (of course, Wickens also included a control group of subjects who received the same kind of stimulus on Trial 4 as they had gotten on the first three trials, to make sure their performance continued to dwindle, which it did). Figure 5-3 illustrates this result.

The interference interpretation here is very clear. Performance deteriorates across trials because of the buildup of proactive interference. If the to-be-remembered stimulus changes, however, then you are released from the interference. Thus, **release from PI** occurs *when the decline in performance caused by proactive interference is reversed because of a switch in the to-be-remembered stimuli.* For example, as shown in Figure 5-3, recall rebounded to about 90%. Wickens's (1972) research over a lengthy period demonstrated conclusively the effect of proactive interference and then the release from PI when the stimulus materials are changed.

For now, the importance of the Wickens's research was that it showed clearly the influence of interference in the process of forgetting information in short-term memory. Although it is possible that simple decay also occurs in short-term memory, it seems almost impossible to give this hypothesis a fair test. But from the practical standpoint, interference caused by intervening material surely characterizes our everyday experiences with short-term memory. As Howard (1983, p. 109) put it, "Unrehearsed material is seldom allowed to remain in working memory long enough to decay, because there is usually something else—if only some daydreaming—to be done with the limited capacity available. To convince yourself of this, try keeping your mind completely blank for 15 seconds."

■ Section Summary

- Short-term or working memory is an intermediate memory system between the sensory memories and long-term memory. Its capacity for holding information is severely limited, on most accounts to only 7 ± 2 units of information. The process of recoding, grouping more information into a single unit, is the means of overcoming this limitation or bottleneck in the information-processing system.
- Whereas decay as an explanation of forgetting from short-term memory is logically possible, most of the research implicates a process of interference or competition as the reason for short-term forgetting. With an attention-consuming distractor task, such as counting backward by threes, even a very simple stimulus can be lost from short-term memory. The research suggests that this loss is a product of two kinds of interference: retroactive interference from the distractor task and proactive interference from multiple trials on the same kind of material.

Short-Term Memory and Recall

What does Howard's (1983) phrase "unrehearsed material" imply? What happens to material sitting in short-term memory that goes unrehearsed? Usually it undergoes interference and so is lost from the short-term store. Let's explore this not from the direction of interference but from the more positive direction of rehearsal. What happens when the material sitting in short-term memory *is* rehearsed?

Of course, we have nibbled at the edges of this question, and you have encountered some indirect answers to it already. The term *rehearsal* has been tossed in occasionally, as in the form of Miller's (1956) recoding, but it has not yet been really defined or explored as a vital, short-term memory process. Furthermore, if you remember the topic of rehearsal from your introductory psychology course, you may have wondered why you have read this far in the chapter without seeing a **serial position curve,** a *graph of item-by-item accuracy on a recall task.* The term *serial position* simply refers to the original position an item had in the list that was studied; for example, *serial position 3* refers to the item presented third in a list being learned. I wanted to save this discussion until dealing with the decay and interference approaches to forgetting because they provide insight into the particular shape of the serial position curve. But now the time has come to talk about serial position. Figure 5-4 shows several time-honored, traditional serial position curves (which you encountered briefly in Chapter 2).

Free Versus Serial Recall

Before studying the evidence in these serial position curves, let's consider the two basic tasks we use to test subjects: **free recall** and **serial recall.** In free recall, subjects are free to *recall the list items in any order,* whereas in serial recall we ask subjects to *recall the list items in their original order of presentation.* Not surprisingly, serial recall is the more difficult task to perform. To be able to recall the items in order, subjects must rehearse the items as they are shown, trying to store not only the stimulus but also its position in the list. As more and more items are shown, subjects are less and less able to do this rehearsal, so they tend to show poorer performance later in the list.

In contrast, free recall provides the opportunity to recall the items in any order. As Atkinson and Shiffrin (1968, 1971) argued, this final recency portion of the list is generally held only in short-term memory and is spewed out, so to speak, as soon as the signal to recall is given to the subjects. This recall strategy works because the recency of the last items ensures that they are still in short-term memory. Clearly, you cannot capitalize on recency in a serial recall task; you must start recalling with the first item in the list. Because you cannot rely on immediate recall for any of the items in serial recall, you must rehearse them as they are shown to store them in a more enduring form.

Serial Position Effects

We generally call the early positions of the list the primacy portion of the serial position curve; these are the early serial positions plotted across the bottom of Figure 5-4. *Primacy* here has its usual connotation of "first": It is the first part of the list that was studied. The term ***primacy effect,*** then, always refers to the *accuracy of recall for the early list positions.* A strong primacy effect means good, accurate recall of the early items on the list, usually because of rehearsal. A weak primacy effect, low accuracy on the early items, usually is caused by insufficient rehearsal. The final portion of the serial position curve is known as the recency portion. ***Recency effect*** refers to *the level of correct recall on the final items of the originally presented list. High recency* means "high accuracy," and *low recency* means that this portion of the list was hardly recallable at all.

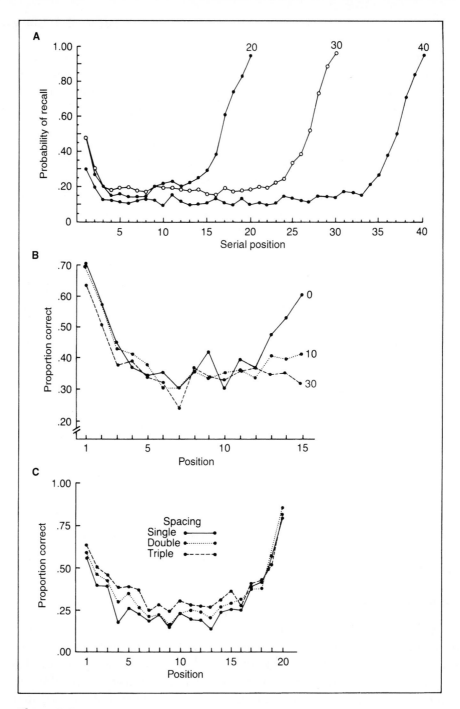

Figure 5-4

A, Serial position curves showing recall accuracy across the original positions in the learned list. Rate of presentation was one item per second.

B, Serial position curves showing the decrease in recency when 10 or 30 s of backward counting is interpolated between study and recall.

C, Three different rates of presentation: single (3 s), double (6 s), and triple (9 s).

As Figure 5-4A shows, a strong recency effect is obtained across a range of list lengths; Murdock (1962) presented 20, 30, and 40 item lists at a rate of one item per second. Note further that there is a slight primacy effect for each list length but that the middle portion of the lists showed very low recall accuracy. Apparently, the first few items were rehearsed enough to make them recallable from long-term memory, but not enough time was available for rehearsing the items in the middle of the list. For all lists, though, the strong recency effect can be attributed to recall from short-term memory.

The experimental manipulation that eliminates the recency effect should be no surprise to you. Glanzer and Cunitz (1966), for instance, showed their subjects 15-item lists, required them to do an attention-consuming counting task for either 10 or 30 s, and then asked them to recall the items. In contrast to the group that was asked for immediate recall (0-s delay), the groups that had to perform the counting task before recalling the list showed very low recency (Figure 5-4B). On the other hand, the primacy portion of the list was essentially unaffected by the counting task. In other words, the early list items must have resided in a more permanent, long-lived memory store for them to endure the 30 s of counting that was interpolated between study and test. These items seemed immune to the interference effects of the distractor task. The most recent items were dramatically susceptible to interference, however, so they must have been stored in a shorter-term, more fragile memory (STM).

Other manipulations, summarized by Glanzer (1972), showed how the two portions of the serial position curve are indeed influenced by different factors. For our consideration of short-term memory, note that providing more time per item during study (spacing of 3 versus 6 versus 9 s, in the figure) had almost no effect on the recency portion of the list but did alter the primacy portion to a significant degree (Figure 5-4C; from Glanzer & Cunitz, 1966). Additional time for rehearsal enabled subjects to store the early items more strongly in long-term memory, it seemed. On the other hand, additional time was not necessary or even helpful for the sort of immediate recall used for the most recent items. These items were presumably held in short-term memory and recalled rapidly before interference could take place.

Rehearsal Buffer

The notion of short-term memory as a **rehearsal buffer,** *a mental recycling system for holding information temporarily,* was a dominant idea through the 1960s. Waugh and Norman's (1965) model explicitly showed rehearsal as a recirculating loop within primary (short-term) memory. The typical interpretation was that rehearsal was an optional control process invoked by short-term memory. Rehearsal was thought to have two properties: it could maintain information in short-term memory by recirculating it through the rehearsal buffer, and at the same time it could increase the likelihood that the rehearsed information would be transferred to long-term memory for more permanent storage (Atkinson & Shiffrin, 1968; Waugh & Norman, 1965). Bear these two

PROVE IT

Tests of Short-Term, Working Memory

Several tests of short-term, working memory can be given with very little difficulty, to confirm the various effects you are reading about in this chapter. Here's a suggestion, along with a few sample lists. Additional demonstrations can be found on the Web page.

Simple Memory Span

Make several lists, being sure that the items do not form unintended patterns. Read the items at a fairly constant and rapid rate (no slower than one item per second) and have the subject name them back in order. Your main dependent variable will be the number or percentage correct.

Lists can be made up of single digits, consonants, nonsense syllables, unrelated words, or simple line drawings. Several easy variations on this procedure are possible:

- To illustrate the importance of interference, have your subjects do an interference task on half of the trials. On an interference trial, give them a number like 437 and have them count backward by threes, out loud, for 15 s, before recalling the list items.
- Keeping list length constant, give different retention intervals before asking for recall (e.g., 5 s, 10 s, 20 s), either with or without backward counting.
- Vary the presentation rate (e.g., 1 word per second versus 1 word per 3 s) to see how the additional time for rehearsal influences recall.
- See whether your subjects notice anything different about lists that have some special pattern to them, like the starred lists here:

870314
71505436
2864612975
584393482561
TSYLQP
CIMWODXA
*QWERTYUIOP
KWUCRALNYWGSJ
*LABONNEMAISON
LEAF GIFT CAR FISH ROCK
PAPER SEAT TIRE HORSE FILM BEACH FOREST BRUSH
BAG KEY BOOK WIRE BOX WHEEL BANANA FLOOR BAR PAD BLOCK RADIO BOY
*LOVE EMOTION PLAN ATTEMPT RULE LAW ANALYSIS SYSTEM FINE PAYMENT
*WHILE I WAS WALKING THROUGH THE WOODS A RABBIT RAN ACROSS MY PATH

properties in mind—recycling and transferring to long-term memory—because they reappear later in the chapter, when we consider working memory span tasks. For now, consider the question, What is short-term memory for? Part of the answer is rehearsal: rehearsal that can transfer information to long-term memory and rehearsal that maintains a short-term memory trace for a brief period of time.

■ Section Summary

• Serial position curves reveal the operation of two kinds of memory performance. Early positions in a to-be-recalled list are sensitive to deliberate rehearsal that transfers information into long-term memory, whereas later positions tend to be recalled with high accuracy in the free recall task; this latter effect is called the recency effect and is due to the subjects' strategy of recalling the most recent items first. Asking subjects to perform some distractor task before recall usually eliminates the recency effect because the distractor task prevents the subject from maintaining the most recent items in immediate memory. The rehearsal that is necessary to transfer information into long-term memory is a short-term, working memory activity.

Retrieval from Short-Term Memory

Our focus so far has been on rehearsal and its effects, especially how we maintain information in short-term memory and how we transfer it to long-term memory. We turn now to a different question: How do we access or retrieve the information stored in short-term memory?

Think of this question as the short-term memory equivalent of a question that seems more sensible to our introspections: How do we access or retrieve information from long-term memory? Such a question is particularly interesting when retrieval, whether from short- or long-term memory, is extremely rapid and out of conscious awareness (e.g., does a robin have feathers?). That is the focus of this section, how the rapid process of retrieval happens in short-term memory. To answer this question, we turn to a second kind of memory task: recognition.

Recognition Tasks

All students are familiar with a common version of a recognition task: multiple choice tests. In this format, you select the one correct alternative, and in the process you reject the others as being incorrect. From the standpoint of cognitive processes, you have said "Yes" to the correct alternative, indicating "Yes, I recognize that as the information I studied for the test." Similarly, deciding that an alternative is wrong is the same as deciding "No, that choice is new. I haven't studied it before." Clearly, making these decisions requires you to access some stored knowledge then compare the alternatives to that knowledge. When one of the alternatives matches your knowledge, then you can respond "Yes, that's the correct alternative."

The important angle in cognitive science, as you have seen several times already, is that we can time people as they make their "yes/no" recognition decisions and then try to infer the underlying mental processes used in the task on the basis of how long they took. It was exactly this procedure Saul Sternberg used in addressing the question of how we access information in short-term memory.

Short-Term Memory Scanning: The Sternberg Task

Sternberg (1966, 1969, 1975) began his work by noting that the use of reaction time (RT) tasks to infer mental processes had a venerable history, dating back at least to Donders's work in the 1800s. Donders had proposed a general method called the subtractive method for determining the time necessary for simple mental events. For example, if your primary task involves processes A, B, and C, you devise a comparison task that has only processes A and C in it. After administering both tasks, you subtract the A + C time from the A + B + C time. The difference should be a measure of the duration of process B because it is the process that was subtracted from the primary task.

Sternberg pointed out a major difficulty in applying Donders' subtractive method. It is virtually impossible to make sure that the comparison task, the A + C task, truly contains *exactly* the same A and C processes as they occur in the primary task. There is always the possibility, Sternberg reasoned, that the A and C components may be inadvertently simplified when you eliminate process B. If so, then subtracting one from the other can't be justified.

Sternberg's solution to this problem was a genuine innovation. Rather than trying to eliminate one process from the primary task, he arranged his experiments so that the critical process would have to *repeat* some number of times during a single trial. Across an entire experiment there would be many trials on which process B had occurred only once, many on which it occurred two times, three times, and so forth. He then examined the RTs for these successive conditions, and inferred the nature of process B by determining how much time was *added* to people's responses for each repetition of process B.

The Sternberg Task The task Sternberg devised was a short-term memory scanning task, now simply called a Sternberg task. Participants first stored a short list of letters, called the memory set, in short-term memory. They then saw a single letter, the probe item, and responded "yes" or "no" depending on whether the probe item was among the letters in the memory set. So, for example, if you stored the set *l r d c* in short-term memory and then saw the letter *d*, you would respond "yes." If the probe item were *m*, however, you would respond by pressing the "no" button.

In a typical experiment, Sternberg's groups were shown several hundred trials, each consisting of these two parts, memory set then probe item, as shown in Table 5-1. Memory sets were from one to six letters long (digits were used in some experiments), well within the span of short-term memory, and they changed on every trial. Probe items changed on every trial too, and were selected so that the correct response was "yes" on half the trials and "no" on the other half. More importantly, across the hundreds of trials, when the probe item did match one of the letters in the memory set, it matched each position in the set equally frequently. This is illustrated by Trials 2 and 3 in Table 5-1. Take a moment to try several of these trials, covering the probe item until you have stored the memory set in short-term memory, then covering the memory set and uncovering the probe then making your "yes/no" judgment. (For a better demonstration, have someone read the memory sets and probe items to you out loud.)

Table 5-1 SAMPLE STERNBERG TASK

Trial	Memory set items	Probe items	Correct response
1	R	R	Yes
2	LG	L	Yes
3	SN	N	Yes
4	BKVJ	M	No
5	LSCY	C	Yes
Before timing starts, store memory set in STM	Timing starts here Probe item	Scan STM	Timing stops here Make response
e.g., E Q H D	J	Compare J to E, compare J to Q, etc.	No

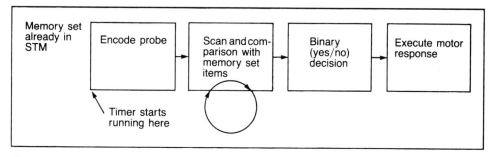

Figure 5-5

The four-stage process model for short-term memory scanning. Adapted from Sternberg (1969).

Figure 5-5 illustrates the **process model** that Sternberg (1969) proposed for this task, simply *a flowchart of the four separate mental processes that occurred during the timed portion of every trial.* At the point marked "Timer starts running here," the individual begins to encode the probe item. Once this process is finished, the search or scan through short-term memory could begin. That is, the mentally encoded probe could then be compared with the items held in memory to see whether there was a match. A simple yes or no decision could then be made, after which the person could make the physical response that stopped the timer, a button press.

In Sternberg's task, it was the search process, the scan through the contents of short-term memory, that was of particular interest. Notice–this is critical–that it was *this* process that was repeated different numbers of times, depending on the size of the memory set. That is to say, when two items were stored in short-term memory, the scan or comparison process would have to occur twice, once for the item in position 1, once for the item in position 2. If five items were stored, likewise, the probe would have to be compared with each of the five. Thus, by manipulating the size of the memory set, Sternberg influenced the number of cycles through the search or scan process. And by

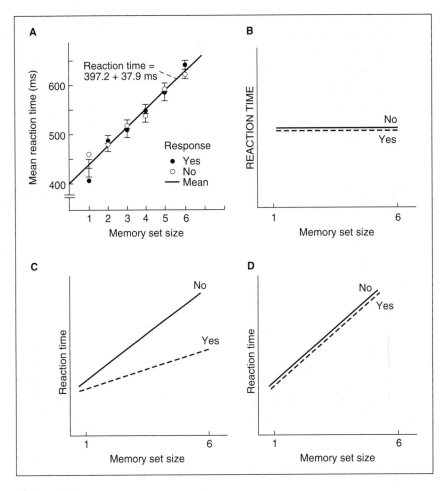

Figure 5-6

A, Reaction time in the short-term memory scanning task, for "yes" (shaded circles) and "no" (unshaded circles) responses. Reaction time increases linearly at a rate of 37.9 msec per additional item in the memory set.
B, The predicted RT effects if short-term memory is scanned in parallel fashion.
C, The predicted RT effects if short-term memory is scanned in a serial self-terminating fashion.
D, The predicted RT effects if short-term memory is scanned in a serial exhaustive fashion, the prediction that matches the obtained results.

examining the slope of the RT results, he could determine how much additional time was necessary for each cycle through that process.

Sternberg's Results Figure 5-6 shows Sternberg's (1969) results. There was a linear increase in RT as the memory set got larger and larger, and this increase was nearly the same for both "yes" and "no" trials. The equation at the top of the figure shows that the *y*-intercept of this RT function was 397.2 msec. Hypothetically, if there had been zero items held in short-term memory, the *y*-intercept would be the combined time for the encoding, decision, and response stages, the stages that occur only once per trial (refer back to Figure 5-5). More importantly, the slope of the equation was 37.9 msec; for each additional item in the memory set, the mental scanning process took an additional 37.9 msec. Putting it slightly differently, the results indicated that the search rate through short-term memory is approximately 38 msec per item—*very* fast.

What kind of mental search would produce such results? Sternberg considered three possibilities. The first and most intuitively appealing alternative was called serial self-terminating search. In this kind of search, the positions in short-term memory are scanned one by one, and the scan stops when a match is found; this is exactly how you search for a lost object, say your car keys. This kind of search predicts that, on the average, the slope of the RT curve for "yes" responses should be smaller than the slope for "no" responses. That is, on "no" trials, all positions have to be searched before you can decide that the probe letter truly was not in the memory set. But on "yes" trials, participants encountered matches at all positions in the memory set, sometimes early, sometimes late, with equal frequencies at all positions. Note the similarities here to the visual search task you read about in Chapter 4 ; in Figure 4-5, the slopes of the positive instance curves ("yes, I found the target") were always smaller than those of the corresponding negative curves ("no, the target was not in the display").

Although this kind of search seems reasonable, both for visual scanning and for short-term memory scanning, Sternberg's data did not match the prediction. A self-terminating search always predicts a smaller slope for "yes" than for "no" trials, yet Sternberg's data showed the same slope for both kinds of trials.

The second possibility he considered was a parallel search through short-term memory, in which each position in the memory set would be scanned simultaneously; that is the meaning of a parallel process (i.e., processes occurring at the same time). If short-term memory were scanned in parallel, in Sternberg's reasoning, then there should be no increase in RT at all. If all the positions can be scanned simultaneously, it should not take longer to scan six items than three, for example. But again, the data did not match this prediction, so parallel search was also rejected.

Instead, Sternberg inferred that short-term memory is searched in a **serial exhaustive** fashion. That is, *the memory set is scanned one item at a time (serial), and the entire set is scanned on every trial, whether or not a match is found (exhaustive).* Notice that exhaustive search has to be correct for "no" trials because the positions have to be scanned exhaustively before you can confidently and accurately make a "no" decision. Because of the similarity of the "yes" and "no" curves in Figure 5-6, therefore, Sternberg argued strongly that both reflect the same mental process, serial exhaustive search through short-term memory (Sternberg, 1969;1975). How quickly can the contents of short-term memory be scanned? Apparently, based on Sternberg's classic results, the contents can be scanned at a rate of about 38 msec per item. And how do we search short-term memory? By means of a serial exhaustive search.

Limitations to Sternberg's Conclusions   Across the years, there have been several critics of Sternberg's conclusions or the assumptions leading to those conclusions. In particular, one criticism involved his interpretation that increasing reaction times necessarily mean serial exhaustive search. For example, it was argued that increasing RTs could be the product of a parallel search in which each additional item to be scanned slows down the rate of scanning for all items (much as a battery can run several motors at once, but each runs more slowly when more motors are connected; see Baddeley, 1976, for a review of such criticisms). Others have objected to a different aspect of Sternberg's work: the embedded assumption that the several stages or processes are sequential and that one must be completed before the next one begins. For instance, McClelland (1979) proposed that the mental stages might overlap partially, in cascade fashion. In a general way, our earlier discussions of automaticity and parallel processing should suggest the nature of this criticism to you. With practice, a process becomes more automatic, thus releasing attentional and processing resources to be devoted to other mental processes. Such outcomes suggest that the assumption of sequential and independent stages of processing is incorrect or at best incomplete.

On the other hand, Sternberg's work inspired the field, pushed it forward toward more useful ways of investigating other cognitive phenomena. Most current research based on RT tasks (e.g., Treisman's visual search task and a variety of long-term memory tasks) owes credit, even if only indirectly, to Sternberg's ground-breaking and insightful work.

■ Section Summary

- Sternberg's important paradigm, short-term memory scanning, provided a technique for investigating how we search through information held in short-term memory. Sternberg's results indicated that this search is accomplished in a serial exhaustive fashion at a rate of about 38 msec per item to be scanned or searched. The Sternberg task illustrated how the short-term memory search processes of different kinds of people (children, adults, people under drug influences) might be investigated and how other kinds of memory search processes might be studied (e.g., long-term memory).

Multiple Codes in Short-Term Memory

We turn now to a somewhat different question about short-term memory. What is the form of the stored information? If the information stored in visual sensory memory is based on a visual code, and the information stored in auditory sensory memory is based on a sound code, then what is the code for short-term memory? Or are there several different kinds of codes that can be held in short-term memory? (The theme here is the representation of knowledge in memory.)

Verbal Codes

Most of the early research on short-term memory, if it considered this question at all, merely assumed that information in short-term memory was held in an acoustic, verbal code. If the experiment asks subjects to report a spoken triad of letters or scan through a short list of letters, it seems only natural to suppose that the memory code for the letters is related to the letter names themselves, a verbal, almost speechlike code. And indeed, several reports demonstrated that short-term memory represents information in an acoustic, verbal-based form. Conrad (1964), for instance, presented strings of letters visually to his subjects and then recorded their errors in immediate recall. He found that when they made mistakes, they were quite likely to "recall" a letter that sounded like the correct one, substituting *D* for *E*, for example. Visual confusions, such as substituting *F* for *E*, were rare. In other words, even though the letters were presented visually, they were apparently stored in short-term memory in an acoustic, sound-based fashion. In a similar study, Wickelgren (1965) presented four letters to his subjects, distracted them by having them copy down eight different letters, then asked them to recall the original four letters. Performance was particularly poor when the eight copied letters rhymed with the four target letters. (Note Wickelgren's use of a retroactive interference task here.)

Such studies demonstrated that short-term memory holds and uses a verbally based code, one related to the spoken names of the stimuli. This code usually is called an **acoustic–articulatory code** because either the actual *sound (acoustic code) or the pronunciation (articulatory code)* could be important. Subsequent research, however, showed that the acoustic–articulatory code was not the only format for storage in short-term memory.

Semantic Codes

A variety of studies were devised to show that short-term memory can retain a semantic, meaning-based code. Among the most famous were the release-from-PI studies reported by Wickens and his colleagues (reviewed in Wickens, 1972). Using the standard Brown–Peterson task, Wickens devised lists to be learned that switched, typically on trial 4, from one semantic category to another. The reasoning was very straightforward: If short-term memory can hold a semantic code, then switching from one category to another should result in release from PI.

This was exactly what Wickens found across a variety of studies (one of which is shown in Figure 5-7; see Wickens & Morisano, reported in Wickens, 1972). All subjects had four successive Brown–Peterson trials, each trial consisting of a triad of words to be remembered. One group saw three trials of triads from the professions category, one group's triads were from the flowers category, and one from the vegetables category. On trial 4, these groups were all switched to a triad from the fruit category. The fourth group served as the control group; these participants saw four consecutive trials from the fruit category, so they did not experience a switch on trial 4.

As you would expect, accuracy for all the groups declined across the first three trials because of the buildup of proactive interference. Whereas this decline in recall continued on Trial 4 for the control group, the other groups showed release from PI on Trial 4, higher recall on the switch trial. Furthermore, the amount of release depended on the similarity of the categories. Because switching from professions to

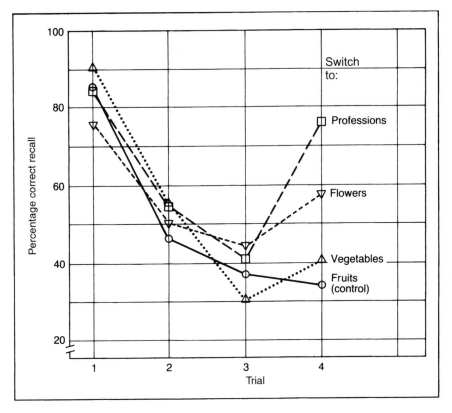

Figure 5-7

Recall accuracy in a release-from-PI experiment by Wickens and Morisano (reported in Wickens, 1972). All subjects received word triads from the fruit category on Trial 4. On Trials 1–3, different groups received triads from the categories *fruits* (control condition), *vegetables, flowers,* and *professions.*

fruits is a major change in category, those subjects showed strong release from PI, compared with the small effect for subjects switched from vegetables to fruits. Because the task relies on short-term memory and because performance on the task depended on the switch in semantic categories, Wickens concluded that short-term memory must hold and use a semantic code too.

Visual Codes

A variety of experiments demonstrated even more flexibility in short-term memory, showing that it can hold and use visual codes as well (e.g., Posner 1978; Posner & Keele, 1967). We will look at just one definitive demonstration of the visual code hypothesis now, and in the process we will begin to see why cognitive psychology started shifting from the traditional term *short-term memory* to the more current *working memory.*

The most dramatic evidence that short-term memory could also use a visual code for information storage came from demonstrations of mental rotation by Shepard and Metzler (1971) and Cooper and Shepard (1973). In the first article, subjects were shown a complex perspective drawing in two forms and had to judge whether the two were the same shape. The critical factor here was that the second drawing was depicted as if it had been rotated from the orientation of the first drawing. Clearly, to make accurate judgments, the subjects had to perform some transformation on the second drawing, mentally rotating it into the same orientation as the first so they could judge it "same" or "different." Figure 5-8 displays several such pairs of drawings and the basic findings of the study.

The overall result was that people took longer to make their judgments as the angular rotation needed for the second drawing increased. In other words, a figure that needed to be rotated 120 degrees to bring it back to the orientation of the first drawing took longer to judge than one needing only 60 degrees of rotation. In the Cooper and Shepard (1973) report, subjects were shown the first figure and were told how much rotation to expect in the second figure. This advance information on the degree of rotation permitted subjects to do the mental rotation ahead of time; in other words, it allowed them time to prepare for the later-presented second figure.

Note that in both studies the subjects were performing a complex, visually based mental task: holding a mental image in short-term memory, then doing difficult, attention-consuming mental work on that image. And because of the short duration of each trial, it was clear that the task was tapping performance based on short-term memory processing. Given the nature of the drawings shown in Figure 5-8, it was almost inconceivable that mental rotation could have been done based only on the traditional acoustic or verbal-based codes. (Ask yourself, what sort of verbal code would be sufficiently detailed to permit such regular rotation without benefit of visual information?) Instead, the mental rotation studies demonstrated conclusively that when we give subjects the chance, they can generate and use visual codes in short-term working memory. And considering the kind of mental processing needed, it certainly seems more natural to call the workplace for this rotation process working memory. Somehow, the notion of 7 ± 2 chunks of information seemed irrelevant to the process of mental rotation.

Other Codes

To conclude this discussion of short-term memory codes, note that other formats for information storage in short-term memory are also possible. For example, most people can conjure up the kinesthetic image of riding a bicycle, of what it feels like physically to lean on your bike as you make a hard right turn (see the Web site demonstrations for a memory span task based on nonverbal codes). For instance, Shand (1982) reported empirical evidence consistent with this intuitive example, evidence of a physical, movement-based short-term memory code.

In his clever study, Shand tested subjects who were congenitally deaf, and skilled at American Sign Language (ASL). They were given five-item lists for serial recall, presented

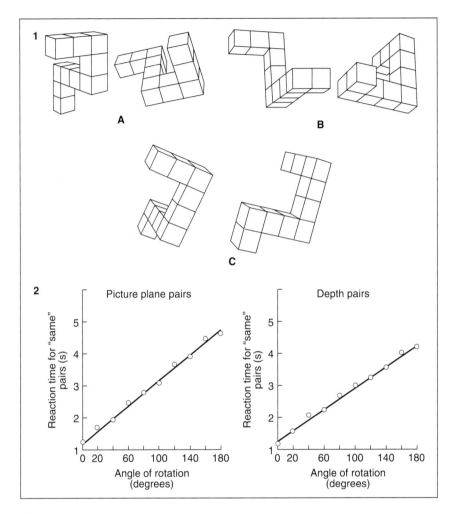

Figure 5-8

1, Three pairs of drawings are shown. For each, rotate the second drawing and decide whether it is the same figure as the first drawing. The *A* pair differs by an 80-degree rotation in the picture plane, and the *B* pair differs by 80 degrees in depth; the patterns in *C* do not match.
2, The RTs to judge "same" are shown as a function of the degrees of rotation necessary to bring the second pattern into the same orientation as the first. Reaction time is a linear function of the degree of rotation.

as either written English words or ASL signs. One kind of list contained English words that were phonologically similar (*SHOE, THROUGH, NEW*) though not similar in terms of the ASL signs. Another list contained words that were cherologically similar in ASL, that is, similar in the hand movements necessary for forming the sign (e.g., wrist rotation in the vicinity of the signer's face), although they did not rhyme in English. The subjects' recall showed confusions based on the cherological relatedness of the list items, even when the list was presented as a series of written, English words. In other words, Shand's deaf subjects were recoding the written words into an ASL-based code and holding *that* code in short-term memory. Their errors naturally reflected the physical movements of that code rather than verbal or auditory features of the words.

In a manner of speaking, cognitive psychology used to be "certain" that short-term memory relied only on acoustic–articulatory coding. It turned out, however, that we had tested short-term memory only with acoustic or verbalizable stimuli. In a very real sense, we had never given subjects the opportunity to show us how they could use other types of codes. In Shand's words, previous arguments for "phonological coding in short-term memory processes may reflect the audiocentricity of the experimenters" (1982, p. 11) rather than the inherent nature of short-term memory. Instead, short-term memory seems capable of holding information in *any* format that can be sensed—auditory, visual, kinesthetic, and so on—and in any format used in the mental system-semantic, imaginal, and so on.

■ Section Summary

- The release-from-PI task, which illustrates interference effects, has been used to document a different point: that short-term memory can hold a variety of informational codes. The evidence suggests that short-term memory often relies on an acoustic–articulatory code but can also hold visual information, semantic information, and even information related to physical movement.

Working Memory

So what kind of system should replace this short-term memory? Adding semantic, visual, and other codes is a step in the right direction, to be sure, but it still seems inadequate. Consider a study by Brooks (1968). Subjects were asked to hold a visual image in short-term memory, a large block capital *F*, and then scan that image clockwise, beginning at the lower left corner. In one condition, they merely said "yes" out loud if the corner they reached while scanning was at the extreme top or bottom of the figure and "no" otherwise; this was the "image plus verbal" condition. The other condition was the "image plus visual" search condition: While the subjects scanned the mental image of the capital *F*, they also had to search through a printed page, locating the column that listed the yes or no decisions in the correct order. Thus, two different secondary tasks were combined with the primary task of image scanning; all the tasks presumably relied on short-term memory. The result was both sensible and damaging to simple models of short-term memory. Making verbal responses while scanning a visual image was easy and yielded few errors. Performing the visual scan of printed columns while scanning the visual image was much more difficult and yielded substantial errors.

But how could that be, if short-term memory is a simple "7 ± 2" system of "slots" into which all information is stored? Why would one kind of information in the slots interfere more with scanning than another kind?

More generally, by the mid-1970s, all sorts of roles and functions were being attributed to short-term memory in tasks involving problem solving, comprehension, reasoning, and the like. Yet as Baddeley pointed out, very little research had actually demonstrated those kinds of roles and functions in STM (Baddeley, 1976; Baddeley & Hitch, 1974; Baddeley & Lieberman, 1980). In Baddeley and Hitch's (1974, p. 48) words, "The empirical evidence for such a view is remarkably sparse." For example, pay attention to how you solve the following problem:

$$\frac{(4 + 5) \times 2}{3 + (12/4)}$$

How can a simple "7 ± 2" system capture both the problem-solving and keeping-track processes here? Didn't you alternate between computing part of the expression and holding the intermediate answers in memory while computing the next part? Likewise, comprehension of sentences can sometimes tax your immediate memory processes almost palpably; for instance,

I know that you are not unaware of my inability to speak German.

Can you feel the burden on your controlled processing when you have to figure out—indeed, almost translate—the meaning of a sentence piece by piece, then put the pieces together? ("not unaware" equals "aware," "inability to speak German" means "cannot speak German," etc.). But notions such as the burden or load on short-term memory or switching between processing and remembering are not addressed by issues such as 7 ± 2 units, recency, and release from PI.

Early Neuropsychological Evidence Going beyond intuitive examples, Baddeley and Hitch (1974) documented their position on the need for an elaborated short-term memory by describing a particularly dramatic case study, originally reported by Warrington and Shallice (1969; also Shallice & Warrington, 1970; Warrington & Weiskrantz, 1970). A series of reports by these authors described a patient "who by all normal standards, has a grossly defective STS. He has a digit span of *only two items*, and shows grossly impaired performance on the Peterson short-term forgetting task. If STS does indeed function as a central working memory, then one would expect this patient to exhibit grossly defective learning, memory, and comprehension. No such evidence of general impairment is found either in this case or in subsequent cases of a similar type" (Baddeley & Hitch, 1974, pp. 48–49, emphasis added; also Baddeley & Wilson, 1988; Vallar & Baddeley, 1984). In a similar vein, McCarthy and Warrington (1984) reported on a patient who could repeat back only a one-item short-term memory list of unrelated words—a memory span of only one word!—but could nonetheless report back six- and seven-word sentences with approximately 85% accuracy. Despite the fact that both types of lists relied on short-term memory processing, performance on one type was seriously affected by the patient's brain damage, and the other was only minimally affected.

How can working memory and short-term memory be the same thing, Baddeley and Hitch reasoned, when a patient with grossly defective STM performance exhibits

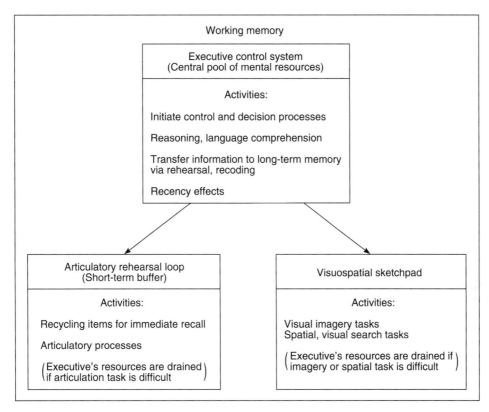

Figure 5-9

Baddeley's working-memory system (e.g., 1986). The executive control system supports reasoning, language comprehension, and other such tasks by using resources from the central pool. Both the articulatory rehearsal loop and the visuo–spatial sketchpad have their own mental resources, but these are insufficient for especially demanding tasks. When necessary, each of these can drain resources from the pool in the central executive system.

no memory deficiencies in other tasks attributed to STM? If unrelated words and the words in sentences are both processed by the same short-term memory system, then how can performance be so good on sentences and so poor on unrelated words? To anticipate Baddeley and Hitch's conclusions, the problem lies with the theory of an undifferentiated STM. In Baddeley's view, traditionally defined STM is but one component of a larger, more elaborate system, **working memory.**

The Components of Working Memory

A description of Baddeley's proposed working memory system provides a useful context for the studies described later; study the diagram of the proposed working memory system in Figure 5-9 as you read (see Baddeley & Hitch, 1974; Salame & Baddeley, 1982).

Note first that Baddeley proposed a working memory system with three major components. The main part of the system was the *central executive* (or sometimes *executive control*) system, assisted by two auxiliary slave systems: the *articulatory or phonological loop* and the *visuo-spatial sketchpad*. Each slave system, in Baddeley's view, had a domain-specific task or set of responsibilities, assisting the central executive by doing some of the lower-level processing involved in a task. Thus, in the arithmetic problem mentioned earlier, the central executive would be responsible for retrieving values from memory (4 + 5, 9 × 2) and applying the rules of arithmetic, whereas a slave system, the articulatory loop, would then hold the intermediate value 18 in a rehearsal-like buffer until it was needed again. The logic of the system was quite appealing: Working memory is easily overloaded, so two subsidiary systems can be given low-level tasks to free the central executive for more serious, pressing work.

The Central Executive The **central executive** system in Baddeley's model was the heart of the working memory system, not appreciably different from the proposed supervisory attentional system (SAS). Think of a large corporation in which the chief executive or executive director is in charge of the difficult tasks such as planning, initiating activities, and making decisions. Likewise in the working memory system, the central executive is in charge of *planning future actions, initiating retrieval and decision processes as necessary, and integrating information coming into the system.* As Figure 5-9 shows, central executive functions also include language comprehension, reasoning, and storage and retrieval operations involving long-term memory. To continue with the arithmetic example, the central executive triggers the retrieval of facts such as "4 + 5 = 9" and invokes the problem-solving rules such as "how to multiply and divide." Furthermore, the central executive also "realizes" that the intermediate value 18 must be held momentarily while further processing occurs. Accordingly, it activates the articulatory or phonological loop, sending it the value 18 to rehearse for a few moments until that value is needed again by the executive. (There is much more to be said about this central component of working memory; see the later section on the individual differences approach to working memory.)

The Slave Systems Assisting the central executive were two subordinate systems: the **articulatory or phonological loop** and the **visuo–spatial sketchpad.** The articulatory or phonological loop was *the speech- and sound-related component responsible for rehearsal of verbal information and phonological processing.* As Figure 5-9 shows, this component recycles information for immediate recall, including articulating the information in auditory rehearsal. Likewise, the visuo–spatial sketchpad is *a system specialized for visual and spatial information, holding or maintaining that kind of information in some short-duration buffer.* When you hold a short list of items for immediate recall—a short-term memory span test, in other words—it would be the articulatory loop that holds the items. If you must generate and hold a visual image for further processing—the capital *F* study, for example—it's the visuo-spatial sketchpad system at work.

Three important limitations about the slave systems are worth emphasizing here. First, the slave systems are responsible for fairly low-level processing: simple articulatory processes and rehearsal for one, simple maintenance of a visual image or spatial representation for the other. Higher-level processing, such as language comprehension and reasoning, is the responsibility of the central executive. Second, the slave systems are domain specific. That is, the slaves are specialized for particular kinds of information or codes: articulation- or sound-based codes for one, visual- and spatial-based for the other. Whereas the central executive can cope with a variety of information types, the slaves are not at all versatile. Third, the slave systems have their own pool of attentional resources, but the pools are very limited. Give either of the slave systems an undemanding task and it can proceed without disrupting activities occurring elsewhere in working memory. On the other hand, if a slave system is given a particularly difficult task, then it either falters or it must drain additional resources from the central executive. Importantly, this give and take in working memory in terms of pools of resources suggests a major way in which Baddeley and many others have investigated working memory: the dual task method.

The Dual Task Method Applied to Working Memory

In general, the dual task method identifies a primary task, the one we are most interested in, and a secondary task, a task to be performed simultaneously with the first one. Both tasks must rely to some significant degree on working memory processes. In general, we are interested in how the two tasks can be performed together and whether there will be competition or interference effects between them. Any two tasks that are performed simultaneously may show either complete independence, complete dependence, or some intermediate level of dependency. If neither task influences the other, then we infer that the two tasks rely on separate mental mechanisms or on separate pools of mental resources. If one task always disrupts the other, then the two tasks presumably use the same mental resources while they are being performed. That is, some common memory component or pool of capacity is being tapped by both.

Finally, if the two tasks interfere with each other in some circumstances but not others, then there is evidence for partial overlap between the two, partial sharing of mental resources. Usually such interference is found when the difficulty of the two tasks reaches some critical point, the point at which the combination of the two tasks becomes too demanding. Researchers manipulate the difficulty of the two tasks just as you would adjust the volume controls on a stereo, changing the left and right knobs independently until the combination hits some ideal setting. In the research, we vary the difficulty of each task separately—we crank up the "difficulty knobs" on the two tasks, so to speak—and then observe the critical point at which performance starts to suffer.

Testing the Working Memory Model

Several standard, long-accepted results fit well with the kind of system Baddeley proposed. For example, in the Brown–Peterson task, we observe interference and poor recall for the triad of list items because of the distractor task, counting backwards by threes. We would assume that the triad of items is being rehearsed in the articulatory loop, thus consuming much of the loop's capacity. Backwards counting not only relies on retrieval of subtraction knowledge into the central executive but also involves articulation. The combination of

rehearsal of the triad and the articulation in backwards counting could easily exceed the articulatory loop's capacity, leading to a decline in performance. Similarly, Brooks's (1968) "capital F" study found the greatest disruption when two visual tasks had to be performed simultaneously, scanning the mental image while searching visually for the correct column of yes or no answers. There was hardly any disruption in performance when the subjects scanned visually while also verbally reporting the yes or no answers; of course the visual and verbal tasks would have relied on different slave systems, leading to little competition for resources.

Working Memory and Reasoning Baddeley presented several sets of results that supported the model he had proposed, results in which a task supposedly dependent on the central executive was paired with a secondary task that tapped one or the other slave system. For example, in one experiment (Baddeley & Hitch, 1974, Experiment 3) subjects were asked to perform a reasoning task. They were shown an initial stimulus such as *AB* and then were timed as they read and responded "yes" or "no" to sentences about the initial stimuli. A simple sentence here would be "*A* precedes *B*," an active affirmative sentence. An equivalent meaning is expressed by "*B* is preceded by *A*," but that's a more difficult sentence because of the passive construction. Making the reasoning task more difficult still, sentences could also be in the negative, such as "*B* does not precede *A*," and could also be passive-negative, such as "*A* is not preceded by *B*" (of course there were also false sentences, e.g., "*B* precedes *A*"). Varying whether the sentence was active or passive and affirmative or negative was Baddeley's way of manipulating the difficulty of the reasoning task.

While doing the reasoning task, subjects also had to perform one of three secondary tasks, called articulatory suppression tasks; subjects either repeated "the the the" over and over, repeated the numbers 1 through 6 over and over, or repeated a random sequence of digits over and over (the random sequence was changed on every trial). Note how the amount of articulation in the three tasks was about the same (a speaking rate of four to five words per second was enforced), but the demands on memory steadily increased up through the random digit task. Indeed, the random digit task was essentially a memory span task, requiring genuine rehearsal. There was also a control condition in which there was no concurrent articulation.

Figure 5-10 shows the reasoning times to the sentences for these four conditions. The control or baseline condition showed that even when reasoning was done by itself, it took more time to respond to the difficult sentences. Adding the articulatory suppression task of saying "the the the" or "one two three four five six" added a bit of time to the reasoning task but did not change the pattern of reasoning times to any great degree; the curves for "the the the" and "one two three . . ." in the figure have roughly the same slope as the control group's pattern. But the random digit condition yielded a very different pattern. As the sentences grew increasingly difficult, the added burden of reciting the random sequence of digits took its toll on reasoning. There was a much steeper increase in reasoning time when subjects had to perform the difficult articulation task, as shown in Figure 5-10. In fact, for the most difficult sentences in the reasoning task, correct judgments took nearly 6 s when random digits had to be recycled through memory at the same time, compared with only 3 s in the control condition.

This was exactly the pattern Baddeley predicted. When the secondary task is very difficult, the articulatory loop must drain or borrow some of the central executive's resources. This means that the central executive, working on the reasoning task, has to slow down or sacrifice accuracy. Exactly as the model predicted, when the slave system drains off attentional resources from the central executive, the executive can no longer maintain its speed or accuracy; the central executive now has to struggle along with its task because it has given up some of its resources to the slave system.

Working Memory and Language Comprehension In a parallel study, Baddeley and Hitch tested language comprehension in a dual-task setting. The results were largely the

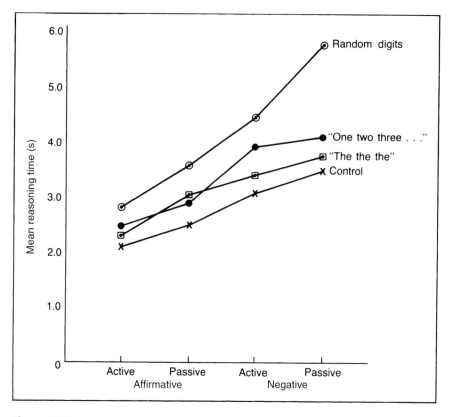

Figure 5-10

Average reasoning time is shown as a function of two variables: the grammatical form of the reasoning problem and the type of articulatory suppression task that was performed simultaneously with reasoning. In the random digits condition, a randomly ordered set of six digits had to be repeated out loud during reasoning; in the other two suppression tasks, either "the the the" or "one two three four five six" had to be repeated out loud during reasoning.

same as were found on the reasoning problems. When participants had to hold six digits in memory while doing the comprehension task, both their comprehension scores and their memory span performance were disrupted significantly. In companion experiments, reasoning and comprehension speed were tested when the stimulus sentences contained phonetically similar words ("*B* precedes *P*"; "Redheaded Ned said Ted fed in bed") versus dissimilar ("*M* precedes *C*"; "Dark-skinned Ian thought Harry ate in bed"). Of course, the phonetic similarity in the sentences should have made it especially difficult for the articulatory loop to perform accurately while it also performed articulatory suppression. This was exactly what the results showed.

Working Memory and Visual Processing Similar research has also been reported on the functioning of the visuo–spatial sketchpad, testing it within a dual task setting. A representative report by Logie, Zucco, and Baddeley (1990) illustrates not only character-istics of the sketchpad system but also its independence of the articulatory loop. In their study, Logie et al. selected two different primary tasks: a visual memory span task and a letter span task. These were paired with two different secondary tasks, one involving mental addition and one involving visual imagery.

In the visual memory span task, participants saw a grid of squares on the computer screen, with a random half of them filled in. After a moment, the grid pattern disap-peared and was then followed by a changed grid pattern where one of the previously filled squares was now empty. Participants had to point to the square that changed, based on their memory of the earlier pattern. Performing adequately on this task presumably was very dependent on the functioning of the visuo–spatial sketchpad. In contrast, the conventional letter memory span task, the other primary task being tested, should have relied very heavily on the articulatory loop and not at all on the sketchpad.

For the secondary tasks, Logie et al. selected a mental addition task thought to be irrelevant to the visuo–spatial system and an imaging task thought to be irrelevant to the articulatory loop. The results of these manipulations are shown in Figure 5-11. First, look at the left half of the graph, which reports the results of the visual span (grid pat-tern) task. Each subject performed the span task by itself, to determine baseline, and then along with the secondary tasks. The graph does not show absolute performance but instead shows the percentage *drop* in dual task performance as compared to baseline. For instance, visual span performance dropped about 15% from baseline when the addition task was paired with it; this means that dual task performance was at 85% of the single-task baseline. In other words, doing mental addition disrupted visual memory to only a modest degree. But when the secondary task involved visual imagery, as shown by the second bar in the graph, visual memory span dropped about 55% from baseline. This is a large interference effect, suggesting that the visuo–spatial sketchpad was stretched beyond its limits when the image-based secondary task was also required.

The right half of the figure shows performance on the letter span task, again sep-arately for the two secondary tasks. Here, the outcome was reversed; mental addition was very disruptive to the letter span task, leading to a 65% decline from baseline, whereas the imaging task depressed letter span scores only a modest 20%. Thus, only minor declines in performance were observed when the secondary task involved pro-cessing in a different domain. But substantial declines resulted when the primary and secondary tasks tapped into the same pool of domain-specific resources (see Baddeley & Lieberman, 1980, for some of the original research on the visuo–spatial sketchpad).

Neuropsychological Evidence

Verbal processes In fact, more recent work has begun to suggest that the several different components of working memory rely on somewhat different brain regions and that the components in Baddeley's model may be further subdivided. In particu-lar, Smith and Jonides (1999; also Smith, 2000) reviewed a number of recent studies that used various brain imaging techniques to identify regions with heightened

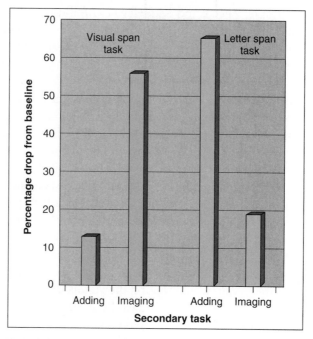

Figure 5-11

Results from Logie, Zucco, and Baddeley's (1990) experiment on the visuo–spatial sketchpad. Two secondary tasks, adding and imaging, were combined with two primary tasks, a visual span or letter span task. The results are shown in terms of the percentage drop in performance measured from baseline; the larger the drop, the more disruption there was from the secondary task.

activity during one or another working memory task. Figure 5-12 shows a diagram of the left hemisphere of the brain, with important areas for verbal storage and executive processes labeled. For what was essentially a Sternberg task, the scanning evidence showed strong activations in a left hemisphere parietal region, noted at the numbered area 40 in the figure (following the standard Brodmann's area map), and three frontal sites, Broca's area (number 44), and the left supplementary motor area (SMA) and premotor areas (number 6).

As you will read in Chapter 9, Broca's area is especially important in the articulation of language, so finding that it was activated in the Sternberg task, in which subjects rehearse the memory set, was not surprising. On the other hand, tasks that emphasize executive control, such as the switching from one task to the other in dual task settings, tend to show especially strong activity in Brodmann's area 46, the dorsolateral prefrontal cortex. In fact, this area has been isolated so frequently in tests involving executive control that it's now commonly referred to by the abbreviation DLPFC.

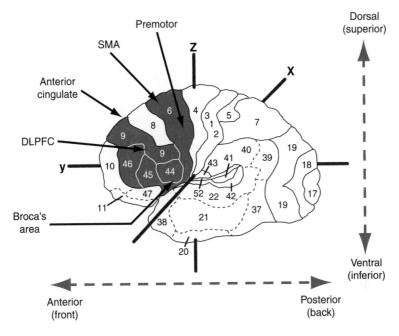

Figure 5-12

The left hemisphere regions of the frontal lobe of the brain that are especially important in verbal working memory tasks: the premotor and supplementary motor area (SMA), Brodmann area 6; the anterior cingulate and the dorsolateral prefrontal cortex (DLPFC), Brodmann area 9; and Broca's area, Brodmann area 44. From Smith & Jonides (1999).

Visual Processes Parallel studies using brain imaging have also shown specific locations and regions involved in visual working memory tasks. In one (Jonides et al., 1993), subjects were first shown a pattern of three random dots, the dots were then removed for 3 s, and then a circle outline appeared; the subject's task was to decide whether the circle surrounded a position where one of the three dots had appeared. In the control condition, the three dots remained visible while the circle was shown, thus eliminating the need for remembering the earlier locations. Positron emission tomography (PET) scans were taken during the full task as well as the control, and then the control pattern of activations was subtracted from the activations in the full task. Because the tasks differed only in the need to remember the dot positions, the difference between the scans presumably showed the region of the brain that had been responsible for remembering the spatial locations in the full task.

Three right hemisphere regions, noted in Figure 5-13, showed heightened levels of activity, so they presumably were the regions especially involved in spatial working memory. They were a portion of the occipital cortex, a posterior parietal lobe region, and the premotor and DLPFC region of the frontal lobe. In related work, when the experimental task required spatial information for responding, it was the premotor

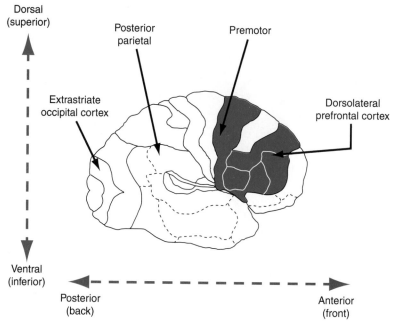

Figure 5-13

The right hemisphere regions of the brain that are especially important in visual and spatial working memory tasks: the extrastriate occipital cortex; the posterior parietal lobe, the premotor area, and the Dorsolateral prefrontal cortex (DLPFC). From Smith (2000).

region that was more active; when the task required object rather than spatial location information, the DLPFC was more active (Jonides et al., 1993; see also Miyake et al., 2000, for a review of various executive functions attributed to working memory).[2]

Individual Differences Approach to Working Memory

A different approach to investigating working memory (although one that is still compatible with the evidence you have been studying here) can be described as an individual differences approach. As in any area of psychology, when we speak of individual differences we're talking about characteristics of individuals—anything from height to intelligence—that differ from one person to the next and can be measured and related to other factors. Traditionally, such approaches have been rather rare in cognitive psychology, probably because of the general assumption that people's cognitive processes do not differ dramatically from one person to the next; the speed, accuracy, or efficiency might differ, of course, but not the basic processes.

---

[2]The procedure of subtracting patterns in the control condition from those obtained in the experimental condition is straightforward conceptually, although the computations are mind-boggling. But notice that conceptually it rests on the same type of logic that Donders used (and Sternberg rejected), finding a control task that contains all of the experimental tasks' components except the one of interest. It would be surprising if this method does not come under attack again, in its newer application to brain imaging.

Since about 1980, however, a growing body of evidence has accumulated based on measured differences in working memory capabilities of different people, where the differences are then related to one or another cognitive process. In particular, this research proceeds by first giving a test to a group of individuals to assess each person's working memory span. Typically, we then divide them into groups, say into high-span and low-span groups, and give the groups a set of standard cognitive tasks. The intent of this research strategy is to interpret group differences in terms of the functioning of working memory.

Consider a program of representative research conducted by Engle and his co-workers (Engle, 2000; Rosen & Engle, 1997). First, subjects are given a working memory span task that is, in essence, a dual task procedure: The task requires simultaneous mental processing and storage of information in working memory. For example, a subject might see the following sentences and words, one at a time (from Engle, 2000):

For many years, my family and friends have been working on the farm. SPOT

Because the room was stuffy, Bob went outside for some fresh air. TRAIL

We were fifty miles out at sea before we lost sight of the land. BAND

The subjects read the first sentence out loud, then said the capitalized word out loud; then they read the second sentence and the word, and then the third. At that point, subjects were asked to recall the three capitalized words they had seen, demonstrating that they had stored those words in working memory. A follow-up question about one of the sentences was also asked to make sure they had spent sufficient time to comprehend (e.g., "Who has been working on the farm?"). Scores on this span task are derived from the number of capitalized words that can be recalled, assuming that the questions are also answered correctly. Thus, someone who recalled "SPOT TRAIL BAND" and answered the question correctly (and was able to do this correctly at least two out of three times with lists of the same length) would have a memory span of 3. To test the limits, such a person was then tested with sets of four sentences and words, and if successful then sets of five, to determine his or her span.

In alternative versions of the test, the sentences might be replaced with arithmetic statements (e.g., "Is $(6 \times 2) - 2 = 10$? BEAR") to be judged true or false or visual patterns requiring some kind of counting (e.g., "count the blue squares in three successive patterns, remembering each of the totals for later recall"). In yet others, subjects answered a brief question about each sentence before moving on to the next sentence, with the storage part of span being tested by having subjects then recall the final word in each sentence. All variations of the working memory span task, regardless of the specific content, involve both *processing* and *storage*: Process the sentence for meaning, for instance, and store the word for recall.

Many investigators have used this kind of span task as a way of estimating subjects' working memory capacity, then testing those subjects on various tasks thought to rely at least in part on controlled attention and working memory processes. The original work that used this method (Daneman & Carpenter, 1980) examined reading comprehension as a function of working memory span. There were significant correlations between subjects' span scores and their performance on the comprehension tasks. One of the most surprising correlations was the correlation between span and verbal Scholastic Aptitude Test (SAT) scores; it was .59, whereas simple memory span scores seldom correlated significantly with SATs. This strong correlation means that there is some important underlying relationship between one's working memory span and the comprehension and verbal processing measured by the SAT.

The strongest correlation in Daneman and Carpenter's work was the .90 correlation between working memory span and performance on a pronoun reference test. Here, subjects read sentences one by one and at some point confronted a pronoun that referred back to a previously encountered noun. In the hardest condition, the original noun had occurred up to six or seven sentences earlier, meaning that drawing the connection from the pronoun back to the noun should have been especially difficult. The results are shown in Figure 5-14. Dramatically, individuals with the highest working memory span of 5 scored 100% correct on the pronoun test, even in the "seven sentences ago" condition. Subjects with the lowest spans (of 2), got 0% correct in that condition. The strong implication was that individuals with higher working memory spans were able to keep more of the relevant information active in working memory as they comprehended the sentences.

Research since this initial report has extended these findings in an astonishing number of ways. Basically, if a task relies on an individual's controlled attentional processes, scores on the task correlate strongly with working memory span. Here are just a few examples (for thorough updates, see Daneman & Merikle, 1996, and Miyake & Shah, 1999).

Conway, Cowan, and Bunting (in press) examined individuals' working memory span, then tested them for the classic cocktail party effect of hearing one's own name while paying attention to some other message. About 65% of the subjects with low working memory spans heard their name in the dichotic listening task, compared with only 20% of those with high spans. The implication was that low-span subjects had difficulty blocking out or inhibiting attention to the distracting information in the unattended message, so they were more likely to hear their own names.

Kane, Bleckley, Conway, and Engle (in press) performed an experiment on eye movements. In one condition, called the prosaccade condition, a visual cue is shown to orient the subject toward a visual location where a target letter will appear (e.g., cue and target on the right). Both high and low working memory span groups did well on this task. But in the antisaccade condition, the cue is shown on one side as a signal that the participant should orient to the *opposite* side, where the target letter will appear. The trick, of course, is that you have to overcome the strong, automatic tendency to orient toward the visual cue. Overcoming that tendency is essentially a test of controlled attention: You have to deliberately inhibit the automatic tendency to focus toward the cue and instead move your eyes to the opposite side. High-span subjects had no particular difficulties in this task; they apparently had sufficient attentional capacity to inhibit the tendency to look toward the cued side. But low-span subjects were much slower and less accurate in the antisaccade task. These subjects also had greater difficulties when they were switched back to the

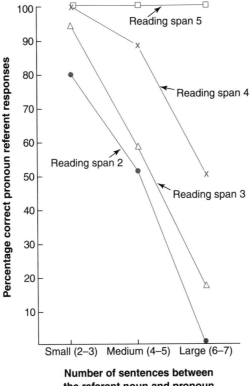

Figure 5-14

The percentage of correct responses to the pronoun reference task when the antecedent noun occurred a small, medium, or large number of sentences before the pronoun, as a function of participants' working memory (reading) span. From Daneman & Carpenter (1980).

prosaccade version of the task. Low-span subjects apparently did not have sufficient controlled attentional resources to inhibit the "same-side" tendency, so they did poorly when the cue signaled the need to shift attention to the opposite side.

The functioning of long-term memory also depends on working memory considerations, as shown by several studies. Rosen and Engle (1997), for instance, had their high- and low-span subjects perform a verbal fluency task: generate members of the animal category as rapidly as possible for up to 15 min. High-span subjects outperformed their low-span counterparts, a difference noticed even 1 min into the task. Intriguingly, in a second experiment, both span groups were tested in the fluency task alone and also in a dual task setting. While naming animals, subjects had to monitor the digits that showed up, one by one, on the computer monitor and press a key whenever three odd digits appeared in the sequence. This attention-consuming task reduced performance on

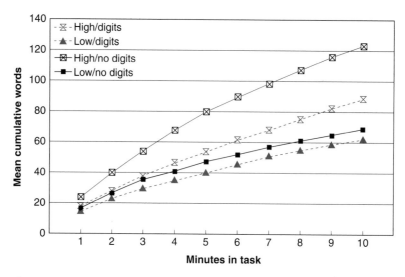

Figure 5-15

The cumulative number of animal names generated by participants of high (open points) or low (filled points) working memory span. Dashed lines indicate performance when participants performed the secondary task of monitoring a stream of digits while generating animal names. From Rosen & Engle (1997).

the animal naming task but only for the high-span subjects, as shown in Figure 5-15. Low-span subjects showed no decrease in their fluency task performance.

Rosen and Engle suggested that the normal process of searching long-term memory for animal names was equivalent in both groups; as you will read in Chapter 7, this seems to be a process of spreading activation through the semantic network. But high-span subjects were able to augment this with a deliberate, controlled strategic search; in other words, along with regular retrieval, the high-span subjects could deliberately ferret out some additional, hard-to-find animal names with this controlled attentional process. This additional "ferreting" process relied on working memory resources, of course. As a consequence, the added digit monitoring task used up the working memory resources that had been devoted to controlled strategic search. This made the high-span group much more like the low-span group had been.

Other studies also show the importance of working memory to both short- and long-term memory processes. Kane and Engle (2000), for instance, found that low-span subjects experience greater proactive interference (PI) in the Brown–Peterson task than high-span subjects. High-span subjects presumably used their controlled attentional processes to combat PI, so they showed an increase in PI when they had to perform a simultaneous secondary task that loaded working memory. In fact, Ericsson and Kintsch (1995) proposed a separate system called long-term working memory to capture the ways in which long-term memory information can be held in a rapidly accessible storage system, available for use on a moment's notice during comprehension and other skilled activities.

Overview

The general conclusion from all these studies is that *working memory* is a more suitable name for the attention-limited workbench system of memory. Working memory is responsible for the active mental effort of reasoning and language comprehension, for transferring information into long-term memory by means of rehearsal, and for retrieving information from long-term memory. In fact, Baddeley (1999) recently suggested that there is a third slave component to working memory, one devoted to two fundamental processes: retrieving information from long-term memory and then integrating that information with the current contents of working memory.

Aside from the central executive of working memory, there is a separate articulatory loop component and a separate visuospatial component. The articulatory loop is partially autonomous in that it can recirculate a small amount of information without interfering with the central executive's performance. When overloaded, however, it begins to drain extra mental resources from the executive component. This disrupts the ongoing executive activity, whether it is reasoning, comprehending, or learning. Likewise, the visuo–spatial sketchpad can do a small amount of processing independently but, when faced with a demanding task, can siphon off mental resources from the executive.

Importantly, there is an overall limitation in the mental resources or capacity available to working memory; it is a closed system, with only some fixed quantity of mental resources to spread around. In other words, when extra resources are drained by the slave systems, they are not replaced into working memory by some other component. Instead, the central executive merely suffers along with insufficient resources for its own work. Naturally, as processes become more automatic, fewer of working memory's resources are tied down by the task (see Hirst & Kalmar, 1987, for an analysis of the "pools of resources" metaphor). The interpretation in the individual differences approach differs a bit from this one. In essence, this approach claims that when individuals do not possess those extra resources, for whatever transient or permanent reason, their capacity to perform adequately in controlled attention tasks suffers.

■ Section Summary

- Working memory, a broader conceptualization of our short-term, immediate memory abilities, consists of a central executive system and two major slave systems. The most commonly investigated subsystem is the articulatory rehearsal loop, the system responsible for memory span performance. Baddeley's results suggest that when the memory span task is difficult, the articulatory loop can drain off mental resources from the central executive component. When this happens, the task being performed by the executive suffers in speed or accuracy. The same arrangement applies to the visuo–spatial sketchpad, the other major slave system. On this theoretical account, the memory span performance tested in classic STM research is the articulatory loop, merely one component of the flexible, multipurpose system known as working memory.

- An alternative research strategy is to test participants' working memory span, then examine differences in cognitive performance as a function of their span (e.g., high- vs. low-span). This approach has revealed a substantial number of tasks that show a strong relationship between span and performance. The implication of these results is that working memory span assesses an individual's controlled attentional processes, which are significant aspects of one's performance all the way from selective attention tasks up through reading comprehension.

Key Terms

acoustic–articulatory code (p. 181)

articulatory or phonological loop (p. 188)

Brown–Peterson task (p. 165)

central executive (p. 188)

chunk (p. 163)

decay (p. 165)

free recall (p. 171)

mnemonic device (p. 164)

primacy effect (p. 171)

proactive interference (PI) (p. 168)

process model (p. 177)

recency effect (p. 171)

recoding (p. 164)

rehearsal buffer (p. 173)

release from PI (p. 170)

retroactive interference (RI) (p. 169)

serial exhaustive search (p. 179)

serial position curve (p. 171)

serial recall (p. 171)

visuo–spatial sketchpad (p. 188)

working memory (p. 187)

C H A P T E R **6**

Episodic Long-Term Memory

Memory is the most important function of the brain; without it life would be a blank. Our knowledge is all based on memory. Every thought, every action, our very conception of personal identity, is based on memory. . . . Without memory, all experience would be useless. (Edridge-Green, 1900)

We must never underestimate one of the most obvious reasons for forgetting, namely, that the information was never stored in memory in the first place. (Loftus, 1980, p. 74)

This is the first of three chapters specifically devoted to long-term memory, the relatively permanent storage vault for a lifetime's worth of knowledge and experience. Why do we need three separate chapters? The first reason, as indicated in the Edridge-Green quotation, is obvious: Long-term memory is fundamental to nearly every mental process, to almost every act of cognition. Clearly, you cannot understand human cognition unless you understand long-term memory. The second reason follows from the first: Long-term memory is an enormous area of research with a long (for psychology) history. In fact, the area is so large that it is impossible to do it justice unless some divisions and subtypes are used to organize the material. The third reason relates to everyone's curiosity about his or her own memory system. Who has not complained, at one time or another, about forgetfulness, about the unreliability of memory? Are these complaints justified? Is there some design flaw in human memory that leads to these problems?

Long-term memory is all about divisions and subdivisions these days; various theorists have argued for one or another scheme by which to categorize the varieties of long-term memory. We used to argue over whether long-term memory was a single, indivisible storage system or whether multiple systems were involved (e.g., McKoon & Ratcliff, 1986; Tulving, 1989). Now, it seems, the arguments are about *how many* long-term memory components there are (Schacter, 1989; Squire, 1986, 1993; Tulving, 1985, 1993), with evidence from cognitive neuroscience playing an especially prominent role. Instead of taking a hard line for or against any particular one of the schemes, we will simply adopt one of the more useful ones as an organizational device, then explore the evidence to see where it leads us.

Look at Figure 6-1, a taxonomy suggested by Squire (1986, 1993). As the figure shows, an overall distinction can be made between **declarative** or **explicit memory** and **nondeclarative** or **implicit memory.** In this system, declarative or explicit memory is *long-term memory knowledge that can be retrieved and then reflected on consciously;* in other words, a byproduct of retrieving such knowledge is that we are consciously aware of it. The two kinds of declarative knowledge, episodic and semantic memory, are the topics of this chapter and the next. In contrast, nondeclarative or implicit memory is *knowledge that can influence thought and behavior without any necessary involvement of conscious awareness.*

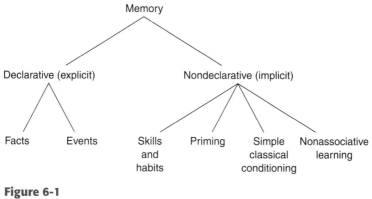

Figure 6-1

A taxonomy of long-term memories. Adapted from Squire (1993).

The key to this distinction is the conscious awareness part—one has it, one doesn't. In Anderson's (1996) straightforward description, "Explicit processes are those that are potentially reportable and implicit processes are those that are not" (pp. 123–124).

Consider a brief example to help clarify the distinction. If I ask you what your mother's maiden name is, I'm asking you to retrieve knowledge from **episodic memory,** *a person's autobiographical memory, memory of the personally experienced and remembered events of a lifetime.* When you retrieve that bit of information, you become conscious of it: you're aware of the name, it's in your consciousness, you can say it out loud, and so forth. Episodic memory not only enables you to record your personal history in memory, it also supports "time travel," the mental ability to "relive experiences by thinking back to previous situations and happenings . . . and to mentally project oneself into the anticipated future" (Wheeler, Stuss, & Tulving, 1997, p. 331). Similarly, if I ask you what a maiden name is, I'm asking you to retrieve knowledge from **semantic memory,** your *general world knowledge, knowledge that relates concepts and ideas to one another, including your knowledge of how to express those concepts and ideas in language.* You retrieve the concept of a maiden name, and it becomes explicit: The concept is now in your conscious awareness. Notice that just as episodic memory is your mental autobiography, semantic memory is your mental encyclopedia, and both involve explicit knowledge that you can become consciously aware of (Tulving, 1972, 1983, 1993).

But there is more going on here than rises to the level of conscious awareness. As you are reading this sentence, you are encountering the term *maiden name* again; in fact, that was the fourth time you encountered it. Although you are not conscious of it, you are now significantly faster at reading that term than you were the first time you read it; the speedup in rereading the word is a form of priming called repetition priming. This effect happens at the nondeclarative, implicit level. Likewise, if I gave you some word stems an hour from now and asked you to fill in the blanks with the first word that comes to mind, you would be more likely than chance to complete "MAI___ " as "MAIDEN" because you have encountered the word recently. Importantly, these effects would occur even if you did not recall having seen the word *maiden* in the previous paragraph (but teasing apart the influences of conscious and unconscious contributions to this, and to recall effects in explicit tasks, is no simple matter; see Buchner & Wippich, 2000; Jacoby, 1991; Jacoby, Toth, & Yonelinas, 1993).

The main focus of this chapter is on the explicit, autobiographical memory system called episodic memory. We'll progress through the evidence about this system, covering what is known about the storage and retrieval factors that influence how we learn and remember. And in the final section of the chapter, we will encounter implicit memory the same way the rest of cognitive psychology encountered it: by coming to terms with the evidence about memory loss in cases of amnesia.

Preliminary Issues

Let's start on the topic of episodic memory by considering three preliminary issues. First, we will talk about a classic, even ancient approach to learning and memory: mnemonic devices. We'll then spend a little time on the first systematic research ever done on human memory, Ebbinghaus's pioneering work, published in 1885. These two topics suggest that people have always been aware of some of the workings—and failings—of memory. Today we call such awareness metamemory, or more generally metacognition; respectively, these terms refer to our understanding and insights into the workings of our own memory and our overall cognitive system. Here's a warning, however: As you read the three chapters on long-term memory, bear in mind that just as your complaints and frustrations about your own memory problems probably are exaggerated, so is your certainty about remembering some kinds of events exactly as they happened, with no distortions or omissions whatsoever. It's a genuine paradox; Our memories are better than we often give ourselves credit for and worse than we are often willing to believe or admit.

Mnemonic Devices

The term *mnemonic* (pronounced "ne-MAHN-ick") means "to help the memory"; it comes from the same Indo-European base word as *remember, mind,* and *think.* A **mnemonic device** is an *active, strategic learning device or method,* a rehearsal strategy. Formal mnemonic devices rely on a preestablished set of memory aids and considerable practice on the to-be-remembered information in connection with the preestablished set. Informal mnemonics, such as those you invent yourself, generally are less elaborate, are more suited to smaller amounts of information that you're trying to remember, and are more idiosyncratic and personalized. The strengths of such mnemonic techniques include the following important principles: (1) The material to be remembered is practiced repeatedly, (2) the material is integrated into an existing memory framework, and (3) the device provides an excellent means of retrieving the information. We will study two of the traditional mnemonic devices first, then turn to the issue of inventing new mnemonics as the need arises.

Classic Mnemonics The first historical mention of mnemonics is in Cicero's *De oratore,* a Latin treatise on rhetoric (the art of public speaking, which in Greek and Roman days meant speaking from memory). In this work, Cicero describes a technique based

Table 6-1 THE METHOD OF LOCI		
Set of Loci	**Words to Be Remembered**	**Grocery List and Images**
Driveway	Grapefruit	Grapefruit instead of rocks along side of driveway
Garage door	Tomatoes	Tomatoes splattered on garage door
Front door of house	Lettuce	Lettuce leaves hanging over door instead of awning
Coat closet	Oatmeal	Oatmeal oozing out the door when I hang up my coat
Fireplace	Milk	Fire got out of control, so spray milk instead of water
Easy chair	Sugar	Throw pillow is a 5-lb bag of sugar
Television	Coffee	Mrs. Olson advertising coffee
Dining-room table	Carrots	Legs of table are made of carrots

on visual imagery and memorized locations, ascribed to Greek poet Simonides (circa 500 B.C.). The mnemonic is commonly called the **method of loci** (*loci* is the plural of *locus*, meaning "a place"; pronounced "LOW-sigh"). The source of Simonides' inspiration, as the story goes, was a personal experience. Simonides was performing a lyric poem at a banquet when he was called out of the hall for a message. While he was outside, the roof of the hall caved in. The disaster was so bad that the bodies of the guests, mangled by the falling roof, were unidentifiable. Simonides, however, realized he could identify the dead by visualizing the banquet table where they had been sitting. Apparently, the scene was impressed strongly enough in Simonides' memory that he was able to remember the faces as they were arranged around the banquet hall locations. (The anecdote trivializes the power of mnemonics, however; among other things, mnemonic devices enabled Greek orators to memorize and recite entire epics such as *The Iliad* and *The Odyssey;* see Yates, 1966.)

There are two keys to the method of loci: first, the memorized physical locations, and second, the mental images of the to-be-remembered items, one per location. In other words, choose a set of places or locations, a set that can be recalled easily and in order. You might select a set of 10 or 12 locations you encounter in a walk across campus, or those you encounter as you arrive home, as your preestablished memory aids. Now form a mental image of the first thing you want to remember, and then mentally place that thing into the first location, continuing with the second item in the second location, and so on. Form a good, distinctive mental image of the item in its place (McDaniel & Einstein, 1986).When it's time to recall the items, all you need to do is mentally stroll through your set of locations, "looking" at the places and "seeing" the items you have placed there. Although there is some evidence that a more bizarre image is more memorable (Burns, 1996; Einstein & McDaniel, 1987), there is also an important role for the distinctiveness of the image (Kroll, Schepeler, & Angin, 1986). Others (e.g., Hirshman, Whelley, & Palij, 1989) suggest that the "surprise response" of encountering something that violates your expectations is part of this distinctiveness effect (wouldn't you be surprised to see a horse up in a tree?). Table 6-1 gives an example of this technique.

Table 6-2 THE PEG WORD MNEMONIC DEVICE

Numbered Pegs	Word to Be Learned	Image
One is a bun	Cup	Hamburger bun with smashed cup
Two is a shoe	Flag	Running shoes with flag
Three is a tree	Horse	Horse stranded in top of tree
Four is a door	Dollar	Dollar bill tacked to front door
Five is a hive	Brush	Queen bee brushing her hair
Six is sticks	Pan	Boiling a pan full of cinnamon sticks
Seven is Heaven	Clock	St. Peter checking the clock at the gates of Heaven
Eight is a gate	Pen	A picket fence gate with ballpoint pens as pickets
Nine is a vine	Paper	Honeysuckle vine with newspapers instead of blossoms
Ten is a hen	Shirt	A steaming baked hen on the platter wearing a flannel shirt

Another mnemonic device is worth mentioning here, partly because it is so commonly known and easy to use. The technique is known as the **peg word mnemonic** (Miller, Galanter, & Pribram, 1960), in which *a prememorized set of words serves as a sequence of mental "pegs" onto which the to-be-remembered material can be "hung."* The peg words rely on rhymes with the numbers one through ten, such as "One is a bun, two is a shoe," and so on (Table 6-2). The material being learned is then hung on the pegs, item by item, making sure that the rhyming word and the to-be-remembered word form a mental image.

For the list "cup flag horse dollar . . .," create a visual image of a flattened tin cup, dripping with ketchup, inside your hamburger bun; for flag, conjure up a visual image of your running shoes with little American flags fluttering in the breeze as you run a marathon; and so on (go ahead and form images for the rest of the list as an exercise to understand the principles of mnemonic devices). Now at recall, all you have to do is first remember what peg word rhymes with one, then retrieve the bun image you created, looking inside to see a cup. Similarly, what peg word rhymes with *two*, and what image do you find along with *shoe?*

Bower (1970) described a study by Ross and Lawrence (1968) to illustrate the effectiveness of such mnemonic devices. In their study, subjects used a set of 40 campus locations as their loci, then had to learn several 40-item lists using the method of loci. The items were presented about one every 13 s and were followed by an immediate recall test; subjects also returned the next day for a delayed recall test. Average performance on immediate recall, using the method of loci, was 38 out of 40 *in their correct order.* One day later, subjects averaged 34 correct, again in order. These levels of accuracy surely are a testimony to the effectiveness of such mnemonic techniques.

The Three Mnemonic Principles The crux of the argument for all mnemonic effectiveness involves three principles, the three things a mnemonic device does to improve memory. First, it provides a structure for learning, for acquiring the information. The structure may be elaborate, as a set of 40 loci would be, or simple, like rhyming peg words. It can even be highly arbitrary if the material is not particularly extensive. (The mnemonic

HOMES for the names of the five Great Lakes, Huron, Ontario, Michigan, Erie, and Superior, isn't related to the to-be-remembered material, but it is quite simple.)

Second, by means of visual images, rhymes, or other kinds of associations and the effort and rehearsal necessary to form them, the mnemonic helps form a durable and distinctive record of the material in memory, one that won't easily be forgotten (what's sticking out of your running shoes?). Therefore, the mnemonic seems to safeguard against interference in storage or against other kinds of loss within memory itself (but see Thomas & Wang, 1996, for somewhat less optimistic results concerning the long-term benefits of some mnemonic systems).

Finally, the mnemonic guides you through retrieval by providing effective cues for recalling the information. As we discuss extensively later in the chapter, this function of the mnemonic device is critically important because much of what we casually call forgetting seems often to be a case of retrieval difficulty.

This three-step sequence may sound familiar to you and will surely become more so throughout this chapter. It is the sequence we talk about every time we consider learning and memory research, when we consider that memory depends on three conceptually distinct stages: the *acquisition* or *encoding* of new information, *retention* of that information across time, and then *retrieval* of the information (Melton, 1963). Logically, your performance in any situation that involves memory depends on all three of these steps. Any one of the three might be the faulty process that accounts for poor performance, and all three must be accomplished successfully for good performance. A good mnemonic device, including those you invent for yourself (e.g., Wenger & Payne, 1995), will ensure success at each of the three stages.

The Ebbinghaus Tradition of Memory Research

We turn now to the first systematic research on human learning and memory, conducted by the first serious human memory investigator, German psychologist Hermann von Ebbinghaus.

As indicated in Chapter 1, the Ebbinghaus tradition of scientific research on human memory began more than 100 years ago, with his publication of *Uber das Gedachtnis* (1885; the English translation, first published in 1913 and reprinted in 1964, is *Memory: A Contribution to Experimental Psychology*). As is commonly known, Ebbinghaus used only himself as a subject in his studies. In the process of his investigations, he had to invent his own memory task, his own experimental stimuli, and his own set of procedures for testing and data analysis. Few, if any, could do as well today without guidance from research and colleagues. As Hilgard put it in his introduction to the 1964 edition, "For the beginner in a new field to have done all of these things—and more—is so surprising as to baffle our understanding of how it could have happened" (p. vii).

Furthermore, Ebbinghaus anticipated a variety of important issues in human memory research, not to mention developments in general scientific methodology. For instance, Nelson (1985, p. 472) notes that the relearning task Ebbinghaus invented was a "radical idea that was far ahead of its time, both methodologically and conceptually" in that it recognized the possible influence of nonconscious factors (as opposed to Wundt's concern with the conscious mind). Ebbinghaus carefully laid out his method of measuring retention of information and thus anticipated Bridgman's (1927) influential notion of the operational definition (Nelson, 1985, p. 474). In devising ways to analyze his results, he even came close to inventing what we now would call a correlated- or within-groups *t* test (Ebbinghaus, 1885/1964, footnote 1, p. 67). We tend to think of Ebbinghaus merely as the inventor of the nonsense syllable, the meaningless consonant–vowel–consonant (CVC) triads that he used as stimuli in all his studies. This is a seriously impoverished view of Ebbinghaus's pioneering contributions.

The Ebbinghaus Research   To begin with, it is instructive to consider *why* Ebbinghaus felt compelled to invent a meaningless stimulus to be used in his studies of memory (or at least, stimuli that varied in meaningfulness; Hoffman, Bringmann, Bamberg, & Klein, 1987). His rationale was that he wanted to study the properties of memory and forgetting, the fundamentals. It was clear to him that words, if used as experimental stimuli, would hopelessly complicate his results. Had he acquired and remembered a list of items by the simple exercise of memory, or had his performance been altered by his existing knowledge of the words? Putting it simply, *learning* seems to imply acquiring *new* information using whatever mental processes are needed. Yet words are not new, so "learning" a list of words in some sense is a misnomer. And a control factor he adopted, to prevent the possible intrusion of mnemonic or nonrote factors, was the very rapid presentation rate of 2.5 items per second (note his accurate metacognition here, that mnemonic and rehearsal processes take time).

The task Ebbinghaus devised for his research, his only experimental task, was the **relearning task,** in which *a list is originally learned, set aside for some period of time, then later relearned to the same criterion of accuracy.* In most cases, this criterion was one perfect recitation of the list, without any hesitations. After relearning the list, Ebbinghaus computed the **savings score** as the primary measure of learning; the savings score was simply *the reduction, if any, in the number of trials (or the time, in other studies) necessary for relearning, compared to original learning.* Thus, if it took 10 original trials to learn a list but only 6 for relearning, there was a 40% savings (4 fewer trials on relearning divided by the 10 original trials). By the method of relearning, *any* information that was left over in memory from original learning could presumably have an influence, conscious or not, during relearning (see Nelson, 1978, 1985; Schacter, 1987). Recent work by MacLeod (1988) indicates that the influence of relearning is on the recall of the material; that is, relearning seems to help retrieve information that was stored in memory yet is not recallable.

Figure 6-2 presents Ebbinghaus's famous forgetting curve, showing the reduction in savings as a function of time until relearning (see Slamecka, 1985, for details on the huge number of learning trials Ebbinghaus subjected himself to in conducting his research; for Figure 6-2, he learned and relearned more than 1,200 lists of nonsense syllables). Ebbinghaus relearned the lists after one of seven intervals: 20 min, 1 hr, 9 hr, 1 day, 2 days, 6 days, or 31 days. As is clear from the figure, the most dramatic forgetting occurs early after original learning. This is followed by a decrease in the rate of forgetting; a full 42% was

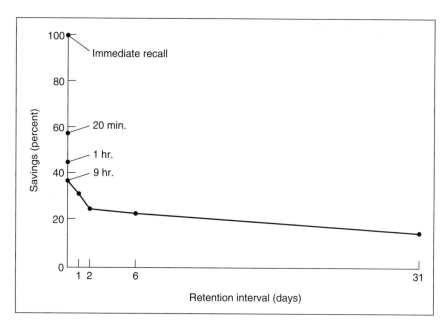

Figure 6-2

The classic forgetting curve from Ebbinghaus (1885/1913). The figure shows the reduction in savings across increasing retention intervals (time between original learning and relearning).

forgotten at 20 min, 56% at 1 hr, 64% after 9 hr, and so on. These forgetting functions have been reanalyzed recently, finding that they follow the same decreasing function as obtained in a variety of other memory tests (technically, a power function; Wixted & Ebbesen, 1991).

Some other fundamental results Ebbinghaus obtained were impressive not because they were surprising but because they were the first empirical demonstrations of the effects. For example, he investigated the effects of repetitions, studying one list 32 times and another 64 times, where the 32-trial condition approximated the standard learning criterion of one perfect recitation. Upon relearning, the more frequently repeated list showed about twice the savings of the less frequently repeated list: in other words, over-learning yields a stronger record in memory. Longer lists were found to take more trials to learn than shorter lists but then showed higher savings upon relearning. In essence, although it is harder to learn a long list originally, the longer list is then remembered better, simply because there was more opportunity to overlearn it (there were more trials in learning before eventual mastery of the whole list).

Finally, in one experiment (Chapter 8), Ebbinghaus continued to relearn the same set of lists across a 5-day period. The savings scores he obtained showed a trend that, if extrapolated, would eventually show perfect savings, that is, no forgetting at all. As an interesting contrast here, Ebbinghaus also reported his results on relearning passages of poetry (kept at 80 syllables). After the fourth day of learning, the savings was 100%. (Is it any wonder that actors overlearn their parts through multiple *rehearsals?*)

Evaluating the Ebbinghaus Tradition There is no disagreement that Ebbinghaus had a tremendous impact on what came to be known as the field of verbal learning and, later, cognitive psychology. In a recent set of papers commemorating the 100th anniversary of the 1885 publication, a consensus began to emerge about the value of Ebbinghaus's work (with some passionate dissenters, of course). In Mandler's (1985) words, Ebbinghaus's contribution represented "a door being opened into the human mind, the realization—contrary to then established wisdom—that it is in fact possible to gain positive knowledge about human memory" (p. 464); Slamecka (1985) simply called him "the founder of our discipline."

On the other hand, he studied the learning of nonsense syllables, thus deliberately excluding meaning from his studies. Much subsequent research, up through the 1960s (and even the 1970s), continued to use nonsense syllables, even as it became clearer that such results were missing the central point: If people will attempt all sorts of mediating, mnemonic, or other rehearsal strategies to make a nonsense syllable sensible and meaningful, then we should be investigating that, not trying to prevent it. A more balanced, temperate view is simply that in the absence of prior research, Ebbinghaus quite properly simplified the experimental situation so as to get interpretable results (Kintsch, 1985), a research strategy that is no longer necessary. Perhaps the fault lies less with Ebbinghaus than with his successors, who slavishly stuck to his methods without questioning their intent or usefulness.

The Current Position If we consider the quite different position that is accepted today and contrast it with the model of Ebbinghaus's research, we arrive squarely at the empirical research on episodic long-term memory. Today's position consists of at least three parts. First, the fact that people invent meaning, regardless of the experimenter's wishes, is taken as evidence that human memory relies very heavily on meaning and that this should be the focus of our research. Second, we also recognize that the participants in our memory experiments are active. They are not content to recite syllables passively and have them eventually make an impression on memory, as Ebbinghaus did, but instead are intent on applying mental resources and strategies to almost every learning situation. In other words, the active participant assumption is quite the opposite from the Ebbinghaus model, although he himself was aware of the tendency (after all, he took great pains to prevent such activity).

The third part of the current position, implied by some of the critics mentioned before, is that results based on meaningless stimuli are themselves meaningless when we attempt to understand how people learn and remember. This is the issue of ecological validity again, saying in essence that our traditional laboratory results do not apply to real-world situations that involve memory for meaningful material. This is too strong a position, of course; much evidence from laboratory tasks has been shown to generalize well to real-world settings. On the other hand, issues such as autobiographical memory, false memories, and thematic influences on memory would not have been investigated by a cognitive science that stuck with relatively impoverished experimental stimuli and list learning paradigms.

Metamemory

Think about these two issues, mnemonics and Ebbinghaus's groundbreaking work, from a larger perspective: They both indicate an age-old sensitivity to the functioning of memory and intuitions about what makes remembering easier or harder. The ancient Greeks knew how difficult it was to remember large amounts of information, so they devised strategies for overcoming those difficulties. Ebbinghaus presented nonsense syllables to himself at a very rapid rate, specifically to prevent himself from rehearsing or using some mnemonic trick to learn faster. This kind of sensitivity, or even insight, into the workings of memory is known as **metamemory,** *knowledge about (meta) one's own memory, how it works, and how it fails to work.* In most researchers' view, metamemory is a part of a broader self-awareness called **metacognition,** *knowledge about one's own cognitive system and its functioning.*

Research on these topics, starting especially with studies on children's memory performance (Brown, 1975; Flavell & Wellman, 1977), has raised at least two important issues. First is the importance of self-monitoring and awareness, or metacognitive awareness. A number of studies have focused directly on metacognitive judgments, such as people's "ease-of-learning" estimates or "feeling-of-knowing" judgments (Leonesio & Nelson, 1990; Nelson, 1988). It seems very clear that part of a person's behavior in a learning task—at least a motivated adult's behavior—involves self-monitoring, assessing how well one is doing. On the other hand, this metacognitive awareness can occasionally mislead us. In experiments on the false fame effect, for example, participants read a list of nonfamous names, which increases the familiarity of those names. Later on, participants were more likely to judge the names to be famous, essentially confusing familiarity with fame (Jacoby, Woloshyn, & Kelly, 1989). Interestingly, this confusion was particularly likely when the participants did not remember reading the original list of names, suggesting that the effect occurred at an implicit level (Kelley & Jacoby, 1996; see also Busey, Tunnicliff, Loftus, & Loftus, 2000).

The second issue involves control or self-regulation, what you do with your metacognitive awareness. That is, if you realize you are not performing some task particularly well, what mental processes or procedures do you follow to improve your performance? How do you select a strategy to apply to the task that will improve your performance? Sometimes the evidence is mixed on this issue. For example, Mazzoni and Cornoldi (1993) report that people often "labor in vain," that is devote more study time to some items than others and yet fail to do better on those selected items (see also Nelson, 1993). On the other hand, Thiede (1999) argues that when study time is tested in appropriate ways, there is a positive, sensible relationship between monitoring and self-regulation on one hand and learning and recall performance on the other (see also Son & Metcalfe, 2000). Reder and Schunn (1996) argue that a large component of this metacognitive effect, the part that controls selecting a strategy to use during performance, is heavily influenced by implicit memory effects. In their view, although we often can explicitly report the strategy we used in a particular task, the actual selection of that strategy is influenced largely by implicit factors.

■ Section Summary

- Long-term memory is now widely viewed as a multicomponent storage system, with a major division between declarative or explicit memories and nondeclarative or implicit memories. Declarative memory consists of two major parts, episodic and semantic memories; nondeclarative or implicit memory includes priming and procedural or motor learning. Explicit memories can be verbalized, but implicit memories cannot; conscious awareness of the memory is unnecessary for implicit memories but always accompanies explicit memories.

- The classic method for improving memory performance involves mnemonic devices, specialized rehearsal strategies that ensure adequate storage of the information and provide a systematic method by which information can be retrieved. The classic mnemonic devices, such as the method of loci, use a variety of techniques, especially visual imagery, to improve performance; familiarity with the mnemonic method provides a useful foundation for understanding both storage and retrieval effects in studies of memory performance.

- Ebbinghaus was the first psychologist to conduct extensive investigations into the processes of learning and forgetting. Working on his own, Ebbinghaus invented methods of conducting such investigations. The relearning task he devised revealed a sensitivity to the demands of simple recall tasks; such tasks tap consciously retrievable information but may underestimate the amount of information learned and retained in memory. The classic forgetting curve he obtained, along with his results on practice effects, inspired the tradition of verbal learning and, later, cognitive psychology. Several of his empirical and methodological insights would be called metacognitive awareness today.

Storing Information in Episodic Memory

How do people store information in episodic memory, the long-term memory system for personally experienced events and information? How is new information recorded in this long-term memory system so that it is preserved until some future time when it is needed? And how can we measure this storage of information? Ebbinghaus's research investigated one principal kind of storage variable, repetition, and one memory task, relearning. He found that an increase in the number of repetitions led to a stronger memory, a *trace* of the information in memory that could be relearned more quickly. This suggests that frequency is a fundamental variable in learning: Information that is presented more frequently is stored more strongly in memory.

A corollary of this idea is that people should be good at remembering how frequently something has occurred. Hasher and Zacks (1984) summarize a large body of research on how sensitive people are to the frequency of events. Because people's estimates of relative frequency generally are good, these authors propose that frequency information is encoded into memory in an automatic fashion, with no deliberate effort or intent. Although the automaticity of such a mechanism has been disputed (Greene,

Why do we rehearse?

1986; Hanson & Hirst, 1988; Jonides & Jones, 1992), there is no doubt that the frequency with which information or events occur has a large impact on long-term memory. (See Anderson & Schooler, 1991, and Schooler & Anderson, 1997, for the intriguing relationship between the need to retrieve some information from memory and the frequency or recency of that information in the environment.)

These effects are interesting, of course, but of limited use if you need to learn and remember something truly new, such as a list of words in an experiment or a list of seven themes in a cognition textbook. How do we acquire this kind of information? We consider three important storage effects here: rehearsal, organization, and imagery. A summary of these three will then lead us to the topic of retrieval and a discussion of forgetting.

Rehearsal

Atkinson and Shiffrin (1968) made a fundamental statement on storage in their influential model of human memory. In their formulation, information that resides in short-term memory may be subjected to **rehearsal,** *a deliberate recycling or practicing of the contents of the short-term store.* Atkinson and Shiffrin proposed that there are two effects of rehearsal. First, rehearsal maintains information in the short-term store, preventing it from being lost or displaced by other information. Second, the longer an item is held in short-term memory by rehearsal, the greater the probability that the rehearsal will also store the item in long-term memory. Basically, this position states that rehearsal "copies" the item into long-term memory, with the strength of the long-term memory

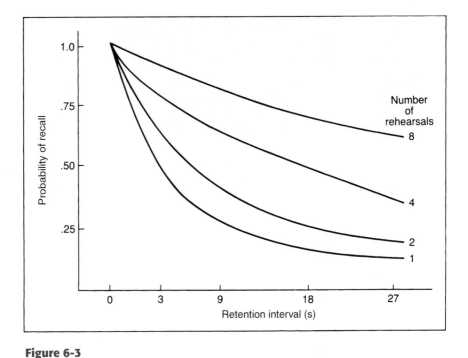

Figure 6-3

Hellyer's (1962) recall accuracy results as a function of the number of rehearsals afforded the three-letter nonsense syllable and the retention interval.

trace depending on the amount of rehearsal. In short, rehearsal transfers information into long-term memory (see also Waugh & Norman, 1965). Of course, in most experimental situations, the items being transferred are words that the subject already knows. Thus "transferring information" generally is taken to mean storing some tag or other indication that a certain word was an item in the list being learned.

What evidence is there of this transfer function for rehearsal? Aside from the classic Ebbinghaus study on repetition, many experiments have shown that rehearsal of information leads to better long-term retention. For example, Hellyer (1962) used the Brown–Peterson task to examine the effects of rehearsal. Subjects were shown a CVC trigram and were asked to perform an arithmetic task between study and recall. The difference in this study was that on some trials the trigram had to be spoken out loud once, on some trials twice, four times, or eight times. Figure 6-3 shows the results of this experiment. The more frequently rehearsed the item was, the better it was retained across the distracting period of arithmetic. Using a somewhat different approach, Hebb (1961; cited in Loftus & Loftus, 1976) presented strings of digits for recall. Whereas performance remained stable and low on the strings that changed from trial to trial, performance improved significantly on the string of digits that was periodically repeated in the learning trials. Although the task seemed to be testing only short-term retention of digit strings, mere repetition of a string led to some transfer of the information into long-term memory.

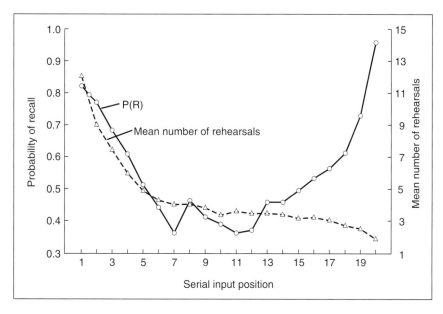

Figure 6-4

In the figure, the probability of recall, P(R), is plotted against the left axis, and the number of rehearsals afforded an item during storage is plotted against the right axis. The similar pattern of these two functions across the primacy portion of the list indicates that rehearsal is the factor responsible for primacy effects.

Although these studies and many others confirmed the general notion that rehearsal leads to an improvement in long-term memory performance, the evidence they presented was somewhat indirect. After all, for evidence about long-term memory, it was slightly odd that two short-term memory paradigms had been used, the Brown–Peterson task and a digit recall task. More direct evidence on rehearsal was soon to follow, however. Among the many such studies, the standard citation on rehearsal is to a series of studies performed by Rundus (1971; Rundus & Atkinson, 1970).

Rehearsal and Serial Position Effects In his experiments, Rundus had his subjects learn 20-item lists of unrelated words, presenting them at a rate of 5 s per word. Subjects were asked to rehearse out loud as they studied the lists, repeating whatever words from the list they cared to during each 5-s presentation. Rundus then tabulated the number of times each of the words had been rehearsed and compared this tally to the likelihood of recalling the word correctly in the free recall task. Figure 6-4 shows his most telling results. In the early primacy portion of the serial position effect, there was a direct positive relationship between the frequency of rehearsal and the probability of recall. In fact, Rundus also examined a proportional measure of rehearsal and found that "for a given amount of rehearsal, items from the initial serial positions have no better recall than items from the middle of the list" (Rundus, 1971, p. 66). In other words, the primacy effect—higher recall of the early items—was viewed as entirely dependent on rehearsal. The early items can be rehearsed more frequently (no doubt because of the experimenter-paced task) and so are recalled better. High recall of the late positions, the recency effect, was viewed as simply recall from short-term memory, which of course is influenced by different factors (e.g., a distractor task before recall). This explained why they were recalled so well despite being rehearsed so little.

Two Kinds of Rehearsal

A more refined view about rehearsal claims that there are two major kinds of rehearsal, each with different effects on storage (Craik & Lockhart, 1972). According to this position, **maintenance rehearsal** (or **Type I rehearsal**) is a *low-level, repetitive kind of information recycling.* This is the kind of rehearsal you would use to recycle a phone number to yourself until you dial it. The essential idea here is that once you stop rehearsing the information, it leaves no permanent record in memory. In Craik and Lockhart's view, maintenance rehearsal merely maintains information at a particular level in the memory system, without storing it more permanently or deeply. As long as an item of information is subjected to maintenance rehearsal, it can be retrieved. Once the maintenance rehearsal stops, however, the item should vanish without a trace.

   Elaborative rehearsal (or **Type II rehearsal**) is a *more complex kind of rehearsal that uses the meaning of the information* to help store and remember it. When information is subjected to elaborative rehearsal, according to Craik and Lockhart, the information is stored more deeply in the memory system, at a level that makes contact with the meaning of the information. As a consequence, material that was rehearsed elaboratively should be more permanently available for retrieval from memory; in short, it should be remembered better. You might include imagery or mnemonic elaboration in your elaborative rehearsal, you might try to construct sentences from the words in a list you are trying to learn, you might impose some organization or structure on the list, or you might even try to convert nonsense syllables like "BEF" into more meaningful items like "BEEF." Stating it differently, maintenance rehearsal maintains an item at its current level of storage, whereas elaborative rehearsal moves the item more deeply, and stores it more permanently, into the memory system.

Depth of Processing

Craik and Lockhart (1972) advanced a notion of the memory system very different from the stage approach of sensory, short-, and long-term memory to which we became accustomed. They embedded their proposal of two kinds of rehearsal into what they called a **levels of processing,** or **depth of processing,** framework. The essence of this framework is as follows. Any perceived stimulus receives some amount of mental processing. Some stimuli, which receive only incidental attention, are processed only to a very shallow level in memory, possibly no deeper than a rather sensory level (as in hearing the sounds of the words without attending to meaning, as a daydreamer might do during a lecture). Other stimuli are subjected to more intentional and meaningful processing. This deeper processing elaborates the representation of that item in memory, for example, by drawing relationships between already-known information and the item being processed.

Thus superficial kinds of processing, which entail little attention to the meaning of an item, correspond to maintenance rehearsal, or shallow encoding into memory; Nairne (1983) draws a strong parallel between Type I rehearsal and the articulatory loop of working memory. Meaningful processing, which takes much more attention and effort, corresponds to elaborative rehearsal, or a deep encoding of the material. An important theme in this depth of processing framework is that the mental activities a subject engages in *during* processing are as important for understanding memory as a determination of the "final resting place" of the information (what we've called short- or long-term memory).

Several predictions from the depth of processing framework were tested with a fair degree of initial success. For example, if information is processed shallowly, with only maintenance rehearsal, then the information should not be particularly memorable on a later recall test; if it is only maintained, then it should not be stored in long-term memory by that maintenance (technically, according to the Craik and Lockhart position, we should say that it is not stored at a deep, meaningful level).

This is exactly the result Craik and Watkins (1973) reported. The subjects in this experiment heard a long series of words on a tape recording. Their task was to monitor the words, listening for those that began with some critical letter, say *G*. When a new "*G*-word" was presented, they were to remember the new one and forget the previous one. At the end of the list, subjects merely had to report the last *G*-word they had heard. This procedure was followed across several trials, with each trial having a different critical letter. Because of the way the lists were constructed, Craik and Watkins could specify exactly how long each of the critical words was maintained by Type I rehearsal. Table 6-3 gives an example of a list like those Craik and Watkins used and illustrates what they called the "i-value," the number of intervening items across which a critical word was maintained.

As you might expect, at the end of the set of trials, subjects were given a surprise recall test in which they were to recall all words they had heard from all the lists. As you might *not* expect, the amount of time an item had resided in short-term memory (the i-value) had no effect on the subjects' recall. Lists that had been presented at a slower rate were recalled more accurately, as in earlier research, but this effect was independent of time in short-term memory per se. As they put it in their conclusion, "Time in short-term store will only predict later long-term store performance when the subject has used the time to encode the items elaboratively" (Craik & Watkins, 1973, p. 603; see also Craik & Tulving, 1975).

Challenges to Depth of Processing

Now that you understand the Craik and Lockhart notion of depth of processing, it's time to pull the rug out from under you—enthusiasm for the depth of processing approach dimmed within several years. Much of this dimming was caused by Baddeley's (1978) important review paper "The Trouble with Levels."

Table 6-3 SAMPLE LIST OF WORDS IN THE CRAIK AND WATKINS STUDY		
Word List	**The "i-Value" for Critical Words**	
	Subject Maintains Critical Word	
Goat	Goat	
Daughter	Goat	
Oil	Goat	
Rifle	Goat	i = 4
Garden	Garden	i = 1
Grain	Grain	
Table	Grain	
Football	Grain	
Anchor	Grain	i = 4
Giraffe	Giraffe	
Brush	Giraffe	i = 2
End of list		

G is the critical letter. The "i-value" is the number of intervening words during which the critical words were held.

A major point in this review concerned the problem of defining levels independently of retention scores, as when defining and manipulating Type I and II rehearsal (see Glenberg & Adams, 1978; Glenberg, Smith, & Green, 1977). In essence, this criticism was that no method existed for deciding ahead of time whether a particular kind of rehearsal would prompt shallow or deep processing. Instead, we simply had to wait and see whether it improved recall. If it did, it must have been elaborative rehearsal; if it did not, it must have been maintenance rehearsal. The circularity of this reasoning should be obvious; the evidence that elaborative rehearsal had occurred, higher recall, was also used as the evidence showing that elaborative rehearsal improves recall.

Task Effects A second point in Baddeley's (1978) review concerned task effects. That is, a genuine difficulty arose with the levels of processing approach when slightly different memory tasks were used. The reason for the difficulty was simply that very different results were obtained using one or another task.

We have known since the time of Ebbinghaus that different memory tasks shed different kinds of light on the variables that affect performance. Ebbinghaus used a relearning task instead of simple recall, so that even material that was difficult to retrieve might have a chance of influencing performance. In a similar vein, a substantial difference generally is found between performance on recall and **recognition tasks.** In recognition tasks, subjects are shown items that were originally studied, known as "old" or target items, as well as items that were not on the studied list, known as "new" or distractor items. They must then decide which items are targets and which are distractors. Accuracy on a recognition task usually is much higher than on a recall task (see Table 6-4 for a list and description of all these tasks).

The reason that recognition is easier, it is generally agreed, is that recognition tasks take much less retrieval effort than recall tasks; indeed, recognition does not seem to

Table 6-4 STANDARD MEMORY TASKS AND TERMINOLOGY

Relearning task

1. Original learning. Learn list items (e.g., list of unrelated words) to some accuracy criterion.
2. Delay after learning list 1.
3. Learn list 1 a second time.

   Dependent variables: Main dependent variable is the savings score: how many fewer trials during relearning relative to number of trials for original learning. If original learning took 10 trials and relearning took 6, then relearning took 4 fewer trials. S score = $\frac{4}{10}$; expressed as a percentage, savings was 40%.

   Independent or control variables: Rate of presentation, type of list items, length of list, accuracy criterion.

Paired-associate learning task

1. A list of pairs is shown, one pair at a time. The first member of the pair is called the stimulus, and the second member is the response (e.g., for the pair "ice–brush," "ice" is the stimulus term and "brush" is the correct response).
2. After one study trial, the stimulus terms are shown, one at a time, and the subject tries to name the correct response term for that stimulus.
3. Typically, the task involves several successive attempts at learning, each attempt including first a study trial then a test trial; the order of the pairs is changed each time. In the anticipation method, there is just one continuous stream of trials, each consisting of two parts, presenting the stimulus alone, then presenting the stimulus and response together. Across repetitions, subjects begin to learn the correct pairings.

   Dependent variables: Typically the number of study test trials to achieve correct responding to all stimulus terms ("trials to criterion") is the dependent variable.

   Independent and control variables: Presentation rate, length of list, the types of items in the stimulus and response term lists, and the types of connections between them. Very commonly, once a list had been mastered, then either the stimulus or response terms would be changed, or the item pairings would be rearranged (e.g., "ice–brush" and "card–floor" in the first list, then "ice–floor" and "card–brush" on the second list).

Recall task

Serial recall task: Learn list information, then recall the items in their original order of presentation.
Free recall task: Learn list information, then recall the items in any order.

1. Learn list items.
2. Optional delay or optional distractor task during delay.
3. Recall list items.

   Dependent variables: Main dependent variable is the number (or percentage) of list items recalled correctly. If multiple lists are presented, recall accuracy often is scored as a function of the original position of the items in the list. Occasionally, other dependent variables involve order, speed, or organization of recall (e.g., items recalled by category—"apple, pear, banana, orange"—before a different category was recalled in a free recall task).

   Independent or control variables: Rate of presentation (usually experimenter paced), type of list items, length of list.

Recognition task (episodic)

1. Learn list items.
2. Optional delay or optional distractor task during delay.
3. Make yes/no decisions to the items in a test list: "yes" the item was on the original list, "no" it was not on the original list. This is often called deciding whether the item is "old," that is, on the original list, or if it is "new," not on the original list. Old items are also called targets, and new items are also called distractors or lures.

   Dependent variables: In episodic tasks, the dependent variable usually is a measure of accuracy, such as the percentage correct on the test list. Correct decisions on old items can be called hits, and incorrect decisions on new items can be called false alarms.

   Independent or control variables: Same as in recall tasks.

require deliberate retrieval at all because the to-be-retrieved answer is presented to the subject, who then only has to make a new versus old decision. Because more information is stored in memory than can be retrieved easily, recognition generally shows greater sensitivity to the influence of stored information.

The relevance of this effect to the issue of depth of processing is simply that most of the early research that supported the levels of processing approach relied on recall tasks. When recognition tasks were used, however, Type I rehearsal was seen to have clear effects on long-term memory.

A clever set of studies by Glenberg, Smith, and Green (1977) confirmed this clearly and became one of the more serious challenges to the depth of processing position. Glenberg et al. used a standard Brown–Peterson task but asked subjects to remember a four-digit number as the (supposedly) primary task. During the variable-length retention intervals, subjects had to repeat either one or three words out loud as a distractor task (don't confuse the distractor task here with distractor items, items tested in recognition that were not shown originally). Because the subjects were led to believe that digit recall was the important task, they presumably devoted only minimal effort to the word repetitions; that is, they probably used only maintenance rehearsal or Type I processing.

At the end of the 60 experimental trials of Experiment 1, the subjects were surprised with a free recall test on the words they had spoken during the distractor periods. Consistent with the levels of processing view, recall of the words showed no effect of the varying amount of rehearsal, that is, of the period of time (2, 6, or 18 s) during which subjects had repeated the words out loud. But when the final memory test was a recognition task, the rehearsal interval *did* influence performance; words rehearsed for 18 s were recognized significantly better than those rehearsed for shorter intervals. And, to ice the cake, a third experiment showed the same beneficial effects of rehearsal in the recognition task, but this time using 3-letter nonsense syllables instead of meaningful words. As in their second experiment, the longer an item had been rehearsed, the better it was recognized. (Given what you know about nonsense syllables and about maintenance rehearsal, think about why this study was icing on the cake.)

Of course, in the depth of processing view, shallow processing (e.g., merely repeating words) should always lead to poorer retention than deep, semantic processing. Yet the Glenberg et al. studies disconfirmed this central prediction; mere repetition and time in short-term memory did affect retention (see Wixted, 1991, for a report on the positive effects of maintenance rehearsal and the metacognitive effects of deciding which type of rehearsal to use). Shallow processing can result in equal or even superior performance. (But in general, elaborate, semantic processing will always help you improve your memory more than shallow, maintenance rehearsal.)

Organization in Storage

Another vitally important piece of the storage puzzle involves the role of **organization,** the *structuring or restructuring of information as it is being stored in memory.* Part of the importance of organization is derived from the powerful influence it exerts: Well-

GOOD ADVICE

Improving Your Memory

Baddeley (1978) was one of the critics of the depth of processing viewpoint, concluding that it was valuable only at a rough, intuitive level but not particularly as a scientific theory. Although that may be true, it is hard to beat Craik and Lockhart's insights if you're looking for a way to improve your own memory. Think of maintenance versus elaborative rehearsal as simple recycling in short-term memory versus meaningful study and transfer into long-term memory.

Apply this now to your own learning. When you are introduced to someone, do you merely recycle that name for a few seconds, or do you think about it, use it in conversation, and try to find mnemonic connections to help you remember it? When you read a text, do you merely process the words at a fairly simple level of understanding, or do you actively elaborate when you are reading, searching for connections and relationships that will make the material more memorable? In other words, incorporate the depth of processing ideas into your own metacognition. Try inventing a mnemonic, applying elaborative rehearsal principles, to something you may need for this course, such as the seven themes of cognition presented in Chapter 2.

organized material can be stored and retrieved with impressive levels of accuracy. Another part of its importance is that the topic furnished dramatic confirmation, during the critical 1950s and 1960s, of the active-subject assumption that we are active participants in learning situations, intentionally seeking ways to make information more memorable.

The earliest program of research on organization (or clustering) was conducted by Bousfield. In his earliest study (Bousfield & Sedgewick, 1944), Bousfield asked subjects to name, for example, as many birds as they could. The intriguing result was that the subjects tended to name the words in subgroups, such as "robin, bluejay, sparrow—chicken, duck, goose—eagle, hawk." To investigate this further, Bousfield (1953) gave subjects a 60-item list to be learned for free recall. Unlike other work at that time, however, Bousfield used related words for his lists, 15 words each from the categories *animals*, *personal names*, *vegetables*, and *professions*. Although the words were presented in a randomized order, the subjects tended to recall them by category; for instance, "dog, cat, cow, pea, bean, John, Bob." Bousfield's modest interpretation of this pattern of recall was that the greater-than-chance grouping of items into clusters "implies the operation of an organizing tendency" (p. 237).

Where did this organizing tendency come from? Not from the words themselves, to be sure—it would be foolish to say that the words exerted the tendency to organize themselves. No, the tendency was in the *participants*, in their unseen mental activities that went on during the learning of the list. Obviously, the participants noticed at some point during input that several words were drawn from the same categories. From that point on, they used the reasonable strategy of grouping the items together on the basis of category membership (there is a nice metamemory effect here as well). This implies that subjects were reorganizing the list as it was presented, by means of rehearsal. The consequence of this reorganization during storage was straightforward: The way the material had been stored governed the way it was recalled.

Investigations of category clustering became very common after Bousfield's initial reports for several important reasons. A widely shared viewpoint, expressed neatly by Mandler (1967, p. 328), was that "memory and organization are not only correlated, but organization is a necessary condition for memory." In this view, *any* information that was stored in memory was organized, almost by definition. Furthermore, standard storage strategies, most prominently rehearsal, came to be viewed as organizational devices with the consequence that anything rehearsed was also organized (at least anything rehearsed elaboratively). In this view, mnemonic devices were no different; for instance, "all organizations are mnemonic devices" (Mandler, 1967, p. 329), and likewise, all mnemonic devices provide organization. We will discuss two reasons for the rash of studies on clustering here, along with examples of the research that supported those reasons. Chapter 7, which covers semantic memory, delves still more deeply into the topic of organization. Indeed, the clustering research, with its focus on how word meaning affects recall, was probably the most important experimental bridge to studies of long-term semantic memory.

Relationship to Chunking   First, researchers came quickly to the realization that category groupings were merely another form of *chunks* of information, similar to Miller's (1956) famous units of information. Thus clustering research was seen to fit in particularly well with another important set of results, those related to the capacity of short-term memory and the formation and transfer of chunks into long-term memory. Clustering was seen as a powerful *recoding* strategy, a means of making a mass of information memorable. Items such as "dog, cat, cow" could be grouped together into a chunk, with the category name *animal* serving as a code for that chunk. Thus memory for a long list could be described in terms of a hierarchical structure, with a code high in the structure serving as the label, in a sense, for the individual items at the bottom of the structure. Mandler (1967) extended the similarities between clustering and chunking even further. He noted that in his studies of clustering, where subjects were free to use as many categories as they wanted, there was a strong preference for using approximately 5 ± 2 categories, a particularly obvious connection to Miller's (1956) work.

The power of such organizational schemes for improving the storage of information into long-term memory was demonstrated convincingly by Bower, Clark, Lesgold, and Winzenz (1969). Four hierarchies of words were presented to subjects in the organized condition, arranged as lists with headers (one of the four hierarchies is shown in Figure 6-5); for instance, under *stones* was *precious*, and under that were *sapphire*, *emerald*, *diamond*, and *ruby*. The control group was shown words in the same physical arrangements, but the words were randomly assigned to their positions. Participants got four trials to learn all 112 words; their performance is shown in Table 6-5. Presenting the words in the hierarchically organized fashion led to 100% accuracy on Trials 3 and 4, an amazing feat given the number and unfamiliarity of the words. In contrast, the control group only managed to recall 70 words out of 112 by Trial 4, 62% accuracy. As Anderson (1985) pointed out, a chapter outline can

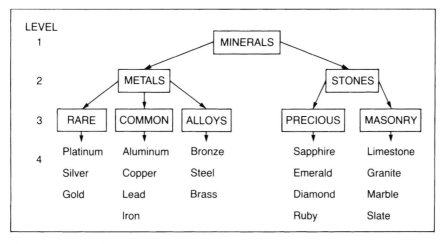

Figure 6-5

One of the hierarchies presented by Bower et al. (1969).

Table 6-5 AVERAGE PERCENTAGE OF WORDS RECALLED OVER FOUR TRIALS AS A FUNCTION OF ORGANIZATION				
Conditions	**1**	**2**	**3**	**4**
Organized	65%	94.7%	100%	100%
Random	18.3	34.7	47.1	62.5

Adapted from Bower et al., 1969.

serve much the same function as the Bower et al. hierarchies, with obvious implications for students' study strategies (*there's* a strong hint).

Rehearsal Strategies A second reason for the popularity of clustering studies was that they demonstrated subjects' strategies for learning in an obvious and objective fashion. Many studies used the standard free recall task, then examined the effects of different degrees of list organization, different numbers of categories, different numbers of items within categories, and so on. Clustering and organization were then examined in terms of a creative array of dependent variables, such as order of recall, degree of clustering, speed and patterning of pauses during recall, and rehearsal (see reviews by Johnson, 1970; Mandler, 1967, 1972). As an example, Ashcraft, Kellas, and Needham (1975) had their participants rehearse out loud as they studied clustered or randomized lists. Interestingly, the results suggested that recalling the words by category was due to reorganization during rehearsal. That is, the participants tended to rehearse by category; for instance, when "horse" was presented, this would trigger the rehearsal of "dog, cat, cow, horse" together. Apparently, when sufficient time is provided during input, subjects can thoroughly reorganize the words as they store them in memory. Furthermore, the number of times a word had been rehearsed during study was predictive of recall order; more frequently rehearsed categories, as well as words within those categories, were recalled earlier than categories and words that received less rehearsal. In other words, rehearsal and organization are intimately related to the nature of recall from memory.

Subjective Organization Don't misunderstand the above section: Organization during rehearsal is *not* limited to lists of words that belong to obvious, known categories. In fact, some of the earliest and most provocative evidence of organization came from a classic study by Tulving (1962) on the organization of unrelated words.

Tulving used what was called the multitrial free recall task, in which the same list of words is presented repeatedly across several trials, where each trial had a new reordering of the words. His analysis looked at the regularities that developed in the subjects' recall orders, that is, the consistent groupings of otherwise unrelated words that subjects adopted over trials. For example, a subject might recall the words "dog, apple, lawyer, brush" together on several successive recall trials. This consistency, despite the experimenter's reordering of the list items from trial to trial, suggested that the subject had formed a cluster or chunk composed of those four items on some idiosyncratic basis. For example, a subject might link the words together in a kind of sentence or story: "The dog brought an apple to the lawyer, who brushed his hair." Regardless of how these links were formed, the clusters were then used repeatedly during the recall trials, serving subjectively as the same kind of organized unit that "dog, cat, horse, cow" would in an experimenter-defined cluster.

Tulving called this **subjective organization**, that is, *organization developed by the subject for structuring and remembering a list of items without experimenter-supplied categories.* In other words, Tulving pointed out that even "unrelated" words become organized because of the mental activity of the subject who imposes this organization. As he put it, "Perhaps paradoxically this suggests that a list of completely *unrelated* words is probably as fictional as is a truly nonsensical nonsense syllable" (p. 352).

Imagery

The last storage variable to be considered here involves **visual imagery**, *the mental picturing of a stimulus that affects later recall or recognition.* Of course, we have discussed two prominent visual imagery effects already: the mental rotation studies, which suggest an imaginal code in working memory, and the imagery-based mnemonic devices. What we are focusing on now, however, is the effect of visual imagery on the storage of information into long-term memory, the possible boost that imagery gives to material you are trying to learn.

The name most closely associated with early research on imagery is Alan Paivio. In his book, Paivio (1971) reviewed scores of studies that illustrated the generally beneficial effects of imagery on learning and retention. These beneficial effects are beyond those caused by other variables, such as word- or sentence-based rehearsal, or meaningfulness (Bower, 1970; Yuille & Paivio, 1967).

As just one example, Paivio described a **paired-associate learning** study by Schnorr and Atkinson (1969; see Table 6-4). In such a study, items are presented in pairs, the first item designated the stimulus item, the second the response item. The subject's task here is to *learn the list so that the correct response item can be reproduced whenever the stimulus item is presented.* Thus, if you saw the pair "elephant–book" during study, you would be tested during recall by seeing the term "elephant" and your correct response would be "book" (the later section on interference describes this task in more detail). Schnorr and Atkinson had their subjects study half of a paired-associate list by means of imagery, forming some visual image of the stimulus and response terms together. The other half of the list was studied by means of rote repetition. On immediate recall, the pairs learned by imagery were recalled at better than 80% accuracy, compared to about 40% for the rote repetition pairs. The superiority of the imagery condition was found even after a 1-week retention interval.

Studies such as this one led Paivio to propose the **dual coding hypothesis** (Paivio, 1971). This hypothesis states that *words that denote concrete objects, as opposed to abstract words, can be encoded into memory twice*, once in terms of their verbal attributes and once in terms of their imaginal attributes. Thus a word like *book* enjoys an advantage in memory studies. Because it can be recorded twice in memory, once as a word and once as a visual image, there are two different ways it can be retrieved from memory, one way for each code. A stimulus term like *idea*, on the other hand, probably has only a verbal code available for it because it does not have an obvious imaginal representation. (This is not to say that people cannot eventually create an image to help remember a word like *idea* but merely that the image is much more available and natural for concrete words.)

There is much more to be said about imagery and, in general, other nonverbal means of representing and remembering information (Kosslyn, 1978, 1981; Marschark & Cornoldi, 1990; Marschark, Yuille, Richman, & Hunt, 1987; Paivio, 1971). For now, consider an episodic memory study by Watkins, Peynircioglu, and Brems (1984), who tested the idea that rehearsal might also have a pictorial or imaginal component aside from the verbal type that has been so extensively studied. They presented picture–word pairs to two groups of subjects, one given verbal rehearsal instructions, the other pictorial rehearsal instructions ("try to maintain an image of the picture in your mind's eye"). After the list of pairs had been presented, subjects were given a cued recall task in which either a fragment of the printed word or a fragment of the picture was presented as a cue. The most important results involved the match between study and test conditions. When subjects had been shown the pictures, their performance was best on the picture fragment test, but only if they had been given a 15-s rehearsal interval. Likewise, those who had rehearsed verbally during the 15-s interval did best on the word fragment test. The other conditions, when there was a mismatch between study and test, and when there had been no time for rehearsal, yielded low performance. In other words, either type of rehearsal improved performance when the recall test was consistent with the participants' type of rehearsal. But neither type improved performance if the retrieval cues were inconsistent with the type of rehearsal.

Storage Summary: Encoding Specificity

We conclude this section on storage with a short summary that also previews several important ideas for the topic of retrieval. What generalizations can we draw from research on rehearsal, organization, and imagery? How are we to understand the phenomenon of storage into episodic memory? The best way to understand storage, it seems, is to consider it in light of retrieval, in terms of how the material will be retrieved from the memory system.

Demonstrate this principle to yourself with a simple example. Time yourself as you name the 12 months of the year; it takes only about 5 s. Now time yourself as you name the 12 months of the year again, but this time in alphabetical order. How long did that take—at least half a minute, if not more, right? It should be obvious that the way this information was acquired and stored—the way it is organized in memory—is based on chronological order. Thus retrieving the information in such a different, incongruent fashion mismatches the storage organization and therefore is difficult.

Compare this to the research you've been reading about. What variables or conditions led to the best performance? There were certainly some experiments in which subjects were able to recall information despite their activity during learning; Hebb's subjects recalled the repeated digit list, for instance, and Glenberg et al.'s subjects recognized words they had originally been told were only part of a distractor task. But for the most part, the research shows that memory performance is enhanced when there is a close correspondence between the study and test conditions, in other words, when the activities during testing *match* those of acquisition. Something that occurs during acquisition facilitates memory performance when retention is tested in a way that matches acquisition. Consistency between acquisition and retention conditions improves our performance, and inconsistency depresses our performance. Why?

In Tulving and Thompson's (1973) view, an important reason is **encoding specificity.** By this phrase, Tulving and Thompson meant that information is encoded into memory *not* as a set of isolated, individual items. Instead, *each item is encoded into a richer memory representation, one that includes any extra information about the item that was present during encoding.* Thus, when you encounter *cat* in a list of words, you are likely to encode not only the word *cat* but also related information about that word. Importantly, this extra information would probably include *animal* and other easily retrievable concepts that are semantically related to *cat*. In this situation, *animal* serves as your higher-order label or code for the clustered items *cat, dog,* and so on.

When your memory is tested, in a free recall task for instance, you attempt to retrieve from memory the record or trace left by your original encoding. In this circumstance, if you encoded *animal* along with *cat*, then the word *animal* should be an excellent **retrieval cue** for recalling *cat—a useful prompt or reminder for the information to be retrieved.* If you study pictures under a picture rehearsal condition, then picture cues will enhance your performance (Morris, Bransford, & Franks, 1977). If the prevailing conditions during the test are quite different, for example, if you are given word fragment cues after pictorial rehearsal, then the likelihood of your retrieving the information decreases. The original context cues will give you the best access to the information during a recall attempt, whether those cues are based on verbal, visual, or other information (Schab, 1990, for instance, has found this effect with odors as the contextual cue).

In summary, storage of information into episodic long-term memory is affected by rehearsal, organization, and imagery. The presence of all three of these leads to a stronger memory trace. Furthermore, congruence between study and test conditions seems critical. Relevant rehearsal, including organizational and imaginal elements, improves performance, as does the provision of retrieval cues that were part of the original encoding of the material. Rehearsal that turns out to be irrelevant for the test conditions generally is of little benefit.

■ Section Summary

- Storage or transfer to long-term memory means tagging or noting in some fashion that a set of words was on the list to be learned. The important variables in storage are rehearsal and organization, whether these involve just verbal concepts or also include visual imagery and other nonverbal features. Maintenance and elaborative rehearsal generally were viewed as having two distinctly different functions, the former for mere recycling of information without increasing its likelihood of retrieval, the latter for more semantically based rehearsal, which was claimed to process the information more deeply into the memory system and make it more memorable. Difficulties in this depth of processing framework involved definitions of the two types of rehearsal and specification of the notion of depth. When memory performance is tested with a recognition task, the results often seem to disconfirm the hypothesis that maintenance rehearsal merely maintains information but does not make it more memorable; the same is true of implicit memory tasks.

- Generally, the amount of rehearsal is positively related to recall accuracy for the primacy portion of a list. Organization, especially by category but also by subjectively defined chunks or clusters, improves memory performance because it stores the information securely and provides a useful structure for successful retrieval. According to the encoding specificity principle, any related information that was encoded along with the studied information should serve as an effective retrieval cue. This is the case even if that related information is normally a lower-strength associate of the to-be-remembered material.

Retrieving Episodic Information

We turn now to the other side of the coin, retrieving information from episodic memory. And as we do, we reencounter the two theories of forgetting that have preoccupied cognitive psychology from the very beginning: decay and interference.

Decay

It's a bit unusual for the name of a theory to imply the content of the theory as clearly as does the term *decay*. Nonetheless, that is what decay theory is all about: The older a memory trace is, the more likely that it has been forgotten, that it has *decayed* away, just as the print on an old newspaper fades into illegibility. The principle dates back to Thorndike (1914), who called it the law of disuse: Habits, and by extension memories, are strengthened when they are used repeatedly, and habits that are not used are weakened through disuse. Thorndike's proposal was a beautiful example of a theoretical hypothesis, easily understood and straightforward in its predictions. Unfortunately, it's wrong, at least as far as long-term memory is concerned.

The basic difficulty with the decay theory of forgetting is that it says that the passage of time is the cause of forgetting. A definitive attack on decay theory was provided by McGeoch (1932), who argued instead that it is the *activities* that occur during a period of time that are responsible for forgetting, not time itself. In other terms, intervening activities produce interference that disrupts retention. Although some theorists argue that there is still some validity to the decay theory (Schacter, 1999), it is difficult to imagine the experiment that would provide a clean, uncontaminated demonstration of this. As a time interval passes in an experiment, there can be any number of opportunities for interference, even if caused merely by the momentary thoughts you focus on while your mind wanders. (The time interval would also give you opportunities for selective remembering and rehearsal of events, which would boost remembering of old information). As Hall (1971, pp. 459–460) put it, "Environmental events themselves, rather than time intervals alone, must be considered in order to account for forgetting."

Interference

Interference theory and tests of interference effects became a staple in the experimental diet of verbal learning psychologists, much to the current dismay of some cognitive psychologists. There were at least two reasons for this trend. First, the arguments against decay theory and for an interference approach were convincing, on both theoretical and empirical grounds. Demonstrations such as the often-cited Jenkins and Dallenbach (1924) study made complete sense within an interference framework: After identical time delays, subjects who had remained awake after learning recalled less than those who slept afterward (Figure 6-6). The everyday activities encountered by the awake subjects seemed to interfere with their memory for the list. Fewer interfering activities intervened for the sleeping subjects, so their performance was better. (Interestingly, this effect may also depend on the amount of rapid eye movement sleep you get after the learning task; see Karni, Tanne, Rubenstein, Askenasy, & Sagi, 1994).

A second reason for the popularity of interference studies is that interference effects were easily obtained in the laboratory, especially with a task already in wide use, the paired-associate learning task. This task was a natural for studying the components of interference—and, by the way, it conformed to the behaviorist *Zeitgeist* or "spirit of the times" prior to the cognitive revolution of the mid- to late-1950s.

Paired-Associate Learning A few moments studying the paired-associate learning task (usually abbreviated as **P–A learning**), will help you understand interference theory and one of the tried-and-true methods of testing memory. The basic elements of a

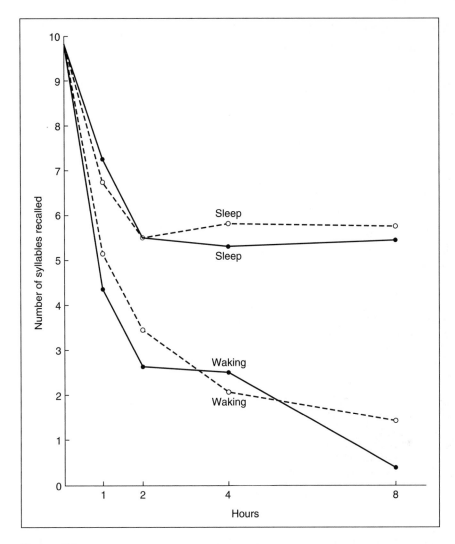

Figure 6-6

The classic Jenkins and Dallenbach (1924) result, showing higher recall of nonsense syllables for two subjects who slept after acquisition versus remaining awake after acquisition.

P–A learning task are as follows (see also Table 6-4). *A list of stimulus terms is paired, item by item, with a list of response terms. After learning, the stimulus terms should prompt the recall of the proper response terms.* The items usually were CVCs or words. In the anticipation method, a subject first saw a stimulus term by itself, tried to name the correct response term that went with that stimulus, and then saw the stimulus–response pair together. Of course, subjects had to guess on the first trial because they had not seen any of the pairs before. After that, however, the number of correct responses made to the stimulus terms

Table 6-6 LISTS OF PAIRED ASSOCIATES

List 1 (A–B)	List 2 (C–D)
tall–bone	safe–fable
plan–leaf	bench–idea
nose–fight	pencil–owe
park–flea	wait–blouse
grew–cook	student–duck
rabbit–few	window–cat
pear–rain	house–news
mess–crowd	card–nest
print–kiss	color–just
smoke–hand	flower–jump

List 3 (A–B$_r$)	List 4 (A–B′)
plan–bone	smoke–arm
mess–hand	mess–people
smoke–leaf	rabbit–several
pear–kiss	park–ant
rabbit–fight	plan–tree
tall–crowd	tall–skeleton
nose–cook	nose–battle
park–few	grew–chef
grew–flea	pear–storm
print–rain	print–lips

grew across repeated trials, showing (in the terminology of behaviorism) that the correct responses had become conditioned to the appropriate stimuli. A typical procedure was to bring a subject up to some predetermined accuracy criterion, one perfect trial, for instance, then ask the subject to learn another list of paired associates.

Table 6-6 presents several P–A learning lists to use as a demonstration. Imagine learning List 1 to the criterion of one perfect trial (try it to get a better idea of what the task is like). After that, you would switch to the second half of the P–A study, which would involve learning another list of paired associates; the similarity of the first and second lists was of critical importance. If you were switched to List 2, you would have experienced little or no interference because List 2 contains stimulus and response terms that are not similar to List 1's terms. In the terminology of interference theory, this was the A–B, C–D condition, where the letters *A* through *D* refer to different lists of stimulus or response terms. This condition represented a kind of baseline condition in terms of interference because there is no similarity between the A–B and the C–D terms (however, you may have needed fewer trials on the second list because of "general transfer" effects from List 1, warmup or learning to learn).

If you were shifted to List 3, there would have been "massive" negative transfer; it would have taken you many more trials to reach criterion on the second learning list. The reason for this is that the same stimulus and response terms were used again but in new pairings. Thus your experience on List 1, forming strong enough associations to reach criterion, interfered with the later activity of learning to re-pair the items. The

Table 6-7 DESIGNS TO STUDY TWO DIFFERENT KINDS OF INTERFERENCE

Proactive interference (PI)			
	Learn	**Learn**	**Test**	**Interference Effect**
PI group	A–B	A–C	A–C	A–B list interferes with A–C
Control group		A–C	A–C	

Retroactive interference (RI)			
	Learn	**Learn**	**Test**	**Interference Effect**
RI group	A–B	A–C	A–B	A–C list interferes with A–B
Control group	A–B		A–B	

standard term for this type of list was A–B, A–B$_r$, where the subscript r stood for "randomized" or "re-paired" items. Finally, if you were switched to List 4 (the A–B, A–B′ condition), there would have been a great deal of positive transfer; you would need fewer trials to reach criterion on the second list because List 4 (designated B′) is highly related to the earlier one (B) you learned. For instance, in List 1 you learned "plan–leaf"; in List 4, "plan" went with "tree."

These are all *proactive* transfer and interference effects; that is, they demonstrate the effects a prior task can have on a current learning task. Of course, we discussed proactive interference (PI) and release from PI at some length in Chapter 5. Table 6-7 gives the general experimental design for a proactive interference study as well as for a retroactive interference (RI) study. To repeat, retroactive interference exists when some learning experience interferes with recall of an *earlier* experience; the newer memory interferes backward in time ("retro").

Both proactive and retroactive interference were examined extensively (or excessively, depending on your viewpoint), with complex theories built on P–A learning results. Although an extensive literature is available, no attempt is made to cover it in depth here (but see standard works such as Postman & Underwood, 1973; Underwood, 1957; Underwood & Schultz, 1960; and Klatzky, 1980, Chapter 11, for a very readable summary). Instead, we summarize a major difficulty encountered in this work, important because it was instrumental in the shift to a cognitive rather than behaviorist approach to memory.

Problems of Meaning   The behaviorist tradition had it that P–A learning was essentially a matter of association formation. In other words, the B terms in an A–B list became associated with their A terms, so that presenting a stimulus from the A list should elicit the B response term. Likewise, if a new list were learned, say A–C, then the A–B associations had to be unlearned even as the new A–C connections were being conditioned (e.g., Kintsch, 1970; Underwood & Postman, 1960). The term *unlearned*, of course, is what we would call forgotten; the original A–B connections are lost while one is learning A–C. A definitive demonstration that this was *not* generally true was provided by Slamecka (1966). Before having his participants learn an A–B and then a A–C list, he had them generate their own free associates to the A words (e.g., to the A word *cat*, you might generate *dog*). According to strict interference theory, learning the A–B list and then A–C should have resulted in unlearning the original free associates. But of course it did not: After showing the normal interference effect in learning A–C, participants had no difficulty recalling their original free associates to the A words. What should have been altered by interference, the preexisting associations, was immune to it. In the face of existing associations in memory, laboratory-induced interference seemed downright puny.

The mismatch between traditional interference predictions and the (obvious) result suggested an unsettling conclusion: that theories based on traditional learning tasks and paradigms were irrelevant to an understanding of memory for words and language. It seemed entirely possible that the P–A learning laws were not general, that they applied fully only to nonsense syllable learning in a P–A task. As Jenkins (1974) put it in the title of his article: "Remember that old theory of memory? Well, forget it!"

Retrieval Failure

Since the mid-1960s, a very different theory has come to dominate cognitive psychology's view of forgetting. Both the decay and interference theories suggested that information in long-term memory can truly be forgotten, that is, lost from memory. This more technical definition of the term *forgetting, loss from memory*, was implicit in the mechanisms thought to account for forgetting, such as unlearning. The current view makes a radically different claim, that in essence there may be no genuine forgetting from long-term memory, except possible loss caused by organic or physical factors, such as stroke or diseases such as Alzheimer's. Instead, so-called forgetting often is a failure of retrieval.

An Everyday Example Everyone is familiar with retrieval failure, although it often parades under a different name. Students claim that they knew the information, but that they "blocked" on it during the exam; if this is not just a rationalization, then it is an example of retrieval failure. The more straightforward (believable) explanation is the classic **tip-of-the-tongue (TOT)** phenomenon.[1] People are in the TOT state when they are *momentarily unable to recall some shred of information, often a person's name, that they know is stored in long-term memory*. Interestingly, even though you may be unable to retrieve a word or name during a TOT state, you usually have access to partial information about the target word, such as the sound it starts with, its approximate length, and the stress or emphasis pattern in pronunciation. (Brown & McNeill, 1966, is the classic TOT paper. Jones, 1989, and Meyer & Bock, 1992, report on words that sound like the unretrievable target as cues for successful retrieval. See Burke, MacKay, Worthley, and Wade 1991, for a state-of-the-art investigation of the TOT effect, including a list of questions that can be used to trigger the TOT state.)

---

[1]TOT is pronounced "tee-oh-tee," not like the word *tot*. Furthermore, it is often used as a verb: "The subject TOTed ("tee-oh-teed") 7 times on the list of 20 names." For another regrettable example of "cognitive verbs," see Chapters 9 and 10, on "garden pathing."

But retrieval failure, like the TOT phenomenon, is not limited to occasional lapses in remembering names or unusual words. In fact, as Tulving and his associates found, it is a fundamental aspect of memory.

Research on Retrieval Failure An early and powerful laboratory demonstration of retrieval failure was provided in a study by Tulving and Pearlstone (1966). In this study, two groups of subjects studied the same list of 48 items, four words from each of 12 different categories (e.g., animals, fruits, sports; other subjects learned shorter lists, or lists with fewer items per category, but we focus only on the two most dramatic groups here). The items were preceded by the appropriate name of the category, such as "crimes—treason, theft; professions—engineer, lawyer," but subjects were told that they had to remember only the items themselves. Because both groups were treated identically until the beginning of the recall period, it can be assumed that both had acquired the same amount of information from the list and both had retained equal amounts in memory. At recall, one group was asked for standard free recall. The other group was asked for free recall but was given the names of the categories as retrieval cues, that is, a cued recall condition.

The results were both predictable and profound in their implications. The free recall group was able to recall 40% of the list items, whereas the cued recall group named 62% of the items. In short, the free recall group had recalled only a portion of the items that were actually learned. We know they learned more than they recalled because the cued group had been exposed to the same learning and retention conditions yet recalled more. As Tulving and Pearlstone (1966, p. 389) put it, "Information about many words must be *available* in the storage . . . even when this information is not *accessible*" (emphasis added) under free recall conditions.

One conclusion we can draw from these results confirms intuitions dating back to Ebbinghaus; the recall task often underestimates the amount of information that was learned. Recognition scores, not to mention savings scores, usually show much higher retention than recall scores.

A much more important implication is that unsuccessful retrieval, say in the absence of cues, might prove to be a critical component of forgetting. In fact, retrieval failure might be the major (or even the only) cause of forgetting. On this view, *information stored in long-term memory remains there permanently*, and so is **available**, just as a book on the library shelf is available. Successful performance, however, depends not just on availability but also on **accessibility**, *the degree to which information can be retrieved from memory*. Items that are not accessible are not immediately retrievable, just as the misshelved book in the library cannot be located or retrieved. This position suggests that information is not lost *from* memory, but instead is lost *in* memory, so to speak. This loss of access persists until some effective retrieval cue is presented, some cue that locates the item that cannot be retrieved.

Retrieval Cues and Encoding Specificity

You already know how access can be increased to an inaccessible memory trace. But you learned the principle under a different name: *encoding specificity*. The way to increase your access to information in memory is to reinstate the original learning context, to

You haven't really forgotten all seven names. If you need a big hint, see the web page.

maximize the congruence between current test conditions and the conditions that prevailed during acquisition. In short, access is increased by effective retrieval cues. Any cue that was encoded along with the learned information should increase the accessibility of that information. This is why the category cues helped Tulving and Pearlstone's subjects recall more than they otherwise would have. Similarly, this is why recognition memory tests usually reveal higher performance than recall tests. In a recognition test, you merely have to pick out which of several alternatives is the correct choice. What better retrieval cue for some piece of information could there be than the very information you are attempting to retrieve?

Subsequent research has demonstrated the power of the encoding specificity principle in quite dramatic fashion. (By far the most convincing demonstration I've ever seen is presented in Tables 6-8 and 6-9, taken from the Bransford & Stein, 1984, book on problem solving; do that demonstration now, before reading further.)

Thomson and Tulving (1970) asked their subjects to learn a list of words for later recall. Some of the list words were accompanied by cue words printed in lowercase letters; subjects were told they need not recall the cue words but that the cues might be helpful in learning the items. Some of the cue words were high associates of the list items, such as "hot–COLD," and some were low associates, such as "wind–COLD." During recall, subjects were tested for their memory of the list under one of three conditions: low- or high-associate cues or no cues at all.

The results were exactly as predicted from the encoding specificity principle. High associates used as retrieval cues benefited the subjects' recall both when the high associate had been presented during study and when no cue word had been presented.

Table 6-8

This demonstration experiment illustrates the importance of retrieval cues. You need a blank sheet of paper and a pencil. Please follow the instructions exactly.

Instructions: Spend 3 to 5 s reading each of the following sentences, and read through the list only once. As soon as you are finished, cover the list and write down as many of the sentences as you can remember (you need not write "can be used" each time). Please begin now.

A brick can be used as a doorstop.
A ladder can be used as a bookshelf.
A wine bottle can be used as a candleholder.
A pan can be used as a drum.
A record can be used to serve potato chips.
A guitar can be used as a canoe paddle.
A leaf can be used as a bookmark.
An orange can be used to play catch.
A newspaper can be used to swat flies.
A TV antenna can be used as a clothes rack.
A sheet can be used as a sail.
A boat can be used as a shelter.
A bathtub can be used as a punch bowl.
A flashlight can be used to hold water.
A rock can be used as a paperweight.
A knife can be used to stir paint.
A pen can be used as an arrow.
A barrel can be used as a chair.
A rug can be used as a bedspread.
A telephone can be used as an alarm clock.
A scissors can be used to cut grass.
A board can be used as a ruler.
A balloon can be used as a pillow.
A shoe can be used to pound nails.
A dime can be used as a screwdriver.
A lampshade can be used as a hat.

Now that you have recalled as many sentences as you can, turn to Table 6-9.

Presumably, when no cue word had been presented, subjects spontaneously retrieved the high associate during input and encoded it along with the list item. In contrast, when low associates had been presented during learning, only low associates functioned as effective retrieval cues. High associates used as retrieval cues were no better for these subjects than no cues at all. In other words, if you had studied "wind–COLD," receiving "hot" as a cue word for "COLD" was of no value. Encoding specificity thus can even override existing associations during a recall attempt. (Note that encoded cues do not cause unlearning of the preexisting association; they simply function as more effective cues during the task.)

More surprising than this, encoding specificity can even override the usual advantage that recognition shows over recall. A series of influential papers by Tulving demonstrated a paradoxical result, called recognition failure of recallable words (Tulving & Thomson, 1973; Watkins & Tulving, 1975). In these studies, a weakly associated cue is presented along with the target word during original learning, as in "glue–CHAIR."

Table 6-9

Do *not* look back at the list of sentences in Table 6-8. Instead, use the following list as retrieval cues, and write as many sentences as you can. Be sure to keep track of how many you can write down, so you can compare this with your earlier recall performance. Begin now.

flashlight	lampshade
sheet	shoe
rock	guitar
telephone	scissors
boat	leaf
dime	brick
wine bottle	knife
board	newspaper
pen	pan
balloon	barrel
ladder	rug
record	orange
TV antenna	bathtub

When a recognition test is presented later, the target "CHAIR" often is not recognized if it appears in a very different context, as in the set "desk, top, chair." In other words, subjects fail to identify "CHAIR" as a word they have seen previously in the experiment because its current context is so different from the original encoding; this is recognition failure. After this, subjects are given a cued recall test. Here they routinely *do* recall "CHAIR" when presented with "glue" as a retrieval cue. Although these experiments used arbitrary contexts (who would spontaneously think of "glue" as a cue for "CHAIR"?), the similarity of the result to the earlier point about congruous study and retrieval contexts is obvious. In short, even simple recognition depends on encoding specificity.

Tulving and Thomson's (1973) principle of encoding specificity claims that the information you encode, target items as well as related information, determines what gets stored in your memory representation and therefore what will be an effective retrieval cue. That is, a retrieval cue is effective if you thought of it and encoded it spontaneously during learning or if it was presented (and you encoded it) during the learning sequence; in other words, the cue can come either from conceptually driven processes (what you already knew) or data-driven processes (what the stimulus item triggered during learning; Micco & Masson, 1991; Nelson, McKinney, Gee, & Janczura, 1998). Retrieval cues that are not effective simply do not match your encoded representation of the item because they were not explicitly presented or spontaneously generated during learning.

Demonstrations of this principle are common in everyday experience: For instance, you hear a "golden oldie" on the radio, and it reminds you of a particular episode (a special high school dance, with particular classmates, and so forth). The effect even extends to general context effects: Marian and Neisser's (2000) bilingual participants remembered more experiences from the Russian-speaking period of their lives when they were interviewed in Russian, and more from the English-speaking period

"I forget the name of the product, but the jingle on TV goes something like 'Ya-dee-dum-dee-rah-te-dum-dee-rah-dee-dum.'"

when interviewed in English (see also Schrauf & Rubin, 2000). And here's a customized example of failure to recall a recallable word. Think of all the words you have read in this chapter and the lists you have learned. Limiting yourself to just these words, can you remember a word that is highly associated with "parade"? No? Maybe it will be easier with a more appropriate retrieval cue, one you encoded specifically along with the target word. Fill in the blank with the following cue: "two–shoe–_____."

■ Section Summary

- Decay and then interference were once thought to cause true forgetting from long-term memory. Although interference is easily demonstrated in the laboratory using proactive or retroactive interference tasks, the evidence now suggests that interference may disrupt retrieval. In this view, retrieval failure is not an issue of true forgetting because information stored in long-term memory remains available in memory. Instead, retrieval failure often is caused by loss of access to the stored information. Effective retrieval cues provide access to otherwise unretrievable information.

Amnesia and Implicit Memory

We study cognitive dysfunctions caused by brain damage, such as the agnosias you read about in Chapter 3, to understand the cognitive system and its organization. Sometimes, the patterns of disruptions and preserved abilities can tell us a great deal about the way the cognitive system works. As you will see, this has been an especially fruitful way to investigate and understand long-term memory, by considering what is damaged and what remains intact in cases of amnesia.

Amnesia is *the loss of memory or memory abilities caused by brain damage or disease.* Amnesia is one of the oldest and most thoroughly investigated mental disruptions caused by brain disorders, as well as one of the more common results of brain injury and damage. Although some amnesias are temporary, due to a strong blow to the head, for example, the amnesias we are interested in here are relatively permanent, caused by enduring changes in the brain.

Many different kinds of amnesias have been studied, and we have space to discuss only a few of these. A few bits of terminology will help you understand the material and alert you to the distinctions in memory that are particularly relevant for neurocognition.

First, the loss of memory in amnesia is always considered in relation to the date of the brain injury. If a person suffers *loss of memory of events before brain injury*, this is called a **retrograde amnesia.** Note that *retro-* here has the same connotation as in the discussion of retroactive interference in the previous section; the loss is backward in time. The other form of amnesia is **anterograde amnesia,** *disruption of memory of events occurring after brain injury, especially a disruption in acquiring new long-term memories.* A person can often show both forms of amnesia, although the extent of the memory loss usually is different for events before and after the damage. The cases we'll talk about here are rather extreme in that the memory disruption seems to be complete: so-called profound or dense amnesia. Most amnesias are not quite as complete as these.

Second, we are trying to understand the architecture of memory, how the various components are interrelated, whether some components are independent of others, and so on. This is an analysis of dissociations, where the term *dissociation* refers to *a disruption in one component of the cognitive system but no impairment of another.* If two mental processes—call them A and B—are dissociated, then A might be disrupted by brain damage while B remains normal; patient K.C., described later, displays this kind of pattern. Sometimes a different patient is discovered who has the reverse pattern: B is disrupted by the brain damage but A is intact. When two such complementary patients are found, with *reciprocal patterns of cognitive disruption*, then the abilities A and B are said to be **doubly dissociated.**

Importantly, a double dissociation implies not only that A and B are functionally independent but also that A and B are implemented in different physical regions of the brain (a simple example would be seeing and hearing, either of which can be damaged without affecting the other). A simple dissociation is not quite as strong. If process A is damaged while B remains normal, it could be that research simply has not yet found a patient with the reciprocal pattern. Or it could be that process A can be selectively damaged without affecting B but that damage to process B would always disrupt A. The opposite of a dissociation is an association, that is, a situation in which A and B are so completely associated that damage to either process would always disrupt the other (e.g., recognizing objects and recognizing pictures of objects).

Finally, the most useful cases to study, from the standpoint of cognitive neuroscience, are those resulting from focal brain lesions, that is, cases in which the damage is to a small, restricted area of the brain. Cases such as that of patient K.C. illuminate the underlying mental processes more clearly because many of his mental processes remain intact despite the dysfunction caused by the focal lesion. Unfortunately, with the kind of widespread damage and neural deterioration characteristic of some injuries or diseases, such as Alzheimer's disease, it is difficult to learn anything about cognitive components and their relationships: So many regions are damaged that no single one can be pinpointed as the region responsible for a particular ability.

Dissociation of Episodic and Semantic Memory

We begin with a case history of a patient whose amnesia speaks directly to the topic of this chapter: episodic memory. Tulving (1989) described a detailed study of patient K.C. (you read a brief account of this in Chapter 2), who experienced serious brain injury, especially in the frontal regions, in a motorcycle accident. As a result of this injury, K.C. shows a seemingly complete loss of episodic memory : He is completely amnesic for his own autobiographical knowledge. In Tulving's words, "K.C.'s case is remarkable in that he cannot remember, in the sense of bringing back to conscious awareness, a single thing that he has ever done or experienced in the past. . . . K.C. does not remember any personally experienced events from either before or after his accident (p. 362).

K.C. has a profound amnesia for events both before and after his brain damage, both retrograde and anterograde amnesia. That is, he shows no evidence of remembering any specific experience he has ever had, including those that have happened since the injury. His most serious memory deficit is one of "massive failure to retrieve . . . previously accessible personal experiences" (Tulving, 1989, p. 363), along with failure to store in long-term memory any new personal experiences. Interestingly, although his episodic memory system no longer works, his semantic memory system does. In fact, he is adept at answering questions about his past by relying on general, semantic knowledge; when asked about his brother's funeral, he responded that the funeral was very sad, not because he remembers attending the funeral (he did not even remember that he had a brother) but because he knows that funerals are sad events.

K.C.'s pattern of memory disruption, intact semantic memory yet damaged episodic retrieval, is evidence of a dissociation between the episodic and semantic systems. This pattern suggests that episodic and semantic memories are indeed separate, distinct long-term memory systems, enough so that one can be severely damaged while the other remains intact. In terms of Squire's (1987) taxonomy (look back to Figure 6-1), K.C. has lost one of the two major components of declarative knowledge, his episodic memory.

Functional imaging evidence As Tulving (1989) acknowledged, there are some limitations on what can be learned about normal cognition from data on patients with brain damage (but see Caramazza, 1986, and Caramazza & McCloskey, 1988, for a spirited defense of case studies). Patient K.C. is unique; no other reports describe patients incapable of recalling *any* personal memories. Because we might worry about the generality of such results—an isolated case such as K.C. could have been atypical before his accident—Tulving presented further support for his conclusions, studies of brain functioning among normal individuals.

Turn to the color illustrations in the front cover of the book, and you will see an amazing set of photographs. In these pictures (color plate #3), the blood flow to the brain is being measured; you read about this imaging technique in Chapter 2. The logic behind such a procedure is that mental activity, say retrieving some particular memory, involves an increase in neural activity—*activation*, quite literally. This increase should show up as an increase in cerebral blood flow to whichever brain regions are being activated. Thus, by injecting a small dose of radioactive material (irradiated gold in Tulving's report) into the bloodstream, the apparatus detects regions of the brain that have higher concentrations of radioactivity on a very short time scale (e.g., 12 separate intervals of 0.2 s each across an 80-s period).

What do the photographs show? In the left panel, the subject was thinking about a fairly generic memory, the history of astronomy that he had read about many years before. In the right panel, the subject was recalling personal memories from a summer nearly 50 years before, that is, a 50-year-old episodic memory. The red area in the pictures show regions where the blood flow was above the baseline level, and the green regions where blood flow was lower than average.

Clearly, *different* brain activity resulted when these two types of memories were retrieved. If the memory of the history of astronomy is assumed to be a genuine semantic memory, then different regions of the brain seem to be active when retrieving semantic versus episodic memories. (The same kind of results were obtained when the subject retrieved recent semantic and episodic memories; see also Wood, Taylor, Penney, & Stump, 1980.) If anything, it appeared that episodic retrieval was accompanied by greater activation in the anterior (front) regions of the brain. This finding agrees with research on patients with amnesia, showing that the frontal lobes are especially important for time-related aspects of memories (see reviews by Kesner, 1998; Schacter, 1987; 1996, and Wheeler et al., 1997). Semantic retrieval, conversely, seemed to activate more posterior (rear) regions of the brain.

Anterograde Amnesia

The modern story of anterograde amnesia begins with a classic, well-known case history. A popular theoretical stance in 1950 was that memories are represented throughout the cortex, distributed widely rather than concentrated in one specific place or region. This position was most clearly articulated by well-known researcher Karl Lashley in his famous 1950 paper. A mere 3 years later, an accidental discovery by a neurosurgeon named William Scoville "revolutionized the study of the memory process" (Kolb & Whishaw, 1996, p. 357; see this source for the complete story). Scoville performed radical surgery on a patient known as H.M., sectioning (lesioning) H.M.'s hippocampus in both the left and right hemispheres in an attempt to gain control over his severe epileptic seizures. To

Scoville's utter surprise, the outcome of this surgery was a pervasive anterograde amnesia; H.M. became unable to learn and recall anything new. Although his memory of events before the surgery remained intact, as did his overall IQ (in fact, his IQ is 118, well above average), he completely lost the ability to store new information in long-term memory. In Kolb and Whishaw's (1996, p. 357) words, "Surgery had interfered with the process of storing or retrieving new memories but had not touched previously stored memories. The case of H.M . . . shifted the emphasis from a search for the location of memory to an analysis of the process of storing memories."

Across the intervening years, H.M. has served as a subject hundreds of tasks (e.g., Milner et al., 1968), documenting the many facets of his pervasive anterograde amnesia. His memory of events before surgery, including his childhood and school days, is quite good. His language comprehension is normal, and his vocabulary is above average. Yet any task that requires him to retain information across a delay shows severe impairment, especially if the delay is filled with an interfering task. These impairments apply equally to nonverbal and verbal materials, a result apparently related to the bilateral (both sides) lesions from his surgery (left hemisphere lesions in the hippocampus tend to yield amnesia for only verbal memories). For instance, after a 2-min interference task of repeating digits, he was unable to recognize photographs of various faces. He is unable to learn sequences of digits that go beyond the typical short-term memory span of seven items. In a conversation reported by Cohen (in Banich, 1997), he cycled back and forth repeatedly between two topics he did remember (a childhood memory about some rifles he had and a related memory about guns) failing to remember that he had already talked about those topics only minutes before.

H.M.'s Implicit Memory   Interestingly, the evidence also suggests strongly that H.M.'s memory is normal when it comes to motor learning. That is, he was able to learn a rather difficult motor skill, mirror-drawing; this task requires that the subject trace between the lines of a double-star pattern while looking at the pattern and pencil only in a mirror (Figure 6-7). H.M.'s performance (the bottom portion of the figure) showed a completely normal learning curve, with very few errors on the third day of practice. Notice, though, that on days 2 and 3 he did not remember ever having done the mirror-drawing task before; he had no explicit memory record of ever having done the task, despite his perfectly normal pattern of performance based on implicit memory.

Likewise, H.M. has also shown systematic learning and improvement on a procedural task, the Tower of Hanoi problem you will read about in Chapter 12. Although he did not remember particular moves in the problem and spoke of not remembering the task itself, his performance nonetheless improved across repeated days of practice (reported in Kolb & Whishaw, 1996). Such empirical demonstrations confirm what clinicians working with amnesia patients have known or suspected for a long time: Despite profound difficulties in what we normally think of as memory, aspects of the patients' behavior do demonstrate a kind of memory—in other words, implicit memory (see Schacter, 1996, especially his Chapter 6, for an eloquent, first-person narrative).

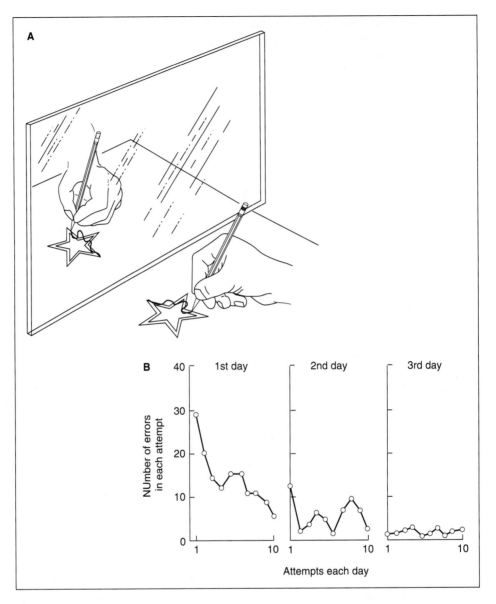

Figure 6-7

A, In this test the subject's task is to trace between the two outlines of the star while viewing his or her hand in a mirror. The reversing effect of the mirror makes this a difficult task initially. Crossing a line constitutes an error. **B,** Patient H.M. shows clear improvement in the motor learning star task, an instance of implicit learning and memory. After Blakemore (1977).

Implications for Memory What do we know about human memory as a function of H.M.'s disrupted and preserved mental capacities? How much has this person's misfortune told us about memory and cognition?

The most apparent source of H.M.'s amnesia is a disruption in the process of transferring information to long-term memory. That is, H.M.'s retrieval of information learned before surgery is intact, indicating that his long-term memory per se, including retrieval, was unaffected by the surgery. Likewise, his ability to attend to questions and answer them and to perform other simple short-term memory tasks indicates that simpler attentional, awareness, and working memory functions also are intact. But he has a widespread disability in transferring new information into long-term memory, a function possibly corresponding to elaborative rehearsal or the role of the central executive component of working memory. Note that this disability seems to affect most or all of H.M.'s deliberate or explicit storage of information in long-term memory (Milner et al., 1968), including real-world episodic material.

It is a mistake to conclude from this that H.M.'s memory disruption—say the process of explicit rehearsal—takes place in the hippocampus. Instead, it seems more likely that the hippocampus is a critical pathway for successful transfer to long-term memory, a route through which the process takes place rather than the actual location of that process. In Squire's (1987, p. 180) view, this route or pathway idea is central to understanding how "amnesia appears to reflect neither direct injury to, nor loss of, those brain regions in which information is processed and stored. Instead, amnesia seems best explained by hypothesizing a neural system, which is damaged in amnesia, that ordinarily *participates* in memory storage without being itself a *site* of storage." Other research on patients with similar lesions (e.g., Penfield & Milner, 1958; Zola-Morgan, Squire, & Amalral, 1986) confirms the importance of the hippocampus to this process of storing new information in long-term, explicit memory. In some sense then, the hippocampus is a gateway into long-term memory. In Squire's (1992) view, the hippocampus is absolutely essential for declarative or explicit memory.

Implicit and Explicit Memory

To repeat a point made at the beginning of this chapter, the operative word in these definitions is *conscious*. Explicit memories, whether episodic or semantic, come to us with conscious awareness and therefore have an explicit effect on performance, an effect that could be verbalized. For example, name the third letter of the word meaning "unmarried man." The very fact that you can say *c* and name the word *bachelor* attests to the fact that this is an explicit memory and an explicit effect on performance. In contrast, fill in the following word stems: "gre__, mai__, fl__." Even without any involvement of conscious awareness, you may have filled these in with the words "green, maiden, flag"—or, more appropriately, across some number of students reading this chapter, a larger percentage may have completed those stems that way than would have been expected by chance. The words *green, maiden,* and *flag* occurred in this chapter; we even made a point, early on, that you were reading *maiden* more rapidly after encountering it in an earlier paragraph, an effect called repetition priming. Importantly, we all demonstrate such implicit effects as repetition priming, whether amnesic or not (Graf & Schacter, 1987; Kolers & Roediger, 1984).

Repetition Priming One general form of the effects of implicit memory is **repetition priming.** In repetition priming, *a previous encounter with information facilitates later performance on the same information, even unconsciously.* Repetition priming effects have been established in any number of different research tasks, such as word identification and lexical decision tasks (Morton, 1979), word and picture naming (Brown, Neblett, Jones, & Mitchell, 1991), and rereading fluency (Masson, 1984). In all these, a previous encounter with the stimulus yields faster performance on a later task, even though you may not consciously remember having seen the stimulus before (see Logan, 1990, for the connection of repetition priming to automaticity).

In a classic demonstration of repetition priming, Jacoby and Dallas (1981) asked their subjects to study a list of familiar words, answering a question about each as they went through the list. Sometimes the question asked about the physical form of the word, as in "Does it contain the letter *L*?" Sometimes the question asked about the word's sound, as in "Does it rhyme with *train*?" And sometimes, the question asked about a semantic characteristic of the word, as in "Is it the center of the nervous system?" This was a direct manipulation of the participants' *depth of processing*, which you studied earlier. Asking about the physical form of the word should induce only shallow processing, according to that framework, leading to poor memory performance later on. Asking about rhymes demands somewhat deeper processing, and asking about semantic characteristics should demand full, elaborative processing on the list words.

At test, the subjects' explicit memory performance was assessed by a yes/no recognition task ("Did this word occur in the study phase?"). Here, their recognition accuracy was affected by the type of question they answered during study. When a question related to the physical form of the word had been asked during study, recognition performance was at chance, 51%; see Figure 6-8. When the question had been asked about the sound of the word, performance improved. And when truly semantic processing had been devoted to the word, recognition accuracy was quite high, 95%.

What made this a test of explicit memory was that subjects had to say "yes" or "no" based on whether they had seen the word earlier during the study phase. As we would expect, more elaborative processing led to better explicit memory performance.

The other test given to subjects, the implicit memory test, was a perceptual test. Here, words were shown one at a time for only 35 msec, followed by a row of asterisks as a mask. Subjects merely had to report the word they saw. In other words, the perceptual test did not require the subjects to remember which words they had seen earlier, or in fact to remember anything about the study phase. They just had to identify the briefly presented words.

In these perceptual recognition tests, identification of the words averaged about 80%, regardless of how the word had been studied. That is, a constant 80% of the previously presented words were identified in the perceptual test, whereas only 65% of

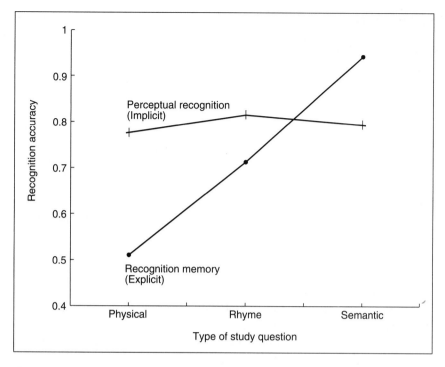

Figure 6-8

Recognition accuracy for words tested with an explicit or implicit memory task. Words were originally studied with questions asking about physical, rhyme, or semantic characteristics of the words. The figure shows that implicit memory performance was unaffected by the original type of learning.

control words that had not appeared earlier were identified. Of special importance, it made no difference how the word had originally been processed (i.e., with physical, rhyme, or semantic questions; Figure 6-8).

This is the typical implicit memory result. Even with no conscious or necessary recollection of the original event, there is facilitation of performance when the stimulus is repeated. Measures of explicit memory, a recall or yes/no recognition task, generally show strong effects of how the information was studied. But measures of implicit memory, say a perceptual or word stem completion task, usually show significant priming or facilitation regardless of how information was studied (see also Roediger, Stadler, Weldon, & Riegler, 1992; Thapar & Greene, 1994).

If we had ignored the cognitive neuroscience evidence from patients such as H. M. and K. C.—indeed, if we had stuck slavishly to Ebbinghaus-inspired nonsense syllables—we would have missed the boat. We would have missed the evidence that there is a second, less obvious kind of long-term memory, a kind not dependent on conscious recollection. We would have missed the whole important issue of implicit memory.

Section Summary

• Studies of individuals with amnesia caused by brain damage have taught us a great deal about the components of long-term memory. Patient K.C. shows total amnesia for episodic information, although his semantic memory is unimpaired, suggesting a dissociation between episodic and semantic memories. Like patient H.M., a person with anterograde amnesia typically is unable to acquire new explicit memories but shows intact implicit learning and memory. The medial temporal area and especially the hippocampus are very important for the formation of new explicit memories, but different brain structures underlie implicit learning.

Key Terms

accessibility (p. 235)
amnesia (p. 240)
anterograde and retrograde (p. 240)
available (p. 235)
declarative and nondeclarative memory (p. 204)
depth of processing (p. 218)
dissociation (p. 240)
doubly dissociated (p. 240)
dual coding hypothesis (p. 227)
elaborative rehearsal (p. 218)
encoding specificity (p. 228)

episodic and semantic memory (p. 205)
explicit memory (p. 204)
forgetting (p. 234)
implicit memory (p. 204)
levels of processing (p. 218)
maintenance rehearsal (p. 218)
metacognition (p. 213)
metamemory (p. 213)
method of loci (p. 207)
mnemonic devices (p. 206)
organization (p. 222)
paired-associate learning (p. 227)

peg word mnemonic (p. 208)
recognition tasks (p. 220)
rehearsal (p. 215)
relearning task (p. 210)
repetition priming (p. 246)
retrieval cue (p. 228)
savings score (p. 210)
subjective organization (p. 226)
tip-of-the-tongue (TOT) (p. 234)
Type I and Type II rehearsal (p. 218)
visual imagery (p. 226)

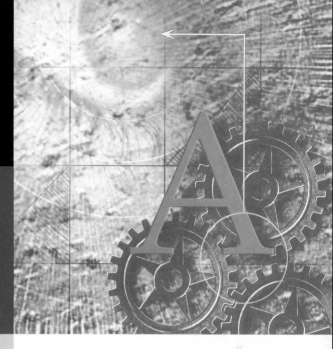

CHAPTER 7

Semantic Long-Term Memory

Semantic memory is the memory necessary for the use of language. It is a mental thesaurus, organized knowledge a person possesses about words and other verbal symbols, their meaning and referents, about relations among them, and about rules, formulas, and algorithms for the manipulation of these symbols, concepts, and relations. (Tulving, 1972, p. 386)

Human concepts are probably . . . like hooks or nodes in a network from which many different properties hang. The properties hanging from a node are not likely to be all equally accessible; some properties are more important than others, and so may be reached more easily or quickly. . . . Thus, a concept would be a set of interrelationships among other concepts . . . everything is defined in terms of everything else . . . like a dictionary. (Collins & Quillian, 1972, pp. 313–314)

This chapter is concerned with a rather different kind of long-term memory from that discussed in Chapter 6. It concerns **semantic memory,** literally "memory for meaning," our *permanent memory store of general world knowledge.* It has been variously described as a thesaurus, a dictionary, and an encyclopedia. Semantic memory is where your knowledge of language and other conceptual information is stored. It is the permanent repository of information you use to comprehend and produce language, to reason, to solve problems, and to make decisions. Whereas episodic memory is a personal, autobiographical store, semantic memory is a generic storehouse of knowledge. In fact, *generic memory* (Hintzman, 1978) might be a better name for this system (although way too boring). That is, whereas your episodic memory differs substantially from mine, our semantic memories are thought to be largely similar—maybe not in exact content, depending on our cultural backgrounds, but certainly similar in terms of structure and processes. Thus you have no idea what *my* mother's maiden name is, but we all share a highly similar semantic concept of a maiden name.

As Tulving (1972) noted, the first usage of the term *semantic memory* appears to have been in M. Ross Quillian's doctoral dissertation in 1966. Quillian set himself the task of programming a computer to understand language, that is, to answer a variety of questions in a reasonably humanlike fashion, and to paraphrase English text. The inspiration for this work came not from psychology but from computer science and artificial intelligence (AI). Machine translation, as it was known, had been a long-standing goal in computer science, yet progress toward this goal had been surprisingly slow. The overly confident predictions of the 1950s had failed to take into account a subtle yet important fact: Even the simplest acts of human comprehension require vast amounts of knowledge, much more than the words to be comprehended suggest. Thus for computers to understand, answer questions, or paraphrase, they needed this kind of knowledge base. This was Quillian's goal: to provide that extensive knowledge base, to see whether the AI system could then "understand." The implicit point, of course, would be that humans also need this vast storehouse of knowledge to comprehend. The study of that vast storehouse is the study of semantic memory.

This chapter covers the basics of semantic memory, the fundamental structures and processes investigated in semantic memory research. This includes topics such as how words and word meanings are stored in memory and how they are retrieved. We consider several models and approaches to semantic memory and two important ideas introduced earlier in the book: priming and automaticity. That plus a treatment of recent neuropsychological evidence sets the stage for Chapter 8, where the divisions of long-term memory are studied together. There, we delve into the question of interactions between the episodic and semantic systems, especially as applied to memory for real-world events and episodes, and to topics such as false memories and memory illusions. Throughout both chapters—indeed, throughout the remainder of the book—the theme we are most concerned with is the representation of knowledge, in Kintsch's (1974) terms, the representation of meaning in memory, and retrieval of that knowledge.

Semantic Memory

A study on leading questions, also discussed in Chapter 8, provides a convenient entry into the topic of semantic memory. Loftus and Palmer (1974) showed their subjects several short traffic safety films that involved car accidents. The participants were asked to describe each accident after seeing the film and then were asked a series of questions. One of the questions asked for an estimate of the cars' speed (which people are notoriously poor at estimating). One group of subjects was asked, "About how fast were the cars going when they hit each other?" The other four groups were asked almost the same question, except that the verb *hit* was replaced with either *smashed, collided, bumped,* or *contacted.* As you might expect, participants who got the stronger verbs such as *smashed* gave higher estimates of speed. The question led them to a biased answer.

Hold it. *Why* would we expect this effect? Why are we not surprised that people estimated higher speeds when the question said *smashed* instead of *bumped* or *hit?* Our intuitive answer here is that *smashed* implies a more severe accident than *bumped.* But consider this intuitive answer again. How did Loftus and Palmer's subjects know that *smashed* implies a more severe accident? It is not enough merely to say that *smashed* implies *more severe.* We are asking a more basic question than that. We want to know what is stored in memory that tells you what *smash* and *bump* mean. How is the difference between those two concepts represented in memory, and how do you retrieve those concepts when you encounter those words? How does memory represent the fact that *smashed* implies a severe accident, that moving cars have drivers, that robins have wings, or that bananas, canaries, and daisies are all yellow? In short, what is the structure and content of semantic memory per se, and how do we access the knowledge stored in it?

As you just read, one of the earliest systematic attempts to answer such questions (aside from philosophical and strictly linguistic analyses) was Quillian's (1968, 1969) work in artificial intelligence. His model of semantic memory, TLC (for *Teachable Language Comprehender*), was not a genuine psychological model but rather a computer program for understanding language. Very shortly, however, Quillian began a collaboration with Allan Collins, and the psychological model they based on TLC became the first serious attempt in cognitive psychology to explain the structure and processes of semantic memory.

The Collins and Quillian (and Loftus) Model

The Collins and Quillian model of semantic memory (1969, 1970, 1972, Collins & Loftus, 1975) was an extensive theory of semantic memory, comprehension, and meaning. At the heart of the model were two fundamentally important assumptions, one about the *structure* of semantic memory and one about the *process* of retrieving information from that structure. Because these two assumptions have been central to many models since the early Collins and Quillian work (e.g., Glass & Holyoak, 1975), including current connectionist models, you need a firm grasp on what they mean.

Nodes in a Network Collins and Quillian viewed the entries in semantic memory, the concepts in semantic memory, as being nodes in a network. In other words, the structure of semantic memory was said to be a **network,** *an interrelated set of concepts or interrelated body of knowledge.* Each concept in the network is represented as a **node,** *a point or location* in the semantic space.

Furthermore, concept nodes are linked together by **pathways,** *labeled, directional associations between concepts.* This entire collection—nodes connected to other nodes by pathways—is the network. Note that in such a structure, every concept is related to every other concept, in the sense that some set of pathways, however indirect and long, can eventually be traced between any two nodes. (By analogy, any two cities are connected either by a direct route or by an indirect series of highways and roads; Reisberg, 1997.)

Spreading Activation The major process that operates on this structure is **spreading activation,** the *mental activity of accessing and retrieving information from this network.* Concepts usually are in a quiet, unactivated state, at baseline. For example, at this very instant, as you are reading this sentence, one of the many concepts in your semantic memory that is probably not activated is "MACHINE." But when you read the word, its mental representation received a boost in activation. "MACHINE" was no longer quiet and unactivated; it was active or primed, awakened, so to speak (actually, it was probably implicitly primed by the "machine translation" phrase earlier). This activation, for Collins and Quillian, was the process of retrieval, the process of accessing the meaning of a concept. (When it is important to make the distinction, words will be italicized, and concept names will be printed in capital letters.)

A key feature of activation is that it spreads through the network along the stored pathways. That is, once a concept becomes activated, it begins to spread that activation to all the other concepts to which it is linked. Thus activation begins at a concept node and then starts spreading throughout the network, activating the nodes it encounters along the way. In Collins and Quillian's description, the "search continually widens like a harmless spreading plague" (1972, p. 326).

Look at Figure 7-1A, a simple diagram of a few concepts and the interconnecting pathways among them. Even such a simple network codes or represents a great deal of information. For instance, some of the facts coded in this network are that "ROBIN" is a member of the category "BIRD," that a "ROBIN" has a "RED BREAST," that a "CANARY" is "YELLOW," and so on. Each of these simple connections records an elementary fact or **proposition,** a *relationship between two concepts.*

Note further that each of the pathways joining two concept nodes is a labeled and directed pathway. Each pathway specifies a certain relationship and the direction of that relationship. Thus "ROBIN *is a* BIRD," *is a member of the category* "BIRD," and "BIRD has the *property* FEATHERS." (The latter statement is called a **property statement.** The *isa* relationship, indicating category membership, was a bit of cognitive jargon contributed by Rumelhart, Lindsay, & Norman [1972] meaning "is a," as in "is a member of the category." The importance of the direction of the relationship is well illustrated by *isa* because the reversed direction is not true, that is "*All BIRDS are ROBINS." By convention, sentences that are intentionally wrong are prefaced by an asterisk.) Moreover, the illustrations in Figure 7-1 show what would happen to this portion of your semantic network when the word *robin* is presented. First, the concept corresponding to *robin* becomes activated, illustrated by boldface in Figure 7-1A. After this, the concept "ROBIN" begins to spread activation to the concepts it is linked to, the boldfaced "BIRD," "RED BREAST," and "BLUE EGGS" concepts in Figure 7-1B. *Those* concepts continue the spread of activation to their associated nodes, as depicted in Figure 7-1C.

Collins and Quillian proposed that such a spread of activation is triggered each time a concept is activated in semantic memory. Thus when *two* concepts become activated, there are *two* simultaneous spreads of activation, one from each concept node. As an exercise, study Figure 7-1A and mark which concept nodes will become activated by a sentence like "A robin can breathe." To keep track of the original source of activation, write a *1* next to pathways and nodes that will be activated by "ROBIN" and a *2* next to those activated by "BREATHE." Take this demonstration through at least two cycles; first, the original node activates its connected nodes, and second, those nodes activate their connected nodes. (In a sense, you are "hand simulating" the computerized memory search in TLC. This is a laborious process, which highlights one of the attractive features of computer simulation and artificial intelligence programming. Let the computer do all the dreary work of spreading the activation and keeping track of the sources, while you merely wait at your terminal for the program to tell you the final outcome of the search.)

Intersection Search What did you discover in that exercise? If you did it correctly, you should have discovered two important properties of spreading activation search. First, you found that the activation originating with "ROBIN" eventually primed a node that was *also* primed or activated by "BREATHE." This is the exact process proposed by Collins and Quillian and originally programmed into Quillian's TLC model to explain how information

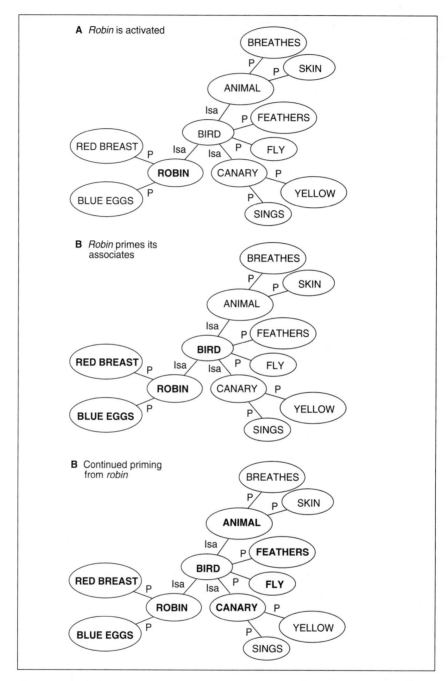

Figure 7-1

A portion of the semantic network is illustrated. **A,** The concept "ROBIN" has been activated and is shown in boldface. **B,** The spreading activation from "ROBIN" has activated concepts linked to "ROBIN," such as the boldface "BIRD," "RED BREAST," and "BLUE EGGS." **C,** The continued spread of activation that originated from "ROBIN" is depicted.

is retrieved from semantic memory. The "harmless spreading plague" eventually encounters another "harmless spreading plague" that came from a different source. When that happens, then a connecting route or set of pathways has been retrieved from semantic memory. In the terminology of the model, *when the two spreads of activation encounter one another,* an **intersection** has been found between the two concepts, "ROBIN" and "BREATHE."

Once an intersection has been found, a decision stage must operate to make sure that the retrieved pathway is valid, to make sure it represents the relationship specified in the sentence. In other words, although a pathway would be found between "ANIMAL" and "RED BREAST," a decision stage would decide that the intersection activated by "all animals have red breasts" is invalid.

Related Concepts   The second characteristic of intersection search that you should have discovered is that other concepts also become activated or primed during the search. That is, the intersection pathway was "ROBIN *isa* BIRD *isa* ANIMAL *property* BREATHE." But many other concepts were also primed during the search; there should also be a *1* next to "RED BREAST" and "BLUE EGGS" from the first cycle, a *1* next to "FLY, FEATHERS, and CANARY" after the second cycle, and so on. Thus a spreading activation search not only retrieves the relevant pathway between two concepts, it also activates related concepts. To be sure, more and more distant concepts, connected by longer pathways, do not receive as much activation as those that are close. And even the close, related concepts do not remain activated forever, of course, because activation is always presumed to decay after some amount of time. Nonetheless, for a short period, nearby related concepts receive a boost in their activation levels, making them temporarily more accessible. This priming of related concepts is key to an understanding of semantic processing; we return to it repeatedly throughout the chapter, and indeed throughout the book.

Smith's Feature Comparison Model

Given the excitement of studying meaning and how it is represented in memory, it is not surprising that other approaches to semantic memory soon appeared. We focus here on one alternative, the Smith feature comparison model, because it offered a clear contrast to the Collins and Quillian model in some basic assumptions and because it was the most successful challenger to that model (see Chang, 1986, for a review of all the major models). We also consider some hybrid approaches found in other models.

Feature Lists   Smith's model (Rips, Shoben, & Smith, 1973; Smith, Rips, & Shoben, 1974) was much simpler than the Collins and Quillian network model in its assumptions about the structure of semantic memory, but as a consequence it was somewhat more elaborate in its assumptions about the process of retrieval. Its most basic structural element was the **feature list.** Rather than postulating extensive networks of concepts and pathways, Smith et al. suggested that we consider semantic memory to be a collection of lists. Each concept in semantic memory would be represented as a list of **semantic features,** *simple, one-element characteristics or properties of the concept.* Thus the concept

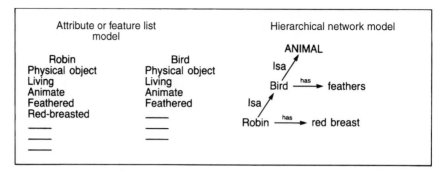

Figure 7-2

Information in semantic memory is represented differently in feature list models and in hierarchical network models. In feature list models, a concept is represented as a list of simple semantic features; in hierarchical network models, concepts are represented as nodes that connect to other nodes via pathways. The Smith et al. (1974a, b) model is a feature list model, and the Collins and Quillian (1972) model is a hierarchical network model. Adapted from Smith (1978).

"ROBIN" would be represented as a list of its features, such as animate, red-breasted, and feathered (Figure 7-2).

Smith et al. suggested that these feature lists were ordered in terms of a factor called *definingness.* That is, the feature lists stored in memory are ordered in a priority ranking, with the most defining features for a concept at the top of the list and the least defining features at the bottom. Thus an essential feature is called a **defining feature,** such as *animate* for "BIRD," and would be stored near the top of the feature list. Conversely, features that are not particularly defining for the concept (e.g., "ROBIN" *perches in trees*) would be placed at the bottom of the list. In fact, Smith et al. proposed that these lower features are more appropriately called **characteristic features** of the concept, *features that are common but not essential to the meaning of the concept.* Thus characteristic features do not define "ROBIN" or "BIRD": Robins may or may not perch in trees. But defining features are essential: If it is a robin, it has to be animate.

Feature Comparison The major process of information retrieval in the Smith model was a feature comparison process; follow along with the sequence of processes illustrated in Figure 7-3 as you read. Suppose you are given the sentence "A robin is a bird" and have to make a true/false judgment. According to the model, you would access the two concepts "ROBIN" and "BIRD" in semantic memory and then compare the features on those two lists. This Stage I feature comparison process involved a rapid, global comparison of the features: Some randomly selected subset of features on each of the two lists is compared to "compute" the similarity between the two concepts. This comparison process yields a feature overlap score, an index or measurement of the similarity of the two concepts. For illustration purposes here, assume that these scores range from 1 to 10.

Of course, for the concepts in "A robin is a bird," the feature lists should overlap a great deal; there are hardly any "ROBIN" features that are not also "BIRD" features.

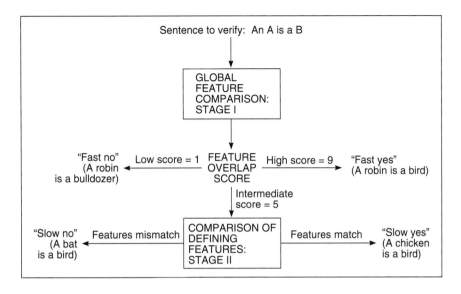

Figure 7-3

The comparison and decision process in the Smith et al. model, with samples sentences.

The outcome of this feature comparison process then would be a very high overlap score (e.g., 8 or 9), so high that you could confidently respond "yes" immediately on the basis of this global comparison of features. Conversely, with a sentence such as "A robin is a bulldozer," there should be so little feature overlap (e.g., 1 or 2) that you could respond "no" immediately without any further processing. Smith et al. call these "fast yes" and "fast no" responses Stage I responses. When overlap scores are very high or very low, there is no need to continue the search, so a response is made immediately.

What about other kinds of sentences, where the stated relationship is not quite so obvious? First, consider "A chicken is a bird." As before, the process of retrieving information is the feature comparison process, now being performed on the "CHICKEN" and "BIRD" features. Most people's intuition is that chickens are a somewhat less representative example of the bird category: They do not perch or make nests in trees, they do not fly, and so on. For such instances, the Stage I comparison process would find only an intermediate degree of overlap between "CHICKEN" and "BIRD." Smith et al. claimed that when the overlap scores indicate only moderate similarity (say, 5 or 6), a second comparison is necessary. The second comparison is called a Stage II comparison.

Unlike the fast, global Stage I comparison, the Stage II comparison is careful and rather slow, and only the defining features are used to compute its evidence. Thus, for the "CHICKEN–BIRD" sentence, only the defining features of the two concepts are compared in Stage II. Because it is true that chickens are birds, presumably there is a match on all the tested features in this stage, yielding a "slow yes" response. The response is slow because it involves Stage II comparison and "yes" because all the defining features from "CHICKEN" match those from "BIRD." Similarly, for the sentence

Table 7-1 RECOGNITION TASKS IN SEMANTIC MEMORY

In Table 6-4, the recognition task consisted of two basic steps; the subject first learned a set of words on a list and then made yes/no decisions on a test list ("yes" if the test word was on the studied list, "no" if it was not on the studied list). The two important features that make a recognition test are as follows:
    Subjects make yes/no or forced-choice decisions.
    The decisions are based on information stored in memory.
For semantic memory research, this task has been generalized to include information already stored in long-term memory before the beginning of the experiment.

Generalized recognition task (Semantic)

Information to be tested is already in long-term memory, such as knowledge of categories ("A robin is a bird") or words.
    Subjects make yes/no decisions to a sequence of test items, presented one at a time. Unlike episodic recognition tasks, here the "yes" response usually means the item is true. For example, in a sentence verification task, subjects say "yes" to "A robin is a bird," that is, to any sentence that is true. In a lexical decision task, subjects respond "yes" if the letter string is a word (e.g., "MOTOR") and "no" if it is not (e.g., "MANTY").
    Dependent variables: Typically, the major dependent variable is reaction time (RT), although accuracy is also important. Because the task usually involves yes/no decisions, guessing rate usually is 50%; if accuracy drops to 70% or 80%, then RT is questionable, often because subjects have traded accuracy for speed (i.e., they are faster than they would have been if they had maintained higher accuracy). Occasionally, subjects are given a response deadline; that is, they are given a signal after some brief interval, say 300 msec, and must respond immediately after the signal. In such a task, error rate becomes the major dependent variable. Recently, different patterns of brain waves have been used instead of RT or errors (see the description of Kounios & Holcomb, 1992, in this chapter).
    Independent variables: An enormous range of independent variables can be tested; such as the semantic relatedness between concepts in a sentence like "An *S* is/has a *P*"; word length, frequency, concreteness, and the like in a lexical decision task; and the number of times a stimulus (word, picture) is repeated in the sequence of trials and how recently it was repeated (called lag).

"A bat is a bird," the overlap score is intermediate, which triggers Stage II. Here, however, there are several important mismatches: The characteristic features that make bats similar to birds are not considered, and the defining features (mammal, furry, teeth, etc.) mismatch. Thus, the Stage II comparison gives convincing evidence that the sentence is false, and the response is a "slow no" response.

Empirical Tests of Semantic Memory Models

Most early tests of semantic memory models adopted the **sentence verification task,** in which *simple sentences are presented for the subjects' yes/no decisions.* The stimuli often used the frame "An *S* is a *P*" (e.g., "A robin is a bird" or "A canary is green"), where *S* stood for *subject* (robin, canary), and *P* stood for *predicate* (bird, green). Accuracy scores for subjects' decisions about these simple sentences would not tell us much, of course; people seldom are in doubt or make mistakes about such simple facts. Thus reaction time (RT) tests were the usual method of testing semantic memory models. Present subjects with simple sentences, some true and some false, and time them as they make their yes/no decisions. What makes this a semantic memory task is the nature of the knowledge being tested. Recall that when we provide a set of stimuli for participants to learn, then test their memory for the stimuli, we are using an episodic memory task. But when we ask subjects to perform based on what

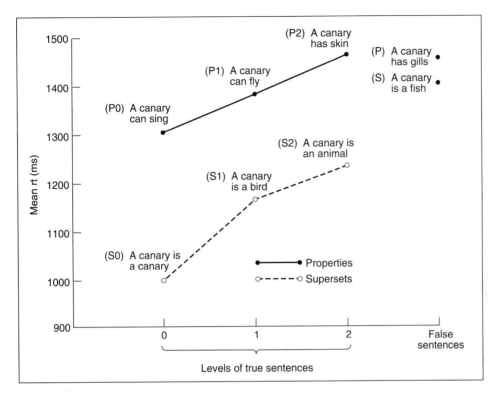

Figure 7-4

Reaction time to superordinate (S) sentences and property (P) sentences is shown as a function of levels within the hierarchy. An S2 sentence involves a superordinate connection two levels up the hierarchy; S1 means one level up in the hierarchy; a 0 level sentence had the predicate stored at the same hierarchical level. From Collins and Quillian (1969).

they already know, we are testing general, semantic knowledge. Table 7-1 lists the characteristics of such yes/no recognition tasks when they are used in semantic memory settings.

Early Results   Collins and Quillian's (1969) earliest report tested an obvious prediction from their model: Two concepts that are closer together in the network should take less time to verify than two that are farther apart. Refer again to Figure 7-1 and to the "hand simulation" you performed. If we assume that your conceptual knowledge about this portion of semantic memory is accurately represented in the figure, then several predictions can be made. An obvious and important one is that you should be faster to verify "A robin is a bird" than "A robin is an animal" simply because it should take less time for activation to spread and intersect when the two concepts are separated by only one pathway rather than two. Likewise, based on the figure, it should take less time to verify that canaries are yellow than that they can fly or breathe, for the same reason.

Figure 7-4 shows the results of Collins and Quillian's (1969) classic test of these predictions. In the figure, S indicates a superordinate statement, or an *isa* sentence, and

P indicates a property statement. Tagged onto the *S* or *P* is a digit from 0 to 2, which indicates how many levels in the hierarchy the search proceeded through to find the stated concept. As you can see, reaction time increased as the semantic distance between the two concepts increased. For the superordinate sentences, searching for an S2 relationship (e.g., "A canary is an animal") took about 75 msec longer than searching for an S1 relationship ("A canary is a bird"). The same increase in time was also found for property sentences going up 1 and 2 levels. (Note that a P0 sentence meant "up 0 levels," that is a sentence in which the predicate was stored at the same level in the hierarchy as the subject; e.g., "A canary can sing"). From these results, Collins and Quillian concluded that the hierarchical nature of semantic memory had been demonstrated: It took longer to retrieve a relationship between two concepts at more distant levels in the hierarchy than those stored closer together. Moreover, it appears from these results that the *isa* pathways are stronger than the *property* pathways because superordinate sentences were retrieved faster than property sentences (see Hampton, 1984, for confirmation).[1]

Clashing Models and Explanations

Although the Collins and Quillian result sounds like strong evidence for their network model, it was by no means a definitive test: The Smith et al. model had a viable explanation of those results, too. The Smith model argued that a pair of concepts such as "ROBIN and ANIMAL," which Collins and Quillian turned into S2 sentences, have lower feature overlap than a pair such as "ROBIN and BIRD" (which formed S1 sentences). If so, then more S2 sentences would need the extra comparison step of Smith et al.'s Stage II, on average. This would tend to slow down the comparison process.

Let's consider three more issues that were heavily investigated in the semantic memory area, not only to evaluate the models that were proposed but also to lead up to a generalization about the structure of semantic memory: the principle of semantic relatedness.

Cognitive Economy A second challenge to the Collins and Quillian approach came from studies that examined one of the model's assumptions, that of cognitive economy. Embedded in their model was the assumption that redundant information is not stored in semantic memory: "The sheer quantity of information involved . . . argues strongly that both the human subject's memory and our model thereof contain as little redundancy as possible and that it [should] contain stored facts only when these cannot otherwise be generated or inferred" (Quillian, 1968, p. 228). This was the principle of **cognitive economy:** to economize in the number of concepts that must be stored, *only nonredundant facts are stored in memory.*

According to this principle, concepts such as "FEATHERS" and "BREATHES" (e.g., in Figure 7-1) only appear at their highest level of generality (with the superordinates

---

[1]Collins and Quillian tested many more concepts than just canaries and robins, of course, although the tradition in this area of research is to illustrate the models using these words. In a depressing example of literal-mindedness, a student of mine once answered an essay question on semantic memory by saying, "Collins and Quillian devised a psychological model to explain what people know about birds."

"BIRD" and "ANIMAL") rather than repeatedly throughout the network (with "ROBIN," "CANARY," etc.) Not only would this principle save space—a critical factor in Quillian's original work, because computers of the day had severely limited memory—but it also yielded a very useful characteristic because of the hierarchical structure of the network. This principle is known as **inheritance,** the notion that *the members of a category possess or inherit the properties of the category itself;* anything true of "ANIMAL" is necessarily true of "BIRD," "ROBIN," "CANARY," and so forth. By this mechanism, the structure allows inferences about higher-level properties rather than forcing the system to store each of them directly and repeatedly. Although Collins and Quillian never took an extreme stand on this principle, most investigators realized that some degree of cognitive economy was intended.

There is clearly some truth to the cognitive economy idea; after all, we surely do not fill our memories with such facts as "The philosopher Aristotle had two hands" and "Robins have skin." But where do we draw the line between information stored directly and information relegated to the inference process?

Research by Conrad (1972) and others provides us with an answer to this question. In her study, Conrad first collected normative data from a sample of college students, asking them to write down properties of a variety of words (e.g., *robin, banjo, onion*), then tabulating how frequently each property was listed; subjects listed them repeatedly, not in the overly tidy fashion predicted by cognitive economy (see also Ashcraft, 1978b). And when she used the words for the sentences in her verification task, she found little evidence of the economical scheme implied by cognitive economy. Instead, the frequency with which properties were listed normatively was a much more powerful predictor of RT than the hierarchical levels Collins and Quillian used. High-frequency properties, such as "WINGS" for the concept "ROBIN," were verified more quickly than low-frequency properties, such as "FEET" for "ROBIN" (see also Ashcraft, 1976; Glass, Holyoak, & O'Dell, 1974). In other words, it seemed very possible that Collins and Quillian obtained their result not because the properties or superordinates were more distant in a hierarchical structure but simply because these concepts were associated more weakly with the concepts.

Property Statements In contrast, as researchers followed up on some of the property statement results obtained by Collins and Quillian (1969), the Smith et al. model began to have some difficulties. Several researchers, along with Conrad (1972), tested statements of the form "An S *has* a P," where the relationship was not a superordinate *isa* pathway but a property or attribute pathway (e.g., "A robin has wings" and "A canary is yellow").

The difficulty for the Smith et al. model here was that it had to claim that there was a feature list stored in semantic memory that corresponded to "THINGS WITH WINGS," one for "YELLOW THINGS," and so forth. Furthermore, to apply the two-stage decision process of the model it had to claim that each of these unusual lists had to have both defining and characteristic features on it. But what feature, besides "WINGS," might be on the feature list of "THINGS WITH WINGS"? (And, for that matter, why compare this feature list with that of "ROBIN" when the feature list for "ROBIN" presumably had "WINGS" listed on it already?) Equally problematic were property statements such as "Ostrich is large." How could there be feature lists in memory titled "LARGE THINGS" when judging this as true or false is a relative matter; after all, ostriches are large for birds but small compared with many other things (elephants, whales, skyscrapers). The revisions made to the model to handle property statements were awkward and, to some, implausible. And, as you will learn later, they still did not explain some other important results.

In contrast, the Collins and Loftus (1975) network approach contained both property and superordinate pathways and thus had no difficulty in explaining how people verify property statements; the same intersection search process applies to both. Furthermore, the troublesome distinction between defining and characteristic properties was not in the Collins and Quillian model, whereas Smith et al. had some difficulties in convincing researchers that such a distinction even existed (but see Malt, 1990, for the influence of *subjects'* beliefs that there are defining features for some categories). And finally, Collins and Loftus (1975) asked why a property as important as the category to which something belongs would not be stored on the feature list; why did the Smith et al. model insist that we "compute" that a robin is a bird, for instance, given all the other features about robin that *are* stored on the feature list? As they put it, "It is an unlikely model which postulates that people use information that is less relevant to make a decision, instead of information that is more relevant" (Collins & Loftus, 1975, p. 426).

Typicality Effects Despite this shortcoming, the Smith et al. model made a lasting contribution to the semantic memory field in its emphasis on **typicality,** *the degree to which items are viewed as typical, central members of a category.* Inspired especially by Rosch's (1973) insightful work, Smith and colleagues (Rips, et al., 1973) demonstrated successfully the need for an explicit consideration of how well category members fit into their categories and, by extension, the importance of work on categorization itself. In essence, Rosch's and Smith et al.'s research demonstrated that all exemplars—all members of a

Typical birds?

category—are not equal. Therefore, the time to make category judgments depends on how typical or central the item is in its category.

Rosch's work began by using the extensive category membership norms collected by Battig and Montague (1969), in which people merely listed members of various categories. The norms showed a similar effect to the property norms mentioned above: Some items are listed as members of a category much more frequently than others. To use our familiar example, *robin* was the most frequently occurring member of the bird category: It was listed by 85% of the subjects. *Chicken*, on the other hand, was listed by only 9% of the subjects. As you might suspect, such a range of occurrence says something important about people's representation of the semantic category "BIRD" (and other categories as well; see footnote 1) and, as a consequence, implies something important about their RT performance. The important result both in Rosch's studies (1973, 1975) and in Smith et al.'s work (1974a; Rips, et al., 1973) was exactly parallel to Conrad's property frequency results: Exemplars listed very frequently as category members yielded significantly faster judgments than those of lower frequency. Putting it simply, you can decide "true" to "Robin is a bird" more rapidly than you can decide that "Chicken is a bird."

Unlike the equal-length pathways depicted in Figure 7-1, such a result (in network terms) suggested that pathways to less frequent category members were longer, making those members farther away in the semantic network. Under the Smith et al. scheme, less frequent category members were said to have lower feature overlap with their superordinate than more frequent members. In fact, it was exactly this kind of result (Rips, et al., 1973; Rosch, 1973) that led Smith et al. (1974a) to their feature comparison model. This important effect is now called the **typicality effect:** *typical members of a category can be judged more rapidly than atypical members* (see also Casey, 1992). Figure 7-5 illustrates the effect obtained in Smith et al.'s research. (We return to typicality soon because it is more important than this short discussion implies.)

Semantic Relatedness

Figure 7-6 illustrates a modified network representation of part of the *bird* category, one that incorporates the three issues we have been discussing. Note first that there is no rigid cognitive economy in the illustration; properties listed for a concept are linked directly to that concept rather than indirectly via multiple pathways. Second, these pathways are of different lengths, reflecting the results that sentences with high-frequency properties are verified faster than those with low-frequency properties (this result was clearly anticipated by Collins and Quillian; see the introductory quotation). Finally, note how typicality effects are represented in the figure: typical or central members of the category are connected to the superordinate node by shorter pathways, whereas atypical or peripheral members are linked by longer pathways. In other words, the network structure of a category is illustrated in the figure, with the length of connecting pathways representing the degree to which two concepts are related. Shorter pathways denote concepts that are closer in semantic space

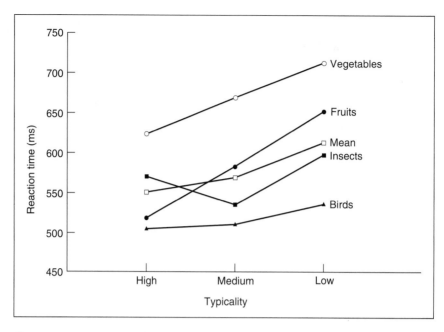

Figure 7-5

Mean RTs to members of categories that are high, medium, or low in typicality. The RTs are much shorter than in comparable studies because the category names were given at the beginning of a block of trials and did not change within the block. Thus each trial consisted of only the target word, and subjects judged whether it belonged to the given category name.

or, to use a different terminology, more strongly related to one another. Longer pathways denote lesser degrees of semantic relatedness.

Unfortunately, it is difficult in a two-dimensional figure to illustrate some other features of networks. For example, most researchers would agree that the strict hierarchical approach is incorrect. This conclusion is based on evidence that statements such as "A beaver is an animal" tend to be verified more quickly than "A beaver is a mammal." Of course, in a strict hierarchy, the latter sentence should be faster to verify or judge because *mammal* is a subset of *animal*. Nonetheless, RTs to such sentences show a different effect than strict logic or hierarchies would imply (Rips, et al., 1973). In the figure, this relaxation of the strictly hierarchical scheme would mean that there should be a connecting pathway from "CHICKEN" to "ANIMAL," for instance, and that this pathway would be shorter than the "CHICKEN *isa* BIRD" pathway. Conceiving of such networks in three-dimensional space makes this easier to imagine but harder to illustrate.

Regardless of how we diagram the illustrations, the empirical prediction from such a network is that performance, particularly RT performance, varies directly as a function of the strength of the connecting pathway. To state it slightly differently, the higher

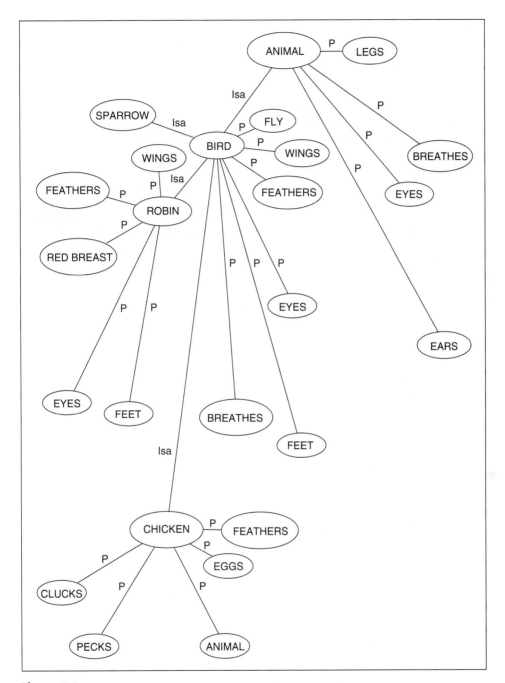

Figure 7-6

A portion of the semantic network is illustrated, taking into account three empirical effects: There is no strict cognitive economy in the hierarchy, so redundant information is stored at several different concepts; typical members of the category are stored more closely to the category name or prototype member; and properties that are more important are stored more closely to the concept than those of lesser importance.

What a typical car used to look like.

the semantic relatedness between concepts, the faster you are able to retrieve the connection between them. This is the **semantic relatedness effect:** *Concepts that are more highly interrelated can be retrieved and judged true more rapidly than those with a lower degree of relatedness.* One important ingredient here is that this semantic relatedness principle applies both to category statements ("An *S* is a *P*") and to property statements ("An *S* has a *P*"; Ashcraft, 1978a; Hampton, 1984). Moreover, this appears to be an important generalization about the overall structure and processing of semantic memories: The closer two concepts are in semantic memory, either in distance or in relatedness, the faster is the set of mental search and decision processes that retrieves and evaluates information about the concepts. The implication here is that semantic memory's structure is based on semantic relatedness among concepts.

Physiological Evidence Some challenging additional evidence on the semantic relatedness effect has been reported recently by Kounios and Holcomb (1992; see Kounios, 1996, for a review). In this experiment, pairs of words varied in their relatedness, either high ("rubies–gems") or low ("spruces–gems"). Half of the time, the category member—the exemplar, in Kounios and Holcomb's term—came before the category ("rubies–gems" is an exemplar–category pair), and half the time the category came first ("gems–rubies" is a category–exemplar pair). Sentences were presented with one of three quantifiers, *all*, *some*, or *no*, thus altering the meaning and true/false status of the sentences (e.g., "All rubies are gems" and "Some gems are rubies" are true, but "No

PROVE IT

Category Retrieval and Episodic Influences

To illustrate that semantic memory is organized according to the principle of semantic relatedness, time some subjects as they generate lists of words for you (e.g., see how long it takes them to generate 20 words); or give the subjects a fixed amount of time (say, 30 s) and tabulate how many words they generate in that period. You should test several well-known semantic categories, such as trees, flowers, vegetables, fruits, insects, or mammals. Now contrast those results with some different categories, such as red things, things that are soft, or things beginning with the letter *m*. You will see some evidence of semantic relatedness even in the latter examples; for instance, in the *red things* category, people are more likely to name *apple* and *tomato* together than *apple* and *fire engine*.

As an added episodic memory twist, at the end of the category retrieval exercise, have your subjects take a new sheet of paper and list as many of the words they generated as they can remember, cautioning them to name *only* words they produced. Do you find more intrusions from the semantic categories?

rubies are gems" is false). The results of the experiment are shown in Figure 7-7. Look at the figure now; you will see the same kind of increasing function as before, for example, when typicality varied from high to low in Figure 7-5.

But look at the figure again. What is the label on the *y*-axis? This is not a standard RT effect for semantic relatedness. Instead, these scores are the amplitudes of brain wave patterns, the **event-related potentials (ERPs)** you learned about in Chapter 2. As a reminder, electrodes are placed on the subjects' scalps during the task, and then specific electrical patterns of brain activity are tracked across time, beginning with the onset of the stimulus (the "event" in "event-related potentials"). In other words, Kounios and Holcomb replicated the standard semantic relatedness effect using a radically different dependent measure: electrical activity in the brain.

As Kounios (1996, 2000) explains, ERPs have become an increasingly useful measurement of cognitive processes in recent years. A major reason for this usefulness is the time-lagged nature just mentioned; present a stimulus, and a certain ERP component occurs within a narrow window of time (e.g., within 300 to 500 msec of the stimulus). By carefully controlling the subjects' muscle movements (including eye blinks), a researcher can be fairly sure that the observed change in electrical potential is a direct result of the stimulus that was presented.

Several different positive and negative ERPs have recently been studied in the intact, functioning brain. For example, an ERP known as *P300* is of interest in some studies; the *P* means it is a positive change in electrical potential, and the *300* means the change peaks roughly 300 msec after the stimulus is presented (it is also called the P3

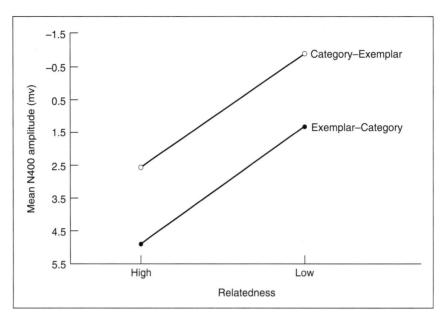

Figure 7-7

Mean N400 amplitude recorded from three midline sites as a function of semantic relatedness and prime–target order.

component because it is the third positive component; Kounios & Holcomb, 1992). This ERP has been linked to activity in working memory (Donchin, 1981). In the Kounios and Holcomb study, the ERP of interest was the N400 component, a *negative* change occurring from about 300 to 500 msec (centered at about 400 msec) after the stimulus, the sentence predicate in their study.

Figure 7-8 shows the actual pattern of recorded N400s, taken from one of the midline electrode sites (recordings were taken from three midline sites and five sites each on the left and right hemispheres). At the 400-msec point, the solid curve for "Exemplar–category, related" stimuli (e.g., "All rubies are gems") continued its drift downward. For all three other sentence types, however, there was a negative peak around 400 msec, especially when the subject and predicate were unrelated. In other words, the N400 component seemed to be particularly sensitive to the relatedness of the two concepts in the sentence or, more accurately, to their *un*relatedness.

Kounios and Holcomb's conclusion is that the N400 ERP component is especially affected by retrieval mechanisms in semantic memory and by coherence and integration processes in language comprehension (see also Holcomb, 1993). When the two words were related (or, in their Experiment 2, when the words had to be categorized as either abstract or concrete), there was a substantial difference in the ERP pattern compared with trials on which the words were semantically unrelated.

One semantic-based result addressed in Kounios (1996) does make particularly good sense, given what we know about lateralization in the cerebral hemispheres. Most

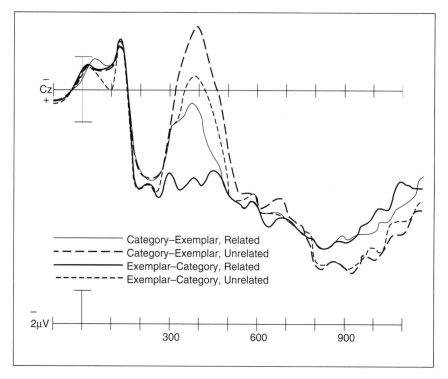

Figure 7-8

The event-related potentials at one midline site (Cz) for four types of trials; "Exemplar–category" and "Category–exemplar" refer to the order of the words. The onset of the target is shown by the vertical bar at the beginning of the time lines.

research suggests that the left hemisphere of the brain is especially important for verbal and language-based tasks, whereas the right hemisphere is somewhat specialized for visual and spatial information. Kounios describes a clear match between ERP results and Paivio's (1990) dual-coding theory. Recall the Paivio work you studied in Chapter 6, that concrete words may be learned and recalled better than abstract words because they can be represented in both a verbal code and an image-based code (Paivio, 1971). In his more recent work, Paivio (1990) suggests that there are two distinct systems for representing knowledge: the verbal system, which contains word meanings, and the concrete system, which contains knowledge based on visual images. His hypothesis, in terms of lateralization, was that the word-based knowledge would be located in the left hemisphere and image-based representations would be located in the right hemisphere. In this theory, concrete words should enjoy an advantage because they can be processed in both hemispheres, once as words and once as images, whereas abstract words can only be dealt with in verbal terms, and principally in the left hemisphere.

Kounios and Holcomb (1994) used a lexical decision task, showing both concrete (e.g., *table*) and abstract (e.g., *justice*) words for simple yes/no decisions. But in addition to measuring RTs, they also examined ERP patterns, providing clear physiological support for Paivio's predictions. As shown in the bottom of Figure 7-9, ERPs for concrete words were equal and high for both hemispheres (see Chapter 9 for further information on Wernicke's area of the brain). In contrast, the amplitude of the ERPs was markedly lower in the right than in the left hemisphere for abstract words, and both of these amplitudes were lower than those found for concrete words.

Kounios's (1996) conclusion is that RT effects in semantic memory research probably reflect processes occurring after retrieval, probably decision processes. This is quite unlike the traditional interpretations of RT results, which almost uniformly have been thought of as revealing differences in retrieval processes. This "Kounios challenge" has yet to be adequately addressed in current models of semantic memory. It seems clear, at a minimum, that future models must consider how semantic relatedness effects might affect decision processes and how left-versus-right-hemisphere representations of abstract and concrete concepts should be captured in our models.

■ Section Summary

- Semantic memory contains our long-term memory knowledge of the world, including our knowledge of words, concepts, and language. Early studies of the structure and processes of semantic memory generated two kinds of models: network approaches and feature list approaches.
- In the Collins and Quillian network model, concepts are represented as nodes in a semantic network, with connecting pathways between concepts. Accessing a concept involved the process of spreading activation: Activation spreads from the originating node to all the nodes connected to it by pathways. Several early studies, using the sentence verification task, supported an early version of this model, although the disconfirmation of the cognitive economy hypothesis was viewed as evidence against the model.
- Smith et al. claim that semantic concepts are lists of semantic features. Verification in their model consists of accessing the feature lists and performing a comparison process on the features. While the Smith et al. model initially seemed more able to explain typicality effects, the model did not provide a plausible account of how we verify property statements, nor did it predict or account for semantic priming. When this phenomenon became a central focus of semantic memory research, the feature list approach fell into neglect.

Categorization, Classification, and Prototypes

A final series of important studies addresses the principle of semantic relatedness and the structure of categories in semantic memory from a slightly different perspective, that of how concepts are classified into categories. This discussion also sets the stage for several important processes to be considered in later chapters, chief among them

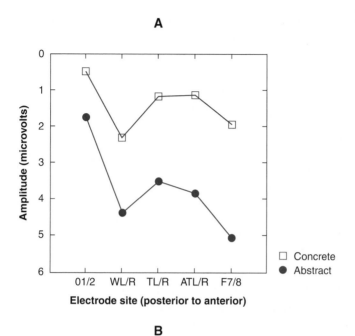

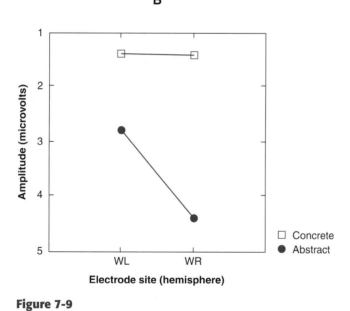

Figure 7-9

A, Mean amplitude of ERPs at five sites (occipital, left and right [01/2]; Wernicke's area, left and right [WL/R], temporal, left and right [TL/R], anterior temporal, left and right [ATL/R], and frontal, left and right [F7/8]), for concrete and abstract words.
B, Mean ERP amplitude for concrete and abstract words at Wernicke's area in the left (WL) and right (WR) hemispheres.

language comprehension. As preparation for this section, you might look up the word *bird* or *flower* in your dictionary and note any illustration that accompanies the definition.

Concept Formation

Traditional research on concept formation (e.g., Bourne & Bunderson, 1963) showed subjects a series of arbitrary patterns and asked them to categorize each pattern as belonging or not belonging to the concept being tested. Oddly enough, subjects were not told what the target concept was ahead of time: They had to develop the concept by guessing and then paying attention to the feedback they received after making their decisions. For example, you might be shown geometric figures of circles and squares, some large and some small, some darkened and some light. The relevant concept here might be "large darkened circle," which you would acquire slowly by paying attention to the feedback you received as you guessed your way through a set of patterns.

An extensive literature exists on this topic, and we know fairly well what factors influence performance (e.g., the number of different dimensions that are relevant and the number that are redundant; see Kintsch, 1970, for a summary). What is not made clear by this literature, however, is how these effects relate to real-world concepts. That is, if "large darkened circle" is the target concept being tested, how does such an arbitrary combination of dimensions relate to concepts such as "GAME," "VEHICLE," or "BIRD"? These categories seem to have nothing comparable to the invariant, arbitrary features used in the laboratory.

Natural Language Concepts

Beginning in the early 1970s, a very different approach to the topic of concept formation and classification appeared, largely through Eleanor Rosch's important research. A central theme in Rosch's reports (1973) was that traditional concept identification research erred in testing stimuli that were not comparable to concepts in the real world.

In classic concept formation tasks, any "large darkened circle" was by definition a member of the category, an instance of the concept being tested, and anything that lacked those three characteristics was not an instance of the concept. Therefore, the question "Which of the category members is a better member of the category or concept?" seems very strange; they are all equal because they are all members.

But Rosch contended that such artificial categories bear little relationship to the natural categories we use in language and thought. **Natural categories,** *concepts and categories that occur in the real world of our experience,* have a complex internal structure, she argued. Questions such as "Which is a better member of the *dog* category: collie or dachshund?" make perfectly good sense for natural categories, suggesting that the category *dog* has an internal structure in which some members are "better" or more representative than others. Given this obvious difference between natural categories and experimenter-defined concepts, Rosch argued that the concept formation literature may have given us "a quite distorted view of how real categories are learned and how they function in cognitive processes" (Rosch, 1973, p. 112).

Rosch is saying that real-world category members do not belong to their categories in simple yes/no, all-or-none fashion; they are not bundles of independent features. Instead, real-world categories show the characteristic of fuzzy boundaries, with ill-defined or uncertain membership for many category instances. For example, is a sled a toy or a vehicle? Is a chicken a better member of the *farm animal* category than of the *bird* category? Furthermore, as Collins and Loftus (1975) pointed out, no single feature seems absolutely necessary as a criterion of membership or classification. For example, having a skin or peel certainly is an important feature of the fruit category, yet a peeled orange is still a fruit.

In short, Rosch claimed that membership in categories is a matter of degree. Some members are highly representative or good instances, close in some sense to an ideal member. Others are poor instances, on the periphery, in the fuzzy area where members seem to blend into another category. This should have a profound influence on how we represent and think about the world.

Perceptual Categories To document her point, Rosch presented a fascinating study conducted with members of the Dani tribe in New Guinea (Rosch-Heider, 1972). She administered both short- and long-term memory tasks, using chips of different colors as the stimuli. She found that the Dani learned and remembered more accurately when the chips were "focal" colors rather than "nonfocal" colors, that is "a really red red" as opposed to "a sort of red red." In other words, the central, perceptually salient, "good" red was a better aid to accuracy than the nonfocal "off-red." One compelling aspect of this study was that the language of the Dani contains only two color terms, one for "dark" and one for "light." Nothing in their language expresses meanings such as "true red" or "off-red," yet their performance was influenced by the centrality of focal versus nonfocal colors.

Given the absence of separate color terms in their vocabulary, Rosch reasoned, it must be that there are structured, mental categories of colors in the subjects' semantic memories, categories that do not rely on the spoken language. Each category has a central tendency, a focal member that represents the "true" or "good" color and also has noncentral, nonfocal members that are less representative. Thus the centrality or "goodness" of a color in its own category made a difference in the memory tasks, even without distinct words to name the different color shades. Using the terms you are already familiar with, these ideas correspond exactly to *typical* and *atypical*.

Semantic Categories Rosch then went on to demonstrate an analogous structure in natural, semantic categories. For example, in one set of studies (Rosch, 1973, 1975), subjects were asked to rate a list of category members on their representativeness or typicality. Categorization results—for instance, RT to verify that "An *S* is a *P*"—depended on the rated typicality of the instance (Rosch, 1973). This is a result you have already encountered, in Figure 7-5. Her later work extended this typicality effect even further.

For example, she found that using the category name prepared people better for a judgment about a typical member than for a judgment about an atypical member (Rosch, 1975; more about this priming effect later). Furthermore, members that are judged typical of a category tend to share more common features than those that are judged atypical. Typical members also tend to share fewer features with members of other categories (Rosch, 1978; Rosch & Mervis, 1975).

Far from finding evidence that category members are equal in the traditional concept formation sense, Rosch's extensive program of research revealed repeatedly that natural concepts and categories have an internal structure. Category members vary in their typicality, in how well they represent or belong to categories. Furthermore, real-world features do not occur independently of one another. Instead, they come in correlated bundles: The things in the real world that have wings often have beaks too. We structure our mental representations of such categories in terms of these correlated features, with typical instances of the category stored centrally, at the core of the concept's meaning, and with atypical instances stored more peripherally. These factors, correlated features and typicality, play a major role in the organization of semantic memory (McRae, de Sa, & Seidenberg, 1997).

Prototypes The term Rosch proposed for *the central, core instance of a category* is ***prototype:*** A "really red red" is a prototypical red, a "doggy dog" (1975, p. 198) is a prototypical dog. Rosch advanced the argument that our mental categories are represented in terms of a prototype, with typical members stored close to the prototype and peripheral members stored farther away. When asked to think of a dog, for example, you generally think of your prototype; few of us would immediately think of a chihuahua, but instead would think of a German shepherd, a golden retriever, or some other more "doggy dog." When you looked up *bird* in your dictionary, did it have a picture of a rather ordinary-looking, typical, yet nondescript bird next to the definition and the same sort of generic picture of a flower? Such neutral, nondistinctive pictures capture closely the idea of a prototype, the central, organizing representation in natural categories.

Besides the studies you read about earlier, what other kind of evidence is there that typicality and prototypes are important issues in the representation of word and category meanings? One of the cleverest studies on typicality was reported by Rips (1975). In his experiment, subjects read a story about an island inhabited by only eight species of animals: sparrows, robins, eagles, hawks, ducks, geese, ostriches, and bats. One group of subjects read that a highly contagious disease had been discovered among all the sparrows; another group read that the robins had the disease, another that eagles were affected, and so on. Subjects were then asked to estimate the percentages of the other animals that would also contract the disease.

The subjects' estimates yielded strong evidence of a typicality or prototype effect. Species that are rated as quite typical or close to the prototype, such as sparrows, were judged very likely to infect almost all the other species. Atypical instances, such as, geese, were judged likely to infect only other atypical members—ducks, for instance—and this to a much lesser degree. The underlying issue was typicality, the representativeness of species within the overall category. Subjects assumed that if a typical instance had an important property, then that was sufficient to predict that all instances, typical and atypical, would share the property as well. If the property was true only of an atypical instance, however, subjects tended to doubt that the property would be shared throughout the category.

Internal Structure and the Power of Categorization

The generalization you should remember from Rosch's research is that categories and concepts in semantic memory are internally structured by semantic relatedness. Categories give us a way to classify objects in our environment, and thereby predict what the objects do, what properties they possess, and how they may be equated under certain circumstances but not under others. We have central, core meanings for each category and concept, and these can be represented as prototypes. Other instances of the concept are arrayed around the prototype, in a semantic distance sense, and can be thought of in terms of their similarities and dissimilarities to the prototype. Bruner, Goodnow, and Austin (1956, p. 12), writing at the very beginning of modern cognitive psychology, claimed that "categorization is the *means by which the objects of the world about us are identified.*" In addition, the process of categorization, relying on existing general world knowledge, is guided or even determined by semantic relatedness and category structure.

There is still much debate on the principles underlying classification and categorization (e.g., Smith & Minda, 2000). One point of view is that feature similarity between concepts provides the foundation for categorization (Tversky, 1977). In such views, robins and sparrows are categorized or classified as birds because of their similarity, where similarity often is defined in the same way as in the Smith et al. (1974a, b) model: in terms of feature overlap. A particularly attractive aspect of basing categorization on such a simple principle is just that—its simplicity. And there is certainly some evidence that semantic similarity is an important component of semantic relatedness (McRae & Boisvert, 1998) and that it can account for a variety of effects, including priming (Thompson-Schill, Kurtz, & Gabrieli, 1998). On the other hand, several authors have challenged, modified, or even rejected this approach, based on theoretical and empirical work (e.g., Medin, Goldstone, & Gentner, 1993; Murphy & Medin, 1985; Rips, 1989; Rips & Collins, 1993). For now, it may be enough simply to note that semantic similarity and relatedness have been "asked," as it were, to provide explanations in settings as simple as verifying "An *S* is a *P*" statements all the way up to tasks that entail slow reasoning, decision making, and problem solving (Ross & Murphy, 1999; Yamauchi & Markman, 2000). In other words, it would not be surprising to find out that similarity by itself predicts priming effects, especially very rapid, automatic priming, but that a variety of other complicating factors enter the picture when slow, deliberate reasoning is involved.

■ Section Summary

- Rosch challenged traditional notions of concept formation by demonstrating that real-world concepts and categories involve fuzzy boundaries; some members of categories are judged as more typical than others. Typical members are said to resemble the prototype of the category. Interestingly, typical members show greater effects of priming than do atypical members. Typicality effects, along with property statements and priming, support the generalization known as the semantic relatedness effect, that semantic memory is structured in terms of concepts' semantic relatedness.

Priming in Semantic Memory

Think back a bit to the section on spreading activation. Four important principles are associated with this idea: Activation spreads, the spreading takes time, activation becomes diffused as it spreads further out from the origin, and the activation decays across time. Researchers immediately began testing these ideas, especially as they related to the principle of semantic relatedness. That is, if semantic relatedness is the organizing principle for semantic memory, then relatedness should determine a great deal about the spread of activation through that structure. Researchers wondered exactly how far out into the network activation spreads, and how long lasting the effect of activation would be. Does more activation spread to highly related concepts? Does it decay faster for less related concepts?

Why all this interest in the process of spreading activation, the mental **priming** of concepts? The reason is straightforward: Priming may be the most fundamental process of retrieval from semantic memory. It has become one of the most frequently tested—and argued about (e.g., McNamara, 1992; Ratcliff & McKoon, 1988)—effects in the study of long-term memory, with dozens of articles appearing yearly. It is absolutely key to an understanding of semantic processing; we return to it repeatedly throughout the entire book, so you need to understand priming, how it affects basic semantic memory processing, and how it has been studied.

Nuts and Bolts of Priming Tasks

In Chapter 2, priming was defined as the activation of words and their meanings. It was part of the automatic process of word access observed in the Stroop task, discussed in Chapter 4 (retrieval cue: name the color of the ink, not the color word itself). But the definition was not limited to just words: Priming can activate concepts and ideas that express the joint meaning of several concepts together. And by the end of this section, we will argue that the effects of context are essentially the same as the effects of priming.

Let's introduce some precise vocabulary for the priming task to facilitate the explanation that follows; Figure 7-10 gives an illustration, and Table 7-2 gives an explanation. To begin with, we have the **prime,** which is *any stimulus that is presented first,* to see whether it influences some later process. The term is also used as a verb, as when we say that a stimulus *primes* some later information. Next is the **target,** *the stimulus that follows the prime;* the target *is* that later information. It is the presumed destination of the activation or priming process, the concept we believe may be affected by the prime. So primes precede the targets, and targets are primed (i.e., are influenced by the primes).

When this influence is beneficial, for instance when the target is easier or faster to process because it was primed, this *positive influence on processing* is called **facilitation;** some-

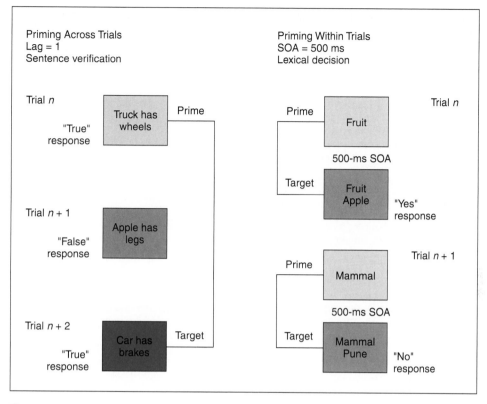

Figure 7-10

A depiction of two types of priming tasks.

times we simply call this **benefits.** Facilitation is almost always a shortening of RTs compared with performance in a baseline condition. Occasionally, the influence is negative, as when a prime is unrelated to the target, and therefore is misleading or irrelevant. When the prime slows down RT performance to the target, the *negative influence on processing* is called **inhibition;** in this case, we also say that there were **costs** associated with the prime.

Priming Across Trials Finally, because we are interested in how long activation takes to dissipate, we often need to keep track of the period of time between the prime and the target. In some studies, this period of time is filled with other stimuli or trials. In this case, the **lag** between prime and target, usually the *number of intervening stimuli*, is our index of the separation between prime and target. For example, *lag 2* would simply mean that two trials came between the prime and the target.

Priming Within Trials In other kinds of priming studies, the prime and target are presented within the same trial. In these studies, you are usually given the prime ahead of time, a hint or warning before the target is shown. The time interval between the prime and the target is especially important here because it is important to keep track of how long you had

Table 7-2 PRIMING TASKS
Essential Terminology
Prime: The stimulus or part of the stimulus expected to have some effect; the prime can either be related to the target (e.g. "bird–robin"), unrelated to the target (e.g., "bird–truck"), or neutral (e.g., "XXXXX–carrot.") *Target:* The stimulus or part of the stimulus expected to be affected by the prime. *Lag:* The spacing between the prime and target in an across-trials priming task; for example, lag 2 means two trials came between the prime and target. *SOA:* Stimulus onset asynchrony, the time interval between the prime and the target in a within-trial priming task, usually measured in milliseconds.
Priming Across Trials
Almost any generalized recognition task (see Table 7-1) can be adapted to a priming task.   Trials are arranged so that the prime trial and the target trial are separated by a fixed number of unrelated trials, for example, at lag 0, or at lag 2. Care must be taken so that an equal number of related targets are true and false so subjects will not respond "yes" merely on the basis of trial-to-trial relatedness.
Priming Within Trials

Most studies of priming within trials use a lexical decision task or another format in which the complete stimulus can be separated into two parts (e.g., Kounios and Holcomb, 1992, presented sentences such as "Some gems are rubies" in two parts: "Some gems are" as the prime and "rubies" as the target).
    Each trial has both a prime and a target. The prime is presented briefly and is followed by the target after some interval of time (SOA).
    Three types of primes—related, unrelated, and neutral—usually are presented at all SOAs. In some studies, the prime is followed by a blank or unfilled (short) interval, and in some the prime is masked before the target is shown.
    For both types of priming tasks, we have the following:
Dependent variables: The dependent variable generally is reaction time, assuming that the error rates for the different conditions are approximately equal. If accuracy is the major dependent variable, then the *hit rate* and the *false alarm rate* are of particular interest. The hit rate is the percentage of true trials responded to correctly (saying "yes" to "yes trials") and the false alarm rate is the percentage of false trials responded to incorrectly (saying "yes" to "no trials").
Independent variables: Aside from using different SOA intervals, the major independent variables are always the types and degrees of relationships between primes and targets. For instance, the prime could be a category name, and the targets would be either high or low typical members of the category; the prime could be a sentence, and the targets would be either high or low semantic associates of the final word in the sentence.

the warning. The time interval is called the **stimulus onset asynchrony (SOA).** If you consider the prime and target to be the two halves of a complete stimulus, then the onset or beginning of the two halves occurs asynchronously, at different times. Thus, we might present a prime and then 500 msec later present the target. This would correspond to an SOA interval of 500 msec. So the **SOA** is *the length of time between the onset of the prime and the onset of the target.*

Empirical Demonstrations of Priming

Let's consider a pair of experiments on word naming, an early report by Freedman and Loftus (1971) and one by Loftus and Loftus (1974) that built on the earlier result. Both were studies of priming within semantic memory.

Freedman and Loftus (1971) were interested in the process of word naming and retrieval and how that process was affected by priming. They asked their participants to name a member of a category that either began with a certain letter or was described by a certain adjective; for example, "name a fruit beginning with *P*," or "name a red flower." On half of the trials, participants saw either the letter or the adjective as a prime and then the category name as the target. In the other half of the trials, the reverse order was used: The category name was the prime, and the letter or adjective was the target.

Freedman and Loftus found clear evidence that the category name is an effective prime. In their data, performance was significantly faster for trials such as "fruit–*P*" than trials when the letter or adjective served as the prime ("*P*– fruit" or "red–fruit"). This suggested that the category name activated its semantic representation and that this activation then spread to the members of the category. When the letter or adjective was presented, a relevant member of the category such as *plum* or *apple* had already been primed, so it was faster to retrieve from semantic memory. Conversely, letter or adjective primes had very little effect, which is another way of saying that there is no category in semantic memory corresponding to "words beginning with *P*" or "red things."

A Demonstration of Priming Across and Within Trials Loftus and Loftus (1974) used this word naming task again, but with two twists. Often during the experiment, a trial such as "fruit–*P*" was followed by another "fruit" trial; the first was the prime, and the second was the target. (Note the double priming manipulation here. Not only was one trial the prime for a target trial, but within each trial there was also a prime and a target, as in "fruit–*P*," just as in the earlier experiment.) Sometimes the target trial followed immediately, at a lag of 0, and sometimes at a lag of 2, when two unrelated trials intervened. The results are shown in Figure 7-11A.

Notice three things about the results. First, seeing the category name as a prime (seeing it first) always yielded faster performance than seeing letter primes: the RT for the line with the open circles is at least 100 msec lower at every point. This is exactly what Freedman and Loftus found. Second, the RTs lag 0 are much shorter than the RTs for the initial prime trial. In other words, seeing two "fruit" trials in a row reduced the necessary processing time for the second one by at least 300 msec. *That* is priming across trials. And third, notice that the priming effect at lag 2 is not as strong as the effect at lag 0; performance was still faster than baseline, but not as fast as in the immediate priming condition. In other words, the priming from the initial trial had dissipated or decayed somewhat at lag 2; there was still a benefit, but it was not as strong.

The second twist in the Loftus and Loftus study is shown in Figure 7-11B priming within trials was also examined when the prime and target were separated in time. This part of the experiment was nearly the same as the first part, except that the prime (the category name or letter) appeared by itself for 2.5 s on every trial and was then followed by the target. This was a manipulation of SOA, the time between the two parts of a stimulus. So Figure 7-11A shows what happened with simultaneous presentation, and Figure 7-11B displays the results with a 2.5-s SOA.

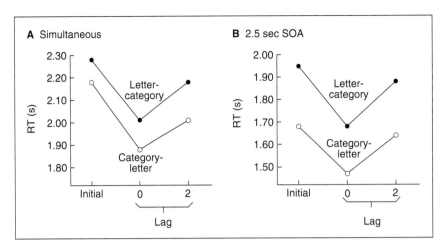

Figure 7-11

Reaction time is shown for simultaneous presentation of the prime and target **A**, and an SOA of 2.5, **B**. In both panels, the curves show RT to the prime ("initial") and the targets at lags 0 and 2. From Loftus and Loftus (1974).

What does Figure 7-11B tell us? All of the curves there are lower than the equivalent curves in Figure 7-11B. In other words, when participants saw the prime for 2.5 s, they could name a word that fit the letter restriction of the target more rapidly than when prime and target were simultaneous. There was more priming, a greater spread of activation, with the additional time; with more time, more members of the primed category became activated. This is exactly what the network model predicted about the spread of activation across time. Just as interesting, the priming also seemed to have decayed or dissipated across intervening trials because lag 2 responses were slower than lag 1 responses.

Priming in Other Tasks

Similar outcomes have been reported in many other tasks. For example, priming across trials has been reported using the sentence verification task (Ashcraft, 1976). A sentence such as "A sparrow has feathers" facilitated another sentence about the same category, such as, "A robin can fly," but only if the target sentence concerned an important property.

Similarly, Rosch (1975) found significant priming within semantic categories, especially if the targets were typical members of the category. She used a matching task in which pairs of words are presented and participants must say "yes" if both words belong to the same category. The primes for these word pairs were either the name of the category or, for the neutral prime condition, the word *blank*. With a 2-s SOA, word pairs that had been primed with the correct category name were significantly faster than those primed with *blank*. Of particular interest were the results for the other variable Rosch investigated: typicality. She found that priming was especially strong when the

Table 7-3 PRIMING IN THE LEXICAL DECISION TASK

			Type of Stimulus Pair		
Top String	Bottom String	Correct Response	Sample Stimuli	Mean RT (ms)	Mean Percentage Errors
Word	Associated word	Yes	Nurse–doctor	855	6.3
Word	Unassociated word	Yes	Bread–doctor	940	8.7
Word	Nonword	No	Book–marb	1,087	27.6
Nonword	Word	No	Valt–butter	904	7.8
Nonword	Nonword	No	Cabe–manty	884	2.6

Source: From Meyer and Schvaneveldt (1971).

words were typical members of the category (e.g., "BIRD; robin, sparrow"). Priming of atypical members was significant but not nearly as strong.

Priming and the Lexical Decision Task   As you read in Chapter 2, a workhorse task in cognitive science is the **lexical decision task,** in which subjects *judge whether a string of letters is a word,* (remember MOTOR and MANTY?); customarily, RT is the primary index of performance. The name of the task comes from the word *lexicon,* meaning a dictionary or a list of words. So in a sense, the lexical decision task asks you whether the string of letters is a genuine entry in your mental lexicon, your mental dictionary.

A huge range of topics has been investigated with the lexical decision task, including the priming and semantic relatedness effects we are interested in now. The task has also shown the intimate and unavoidable relationship between our semantic concepts and the words we use to name them—in other words, the relationship between the semantic and the lexical entries in memory.

The groundbreaking work on this task was reported by Meyer and Schvaneveldt (1971; also Meyer, Schvaneveldt, & Ruddy, 1975). These investigators presented two letter strings at a time and told their participants to respond "yes" only if both were words. In addition to trials with unrelated words such as "TRUCK PAPER," they included trials with related words ("yes" trials were matched with an equal number of "no" trials, on which at least one of the letter strings was not a word; e.g., "CHAIR ZOOPLE").

The related condition yielded the most dramatic result in this study. Two related words such as "BREAD BUTTER" are judged more quickly as words than two unrelated words such as "NURSE BUTTER." Table 7-3 displays Meyer and Schvaneveldt's results and shows this priming effect clearly. Related words were judged in 855 msec, compared to 940 msec for unassociated words.

One particularly interesting aspect of these results—in fact, of all results with the lexical decision task—is the following. It is not logically necessary for participants to access the meanings of words in the lexical decision task. Technically, they need only "look up" the words in the mental lexicon to determine whether the word is there. Yet the results repeatedly show the influence of the meanings of the words: It is the *meaningful* connection

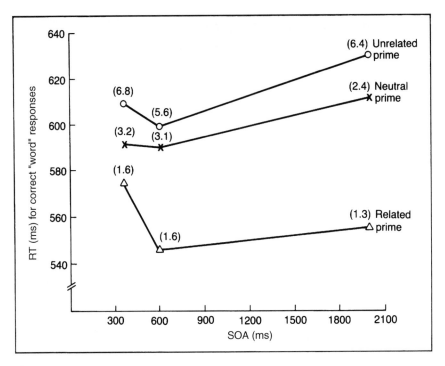

Figure 7-12

Reaction time to lexical decision targets is shown across SOA intervals for unrelated, neutral, and related prime conditions. The numbers in parentheses are the error rates in each condition. From Neely (1976).

between "BREAD" and "BUTTER" that facilitates this decision, rather than some lexical connection (you might think because both begin with *B* that there is a lexical basis for the facilitation, but the same benefits are found with word pairs that are dissimilar in spelling, such as "NURSE DOCTOR"). It seems as if we cannot look up the lexical entry for a word without also accessing the word's meaning.

Priming Is Automatic

Interestingly, this facilitation appears to be automatic; that is, it happens extremely rapidly, and with no deliberate intention on your part. In fact, it is exactly the same effect that Stroop (1935) found with his color words (see Chapter 4). When you see a word, you access the word's meaning automatically, even though you are not required to by the task.

Here's an example. Neely (1976, 1977; Neely, Keefe, & Ross, 1989) selected word pairs so that one of the members was the primary associate to the other at least 40% of the time (based on free association norms). These related pairs were contrasted with unrelated word pairs, and also with a condition in which the neutral letter *X* was paired with a word. For all trials in the experiment, subjects had to judge whether the target

Table 7-4 CONDITIONS AND STIMULI FOR NEELY'S (1977) STUDY

Condition	Sample stimulus[a]
No Category Shift Expected	
No shift	BIRD–robin
Shift	BIRD–arm
Category Shift Expected from "Building" to "Body Part"; from "Body" to "Part of a Building"	
No shift	BODY–heart, BUILDING–window
Shift to expected category	BODY–door, BUILDING–leg
Shift to unexpected category	BODY–sparrow

[a]Prime is in capital letters.

string, the second member of each pair, was an English word (the standard lexical decision task). As Figure 7-12 shows, the processes involved in making these lexical decisions were greatly facilitated when the prime was a related, associated word. Benefits of priming grew from 17 msec at the shortest SOA to 56 msec with a 2,000-msec (2 s) SOA. And inhibition was observed for the unrelated word pairs; there was a nearly constant 16-msec cost of receiving an unrelated word as a prime.

But how do we know this priming is automatic? In a more thorough examination of priming, Neely (1977) tested not only the effects of semantic relatedness on performance in the lexical decision task but also the effects of SOA. The thinking here is that expecting to see a related word probably reflects a very conscious process, one that takes place slowly. But responding more quickly to a related word when you have had very little time to prepare or develop an expectancy should be evidence of automatic priming, literally automatic spread of activation.

Neely (1977) tested these ideas with a lexical decision task. On each trial, participants saw a letter string and had to make a standard lexical decision. Each letter string was preceded by a prime, either a related word, an unrelated word, or a neutral prime, the baseline condition. Table 7-4 summarizes the experiment and shows sample stimuli. Because the results are a bit complicated, we'll take them in stages.

First, Neely found standard semantic priming in his experiment. For prime–target trials such as "BIRD–robin," there was significant facilitation, as shown in the left panel of Figure 7-13 (notice that any point above the dashed baseline at 0 msec indicates facilitation, and any point below baseline indicates inhibition). Because he found this speed up even at very short SOAs, the conclusion is that normal semantic priming is automatic: The spread of activation happens very rapidly. Notice also that this curve showed more facilitation as the SOA got longer. This suggests that with more and more time to prepare for the letter string, priming grew stronger because of the additional effect of conscious factors.

Second, he found significant inhibition, a slowing down of RT, when the prime was unrelated to the target. If you had seen "BIRD" as a prime, you were then slower than

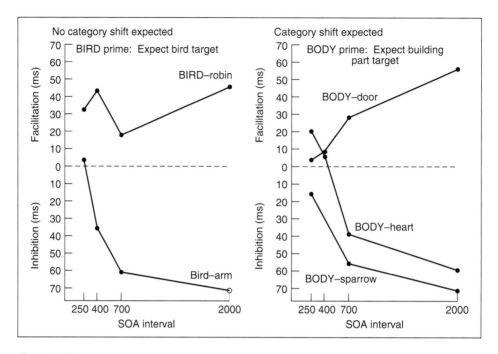

Figure 7-13

Reaction time to lexical decision targets. In the left half, subjects saw a prime and did not expect a shift in category; sample stimuli are "BIRD–ROBIN" for a relevant prime and "BIRD–ARM" for an irrelevant prime. In the right half, subjects expected the target to come from the building category if they saw "BODY" as a prime and from the body part category if they saw "BUILDING" as a prime. When the shift in category occurred as expected, RT was facilitated at longer SOAs. When the expected shift did not occur, there was facilitation at the short SOA when the prime was relevant ("BODY–HEART"). Inhibition occurred when the shift was completely unexpected ("BODY–SPARROW"). From Neely (1977).

baseline to decide that *arm* was a word. Not surprisingly, this inhibition effect grew stronger across longer and longer SOAs: Again, the conscious preparation for a member of the *bird* category worked against you when you saw *arm* as the target.

The truly impressive (and complicated) part of Neely's study comes next. He told his participants that when they saw one particular prime, such as the category name "BODY," they should expect to see a target from a different category, such as a part of a building (e.g., *door*). Likewise, they were told that if they saw "BUILDING" as a prime, they expect to see a body part such as *arm* as the target. In other words, participants were essentially told "Expect a switch to a *different* category when we show you these particular primes."

What happened with these expectations? When the switch from one category ("BODY") to a different one (*door*) really happened, there was significant priming only at the long SOAs, as shown in the top curve on the right of Figure 7-13. This makes perfectly good sense; you see "BODY," and it takes you a bit of time to remember that you should see an item from the building category next. When you are given that bit of time, you are ready for *door, window,* and so forth. But notice in the figure that at the shortest SOA, there was no facilitation on this kind of trial: "BODY–door" was no faster than baseline. Clearly, at short SOAs there was not enough time to prepare for the category shift.

Finally, what about that small percentage of trials when the category switch did not occur; that is, when you saw "BODY" but then saw *arm* or *heart* as the target? The clever thing about this condition, of course, is that it should tap into normal semantic priming because *arm* and *heart* are in the "BODY" category. This was exactly what Neely found, but only at short SOAs. When longer preparation time was given, with longer SOAs, participants could and did prepare for the category switch. Then, when the switch *didn't* happen, they were slowed down, as shown in the bottom curve of the right panel in the figure.

Priming Is an Implicit Process

Accessing a word's meaning is automatic (e.g., Friedrich, Henik, & Tzelgov, 1991). Can it occur even without conscious awareness of having seen the word? Marcel (1980, 1983) reported an impressive set of results that seems to answer "yes" to this question. Marcel examined word recognition in a lexical decision task with priming. He presented the primes in a different way than was typical, however: The prime was immediately followed by a scrambled visual pattern, a visual mask. The purpose of this was to present the masking pattern so soon after the prime that subjects were not consciously aware of the prime word at all, a form of backward masking (remember the circle marker study on visual sensory memory in Chapter 3?).

The task worked. Subjects claimed they had not seen a prime at all: There was no conscious awareness of the prime. Yet relevant primes such as "CHILD" facilitated lexical decisions about words such as *infant.* Although some controversy grew up around these results (see also Carr & Dagenbach, 1986; Carr et al., 1982; Merikle, 1982), recent work indicates that the effect is genuine and important (Hirshman & Durante, 1992; McRae & Boisvert, 1998). Semantic priming, in the lexical decision task and other settings, can indeed occur automatically, without identification of the prime and without conscious awareness. In terminology introduced at the beginning of Chapter 6, we also refer to such effects as implicit, processes that can occur without any necessary involvement of conscious awareness.

For now, think of priming as a two-component process. As you have been reading, a significant degree of priming is obtained under very rapid conditions (e.g., SOAs less than 250 msec). Such a rapid effect suggests strongly that priming can operate automatically, without the need for conscious awareness or recollection. Participants in Neely's (1977) experiment showed this kind of automatic priming effect when they saw normal, straightforward primes and targets, such as "BIRD–robin," at very rapid SOAs. This is the essence of implicit memory.

Explicit memory, on the other hand, refers to intentional, deliberate, and conscious mental processing, including recollection and awareness (Schacter, 1989). In

Neely's (1977) "expect a switch" conditions, it took some extra amount of time for participants to switch from "BUILDING" to the conscious expectation of *body part*. But once they did, there was also a priming effect, this caused by more conscious processing. Because they had to deliberately remember to switch, this was an explicit memory priming effect.

We are still figuring out how all the pieces fit together in this distinction between implicit and explicit memory, exploring which aspects of performance can be attributed to implicit processes. There has been some concern over the measurement of implicit processes and experimental and statistical ways of separating implicit and explicit processes (Buchner & Wippich, 2000; Cowan & Stadler, 1996; Jacoby, Toth, & Yonelinas, 1993; Palmeri & Flanery, 1999). But even now, there seems to be agreement that priming has a clear implicit basis and that implicit and explicit memories are separate entities. Indeed, there can be (implicit) priming effects even in cases when the participants have lost the (explicit) ability to recall information consciously (i.e., in cases of amnesia).

■ Section Summary

- In the priming task, a prime of some degree of relationship to a target is presented first, and then RT to the target is measured. When the prime is relevant, RT to the target usually is speeded up, even at very short time intervals (SOAs). This is generally taken as evidence that semantic priming is an automatic process. When the prime is irrelevant to the target, RT is generally slowed down at longer SOAs. This is usually interpreted as evidence that irrelevant primes generate a conscious expectation that slows down processing when the expectation is misleading. Among the tasks used to examine priming in semantic memory are word naming, sentence verification, and lexical decision tasks. Evidence also suggests that priming is an implicit memory process.

Context, Connectionism, and the Brain

As mentioned earlier, the original Collins and Quillian (1972) model needed a few revisions to account for results that accumulated shortly after its publication. But interestingly, no major revision was ever attempted for the Smith et al. (1974a,b) model. The reason was clear in retrospect: Nothing in the Smith model, no mechanism or process, seemed able to account for the all-important effect of priming. In essence, the major contender to the network approach seemed to drop out of the running. This is not to say that the feature-based approach to semantic concepts was also abandoned. In fact, the feature and network approaches can be complementary (Hollan 1975), and both are integral to the connectionist models you will read about in a moment.

Shortly after the initial semantic memory model debate, investigators in the mid- to late 1970s began to examine much more complex semantic relationships and representations than the simple semantic categories you have been reading about. Research began on the comprehension of complex sentences and paragraphs, connected text, and spoken conversations. People became interested in large-scale semantic representations that involved distinctly episodic as well as semantic knowledge. The unspoken consensus in most of this work was that network approaches, especially when coupled with the process of priming, provided a convenient, flexible, and powerful way of attacking these psychological processes (see Anderson, 1983; Anderson & Lebiere, 1998; Gentner, 1975; Gross, Fischer, & Miller, 1989). In a sense, networks and priming had proved their usefulness in understanding the basics of semantic memory, so they were expanded into more complex areas. We turn now to a prime example of this, a discussion of context and connectionism.

Context

Webster's New Universal Dictionary defines *context* as (1) the parts of a sentence, paragraph, discourse, etc. immediately next to or surrounding a specified word or passage and determining its exact meaning; (2) the whole situation, background, or environment relevant to a particular event, personality, creation, etc.

Ambiguity and Priming Let's consider two examples. What does the word *count* mean? Well, you can't really say, can you, because it's **ambiguous,** it *has more than one meaning.* Maybe putting the word in a sentence will help: "We had trouble keeping track of the count." Most of us would agree that the sentence does not help much; you still can't tell which meaning of the word is intended.

What's missing here is context, some conceptual framework to guide you to an interpretation of the ambiguous word. With an adequate context, you can determine which sense of the word *count* is intended in these two different contexts:

My dog wasn't included in the final count.

The vampire was disguised as a handsome count.

These sentences, taken from Simpson's (1981, 1984) work on ambiguity (you read about this briefly in Chapter 2), point out the importance of context: With adequate context, one that helps you determine the intended meaning, the correct word meaning can be retrieved from memory, even when the word is ambiguous in isolation. In fact, Simpson found that with neutral contexts, such as the "We had trouble" sentence, word meanings are activated as a simple function of their commonness: The number sense of *count* is more common, so that meaning becomes activated to a greater degree. But a context sentence that biases the interpretation one way or the other results in much stronger activation for the biased meaning: With *vampire* you activated the meaning of *count* related to royalty and Count Dracula (see also Balota & Paul, 1996; Paul, Kellas, Martin, & Clark, 1992; Piercey & Joordens, 2000; Smith, Besner, & Miyoshi, 1994).

Think about this again; the context sentence led to activation of one or the other meaning of the ambiguous word. Isn't that *exactly* what happens when you see a prime? Does the prime "BIRD" activate typical members of that category in semantic memory, allowing faster retrieval of *robin* and *sparrow*? Yes, the effect of context seems to be precisely the effect of priming that you have been reading about.

Context and ERPs Let's consider a second example, an offshoot of the Kounios and Holcomb work with ERPs that you read about earlier. In a recent article, Holcomb, Kounios, Anderson, and West (1999) recorded ERPs in a simple sentence comprehension task. Subjects saw sentences one word at a time and were asked merely to respond after seeing the last word in the sentence, saying "yes" if the sentence made sense and "no" if it did not. The stimulus sentences varied along two dimensions; whether the last word in the sentence was concrete or abstract and whether it was congruent with the sentence meaning or anomalous (i.e., made no sense). As an example, "Armed robbery implies that the thief used a weapon" was a concrete–congruent sentence; substituting *rose* for *weapon* made it a concrete but anomalous sentence. Likewise, "Lisa argued that this had not been the case in one single instance" was abstract–congruent sentence, and substituting *fun* for *instance* made it an abstract-anomalous sentence.

Figure 7-14 shows some of the ERP patterns Holcomb et al. obtained in this experiment. In the left panel, you see the "normal" ERP patterns, that is, patterns recorded for congruent, sensible sentences; the three profiles, from top to bottom, came from the three midline electrode sites shown in the schematic drawing (frontal, central, and parietal). In the right panel are the ERP patterns when the sentences ended in an anomalous word.

Notice first in the left panel that the solid and dotted functions, for concrete and abstract sentences, tracked each other very closely: Whatever neural mechanisms operated during comprehension, they generated very similar ERP patterns. But now make a left-to-right comparison of the patterns, seeing the differences in the right panel when the sentences ended in a nonsensical, anomalous word (*rose* in the armed robbery sentence, for example). Here there were marked changes in the ERP profiles. At the central location, for example, there was a steadily downward trend (in the positive direction, in terms of electrical potentials) for sensible sentences but a dramatic reversal of direction for anomalous words. In short, the neural mechanisms involved in comprehension generated dramatically different patterns when an anomalous word was encountered. The mismatch between the context, the already-processed meaning of the sentence, and the final word yielded not only an overt response from the subjects (the response indicating "no, that sentence makes no sense") but also a neural response, signifying the brain-related activity that detected the anomalous ending of the sentence. (Don't get confused about directions here. The functions underneath the gridline are electrically positive, so deflection upward in these graphs is a deflection toward the negative, a deflection going in a negative direction; this is what the *N* in *N400* signifies, a "negative going" pattern.)

In a very real sense, the context of the sentence primes concepts, activates words and concepts that fit into the sentence; for armed robbery, you would expect *weapon*, *gun*, or some similar word. Putting it another way, the topic enables you to prime relevant knowledge in semantic memory and thus guides your comprehension and enhances your memory. What we are concluding here is that context effects serve the same function as priming, activating relevant knowledge, facilitating performance. In a real sense, context is priming.

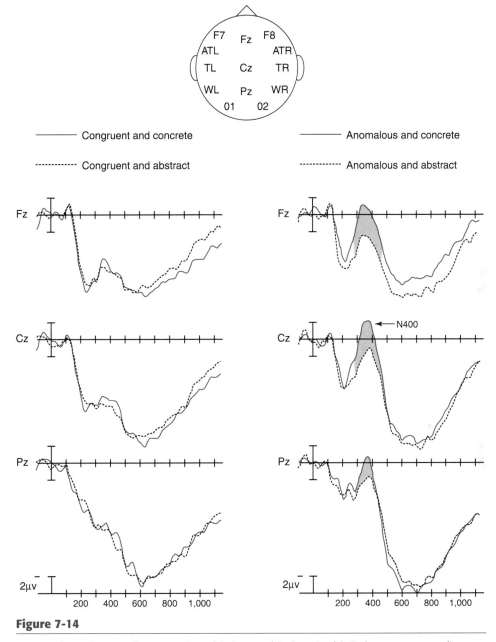

Figure 7-14

ERP profiles at three midline sites (frontal [F_z], central [C_z], parietal [P_z]) for sentences ending with a congruent (left panel) or contextually anomalous (right panel) word. Adapted from Figures 3 and 4 in Holcomb et al. (1999).

Connectionism

A way to model the effect of priming in a semantic network is to use the modern computer-based approach to theorizing in cognitive science. This approach is **connectionism,** a framework in which interconnected nodes in a network, pathways, and priming can be studied. You have had small doses of this approach already, for example when we considered word recognition in Chapter 3. Recall that the computer system was trying to recognize the word "WORK" but that the final *K* was obscured. Because of connections between letter-level and word-level nodes, the system ended up identifying the word correctly.

At the most fundamental level, **connectionist models** (also known as **PDP models** and **neural net models**) contain a massive network of interconnected nodes. The nodes can represent almost any kind of information, from the simple line segments and patterns considered for letter recognition to the more complex features and characteristics we have discussed here, such as "has wings," "red breast," and "can fly." Indeed, what makes connectionist models attractive is that, in principle, any type of knowledge can be represented by the nodes and their weighted, interconnecting pathways.

Examine Figure 7-15, a sample connectionist network for part of the "FURNITURE" category (Martindale, 1991). First, you will notice that each concept node is connected to other nodes by pathways, just as in all network models. The difference here is that each pathway has a number next to it, the path weights or weightings mentioned earlier. The weightings are the indicators of how strongly or weakly connected two nodes are; generally, the weighting scale goes from -1.0 to $+1.0$, with positive numbers indicating pathways that facilitate and negative numbers indicating inhibition. So, for example, the weighting between "FURNITURE" and "CHAIR" is $+0.8$, indicating that "CHAIR" is an important, central member of the category; "ASHTRAY," however, with its $+0.1$, is very weakly associated with "FURNITURE."

If we present the category name "FURNITURE" to the model, heavily weighted members such as "CHAIR" and "SOFA" are highly activated, and the system can thus make decisions about them quite rapidly. This is exactly like the priming experiments you've read about: "FURNITURE" would prime "CHAIR." But "RUG" might actually be slower than baseline if primed by "FURNITURE." To understand this, note first that the weighted connection from "FURNITURE" to "RUG" is quite weak. Second, because "FURNITURE" primes "CHAIR" and "SOFA" a great deal, these nodes tend to inhibit, tend to spread negative activation, to "RUG"; see the weight of -0.8 between "CHAIR" and "RUG." (When neighbors at the same level inhibit one another, this is called lateral inhibition.)

Recently, much effort has gone into building connectionist models of various cognitive structures and processes in letter identification (McClelland & Rumelhart, 1981) and word recognition (Seidenberg & McClelland, 1989). And in the area of semantic memory, there is a model of semantic priming (Masson, 1995), and a connectionist model of word meaning (McRae et al., 1997).

As Masson's discussion makes clear, the glimpse at connectionism here is rather simplified. In many respects, connectionist models make different assumptions—

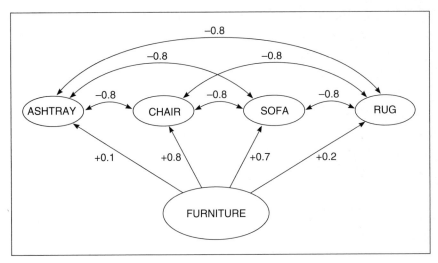

Figure 7-15

A small portion of a connectionist network. Note that the nodes at the same level exert an inhibitory influence on each other and receive different amounts of facilitation from the category name. Adapted from Martindale (1991).

though similar predictions—from those of more typical spreading activation models. For instance, activating a node in a network model means activating that particular point in the network, followed by a spread of the activation to surrounding nodes. In a connectionist model (or, more precisely for Masson's approach, a distributed memory model), however, a concept is defined as a pattern of activation across units in the network. In this model, priming is explained by the similarity of activation patterns between a prime and a target: The "FURNITURE" concept has an overwhelmingly similar pattern of activation to the pattern for "CHAIR," so the one serves as an effective prime for the other.

Connectionism and the Brain

What is exciting about connectionist models, despite their differences (and despite the debate about their usefulness; e.g., Massaro, 1988; McCloskey, 1991; Seidenberg, 1993), is that the approach gives us a tool for understanding the richness of cognition, a working "machine" in a sense that lets us see what happens when multiple layers of knowledge influence even the simplest acts of cognition.

Particularly compelling (Seidenberg, 1993) are four frequently mentioned advantages of using connectionism to model cognitive processes. First, connectionist models are structurally similar to the network of neurons in the brain. That is, the brain is a massive set of interconnected neurons, just as a connectionist network is a massive set of interconnected units. Second, the individual units in connectionism are similar to those in the brain. That is, in the nervous system, a neuron either fires or it does not, and when it does fire, it affects the neurons it synapses on. This yes/no, binary aspect of neural firing is exactly parallel to the fire/no fire nature of connectionist units. Third, the positive and negative weights between units in connectionist models mimic the action of excitatory and inhibitory neural synapses. Fourth, the best description of the activity of a connectionist model is that it is massively parallel: Multiple processes, including spreads of activation and inhibition, are co-occurring in a connectionist model at various levels, much as there is overwhelming evidence of parallel processing in the brain (McClelland, Rumelhart, & Hinton, 1986; Rumelhart, 1989).

Let's take a final look at this richness of cognition, from the perspective of brain damage. You read in Chapter 6 how one possible result of brain damage is amnesia: losing memories acquired before the damage, or losing the ability to acquire new information after the damage. Did you notice in that chapter that the patients' memory losses were for episodic information? Even in cases of profound amnesia, there was no loss of semantic knowledge. Patients H.M. and K.C., for example, were still able to understand and produce meaningful language; in fact, K.C. was adept at "faking" episodic memories by relying on his semantic memory, by knowing rather than remembering (e.g., that his brother's funeral was sad; Tulving, 1989).

Lexical Memory and Anomia But there are also brain disorders that affect the semantic system, and especially the part of semantic memory known as **lexical memory,** *the mental lexicon or dictionary where our word knowledge (as distinct from conceptual knowledge) is stored.* One is *a deficit in word finding,* known as **anomia** (or sometimes **anomic aphasia**). At a superficial level, anomia is quite similar to a tip-of-the-tongue (TOT) state in which you are unable to name the word even though you are certain you know it (see Chapter 6). Peering beneath the surface, however, suggests that anomia is unlike the TOT phenomenon. Whereas people in a TOT state generally have partial knowledge about the unrecallable word, such as the number of syllables or the first sound, anomic patients have no such partial knowledge. Instead, the phenomenon appears to be complete and successful retrieval of the semantic concept, followed by inability to find the word that names the concept (Ashcraft, 1993). For example, Kay and Ellis's (1987) anomic patient was unable to name the word *president* but in attempting to find the word blurted out "Government . . . leader . . . John Kennedy was one." Cases such as these suggest strongly that the mental representation of a concept is distinct from the representation of that concept's name, such that the concept itself can be retrieved even though the concept's name may be blocked.

A Connectionist Model of Semantic Memory Impairment A particularly puzzling disorder in semantic memory is called a **category-specific deficit.** This is *a disruption in which the person loses access to one semantic category of words or concepts while not losing others.* Warrington and McCarthy (1983; also Warrington & Shallice, 1984) reported the case histories of four brain-damaged patients who showed this strange dissociation. The patients they described had serious difficulties in identifying living things but little or no difficulty in identifying nonliving things. For instance, patient J.B.R. could identify only

6% of a set of pictures of living things and could define only 8% of the words that named those living things (*parrot, daffodil*). But when shown pictures of nonliving things, J.B.R. was successful at naming 90% of them and could define 79% of the words that named those nonliving things (*tent, briefcase*).

How could semantic memory be splintered to the extent that a person's access to categories of living things would be disrupted while access to nonliving things would be preserved? Or, more to the point, could semantic memory be organized into just these two very broad categories, living and nonliving things? This may be a bit too convenient; we might wonder, "Why living versus nonliving things? Why not concrete versus abstract, high versus low frequency, or some other distinction?"

Warrington and Shallice (1984) suggested a more plausible explanation. Suppose that the bulk of your knowledge about living things is coded in semantic memory in terms of sensory properties: A parrot is a brightly colored animal that makes a distinctive sound. Likewise, suppose that most of what you know about nonliving things involves their functional properties: A briefcase is for carrying around papers and books. Warrington and Shallice suggested that a possible reason for the dissociation in their patients could be a selective loss or blocking of sensory knowledge. If so, that might explain the patients' impairments in naming and defining living things.

Going one step further, Farah and McClelland (1991) decided to build a connectionist model that would evaluate the Warrington and Shallice hypothesis; their work gives us a glimpse at how connectionism and neurocognition can join forces in explaining this kind of memory impairment. In their model, semantic memory contained two basic types of knowledge or features about concepts—visual features (sensory) and functional features—with this knowledge being acquired by verbal or visual input to the semantic system. After constructing and training the model (establishing its memory, in a sense), Farah and McClelland "lesioned" it. That is, they "damaged" the visual units in the semantic memory network by altering the connection weights or disconnecting the visual units from the rest of the network.

The outcome of this procedure was strikingly similar to the patients' dissociations. That is, when the visual units were lesioned, the network showed extremely poor accuracy in associating names and pictures of living things; this is shown in the left panel of Figure 7-16, as is the modest decline in accuracy for the *nonliving thing* category. Conversely, when the network's functional units were lesioned rather than the visual units, it was the *nonliving* category that suffered (right panel, Figure 7-16).

Does this demonstration prove that impairment of patient J.B.R.'s visual semantic knowledge accounts for the dissociation? No, of course not; the model makes the correct prediction, certainly a big point in its favor, but such evidence is never taken as proof that the model is correct. Instead, think of the Farah and McClelland demonstration in this way. Warrington and Shallice asked, in essence, "Is it possible that impairment of sensory knowledge could produce the dissociation between living and nonliving things?" An appropriate answer to this question is: "Yes, it is entirely possible, because just such a dissociation was produced or simulated in a connectionist model." In other words, the connectionist model provides a degree of assurance, probably a large degree,

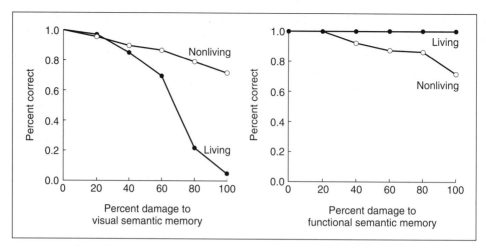

Figure 7-16

Performance of the basic model, as measured by probability of correctly associating names and pictures for living and nonliving things, after different amounts of damage to visual and functional semantic units.

that the Warrington and Shallice hypothesis is reasonable and should be pursued further with both the impaired patients and connectionist modeling.

Shelton & Caramazza (1999) recently reviewed and summarized such case studies and the semantic disruptions that have been documented, and suggest that some refinements must be made to the visual versus functional discrimination suggested by Farah and McClelland. They note the myriad dissociations described in the literature, including those in which patients' spoken output is disrupted despite intact written output (and vice versa) and those in which only some part (say, animals) of the *living things* category is disrupted. They suggest that the visual versus functional distinction may not be powerful enough to capture all the evidence. In an intriguing proposal, they speculate that a plausible distinction in semantic storage might be one between things that are evolutionarily significant, such as food and animals—both from the *living* category—and nonliving things, objects that have functional but not survival importance. Such a dissociation, if it characterized both anatomical and functional organization of memory, could then be the basis for the semantic dissociations observed in patients with brain damage; we would just need to document that one portion of the *living things* category—the evolutionarily important category—had been damaged to account for patients' naming deficits.

We conclude on this theoretical note, that the suggested distinction in Shelton and Caramazza (1999) represents a form of modularity (Fodor, 1983). Modularity is a theoretical perspective in which different abilities, characteristics, types of cognitive processes, and so forth are theorized to be represented in separate components or modules in memory. Modules, in this sense, are autonomous mechanisms, designed biologically to be standalone, independent processors, highly specialized for only one task or process. In important respects, modules are thought to operate much like reflexes do, specialized for one particular kind of process, responsive to one particular kind of stimulus. In terms of evidence you have been studying, it is conceivable that word knowledge—knowledge of which word is the name of a particular concept—might be considered a separate module from knowledge of the concept itself. On the evidence summarized by Shelton and Caramazza (1999), we might postulate a separate module for written output (an orthographic module) and spoken output (a phonological module). You will read about other dissociated processes and abilities later, especially when we consider language in Chapter 9. For now, bear in mind that the answer to the question "How is memory organized?" might be some combination of connectionist-inspired networks and separate, modularity-inspired components, all of which interact smoothly (except in people with brain damage) to support cognition.

■ Section Summary

• Cognitive psychology has devoted much attention to the network approach to semantic memory. This approach is found in a wide variety of topics and has been extended far beyond the simple noun concepts that were so heavily investigated in the 1970s. Priming and spreading activation appear to be central constructs in theories of semantic memory, especially in connectionist approaches. These approaches even furnish persuasive analyses of semantic disruptions caused by brain damage, so-called category-specific deficits. The differences between connectionist and modular approaches to the mind have not been resolved.

Key Terms

ambiguous (p. 287)

anomia (p. 292)

anomic aphasia (p. 292)

benefits (p. 277)

category-specific deficit (p. 292)

characteristic features (p. 256)

cognitive economy (p. 260)

connectionism (p. 290)

connectionist mode (p. 290)

cost (p. 277)

defining feature (p. 256)

event-related potentials (ERPs) (p. 267)

facilitation (p. 276)

feature list (p. 255)

inheritance (p. 261)

inhibition (p. 277)

intersection (p. 255)

lag (p. 277)

lexical decision task (p. 281)

lexical memory (p. 292)

natural categories (p. 272)

networks (p. 252)

neural net model (p. 290)

nodes (p. 252)

pathways (p. 252)

PDP model (p. 290)

prime (p. 276)

priming (p. 276)

property statements (p. 253)

proposition (p. 253)

prototypes (p. 274)

semantic features (p. 255)

semantic memory (p. 250)

semantic relatedness effect (p. 266)

sentence verification task (p. 258

stimulus onset asynchrony (SOA) (p. 278)

spreading activation (p. 252)

target (p. 276)

typicality (p. 262)

typicality effect (p. 262)

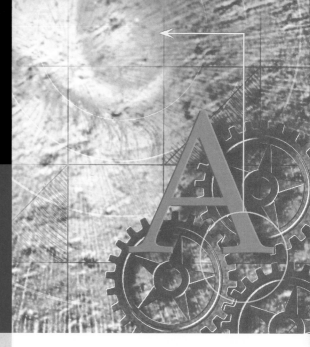

CHAPTER 8

Interactions in Long-Term Memory

The first notion to get rid of is that memory is primarily or literally reduplicative, or reproductive. . . . Remembering is not the re-excitation of innumerable fixed, lifeless and fragmentary traces. It is an imaginative reconstruction, or construction, built out of . . . a whole active mass of organised past reactions or experience, and . . . a little outstanding detail which commonly appears in image or in language form. (Bartlett, 1932, pp. 204, 213)

Indeed, the primary reason for the widespread acceptance of the notion of schematic knowledge structures is that it is almost impossible to imagine how mental life could be managed without them. (Nisbett & Ross, 1980, p. 38)

Having studied episodic and semantic memory separately in the previous two chapters, we must now put them back together again. You read about the evidence of a dissociation between episodic and semantic memories, showing how they are separate in several important respects; after all, patient K.C. seems to have lost his entire episodic memory, suffering brain damage that nonetheless preserved his semantic memory. Be that as it may, we also need to understand the normal, everyday operation of long-term memory, the continual, coordinated, cooperative processes of interaction between the episodic and semantic systems that let us understand and remember our experiences. Thus, this chapter is about these interactions.

In Chapter 7, you read of a distinguishing feature of semantic memory research, that we test the subjects on the knowledge they already have, knowledge they bring to the laboratory. Episodic tasks, in contrast, present the to-be-learned material to the subjects, then test their memory of that material. Although most of the research presented in this chapter also presents specific materials to the subjects, there are at least two major differences from standard episodic memory situations. First, the material to be learned is deliberately meaningful. This means we will not be presenting lists of words for recall or simple yes/no sentences for semantic verification. Instead, we are interested in people's memory for passages of text they read or hear, memory for natural events that happen to them, and so forth. As you will see, what we remember from our everyday experiences is significantly influenced by semantic knowledge, our knowledge of concepts, relationships, and general information about the world. The term for this effect, when already-known information influences our memory of new events, is conceptually driven processing.

A second difference in this chapter is that there is a far greater emphasis on accuracy of performance rather than the speed (RT) of performing; in fact, in many cases the emphasis is on *inaccuracy*. A stunning aspect of many of the results you will read about is inaccurate, error-prone memory performance, such as eyewitness recollection of the details of an event that are just plain wrong. Schacter (1996) writes eloquently of the "fragile power" of memory, the paradoxical situation in which we are capable of remembering amazing quantities of information yet have a strong tendency to *mis*remember under a variety of circumstances. We focus on the fragile part of this description in this chapter.

The Seven Sins of Memory

In a recent, very approachable essay, Schacter (1999) provides some specifics about the fragile nature of memory by enumerating Seven Sins of Memory, seven ways in which our long-term memory lets us down (see Table 8-1). Material about the first three of the Seven Sins was covered in Chapter 6. First, there is a transience to long-term memory, a tendency to lose access to information over time. Although we attributed that to interference and retrieval failure in Chapter 6, Schacter asserts that there may also be genuine forgetting from long-term memory, especially when a memory is not used and hence not rehearsed. Second, we tend to be absent-minded, losing track of information, details, intended activities, and so on. In Schacter's view, absent-mindedness is largely a failure of attention during encoding, especially because we may have been relying on automatic processing, thus failing to encode information at a deeper, more elaborate level. Third, we sometimes experience blocking, a temporary loss of access to information, say in a stressful situation such as an exam. The most common example of such blocking is the tip-of-the-tongue (TOT) phenomenon. Interestingly, blocking appears to be a special problem for older adults and especially when one is attempting to retrieve a name (Maylor, 1997).

Schacter describes the first three as sins of omission: Just when you need to remember something, you can't. The next three of the Seven Sins, all of which appear repeatedly throughout this chapter, are better described as sins of commission; situations in which you

Table 8-1 THE SEVEN SINS OF MEMORY	
Sin	**Description**
Transience	The tendency to lose access to information across time, whether through forgetting, interference, or retrieval failure.
Absent-mindedness	Everyday memory failures in remembering information and intended activities, probably caused by insufficient attention or superficial, automatic processing during encoding.
Blocking	Temporary retrieval failure or loss of access, such as the tip-of-the-tongue state, in either episodic or semantic memory.
Misattribution	Remembering a fact correctly from past experience but attributing it to an incorrect source or context.
Suggestibility	The tendency to incorporate information provided by others into your own recollection and memory representation.
Bias	The tendency for knowledge, beliefs, and feelings to distort recollection of previous experiences and to affect current and future judgments and memory.
Persistence	The tendency to remember facts or events, including traumatic memories, that one would rather forget, that is, failure to forget because of intrusive recollections and rumination.

From Schacter (1999).

remember something, but the memory involves an error, maybe an incorrect time or person, maybe a detail you picked up from a different source. In brief, these three sins are misattribution, suggestibility, and bias. As you will learn in this chapter, misattribution consists of remembering something but being mistaken about the correct source of the information. Suggestibility is closely related to this and involves incorporating information supplied by other sources into your own memory of an event. And bias is a version of top-down processing; it involves "the distorting influences of present knowledge, beliefs, and feelings on recollection of previous experiences" (Schacter, 1999, p. 193). (Schacter's final Sin of Memory is persistence, by which he means the intrusive recollection of past events, especially traumatic ones—quite literally, failures to forget. We run into this briefly in the section on repressed and recovered memories.)

Let's launch into the sins of commission, into the evidence for both the powerful mechanisms that enable us to understand and the fragile processes that lead to mistaken memories (consult the original Schacter, 1999, article for the accumulating neuroscience evidence on these sins).

Reconstructive Memory and Semantic Integration

Table 8-2 contains a story called "The War of the Ghosts." The story is important not only because of the psychological points it raises but also for historical reasons: Bartlett (1932) used it in one of the earliest research programs on remembering meaningful material. Do the demonstration in the table now, before reading any further.

Table 8-2 BARTLETT'S (1932) "THE WAR OF THE GHOSTS"

Read the following, then attempt to reproduce the story by writing it down from memory.

One night two young men from Egulac went down to the river to hunt seals, and while they were there it became foggy and calm. Then they heard war-cries, and they thought: "Maybe this is a war-party." They escaped to the shore, and hid behind a log. Now canoes came up, and they heard the noise of paddles, and saw one canoe coming up to them. There were five men in the canoe, and they said:

"What do you think? We wish to take you along. We are going up the river to make war on the people."

One of the young men said: "I have no arrows."

"Arrows are in the canoe," they said.

"I will not go along. I might be killed. My relatives do not know where I have gone. But you," he said turning to the other, "may go with them."

So one of the young men went, but the other returned home.

And the warriors went on up the river to a town on the other side of Kalama. The people came down to the water, and they began to fight, and many were killed. But presently the young man heard one of the warriors say: "Quick, let us go home: that Indian has been hit." Now he thought: "Oh, they are ghosts." He did not feel sick, but they said he had been shot.

So the canoes went back to Egulac, and the young man went ashore to his house, and made a fire. And he told everybody and said: "Behold I accompanied the ghosts, and we went to fight. Many of our fellows were killed, and many of those who attacked us were killed. They said I was hit, and I did not feel sick."

He told it all, and then he became quiet. When the sun rose he fell down. Something black came out of his mouth. His face became contorted. The people jumped up and cried.

He was dead.

Now that you have read and recalled the story, spend a moment jotting down some of the thoughts that occurred to you as you read and then tried to recall it. For example, if you remembered some specific details, comment on what made those details more memorable to you. Did you get most of the story line correct, or did you have to do some guessing? What was your sense of the story as you read it? You no doubt reflected on how peculiar the story was, with unfamiliar names and characters, vague and hard-to-understand twists of the story line, and unexplainable events. The story is a North Pacific Indian (Eskimo) folktale, so it is not surprising that it differs so much from other stories with which you are familiar.

Once you have exhausted your intuitions, look at Table 8-3 and compare your recalled version with the retellings in the table. Although your version may be closer to the original, because so little time passed between reading and recalling, you should be able to see points of similarity to the tabled retellings.

Table 8-3 TWO RETELLINGS OF BARTLETT'S (1932) "THE WAR OF THE GHOSTS"

First recall, attempted about 15 min after hearing the story:

Two young men from Egulac went out to hunt seals. They thought they heard war-cries, and a little later they heard the noise of the paddling of canoes. One of these canoes, in which there were five natives, came forward towards them. One of the natives shouted out: "Come with us: we are going to make war on some natives up the river." The two young men answered: "We have no arrows." "There are arrows in our canoes," came the reply. One of the young men then said: "My folk will not know where I have gone"; but, turning to the other, he said: "But you could go." So the one returned whilst the other joined the natives.

The party went up the river as far as a town opposite Kalama, where they got on land. The natives of that part came down to the river to meet them. There was some severe fighting, and many on both sides were slain. Then one of the natives that had made the expedition up the river shouted: "Let us return: the Indian has fallen." Then they endeavored to persuade the young man to return, telling him that he was sick, but he did not feel as if he were. Then he thought he saw ghosts all round him.

When they returned, the young man told all his friends of what had happened. He described how many had been slain on both sides.

It was nearly dawn when the young man became very ill; and at sunrise a black substance rushed out of his mouth, and the natives said one to another: "He is dead."

Second recall, attempted about 4 months later:

There were two men in a boat, sailing towards an island. When they approached the island, some natives came running towards them, and informed them that there was fighting going on on the island, and invited them to join. One said to the other: "You had better go. I cannot very well, because I have relatives expecting me, and they will not know what has become of me. But you have no one to expect you." So one accompanied the natives, but the other returned.

Here there is a part I can't remember. What I don't know is how the man got to the fight. However, anyhow the man was in the midst of the fighting, and was wounded. The natives endeavored to persuade the man to return, but he assured them that he had not been wounded.

I have an idea that his fighting won the admiration of the natives.

The wounded man ultimately fell unconscious. He was taken from the fighting by the natives.

Then, I think it is, the natives describe what happened, and they seem to have imagined seeing a ghost coming out of his mouth. Really it was kind of materialisation of his breath. I know this phrase was not in the story, but that is the idea I have. Ultimately the man died at dawn the next day."

Bartlett's Research

Bartlett (1932), not unlike Ebbinghaus, wanted to study the processes of human memory with the methods of experimental psychology. Very much *unlike* Ebbinghaus, however, he wanted to study memory for *meaningful* material, so he used folktales, ordinary prose, and pictures in his investigations. His typical method had subjects study the material for a period of time, then recall it several times, once shortly after study and then again at later intervals. By comparing the subjects' successive recalls, Bartlett examined the progressive changes in what his subjects remembered. (Interestingly, if you test your memory several times, with only short periods between tests, your performance typically improves across tests, a phenomenon known as hypermnesia [Wheeler & Roediger, 1992]. If substantial time intervenes between tests, however, then we see the more customary effect, greater forgetting across time.)

Using these methods, Bartlett obtained evidence that human memory for such meaningful material is not especially reproductive, that is, does not reproduce the original passage in any strict sense of the term. Instead, Bartlett characterized this sort of remembering as "an effort after meaning." The modern term for this is **reconstructive memory,** in which *we construct a memory by combining elements from the original material together with existing knowledge.*

Two particularly notable aspects of Bartlett's results led him to this conclusion. The first aspect concerns omissions, information the subjects failed to recall. For the most part, people in Bartlett's studies did not recall many details of the story, either specific names (e.g., Egulac) or specific events in the narrative (e.g., the phrase "His face became contorted"). The level of recall for the main plot and sequence of events was not too bad, but minor events often were omitted. As a result, the retellings of the story are shorter than the original. Of course, the subjects were not asked for *verbatim* (word-for-word) recall, so rephrasing and condensing are to be expected. Nonetheless, there were significant losses of information in the recall protocols.

The second aspect of Bartlett's results is more interesting. There was a strong tendency for the successive recalls to normalize and rationalize the occurrences in the story. That is, subjects showed an overwhelming tendency to add to and alter the stories, to supply additional material that was not contained in the original (the island mentioned after 4 months, for example). These changes often had the effect of making the story more "normal," conventional, or reasonable. Because the story surely was strange to Bartlett's subjects, his friends and colleagues in Great Britain, it is not especially surprising that their retellings modernized and demystified the original. For example, note how the ghost theme becomes progressively less prominent in the two retellings in Table 8-3, even though *ghosts* is in the title of the story. What is fascinating about this result is the *source* of this additional material. Where did it come from, if not from the story itself? It came from the subjects' memories: This is Schacter's point about bias and top-down processing.

Schemata

Bartlett borrowed the idea of a **schema** to explain the source of these adjustments and additions (although he complained about the vagueness of the term). In his view, a schema was "an active organisation of past reactions or past experiences" (1932, p. 201), essentially what we have been calling general world knowledge. More generally, a schema is *a stored framework or body of knowledge about some topic;* we also use the term ***script*** as a synonym of *schema*. Bartlett claimed that when we encounter new material, such as the "Ghosts" story, we try to relate the material to existing schemata (the plural of "schema"). If the material does not match an existing schema, then we tend to alter the material to make it fit (similar in spirit to Piaget's *assimilation*). Therefore recall is not a true, exact recall or reproduction of the original material. Instead, it is a reconstruction based on elements from the original story and on our existing schemata.

Reconstruction Versus Episodic Recall What do we have here? We have a seemingly simple task, "read this story then recall it," which we might expect to lead to a pure episodic memory ("I remember reading the story about ghosts, and it goes like this."). But when we turn to the results, we find that, unlike typical recall results in episodic tasks, subjects are remembering things that were not there. The source of these remembered things must be the subjects' memories, their knowledge, however vague, of events such as "Indian warriors doing battle."

An unimaginative way of looking at these results would be to claim that information already stored in memory is exerting an interfering effect on current memory performance. We called it proactive interference in Chapter 6 (see also Dempster, 1985). A much more intriguing perspective is that normal comprehension takes place within the context of a person's entire knowledge system. Therefore efforts to understand and remember meaningful material involve one's own meaning system or general knowledge of the world. In short, what we already know exerts a strong influence on what we remember about new material.

Extensions of Reconstructive Effects More recent research has fleshed out some of the details of this generalization and has added to our understanding of the importance of existing knowledge or schemata. For example, knowledge of the theme or topic of a passage improves people's memory of the passage (Bransford & Johnson, 1972; Dooling & Lachman, 1971). On the other hand, providing a theme, say, by attaching a title to a story, can also distort recall or recognition in the direction of the theme.

A clever demonstration of this distortion effect was provided by Sulin and Dooling (1974). One group of subjects read a paragraph about a fictitious character: "Gerald Martin's seizure of power. Gerald Martin strove to undermine the existing government to satisfy his political ambitions. Many of the people of his country supported his efforts" (p. 256). A second group read the same paragraph, but the name *Adolf Hitler* was substituted for *Gerald Martin*. After a 5-minute waiting period, subjects were shown a list of sentences and had to indicate whether each was exactly the same, nearly the same, or very different from one in the original story.

Preexperimental knowledge—that is, existing knowledge about Hitler—led to significant distortions in the subjects' recognition of sentences. Subjects who read the Hitler paragraph rated sentences as "the same" more frequently when the sentences matched their existing knowledge about Hitler, even though the original passage contained no such information (e.g., "Hitler was obsessed by the desire to conquer the world," p. 259). Furthermore, these *thematic effects*, as they were called, grew stronger in the group that was tested 1 week after reading the story.

This thematic effect was particularly striking in a second experiment Sulin and Dooling conducted. One group read an account about Carol Harris ("Carol Harris was a problem child from birth. She was wild, stubborn, and violent"). Only 5% of the subjects in this group said "yes" 1 week later when asked if the sentence "She was deaf, dumb, and blind" had been part of the passage. In a contrasting group, the same paragraph was presented, but the name *Helen Keller* was used. Fully 50% of these subjects said "yes" 1 week later to the same critical question. The same pattern of results was also obtained by Dooling and Christiaansen (1977), in which subjects were told that the paragraph about Carol Harris that they had read a week before had in fact been about Helen Keller. Just as before, subjects responded "yes" to statements that referred to thematically consistent information, as if they were drawing inferences from their existing knowledge rather than remembering the passage on its own terms. Dooling and Christiaansen concluded that thematic effects are prominent during retrieval, at the time of test, because they were observed a full week after exposure to the passage.

Kintsch (1977) points out that such results argue that recall of connected, meaningful passages is "neither reproductive nor constructive nor reconstructive, but all three" (p. 363). Immediately after reading, recall is fairly accurate—in other words, reproductive—especially for less exotic passages than "The War of the Ghosts." Note, however, that thematic inferences are still observed here, particularly when the title or topic of the passage invites the reader to draw such inferences. Later testing, especially when the topic or theme is already familiar to the subject, shows even more prominent reconstructive effects.

Finally, constructive effects, to use Kintsch's (1977) term, consist of drawing inferences from the passage *during* the original comprehension process. For instance, Sulin and Dooling's subjects probably inferred that it was the German government being undermined in the Hitler story. If they did so at the time of original reading, then the constructive memory effect should influence all later retrieval attempts. If the inference was drawn only at the time of retrieval, however, then the thematic effects would be part of reconstructive memory. In general, it can be difficult to disentangle inferences drawn during original comprehension from those drawn during retrieval (but see Frederiksen, 1975) unless performance is tested both immediately after comprehension and again at a later time (and even this introduces another complexity because recalling a passage once influences a second recall attempt).

These are complex and important ideas, and we return to them again throughout this chapter and in Chapter 10, where the combination of semantic and linguistic knowledge is discussed. For now, just remember the most prominent feature of the results:

Existing knowledge can exert a tremendous influence on our memory for meaningful material. As a normal byproduct of understanding, we relate new information to general knowledge already stored in memory. Subsequently, our performance in a memory task is based both on the new information and on general knowledge. It is probably impossible to find a more convincing example of conceptually driven processing than the effect of existing knowledge on current comprehension. And because a new *episode* is being influenced by existing *semantic* knowledge, this line of research demonstrates clearly a major topic of this chapter—the interaction of episodic and semantic memories.

Semantic Integration

Let's study another research program within this general topic of reconstructive memory, a demonstration that related pieces of information become linked or fused in memory. This line of evidence is the well-known set of studies by Bransford and Franks (1971, 1972). As before, this important set of results will make more sense to you if you begin with the demonstration in Table 8-4.

Bransford and Franks (1971) were interested in the general topic of how people acquire and remember ideas, not merely individual sentences but integrated, semantic

---

Table 8-4 SAMPLE EXPERIMENT OF BRANSFORD AND FRANKS (1971)

Instructions: Read each sentence in the table individually. As soon as you have read each one, close your eyes and count to five. Then look at and answer the question that follows each sentence. Begin now.

The girl broke the window on the porch.	Broke what?
The tree in the front yard shaded the man who was smoking his pipe.	Where?
The hill was steep.	What was?
The sweet jelly was on the kitchen table.	On what?
The tree was tall.	Was what?
The old car climbed the hill.	What did?
The ants in the kitchen ate the jelly.	Where?
The girl who lives next door broke the window on the porch.	Lives where?
The car pulled the trailer.	Did what?
The ants ate the sweet jelly that was on the table.	What did?
The girl lives next door.	Who does?
The tree shaded the man who was smoking his pipe.	What did?
The sweet jelly was on the table.	Where?
The girl who lives next door broke the large window.	Broke what?
The man was smoking his pipe.	Who was?
The old car climbed the steep hill.	The what?
The large window was on the porch.	Where?
The tall tree was in the front yard.	Was what?
The car pulling the trailer climbed the steep hill.	Did what?
The jelly was on the table.	What was?
The tall tree in the front yard shaded the man.	Did what?
The car pulling the trailer climbed the hill.	Which car?
The ants ate the jelly.	Ate what?
The window was large.	What was?

ideas. They asked their subjects to listen to sentences like those in Table 8-4 one by one, and then (after a short distractor task) answer a simple question about each sentence. After going through this procedure for all 24 sentences and taking a 5-minute break, subjects were given another test. During this second test, subjects had to make yes/no recognition judgments, saying "yes" if they remembered reading the sentence in the original set and "no" otherwise. They also had to indicate, on a 10-point scale, how confident they were about their judgments: Positive ratings (from 1 to 5) meant they were sure they had seen the sentence, negative ratings (from -1 to -5) meant they were sure they had not. *Without* looking back at the original sentences, take a moment now to make these judgments about the sentences in Table 8-5; "OLD" means "Yes, I've seen it before" and "NEW" means "No, I didn't see it before."

All 28 sentences in this recognition test are related to the original ideas in the first set of sentences. The clever aspect of the recognition test that Bransford and Franks

---

Table 8-5 SAMPLE EXPERIMENT BY BRANSFORD AND FRANKS (1971)

Instructions: Check "OLD" or "NEW" for each sentence, then indicate how confident you are on a scale from 1 to 5 (5 is "very high confidence").

	OLD/ NEW	Confidence (-5 to $+5$)
1. The car climbed the hill.	_____	_____
2. The girl who lives next door broke the window.	_____	_____
3. The old man who was smoking his pipe climbed the steep hill.	_____	_____
4. The tree was in the front yard.	_____	_____
5. The ants ate the sweet jelly that was in the kitchen.	_____	_____
6. The window was on the porch.	_____	_____
7. The barking dog jumped on the old car in the front yard.	_____	_____
8. The tree in the front yard shaded the man.	_____	_____
9. The ants were in the kitchen.	_____	_____
10. The old car pulled the trailer.	_____	_____
11. The tree shaded the man who was smoking his pipe.	_____	_____
12. The tall tree shaded the man who was smoking his pipe.	_____	_____
13. The ants ate the jelly on the kitchen table.	_____	_____
14. The old car, pulling the trailer, climbed the hill.	_____	_____
15. The girl who lives next door broke the large window on the porch.	_____	_____
16. The tall tree shaded the man.	_____	_____
17. The ants in the kitchen ate the jelly.	_____	_____
18. The car was old.	_____	_____
19. The girl broke the large window.	_____	_____
20. The ants ate the sweet jelly that was on the kitchen table.	_____	_____
21. The ants were on the table in the kitchen.	_____	_____
22. The old car pulling the trailer climbed the steep hill.	_____	_____
23. The girl broke the window on the porch.	_____	_____
24. The scared cat that broke the window on the porch climbed the tree.	_____	_____
25. The tree shaded the man.	_____	_____
26. The old car climbed the steep hill.	_____	_____
27. The girl broke the window.	_____	_____
28. The man who lives next door broke the large window on the porch.	_____	_____

STOP. Count the number of sentences judged OLD.

devised is that only 4 of the 28 sentences had in fact appeared on the original list; as in Table 8-5, the other 24 are new. As you no doubt noticed in the tables, the separate sentences were all derived from four basic idea groupings, such as "The ants in the kitchen ate the sweet jelly that was on the table." Each of the complete idea groupings consisted of four separate simple propositions; for example,

The ants were in the kitchen.

The ants ate the jelly.

The jelly was sweet.

The jelly was on the table.

The original set of sentences (Table 8-4) presented six sentences from each idea grouping. Two of the six were called "ones," simple, one-idea propositions such as "The jelly was on the table." Another two sentences were "twos," where two simple propositions were merged, as in "The ants in the kitchen ate the jelly." Finally, the last two were "threes," as in "The ants ate the sweet jelly that was on the table." In Bransford and Franks's first two experiments, only ones, twos, and threes were presented on the original list; in the third experiment, a few fours also appeared during learning, but this made no difference in the results. In all three experiments, the final recognition test (Table 8-5) presented ones, twos, threes, and the overall four for each idea grouping.

So what did they find? Just as your performance probably indicated, Bransford and Franks's subjects overwhelmingly judged threes and fours as old; in other words, they judged that they had seen them on the study list (just as you probably judged question 20, the four, as old). Furthermore, they were very confident in their ratings, as shown in Figure 8-1 (taken from Experiment 3). That is, people were recognizing the sentences that expressed the overall idea grouping most thoroughly, even when they had not seen exactly those sentences during study. Such responses are called *false alarms* or *false positives*, saying "OLD" when the correct response is "NEW."

Moreover, subjects were not especially confident about having seen genuinely old sentences (e.g., sentences 11, 17, 23, and 26 in Table 8-5); the only sentences they were sure about were noncase sentences (e.g., sentences 3, 7, 24, and 28 in Table 8-5), in which ideas from different groupings had been combined. Furthermore, they were fairly confident that they had not seen ones, as shown by the strong negative ratings in the figure (between −1 and −3), even though they had seen several sentences of that short length (e.g., sentence 9 in Table 8-5). Apparently, because the shorter sentences did not express the whole idea, subjects believed that they had not seen them before.

These results (Bransford and Franks, 1971, 1972) suggest that subjects had acquired a more general idea than any of the individual study sentences had expressed; they "integrated the information communicated by sets of individual sentences to construct wholistic semantic ideas" (1971, p. 348). In essence, Bransford and Franks's subjects were reporting a *composite* memory, one in which related information was stored together in memory. All the related ideas seem to have been fused together into one

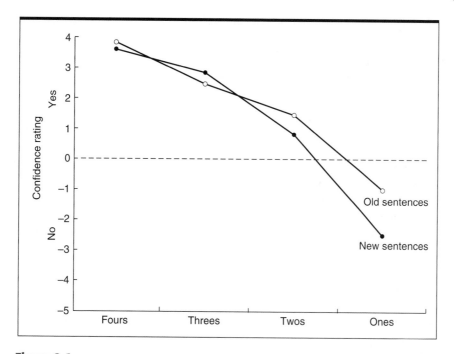

Figure 8-1

Confidence ratings for subjects' judgments of new and old sentences. From Bransford and Franks (1971).

semantic representation, forming one memory record of the whole idea. Therefore, the subjects' later recognition performance was entirely reasonable: They were matching the combined ideas in the recognition sentences to their composite memory representations. Rather than finding verbatim memory, Bransford and Franks found "memory for meaning," memory based on the **semantic integration** of related material (see also Richardson, 1985; Radvansky & Zacks's 1991 data indicate that subjects can structure the input sentences based on situation-specific "situation models"; see also Radvansky, Spieler, & Zacks, 1993; Zwaan & Radvansky, 1998).

Technical and Content Accuracy

Note two general points here. First, recall or recognition of meaningful material seems quite unlike the recall and recognition we discussed in Chapter 6. That is, the episodic memory tasks you read about there generally looked for, and found, performance based solely on the items presented as stimuli. Let's refer to this very heavily data-driven kind of processing as **technical accuracy**, *recalling or recognizing exactly what was experienced.* When scored according to strict, verbatim criteria, technical accuracy ranges from not especially impressive (Bartlett's results) to dramatically inaccurate (Bransford and Franks's results)—"abysmally awful" in one researcher's words.

But in some important ways, technical accuracy is an unsatisfactory way of evaluating memory for meaningful material. For one thing, it misses the important fact that subjects are remembering with a fairly high degree of accuracy; it is just a different kind of accuracy. Let's call this different kind of accuracy **content accuracy**, defined as *recalling or recognizing the meaning or content of what was experienced.* The difference between these two terms is that technical accuracy stresses verbatim memory, whereas content accuracy stresses memory of concepts and ideas, the meaningful, semantic content of the material.

Which of these kinds of accuracy is more important? Well, it seems clear that each kind is important for different memory situations and demands. We should not dismiss technical accuracy too casually. Despite Bartlett's view that "literal recall is extraordinarily unimportant" (1932, p. 204), there are many situations in the real world in which technically accurate memory is important. A prime example of this is eyewitness testimony, which you will read about in a moment. More everyday examples exist as well: Knowing the concept of "the personal identification number for my ATM card" does not help much if I can't remember the number itself.

On the other hand, there are also countless situations in which technical accuracy is not called for or even would be considered very inappropriate. For instance, if you ask a friend what your professor said yesterday in class, you do not expect your friend to give you a verbatim retelling of the lecture. In such situations, instead, recalling the *gist* or overall meaning of an event is important. Your ability to paraphrase correctly, for example, is a demonstration of content accuracy. It's pretty unlikely that you will be asked for verbatim recall of this text on your exams, although you may memorize verbatim definitions of certain key concepts and terms. Instead, you are usually tested on content accuracy, on how well you have retained the ideas and concepts, and on how well you can express these ideas in your own words.

Consider Bransford and Franks's subjects again, and the kind of memory system that produces false alarms to related sentences that have never been shown. Bransford and Franks's subjects made false alarms to fours such as "The ants in the kitchen ate the sweet jelly that was on the table." But isn't that the whole point of memory? Isn't this an instance of high—even perfect—content accuracy? In other words, what good would a memory system be to us if it did not combine related information together into a unified, composite idea? It would be debilitating if our memories didn't pull related information together, if we didn't notice the semantic relationships among separate ideas, and if we didn't store them together. If our memories could not do this, then in a sense we could never understand—we could only record isolated fragments in memory without drawing connections among them. To reduce it to concrete terms, think how useless your memory would be if you did not realize that the jelly that the ants ate was the same jelly that was on the kitchen table!

Integrative Memory By focusing on content accuracy, a different perspective on memory and cognitive processes emerges, one that emphasizes how the memory system deals with meaningful, related information. We store separate bits of information together to the extent that those separate bits are related to each other (the principle of semantic relatedness). We use what we already know—call it schemata, general world knowledge, or semantic memory—to understand new experiences in a conceptually driven fashion. Those new experiences then become part of our elaborated knowledge structures and continue to assist later cycles of conceptually driven processing.

Let's call this the integrative memory tendency. One negative consequence of this tendency is that the separate bits of information may not match our existing knowledge completely, leading to certain kinds of distortions when we attempt to remember (Bartlett, 1932). Moreover, later retrieval may be technically inaccurate, a definite problem in situations such as eyewitness testimony where verbatim accuracy is the goal (Neisser, 1981). An overwhelmingly positive consequence of this tendency, however, is that content accuracy is enhanced, that we can understand and remember complex, meaningful events and episodes.

■ Section Summary

- Bartlett's (1932) early research demonstrated an important fact that motivates the topic integrating semantic and episodic memory. When meaningful material is to be remembered, we tend to reconstruct the memory from two sources: the presented information and our existing knowledge. Bartlett used the term *schema* to refer to this existing knowledge base and found that the subjects' schemata led to various omissions, distortions, and alterations of the originally presented material. This research, and most of the rest of the topics studied here, give specific evidence of three of the Seven Sins of Memory discussed by Schacter (1999): misattribution, suggestibility, and bias.
- Research on schemata and semantic integration suggests that memory for meaningful material is not particularly accurate in a technical sense because related information is either integrated in memory or accepted and then stored as having occurred in the original. Content accuracy, however, is enhanced by such a tendency to integrate related information.

Propositions

If you think for a moment about the kinds of experiments we have just been discussing, you will notice an interesting fact: In most or all reconstructive memory studies, we intentionally lure subjects into making mistakes (at least in the sense of technical accuracy). That is, we present meaningful material such as a story or a set of related sentences, then do something that invites mistakes of one sort or another. Bartlett gave his subjects a peculiar story, much too long to be remembered verbatim, and filled with unusual events; however reasonable semantic integration is, it was clearly a setup for Bransford and Franks to present sentences that were so unmistakably related and easily confused.

This is not to say that such research is unrepresentative, biased, or in some other way unfair or misleading. There are many situations in everyday affairs in which related information lures us into remembering something that was not in the original. Furthermore, it is obviously important to understand how human memory can be influenced by such factors. On the other hand, there is a more general kind of research in which semantic and episodic factors are combined, but the subjects are not deliberately misled or lured into mistakes. In this other kind of research, to which we now turn, we are merely interested in what subjects can recall when presented with ordinary connected prose. Putting it simply, aside from the occasionally distorting or misleading effects that existing knowledge can exert, what are the more ordinary effects of existing knowledge as we understand simple sentences, stories, and other forms of connected discourse?

The Nature of Propositions

We will conclude in this section that what people remember from meaningful material is the idea or gist, the basic semantic relationships embedded in a sentence or paragraph. But to talk about remembering ideas, we need a way to represent those ideas so we will know what we mean by *meaning*. We need some way to diagram a sentence's meaning, to pin down what the vague term *meaning* means. And to do research on content accuracy, we need some way to score subjects' recall to see how well they remembered the meaning of a sentence.

By nearly unanimous agreement, the semantic unit that codes meaning is called a proposition. A proposition is a representation of meaning that can be stored in and retrieved from memory. Usually, a proposition represents the meaning of a single, simple sentence, a simple idea. In Anderson's (1985, p. 114) terms, "A proposition is the smallest unit of knowledge that can stand as a separate assertion," for example, the smallest unit about which you can make true/false judgments. Let's begin with this basic unit of meaning by learning the terminology of propositions and learning how they are structured.

The Basics In Chapter 7, the term *proposition* was defined as a simple relationship between two concepts, one that can be expressed by a simple, declarative sentence, such as, "A robin has wings." Figure 8-2A diagrams this relationship in the familiar way, using network nodes and pathways. In Figure 8-2B the sentence is also diagrammed as a proposition. If you compare the two, you will see that the propositional representation is only slightly different. First, we place a central node in the diagram to represent the overall sentence. Then each concept in the simple sentence is attached to the node by its own labeled pathway. The differences between the left and right diagrams are largely superficial.

But because sentences often express more than a relationship between two concepts, we are going to drop that limitation and redefine **proposition** as the *set of semantic nodes connected by labeled pathways, where the entire collection of concepts and relationships expresses the meaning of a sentence or coherent phrase*. And, as you will soon see, we will no longer limit ourselves to diagramming relationships that are already stored in semantic memory. Instead, any set of meaningful relationships among concepts can be represented in propositional format. (Try sketching the propositions from the Bransford and Franks study, for example, "The ants ate the jelly." The propositional approach is exactly the one they used in constructing the ones, twos, and so on.)

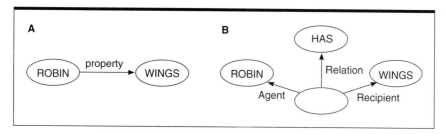

Figure 8-2

A simple network representation (**A**) and propositional representation (**B**) of "A robin has wings."

Semantic Cases as Pathway Labels A genuine difference between simpler semantic networks and the propositional approach involves the labels on the pathways. In semantic memory, we limited ourselves to a small handful of types of relationships; in fact, we used only *isa* and *property* pathways. But a sentence can have many different kinds of relationships among the words, so we need a longer list of labels for the pathways in propositional notation.

Technically, the source of these relationships was a theory in psycholinguistics known as **case grammar**, an important approach advanced by Fillmore (1968) and others. In this theory, the *sentence is analyzed in terms of the semantic roles played by each word*; just as an actor or actress plays a certain role in a play, each content word in a sentence plays a role in the meaning of the sentence. These different semantic roles are essentially the different labels we will use in our propositional diagrams. The theory itself is covered at greater length in Chapters 9 and 10. For now, we need only a basic understanding of the different semantic roles, to get going on the topic of propositions.

Consider a very simple sentence: "Laura eats spaghetti." To state the obvious, "Laura" is the person doing something in this sentence, "spaghetti" is the thing it is done to, and "eat" is the thing Laura does to the spaghetti. In propositional terminology, Laura is the *agent* or *actor* in this sentence, the person (or sometimes the thing) performing the overall action in the sentence. What role is played by the spaghetti? It is the *recipient* of the overall action, or alternatively, the *patient* (just as you are the patient in a procedure performed in the doctor's office). And the overall action, the basic relationship being expressed in the sentence—eating—is called the *relation* in this approach, not a particularly memorable label but useful because of its generality.

Consult Figure 8-3 to see a propositional diagram of "Laura eats spaghetti," along with a listing of the semantic cases used as labels in the propositional approach to meaning. A slight modification of the sentence, "Laura ate spaghetti with a fork," is also diagrammed, to show some of the other typical case roles in this approach. Bear in mind here that what we are doing is simply devising a way to diagram or represent the meaning of a sentence (unlike what you did in seventh-grade English, when you diagrammed the grammatical roles of the words). The more constituents there are in a sentence, the more concepts and pathways we need to represent the full meaning.

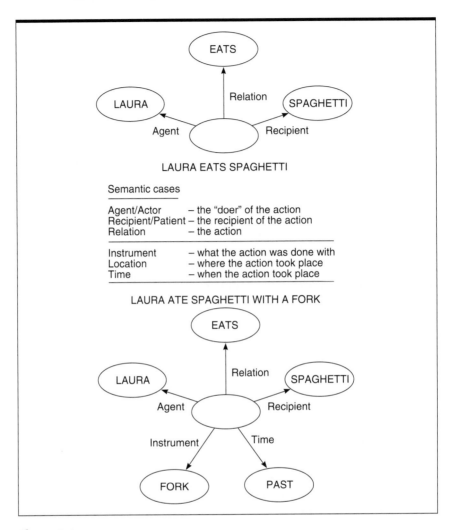

Figure 8-3

Propositional representations of two sentences, "Laura eats spaghetti" and "Laura ate spaghetti with a fork." The various semantic cases that appear in the sentences are listed along with a brief explanation.

Nonetheless, the entire meaning still is shown by the proposition or set of propositions that represent the sentence.

Elaborated Propositions Just as we attempted to account for semantic knowledge in terms of a network structure, propositional theories attempt to account for our mental representation of the meanings of sentences as networks of interconnected propositions. To illustrate, consider a particularly memorable sentence and its propositional representation,

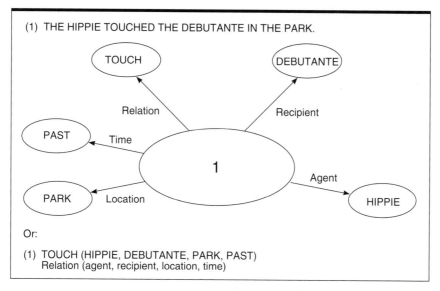

Figure 8-4

A propositional representation, in "node-plus-pathway" notation and in written form, of the sentence "The hippie touched the debutante in the park." Network notation after Anderson (1980) and Anderson and Bower (1973); written proposition after Kintsch (1974).

as presented in Figure 8-4 (sentence from Anderson & Bower, 1973, notational scheme based on Anderson, 1985). The sentence,

(1) The hippie touched the debutante in the park,

is represented here as a set of interrelated concepts, one for each main word in the sentence. Each relationship among the words is specified by the type of pathway that connects the nodes (e.g., agent, recipient or patient, location). Thus sentence 1 is composed of five *relationships or connections of meaning,* five **semantic cases:**

"TOUCH" is the **relation** in the sentence, the *topic or major event* in the sentence.

"HIPPIE" is the **agent** for this event, the *actor or person* who did the touching.

"DEBUTANTE" is the **patient** (or **recipient**) of the event, the *one who received the action* of touching.

"PARK" is the **location** of the event, and the

"PAST" is the **time** at which the touching occurred.

An alternative format for representing propositions involves a *relation,* usually the verb, followed by *an ordered list of concepts,* the **arguments** of the relation (e.g., Kintsch, 1974; see bottom of Figure 8-4).

Strengths of Propositional Theories

What are the advantages of a proposition-based theory of long-term memory for meaning? First, note that the proposition accurately reflects the meaning of the sentence. Although this may seem true just by definition, consider a more subtle point: a propositional representation is unaffected by superficial aspects of the sentence. For instance, look at Figure 8-4 and decide how the following sentences would be diagrammed:

(1a) In the park, it was the debutante who was touched by the hippie.

(1b) The hippie, who was in the park, touched the debutante.

If you concluded that Figure 8-4 represents *all* these sentences, you're right: Each is just a superficially different way of saying the same thing (this glosses over subtle differences in active and passive sentences; see Chapters 9 and 10).

As it happens, people tend to be fairly inaccurate when it comes to remembering the surface form of sentences, whether they were active or passive, whether the prepositional phrase came first or last, and so on (e.g., Sachs, 1967). This is exactly what we would expect if people store and then remember the propositions specified by sentences rather than the verbatim sentences themselves. (Can you see the relationship to Bransford and Franks's results?)

Now consider a much more important advantage. We are interested in understanding what people store in memory when they comprehend complex meanings. This is a much more difficult task than representing the kind of relationship that stands between "ROBIN" and "WINGS." One attractive feature of proposition-based theories is that the basic elements of nodes and pathways are flexible and powerful enough to represent the whole range of complexity in which we are interested. With propositions, we can represent simple semantic connections ("ROBIN has WINGS") all the way up to complex, sentence-based connections ("The hippie touched the debutante in the park").

Another demonstration of this power is that a second sentence that is related to the first can be incorporated into our representation, so that the relationship between the sentences is also coded. Consider an expanded set of sentences in the hippie story:

(1) The hippie touched the debutante in the park.

(2) So

(3) she slapped him.

Figure 8-5 diagrams both sentences in propositional format and connects them by means of a higher node, which represents the idea of causation. That is, it should be clear from the figure that the two separate ideas or events are specified as nodes 1 and 3. Furthermore, because the meaning of 1 is the cause for the action in 3, another node (2) must connect them with the idea of cause-and-effect. That is, because the idea of causation is a separate meaning from "TOUCH" and "SLAP," we have given it its own separate node in the structure. (We will ignore for now that some process must deter-

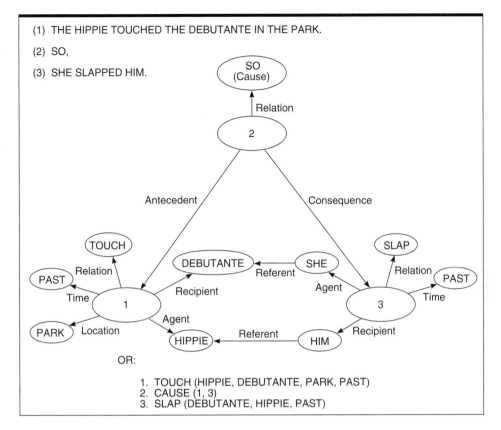

(1) THE HIPPIE TOUCHED THE DEBUTANTE IN THE PARK.

(2) SO,

(3) SHE SLAPPED HIM.

OR:

1. TOUCH (HIPPIE, DEBUTANTE, PARK, PAST)
2. CAUSE (1, 3)
3. SLAP (DEBUTANTE, HIPPIE, PAST)

Figure 8-5

A propositional representation, in network and written form, of "The hippie touched the debutante in the park. So she slapped him." Network notation after Anderson (1980) and Anderson and Bower (1973); written proposition after Kintsch (1974).

mine that *she* refers to the debutante and *him* to the hippie [O'Brien & Albrecht, 1991]. These forms of reference are discussed in Chapter 10.)

Try paraphrasing these sentences, rearranging phrases, substituting different words (e.g., "therefore" instead of "so"), and the like, and then see how your paraphrase compares with the meaning represented in Figure 8-5. Because the entire meaning of the story is completely specified as nodes 1, 2, and 3, any paraphrase is also represented by the same set of propositions.

Equally important, several different ideas, expressed across more than one sentence, can all be related to one another in a single representation. This ability to relate propositions to one another is crucial to the importance of propositional theories. Without this ability, such theories could never account for our understanding of a simple paragraph or story, in which one idea leads to the next, where one idea elaborates another, and so on. And you will notice that the higher nodes that connect separate sentences serve a similar

---

Table 8-6 SAMPLE SENTENCES FOR FORMING PROPOSITIONAL REPRESENTATIONS

Begin with some very simple sentences, such as
   (a) Mary bought a book.
   (b) John drives a Jeep.
Then progress to somewhat more complex sentences, such as
   (c) Mary bought a German book.
   (d) John drives a Jeep that he bought in Texas.
     Note that (c) consists of a verb relation and an adjective relation, and (d) has two verb relations that involve both John and Jeep (but only one of them necessarily involves Texas).
     Think of some variations on these sentences and how you would alter the propositional structures to incorporate the changes. For instance, add to your structure for (d) to get
   (e) After John went to Texas, he bought a Jeep. (It probably makes no difference if you diagram this using the relation "AFTER" or the relation "THEN".)
Finally, a challenging example from Anderson (1980) is the sentence
   (f) "Nixon gave a beautiful Cadillac to Brezhnev, who is leader of the USSR."
     To get started on this one, note that Anderson identifies three propositions here: *give, beautiful,* and *leader of.* Be sensitive to implied concepts, such as the implied causation in the expanded "hippie" sentence, or the implied sequence in
   (g) John went to Texas and bought a Jeep.

---

purpose as category nodes in semantic networks: They yield a hierarchical structure for the nodes, where higher nodes can be broken down into separate elements or parts.

Rules for Deriving Propositions

Proposition-based theories, as mentioned, are almost universally accepted within cognitive psychology as the way to represent complex meanings. Because meaning is so critical to an understanding of human cognition and because you need to understand this important approach, we will spend some time dealing with propositions, learning how to derive them from connected discourse. Table 8-6 presents some sample sentences to use in practicing the rules; the rules themselves are somewhat modified from Anderson's (1980, pp. 106–107) list. Spend a few minutes deriving a propositional representation based on those rules for the sentence

(4) The hungry lion ate Max, who starved it.

    Figure 8-6 contains corresponding steps to the rules that follow, illustrating the process of constructing a propositional representation of sentence 4. (Network diagrams are far easier to understand than list format propositions, so I'd encourage you to stick with the "node and pathway" notation.) Any rule preceded by an asterisk is an elaboration or modification to Anderson's scheme (but paraphrases are not starred). All rules should be applied to each sentence being analyzed.

    1. Find all the relational terms in the sentence. These usually are verbs, sometimes adjectives or relational expressions such as *father of* or occasionally prepositions such as *above* or *on top of.* In sentence 4, the relations are *hungry, eat,* and *starve.*

    2. Write a simple sentence or phrase for each relation, and give each one a number. Each sentence will contain only the one relation and its noun arguments. Each sentence

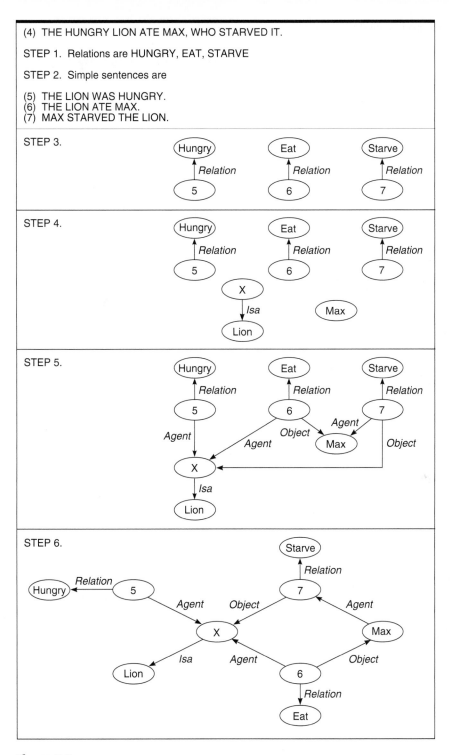

(4) THE HUNGRY LION ATE MAX, WHO STARVED IT.

STEP 1. Relations are HUNGRY, EAT, STARVE

STEP 2. Simple sentences are

(5) THE LION WAS HUNGRY.
(6) THE LION ATE MAX.
(7) MAX STARVED THE LION.

STEP 3.

STEP 4.

STEP 5.

STEP 6.

Figure 8-6

Steps in deriving a propositional representation for "The hungry lion ate Max, who starved it." Adapted from Anderson (1980).

will be one of the propositions from the original sentence. For sentence 4, you should get three separate simple sentences:

(5) The lion was hungry.

(6) The lion ate Max.

(7) Max starved the lion.

3. Draw an oval to represent the overall node for each proposition, sentences 5 through 7, and number it to correspond to the simple sentence. Write the relation next to its oval, and connect the node to the relation by an arrow labeled *relation*.

4. Add a node to each proposition for each argument, each noun or noun-like word in the proposition (ignore function words such as *the*). Two classes of nouns should be distinguished here. If a noun refers to a specific person or object, such as Max, simply write the noun. If a noun refers only to an instance of a category, such as *lion*, then create a new node and give it an arbitrary name such as *X*. The *X* will stand for this particular instance of the category. Connect the *X* to its class noun with an *isa* arrow. Do not create different nodes for the same noun, but use the same node for both instances; *there should only be one *Max* node, even though *Max* occurs in propositions 6 and 7.

5. Connect all the arguments to the numbered oval with arrows. Label the arrows with an appropriate semantic label, such as *agent*, *patient/recipient*, or *location*.

6. Rearrange the network to make it neat. *In other words, there is no significance at all to the position of the nodes. The meanings are coded in terms of nodes that are connected and the nature of the pathway or arrow that connects them.

Are Propositions Real?

However theoretically elegant the propositional approach is in representing the meaning of connected discourse, the ultimate test of the validity and usefulness of propositions is empirical. It is fine to have an objective, systematic, and reasonable way of representing meaning, as is provided by propositional-based theories of meaning (e.g., Anderson, 1976; Kintsch, 1974). Yet, if this approach were not supported by research results, it would be little more than an intellectual curiosity to cognitive psychology. Fortunately, a score of research reports have documented the psychological validity and utility of these hypothesized propositional structures. We discuss a few to give you the flavor of this important kind of research.

The basic idea in all these tests is fairly straightforward. First, choose the samples of connected text that are going to be presented and derive their propositional structure. Having determined this structure, determine which portions of the structure are more important to an understanding of the passage and which are less important; details of a minor episode, for instance, are relatively unimportant, but the overall outcome of a main episode is very important. Draw some predictions about recall, given what we know about the capacity of the memory system and the structure and importance of the elements in the passage. Finally, give the passages to subjects and, using the rules just described, score their recall to see what is and is not remembered, what is and is not distorted, and what is and is not invented.

Remembering Propositions   Let's begin with a classic study, one performed by Sachs (1967) before the advent of propositional theories. Sachs was testing a very general notion about memory; that people tend to remember meaning rather than superficial, verbatim information in the sentences they hear or read. Her subjects heard passages of connected text and were then tested on one critical sentence in the passage 0, 80, or 160 syllables after the critical sentence had been heard. (See Table 8-7 for an example; why not read it now and confirm Sachs's results for yourself?)

The test was a simple recognition test among four alternatives. One alternative was a verbatim repetition, another choice represented a change both in surface form and in meaning, and the other two represented changes only in surface form. When recognition was tested immediately, subjects were very good at recognizing the exact repetition; in other words, they rejected changes in superficial structure and changes in meaning. After comprehending the next 80 syllables in the passage, however, performance was accurate only in rejecting the alternative that changed the meaning. In other words, subjects showed no preference for the repetition (*d*, the correct answer) over the paraphrases (*a* and *c* in the table) when the extra material intervened.

Sachs's conclusions were straightforward; we quickly lose information about the actual, verbatim string of words that we hear (or read), but we do retain the meaning. Our memory of the input is then based largely on the propositions. We reconstruct what must have been said based on the meaning that is stored in the propositional structure. Only in

---

Table 8-7 SAMPLE PASSAGE FROM SACHS (1967) INCLUDING MULTIPLE-CHOICE RECOGNITION TEST FOR CRITICAL SENTENCE

Read the passage below at a comfortable pace but without looking back. After you have finished reading, your memory of one of the sentences in the paragraph will be tested.

There is an interesting story about the telescope. In Holland, a man named Lippershey was an eyeglass maker. One day his children were playing with some lenses. They discovered that things seemed very close if two lenses were held about a foot apart. Lippershey began experimenting and his "spyglass" attracted much attention. He sent a letter about it to Galileo, the great Italian scientist. Galileo at once realized the importance of the discovery and set about to build an instrument of his own. He used an old organ pipe with one lens curved out and the other in. On the first clear night he turned the glass toward the sky. He was amazed to find the empty dark spaces filled with brightly gleaming stars! Night after night Galileo climbed to a high tower, sweeping the sky with his telescope. One night he saw Jupiter, and to his great surprise discovered near it three bright stars, two to the east and one to the west. On the next night, however, all were to the west. A few nights later there were four little stars.

Now, without looking back, decide which of the following sentences occurred in the paragraph.
   a. He sent Galileo, the great Italian scientist, a letter about it.
   b. Galileo, the great Italian scientist, sent him a letter about it.
   c. A letter about it was sent to Galileo, the great Italian scientist.
   d. He sent a letter about it to Galileo, the great Italian scientist.
Check to see whether your answer was correct by referring back to the paragraph.

situations where there is something "special" about the verbatim string, say, in recalling a joke, do we appear to retain surface form as part of our ordinary memory for meaningful discourse (but see Masson, 1984). Note that Sachs's results are entirely consistent with the propositional approach to meaning: Sachs's subjects, as a current reinterpretation would say, were deriving the propositional structures of the passage they heard. They then retained only those structures, rather than the surface form of the sentences.

Confirmation of this last point was offered by Kintsch and Bates (1977), who gave a surprise recognition test to students either 2 or 5 days after a classroom lecture. Some evidence of verbatim memory was present after 2 days, but very little persisted 5 days afterward. As expected, verbatim memory for details and extraneous comments was somewhat better than verbatim memory for general lecture statements. This was no doubt a **von Restorff effect,** *improved retention of one piece of information that is made distinct or different from the information around it* such as underlining one word in a list in red ink (Cooper & Pantle, 1967). That is, because there were very few detail and extraneous statements in comparison to lecture statements, memory of those infrequent (and therefore distinctive) statements was fairly good (see also Bates, Masling, & Kintsch, 1978). Even here, however, reconstructive memory seemed to play a role in remembering; students were better at rejecting items such as jokes that had not been presented than they were at recognizing jokes and announcements that had been heard (see also Brewer & Hay, 1984, on reconstruction of different linguistic styles).

Gernsbacher (1985) addresses the same phenomenon explicitly within the framework of propositional theories. In essence, she found the same results as Sachs did for both verbal passages and sequences of pictures that told a story nonverbally. Furthermore, Gernsbacher's research tested several explanations of why we lose the more superficial aspects of what we hear or see. Her conclusion, for both kinds of passages, was that people have poor memory of surface information because of processing shifts during comprehension. That is, as we comprehend the successive elements of a passage, we shift from building one propositional element to building the next one, then the next, and so on. Each time we shift in this manner, information from the previous substructures that were built becomes less and less available, so that eventually the only information that remains is the propositional structure that represents meaning. (This work is pursued more thoroughly in Chapter 10.)

Kintsch reported several direct tests of propositional theory, particularly the notion that a sentence with more underlying propositions is a more difficult sentence and thus harder to remember. In one set of studies, Kintsch (1974) presented short sentences for simple free recall (five sentences were presented, followed by a 2-minute recall interval, followed by another five sentences, etc.). The sentences had between two and four content words each and from one to three propositions each; for instance, "The crowded passengers squirmed uncomfortably" and "The horse stumbled and broke a leg." Both sentences have four content words, but the first sentence has three propositions whereas the second sentence has only two. Kintsch's general predictions, based on propositional analysis, were upheld. Whereas subjects tended to recall about the same amount from all sentences, recall of the elements of any single proposition went down as the total number of propositions increased. Thus the more complex a sentence is, as indicated by the number of propositions it contains, the more there is to remember. Of course, with more to remember, less is recalled.

Propositions and Priming At a more detailed level, several experiments have both confirmed the psychological reality of propositions and tied them to a phenomenon you are quite familiar with: priming. Ratcliff and McKoon (1978, Experiment 2; see also McNamara & Diwadkar, 1996), for example, tested the possibility of priming effects within the propositions formed when we comprehend sentences. They presented sentences to their subjects and told them to learn the sentences for a later unspecified memory test. The test sentences were written so that each would contain two propositions, for example,

Geese crossed the horizon as wind shuffled the clouds.

The chauffeur jammed the clutch when he parked the truck.

After a 20-minute interval filled with an unrelated task, subjects were shown single words in a recognition task and had to say "yes" if the word had been in one of the learned sentences and "no" otherwise.

The priming manipulation in the studies was in the sequencing of the trials during recognition. Sometimes the word on one trial (the prime) was immediately followed on the next trial by a word (the target) from a different sentence, and sometimes primes were followed by a target word from the same sentence. When the prime and target were from the same sentence, they had either occurred in the same proposition or in different propositions. For example, in the "geese" sentence above, the pair *geese–horizon* came from the same proposition, whereas the pair *geese–clouds* came from different propositions.

In the baseline condition, where primes and targets were from completely different sentences (e.g., *geese–clutch*), mean RT to targets was 847 msec (Experiment 2), as shown in Table 8-8. This is the *unprimed* condition because the unrelated propositions from different sentences would not be stored together during learning. But when the prime and target words did come from the same sentence, the RT to the target was shorter: 709 msec when they had been in the same proposition and 752 msec when they

Table 8-8 PRIMING RESULTS FROM RATCLIFF AND MCKOON (1978)		
Condition	**RT to Target**	**Priming Effect**
Across sentences	847 msec	None; baseline
Between two propositions in the same sentence	752 msec	95 msec facilitation
Within a single proposition	709 msec	138 msec facilitation
Examples		
Across sentences:	geese–clutch	
Between two propositions in the same sentence:	geese–clouds	
Within a single proposition:	geese–horizon	

were in different propositions within the same sentence; again, see Table 8-8 for examples. In other words, a prime–target pair such as *geese–horizon* was 138 msec faster than baseline (847 msec − 709 msec), because of priming within the proposition. A pair such as *geese–clouds* was 95 msec faster than baseline (847 msec − 752 msec), because of priming between the two propositions.

The support for propositional theories in these data should be clear. Words from the same sentence should be represented together in the propositions that are stored in memory. And words from the same phrase or clause should be even more closely related in the stored propositions. Thus even though the words were not related in the strict sense of semantic memory—*horizon* is not a semantic property of *geese*, after all—words stored together in a sentence's proposition still prime one another. Therefore, these results are viewed as strong support for the psychological reality of propositions, the idea that we comprehend by constructing propositional representations of sentences, then remembering those propositions.

■ Section Summary

- Comprehending and remembering ideas involve constructing propositional representations in which meaningful elements are represented as nodes connected by various pathways (e.g., agent, recipient). Much evidence has been reported in support of this notion; we tend to remember the gist or general meaning of a passage, rather than superficial aspects, and we routinely "recognize" a sentence as having occurred before even if the sentence is a paraphrase. Propositions form the base of several important lines of research, including studies of semantic memory performance, recall of connected prose, and comprehension and recall of stories.

Propositions, Semantic Networks, and Scripts

Look back for a moment at Figure 8-6, the propositional representation of the "Max" sentence. Do you see anything that resembles a semantic memory entry or concept in this network? Not really; we have the elements of the sentence diagrammed as three basic idea units, with the relationship among the three clearly indicated, yet nothing in the figure gives a clue as to what a lion is, what *starving* means, or what kind of creature Max is. We have claimed that when people read or hear connected discourse, they construct a propositional representation of the input, yet there seems to be something missing. How would you know that a lion is a ferocious enough animal that it might eat someone who starved it, based on the diagram in Figure 8-6? And yet, knowing that lions are big and ferocious *must* be part of your comprehension because of your reaction to a slightly different sentence:

(8) The mouse ate Max, who starved it.

Clearly, when you comprehend a sentence, you do more than merely construct the correct propositional representation of the ideas in the sentence. The process must also include looking up the concepts mentioned in the sentence, retrieving them from semantic memory. This is a critical aspect of comprehension because your semantic knowledge enables you to determine which semantic roles can be played by the different concepts.

Putting it simply, you access your semantic concepts for "LION," "EAT," and presumably "MAN" or "HUMAN," the node with which *Max* is associated. Having retrieved those concepts, you then can determine that a lion is big and ferocious enough to eat a man, that eating is something that lions do, and so on. Likewise, the semantic concepts you retrieved for "Laura ate spaghetti with a fork" guided your interpretation of that sentence, guided your analysis that "SPAGHETTI" is a food that can be eaten, and so on (compare with "Laura ate spaghetti with a friend").

How do we know that this kind of semantic retrieval takes place during comprehension? We know because of your reaction—"this isn't quite right" —when we substitute concepts that cannot play those semantic roles, as in sentence 8 or something even more unacceptable (*"The textbook ate Max, who starved it"). We also know because of the reconstructive manner in which you recall sentences, stories, or other kinds of connected discourse; you often fill in your recall with details that were not mentioned in the original passage.

Scripts

To understand this point, we need to consider the much larger representations of knowledge that are stored in memory, representations of entire episodes or events that guide our comprehension and behavior. These are called **scripts**, *the large-scale semantic and episodic knowledge structures that guide our interpretation and comprehension of daily experience.* These structures must be much more detailed than the simple semantic memory concepts and propositions we have discussed because people know much more about the world than just the bare meanings of words and how the words go together in sentences. For example, consider the large amount of knowledge you have in memory that guides your comprehension of even a simple story:

> Billy was excited about the invitation to his friend's birthday party. But when he went to his room and shook his piggy bank, it didn't make a sound. "Hmm," he thought to himself, "maybe I can borrow some from Mom."

Scripts in Memory Think for a moment about the common meaning of the word *script:* the dialogue and actions that are to be performed by the actors and actresses in a play. The script for a play details exactly what is supposed to happen in a stage production. In similar fashion, a mental script is a general knowledge structure about ordinary events and situations. In other words, a script is a mental representation of what is supposed to happen in a particular circumstance. Are you going to a restaurant? Your mental script tells you what to expect, what order the events will take, who the central characters are, and what you and they are supposed to do. Are you invited to a birthday party, taking an airplane flight, or sitting in a class on human memory and cognition?

Your generalized knowledge of what happens in these settings guides your comprehension as the events unfold, and leads to certain expectations.

The overall theory behind the notion of scripts is quite straightforward. People record in memory a generalized representation of events they have experienced, and this representation is invoked, or retrieved, when a new experience matches an old script. One function of a script, in a written or spoken story, is that it provides a kind of shorthand for the whole event; you need not describe every element of the experience but can merely refer to the whole event by invoking the script. More importantly, the activated script provides a framework or context within which new experiences can be understood and within which a variety of inferences can be drawn to complete your understanding (Abbot, Black, & Smith, 1985; Reiser, Black, & Abelson, 1985; Seifert, Robertson, & Black, 1985).

Let's develop this notion of scripts with a few examples. Consider the following abbreviated stories (taken or adapted from Schank & Abelson, 1977, pp. 38–40):

(9) John went to a restaurant. He asked for a hamburger. He paid the check and left.

(10) John went to a restaurant. He asked the waiter for a hamburger. He paid the check and left.

(11) John went into the restaurant. He ordered a Big Mac. He paid for it and then ate it while driving to work.

According to Schank and Abelson (1977), our understanding of stories 9 and 10 is guided by our scripted knowledge of a particular situation: going to restaurants. Story 11 is understood by a particular variant or track in the restaurant script, the "fast food" track. In memory, these authors claim, are recorded a tremendously large number of separate scripts, generalized knowledge structures pertaining to routine, frequently encountered situations or events such as going to restaurants. The average adult, having experienced many different instances of eating in restaurants, has a generalized script representation of this situation (and scripts for countless other situations, too). Whenever we encounter a story like 9, elements of the story trigger or activate the appropriate script; in a real sense, the script is primed. As a consequence, all subsequent events in the story (or events in a real-world experience) are interpreted with reference to the script that is activated in memory. In Schank and Abelson's model, *phrases or words that activate a script* are called **headers,** which either name the script or refer to some semantically related concept that is part of the script. In a general sense, a header is nothing more than a prime, a concept that activates a related body of knowledge. Thus headers such as "HUNGRY" or "WAITER" activate the restaurant script, providing access to the entire body of restaurant knowledge.

In story 9 the explicit script name *restaurant* and the reference to a kind of food are sufficient to activate the script. Thus the explicit reference to the waiter in story 10 is in some sense unneeded: *Restaurant* and *hamburger* are sufficient to activate the restaurant script. Schank and Abelson (1977) claim that, in general, two concepts are necessary to convince the reader that the restaurant script is indeed the focus of the story. In other words, it takes two headers to determine which script should be activated. Contrast 9 with "I met a bus driver in the restaurant," in which it is not at all clear whether the rest of the story will be about a restaurant or a bus driver (but note that both concepts must be kept in mind, just in case one of those details becomes important later on).

Furthermore, a story such as 11 requires somewhat more specialized scripted knowledge than a general restaurant script. After all, a typical restaurant doesn't usually let you eat in your car. Clearly, the *Big Mac* header is instrumental here in activating a particular version or track in the overall script. If you have specific knowledge of that track, you will not be surprised that John ate his lunch on the way to work. If you have never heard of a Big Mac before, you will have some difficulty in understanding why that event takes place.

Finally, consider a somewhat longer story (from Abelson, 1981):

(12) John was feeling very hungry as he entered the restaurant. He settled himself at a table and noticed that the waiter was nearby. Suddenly, however, he realized that he'd forgotten his reading glasses.

Although this story does not necessarily call up any particular track of the general restaurant script, it does illustrate some of the predictive and interpretive power of script theory for explaining human comprehension. Almost all readers (or listeners) will understand John's problem as "unable to read the menu." It makes little difference that "the menu" or even "a menu" was never mentioned. The restaurant script is activated by the headers "HUNGRY" and "RESTAURANT," which in turn activate the whole set of **frames** (also called slots), *details about specific events within the script*. This prepares you to receive specific information about those frames. When the detail comes along, such as "the waiter," that particular detail is stored in the appropriate frame. If the detail does not come along (e.g., "the menu"), it is simply inferred from the generalized script knowledge. Your comprehension then proceeds normally after "forgotten his reading glasses" because the unmentioned "thing you read in a restaurant" is supplied by the script.

In script terminology, the menu is a **default value** for the frame, the *common, typical value or concept that occupies the frame*. In the restaurant script, the default value "MENU" is the ordinary way that patrons find out what is available for dinner. Thus unmentioned details in the story are filled in by the default values. This means that a storyteller does not need to mention everything. We merely assume that the listener will supply any missing details from the stored script. In intuitive terms, the rule goes something like this. If no detail was mentioned, assume the normal, default values as specified by the script. If a detail was mentioned, replace the default value with the detail. Thus two plausible continuations of 12, one assuming the default value, and one not, might be

(12a) Rather than go to his car to get his glasses, John asked the waiter to tell him what kinds of sandwiches they had.

(12b) But then the waiter told him that he wouldn't need his glasses because tonight's dinner was a buffet.

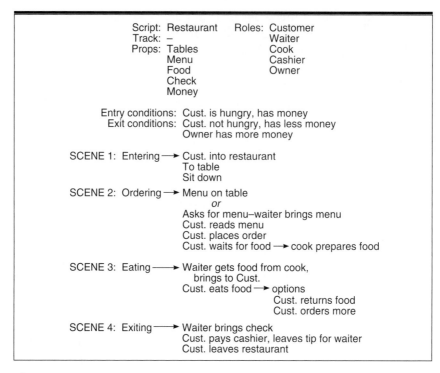

Figure 8-7

A depiction of a standard restaurant script. Adapted from Schank and Abelson (1977).

Predictions Figure 8-7 presents a generic restaurant script, based on Schank and Abelson's (1977) work, as an indication of the generalized knowledge represented in scripts. If you have such a conventional restaurant script, this enables you to understand and predict the various events in the sequence. An individual with different experiences, however, may have some difficulties in understanding what is going on, for example, a small child who has only been to fast food restaurants. Thus comprehension should suffer to the degree that your current experience mismatches your script.

A well-known example of such processing difficulties is presented in the story in Table 8-9 (Bransford, 1979); be sure to make an honest effort to understand the story before you read the explanation in the bottom portion of the table. As this passage shows, a story may activate a script but then mismatch the expected events in the script. Depending on the severity of the mismatch, we would predict difficulties in comprehension and recall. On the other hand, if a person lacks a specialized track within the script, we would predict comprehension based on the more general script that is in memory.

A final prediction from script theory is important enough that it must be developed in greater detail. Note from the shorthand and default ideas mentioned earlier that everything need not be mentioned in a story for a person to understand. In fact, as Schank and Abelson (1977, p. 38) put it, "When someone decides to tell a story that references a script,

Table 8-9 RESTAURANT EPISODE WITH EXPLANATION

Jim went the restaurant and asked to be seated in the gallery. He was told that there would be a one-half hour wait. Forty minutes later, the applause for his song indicated that he could proceed with the preparation. Twenty guests had ordered his favorite, a cheese soufflé.

Jim enjoyed the customers in the main dining room. After two hours, he ordered the house specialty-roast pheasant under glass. It was incredible to enjoy such exquisite cuisine and yet still have fifteen dollars. He would surely come back soon.

Assume, therefore, that Jim went to a very special type of restaurant. The owner allows people who can cook at least one special meal to compete for the honor or preparing their specialty for other customers who desire it. These who wish to compete sit in the gallery rather than the main dining room (although a central stage is accessible to both).

The competition centers on the competitor's entertaining the crowd, by singing, for example, or dancing or playing an instrument. The approval of the crowd is a prerequisite for allowing the person to announce his or her cooking specialty. The rest of the crowd then has the option of ordering it, and the person receives a certain amount of money for each meal prepared. After doing the cooking and serving the meal to the customers, the person can then order from the regular restaurant menu and pay for it out of the money received for cooking. In general, this arrangement benefits the manager as well as the person. The manager obtains relatively inexpensive entertainment, and the person is usually able to make more than enough money to pay for an excellent meal.

From Bransford (1979).

he recognizes that he need not (and because he would otherwise be considered rather boring, should not) mention every detail of his story. He can safely assume that his listener is familiar with the referenced script and will understand the story as long as certain crucial items are mentioned." In other words, the shorthand function of scripts relieves us of mentioning all the slots or frames in the script. We can assume that the reader or listener will *infer* those unmentioned details by means of the stored script.

A strong prediction of script theory is that people's recall of a story is influenced not merely by the details that were mentioned but also by the events and details that were inferred based on scripted knowledge. As a simple example, if we developed a longer restaurant story, you might "recall" that the customer left a tip for the waiter, even though no tip was ever mentioned in the original passage. Where does the tip come from? It comes from your script, from your long-term semantic and scripted knowledge (in a few moments, you will read about some research by Loftus and Palmer; the broken glass there came from the same place). And, importantly, such "recall" reflects reconstructive memory processes.

Evidence of Scripts

Convincing evidence of these predictions has been collected in the past several years, and we will spend a few moments discussing that evidence. In fact, we have already encountered some evidence of this nature in the first section of the chapter on reconstructive memory. Why did Sulin and Dooling's subjects "remember" that they had read "She was deaf, dumb, and blind"? Because they were given the information that the story was about Helen Keller, and this triggered the subjects' memory of information on Helen Keller.

Evidence specific to the script theory approach has been reported by a variety of researchers (Bower, Black, & Turner, 1979; Graesser, 1981; Graesser & Nakamura, 1982; Long, Golding, Graesser, & Clark, 1990; Maki, 1989). The article by Smith and Graesser (1981) is a good representative of such data. Smith and Graesser were investigating the role of typicality or relevance of specific events and actions in people's memory for script-based passages: Do we remember predictable events and actions better than unpredictable ones, or is it the other way around? They presented 10 passages to their subjects, each one related to a different scripted activity (e.g., taking the dog to the vet, washing a car, cleaning an apartment), and tested them with a recall or recognition task. Tests were conducted 30 min after subjects heard the passages, then again after 2 days, 1 week, and 3 weeks.

What made the Smith and Graesser evidence so compelling was the care they took in constructing their passages. Stories mentioned both typical and atypical actions within each script situation; Smith and Graesser collected norms in order to know what is typical and what is not. In their standard analyses of recall and recognition performance, typical information was remembered better than atypical information. These scores, however, were then corrected for guessing because the high accuracy on typical information probably included both events that were genuinely remembered as well as events that were merely reconstructed from the script knowledge.

When the scores were corrected for reconstructed guesses, recall and recognition were higher for atypical events than for typical events. In other words, in a story about taking the dog to the vet, subjects showed more accurate memory for the unusual, atypical events that occurred (e.g., "While waiting for the vet, Jack dropped his car keys"). Typical events, those anticipated by the script (e.g., "Jack led the dog into the waiting room"), were recalled more poorly once the scores had been corrected for guessing (note that correcting the scores for guessing makes this a technical accuracy score because content accuracy would not distinguish the presented from the reconstructed information). Thus memory for the stories conformed to the schema-copy-plus-tag hypothesis: You store a copy of the generic script as your main memory for the story and then tag onto that generic script the specific, atypical details that occurred (Graesser, 1981; Smith & Graesser, 1981; see Pezdek, Whetstone, Reynolds, Askari, & Dougherty, 1989, for the same effect in memory for real-world scenes).

Rounding out this sort of evidence, Nakamura, Graesser, Zimmerman, and Riha (1985) tested this hypothesis in a more naturalistic setting, using a classroom lecture as the input and a later memory test as the evidence. As was found with the prose passages, memory was better for the atypical or irrelevant information (e.g., sipping a cup of coffee) than for more typical information (e.g., underlining a word on the blackboard). Part of the strength of the Nakamura et al. article is that it extends the script approach to settings beyond written or spoken passages. Another strength is that the results were obtained in a natural, nonmemory setting. The students were unaware at the time of the lecture that their memory would be tested for events that happened during the lecture. In other words, *incidental* memory in the Nakamura et al. study seemed largely the same as more *intentional* memory in the laboratory studies.

■ Section Summary

- Scripts are large-scale representations of complex events and episodes, such as going to a restaurant or attending a birthday party. Script knowledge can be represented in the same kind of network structure as propositions and is assumed to be accessed by similar processes, such as spreading activation. A story invokes a script by mentioning headers, and these in turn activate the entire script. Script theories make a variety of predictions about comprehension and retrieval and provide a useful way to explain how people understand and interact with the real world.

False Memories, Eyewitness Memory, and "Forgotten Memories"

Schacter (1996) spoke of the fragile nature of memory and the Seven Sins of Memory, discussing how our memories can fail us in certain situations. Where is the weakness—the sin—in a memory system that functions according to the principle of semantic relatedness and integration? The answer is—in exactly those situations that call for technical accuracy. The weakness of such a memory system is that there are situations when it is important to be able to distinguish between what really happened and what our existing knowledge and comprehension processes might have contributed to recollection. We discuss two research programs that show incorrect or distorted memory, then tackle the difficult issues raised by these results.

False Memories

A simple yet powerful laboratory demonstration of **false memory,** *memory of something that did not happen,* is reported by Roediger and McDermott (1995), based on a demonstration by Deese (1959; go to the Web site to see the suggested readings for some of the many studies that have replicated and extended this now-popular paradigm). Roediger and McDermott's participants studied 12 item lists made up of words such as *bed, rest, awake,* and *pillow,* words highly associated with the word *sleep.* Importantly, *sleep* was never presented in the list. Instead, it served as the *critical lure* word, a word that was highly related to all the other words in the list but that never appeared in the list. In immediate free recall, 40% of the participants recalled *sleep* from the list and then later recognized it with a high degree of confidence. This is a false memory, of course.

In a second study, participants studied multiple lists, constructed in the same fashion, either recalling the list of words immediately or performing a distractor task (arithmetic). Everyone then was given a recognition task. During free recall, an even larger percentage of the participants, 55%, recalled the lure than in Experiment 1. The recognition results, shown in Figure 8-8, were even more dramatic. Of course, a few people "recognized" nonstudied words, words that were unrelated to the lists they had studied (e.g., *thief* for the *sleep* list). More importantly, correct recognition for studied words increased to well above chance for the study/arithmetic lists and even higher for study/recall lists. But false recognition of the critical lure was slightly

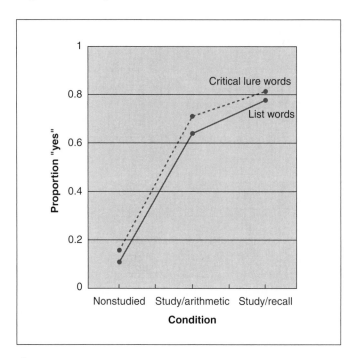

Figure 8-8

Roediger and McDermott's (1995) results.

higher than correct recognition of words actually shown on the list, showing the same pattern of increases across conditions. Indeed, there was an 81% false alarm rate for critical lures when the lists had been studied and recalled. In other words, falsely remembering the lure during recall strengthened participants' memories of the lure word, leading them to an even higher false recognition rate. When questioned further, most of the participants claimed to "remember" the critical lure word rather than merely "know" it had been on the list.

In terms of content accuracy, of course, this performance is good, exactly what we would expect; you see a list of words such as *bed*, *rest*, *awake*, and *pillow*, and because the list is "about" sleep, you then recall *sleep*. But in terms of technical accuracy, this performance is poor, because the participants came up with the word *sleep* based on their understanding of the list and then could not distinguish between what had really been on the list and what had been supplied from memory. Roediger and McDermott's (1995, p. 812) conclusion about this compelling memory illusion summarized the situation aptly:

> All remembering is constructive in nature. . . . The illusion of remembering events that never happened can occur quite readily. Therefore, as others have also pointed out, the fact that people may say they vividly remember details surrounding an event cannot, by itself, be taken as convincing evidence that the event actually occurred.

PROVE IT

False Memory

This is a fairly easy demonstration to perform if you have several volunteers and about 15 min available. It is an adaptation of the Roediger and McDermott (1995) method, shorter than the original experiment while demonstrating the same effect. Prepare enough copies of your distractor task, (e.g., a page full of simple arithmetic problems) to have one for each volunteer.

1. Tell your volunteers they will hear three lists and afterwards will be asked to recall as many of the words as they can; order of recall is not important.
2. Read the three lists to your volunteers at an "easy" speaking rate, about one word per 2 s. Pause only briefly between lists.
3. After finishing the third list, have your volunteers do 2 min of arithmetic, finishing as many problems as they can.
4. Ask your volunteers to write down as many words as they can remember from the three lists. Give ample time (approximately 3 min) so they can get as many words as possible.
5. When everyone is done, have them turn over their sheet of paper, and make recognition decisions, one by one, to the 20-word recognition test. For each word, they should say "no" if the word was not on the list and "yes" if it was on the list. When they say "yes," also have them note whether they remember the word specifically or whether they just "know" it was on the list.
6. Look especially for recall of the words *sleep*, *thief*, and *chair*, because these are the nonpresented, critical lures. On recognition, look for false alarms (saying "yes") to the critical lures in positions 5, 13, and 16.

Word Lists

1. bed, rest, awake, tired, dream, wake, snooze, blanket, doze, slumber, snore, nap, peace, yawn, drowsy
2. steal, robber, crook, burglar, money, cop, bad, rob, jail, gun, villain, crime, bank, bandit, criminal
3. table, sit, legs, seat, couch, desk, recliner, sofa, wood, cushion, swivel, stool, sitting, rocking, bench

Recognition List

1-dream, 2-fork, 3-weather, 4-bracelet, 5-chair, 6-robber, 7-stool, 8-traffic, 9-snooze, 10-couch, 11-radio, 12-jail, 13-sleep, 14-sand, 15-blanket, 16-thief, 17-bed, 18-boy, 19-skin, 20-cushion

Scoring Key

"Yes" words	1, 6, 7, 9, 10, 12, 15, 17, 20
No" words	2, 3, 4, 8, 11, 14, 18, 19
Critical lures	5, 13, 16

In eyewitness memory and testimony, any new information about an event is integrated with relevant existing knowledge. Thus, we are less than accurate when we attempt to retrieve such knowledge, since we are often unable to discriminate between new and original information.

Leading Questions and Memory Distortion

The second line of research is another simple yet powerful demonstration of how inaccurate our memories can be. This is the deservedly famous program of research begun by Elizabeth Loftus and her colleagues on the topic of leading questions and memory distortion. Loftus started by examining the effects of leading questions, that is questions that tend to suggest to the subject what answer is appropriate. She wondered whether there were long-term consequences of leading questions in terms of what people remember about events they have witnessed.

In an early study, Loftus and Palmer (1974) showed several short traffic safety films to college classes, with films depicting car accidents. The students were asked to describe each accident after seeing the film and then answer a series of questions about what they had seen.

One of the questions asked for an estimate of the car's speed, something people are notoriously poor at. One group of students responded to the question, *"About how fast were the cars going when they hit each other?"* The other four groups were asked almost the same question, except that the verb *hit* was replaced with *smashed, collided, bumped,* or *contacted.* As you might expect, those who got the stronger verbs such as *smashed* in their questions gave higher estimates of speed; the question led them to a biased answer.

Hold it. *Why* would we expect this effect? Why aren't we surprised that people estimated higher speeds when the question said *smashed* instead of *bumped* or *hit?* The answer is straightforward—and you know the answer already. When you are asked a question, you understand the question by retrieving the meanings of the words from semantic memory. Your concept node for "SMASH" includes semantic information about car speeds and damage from accidents. We understand by accessing our conceptual, semantic knowledge, including whatever scripted knowledge we have about car accidents. So the phrasing of the question leads you to respond based on your semantic interpretation of "SMASH." This is a straightforward demonstration of leading questions and a combination of all three of Schacter's (1999) "sins of commission": misattribution, suggestibility, and bias.

The longer-term importance of this effect gets to the heart of issues about eyewitness testimony and memory distortion. Loftus and Palmer wondered whether the question about speed had in some way altered the subjects' memory representation of the filmed scene. In other words, if participants are exposed to the implication that the cars had "smashed" together, would they remember a more severe accident than they had actually seen? This kind of effect would be called a **memory impairment:** *a genuine change or alteration in memory of an experienced event as a function of some later event.* (Note that the episodic memory literature also has a name for this kind of effect: retroactive interference.)

This is exactly what Loftus and Palmer found in their second experiment. A week after the original film and questions, the participants were given *another* set of questions about the original film (but they did not see the film again). One of the questions asked, "Did you see any broken glass?" Many of the participants in the "smashed" group said "yes," even though there had been no broken glass in the film. In fact, 34% of the "smashed" group said "yes," compared with only 14% of the group who saw *hit* (and 12% of those who had not been asked for a speed estimate). Furthermore, the likelihood of saying "yes" grew stronger and stronger as the estimates of speed went up, as shown in Figure 8-9. At each point in the graph, "remembering" broken glass was more common for the participants who had seen "smashed."

Think about that again. Despite the fact that they had not seen any broken glass in the original film, they remembered broken glass, partly as a function of their own speed estimate and partly as a function of the verb they had been questioned with a week earlier. It genuinely seemed that what happened *after* the memory was formed altered the nature of that memory. The question about "smashed" was not just a leading question; it was a source of misleading information.

The Misinformation Effect

Investigators have now developed a standard task to test for the effects of misleading information. In the typical experiment, the participants see the original event in a film or set of slides (e.g., slides depicting a car accident, with one slide showing a stop sign). Later, they are exposed to some additional information, such as a narrative account of the car accident. Some of the participants receive only neutral information at this stage, whereas others are given a specific bit of misinformation (the narrative mentions "the yield sign," for instance). Finally, there is a memory test, often a yes/no recognition task that asks about the critical piece of information: Was there

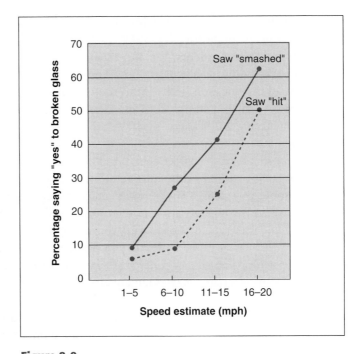

Figure 8-9

Loftus and Palmer's (1974) results.

a stop sign or a yield sign? (See also Zaragoza, McCloskey, & Jamis, 1987, who used a recall task.)

The common result is that some *people incorrectly claim to remember the misinformation*, the yield sign here; this is the standard **misinformation effect.** Belli (1989), for instance, found that misled subjects showed more than 20% lower accuracy than did control groups who were not exposed to the misinformation. Furthermore, Loftus, Donders, Hoffman, and Schooler (1989) found that misled groups were faster in their incorrect judgments—picking the yield sign—than in their correct decisions, as shown in Figure 8-10. This suggests a surprising degree of misplaced confidence on the part of the misled subjects.

Although these results implied that memory might truly be impaired or altered by the misinformation, several later studies called into question the original methods of testing and hence the conclusion of memory impairment. The crux of the debate involves the nature of the recognition test, and the "different ways of arriving at the same memory report" (Loftus & Hoffman, 1989, p. 103). In particular, it is always possible that the subjects did not actually encode the original item (stop sign) when they saw the slides. If so, then the misinformation effect could reflect guessing or remembering the yield sign from the narrative (McCloskey & Zaragoza, 1985). In either case, the misinformation effect would not signify true memory impairment at all, but instead some other process. In fact, several studies (McCloskey & Zaragoza, 1985; Zaragoza &

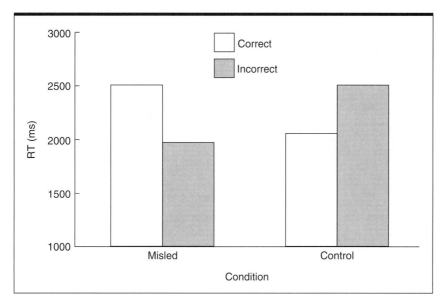

Figure 8-10

Mean reaction time to correct and incorrect targets (e.g., stop sign, yield sign) depending on whether the subject had been misled. Note that misled subjects were faster on "incorrect" responses, that is, saying "yes" to the yield sign.

Koshmider, 1989) used a modified task that corrected for this problem; the results seemed to support the nonimpairment interpretation.

Source Misattribution and Misinformation Acceptance

Several recent reviews and summaries (Ayers & Reder, 1998; Loftus, 1991a; Loftus & Hoffman, 1989; Roediger, 1996) outline the overall message of this research. As Loftus (1991) noted, genuine alteration of the original memory may be only one part of the memory distortion explanation. Based on the accumulated evidence, in fact, there seem to be three important effects: source misattribution, misinformation acceptance, and overconfidence in the accuracy of memory.

Source Misattribution   Sometimes people do come to believe that they remember something that never happened. This has been called **source misattribution,** *the inability to distinguish whether the original event or some later event was the true source of the information.* In essence, the source misattribution effect suggests a confusion in memory in which we cannot clearly remember the true source of a piece of information (Zaragoza & Lane, 1994). Using the stop sign/yield sign example, the source misattribution effect basically says that we cannot correctly distinguish whether memory of the yield sign came from the original film or from some other source, maybe the narrative that was read later, or maybe from existing knowledge and memory.

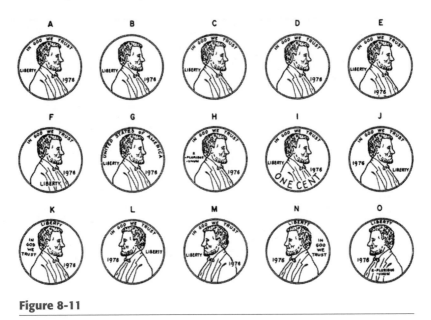

Figure 8-11

Which penny drawing is accurate? From Nickerson and Adams (1979).

Misinformation Acceptance According to Loftus (1991a), a second, possibly larger component of memory distortion is at least as disturbing as genuine memory impairment. This is called **misinformation acceptance,** in which participants *accept additional information as having been part of an earlier experience without actually remembering that information.* For example, the participant in a misinformation experiment may not remember seeing a stop sign at all but is nonetheless quite willing to accept that there was a yield sign when the narrative mentions it. Later on, the participant reports having seen the yield sign. In short, people seem quite willing to accept information presented after the fact and then often become quite certain about these "second-hand" memories. Disturbingly, these tendencies probably grow stronger as more and more time elapses since the original event and the original memory becomes less accessible (Payne, Toglia, & Anastasi, 1994).

Overconfidence in memory Despite our feeling that we remember events accurately ("I saw it with my own eyes!"), we often misremember what we have experienced, or we form memories on the basis of suggestion from some other source besides the original event.

And as if this weren't bad enough, we often become unjustifiably confident in the accuracy of our own memories and surprisingly unaware of how unreliable memory can be (a classic illustration is shown in Figure 8-11). As you read a moment ago, Roediger and McDermott's (1995) participants not only (falsely) recalled and recognized the critical lure, the majority of them claimed that they genuinely remembered it, claiming to have explicit, "vivid memory" of hearing the word in the list. The ultimate reason for

this overconfidence, aside from a basic belief in ourselves, seems to involve two factors. The first is **source memory,** our *memory of the exact source of information.* As several investigators note (e.g., Schacter, 1996), our source memory often is very flawed; we cannot accurately distinguish whether the source of some piece of information was the original event, some later event, or even our own general knowledge of the relevant situation. A second reason may have something to do with **processing fluency,** the *ease with which something is processed or comes to mind,* as if you thought to yourself "I remembered 'sleep' too easily to have just imagined that it was on the list, so it must have been on the list" (see Kelley & Lindsay, 1993). As Loftus and Hoffman (1989, p. 103) put it, both memory psychologists and the courts should find it interesting that such memories can arise through the process of suggestion or exposure to misinformation, and then become "as real and as vivid as a memory that arose from . . . actual perception."

Stronger Memory Distortion Effects

But can something as simple as this in the laboratory explain real-world inaccuracies in memory? Probably so. Consider just a sampling of recent experiments on false memories and memory distortions.

- Repeated exposure to misinformation increases memory reports of the misinformation (Mitchell & Zaragoza, 1996). Repeated recall of misinformation strengthens later recall and confidence about the misinformation (Roediger, Jacoby, & McDermott, 1996). And repeated questioning about an event can enhance recall of certain details and induce forgetting of others, even when no misinformation was present (Shaw, 1996; Shaw, Bjork, & Handal, 1995). Repeated questioning also increases confidence in one's memories, whether they are correct or incorrect (Shaw, 1996).

- Imagining that something happened increases later memory reports that it actually did happen (Garry, Manning, Loftus, & Sherman, 1996; Hyman & Pentland, 1996), as can instructions to accept consistent information as having happened (Brainerd & Reyna, 1998).

- Misinformation effects are found even when participants are warned that misleading information might be presented (Belli, Lindsay, Gales, & McCarthy, 1994).

It doesn't take much to realize the implications of this work: Memory is suggestible. People's memory of events can be altered and influenced, both by the knowledge they have when the event happens and by information they encounter afterward. People report that they remember events that did not happen. And in many cases, they become confident about the accuracy of their memory for those events.

Repressed and Recovered Memories

There are broad, seriously disturbing implications of these findings. If we can "remember" things with a high degree of confidence and conviction, even though the remembered things never happened, then how seriously should eyewitness testimony be weighed in court proceedings? Juries usually are heavily influenced by eyewitnesses. Is this justified? Should a person be convicted of a crime based solely on someone's memory of a criminal act? The current controversy over recovered memories is an obvious and worrisome arena in which our understanding of human memory is critical.

Here is a summary of a recovered memory case. A person "recovers" a memory, possibly a horrible childhood memory of abuse. The absence of that memory for many years is said to indicate that the experience was repressed, or intentionally forgotten. Although the recovery sometimes is spontaneous, it can also be an outcome of psychotherapy, in which the individual and therapist have done "memory work" to bring the memory into awareness. Now that the awful memory is "recovered," the person sometimes seeks restitution, such as having the remembered perpetrator brought to trial. It goes without saying that there is often no objective way to determine whether the recovered memory is real, no sure way to determine whether the remembered event actually happened. Therefore these cases often simply become one person's word against another's, both people claiming to be telling the truth.

The past few years have seen a huge rise in court cases involving recovered memories, and several people have been convicted of crimes based on someone's recovered memory (Loftus, 1993; Loftus & Ketcham, 1991). Cognitive science has become involved in this controversy for the obvious reason, our understanding of how memory works. As the research has developed, certain aspects of the recovered memory situation have fallen under greater scrutiny.

Of these, two are especially important. First is the notion of **repression,** *intentional forgetting of painful or traumatic experiences* (Freud, 1953/1905). From the clinical standpoint, "the evidence for repression is overwhelming and obvious" (Erdelyi & Goldberg, 1979, p. 384). There is little hard, empirical evidence on the nature of this type of forgetting, however, often not even reliable estimates on how often it occurs. And some data suggest that the opposite reaction may occur in some cases of trauma: Painfully clear and explicit memory of the trauma (Schacter's seventh sin, persistence). Cognitive science is no closer than clinical psychology in determining whether the evidence weighs more heavily for or against the process of repression (but see Nadel & Jacobs, 1998, on possible neurobiological differences for traumatic memories, and Arrigo & Pezdek, 1997, for a useful perspective on studying repressed memories).

More worrisome is that some of the therapeutic techniques for helping a client recover a memory are disturbingly similar to variables shown to increase false memories, including imagery, suggestive questioning, and repetition. In fact, essentially these techniques were used in a case that documents how a completely false, fabricated memory can be "implanted" in a susceptible person (Ofshe, 1992). And as several laboratory studies have shown, it is not necessary to go to extreme lengths to implant a memory (Loftus & Coan, 1994). Indeed, on a minor scale, all you have to do is present a list of words such as *bed*, *rest*, *awake*, and *pillow*, and the word *sleep* emerges.

No one doubts that child abuse and other personal traumas occur. And no one questions the need for genuine victims to grapple with and overcome such tragedy. But it is equally important that cognitive science provide its expertise on issues that hinge so critically on memory. And we should be especially mindful that memories are (sadly) prone to distortion and error, perhaps especially so for genuine victims of abuse (Bremner, Shobe, & Kihlstrom, 2000). The very reconstructive processes that bestow power on long-term memory bring with them a degree of fragility.

■ Section Summary

- Several paradigms give clear evidence of false memories, such as the Roediger and McDermott (1995) list presentation studies (seeing a list such as *bed*, *rest*, *awake*, *tired*, etc., then remembering the nonpresented word *sleep*) and eyewitness memory research by Loftus and others. "Remembering" in such situations is affected by source misattribution, the acceptance of misinformation, and bias. People tend to be overconfident about their memories, regardless of the distortions that might be involved. Cases of "forgotten" and "recovered" memories are particularly difficult to assess because of the fragile, reconstructive nature of memories.

Autobiographical Memories

Let's conclude this chapter on a somewhat less controversial topic: *the study of one's lifetime collection of personal memories*, or **autobiographical memory.** In the past few years there has been a huge increase in the number of studies about genuine autobiographical memory, real-world investigations of memory for more natural experiences and information, and some important theoretical advances on what might be called the self-memory system (Conway & Pleydell-Pearce, 2000). A set of impressive investigations by Bahrick and his colleagues illustrates the nature of real-world memory for personal events.

Recognition memory for information acquired across an extended period is remarkably accurate across many years, whereas recall performance begins to decline within months.

The Bahrick Work

Bahrick, Bahrick, and Wittlinger (1975) reported a fascinating study titled "Fifty Years of Memory for Names and Faces." Nearly 400 subjects, ranging in age from 17 to 74, were tested for their retention of name and face information about members of their own high school graduating classes. For the youngest subjects, this represented a retention interval of only 2 weeks; for the oldest, the retention interval was 57 years. Pictures and names were taken from the subjects' high school yearbooks and were used in a variety of retention tests. In particular, subjects were asked for simple free recall of names and then were given five other tests: name recognition, picture recognition, picture-to-name matching, name-to-picture matching, and cued recall of names using pictures as cues.

Figure 8-12 shows the average performance on these six tests across the retention intervals, that is, time since graduation. The free recall curves on the right show an average of just under 50 names accessible for free recall a mere 3 months after graduation. Because the average size of graduating classes for all subjects was 294 (and no subjects had fewer than 90 in their classes), this level of free recall is quite low: It works out to only about 15% of classmates' names. This number then dwindles further, so that the oldest group, having graduated an average 48 years earlier, recalled only about 18 names, something like 6% recall. Cued recall, with pictures as cues, was largely the same as free recall.

In obvious contrast, however, all four recognition tests showed impressive levels of retention. Simple recognition of names and faces was 90% at the 3-month retention

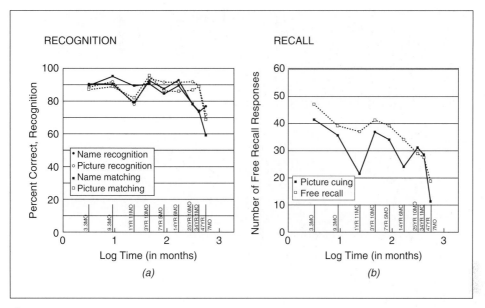

Figure 8-12

Results from the Bahrick et al. (1975) study of memory of faces and names across 50 years. From Bahrick, Bahrick, and Wittlinger (1975).

interval. Name recognition did not begin to decline noticeably until about 15 years later, and picture recognition remained in the 80–90% range until about 35 years later. And, as Bahrick et al. point out, the decline in the very oldest group may have been influenced by factors related to physical aging, possibly introducing a negative bias for the oldest group.

What leads to such impressive levels of retention, particularly when we compare them with the lower performance of subjects in laboratory memory studies? As Bahrick et al. note, in the typical situation, people have learned the names and faces of their classmates across a 4-year (or longer) period. This situation is called prolonged acquisition. According to the authors, this principle has two important components: overlearning and distributed practice. First, the information tested in the Bahrick et al. study was overlearned, in fact to a much higher degree than laboratory studies have examined (even Ebbinghaus didn't test the effects of a 4-year learning phase). The result of such overlearning is much-improved retention. (Will you remember 80–90% of your cognitive psychology course material 35 years from now?)

Second, prolonged acquisition represents learning that was distributed across a very long period of time, in contrast to typical memory experiments in which learning opportunities are massed together over a short period. This neatly confirmed the standard laboratory finding that distributed practice leads to much better retention than massed practice (Underwood, Keppel, & Schulz, 1962). Bahrick's work, including memory of foreign language (1984; Bahrick, Bahrick, Bahrick, & Bahrick, 1993) and math (Bahrick & Hall, 1991)

Do you remember when you saw this movie? whom you saw it with? where you saw it?

learned in school and of a city's streets and locations 50 years later (Bahrick, 1983) shows this to be one of the soundest bits of advice cognitive psychology gives to students. Distribute your practice and learning rather than massing it together (better known as cramming). Indeed, the Bahrick results suggest that the laboratory-based effect not only is general to more naturalistic settings but is greatly magnified when naturalistic, everyday memories are tested (see also Hyman & Rubin, 1990; Smith & Rothkopf, 1984).

Psychologists as Subjects Finally, several modern-day Ebbinghauses have adopted the procedure of testing their own memories in carefully controlled, long-term studies. One major difference from Ebbinghaus's procedure was that Linton (1975, 1978), Wagenaar (1986), and Sehulster (1989) tested their memories for naturally occurring events, not artificial laboratory stimuli. For instance, Wagenaar recorded daily events in his own life for more than 6 years, some 2,400 separate events, and then tested his recall with combinations of four different cue types: what the event was, who was involved, and where and when it happened. Although he found that pleasant events were recalled better than unpleasant ones at shorter retention intervals, his evidence also showed that none of the events could truly be said to have been forgotten (but contrast this with the Bahrick, Hall, & Berger, 1996, evidence that bias toward pleasant things affects our memories of high school grades).

Time-based cues, furthermore, were particularly useful in recalling events. Interestingly, the time lag since an event, while important, had a less powerful effect on recall than the salience or importance of the event and the degree of emotional involvement. Sehulster's data, on memory of 25 years of performances at the Metropolitan Opera, showed very similar effects; that is, the importance or intensity of the performance was a predictor of superior recall.

The Relationship of Laboratory to Real-World Memory

A debate arose in the late 1970s as to the value of traditional laboratory research on episodic memory compared with the new autobiographical memory approach. One side of the debate was represented by the claim that little seemed to have been discovered about the "real" functioning of memory in 100 years of laboratory research (Neisser, 1978, p. 4; "If X is an interesting or socially significant aspect of memory, then psychologists have hardly ever studied X." See also Haber's 1983 critique of iconic memory research in Chapter 3). The argument was largely one of ecological validity: How can we discover how memory really works when we test it only with arbitrary tasks and arbitrary stimuli in sterile, unrepresentative laboratory settings?

The other side in the debate provided a strong defense of the laboratory approach (see especially Loftus, 1983; Mook, 1983; Utta, 1983). One of the better known of these counterarguments, by Banaji and Crowder (1989), offered two basic comments on the "real-world research" movement. First, there is the undeniable fact that memory is a complex topic, influenced by a large number of variables in ways we only partly understand. In the face of this complexity, Banaji and Crowder argued, it makes no sense to abandon the laboratory setting, where extraneous variables and influences can be eliminated or held constant. Second, Banaji and Crowder criticized the new approach, saying that the promise of everyday memory research was unfulfilled; the "bankruptcy of everyday memory" research, in their words. They argued that no important insights or new discoveries had been made in the studies of everyday memory in the decade after Neisser's original remarks and that what little had been discovered was already known from traditional laboratory research.

Somewhat of a truce seems to have developed in this debate. On one hand, a more temperate position has emerged about the value of controlled laboratory studies (Conway, 1991; Neisser, 1988, 1991; Tulving, 1991). There is also now a greater openness and acceptance of some of the real-world research efforts, especially given some of the more recent, impressive applications of these methods (Rubin, 1996; Rubin, Rahhal, & Poon, 1998; Schulkind, Hennis, & Rubin, 1999). All in all, this is probably like many other disputes on the appropriate ways of doing research: Give a new method time to develop and prove itself and remain open to the possibility that it will ultimately contribute important new evidence.

The Irony of Memory

We conclude on the topic of the irony of memory: the question of how this powerful, flexible system can also be so fragile, so prone to errors.

Is Human Memory So Awful? We complain about how poor our memories are, how forgetful we are, how hard it is to learn and remember information. We deal with difficulties of the transience of our memories, our absent-mindedness, the occasionally embarrassing blocking we experience when trying to remember. Are these accurate assessments of our memories, valid metacognitions?

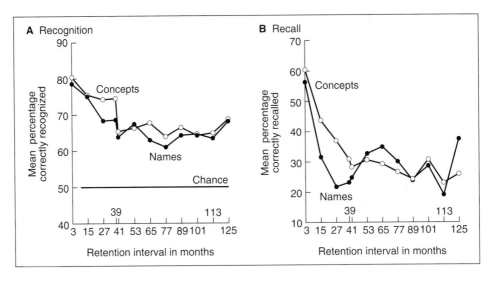

Figure 8-13

A, Mean percentages of correctly recognized names and concepts across retention intervals.
B, Mean percentages of correctly recalled names and concepts across retention intervals.
From Conway, Cohen, and Stanhope (1991).

Well, they're probably exaggerated. First, as Anderson and Schooler (1991) note, when we complain about memory failures, we neglect the huge stockpile of facts and information that we expect memory to store and to provide immediate access to. We underestimate the complexities, not to mention the sheer volume, of information stored in memory (e.g., some have estimated that the typical adult has at least a half-million-word vocabulary, and it is almost impossible to estimate how many people we have known across the years). Second, we fall into the trap of equating remembering with recall. When we say we have forgotten something, we probably mean we are unable to recall it right now. But as you have read repeatedly, recall is only one way of testing memory. Recognition and relearning are far more forgiving in terms of showing that information has indeed been retained in memory. (And third, we focus on the failures of retrieval, without giving credit for the countless times we remember accurately; see also Chapter 11, on our tendency to search for confirming evidence.)

How much cognitive psychology will you remember in a dozen years? Your honest estimate is (probably) "not much at all." If so, then you have seriously underestimated your memory. A study by Conway, Cohen, and Stanhope (1991) examined exactly that: students' memory of the concepts, specific facts, names, and so on from a cognitive psychology course taken up to 12 years earlier. Figure 8-13 shows their results. Recall of material dwindled quite a bit across the 12 years, from 60% to 25% for concepts, for example. But recognition for the same material dropped only a bit, from 80% to around 65–70%. Correct recognition for all categories of information remained significantly above chance across all 12 years. Your honest estimate—your metacognitive awareness of having information in storage—can be quite inaccurate.

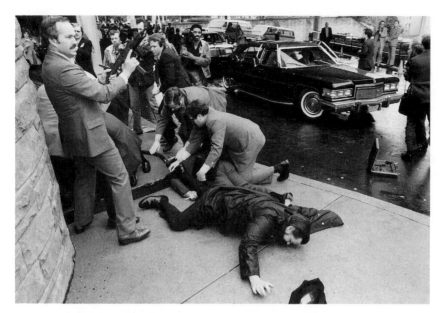

Distinctiveness or rated memorability is an important determinant of how accurately we remember an event, such as President Reagan's attempted assassination.

Special Flashbulb Memories On the other hand, we often seem to have—or believe we have—extremely accurate and very detailed memories of particular events, especially when the events were surprising or highly unusual. For example, Winograd and Killinger (1983) examined the flashbulb memories (Brown & Kulik, 1977) of college students for a significant event, the assassination of President Kennedy in 1963 (note that subjects were asked to recall their own particular circumstances when they heard news of the event, not whether they remembered the event itself). The data showed an increase in the amount of recallable information as a function of the subject's age in 1963, but the evidence also showed that the surprise or shock involved in such events may not be necessary for high levels of retention; subjects showed high recall for the Nixon resignation and the moon landing of the U.S. astronauts, neither of which was an unexpected, surprise occurrence.

Distinctiveness of the event, however, seems quite important (Schmidt, 1985). This is more than a little reminiscent of the old-fashioned von Restorff effect you encountered earlier. And it is strikingly similar to the surprise response idea discussed in Chapter 6 in connection with the effects of bizarre imagery on mnemonics (Hirshman, Whelley, & Palij, 1989).

Some early studies suggested that flashbulb memories probably do not differ in kind from more ordinary types of memories (McCloskey, Wible, & Cohen, 1988). For instance, Christianson (1989) tested Swedish subjects' memories for the assassination of their prime minister in 1986, once barely 6 weeks after the assassination and again a year later. He found that only the general information was recalled with accuracy. Details that were recalled, in contrast, seemed to be a creative mixture of a few specifics plus more general knowledge, exactly the kind of memory first identified by Bartlett (1932; see also Neisser, 1982; Weaver, 1993).

In contrast, Conway et al. (1994) did a similar, extensive study and found evidence of special, flashbulb-like memories. They tested subjects on their personal recollections at the time of British prime minister Margaret Thatcher's resignation, first just 2 weeks after the event, then again nearly a year later. More than 86% of their sample from the U.K had accurate, detailed recollections of the event, including specific personal details (e.g., what they had eaten for breakfast that day). Because fewer than 30% of the non-U.K. subjects had such memories, the authors conclude that vivid, accurate flashbulb memories can be formed. Furthermore, whether you form such memories depends critically on "the level of importance attached to the event and level of affective response to the news"; in other words, you are more likely to form a flashbulb memory if you view the event as especially important to you and if it has an emotional effect on you (see also Libkuman, Nichols-Whitehead, Griffith, & Thomas 1999, on the role of emotional arousal in remembering).

But here's the irony again: Is memory good, even flashbulb-quality good, or is it widely subject to the sins of misattribution, suggestibility, bias, and the rest? The circumstances Conway et al. (1994) isolated as important for forming flashbulb memories—high level of importance, high affective response to the event—should also characterize memories of traumatic events, exactly those that are in dispute in cases of repressed and recovered memories.

■ Section Summary

- Studies of autobiographical memory, or memory in real-world settings, show the same kinds of effects as laboratory studies, but sometimes more strongly. Recognition memory for information acquired across an extended period is remarkably accurate across many years, whereas recall begins to decline within months. Distinctiveness, importance of the event to oneself, and the level of one's affective response are all important factors in remembering real-world events, especially those that seem to produce flashbulb memories. The ironies of memory—a powerful, large-capacity system that is nonetheless quite prone to error—have not been completely explained.

Key Terms

agent (p. 313)
argument (p. 313)
autobiographical memory (p. 339)
case grammar (p. 311)
content accuracy (p. 308)
default values (p. 325)
false memory (p. 329)
frames (p. 325)
headers (p. 324)
location (p. 313)
memory impairment (p. 333)

misinformation acceptance (p. 336)
misinformation effect (p. 334)
patient (p. 313)
processing fluency (p. 337)
proposition (p. 310)
reconstructive memory (p. 301)
recipient (p. 313)
relation (p. 313)
repression (p. 338)

schema (p. 302)
script (p. 323)
semantic cases (p. 313)
semantic integration (p. 307)
source memory (p. 337)
source misattribution (p. 335)
technical accuracy (p. 307)
time (p. 313)
von Restorff effect (p. 320)

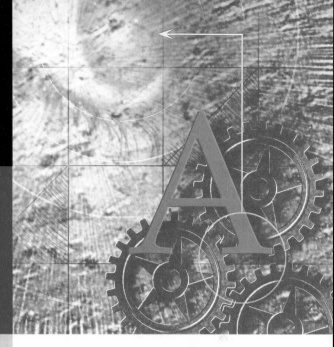

CHAPTER 9

Language

The beginning of wisdom is learning the names of things. (Confucius)

Man is known . . . as "the talking animal"; and language is assuredly a capital distinction between man and brute. . . . Language is a system of signs, *different from the things signified, but able to suggest them. (James, 1890, p. 980)*

I personally think we developed language because of our deep inner need to complain. (Lily Tomlin, "The Search for Signs of Intelligent Life in the Universe," TIME, *October 7, 1985)*

anguage *is* the most common and universal feature of human society. More than any other aspect of human knowledge, language pervades every facet of our lives, from our most public behavior to our most private thoughts. We might imagine a society that has no interest in art, music, or biology, for example, or even one with no formal system of numbers and arithmetic. But it is inconceivable that a society would have no language, no means of communication. Every culture, no matter how primitive or isolated, has language, and every person, unless deprived by nature or accident, develops skill in the use of language. The reason is obvious: Language gives us power.

This is a chapter on the basics of language, its characteristics, functions, structure, and form. **Linguistics** is the academic discipline that takes language as its topic, and a good deal of what you'll read has come to us from that discipline. As you learned in Chapter 1, linguistics had a profound influence on cognitive psychology. It was a major turning point in the development of cognitive psychology when Chomsky rejected behaviorism's explanation of language; according to Wasow (1989), Chomsky's influence on the field of linguistics was equally dramatic. Because approaches such as Chomsky's seemed likely to yield new insights and understanding, psychology renewed its interest in language research in the late 1950s and early 1960s, borrowing heavily from linguistic theory.

And yet, as psychologists began to apply and test linguistic theory, they discovered an important limitation in the purely linguistic approach. Language is a purposeful activity. It's there to *do* something; to communicate, to express thoughts and ideas, even to complain. Linguistics, however, focused on language itself as a formal, almost disembodied system. In such an approach, the *use* of language by humans was somehow seen as less interesting, tangential, or even irrelevant. Upon reflection, this view denied a fundamental interest in psychology—behavior. The notion that language behavior was somehow less interesting than language itself was unacceptable to psychology, even contradictory. Thus a new branch of cognitive psychology evolved, called **psycholinguistics,** *the study of language as it is used and learned by people.*

We have time only for a brief survey of linguistics and psycholinguistics here. This chapter and the next focus on the nature and structure of language and cover two of the three traditional concerns in psycholinguistics: language comprehension and production. The third concern, language acquisition, is beyond the scope of this book, although several useful sources on that topic are cited in the Suggested Readings. Throughout this treatment, we are especially concerned with the relationships between language and the human cognitive system responsible for its use and acquisition.

Linguistic Universals and Functions

Defining Language

Webster's defines *language* as "the expression or communication of thoughts and feelings by means of sounds, and combinations of such sounds, to which meaning is attributed; human speech." That's not a bad start. For example, one particularly critical idea in the definition is that meaning is *attributed* to the sounds rather than residing in or being part of those sounds. As an illustration, the difference in sound between the words *car* and *cars* is the "s" sound, denoting plural in English. As often as not, this is the meaning of a final "s" sound; "more than one of something." But this meaning is not inherent in the "s" sound, any more than the word *chalk* necessarily refers to the white stuff used on blackboards. This is an

A language does not have to be spoken to be a true language, as sign language for the deaf and symbolic computer languages show.

important idea in the study of language: Language is based on usually arbitrary connections between linguistic elements, such as sounds, and the meanings denoted by those sounds.

On the other hand, the definition is a bit confining. For instance, it restricts language to sounds, to human speech. By this rule, writing would be excluded from a consideration of language, as would sign language for the deaf. It is true that writing is a recent development in the history of language, dating back only about 5,000 years, and it is equally true that the development of writing depended critically on the existence of a spoken language. Thus the spoken, auditory form of a language is more basic than the written version; is there any doubt that children would fail to acquire language if they were exposed only to books instead of speech? Nonetheless, we include written language in our definition for the indisputable reason that reading and writing are major forms of communication in modern society.

Let's offer a definition that is more suitable for our purposes. **Language** is *a shared symbolic system for communication.* First, language is symbolic. It consists of linguistic units, sounds that form words and other meaningful units that symbolize or stand for the referent of the word; the referent, the thing referred to by the final "s," is the meaning *plural.* Second, the symbol system is shared by all speakers of a language culture. Speakers and listeners all learned the same set of arbitrary connections between sound and meaning, and they also share a common rule system that translates the sound-to-meaning connections in the appropriate direction. Third, the system enables communication. The speaker translates from the thought into a public message, according to the shared rule system. This enables the listener to retranslate the public, spoken message back into the underlying thought or meaning. (Except in situations that deal with sounds and speech exclusively, the terms *speaker* and *listener* can also be interpreted to include *writer* and *reader.*)

Universals of Language

Hockett (1960a, 1960b, 1966) proposed a list of 13 **linguistic universals,** *features or characteristics that are common to all known languages.* As distinct from various animal communication systems, Hockett proposed that only human language contains all 13 of these features. Several of the universals or "design features" he identified, such as the vocal–auditory requirement, are not now considered essential characteristics of language, although they may have been essential to the evolution of the language. Other features are critically important to our analysis here. Hockett's full list of 13 linguistic universals is presented in Table 9-1, along with short explanations. We limit our discussion here to just four of these, plus two other features implied by Hockett's list, because they are of greatest importance to our study.

Semanticity As you already know, the term *semantic* means "meaning." It is an obvious yet important point that language exhibits **semanticity,** that *language conveys meaning.* Hockett's point here is that the sounds of human language carry meaning, whereas other sounds that we make, say coughing or clearing our throats, are not part of our language

Table 9-1 HOCKETT'S LINGUISTIC UNIVERSALS

- **Vocal–auditory channel.** The channel or means of transmission for all linguistic communication is vocal–auditory. Hockett excluded written language by this universal because it is a recent invention and because it is not found in all language cultures.
- **Broadcast transmission and directional reception.** Linguistic transmissions are broadcast, that is transmitted in all directions from the source, and can be received by any hearer within range; therefore, the transmission is public. By virtue of binaural hearing, the direction or location of the transmission is conveyed by the transmission itself.
- **Transitoriness: rapid fading.** The linguistic transmission is of a transitory nature; it has to be received at exactly the right time, or it will fade (as contrasted with, say, a message transmitted to a recording device, which preserves the information). This implies that the hearer must perform the message preservation task by recording the message on paper or storing information in memory.
- **Interchangeability.** "Any speaker of a human language is capable, in theory, of saying anything he can understand when someone else says it. For language, humans are what engineers call 'transceivers': units freely usable for either transmission or reception" (Hockett 1960a). In other words, because I can understand a sentence you say to me, I can therefore say that sentence back to you: I can both receive and transmit any message. Contrast this with certain animal systems in which males and females produce different calls or messages that cannot be interchanged.
- **Total feedback.** The human speaker has total auditory feedback for the transmitted message, simultaneous with the listener's reception of the message. This feedback is used for moment-to-moment adjustments to the production of sound.
- **Specialization.** The sounds of language are specialized to convey meaning, that is, linguistic intent, as opposed to nonlanguage sounds. Consider a jogger saying "I'm exhausted," when the speech act conveys a specific meaning. Contrast this with a jogger panting loudly at the end of a run, when the sounds being produced have no necessary linguistic function (although a hearer might infer that the jogger is exhausted).
- **Semanticity.** Linguistic utterances, whether simple phrases or complete sentences, convey meaning by means of the symbols we use to form the utterance.
- **Arbitrariness.** There is no inherent connection between a symbol and the concept or object to which it refers; there is only an arbitrary connection between sound and meaning. Contrast this with iconic communication systems, such as the bee's waggle dance.
- **Discreteness.** Although sound patterns can vary continuously across several dimensions (e.g., duration of sound, loudness of sound), language uses only a small number of discrete ranges on those dimensions to convey meaning. Thus languages do not rely on continuous variation of vowel duration, for instance, to signal changes in meaning.
- **Displacement.** Linguistic messages are not tied in time or space to the topic of the communication; this implicates an elaborate memory system within the speaker or hearer to recall the past and anticipate the future.
- **Productivity.** Language is novel, consisting of utterances that have never been uttered or comprehended before; new messages, including words, can be coined freely by means of rules and agreement among the members of the language culture.
- **Duality of patterning (duality of structure).** A small set of sounds, or phonemes, can be combined and recombined into an infinitely large set of sentences, or meanings. The sounds have no inherent meaning; the combinations do have meaning.
- **Cultural or traditional transmission.** Language is acquired by exposure to the culture, to the language of the surrounding people. Contrast this with various courtship and mating communications of animals, in which the specific messages are genetically governed.

because they do not usually convey meaning in the normal sense of the word. (I'm ignoring here the example of a roomful of students coughing in unison at, say, a professor's boastful remark, to indicate a collective opinion. In this situation, the coughing sound is called *paralinguistic* and functions much the way rising vocal pitch indicates anger. Then again, it could just be a roomful of coughing students.)

Arbitrariness Hockett's feature of arbitrariness is one we just encountered in the dictionary definition of language. ***Arbitrariness*** means that *there is no inherent connection between the units (sounds, words) used in a language and the meanings referred to by those units.* There are a limited number of exceptions to this, such as the onomatopoeia of *buzz, hum, zoom,* and the like, but these are few indeed (and as Pinker, 1994, notes, some units we think are onomatopoetic, like a pig's *oink,* aren't; that sound is named "boo-boo" in Japanese). Far more commonly, however, the symbol we use to refer to something bears no relationship to the thing itself. The word *dog* has no inherent resemblance or correspondence to the four-legged furry creature named by the word, just as the spoken symbol *silence* does not resemble its referent, true silence. Hockett's clever example drives the point home; *whale* is a small symbol for a very big thing, and *microorganism* is a big symbol for an extremely small thing.

Because there are no built-in connections between symbols and their referents, knowledge of language must involve learning and remembering the arbitrary connections. It is in this sense that we speak of language being a shared system. We all have learned essentially the same connections, the same set of word-to-referent associations, and stored them in memory as part of our knowledge of language. Thus by convention—by agreement with the language culture—we all know that *dog* refers to one particular kind of physical object rather than another. Obviously, we have to know what word goes with what referent because there's no way to look at an object and decide what its name must be (see the humorous passage from Mark Twain, on just this point, in the Suggested Readings for this chapter).

Two important consequences of the arbitrariness of language deserve special attention, partly because they help to distinguish human language from several animal communication systems and partly because they tell us about the human language user. These two consequences concern the flexibility of the symbol system and the principle of naming. Neither of these was listed by Hockett, although it is clear that they are derived from his point about arbitrariness.

Flexibility of Symbols Note that the principle of arbitrariness makes language entirely symbolic. *Desk* and *pupitre* are simply the English and French symbols for a particular object. Were it not for the history of our language, we might call it a *zoople* or a *manty.* A consequence of this symbolic aspect of language is that the system demonstrates tremendous **flexibility.** That is, *because the connection between symbol and meaning is arbitrary, we can change those connections and invent new ones.* We routinely shift our terms for the things around us, however slowly such change takes place; the archaic term *automobiles* became *cars,* and people stopped playing records on their phonographs and started playing LPs on their hi-fis.

Calvin and Hobbes

by Bill Watterson

Contrast this degree of flexibility with the opposite of a symbolic system, called an iconic system. In an iconic system, each unit has a physical resemblance to its referent, just as a map is physically similar to the terrain it depicts. In such a system there is no flexibility because changing the symbol for a referent would make the connection arbitrary.

In fact, the human language that comes closest to being iconic is sign language because it originally devised units, the sequences of hand movements, to resemble the thing being referred to. But even sign language now goes far beyond its original iconic scheme. Some of the American Sign Language (ASL) vocabulary remains physically similar to the referent (Figure 9-1), but many more ASL words blend, simplify, and combine signs or rely on rules that violate simple iconic connections. For example (Howard, 1983), ASL intensifies meaning by making the sign more rapidly than usual. Thus to sign the concept "VERY QUICKLY," you would sign "QUICKLY" in a rapid, tense fashion. This seemingly iconic relationship is undermined with "VERY SLOWLY"; you would apply the normal rule for intensifying, making the sign for "SLOWLY" in a rapid, tense fashion.

Naming A corollary point to arbitrariness and flexibility of symbols involves **naming** (Glass & Holyoak, 1986). *We assign names to all the objects in our environment, to all the feelings and emotions we experience, to all the ideas and concepts we conceive of.* Obviously, wherever it is you are sitting right now as you read this book, each object in the room has a name. Of course, in an unfamiliar or unusual place (an airport control tower or a car repair shop) you may not know the name of something, but it never occurs to you that the thing might have no name.

Furthermore, we don't stop by naming just the physical objects around us. We have an elaborate vocabulary by which we refer to unseen characteristics, privately experienced feelings, and other intangibles and abstractions. Terms such as *perception, mental process, spreading activation,* and *knowledge* have no necessary physical referent, nor do words such as *justice, cause, frivolousness, likewise,* and *however* refer to concrete objects. Indeed, we even have words such as *abstractions* and *intangibles* that refer to the *idea* of being abstract. And going one step further, we generate or invent names for new objects, ideas, and activities, and so forth. Think of the new vocabulary that had to be invented

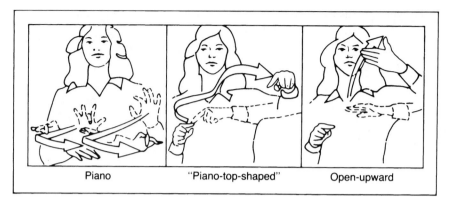

Piano — "Piano-top-shaped" — Open-upward

Figure 9-1

A signer creates an American Sign Language depiction of a grand piano. The sign is partially iconic because it resembles the physical object. *Source.* Newport and Bellugi (1978).

and mastered to describe the various actions and operations in word processing, for instance. Because we need and want to talk about new things, new ideas, and new concepts, we invent new terms.

Displacement One of the most powerful devices our language gives us is *the ability to talk about something other than the present moment*, a feature called **displacement.** By conjugating verbs to form past tense, future tense, and so on, we can communicate about objects, events, and ideas that are not present but are remembered or anticipated. And when we use constructions such as "If I go to the library tomorrow, then I'll be able to . . .," we demonstrate a particularly powerful aspect of displacement: We can communicate about something that has never happened, and indeed might never happen, while anticipating future consequences of that never-performed action. To illustrate the power and importance of displacement to yourself, try speaking only in the present tense for about 5 minutes. You'll discover how incredibly limiting it would be if we were "stuck in the present."

Productivity By most accounts, this final principle of productivity (also called generativity by some authors) is the most important of all the linguistic universals because it gives language its most notable characteristic—novelty. Although it is featured in Hockett's list of universals, he was by no means the first to appreciate its importance. Indeed, the novelty of language, and the productivity that novelty implies, form the basis of Chomsky's (1959) critique of Skinner's book (see Chapter 1) and the foundation for Chomsky's own influential theory of language (1957, 1965). It is an absolute article of faith in both linguistics and psycholinguistics that the key to understanding language and language behavior lies in an understanding of novelty, an understanding of the productive nature of language.

Consider the following: Aside from trite phrases, customary greetings, and so on, hardly any of our routine language is standardized or repetitive. Instead, the bulk of what we say is novel. Our utterances are not memorized, are not repeated, but are new. This is the principle of **productivity,** that *language is a productive and inherently novel activity, that we generate sentences rather than repeat them.* I lecture on the principle of productivity every time I teach my memory and cognition class, each time uttering a stream of sounds, a sequence of words and sentences, that is novel, new, invented on the spot. Even in somewhat stylized situations, as in telling a joke, the language is largely new. Only if the punchline requires a specific word, say because of a double meaning or rhyme, do I try to remember the exact wording of a previously used sentence (and recall from the last chapter that we seldom remember language word for word).

What does this mean? It means that language is a *creative* system as opposed to a repetitive system. We do not recycle sentences, so to speak. Instead, we create them on the spot, now in the active voice, now in the passive, with a prepositional phrase sometimes at the beginning, sometimes at the end, and so on. In a very real sense then, applying our productive rules of language to the words in our vocabulary permits us to generate an infinite number of utterances.

How can we understand any and all of the infinite set of sentences; what does it mean for a theory of language that speakers and listeners can generate and comprehend any one of this numberless set? In brief, it means that speakers of the language must have some flexible basis for producing or generating novel speech, for coming up with the different sequences of sounds and words that can be comprehended by listeners. And, likewise, hearers must have the same flexible basis to hear the sequence of words and recover from them what the intended meaning is. By most accounts, the basis for such productivity is a set of rules. To anticipate later sections of the chapter, rules form the basis for each level of language we discuss, from our phonological system up through the highest level of analysis, the conceptual and belief systems we hold as we comprehend language.

Animal Communication Systems

The contrast between the flexible, productive human language system and the various animal communication systems is staggering. Consider the chimpanzee signaling system (Marler, 1967), for example. This system consists of several distress and warning calls, alerting an entire troupe of chimps to imminent danger. Chimpanzees produce a guttural "rraup" sound to warn others in the troupe of an eagle, one of the chimp's natural predators; they "chutter" to warn of snakes and "chirp" to warn of leopards. The system thus exhibits semanticity, an important characteristic of human language. That is, each signal in chimpanzee has a different, specific referent (eagle, snake, and leopard). And furthermore, these seem to be arbitrary connections: "Rraup" doesn't resemble eagles in any physical way.

But as Glass and Holyoak (1986) note, the troupe of chimpanzees cannot get together and decide to change the meaning of "rraup" from *eagle* to *snake.* The arbitrary connections to meaning are completely inflexible in these systems. (Moreover, this inflexibility probably results at least in part from genetic influence; compare this with Hockett's last universal, cultural transmission.) Furthermore, there is a vast difference

"Matthews ... we're getting another one of those strange 'aw blah es span yol' sounds."

between naming in human languages and in the animal systems. For instance, there seem to be no words in chimpanzee for other obviously important objects and concepts in their environment, such as "tree" (or presumably for more emotional or abstract concepts, given Harlow's [1953] famous demonstrations of the security and comfort needs of baby chimps). And as for displacement and productivity, consider the following delightful quotation from Glass and Holyoak (1986, p. 448): "The monkey has no way of saying 'I don't see an eagle,' or 'Thank heavens that wasn't an eagle,' or 'That was some huge eagle I saw yesterday.' "

In short, beyond the level of arbitrariness, no animal communication system seems to exhibit the characteristics that appear to be universally true of and vitally important to human language. In the wild, at any rate, there appear to be no genuine languages. In human cultures, genuine language is the rule, apparently with no exceptions.

Five Levels of Analysis, a Critical Distinction, and Whorf's Hypothesis

We conclude this introduction with three points. The first concerns the five levels of analysis necessary for a full exploration of language. The second is a traditional distinction

Table 9-2 MILLER'S (1973) FIVE LEVELS OF LANGUAGE ANALYSIS

Level	Explanation
1. Phonology	Analysis of the sounds of language as they are articulated and comprehended in speech
2. Syntax	Analysis of word order and grammaticality (e.g., rules for forming past tense, plurals, rules for determining word ordering in phrases and sentences)
3. Lexical or Semantic	Analysis of word meaning and the integration of word meanings within phrases and sentences
4. Conceptual	Analysis of phrase and sentence meaning with reference to knowledge in semantic memory
5. Belief	Analysis of sentence and discourse meaning with reference to one's own beliefs and one's beliefs about a speaker's intent and motivations

between one's performance in language and one's internal competence. As it happens, this distinction has some important implications for the kinds of tasks we can use in psycholinguistic research. And finally, we talk briefly about the relationship between language and cognition, specifically the question of how strongly our language influences our thinking, known as Whorf's linguistic relativity hypothesis (1956).

Five Levels of Analysis The traditional view of language, a characteristically linguistic point of view, is that language is the set of all acceptable, well-formed sentences in the language. In this scheme, sets of rules are said to generate the sentences, and the entire set of rules is called a **grammar.** In other words, the grammar of a language is *the complete set of rules that will generate or produce all the acceptable sentences and will not generate any unacceptable, ill-formed sentences.* According to most linguists (e.g., Chomsky, 1965), such a grammar operates at three levels: Phonology of language deals with the sounds of language, syntax deals with word order and grammaticality, and semantics deals with accessing and combining the separate word meanings into a sensible, meaningful whole.

In his highly readable introduction to a book on psychology and language, Miller (1973; incidentally, the same Miller of "Magic Number Seven" fame) proposes that language is organized on five distinguishable levels, not just three (Table 9-2). In addition to the three traditional levels of phonology, syntax, and lexical or semantic knowledge, Miller suggests that a psychological approach to language must include two higher levels as well. He calls these the level of conceptual knowledge and the level of beliefs. As he points out, "Grammar, of course, deals with only the first three of these levels . . . and with the relations between them. A psychologist interested in language, however, must also remember that a person's concepts and beliefs play an essential role in his use and understanding of linguistic messages" (p. 8). For organizational purposes, we focus primarily on the first three of the levels in this chapter, the basics of phonology, syntax, and semantics in language. The last two levels of analysis, the conceptual knowledge and belief systems that speakers and listeners use while using language, are addressed in Chapter 10.

A Critical Distinction Chomsky (1957, 1965) has long insisted that there is an important distinction to be drawn at the outset of any investigation into language, the distinction between **competence** and **performance.** Competence is *the internalized knowledge of language and its rules that fully fluent speakers of a language have.* It is an ideal knowledge, to an extent, in that it represents a person's complete knowledge of how to generate and comprehend language. Performance is *the actual language behavior a speaker generates*, the string of sounds and words that the speaker utters.

Chomsky argues that competence is a purer basis for understanding linguistic knowledge and that performance is a less secure basis. The reasons for this should be obvious. When we produce language, not only are we revealing our knowledge of language, but we are also passing that knowledge through the human information-processing system. Therefore, it is not surprising that performance reveals imperfections; after all, memory is fallible. Speakers may lose the train of thought as they proceed through a sentence and thus may be forced to stop and begin again. We pause, repeat ourselves, stall by saying "ummm," and so on. All these **dysfluencies,** these *irregularities or errors in otherwise fluent speech*, can be attributed to the language user. Lapses of memory, momentary distractions, intrusions of new thoughts—all these are imperfections in the language user rather than in the user's basic knowledge of the language.

Thus the discipline of linguistics, not particularly concerned with the psychology of memory limitations, imperfect attention, and the like, relies on the abstract competence that can be exhibited. Chomsky's strategy was to rely on speakers' **linguistic intuitions,** asking people to judge whether a sentence was acceptable or "a good sentence" and accepting their judgments as reflecting their competence. For instance, which of these is a better sentence?

(1) The office was cluttered with large, empty plastic bottles.

*(2) The office was cluttered with plastic, empty large bottles.

(By convention, sentences that are deliberately incorrect are preceded by an asterisk.) In Chomsky's view, we can come closer to knowing about speakers' linguistic competence by asking them to judge sentences than by relying on their online spoken language performance. But, as indicated earlier, *psycho*linguists cannot afford to throw out performance; in fact, they aren't even tempted to throw it out. After all, we are in the business of investigating human behavior and the mental processes that lead to that behavior. As Miller (1973) points out, if we exclude too much of the language user, then we miss many important characteristics of the very language we are trying to understand.

Whorf's Hypothesis. Here's a part of the language user that has often been—and to an extent continues to be—either excluded or ignored, the part influenced by cultural and language differences. We tend to think of mental processes, including those related to language, as universal, as being equally true of all languages. Even slight familiarity with another language, however, reveals at least some of our beliefs to be misconceptions.

A clear example involves spelling, particularly English spelling. Much theoretical work discusses regular and irregular words in English and the possible mental mechanisms

by which readers detect irregularly spelled words. This is important because English spelling is so difficult; think of cases in which the same spelling has different pronunciations (e.g., *through, though, tough*), cases in which different spellings have the same pronunciation (e.g., *road, rode*), and completely irregular words for which the spelling seems barely related to pronunciation at all (e.g., *yacht, colonel*). In English, sadly, spelling is simply not a sure guide to pronunciation. (Where I live, there once was a chain of Hough Bakeries. How was it pronounced?) Contrast this with Korean, a language in which the spelling of a word is an absolutely certain guide to its pronunciation and vice versa. As Simpson (2000) put it, Koreans think that a spelling bee, common in the United States, is "about the silliest thing they've ever heard of"; if you can say the word in Korean, you can spell it, and if you can spell it, you know how it's pronounced. (The name of the bakery rhymed with "tough.")

An organizing issue in studies of cultural influences on language and thought is how one's language affects one's thinking. This topic is commonly called the Whorfian hypothesis, or more formally the **linguistic relativity hypothesis** by Whorf (1956). Whorf's basic idea was that *the language you know shapes the way you think about events in the world around you*. In its strongest version, the hypothesis claims that language controls both thought and perception to a large degree; that is, you cannot think about ideas or concepts that your language does not name. In its weaker version, the hypothesis claims that your language influences and shapes your thought, making it more difficult to think about ideas without having a name for them.

Current thinking finds some merit in the weaker form of the Whorfian hypothesis, that language does indeed influence our thoughts to a degree. For example, "English speakers have no difficulty expressing the idea that, if there are 49 men and 37 pairs of shoes, some men will have to go without shoes. There are nonliterate societies where this would be a difficult situation to describe, because the language may have number terms only for 'one-two-many' (Greenberg, 1978)" (Hunt & Agnoli, 1991, p. 385; see also Hoffman, Lau, & Johnson, 1986). As another example, Hunt and Agnoli note the effect of language on working memory resources. If your language has a simple, one-word label for an idea, then expressing that idea in spoken language would not tax working memory very heavily because articulation of the word would be fairly rapid. Contrast this with a study in which Welsh subjects, whose working memory was tested in Welsh, had lower working memory spans, presumably because of the longer (hence slower to articulate) words. The same subjects had higher working memory spans when they were tested in English. (See Baddeley, 1992a, and Ellis & Hennelly, 1980, for details, and Whitney, 1998, for a full discussion of language and cultural effects. For the effects of an individual difference—blindness—on language, see Shepard & Cooper, 1992.)

■ Section Summary

- Language is our shared system of symbolic communication, a system quite unlike naturally occurring animal communication systems. True language involves a set of characteristics, linguistic universals, that emphasize the arbitrary connections between symbols and referents, the meaningfulness of the symbols, and our reliance on rules for generating language. No known animal communication system contains these critical features.
- Three traditional levels of analysis—phonology, syntax, and semantics—are joined by two others in psycholinguistics; the level of conceptual knowledge and the level of one's beliefs. Linguists focus on an idealized language competence as they study language, but psycholinguists are also concerned with language performance. Therefore the final two levels of analysis take on greater importance as we investigate language users and their behavior. To some degree, we can use people's linguistic intuitions to discover what is known about language; to the extent that language processes are automatic, however, our intuitions provide little insight into the processes behind our performance.

Phonology: The Sounds of Language

In any language interaction, the task of a speaker is to communicate an idea by translating that idea into spoken sounds. The hearer goes in the opposite direction, translating from sound to intended meaning. Among the many sources of information available in the spoken message, the most obvious and concrete one is the sound of the language itself, the stream of speech signals that must be decoded. Other sources of information, say the gestures and facial expressions of the speaker, can be eliminated, as in a telephone conversation, with little or no disruption of the communication; in fact, gestures carry far less information than you might suspect (Krauss, Morrel-Samuels, & Colosante, 1991). But you can't do without the words and the sounds that form those words. Thus our study of the grammar of language begins at this basic level of **phonology,** *the sounds of language and the rule system for combining them.*

Sounds in Isolation

To state an obvious point, different languages sound different: They are composed of different sets of sounds. The basic sounds that compose a language are called phonemes. If we were to conduct a survey, we would find around 200 different phonemes present across all known spoken languages. No single language uses even half that many, however. English, for instance, contains about 46 phonemes (experts disagree on whether some sounds are separate phonemes or blends of two phonemes; the disagreement centers on diphthong vowel sounds, as in *few,* seemingly a combination of "ee" and "oo"). Hawaiian, on the other hand, uses only about 15 phonemes (Palermo, 1978). Note here that there is little significance to the total tally of phonemes in a language; no language is superior to another because it has more (or fewer) phonemes.

Table 9-3 shows the Glucksberg and Danks (1975) typology of the phonemes of English, based on the characteristics of their pronunciation. For consonants, three

Table 9-3 ENGLISH CONSONANTS AND VOWELS

English consonants

Manner of Articulation		Bilabial	Labiodental	Dental	Alveolar	Palatal	Velar	Glottal
Stops	Voiceless	p (*pat*)			t (*tack*)		k (*cat*)	
	Voiced	b (*bat*)			d (*dig*)		g (*get*)	
Fricatives	Voiceless		f (*fat*)	Θ (*thin*)	s (*sat*)	š (i*ss*h)		h (*hat*)
	Voiced		v (*vat*)	∂ (*then*)	z (*zap*)	ž (a*z*ure)		
Affricatives	Voiceless					č (*church*)		
	Voiced					ǰ (*judge*)		
Nasal		m (*mat*)			n (*nat*)		η (si*ng*)	
Liquids					l (*late*)	r (*rate*)		
Glides		w (*win*)				y (*yet*)		

English vowels

	Front	Center	Back
High	i (*beet*)		u (*boot*)
			U (*book*)
	i (b*i*t)		
Middle		əl (b*ird*)	o (b*o*de)
	e (b*a*by)	ə (sof*a*)	
	ε (b*e*t)		ɔ (b*ought*)
	æ (b*a*t)	ʌ (b*u*t)	
Low			
		a (p*a*lm)	

Source. Glucksberg and Danks (1975).

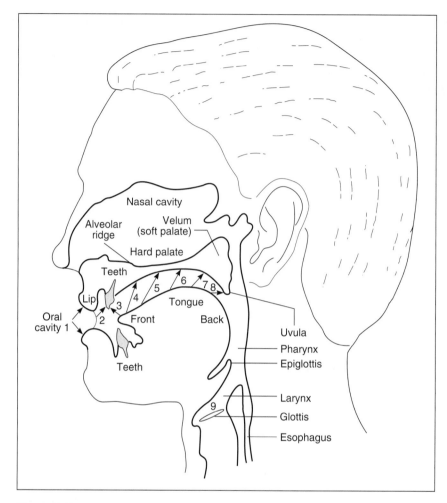

Figure 9-2

The vocal tract, illustrating places of articulation: 1, bilabial; 2, labiodental; 3, dental; 4, alveolar; 5, palatoalveolar; 7, velar; 8, uvular; 9, glottal. *Source.* From Fromkin and Rodman (1974).

variables are relevant: place of articulation, manner of articulation, and voicing. Place of articulation is the place in the vocal tract where the disruption of airflow takes place; as shown in Figure 9-2, a bilabial consonant such as /b/ disrupts the airflow at the lips, whereas /h/ disrupts the column of air at the very rear of the vocal tract, at the glottis. Second, manner of articulation is how the airflow coming up from the lungs is disrupted. If the column of air is completely stopped and then released, it's called a stop consonant, such as the consonant sounds in *bat* and *tub*. A fricative consonant, such as the /f/ in *fine*, involves only a partial blockage of airflow. Finally, *voicing* refers to whether the vocal cords begin to vibrate immediately with the obstruction of airflow (for example, the /b/ in *bat*) or whether the vibration is delayed until after the release of air (the /p/ in *pat.*).

Vowels, by contrast, involve no disruption of the airflow. Instead, they differ on two dimensions: placement in the mouth (front, center, or back) and tongue position in the mouth (high, middle, or low). Scan Table 9-3, pronouncing the sample words, and try to be consciously aware of the characteristics that you (if you're a native or fluent English speaker) know so thoroughly at an unconscious, automatic level.

Let's develop a few more conscious intuitions about the basic sounds of language. Stop for a moment and put your hand in front of your mouth. Say the word *pot* and then *spot*. Did you notice a difference between the two /p/ sounds? Most speakers produce a puff of air with the /p/ sound as they say *pot"*; we puff very little (if at all) for the /p/ in *spot* if it's spoken normally. Given this, you would have to agree that these two /p/ sounds are different at a purely physical level. And yet you hear them as the same sound in those two different words; you treat them as the same sound when you hear and comprehend those words. Figure 9-3 shows actual spectrograph patterns for two families of syllables, the /b/ family on the left, the /d/ family on the right. Note how remarkably different "the same" sound can look.

In the terminology of psycholinguistics, the two /p/ sounds, despite their physical differences, are both instances of the same phoneme, the same basic sound group. That is, the fact that these two different sounds are treated as if they were the same in English means that they represent one phoneme. Thus a **phoneme** is a *category or group of language sounds that are treated as the same sound, despite any physical differences among the category members*. In other words, the English word *spot* does not change its meaning when pronounced with the /p/ sound in *pot*.

A classic illustration of phoneme boundaries is shown in Figure 9-4, from a study by Liberman, Harris, Hoffman, and Griffith (1957). When the presented sound crossed a boundary, that is, between stimulus values 3 and 5 and between 9 and 10, subjects' identifications of the sound switched rapidly from /b/ to /d/, and then from /d/ to /g/. Variations within the boundaries, did not lead to different identifications: Despite the variations, all the sounds from values 5 to 8 were identified as /d/.

There are two critical notions here. The first is that *all the sounds falling within a set of boundaries are perceived as the same, despite physical differences among them.* This is the phenomenon of **categorical perception.** Because English speakers discern no real difference between the hard /k/ sounds in *cool* and *keep*, they are perceived categorically, that is, perceived as belonging to the same category, the /k/ phoneme.

The second notion is quite straightforward: Different phonemes are the sounds that are perceived as being different by speakers of the language. The physical differences between /s/ and /z/ are important in English; changing from one to the other gives you different words, such as *ice* and *eyes*. This is no more, and no less, than saying that the /s/ and /z/ sounds in English are different phonemes. An interesting side effect of such phonemic differences is that you can be insensitive to the phonemic differences of other languages if your own language doesn't use the distinguishing difference. Spanish does not use the /s/ versus /z/ contrast, so native speakers of Spanish have difficulty distinguishing

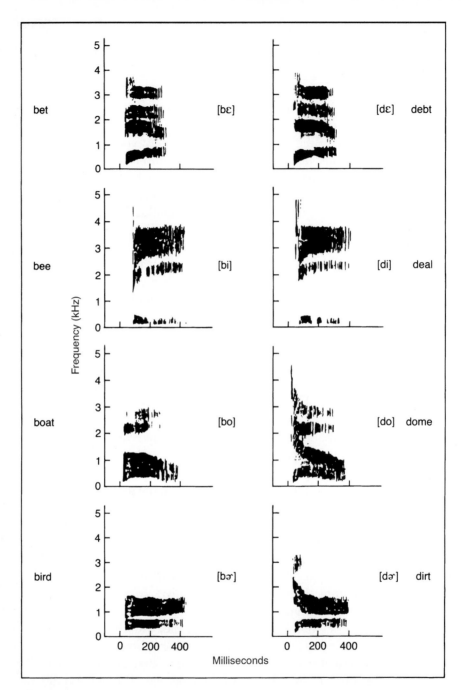

Figure 9-3

Spectrographic patterns of two families of syllables, showing the changes across time in the physical sound patterns. Depicted is the problem of invariance for consonants. There are dramatic changes in the initial portions of the patterns, induced by the following vowel, even though the consonant sounds from top to bottom are all classified as the same phoneme. For instance, the /b/ in *bet* and *bird* are physically very different, yet both are perceived as /b/. In contrast, the /b/ and /d/ sounds in *bet* and *debt* are very similar physically but are perceived as different phonemes. *Source.* Jusczyk et al. (1981).

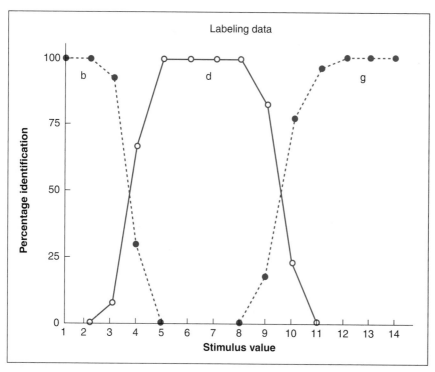

Figure 9-4

One subject's labeling data for synthesized consonants ranging from /b/ to /g/. Note that small changes in the stimulus value (e.g., from values 3 to 4) can result in a complete change in labeling, whereas larger changes (e.g., from values 4 to 8) that do not cross the phoneme boundary do not lead to a change in labeling. *Source.* Liberman et al. (1957).

ice and *eyes* in English. Conversely, the hard /k/ sounds at the beginning of *cool* and *keep* are interchangeable in English: They are the same phoneme. But as Glucksberg and Danks (1975) note, this difference is phonemic in Arabic; the Arabic words for *heart* and *dog* differ only in their initial sounds, exactly the two different hard /k/ sounds in *cool* and *keep*.

Combining Phonemes into Words

From a stock of about 46 phonemes, English generates all its words, however many thousands that might be. This fact, that a small number of units can be combined so flexibly into so many words, is essentially the linguistic universal of productivity, at the level of phonology. Thus from a small set of phonemes we can generate an essentially infinite number of words. Recall further that the essential ingredient of productivity is rules. We turn now to the issue of combining phonemes into words and to the rules by which this is accomplished.

Let's work with a simple example here. There are three phonemes in the word *bat:* the voiced stop consonant /b/, the short vowel sound /ae/, and the final voiceless /t/.

Substitute the voiceless /p/ for /b/, and you get *pat*. Now rearrange the phonemes in these words, and you'll discover that some of the arrangements don't yield English words, such as **abt, *tba,* and **atp.* Why? What makes **abt* or **atp* illegal pronunciation strings in English?

Although it's tempting to say the reason is that syllables like **abt* cannot be pronounced, a moment's reflection suggests that this is false. After all, any number of such "unpronounceable" strings are pronounced in other languages; for example, the initial *pn-* in the French word for *pneumonia* is pronounced, whereas English makes the *p* silent. Instead, the rule seems to be a bit more specific. English usually does not use a "voiced–voiceless" sequence of two consonants within the same pronounced syllable; in fact, it only seldom uses any two-consonant sequence when both are in the same "manner of articulation" category. (Of course, if the two consonants fall in different syllables, then the rule doesn't apply.)

Phonemic Competence and Rules   Why does this seem to be an unusual explanation? The reason is that our knowledge of English phonology and pronunciation is not particularly verbalizable or expressible. You can look at Table 9-3, try to think of words that combine consonants, and eventually come up with tentative pronunciation rules. But this is different from knowing the rules in an easily accessed and expressible fashion. And yet you are a true expert at deciding what phoneme sequences can and cannot be used in English. Your implicit knowledge of how sounds are combined in English tells you that **abt* is illegal because it violates a rule of English pronunciation.

This *extensive knowledge of the rules of permissible English sound combinations* is your **phonemic competence.** These rules tell you what is and isn't permissible; *bat* is, but **abt* isn't. No one ever explicitly taught you these rules, of course; you abstracted them from your language environment as you acquired language. This competence tells you that a string of letters like "pnart" is legal only when the *p* is silent but that "snart" is a legal string—not a word, of course, but a legal combination of sounds. Speakers of the language have this phonemic competence as part of their knowledge of language, an implicit, largely unverbalizable part to be sure, but a part nonetheless.

Speech Perception and Context

We are now ready to approach the question of how people produce and perceive the speech signal. Do we merely hear a word and segment it in some fashion into its separate phonemes, or is this even a possibility given the nature of spoken speech? When we speak, do we merely string phonemes together, one after another, like stringing beads on a necklace?

Categorical Perception and the Problem of Invariance   The answer to both questions is "No." Even when the "same" sound is being pronounced, it is not physically identical to other examples of that "same" sound. The sounds *change*—they change from speaker to speaker and from one time to the next within the same

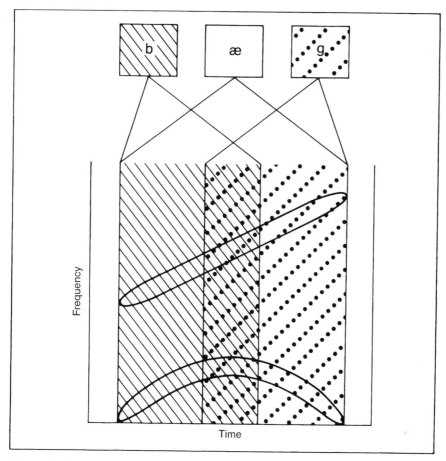

Figure 9-5

Coarticulation is illustrated for the three phonemes in the word *bag;* solid diagonals indicate the influence of the /b/ phoneme, dotted diagonals, the influence of /g/. *Source.* Liberman (1957).

speaker. Most prominently, they change or vary from one word to another, depending on what sounds precede and follow.

This *variability in sounds* is called the **problem of invariance.** This term is somewhat peculiar because the problem in speech perception is that the sounds *are not* invariant; they change all the time. You saw an illustration of this changeability in Figure 9-3, where the initial /b/ and /d/ sounds looked very different in the spectrographic patterns depending on the vowel sound that followed. A second illustration of the problem of invariance is in Figure 9-5, which shows the influence of each of the three phonemes in the word *bag.* To pronounce *bag,* do you simply articulate the /b/, then /ae/, then /g/? No! As the figure shows, the /ae/ sound influences both /b/ and /g/, the /g/ phoneme (dotted lines) exerts an influence well back into the /b/ sound, and so on. The technical term for these effects is **coarticulation:** *More than one sound is articulated at the same time.* As you type the word *the,* your right index finger starts moving toward *h* before your left index finger has struck the *t.* In like fashion, your vocal tract begins to move toward the /ae/ before you have articulated /b/, and toward /g/ before even finishing the /b/. This is yet another illustration of the problem of invariance: Each phoneme changes the articulation of each other phoneme and does so differently depending on what the other phonemes are.

In short, the sounds of language, the phonemes, vary widely as we speak them. Yet we tolerate a fair degree of variability for the sounds within a phoneme category, both when listening and decoding from sound to meaning and also when speaking, converting meaning into spoken sound. How do we do this; how do we tolerate this variability and still decipher the changeable, almost undependable spoken signal?

The answer is *context.* Putting it another way, the answer is *conceptually driven processing.* If we had to rely entirely on the spoken signal to figure out what was being said, then we would be processing speech in an entirely data-driven fashion, a bottom-up process. We would have to find some basis for figuring out what every sound in the word was and then retrieve that word from memory based on the analysis of sound. This is almost impossible, given the variability of phonemes. Instead, context—in this case the words, phrases, and ideas already identified—leads us to correct identification of new, incoming sounds.

A clever demonstration of this was performed by Pollack and Pickett (1964). They tape recorded several spontaneous conversations, spliced out single words from the tapes, then played the spliced words to subjects. When the words were presented in isolation, subjects identified them correctly only 47% of the time. Performance improved when longer and longer segments of speech were played because more and more supportive syntactic and semantic context was then available.

In a related study, Miller and Isard (1963) presented three kinds of sentences to subjects: fully grammatical sentences such as "Accidents kill motorists on the highways," semantically anomalous sentences such as "Accidents carry honey between the house," and ungrammatical strings such as "Around accidents country honey the shoot." They also varied the loudness of the background noise, from the difficult −5 ratio, when the noise was louder than speech, to the easy ratio of +15, when the speech was much louder than the noise. Participants shadowed the strings they heard, and correct performance was the percentage of their shadowing that was accurate. As shown in Figure 9-6, accuracy improved significantly going from the difficult to easy levels of speech-to-noise ratios. More interestingly, the improvement was especially dramatic for grammatical sentences, as if grammaticality helped counteract the background noise. For instance, at the ratio labeled 0 in the figure, 63% of the grammatical sentences were shadowed accurately, compared with only 3% of the ungrammatical strings. Indeed, even at the easiest ratio of +15, fewer than 60% of the ungrammatical strings could be repeated correctly.

More recent evidence is largely consistent with these early findings. That is, the evidence points toward a combination of data-driven and conceptually driven processing in speech recognition, a position now called the integrative or interactive approach

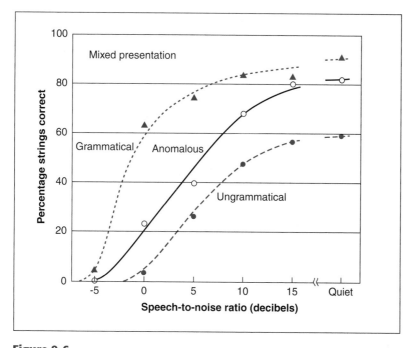

Figure 9-6

Percentage of strings shadowed correctly. *Source.* Miller and Isard (1963).

(Rapp & Goldrick, 2000). At a general level, this approach claims that a variety of conceptually distinct language processes, from the perception of the sounds up through integration of word meanings, operate simultaneously, each having the possibility of influencing the ongoing activity of other processes. While features of the speech signal are analyzed perceptually, listeners' other linguistic knowledge is also being called into play. These higher levels of knowledge and analysis operate in parallel with the phonemic analysis and help the perceptual mechanism identify the sounds and words (Dell & Newman, 1980; Pitt & Samuel, 1995; Samuel, 1996).

As a concrete example, imagine a sentence that begins "The grocery bag was . . ." You are processing the *bag* segment of this speech signal. Having already processed the previous word to at least some level of semantic interpretation, you have developed a useful context for the sentence. To be simple about it, *grocery* limits the number of possibilities that can be mentioned in the sentence. (Recall Chapter 3, where we considered the Warren & Warren [1970] phoneme restoration effect in which subjects "restored" the missing /p/, based on overall meaning, in the sentence "The *eel was on the orange"; see Table 3-2.) Similar evidence of the role of context has been reported by Marslen-Wilson and Welsh (1978) in a task that asked subjects to detect mispronunciations, and by Dell and Newman (1980) in a task that asked subjects to monitor spoken speech for the occurrence of a particular phoneme (recall also the demonstrations of context effects in Treisman's shadowing experiments, e.g., 1960, 1964).

Such results are so powerful that any reasonable theory of speech recognition must account for both aspects of performance: the data driven and the conceptually driven. A specific connectionist model that does exactly that was proposed by McClelland and Elman (1986). In their TRACE model, information is continually being passed among the several levels of linguistic analysis in a spreading activation fashion. Lexical or semantic knowledge, if activated, can thus alter the ongoing analysis at the perceptual level by "telling" it what words are likely to appear next; the model's predictions of what words are likely to appear are based on semantic knowledge. At the same time, phonemic information is being passed to higher levels, thus altering the patterns of activation there (see Dell, 1986, for a spreading activation network theory of sentence production, and Tyler, Voice, & Moss, 2000, for a useful review).

A Final Puzzle

As if the preceding sections weren't enough to convince you of the need for conceptually driven processing, consider one final feature of the stream of spoken speech. Despite coarticulation, categorical perception, and the problem of invariance, we naively believe that words are somehow separate from each other in the spoken signal, that there is some physical pause or gap between spoken words, just as there is a blank space between printed words.

This is not true. Our intuition is entirely wrong. Analysis of the speech signal shows that there is almost no consistent relationship between pauses and the ends of words. Indeed, if anything, the pauses we produce while speaking are longer *within* words than between words. As evidence of this, see Figure 9-7, a spectrograph recording of a spoken sentence. Careful inspection of the patterns in correspondence to the words listed at the bottom illustrates the point: The pauses in the spectrograph bear no particular relationship to the ends of words. There must be other kinds of information that the human information processor uses to decode the spoken language signal.

How can our intuitions about our own language, that words are articulated as separate units, be so wrong? (Note that our intuitions about foreign languages—they sound like a continuous stream of speech—are much more accurate.) How do we segment the speech stream and come to know what the words and phrases are? Part of the answer is our current knowledge of words in the language and the fact that some phoneme combinations simply cannot or do not form words in English (Norris, McQueen, Cutler, & Butterfield, 1997). Another part of the answer to these questions is syntax, the second level of language analysis and the topic we address next.

■ Section Summary

- Phonology is the study of the sounds of language. Spoken words consist of phonemes, the smallest units of sound that speakers of a language can distinguish. Surprisingly, a range of physically different sounds are classified as the same phoneme; we tolerate a fair degree of variation in the sounds we categorize as "the same." This is particularly important in the study of speech recognition because the phonemes in a word

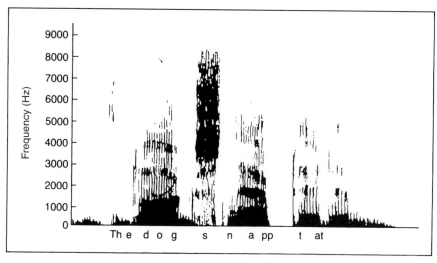

Figure 9-7

A spectrogram from the sentence "John said that the dog snapped at him," taken from fluent spoken speech. Note that the pauses or breaks do not occur regularly at the ends of words; if anything, they occur more frequently *within* the individual words (e.g., between the /s/ and /n/ sounds, between the /p/ and /t/ sounds; compare with the end of *the* and the beginning of *dog*). *Source.* Foss and Hakes (1978).

exhibit a characteristic known as coarticulation. There is much overlap among successive phonemes, such that an initial sound is influenced by the sounds that follow and the later sounds are influenced by what came before. Therefore, speech recognition relies heavily on conceptually driven processes.

Syntax: The Ordering of Words and Phrases

At the second level of analysis we have **syntax,** *the arrangement of words as elements in a sentence to show their relationship to one another; or sentence structure.* We've already studied how sounds are combined to form meaningful words. At this next level of analysis, we are interested in how the words are sequenced to form meaningful utterances, the study of syntax. Just as in phonology, where the rules for combining sounds might be called a phonological grammar, our syntactic grammar is a set of rules for ordering words into acceptable, well-formed sentences.

If you have a connotation associated with the word *syntax,* it probably is not the psycholinguistic sense of *grammar* but the "school grammar" sense of the word instead. In school, if you said "He ain't my friend no more," your teacher might have responded, "Watch your grammar." To an extent, this kind of school grammar is irrelevant to the psycholinguistic study of syntax and grammar. Your teacher was being prescriptive by teaching you what is proper or prestigious according to some set of cultural values. In another way, though, school grammar does relate to the psycholinguistic study of language; language is for expressing ideas, and anything that clarifies this expression, even arbitrary rules about "ain't" and double negatives, improves the communication of meaning. (And finally, your teacher was sensitive to another level of language: People judge others on the quality of their speech.)

Word Order.   Unlike the school grammar idea, the psycholinguistic study of syntax is descriptive; that is, it takes as its goal a description of the rules by which words are arranged to form sentences. Let's take a simple example, one that taps into your syntactic competence. Which is better, sentence 3 or 4?

(3) Beth asked the man about his headaches.

(4) *About the Beth headaches man asked his.

Your "school grammar" taught you that every sentence must have a subject and a verb. According to that rule, sentence 4 is just as much a sentence as 3. Your syntactic competence, on the other hand, tells you that sentence 4 is an ill-formed, unacceptable sentence. You can even specify some of the rules that are being violated in sentence 4; for example, definite articles such as *the* do not usually precede a person's name, and two nouns may not follow one another in the same phrase or clause.

An obvious point here is that the meaning of a sentence is far more than the meanings of the individual words in that sentence. The "far more" here is the arrangement or sequencing of the words. We're speaking now of word order rules, a critical part of English syntax. More than some languages (e.g., Latin), English relies heavily on word order to specify meaning. Consider "red fire engine" versus "fire engine red" (or even "red engine fire"). Despite the fact that *red* and *fire engine* can be nouns, our word order knowledge of English tells us that the first word in these phrases is to be treated as an adjective, modifying the following noun. Thus by varying word order alone, "red fire engine" is a fire engine of the usual color, and "fire engine red" is a particular shade of red.

Phrase Order.   There's more to it than just word order, however. We also rely on the ordering of larger units such as phrases or clauses to convey meaning. Consider the following sentences:

(5) Bill told the men to deliver the piano on Monday.

(6) Bill told the men on Monday to deliver the piano.

In these examples, of course, the positioning of the phrase "on Monday" helps us figure out what meaning was intended; whether the piano was to be delivered on Monday or whether Bill had told the men something on Monday. Thus the sequencing of words and phrases contains clues to meaning, clues that speakers use to express meaning and clues that listeners use to decipher meaning. In general, we need to understand what these clues are and how they are used. We need to explore the various sets of syntactic rules that have been proposed to understand the influence of syntactic factors on comprehension.

We begin by looking at the underlying syntactic structure of sentences, taking a piece-by-piece approach to Chomsky's important work. We then progress to the more current psycholinguistic approach.

Chomsky's Transformational Grammar

At a very general level, Chomsky's intent was to "describe the universal aspects of syntactic knowledge" (Whitney, 1998), that is, to capture the syntactic structures of language. He noted that language has a hierarchical, phrase structure to it: The words do not simply occur one after the other, each with equal status. Instead, words come in groupings, groupings such as "on Monday," "the men," and "deliver the piano." Furthermore, these groupings can be altered, either by moving them from one spot to another in the structure or by modifying them to express somewhat different meanings (e.g., by changing the statement into a question). These two ideas—words come in phrase structure groupings, and the groupings can be modified or transformed—correspond to the two major syntactic rule systems in Chomsky's theory, as shown in Figure 9-8.

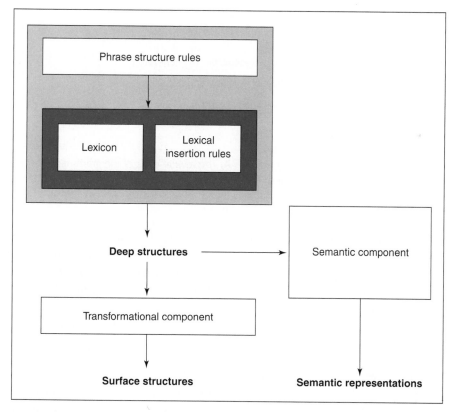

Figure 9-8

A depiction of Chomsky's "transformational grammar." *Source.* Whitney (1998).

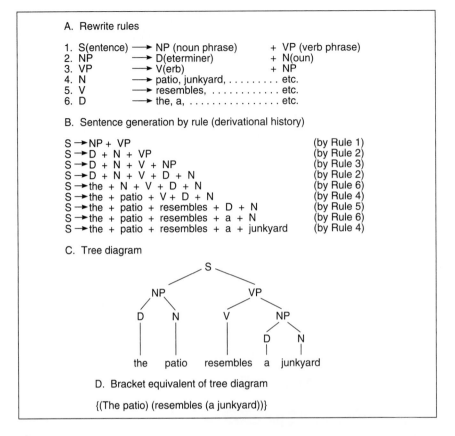

A. Rewrite rules

1. S(entence) ⟶ NP (noun phrase)   + VP (verb phrase)
2. NP ⟶ D(eterminer)   + N(oun)
3. VP ⟶ V(erb)   + NP
4. N ⟶ patio, junkyard, ... etc.
5. V ⟶ resembles, ... etc.
6. D ⟶ the, a, ... etc.

B. Sentence generation by rule (derivational history)

S → NP + VP   (by Rule 1)
S → D + N + VP   (by Rule 2)
S → D + N + V + NP   (by Rule 3)
S → D + N + V + D + N   (by Rule 2)
S → the + N + V + D + N   (by Rule 6)
S → the + patio + V + D + N   (by Rule 4)
S → the + patio + resembles + D + N   (by Rule 5)
S → the + patio + resembles + a + N   (by Rule 6)
S → the + patio + resembles + a + junkyard   (by Rule 4)

C. Tree diagram

D. Bracket equivalent of tree diagram

{(The patio) (resembles (a junkyard))}

Figure 9-9

A depiction of a phrase structure grammar: **A,** The rewrite rules of the grammar;
B, Sentence generation by the rules; **C,** A tree diagram or hierarchical representation;
D, A "bracket equivalent" diagram of the sentence. *Source.* Lachman et al. (1979).

Phrase Structure Grammar Let's start by discussing the phrase structure grammar, the rules (grammar) that generate the overall structure or form of sentences. An important point in Chomsky's system is that the **phrase structure** grammar accounts for the *constituents of the sentence, the word groupings and phrases that make up the whole utterance, and the relationships among those constituents.* To illustrate the nature of a phrase structure grammar, consider a well-known example sentence from Lachman et al. (1979):

(7) The patio resembles a junkyard.

In a phrase structure grammar, the entire sentence is symbolized by an *S*. In this particular grammar, the sentence *S* can be decomposed into two major components, a noun phrase (*NP*) and a verb phrase (*VP*). Thus the first line of the grammar illustrated in Figure 9-9A shows *S→ NP+VP*, to be read, "The sentence can be rewritten as a noun phrase plus a verb phrase." In the second rule, the *NP* can be rewritten as a determiner

(D), an article such as *the* or *a*, plus a noun (N): $NP \rightarrow D+N$; in other words, a noun phrase can be rewritten as a determiner and a noun. In rule 3 we see the structure of a verb phrase; a *VP* is rewritten as a verb (V) plus an *NP*: $VP \rightarrow V+NP$.

As Figure 9-9B shows, six rewrite rules are necessary for generating the sentence "The patio resembles a junkyard." A different but largely equivalent depiction of the grammar is shown in Figure 9-9C, in which a tree diagram shows the most general components at the top and the specific word components at the bottom. An advantage of the tree diagram is that it reveals the hierarchical structure of the sentence as well as the internal structure of the various parts as they relate to each other. Finally, a bracket equivalent is shown in Figure 9-9D.

The Inadequacy of Using Phrase Structure Grammar Alone Chomsky's theory relies heavily on a phrase structure approach because it captures an important aspect of language—its productivity. That is, this kind of grammar is generative; by means of such phrase structure rules, an entire family of sentences can be generated by the grammar. Furthermore, the phrase structure grammar is joined with two other components in Chomsky's theory, the lexical entries (the words we insert into a sentence) and the lexical insertion rules (the rules for putting the words into their slots). These components, as shown in Figure 9-9, generated the first representation of the sentence in Chomsky's theory, the **deep structure** representation. In Chomsky's view, the deep structure is *an abstract syntactic representation of the sentence* being constructed, with only bare-bones lexical entries (words).

The deep structure of a sentence is viewed as critical for two reasons. First, the deep structure is the representation that is passed along to the transformational "fix-it" rules to yield the surface structure of the sentence; we deal with those in a moment. Second, the deep structure is also submitted to a semantic component in the model, the component that "computes" sentence meaning. This component takes the deep structure as its input and produces a semantic representation of the sentence, a representation that reflects the true meaning of the sentence being constructed. Notice that because of the separate treatment of the semantic component, a sentence's true meaning might not be reflected accurately in the surface structure; a surface structure might be **ambiguous,** *or have more than one meaning.* For instance, consider two classic (overworked?) examples of ambiguous sentences:

(8) Visiting relatives can be a nuisance.

(9) The shooting of the hunters was terrible.

A moment's reflection reveals the ambiguities here. The first sentence could mean "Going to visit one's relatives can be a nuisance" or "Having one's relatives come to visit can be a nuisance"; sentence 9 could be referring to lousy hunters or to wounded hunters. These alternative meanings are revealed when we **parse** the sentences, when we *separate or divide the sentence into phrases and groupings,* much the way the phrase structure grammar does. The two meanings of sentence 8—that is, the two deep structures—correspond to two different phrase structures. For sentence 8, the ambiguity boils down to the grammatical function of *visiting*, whether it is used as an adjective or as a verb. These two grammatical functions translate into two different phrase structures (*verb+noun* versus *adjective+noun*).

Sentence (9), however, has only one phrase structure; there is only one way to parse it: {[*the shooting of the hunters*] [*was terrible*]}. Thus sentence 9 is genuinely ambiguous at the level of **surface structure:** It has only one surface structure (one syntactic parsing), yet it is ambiguous. Because phrase structure rules by themselves can generate such ambiguous sentences, Chomsky felt that this illustrated the limitation of the pure phrase structure approach. The reasoning was simple: There must still be something missing in the grammar, because if it were complete, it wouldn't generate ambiguous sentences.

A second difficulty Chomsky pointed out involves examples such as the following:

(10a) Patrick bought a fine French wine.

(10b) A fine French wine was bought by Patrick.

According to phrase structure rules, there is almost no structural similarity at all between these two sentences; they differ radically in their surface structure. And yet they mean virtually the same thing, so at some level they are the same sentence, just different versions of it. People's intuitions, that active and passive paraphrases are more or less identical at the level of meaning, are not captured by the phrase structure approach. According to the phrase structure grammar, sentences 10a and 10b are different.

Transformational Rules Chomsky's solution to such problems was to postulate a second component to the grammar, a set of **transformational rules** that handle the many specific surface forms that can express an underlying idea. These transformational rules *convert the deep structure into a surface structure, a sentence ready to be spoken.* By applying different transformations, we can form an active declarative sentence, a passive voice sentence, a question, a negative, a future or past tense, and so on. With still other transformations, phrases can exchange places, and words can be inserted and deleted. In this view, sentences 10a and 10b differ only in their surface structures; one deep structure is merely transformed in two different fashions. Thus the sentences have different *transformational histories* in that different transformational rules are applied to the deep structure, one set including the active voice, one the passive voice. Likewise, for a simple deep structure idea such as {(boy kisses girl)}, the transformational grammar could generate any of the following, depending on which particular grammatical transformations were selected:

(11a) The boy kissed the girl.

(11b) The girl was kissed by the boy.

(11c) Was the girl kissed by the boy?

More elaborate rules are also applied by this transformational component, including rules that allow us to combine ideas, such as the idea that {(boy kisses girl)} and the idea that {(girl is pretty)}:

(12a) The boy kissed the pretty girl.

(12b) The boy kissed the girl who was pretty.

(12c) The girl who the boy kissed was pretty.

(12d) Will the girl who is pretty be kissed by the boy?

(Recall from Chapter 8 that such sentences would be viewed as having two propositions.) Thus one surface structure for the {(girl) (is) (pretty)} idea is merely "the pretty girl"; an equivalent structure, in terms of meaning, is "the girl who is pretty." On the other hand, sentences 12c and 12d are the most difficult to comprehend, largely because of the passive voice and the embedded relative "who" clauses.

Limitations of the Transformational Grammar Approach

A great deal of research in the 1960s was devoted to the structural aspects of language we have been discussing. For example, some of the most serious work that tested linguistic theory in psychology involved the derivational complexity hypothesis. Much as we suggested for sentences 12a through 12d, this hypothesis suggests that the difficulty of comprehending a sentence is directly related to the number of grammatical transformations applied. In other words, if a deep structure has two transformations applied to it, it is more difficult to comprehend than if only one transformation is applied. As several authors note (e.g., Palermo, 1978), early results in this line of research tended to support the overall theory.

As the 1960s ended, however, psychology became increasingly dissatisfied with this linguistically motivated approach. Work by Fodor and Garrett (1966) was especially instrumental in dimming psychology's enthusiasm for the borrowed syntactic approach of linguistics. These researchers note that much of the support for the derivational complexity hypothesis failed to control potentially important factors in the stimuli. For instance, a derivationally more complex sentence generally has more words in it than a simpler one (contrast sentences 12a and 12c).

At least as persuasive as these criticisms, however, was a metatheoretical point of view. As more research was done, psychology became dissatisfied with the heavily syntactic focus of linguistic theory. To oversimplify just a bit, as Figure 9-8 shows, the major components were said to be syntactic, the syntactic rules for generating first a deep then a surface structure. Components dealing with the meanings of the sentences were literally off to the side, tangential to the central thrust of the theory. In a very real sense, this illustration depicts the difficulty psychology had with linguistic theory: It seemed that meaning was a secondary factor to the syntactic component. It's almost as if the theory, as it was applied directly to language *use*, suggested that we first make up our minds what phrase constituents we're going to use in a sentence, and only then decide what we're going to talk about. The emphasis on syntax clearly slighted the importance of semantics, the centrality of meaning. For psychologists concerned with how we use language to express meaning, this seemed to be heading in the wrong direction.

Actually, this is a somewhat oversimplified view, making it sound as if Chomsky encouraged linguists to avoid meaning. It was not that extreme, of course. In fact, Chomsky repeatedly emphasized the joint importance of syntax and semantics. He pointed out that even a perfectly grammatical sentence may have no genuine meaning; that is, a sentence might be both syntactically acceptable and semantically anomalous. His most famous example of such a sentence is "Colorless green ideas sleep furiously." It's clear that the sentence is grammatically acceptable—consider a sentence with completely parallel syntax, such as "Tired young children sleep soundly." But of course, Chomsky's sentence has no meaning in any ordinary sense of the word. On the other hand, Chomsky's work never dealt satisfactorily with meaning for many psychologists. And trying to apply his theory to the actual use of language—that is, turning his competence-based theory into a performance theory of language production and comprehension—only made it more apparent that a different approach was necessary.

We turn to the major focus of this research, the semantic level of analysis, in a moment. But first, we must conclude this section on syntax with the current psychological view of syntactic processing.

The Cognitive Role of Syntax

From a psychological perspective, what is the purpose of syntax? Why do our sentences have to follow a set of syntactic rules? The answers are obvious: We need syntax to help the listener figure out meaning, to minimize the processing demands of comprehension as much as possible. In a very real way, this purpose was neglected by linguists, which is not surprising given their lack of interest in performance. But from our perspective, it's useful to remind ourselves of this simple fact: If an infinite number of sentences are possible in a language, then the one sentence the speaker is saying to us right now could be about *anything*. Syntax helps listeners determine meaning and helps speakers convey it.

Bock's (1982) excellent article on a cognitive psychology of syntax discusses several important issues that the cognitive approach to language must explain. She notes that the syntactic burden falls somewhat more heavily on the speaker than the listener. That is, when you have to produce a sentence rather than comprehend it, you must create a surface structure, a string of words and phrases that will communicate your idea as well as possible. In Bock's words, your sentence "requires the paraphernalia of the correct morphology, constituent structure and order, and clause structure and order, that is, the correct syntax" (p. 2). Thus syntax becomes a feature of language that is particularly related to the speaker's mental effort, the information processing involved in producing the sentence.

Automatic Processing Two points Bock raises should illustrate some of the current directions in psycholinguistics toward the study of syntax. First, Bock considered the issues of automatic and conscious processes as they apply to language production. As we know, automatic processes are the product of a high degree of practice or overlearning. Bock notes that several aspects of syntactic structure are consistent with the notion of automaticity. For instance, children rely heavily on regular word orders, even if the native language they are learning has irregular word order. The purpose for this is fairly obvious: By relying over and over on the same syntactic frames, those frames can be generated and used more automatically. Similarly, adults tend to use only a very few syntactic structures with any regularity, suggesting that these few can be called into service rapidly and automatically. Interestingly, the syntax you use can be strongly influenced by a previous sentence, quite literally, the priming of syntactic usage (Bock, 1986; West & Stanovich, 1986). In fact, Bock's recent work (Bock & Griffin, 2000) has found evidence that using a particular syntactic construction can prime later constructions even up to lag 10 (i.e., with 10 intervening sentences). Interestingly, such priming effects can be identified in written language as well (Branigan, Pickering, & Cleland, 1999).

Planning In Bock's second point, she reviews evidence that shows an important interaction between syntax and meaning. In general, it seems that we tailor the syntax of our sentences to the accessibility of the lexical or semantic information being conveyed by the sentence. Phrases that contain more accessible information tend to occur earlier in a sentence. If a word is rare or difficult to retrieve, however, then the phrase it appears in tends to occur later in the spoken sentence.

These effects tell us something interesting about the mental mechanism that plans sentences. Earlier theories of sentence planning, such as Fromkin's (1971) theory (Table 9-4), described planning as a sequential process; first you identify the

Table 9-4 FROMKIN'S (1971) MODEL FOR THE PLANNING AND PRODUCTION OF SPEECH

Stage	Process
1	Identify meaning; generate the meaning to be expressed
2	Select syntactic structure; construct a syntactic outline of the sentence, specifying word slots
3	Generate intonation contour; assign stress values to different word slots
4	Insert content words; retrieve appropriate nouns, verbs, adjectives, and so on from the lexicon and insert into word slots
5	Add function words and affixes; fill out the syntax with function words (articles, prepositions, etc.), prefixes, suffixes
6	Specify phonetic segments; express the sentence in terms of phonetic segments according to phonological (pronunciation) rules

meaning to be conveyed, then you select the syntactic frame, and so on. More recent research, however, shows how interactive the planning process is and how flexible syntax is (Ferreira, 1996). Difficulties in one component, word retrieval, can prompt a return to an earlier planning component, say to rework the syntax of the sentence. By selecting an alternative syntax, the speaker buys more time for retrieving the intended word (see also Kempen & Hoehkamp, 1987). Of course, such an interactive system contradicts the strictly hierarchical or sequential approaches to syntax, such as Chomsky's.

In general, recent data show that we begin our utterances when the first part of the sentence has been planned but before the syntax and semantics of the final portion have been worked out or selected. Hesitations in our spoken speech are clues to the nature of planning, as are the effects of momentary changes in priming, lexical access, and working memory load (Bock & Miller, 1991; Eberhard, 1999; Lindsley, 1975). In fact, several recent reports detail how the false starts, hesitations, and restarts in our speech often reflect both the complexity of the intended sentence and a genuine online planning process that unfolds as the sentence is developed (Clark & Wasow, 1998; Ferreira, 1996; Ferreira & Dell, 2000; see Bock, 1996, for a review of methods of studying language production).

■ Section Summary

- Syntax involves the ordering of words and phrases in sentence structure and features such as active versus passive voice. Chomsky's theory of language was a heavily syntactic scheme with two sets of syntactic rules. Phrase structure rules were used to generate a deep structure representation of a sentence, and then transformational rules converted the deep structure into the surface structure, the string of words that makes up the sentence.
- There are a variety of syntactic clues to the meaning of a sentence, so an understanding of syntax obviously is necessary to psycholinguists. On the other hand, psycholinguistics has developed its own theories of language, at least in part because of linguists' relative neglect of semantic and performance characteristics.

Speech Errors

Fascinating work by Fromkin (1971), Garrett (1975), and others has tabulated and made sense of speech errors that occur when we substitute or change sounds, syllables, words, and so on. Speech errors are not random but are quite lawful. For instance, when we make an exchange error, the exchange is between elements at the same linguistic level; initial sounds exchange places with other initial sounds, syllables with syllables, words with words (e.g., "to cake a bake"). If a prefix switches places, its new location will be in front of another word, not at the end.

Collect a sample of speech errors, say, from radio news broadcasters or your professors' lectures, then analyze them in terms of the linguistic level of the elements involved and the types of errors such as (intended phrase in parentheses):

Shift	She decide to hits it. (decides to hit it)
Exchange	Your model renosed. (your nose remodeled)
Perseveration	He pulled a pantrum. (tantrum)
Blend	To explain clarefully. (clearly/ carefully)

Lexical and Semantic Factors: The Meaning in Language

We turn finally to lexical and semantic factors, the third traditional level of linguistic analysis after phonology and syntax. This is the level of meaning in language, the level at which word and phrase meanings are "computed," to use the psycholinguistic jargon; in cognitive psychology, we call this retrieval from memory.

A major component of this level of analysis is simply that: retrieving word meanings from memory. In particular, we refer to retrieval from the **mental lexicon,** *the mental dictionary of words and their meanings.* After rapid perceptual and pattern recognition processes input the stimulus, the encoded word provides access to the word's entry in the lexicon and also to the semantic representation of the concept. The evidence you've read about throughout this book, such as results from the Stroop task and the lexical decision task, attests to the close relationship between the word and its meaning, and the seemingly automatic accessing of one from the other. Recall in the Stroop task that seeing the word *red* printed in green ink triggers an interference process with naming the ink color, clear evidence that *red* was processed to the level of meaning (MacLeod, 1992). Likewise, the lexical decision task does not require that you access the word's meaning but only that you identify a letter string as a genuine word. Nonetheless, identifying *doctor* as a word speeds your decision to *nurse*, clearly showing that semantic knowledge is accessed and activated merely by the printed word (e.g., Table 7-3).

But the retrieval of a word's name and meaning is just the beginning of the process. After the lexical entry has been found in memory, the words and phrases in a sentence must still be related to one another. To take a simple example, "Jill saw Bill" means something quite different from "Bill saw Jill," even though the individual words retain their meanings in both sentences. How listeners extract meaning from such sequences of words in a sentence is also the concern of this third level of linguistic analysis. Let's start with the building blocks of meaning and work up through sentence-level processes.

Morphemes We've been speaking throughout the chapter about words and word meanings. These terms are technically inaccurate if we want to refer to the basic units of meaning in language. The correct term, instead, is *morpheme:* a **morpheme** is *the smallest unit of language that has meaning.* To return to the example we gave at the beginning of the chapter, the word *cars* is actually composed of two meaningful units, two morphemes: *car* refers to a semantic concept and a physical object, and *-s* is a meaningful suffix, denoting "more than one of." Likewise, the word *unhappiness* is composed of three separate morphemes: *happy* as the base concept, the prefix *un-* meaning "not," and the suffix *-ness* meaning "state or quality of being." For our purposes here, it usually makes little difference whether we speak of words or morphemes as they occur in sentences, although there is a debate whether the meaning of a word such as *unhappiness* is literally stored in memory or "computed" from the three individual morphemes (see Carroll, 1986; Whitney, 1998). On the other hand, we'll need this terminology in a few moments when we consider neurological impairments of language skill. In particular, we'll need the distinction between free morphemes, such as *happy, car,* and *legal,* and bound morphemes, such as *un-, -ness,* and *-s.*

The Lexical Representation Think about the word *chase* as an example of how base morphemes or concepts might be represented in the mental lexicon. The lexical representation of *chase* must specify the meaning of this morpheme, must indicate that *chase* means "to run after or pursue, in hopes of catching." Like any other semantic concept, *chase* can be represented as a node in memory, with pathways connecting it to related information, say *run, pursue,* the idea of a high degree of *speed,* and the like. Given this information, along with what you know about situations in the real world, you can easily understand a sentence like

(13) The policeman chased the burglar through the park.

From a more psycholinguistic perspective, however, you know a great deal more about *chase* than just its basic meaning. For one thing, you know it's a verb, specifying a kind of physical action. Related to that, you have a clear idea of how *chase* can be used in sentences, the kinds of things that can do the chasing, and the kinds of things that can be chased. Imagine, then, that your lexical representation of *chase* also includes this additional knowledge; *chase* requires some animate thing or being to do the chasing, some other kind of thing to be chased, and possibly a location where the chasing takes place. Using the terms we discussed in the last chapter for propositions, this additional information could be listed as follows:

	Relation	(agent	patient	optional location)
	Chase	(Animate being	thing or being	location)
(13)	Chase	(Policeman	burglar	park)

Our policeman sentence fits this scheme perfectly.

Case Grammar

You've already encountered the approach we're taking here in the section on propositions in Chapter 8 (remember the "hippie–debutante" sentence?). At a general level, this approach is called **case grammar.** The ideas came originally from Fillmore (1968), and have been developed as a psycholinguistic alternative to the heavily syntactic approaches in linguistics. The basic idea is that *the semantic analysis of sentences involves figuring out what semantic role is being played by each word or concept in the sentence and computing sentence meaning based on those semantic roles.* Two sample sentences illustrate this notion.

(14) The key will open the door.

(15) The janitor will open the door with the key.

Fillmore first pointed out that syntactic aspects of sentences—which words serve as the subject, direct object, and so on—often are irrelevant to the meaning of the sentence. For example, in sentences 14 and 15 the word *key* plays very different grammatical roles; subject of the sentence in 14 but object of the preposition in 15. Focusing on this difference, in Fillmore's view, misses a critical point for language; regardless of its different grammatical roles, the key is doing exactly the same thing in both sentences. In both sentences, *key* plays the same semantic role: It's the instrument, the thing that did the opening. A purely syntactic analysis misses this, but a semantic analysis captures it perfectly.

Fillmore's theoretical position was called case grammar, or sometimes semantic case grammar. He, along with many since his early work, proposed that a sentence is best understood "as made up of a verb and a collection of nouns in various 'cases' in the deep structure sense" (p. 375), that is, in the sense of meaning. In other words, Fillmore proposed that sentence processing involves a semantic parsing, in which we focus on the *semantic roles played by the content words in the sentences.* These semantic roles are called **semantic cases,** or simply **case roles.** Thus *door* is the recipient or patient of the action of *open* in sentences 14 and 15; *janitor* is the agent of *open,* *key* is the instrument, and so on. Stated simply, each content word in the sentence plays a semantic role in the meaning of the sentence. That role is called the word's *semantic case.* The significant—indeed, critical—point about such a semantic parsing is that it relies on people's existing semantic and lexical knowledge, their knowledge of what kinds of things will open, who can perform the opening, and so on.

Reconsider the *chase* sentence 13, "The policeman chased the burglar through the park," and three variations, thinking of the content words in terms of their semantic roles.

(16) The mouse chased the cat through the house.

(17) His insecurities chased him even in his sleep.

*(18) *The book chased the flower.*

Your lexical and semantic knowledge of *chase,* the overall relation in the sentence, is that some animate being does the chasing, the agent case. Some other thing is the recipient of the chasing, the patient, but that thing need not be animate, just capable of moving rapidly (e.g., you can chase a piece of paper being blown by the wind). On just this analysis, it is clear that sentence 13 conforms to the normal situation stored in memory, so it is easy to comprehend. Sentence 16, however, mismatches the customary state of affairs between mice and cats. Nonetheless, either of these creatures can serve as the required animate agent of the relation *chase*, so sentence 16 is sensible. Because of other semantic knowledge, you know that sentence 17 violates the literal meaning of *chase* but could still have a nonliteral, metaphorical meaning. But your semantic case analysis provides the reason why sentence 18 is unacceptable. A book is inanimate, so it mismatches the required animate agent role for *chase; book* cannot play the role of agent for *chase*. Likewise, *flower* seems to violate the movable restriction on the patient case for *chase*.

Recent work by Bresnan (1978; Bresnan & Kaplan, 1982) and Jackendoff (1992) has amplified and extended this important work on case grammars. For example, in Jackendoff's theory of a cognitive grammar (1992; see Figure 9-10), the goal is to build a conceptual structure, an understanding of the sentence. We use the syntax of the sentence and a set of correspondence rules to get from the spoken or written sentence to the conceptual structure. Each lexical entry in the system includes the meaning of the word, and for verbs, a list of the arguments or semantic cases that go along with it. Thus as shown, the lexical entry *chase* would state that *chase* requires an animate agent, that some recipient or patient is needed, and so on. Likewise, for the relation *give*, the case arguments would state that an animate agent and recipient are needed for the *give* relation, and some *object* is the thing being given (for an excellent summary of these positions, see Whitney, 1998).

According to these lexical–semantic grammars, when we perceive words in speech or writing, we look up the concepts in the lexicon. This look-up process accesses not only the word's meaning but also its syntactic and semantic case roles and any case restrictions that apply as well. Each word in the sentence is processed similarly, as it is encountered, with each content word being assigned to the semantic role. If all goes well, the sentence conveys an exact, specified meaning that is captured accurately by the analysis of the cognitive grammar.

Interaction of Syntax and Semantics

Note that semantic factors do not stand alone in language, just as syntactic factors are not independent of semantics. Syntax is more than just word and phrase order rules; it's a clue to how to understand sentences. For example, O'Seaghdha's (1997) evidence shows separable effects of syntactic assignment and semantic integration of word meanings, with syntactic processes occurring before semantic integration. His results, based on RTs, are largely consistent with those in other studies, including ERP investigations of syntactic and semantic processing (Ainsworth-Darnell, Shulman, & Boland, 1998; Friederici, Hahne, and Mecklinger, 1996). And, as you just read, syntax in speech production is sensitive to a word's accessibility; words that can be easily retrieved right now tend to appear earlier in a sentence.

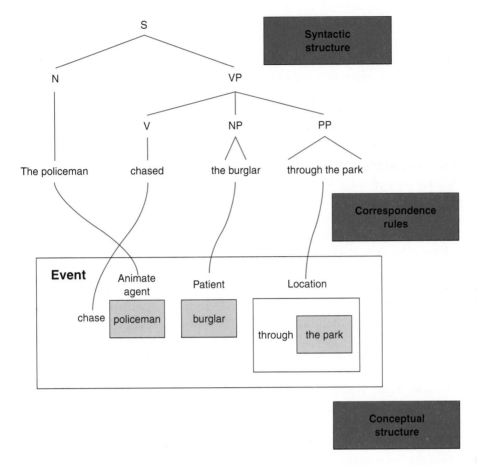

Figure 9-10

In Jackendoff's (1992) conceptual semantics approach, comprehension of meaning is the process of arriving at a conceptual structure for the sentence. To accomplish this, we use both the syntactic structure of the sentence and a set of correspondence rules; the correspondence rules translate from syntactic roles (e.g., noun and verb) into semantic roles (agent, patient, and so forth). *Source.* Adapted from Whitney (1998).

Likewise, semantic factors refer to more than just word and phrase meanings because different syntactic devices can be clues to meaning. To anticipate just a bit, note how syntactic differences in the following sentences influence the semantic interpretation:

(19a) I'm going downtown with my sister at four o'clock.

(19b) It's at four o'clock that I'm going downtown with my sister.

(19c) It's my sister I'm going downtown with at four o'clock.

Sentences 19b and 19c differ subtly from 19a in what might be called the focus of the utterance. In a genuine sense, the focus of each sentence is different, so each means something slightly different. Imagine how inappropriate sentence 19c would be, for instance, as a response to the question "Did you say you're going downtown with your sister at three o'clock?" Our judgments about appropriateness make an important point: Our theories of language performance must be as sophisticated as our own knowledge of language is. We are sensitive to the focus or highlighted aspects of sentences and subtleties of the ordering of clauses, so our theory of language must reflect this in a psychologically relevant way.

Semantic Knowledge Can Overpower Syntax Semantic features can do more than merely alter the syntax of sentences. Occasionally semantic characteristics overpower the syntax of a sentence. Although many examples could be offered here, let's focus on a classic study by Fillenbaum (1974). As you read, note how current terminology would label this an effect of top-down processing.

Fillenbaum presented several kinds of sentences to his subjects and asked them to write paraphrases that preserved the original meaning. Ordinary "threat" sentences such as "Don't print that or I'll sue you" were then reordered into "perverse" threats, such as "Don't print that or I won't sue you." Regular "conjunctive" sentences such as "John got off the bus and went into the store" were then changed into "disordered" sentences, such as "John went into the store and got off the bus." When Fillenbaum scored the paraphrases, he found remarkably high percentages of changes, as shown in Figure 9-11. More than 50% of his subjects "normalized" the perverse threatening sentences, making them conform to the more typical state of affairs, and more than 60% normalized the "disordered" conjunctive sentences. He then asked his subjects to reread their paraphrases to see whether there was even a "shred of difference" from the originals. More than half the time, subjects saw no discrepancies at all. Apparently, the subjects' general knowledge was influential enough that it easily overpowered the syntactic and lexical aspects of the sentences. Sometimes we comprehend not what we hear or read, but what we *expect* to hear or read. (Try these: "Nice we're having weather, isn't it?" and "Ignorance is no excuse for the law.")

This should sound very familiar to you, that our existing knowledge exerts an influence on our current mental processing. Chapters 7 and 8 dealt extensively with general world knowledge, exactly the kind of knowledge Fillenbaum's subjects were consulting when they misinterpreted the perverse sentences. This is the same phenomenon Bartlett (1932), Loftus and Palmer (1974), and others have identified too, though not in the context of experiments on language use per se. Given these similarities between semantic and psycholinguistic ideas, you won't be surprised to find out that the current psycholinguistic view on semantic analysis of language is already familiar to you as well. In short, the psycholinguistic approach to lexical and semantic factors in language relies heavily on two important notions: conceptually driven processing and mental representations called propositions.

Evidence for the Semantic Grammar Approaches

A major prediction of the semantic grammar approach can be stated in two parts. First, we assume that listeners (and readers) begin to analyze the sentence immediately, as soon

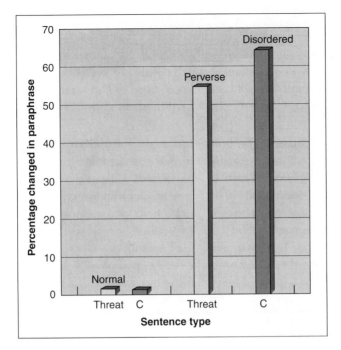

Figure 9-11

Fillenbaum's (1974) results.; Two kinds of normal sentences were shown, threats and conjunctives (labeled C) such as "John got off the bus and went into the store." Threats were then altered to be "perverse," and conjunctives were disordered (e.g., threat C, "John dressed and had a bath"). *Source.* Fillenbaum (1974).

as the words begin. Second, this analysis is a process of assigning each word to a particular semantic case role, with each assignment contributing its part to overall sentence comprehension. As an example, read sentence 20.

(20) After the musician had bowed the piano was quickly taken off the stage.

Your analysis of this sentence proceeds easily and without disruption; it's a fairly straightforward sentence. Now read sentence 21.

(21) After the musician had played the piano was quickly taken off the stage.

What's different about sentence 21? The verb *played* suggests that *the piano* is the semantic recipient of *play*. When you read *played*, your semantic role assignment for *piano* was *recipient*. But then you read *was quickly* and realized you had made a mistake in interpretation. Sentences such as 21 are called *garden path sentences*; the early part of the sentence sets you up so that the later phrases in the sentence don't make sense given the way you assigned case roles in the first part. Figuratively speaking, the sentence leads you down the garden path; when you realize your mistake, you have to retrace your steps

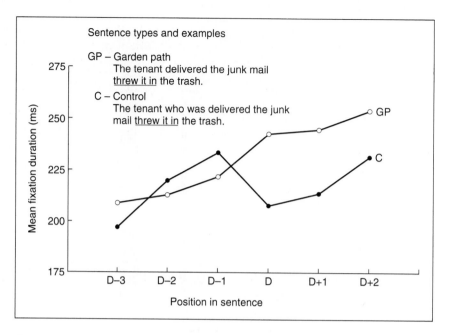

Figure 9-12

A depiction of the effect of garden path sentences on reading time. The curves show eye fixations on phrases before and after D, the point in the sentence where the ambiguity is noticed and Disambiguated. The top curve shows the data from garden path sentences; eye fixation time grows noticeably longer for these curves at D, when the ambiguity is noticed (the D phrase is underlined in the sample sentences). The bottom curve shows data from the control sentences and no increase in reading time at point D. *Source.* Data from Rayner et al. (1983).

back up the path to reassign earlier words to different cases. Additional examples (from Singer, 1990) of this effect are shown in sentences 22 and 23.

(22) The groundsman chased the girl waving a stick in her hand.

(23) The old train the young.

Many research reports have studied how people comprehend such garden path sentences as a way of evaluating the case grammar approach to sentence comprehension (Frazier & Rayner, 1982; Mitchell & Holmes, 1985). For the most part, the results have been quite supportive of that explanation. For example, when subjects read such sentences, their eyes tend to fixate much longer on the later phrases that signal their error in comprehension (e.g., on "was quickly taken off" in sentence 21). As shown in Figure 9-12, subjects spent 40 to 50 msec longer when they encountered their error (at point D in the figure; D stands for the disambiguating part of the sentence that reveals the earlier misinterpretation). This is a kind of recovery time effect; it takes additional time to recover from the initial role assignment when that turns out to be incorrect (see Ferreira, Henderson, Anes, Weeks, & McFarlane, 1996, for comparable results in spoken language comprehension).

A final point to note is that the case restrictions sometimes can be violated intentionally, although there are still constraints on that violation. For instance, consider sentence 17 again: "His insecurities chased him even in his sleep." Such a sentence is understood as a technical but permissible violation of the animate restriction for the agent role of *chase*. In a metaphorical sense, we can "compute" how insecurities might behave like an animate agent; thoughts can behave as if they were animate and can take on the properties of pursuing relentlessly, catching, and so on. A particularly fascinating aspect of language involves such figurative uses of words and how case grammar accommodates such usage (see Gibbs & Nayak, 1991; Glucksberg & Keysar, 1990; Tourangeau & Rips, 1991; and the Suggested Readings).

Case Grammar, Propositions, and Comprehension

The case grammar approach was the theoretical ancestor for the propositional approaches to semantics you studied in the last chapter and the cognitive or semantic grammar you read about a few moments ago. According to these approaches, comprehension requires the listener to do three things. First, the basic word meanings must be retrieved from the mental lexicon and conceptual information from semantic memory. Second, the words are assigned to the various case roles required by the relation expressed in the sentence; this is the same process as deriving a propositional structure for a sentence. Finally, the propositional structure or semantic case assignments must be related to the other structures within the sentence as well as across sentences in connected discourse.

Language production involves largely the same issues. An idea or set of ideas exists in the form of a propositional representation. This meaning structure is manipulated both syntactically and semantically to yield a string of words that conveys the intended meaning. Semantic retrieval must logically occur before the syntactic stage, at least to some degree, because we must know what we're going to talk about before we start casting the sentence into a particular syntactic form and because lexical information helps shape the syntax of the sentence. On the other hand, the evidence (Bock, 1982) suggests that the whole syntactic structure of a sentence is not necessarily finalized as we start to utter the beginning of the sentence. And as you'll read in a moment, lexical retrieval, finding the word in memory, may indeed be a separate process from semantic retrieval, finding the relevant concept or idea.

■ Section Summary

- Semantic factors in language are so powerful that they can sometimes override syntactic and phonological effects. The study of semantics breaks words down into morphemes, the smallest meaningful units in language; *cars* contains the free morpheme *car* and the bound morpheme *-s* signifying a "plural."
- As the study of language comprehension has matured, the dominant approach to semantics claims that we perform a semantic parsing of sentences, assigning words to their appropriate semantic case roles as we hear or read. This case or cognitive

grammar approach is very similar to the propositional approach to meaning described in Chapter 8 and represents the current status of semantic theory in language.

Brain and Language

A particularly large literature exists on brain-related disorders of language, based on people who through the misfortune of illness or brain injury have lost the ability to use language. Formal studies of such disorders date back to the mid-1800s, although records dating back to 3500 B.C. mention language loss caused by brain injury (see McCarthy & Warrington, 1990). Table 9-5 provides a list and short explanation of these disruptions and some others you've already encountered. Despite the variety of mental abilities that can be damaged, none of the impairments cuts to the heart of our humanness as does the loss of language, the loss of our very ability to communicate with others. In this final section, we discuss disruptions of language caused by brain damage and then turn to some new research using various imaging techniques to study how the brain processes language.

Aphasia

The disruption of language caused by a brain-related disorder is known as **aphasia.** Aphasia is always the product of some sort of physical injury to the brain, either brain damage sustained in an accident or blow to the head or diseases and medical syndromes such as stroke. A major goal in neurology is to understand the aphasic syndromes more completely so that people who suffer aphasia may be helped more effectively. From the

Table 9-5 **BRAIN-RELATED DISRUPTIONS OF LANGUAGE AND COGNITION**	
Disorder	**Disruption of**
Language Related	
Broca's aphasia	Speech production, syntactic features
Wernicke's aphasia	Comprehension, semantic features
Conduction aphasia	Repetition of words and sentences
Anomia (anomic aphasia)	Word finding, either lexical or semantic
Pure word deafness	Perceptual or semantic processing of auditory word comprehension
Alexia	Reading, recognition of printed letters or words
Agraphia	Writing
Other Symbolic Related	
Acalculia	Mathematical abilities, retrieval or rule-based procedures
Perception, Movement Related	
Agnosia	Visual object recognition
Prosopagnosia	(Visual) face recognition
Apraxia	Voluntary action or skilled motor movement

standpoint of cognitive neuroscience, the language disruptions observed in aphasic patients can also help us understand language and its neurological basis.

Although there are many different kinds of aphasic disorders, with great variety in their effects and severity, three basic forms are the most common: *Broca's aphasia*, *Wernicke's aphasia*, and *conduction aphasia*.

Broca's Aphasia.   As described by Kertesz (1982), **Broca's aphasia** is characterized by *severe difficulties in producing speech;* it is also called expressive or production aphasia. Patients with Broca's aphasia show speech that is hesitant, effortful, and phonemically distorted. Aside from automatic sequences such as "I don't know," such patients generally respond to questions with only one-word answers. If words are strung together, there are few if any grammatical markers present in the utterance, bound morphemes such as *-ing,-ed,* and *-ly.* Interestingly, such patients typically show less impairment of comprehension, for both spoken and written language.

This syndrome was first described by French neurosurgeon Pierre Broca in the 1860s, who also identified the damaged area responsible for the disorder. The site of the brain damage, an area toward the rear of the left frontal lobe, is therefore called Broca's area. As shown in Figure 9-13 (see also the color plate illustrations), Broca's area lies adjacent to a major motor control center in the brain. This no doubt accounts for the motor difficulties typical of the aphasia, the inability to produce fluent spoken speech.

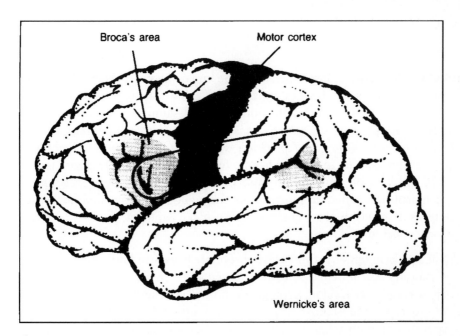

Figure 9-13

Broca's area and Wernicke's area in the cerebral cortex.

Table 9-6 CLASSIC IMPAIRMENTS IN BROCA'S AND WERNICKE'S APHASIAS

Broca's Aphasia	Wernicke's Aphasia
Quality of Speech	
Severely impaired; marked by extreme effort to generate speech, hesitant utterances, short (one-word) responses.	Little, if any, impairment; fluent speech productions, clear articulation, no hesitations.
Nature of Speech	
Agrammatical; marked by loss of syntactic markers and inflections and use of simple noun and verb categories.	Neologistic; marked by invented words (neologisms) or semantically inappropriate substitutions; long strings of neologistic jargon.
Comprehension	
Unimpaired compared with speech production. Word-finding difficulty caused by production difficulties.	Severely impaired; marked by lack of awareness that speech is incomprehensible; comprehension impaired also in nonverbal tasks (e.g., pointing).
Speech Samples	

Broca's aphasia. Experimenter asks the patient's address.
"Oh dear. Um. Aah. O! Oh dear. very-there-were-ave. avedeversher avenyer." (Correct address was Devonshire.)
Wernicke's aphasia. Experimenter asks about the patient's work before hospitalization. "I wanna tell you this happened when happened when he rent. His-his kell come down here and is—he got ren something. It happened. In these ropliers were with him for hi-is friend—like was. And he roden all o these arranjen from the pedis on from iss pescid."

Source. Adapted from Kertesz (1982).

Wernicke's Aphasia Loosely speaking, the impairments in **Wernicke's aphasia** are the opposite of those in Broca's aphasia; see Table 9-6 for a listing of the typical impairments in both aphasias, including speech samples. In patients affected by Wernicke's aphasia, *comprehension is impaired, as are repetition, naming, reading, and writing, but the syntactic aspects of speech are preserved*; it is sometimes called receptive or comprehension aphasia. In this syndrome, "copious unintelligible jargon is produced" (Kertesz, 1982, p. 30), either with unrecognizable content words, recognizable but often inappropriate semantic substitutions, or neologisms, invented nonsense words. In Kertesz's description of a woman with Wernicke's aphasia, the nature of the disorder is very apparent:

> She speaks in sentences and uses appropriate pauses and inflectional markers separating lexical items . . . without articulatory errors or hesitations. . . . In an extraordinary fashion, neologisms of variable length and phonemic complexity replace substantive words, mostly nouns and verbs. She talks as if she spoke without mistakes. . . . There is a rather curious cool and calm manner about her speech as if she did not realize her deficit . . . a very characteristic feature of this disturbance. (pp. 41–42)

German investigator Carl Wernicke identified this disorder and the left-hemisphere region that is damaged, in 1874. This region is thus known as Wernicke's area, also illustrated in Figure 9-13. Note that the area, toward the rear of the left temporal lobe, is adjacent to the auditory cortex, in the left temporal lobe.

If you think about these two aphasias for a moment, you'll notice that several rough distinctions can be drawn between them in terms of linguistic characteristics you've studied in this chapter. A Broca's aphasic, with neurological damage near the motor control area, demonstrates disorders in the motoric and syntactic aspects of language—fluent, coordinated, grammatical speech—but relatively normal comprehension at a semantic level. Syntactic markers are especially absent here, as if bound morphemes such as *-er* and *-ing* had become unavailable. Indeed, this aphasia sometimes is called agrammatic aphasia, referring to the lack (prefix *a-*) of grammatical form that is evidenced. In contrast, free morphemes, word stems and content words, seem relatively unaffected.

On the other hand, a Wernicke's aphasic can generate speech fluently and grammatically, but the semantic aspects of the speech are severely impaired: Invented nonsense words substitute for genuinely semantic words. As a product of brain damage in different locations, in other words, opposite aspects or components of linguistic ability seem to be lost and preserved. This is a classic demonstration of double dissociation. It also reflects a basic distinction, at the level of brain organization, between syntax and semantics (see Breedin & Saffran, 1999, for a case study showing loss of semantic knowledge but preserved syntactic performance).

Conduction Aphasia Much less common than Broca's and Wernicke's aphasias, **conduction aphasia** is a more narrow disruption of language ability. Both Broca's and Wernicke's areas seem to be intact in conduction aphasia, and people with conduction aphasia can understand and produce speech quite well. Their language impairment is that they are *unable to repeat what they have just heard*. In intuitive terms, the intact comprehension and production systems seem to have lost their normal connection or linkage. And indeed, the site of the brain lesion in conduction aphasia appears to be the primary pathway between Broca's and Wernicke's areas, called the *arcuate fasciculus* (Geschwind, 1970). Quite literally, the pathway between the comprehension and production areas is no longer able to conduct the linguistic message.

Anomia Another type of aphasia deserves brief mention here because it relates to the separation of the semantic and lexical systems discussed earlier. **Anomia** or **anomic aphasia** is a disruption of word finding, an *impairment in the normal ability to retrieve a semantic concept and say its name*; you encountered this briefly back in Chapter 7. In anomia, some aspect of the normally automatic semantic or lexical components of retrieval has been damaged. Although moderate word-finding difficulty can result from damage almost anywhere in the left hemisphere, full-fledged anomia seems to involve damage especially in the left temporal lobe (Coughlan & Warrington, 1978; see McCarthy & Warrington, 1990, for details). Although there is a similarity between anomia and the tip-of-the-tongue (TOT) phenomenon, the similarity may be only superficial. For instance, several researchers (e.g., Geschwind, 1967; Goodglass, Kaplan, Weintraub, & Ackerman, 1976) found no evidence among their anomic patients of the partial knowledge that characterizes a TOT state. Newer evidence indicates that anomia can involve retrieval blockage only for the lexical component of retrieval, leaving semantic retrieval of the concept intact (e.g., the patient described in Chapter 7; Kay & Ellis, 1987). This, along with other cases (e.g., Ashcraft, 1993) suggest preserved semantic retrieval but a blockage in finding the lexical representation that corresponds to the already retrieved semantic concept.

Other Aphasias As Table 9-5 shows, a variety of highly specific aphasias are also possible. Although most of these are quite rare, they nonetheless give evidence of the separability of several aspects of language performance. For instance, in *alexia* (or dyslexia), there is a disruption of reading without any necessary disruption of spoken language or aural comprehension. In *agraphia*, conversely, the patient is unable to write. Amazingly, a few reports describe patients with alexia but without agraphia—in other words, patients who can write but then cannot read what they have just written (Benson & Geschwind, 1969). In *pure word deafness*, a patient cannot comprehend spoken language, although he or she is still able to read and produce written and spoken language.

Even such a short list conveys an important point: Language skills and abilities consist of many different components, some quite independent or dissociated from others. Often, the only way to observe this independence is to test a brain-damaged patient whose particular injury has led to a breakdown of the normally coordinated system.

Generalizing from Aphasia

Although it is a mistake to believe that our eventual understanding of language will be reducible to a catalog of biological and neurological processes (e.g., Mehler, Morton, & Jusczyk, 1984), knowledge of the neurological aspects of language should nonetheless be useful for something beyond the rehabilitation and treatment of aphasia. What do studies of such abnormal brain processes tell us about normal cerebral functioning and language?

Well for one, the very different patterns of behavioral impairments in Broca's and Wernicke's aphasias, stemming from different physical structures in the brain, certainly imply that these two physical structures are responsible for different aspects of linguistic skill. Furthermore, these selective impairments and different brain locations also reinforce the notion that syntax and semantics are two separable but interactive aspects of normal language (e.g., O'Seaghdha, 1997; Osterhout & Holcomb, 1992). That is, the double dissociations indicate that different, independent modules govern comprehension and speech production. Other dissociations indicate yet more independent modules of processing, such as separate modules corresponding to reading and writing.

An intriguing inference from such studies is that the specialized cerebral regions signal an innate, biological basis for language; that is, the human nervous system is rather specifically adapted to learn and use language, as opposed to simply being generally able to do so. Several theorists have gone a significant step further in this issue, discussing the possible evolutionary mechanisms responsible for lateralization, hemispheric specialization, the dissociation of syntax and semantics revealed by Broca's and Wernicke's aphasias, and even cognition in general (Corballis, 1989; Geary, 1992; Lewontin, 1990). These are fascinating lines of reasoning on the nature of language and cognition as represented in the brain.

Language in the Intact Brain

With the advent of modern imaging devices and methods, we have begun to learn an extraordinary amount about how the brain processes language from neurologically intact people. Especially because of some inherent limitations on evidence drawn from isolated, single cases of brain damage, the newly reported evidence on intact individuals enables us to go much further in understanding how the brain processes language.

Consider a representative study, looking at people's sensitivity to the syntactic structure of sentences. Osterhout and Holcomb (1992) presented sentences to their subjects and recorded the changes in their brain wave patterns (ERPs) as they comprehended. In particular, the authors examined ERP patterns for sentences that violated syntactic or semantic expectations, comparing these with the patterns obtained with control sentences. When sentences ended in a semantically anomalous fashion ("John buttered his bread with socks"), a significant N400 ERP pattern was observed, much as reported in Kounios and Holcomb's (1992) study of semantic relatedness (see Chapter 7). But when the sentence ended in a syntactically anomalous fashion ("John hoped the man to leave"), a strong P600 pattern occurred (a positive electrical potential) 600 msec after the anomalous word "to" was seen; see Figure 9-14. This is dramatic confirmation of the important and seemingly separate role of syntactic processing during language comprehension.

A wealth of new evidence illustrates the importance to cognitive science of such imaging and neuropsychological techniques and strongly suggests that the upcoming wave of research on language processing will feature techniques such as imaging and ERP methods very prominently. Here are three brief examples.

Learning Language. McCandliss, Posner, and Givon (1997) taught subjects a new, miniature artificial language and recorded ERPs during the learning process. Early in training, words in the new language showed ERP patterns typical of nonsense material. But after 5 weeks of additional training, the ERP patterns looked like those obtained with English words. Furthermore, left hemisphere frontal areas reacted to semantic aspects of the language, whereas posterior areas were sensitive to the visual characteristics of the words, the orthography.

Syntactic Processing. Rosler, Pechmann, Streb, Roder, and Hennighausen (1998) performed a very ambitious study on syntactic processing, using the ERP methodology.

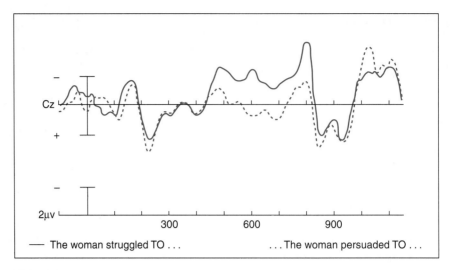

Figure 9-14

Mean ERPs to syntactically acceptable sentences (solid curve) and syntactically anomalous sentences (dotted curve). The P600 component, illustrated as a downward dip in the dotted curve, shows the effect of detecting the syntactic anomaly. Note that in this figure, positive changes go in the downward direction.

Sentences were presented word by word; to make sure subjects were comprehending, they had to answer a question about the sentence 5 s after they saw the last word. The sentences were all grammatical, but some of them differed from normal, canonical word order. The extensive ERP patterns demonstrated a variety of effects; for example, the patterns differed appreciably when the sentences violated canonical word order and when elements in the sentence cued the subjects that an unusual word order would follow. The especially compelling aspect of these results is that the ERP patterns tapped into purely mental processes that are not revealed by outward, behavioral measures such as RT or accuracy.

Individual Differences Reichle, Carpenter, and Just (2000) used functional magnetic resonance imaging (fMRI) to look at brain activity while subjects verified sentence–picture stimuli (e.g., "The star is above the plus," followed by a picture that did or did not match the sentence). When subjects were asked to use a verbal strategy to make their decisions, brain regions associated with language processing (especially Broca's area) were active; when subjects were instructed to use a visual imagery strategy, regions in the parietal lobe were active, the same regions that are active when visual–spatial reasoning tasks are given. Interestingly, the language area activity was somewhat lower when high-verbal subjects were tested, and likewise for visual areas in subjects high in visual–spatial abilities, as if high verbal or spatial ability reduced the amount of brain work needed to perform the task.

■ Section Summary

• Extensive evidence from studies with brain-damaged people and more modern work using imaging and ERP methods reveals several functional and anatomical dissociations in language ability. The syntactic and articulatory aspects of language seem centered in Broca's area, in the left frontal lobe, whereas comprehension aspects are focused more on Wernicke's area, in the posterior left hemisphere junction of the temporal and parietal lobes. The study of these and other deficits, such as anomia, converges with evidence from imaging and ERP studies to illustrate how various aspects of language performance act as separable, distinct components within the overall broad ability to produce and comprehend language.

Key Terms

ambiguous (p. 375)
anomia (p. 393)
anomic aphasia (p. 393)
aphasia (p. 390)
arbitrariness (p. 352)
Broca's aphasia (p. 391)
case grammar (p. 383)
case roles (p. 383)
categorical perception (p. 363)
coarticulation (p. 368)
competence (p. 358)
conduction aphasia (p. 393)
deep structure (p. 375)
displacement (p. 354)
dysfluency (p. 358)

flexibility of symbols (p. 352)
grammar (p. 357)
language (p. 350)
linguistic intuitions (p. 358)
linguistic relativity hypothesis (p. 359)
linguistic universals (p. 350)
linguistics (p. 348)
mental lexicon (p. 381)
morpheme (p. 382)
naming (p. 353)
parse (p. 375)
performance (p. 358)
phoneme (p. 363)

phonemic competence (p. 366)
phonology (p. 361)
phrase structure (p. 374)
problem of invariance (p. 367)
productivity (p. 355)
psycholinguistics (p. 348)
semantic cases (p. 383)
semanticity (p. 350)
surface structure (p. 376)
syntax (p. 371)
transformational rules (p. 376)
Wernicke's aphasia (p. 392)

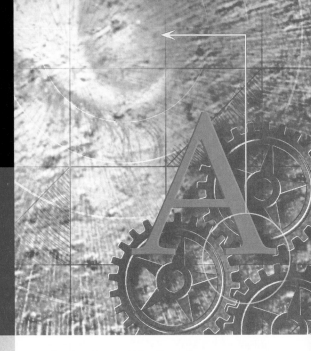

CHAPTER 10

Comprehension: Written and Spoken Language

Language simply does not work in isolation. . . . Understanding what one has heard is a complex process that . . . cannot be reasonably isolated into [separate] linguistic and memory components but must be a combined effort of both. (Schank, 1972, pp. 626–628)

If we place practical knowledge outside the basic machinery of linguistic comprehension, we create the problem of explaining when and how it is invoked for interpretive purposes. . . . The usual resolution of this problem consists of waving the hands vaguely toward a distant bridge that may someday need to be crossed. . . . [But] a language machine that does not interact smoothly with a person's practical knowledge will say little or nothing of importance about the central problems of cognitive psychology. (Miller, 1977, p. 401)

There's more to language than just the words. (Jean Redpath, on A Prairie Home Companion, *May 4, 1985)*

omprehension—even the title of this chapter must be explained a bit, if only because much of Chapter 9 dealt with language comprehension too. What does the word *comprehension* mean here that it didn't imply in Chapter 9? Basically, the expanded meaning here includes not only the fundamental language processes we studied in Chapter 9 but also the additional processes we use when comprehending realistic samples of language, say a passage in a book or a connected, coherent conversation. How do we comprehend? What do we *do* when we read, understand, and remember connected sentences? By taking a larger unit of analysis than simple, isolated sentences, we confront a host of intriguing questions and issues that are central to communication and to cognitive psychology. And by confronting Miller's (1973) highest two levels of analysis, conceptual knowledge and beliefs, we address the important issues Miller (1977) describes as the "distant bridge that may someday need to be crossed." In short, it's time to cross the bridge.

Getting Started: An Overview

Conceptual and Rule Knowledge

You read about the first three levels of language analysis—the phonological, syntactic, and lexical and semantic levels—in Chapter 9. Let's start digging into comprehension by discussing Miller's (1977) fourth and fifth levels, the conceptual and belief levels. Here's the sentence Miller uses to illustrate these final, important levels of language understanding:

(1) Mary and John saw the mountains while they were flying to California.

If this sentence were spoken out loud, your comprehension would begin with phonological processes, translating the stream of sounds into words. Your syntactic knowledge would parse the sentence into phrases and would assist the semantic level of analysis as you determined the case roles for each important word: Mary and John are the agents of *see*, the word *mountains* is assigned the patient or recipient role, *they* is the agent of *fly* in the second main clause, and so forth.

So far so good. But Miller's sentence is more challenging than that. It's ambiguous, has more than one meaning. There's the obvious one, that Mary and John looked out the plane window and saw mountains during a flight to California. But there's also the possibility that *they* refers to the mountains. *They* merely denotes something plural, after all, so syntactically, the *they* could refer to the mountains.

Those of you who noticed this ambiguity probably rejected it immediately for the obvious reason: Mountains don't fly. We're getting close to the exact point Miller is making here. Knowing that mountains don't fly is part of your semantic, conceptual knowledge, part of your encyclopedic knowledge of the world. It is not a part of your mental lexicon, your simpler lexical knowledge about the word *mountains*. As he put it, look in as many dictionaries as you'd like, and you won't find "mountains don't fly" in any of them. Accordingly, your comprehension of sentence 1 must have included not only those first three levels of analysis, up through the mental lexicon, but also a conceptual level of analysis, in which you compared your interpretation with your semantic knowledge.

Miller also argues that beliefs are important to a complete understanding of comprehension. I could tell you "No, I'm not saying that Mary and John were flying to California. I'm saying that it was the *mountains* that were flying." Although you can understand that *I* might think mountains can fly, you obviously wouldn't change your mind about the issue; your belief in your own knowledge and your feeling that I'm lying or playing some kind of trick (or just plain crazy) are an important part of your comprehension. The purely linguistic analysis of language misses this occasionally critical aspect of language comprehension as well: Think how prominent your beliefs are, and how critical to comprehension and memory, when you hear advertisements or speeches in political campaigns.

Rules form yet another part of the knowledge that must be taken into account. In Chapter 9 we discussed the tacit rule knowledge people have at the phonological and syntactic levels and the distinctly semantic knowledge of case rules. These are all used to understand a sentence, of course. But additional levels of rules are operating when we deal with more complex passages of text or with connected conversation. Some rules have the flavor of strategies; for example, we tend to interpret sentence 2 as focusing on Tina, largely because she is mentioned first in the sentence (Gernsbacher, 1990).

(2) Tina gathered the kindling as Lisa set up the tent.

Several lines of evidence speak to this idea, that we provide a focus to our sentences by using mechanisms such as first mention and certain kinds of reference (e.g., "There was this guy who . . ." instead of "A guy . . .").

Other rules have to do with reference, building bridges between words referring to the same thing. For example, after reading sentence 2, how do you know that the phrase "After she got the fire started" refers to Tina? Still more rules parade under the name *pragmatics* and refer to a variety of extralinguistic factors in a sentence. As an example, indirect speech acts such as "Do you have the time?" or "Can you open the window?" mean something different from what a literal reading would suggest. And finally, high-level rules operate in conversational interactions, rules that specify how the participants in a conversation structure their remarks, and how they understand the remarks of others. As always, simply because you can't state the rule or were never explicitly taught the rule doesn't mean that the rule isn't there. On the contrary, it simply means that the rules are part of your implicit, tacit knowledge.

Traditional Comprehension Research

Much of the traditional evidence about comprehension relied on people's linguistic intuitions, their (leisurely) judgments about the acceptability of sentences, or simple measures of recall and accuracy. The Sachs (1967) study you read about in Chapter 8 was a classic example of early comprehension research, with a straightforward conclusion. Recall that as subjects were reading a passage, they were interrupted and tested on a target sentence, either 0, 80, or 160 syllables after the end of the target. Their recognition of the target sentence was very accurate at the immediate interval. But beyond that, they were accurate only at rejecting the choice that changed the meaning of the sentence. That is, the subjects could not accurately discriminate between the true target sentence and the two choices that were paraphrases: If the choice preserved the original meaning, then the subjects mistakenly "recognized" it. Clearly, these results showed that memory of meaningful passages does not retain verbatim sentences for very long but does retain meaning quite well.

Another example of such pioneering research is work by Jarvella (1970, 1971). Jarvella had subjects listen to lengthy passages but interrupted them at various unpredictable times. When they were interrupted, they were supposed to write down whatever they could remember from the end of the passage immediately before the interruption. Jarvella was testing the hypothesis that people hold information about a sentence in memory until that sentence or meaningful clause is completed; once the sentence is completed, however, they "file away" the overall meaning or gist of the sentence and turn their attention to the next, incoming sentence (very much in the same tradition as Sachs, 1967; see also Gernsbacher, 1985, 1990; Glanzer, Fisher, & Dorfman, 1984). To test this hypothesis, Jarvella constructed pairs of sentences that varied in sentence structure, whether the middle clause did or did not complete a sentence, as in sentences 3 and 4:

(3) *The tone of the document was threatening.* **Having failed to disprove the charges,** *Taylor was later fired by the President.*

(4) *The document had also blamed him for* **having failed to disprove the charges.** *Taylor was later fired by the President.*

Although the first clauses in the sentence are different, note that the second (in boldface) and third clauses (italicized) are the same. The difference is that the middle clause is part of the final sentence in 3, but part of the first sentence in 4.

If we remember sentences in a simple, recency–based fashion, then recall accuracy for the clauses should resemble the final portion of a standard serial position effect: The first clause should be remembered poorly, the middle one somewhat better, and the final one best. And in fact, recall of the first and last clauses was almost indistinguishable regardless of sentence structure; the first clause was "a long time ago," and the last one was the most recent. But as Figure 10-1 shows, recall of the critical middle clause depended significantly on sentence structure in the passages, not on simple serial position and recency. When "having failed to disprove the charges" was part of the second sentence, as in 3, recall was of that clause was high, at 54%. But when that same phrase was part of the first sentence, it was recalled only 21% of the time.

Jarvella's hypothesis was supported: Once a sentence has ended, it seems to be purged from working memory as a verbatim or active memory and therefore no longer accessible for word-by-word recall. Sentence structure of the passages was a salient cue for subjects to wrap up comprehension of one sentence and then move on to the next. In other words, memory for sentences, or more generally for discourse, does not follow the standard serial position curve, does not invariably obey the rules of primacy and recency discovered in list-learning experiments. Instead, what we remember is affected by the structure of the sentences and the role the ideas play in the overall meaning of the sentence.

Limitations of the Traditional Research As powerful as they may have been, studies such as those by Sachs and Jarvella raised more questions than they answered. For the Sachs experiment, we wondered when and how rapidly the verbatim memory record

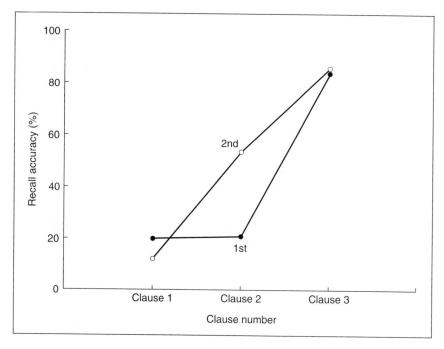

Figure 10-1

Recall accuracy for the first, second, and third clauses in pairs of sentences. The important effect is that the second clause was recalled very poorly when it was part of the first sentence but well when it was part of the second sentence. *Source.* Data from Jarvella (1970).

started declining, and how subjects managed to retain the meaning so well despite forgetting the exact wording of the target. For Jarvella's work, how could sentence structure so overpower the standard serial position effect in recall, and what did that say about memory of sentences? As work like this continued, it became apparent that cognitive psychology needed better, more precise methods of investigating questions about comprehension. We wanted to investigate more about comprehension processes than people's linguistic intuitions or recall scores could reveal. But what methods could be used, for example, in sentences such as the following one (from Miyake, Just, & Carpenter, 1994)?

(5) Since Ken really liked the boxer, he took a bus to the nearest pet store to buy the animal.

When you read (or hear) a sentence with an ambiguous word such as *boxer,* do you access both meanings of the word, or just the dominant meaning? If you access both meanings, do you then keep both of them active in working memory until another word (*pet*) comes along to resolve the ambiguity? Because comprehension processes operate very rapidly and automatically, none of the traditional measures is very useful in giving us the detailed evidence we need to answer such questions.

The difficulty of language comprehension when working memory is overloaded.

Online Comprehension Tasks

What's needed instead is a *task that measures comprehension as it happens*, or **online comprehension tasks.** Online comprehension tasks involve the same cognitive approach you've been reading about throughout this book: Find a dynamic, time- or action-based task that yields measurements of the underlying mental processes as they occur. Contrast performance in a variety of conditions, pitting factors against each other to see how they affect comprehension speed or difficulty. Then draw conclusions about the underlying mental processes, based on the performance measures.

Written language In one commonly used method, a sentence appears on a computer screen and is immediately followed by a word. Sometimes the subjects must make a "yes" or "no" response to the word, indicating whether the word was in the just-read sentence. Sometimes the subject must simply name the word or perform a lexical decision task on it. Look at Table 10-1 to see some sample stimuli and test words for these tasks.

Naturally, your performance would be timed and would lead us to inferences about the nature and operation of cognitive processes. For example, if the ambiguous word *boxer* activates both the *dog* and the *fighter* meanings of the word, then we might expect RT to *dog* and *fight* to be about the same and both of these faster than to the neutral word *plate*. But if *boxer* is interpreted during comprehension only in one of its two senses, then *dog* would be faster than *fight* (or the other way around, depending on which meaning is dominant).

Table 10-1 SAMPLE STIMULI AND TEST WORDS FOR ONLINE COMPREHENSION TASKS

Task	Sentence	Yes	Related	Unrelated	No
Was this word in the sentence?	Ken really liked the boxer.	Ken			Bill
Naming	Ken really liked the boxer.		Dog/fight	Plate	
Lexical decision	Ken really liked the boxer.		Dog/fight	Plate	Lamt

Spoken language Online tasks for comprehension of spoken language have typically depended on rather different procedures, although they rely on the same kind of logic and reasoning. One approach uses an interruption procedure in which we interrupt subjects during presentation of a sentence and ask for some sort timed memory performance based on what was just heard; this would be an auditory equivalent of the tests shown in Table 10-1. Another uses the technique of monitoring, where subjects listen to a sentence and must detect a prespecified target (e.g., "listen for the sound /b/" in this sentence). When the target is detected, the subject presses a key as rapidly as possible, and again an RT measurement is taken. For example, detection of /b/ in *boxer* might be slower than normal because the subject was grappling with the ambiguous concept "BOXER"; *normal* here refers to a baseline condition, say detecting the /b/ in a nonambiguous word such as *baseball* or *blanket*. In general, we would expect that phoneme detection would be slower if the target phoneme occurs in a difficult part of the sentence, a part where comprehension was especially difficult. Additional techniques have used cross-modality tasks, that is, tasks in which a sentence is *heard* by the subject up until the last word, at which point the last word is shown visually on a computer screen.

Let's study some results from online comprehension tasks within the context of a unifying theory of comprehension. You'll see how this research technique is used to study the comprehension of sentences and whole passages of text and how models incorporate this kind of evidence.

Comprehension as Mental Structure Building

Gernsbacher's overall theory of discourse comprehension is called the structure building framework. It combines familiar ideas—for example, spreading activation and propositions—with online techniques and provides a useful approach for understanding many of our recent discoveries about comprehension. The theory is summarized in Table 10-2; a full explanation is provided in Gernsbacher's book (1990; see also overview chapters in 1991 and 1997). Her basic theme is that language comprehension—indeed, *any* comprehension of coherent material—is a process of building mental structures. Laying a foundation, mapping information onto the structure, and shifting to new structures are the three principal components of this structure-building process.

Laying a Foundation According to Gernsbacher, as we read sentences we begin to build a mental structure that stores the meaning of the sentence in memory. A foundation is

Table 10-2 SUMMARY OF GERNSBACHER'S STRUCTURE BUILDING FRAMEWORK

Process	Explanation
1. Laying a foundation	Initiate a structure for representing clause or sentence meaning
2. Mapping information	Map or store congruent information into the current structure
3. Shifting	Initiate a new structure to represent a new or different idea

Control Mechanisms	Function
1. Enhancement	Increase the activation of coherent, related information
2. Suppression	Dampen the activation of information no longer relevant to current structure

initiated as the sentence begins and most commonly is built around the first character or idea in the sentence. This is equivalent to saying that sentence 6,

(6) Dave was studying hard for his statistics midterm.

is about the character named Dave. More formally, we would say that the discourse focus (Rayner, Garrod, & Perfetti, 1992) of sentence 6 is "Dave and his exam." Assume, in short, that the initial foundation involves the overall relation being expressed ("STUDY") and the agent ("DAVE"). A new sentence structure—a proposition—is initiated, focused on the central character Dave. As the words *was studying* are read, their meanings are accessed in lexical and semantic memory, and memory nodes corresponding to those meanings become part of the current "Dave structure." In the format you encountered in the last chapter, this might be represented as "STUDY (Dave)."

Mapping Information   As more elements appear in the sentence, they too are added to the structure, by the process called mapping. *Mapping* here simply means that additional word and concept meanings are now added to the "DAVE" structure, elaborating that structure by specifying Dave's activities. For instance, the prepositional phrase "for his statistics midterm" is processed. Because the concept "MIDTERM" is a coherent idea in the context of studying, these words or memory nodes are added to the structure. Inferences that you draw as you read would also be added to the structure. For instance, when your conceptual knowledge about "MIDTERM" was activated, you surely drew the inference that Dave probably was enrolled in a statistics course. Generally then, mapping is the process by which recurring terms and inferred ideas are related to each other and to the meaning of the whole passage, and stored as part of the structure under construction.

Shifting to a New Structure   We continue trying to map incoming words to the current structure on the assumption that those words belong to the first idea unit, the structure under construction right now. But at some point, a different idea is encountered, an idea that signals a change in focus or topic shift. As an example, consider this continuation of the Dave story.

(7) Because the professor had a reputation for giving difficult exams, the students knew they'd have to be well prepared.

In the model, when you read "Because the professor," some coherence component detects the change in topic or focus. One clue to this change is the word *because* or other connectives (e.g., *later, although, meanwhile*), especially those that indicate a shift in time (e.g., "around 6 o'clock"; Bestgen & Vonk, 2000). Another clue involves the introduction of a new character in the story and the chain of inferences you need to draw to figure out who the professor is; you inferred that Dave must be enrolled in a statistics class, and because midterms are exams given in college classes that are taught by professors, the professor must be the professor who teaches the statistics class Dave is enrolled in.

At such moments, you react by closing off or finishing the "Dave structure" and beginning a new one, one about the professor. Although the "Dave structure" still retains its prominence in your overall memory of the story, you are now working on a new current structure, mapping the incoming ideas (e.g., reputation, difficult exams) onto that structure. And at the end of that phrase, you will have constructed two related but separate structures, one for each meaning (the phrase beginning "the students" will trigger yet another structure to be built, yielding three distinct substructures).

Evidence of Structure Building What evidence supports these claims about the comprehension process? In Gernsbacher's early work, two major effects provided support for these mechanisms: the **advantage of first mention** and the **advantage of clause recency.** In the advantage of first mention, *characters and ideas that were mentioned in the very first sentence, at the beginning of the entire episode, retain a special significance.* This special significance showed up clearly in a study by Gernsbacher and Hargreaves (1988). In the task, a name appeared on the computer screen after the subject finished reading the last word of a sentence. Subjects had to respond, as rapidly as possible, "yes" if the name had been in the sentence and "no" if it had not (obviously, there were control conditions in which other names were shown during the test). Thus, after reading a sentence such as "Tina gathered the kindling as Lisa set up the tent," you'd be shown *Tina, Lisa,* or some other name (to control for guessing). As Figure 10-2 shows, when the test item was the first-mentioned participant, it took subjects about 900 msec to say "yes," compared with more than 950 msec for responding to the second-mentioned agent. Thus there was a 50-msec advantage of first mention.

The effect is also shown in Figure 10-3, along with the second major effect, the advantage of clause recency (Gernsbacher, Hargreaves, & Beeman, 1989). Here, *the most recently mentioned character showed an advantage* in the "Coincident" condition: If you have to make a decision immediately after hearing the sentence, then there is about a 50-msec advantage for names that occurred in the most recent clause (*Lisa* in the just-mentioned sentence). This advantage disappeared when the decision was delayed even by 150 msec. And at the later delay conditions, the stronger effect of first mention prevailed.

Thus, beyond a very transitory recency effect, characters who appeared early in the story, who are in the main discourse focus, retain an advantage in performance; they remain accessible (McKoon, Ratcliff, Ward, & Sproat, 1993). This implies that

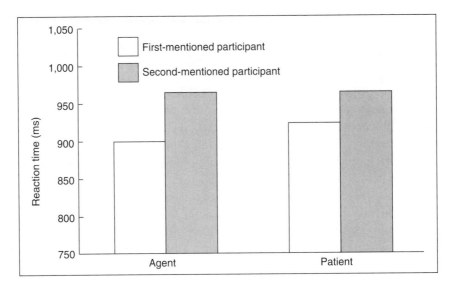

Figure 10-2

Mean reaction time to names that had appeared in the studied sentences when the name was the first- or second-mentioned participant and when the name played the agent or patient case role in the sentence. *Source.* Data from Gernsbacher and Hargreaves (1988). From Gernsbacher (1990).

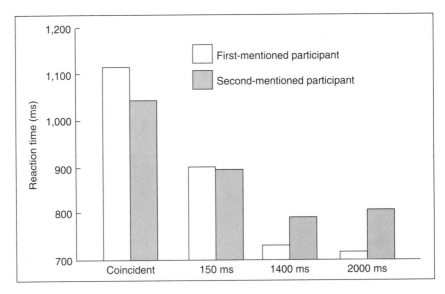

Figure 10-3

Mean reaction time to names that had appeared in the studied sentences when the name was the first- or second-mentioned participant. Names were tested immediately at the end of the sentence (Coincident) or at varying delays after the end of the sentence (150, 1,400, or 2,000 msec later). *Source.* Data from Gernsbacher et al. (1989). From Gernsbacher (1990).

Table 10-3 SAMPLE SENTENCES WITH INDEFINITE AND DEFINITE ARTICLES

Indefinite	Definite
A grandmother sat at a table.	The grandmother sat at the table.
A child played in a backyard.	The child played in the backyard.
Some rain began to pour down.	The rain began to pour down.
An elderly woman led some others outside.	The elderly woman led the others outside.

Source. Robertson et al. (2000).

the first-mentioned character is central to the structure that was built, to the memory representation of the meaning of the sentences. Furthermore, it makes no difference if the first-mentioned character was the agent or patient in the structure, whether the sentence was in the active or passive voice, or whether the character was the syntactic subject of the sentence; the effect even generalizes to Spanish, which has much greater flexibility than English in its word order rules (Carreiras, Gernsbacher, & Villa, 1995). What mattered was first mention, and being in the foundation of the structure that represents sentence meaning.

In other words, the first participant or idea is in the discourse focus, and later clauses are represented in substructures; they're important, of course, but they're subservient to the focus of the first clause, the most important idea in the sentence. Interestingly, we are not only sensitive to discourse focus when we read and comprehend (Birch & Garnsey, 1995; Birch & Rayner, 1997; Morris & Folk, 1998); we also deliberately manipulate the structure of our sentences to highlight discourse focus when we speak (Ferreira, 1994).

In subsequent work, Gernsbacher examined a different factor in comprehension, the effect of using the definite article *the*. When we read sentences that describe characters, objects, and events with the article *the*, the sentences seem more coherent and sensible than sentences using *a*, *an*, and *some* (Gernsbacher & Robertson, in press; see Table 10-3 for sample sentences). Furthermore, such sentences are understood better and are remembered better later on (Haviland & Clark, 1974). Gernsbacher's (1997) view is that *the* is a cue for discourse coherence, enabling us to perform the mapping process more efficiently and accurately.

In a recent article (Robertson et al., 2000), Gernsbacher and her colleagues presented such sentences for subjects to read and comprehend, followed by a recognition test (to make sure they actually processed the sentences). In all cases, sentences using *the* showed greater evidence of coherent processing than those with the indefinite *a*, *an*, and *some*. What was especially fascinating about this study was that subjects were tested in a functional magnetic resonance imaging (fMRI) procedure, and the levels of activity of different brain regions were measured. As Figure 10-4 shows, sentences that used the definite article showed greater activation levels than those with indefinite articles. Equally interesting, these activations were greater in right hemisphere regions than in left hemisphere regions. Recall from Chapter 9 that the left hemisphere is considered specialized for language processing. But the Robertson et al. data actually showed

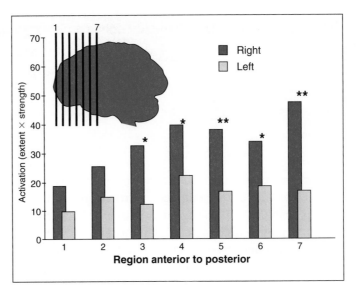

Figure 10-4

Activation levels for sentences presented with definite versus indefinite articles (levels in the figure are difference scores, showing how much greater the activations for definite than indefinite article sentences were), for seven left and right hemisphere locations in the brain. *Source.* From Robertson et al. (2000).

greater *right* hemisphere activity for the comprehension task with definite articles. Thus these results added to the collection of evidence that the right hemisphere of the brain may be especially important for coherence and inference processes in language comprehension. This is especially the case when the task requires comprehension of discourse (i.e., integration of the meanings of several related sentences rather than processing single, isolated sentences).

Enhancement and Suppression Finally, two control mechanisms in Gernsbacher's model connect her work to the familiar process of spreading activation, and they also lead us into the next major topic in comprehension, the problem of reference and inference. Let's add one more sentence to the Dave story to discuss full-blown comprehension in Gernsbacher's model.

(6) Dave was studying hard for his statistics midterm.

(7) Because the professor had a reputation for giving difficult exams, the students knew they'd have to be well prepared.

(8) Dave wanted an A on that test.

As noted earlier, when you encounter sentence 7, you initiate a new substructure because there has been a change in focus. Although the new substructure carries different information, it is still related to the first one. That is, two prominent ideas in sentence 7 map onto the ideas from sentence 6; *exams* refers with a different name to the same concept as *midterms,* and *the professor* maps onto the statistics course implied by sentence 6. According to Gernsbacher, such mappings reflect the activation of related memory nodes, especially those mapped into the foundation of the first structure (Millis & Just, 1994). That is, the "PROFESSOR" memory node becomes activated. This activation then combines with the activation from *midterm* and *statistics course* because of their semantic relatedness. This is the process of **enhancement,** that the many related *memory nodes are now being boosted or enhanced in their level of activation.* Of course, the enhancement process is essentially the same as the spreading activation process in semantic memory. Concepts that are semantically related to the words in the sentences become activated: Their level of activation is enhanced. It is the *degree* of enhancement and activation among concepts that predicts which concepts will be remembered better or responded to more rapidly. And the more frequently the same set of nodes is enhanced across the entire sentence, the more coherent the passage is.

Note, however, that the enhancement of some memory nodes implies that other nodes will lose activation. That is, while sentence 7 enhances the activation of memory nodes related to "PROFESSOR, EXAM," and so on, there is a simultaneous **suppression** of memory nodes that are now out of the main discourse focus. In other words, *activated nodes that become unrelated to the focus decrease in activation* by the process of suppression. Figure 10-5 is an illustration of these competing tendencies. Note that as the professor clause is being processed (ideas 3 and 4), the activation level for "DAVE" drops; the "DAVE" node undergoes suppression because it's no longer the main discourse focus. Then, as the story unfolds further (ideas 5 to 7), the memory nodes for "DAVE" regain their enhancement, and the "PROFESSOR" nodes dwindle. Thus the original Dave structure from sentence 6 receives renewed enhancement when you read in sentence 8 that Dave wanted an A on the test. The original "DAVE" and "EXAM" concepts are reactivated, as if your comprehension process signals "Dave is back again, so get ready for more information about studying for his midterm" (De Vega, 1995; Huitema, Dopkins, Klin, & Myers, 1993; Klin, 1995; O'Brien, Albrecht, Hakala, & Rizzella, 1995).

A Situation Model Approach to Comprehension

What happens to such connected stories? How are such passages saved in memory for later use? An intriguing idea, applicable at least to some kinds of stories, is that we store a **situation model** of the passage (Johnson-Laird, 1983; Van Dijk & Kintsch, 1983). A situation model is *a representation of the real-world situation described in a passage of text;* it's not the propositions or structures that code the meanings of the sentences, but the higher-level representation of the situation described in those sentences. Importantly, such situation models include temporal and spatial information, information about the objects, people, and locations mentioned in the stories, and inferences drawn while comprehending (Radvansky, 1998). Thus with our "Tina–Lisa" sentences, you'd not only form structures that coded the meanings, focus, and so forth, but also a higher-level representation of the situation: Tina

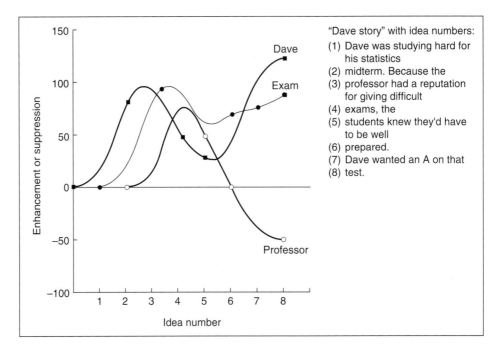

Figure 10-5

Hypothetical activation curves for the concepts *Dave, exam,* and *professor* from the "Dave story" in the text. As concepts are introduced or mentioned again (*Dave, exam*), their activation becomes enhanced. When the focus shifts, old concepts (*professor*) become suppressed; that is, their activation dwindles.

searching through the woods for kindling, Lisa in some kind of clearing, hammering tent pegs, and the like. When you retrieve information about the passage of text, your retrieval from the situation model is influenced by its structure (e.g., whether you stored a person-based or a location-based model).

For example, Rinck and Bower (1995) had subjects memorize a diagram of a research lab, where each room had four different things in it (e.g., the main office had a desk, a water fountain, etc.; the library had shelves, a couch, etc.). They then read a narrative about the lab director preparing the lab for some important visitors, moving from room to room to check on things. Reading times were recorded on the assumption that reading and comprehension would be faster when sentences matched the lab director's location, that is, when the reader was taking the perspective of the lab director. Special target sentences were inserted in the narrative to test the subjects' situation model. A sample target sentence was "He thought that the shelves in the library still looked like an awful mess." If subjects had just read that the director went from the main office, through the conference room, and into the library, their target reading times were quite rapid, approximately 160 msec per syllable. Because the shelves were in the library and the director had just entered the library, the target sentence matched the subjects' situation model very closely and thus was faster to read; in a sense, the reader and the lab director were in the library together, looking at the messy shelves. But reading times slowed down progressively as the target sentence said something about the director's (and readers') previous locations, such as the conference room, the main office, or even earlier locations. And although the times were slower when the room name wasn't mentioned, the same basic pattern of reading times applied nonetheless; when the target sentence was about a room further away from the director's current location, reading time suffered (see also Radvansky, Wyer, Curiel, & Lutz, 1997; Zwaan, 1996).

■ Section Summary

- A variety of online tasks have been devised to investigate comprehension of language, such as tasks involving interruption during reading or hearing and tasks requiring the subject to monitor a spoken passage for a particular target sound or word. These online tasks generally have supported the view that comprehension is an interactive process in which phonetic, syntactic, lexical, and semantic or conceptual factors are in continual operation, each assisting the others during the comprehension process.

- Sentence comprehension has been described as a process of structure building in which you map incoming concepts onto the structure under construction until a new concept switches the discourse focus. Concepts enjoy an advantage of first mention in later tests of memory and for a brief time enjoy a recency advantage. This framework is also compatible with comprehension based on situation models.

Reference, Inference, and Memory

So far in this chapter we have avoided a specific discussion of two critically important language devices, reference and inference, and the mental processes necessary to deal with them. We simply took it for granted that readers will infer that "the professor" in sentence 7 referred back to Dave's statistics professor, that a midterm is an exam, and so on. But now we must confront the reference and inference steps because they are critical to comprehending in a coherent fashion. How do we comprehend a sentence that does not stand on its own, a sentence that requires reference to another sentence to be understood? Equally interesting is the topic of inference. What kinds of inferences are drawn during comprehension? How do we tailor our written and spoken language to the inferences that a listener or reader is likely to draw?

Reference Reference involves finding the connections between elements in a sentence or passage of text, finding the words that refer to other concepts in the sentence. In sentence 6, "Dave was studying hard for his statistics midterm," the word *his* refers back to *Dave*. In this situation, *Dave* is the **antecedent** of *his*, because *Dave* comes before the pronoun. And *the act of using a pronoun or possessive later on* is called **anaphoric reference.** Definitionally then, **reference** is the *linguistic process of alluding to a concept by using another name*. Most commonly, we use pronouns or synonyms to refer to the antecedent, although there are several other types of reference.

Implication and Inference   Implication, on the other hand, is not as obvious as reference. In **implication,** there is *an intended reference in a sentence or utterance, but it is not mentioned explicitly.* The intention here is on the part of the speaker (or writer), who implies but does not state some conclusion or connection; in a sense, implication is in the mind of the speaker. If the listener (reader) draws the appropriate conclusion or connection during comprehension, then we say that the listener has drawn an inference, has drawn the appropriate conclusion. Thus, **inference** is *the process by which the listener or reader draws connections between concepts, determines the referents of words and ideas, and derives conclusions from a message.* Implication is something that speakers do, and drawing inferences is something hearers do. If I say to my class, "The next exam is on Wednesday, and it covers a lot of material," I'm probably implying something about the difficulty of the exam, but I leave it to my students to draw that inference.

Simple Reference and Inference

To begin with, reference and inference are as common in language as any other feature we can identify. Part of the reason for this, no doubt, involves redundancy. Contrast a normal passage such as 9a with 9b to see how boring and repetitive language would be without the use of synonyms, pronouns, and so on:

(9a) Mike went to the pool to swim some laps. After his workout, he went to his psychology class. The professor asked him to summarize the chapter that he'd assigned the class to read.

(9b) Mike went to the pool to swim some laps. After Mike swam some laps, Mike went to Mike's psychology class. The professor of Mike's psychology class asked Mike to summarize the chapter that Mike's psychology professor had assigned Mike's psychology class to read.

The sentences in 9b also illustrate a second aspect of reference. It is almost impossible to specify each component in a sentence; *no* sentence stands on its own completely. Sentence 9b avoids pronouns of all sorts, referring to *Mike* instead of *he,* for instance. Yet even 9b is incomplete in that the full meaning of each term is not specified in the sentence itself. Instead of specifying everything, we rely on listeners to know the meanings of our words, to know about syntactic devices that structure our discourse, and to share our general conceptual knowledge of the world (e.g., to know that swimming laps can be a workout, that professors assign chapters for their students to read). In fact, as you'll read in the last section of this chapter, if you *do* specify everything exactly, you're breaking an important conversational rule.

In naturally occurring discourse, several different kinds of reference occur; Clark's (1977) useful list is shown in Table 10-4. Consider three simple forms of reference:

(10) I saw a convertible yesterday. The convertible was red.

(11) I saw a convertible yesterday. The car was red.

(12) I saw a convertible yesterday. It was red.

Table 10-4 TYPES OF REFERENCE AND IMPLICATION
Direct Reference
Identity. Michelle bought a computer. The computer was on sale.
Synonym. Michelle bought a computer. The machine was on sale.
Pronoun. Michelle bought a computer. It was on sale for 20% off.
Set membership. I talked to two people today. Michelle said she had just bought a computer.
Epithet. Michelle bought a computer. The stupid thing doesn't work.
Indirect Reference by Association
Necessary parts. Eric bought a used car. The tires were badly worn.
Probable parts. Eric bought a used car. The radio doesn't work.
Inducible parts. Eric bought a used car. The salesperson gave him a good price.
Indirect Reference by Characterization
Necessary roles. I taught my class yesterday. The time I started was 1:30.
Optional roles. I taught my class yesterday. The chalk tray was empty.
Other
Reasons. Rick asked a question in class. He hoped to impress the professor.
Causes. Rick answered a question in class. The professor had called on him.
Consequences. Rick asked a question in class. The professor was impressed.
Concurrences. Rick asked a question in class. Vicki tried to impress the professor too.

Source. Adapted from Clark (1977).

In sentence 10, the reference is so direct that it seems to require no inference on the part of the listener whatsoever; this is an instance of identity reference, using the definite article *the* to refer back to a previously introduced concept, *a convertible*. Likewise, synonym reference requires that you consider whether the second word is an adequate synonym for the first, as in sentence 11; can a convertible also be referred to as "the car"? Pronoun reference requires similar reference and inference steps. In sentence 12, *it* can refer only to the word *convertible*, because the only concept introduced in the earlier phrase that can be equated with *it* is "CONVERTIBLE." That is, in English, the word *it* must refer to an ungendered concept, just as *he* must refer to a male, and so forth. Contrast this with languages in which nouns have gender and pronouns must agree with the gender of the noun; translated literally from French, we get "Here is the Eiffel Tower. She is beautiful."

Bridging Clark (1977) uses the term ***bridging*** to refer to the underlying mental processes we're discussing. That is, Clark describes all forms of reference, implication (he calls it implicature, after Grice, 1975), and inference as bridging, *a process of constructing a connection between concepts*. Metaphorically, this is a process of building a *bridge* across which comprehension can pass. Bridging clearly is a two-party process. Speakers and listeners must both build the same bridges if communication is to be successful (and writers and readers too, of course). Consider the explicit bridges you need to draw to understand the remaining examples in Table 10-4, such as the reference by epithet that equates *the stupid thing* with *a computer*, or the heavily inferential connection between the chalk tray and the statement "I taught my class yesterday."

In bridging, according to Clark, the speaker uses reference of one sort or another to indicate the kinds of implications that are intended by an utterance. For their part, hearers interpret the utterance in the same fashion, both computing the references in the utterance and drawing inferences necessary for comprehension. When the speaker genuinely intends an implication, we call it an authorized implication, and if the listener draws the intended inference, it's an **authorized** inference. On the other hand, an **unauthorized** implication is an accidental implication on the part of the speaker, and an **unauthorized** inference is a mistaken inference on the listener's part, as when I say, "Your hair looks pretty today," and you respond, "So you think it was ugly yesterday?" (see also McKoon & Ratcliff, 1986).

Inferences During Comprehension

The examples in Table 10-4 make it clear that the bridges we need to build for comprehension vary tremendously in their complexity, from very simple and direct to very difficult and remote. Even on intuitive grounds, consider how the following sentences differ in the ease of comprehension:

(13) Marge went into her office. It was very dirty.

(14) Marge went into her office. The floor was very dirty.

(15) Marge went into her office. The African violet had bloomed.

Whereas sentence 13 is a simple case of pronoun reference, sentence 14 refers back to *office* with the word *floor*. Because an office necessarily has a floor, it is clear that the implication in sentence 14 is that it was Marge's office floor that was dirty; in other words, Marge's office is indeed the antecedent (likewise for *the professor* referring back to the inferred statistics class in our earlier example). One of the properties you retrieve from your semantic memory is that an office has a floor, although that property of "OFFICE" probably is a very weakly related one. Thus, if you comprehend that the office floor was dirty, you must have drawn this inference. But it's an even longer chain of inference to draw the inference in sentence 15 that Marge happens to have an African violet in her office; a floor is necessary, but an African violet isn't.

Think back to our discussion of semantic memory and the typicality of instances in a category as well as the typicality of properties of those instances. Given that the associated pieces of information are associated in the speaker's and listener's semantic memories, it seems likely that the structure of concepts in semantic memory would at least partly determine what can and can't be inferred, how acceptable or understandable a referring sentence might be judged, and how quickly people would comprehend or verify a referring sentence. That is, a very predictable piece of information would be a very typical concept or property (McKoon & Ratcliff, 1989; O'Brien, Plewes, & Albrecht, 1990); Marge's office necessarily has a floor but probably also has a desk, a chair, some shelves, and so on. It's conceivable that it has some plants, of course, but that is optional enough that sentence 15 seems less definite and would probably take more time to comprehend.

The Processes and Extent of Drawing Inferences

We've been describing comprehension in terms of the knowledge stored in memory and the retrieval of that knowledge to draw inferences. Retrieving information such as *a midterm is an exam* and *offices have floors* allows you to understand the various forms of reference that are so common in language.

Multiple Processes in Drawing Inferences But we've actually made the process sound simpler than it really is. At a minimum, the process of comprehending references and drawing inferences involves at least three distinct steps. First, as you read, you start retrieving related information from memory, using both syntactic and semantic cues: Gendered pronouns, the singular or plural status of the verb, the concepts in the focus of the discourse, and so forth, help us know what information should be retrieved. Second, the retrieved information must be kept in memory, probably in working memory, so it's available as you make the connections and draw inferences. And finally, you integrate the meanings together; you make the connections between antecedents and referents (*he* is Mike), draw the inferences from one phrase to another (offices have floors), determine which meanings are relevant (the dog meaning of *boxer*), and so on. But we aren't limited to retrieving information only from conceptual or semantic memory. In principle, all of our long-term memory knowledge, including script knowledge and our personal episodic store, can contribute to the comprehension process.

What research supports all these claims about reference and inference? In fact, dozens of studies have examined language comprehension from the standpoint of bridging or drawing inferences in written and spoken language. In general, the results of these studies confirm the broad outlines of models such as Gernsbacher's (1990) structure building framework or any model that includes drawing inferences in the list of online comprehension processes. Let's review some of the evidence to give you an idea about this important process.

The Extent of Drawing Inferences Given that some forms of reference and inference are simple and straightforward but some are complex, we need to consider just how extensively people draw inferences when they comprehend. This has been at the center of an important, active debate in the past 10 to 15 years. Everyone agrees that some degree of inference drawing is essential to normal comprehension, given the issues of reference and inference we've been discussing. That is, even the minimalist hypothesis (McKoon & Ratcliff, 1992) would claim that when you read sentence 13, you'd draw the connection between *it* and *office* online, as you would between *floor* and *office* in sentence 14. Every theory of comprehension must include at least some degree of reference and inference processing because failing to draw those connections would mean you hadn't really comprehended the sentences at all.

The debate centers on how much further the normal reader goes in drawing inferences. We surely don't draw all possible inferences as we read; our cognitive resources would be quickly overwhelmed if we did, as several researchers have pointed out (Singer, Graesser, & Trabasso, 1994). For example, when you read a sentence like 13 or 14, you surely would not draw an inference immediately that Marge decided to clean her office, although if the next sentence in the story said that, you'd certainly understand the continuation. But you wouldn't draw the "so she cleaned it" inference online when you comprehended the original sentences (Millis & Graesser, 1994). The McKoon and Ratcliff (1992) position is that we draw inferences online only to the extent that the information can be retrieved automatically, and only to make the local discourse, the immediate phrase or sentence, coherent.

Several researchers argue against the minimalist position, however, saying that it underestimates the extent of inference drawing during normal comprehension (Singer et al., 1994). And ample evidence shows that in many circumstances, we do draw inferences routinely as we comprehend. For example, many studies have shown that readers draw elaborative inferences from text in an online fashion and then store those inferences as part of their long-term memory of the material that was read (Long, Golding, & Graesser, 1992; Noordman, Vonk, & Kempff, 1992; O'Brien, Shank, Myers, & Rayner, 1988). This is particularly the case when the inference stems from a concept that was in the focus of the discourse (Whitney, Ritchie, & Crane, 1992).

In a recent example, Garrod and Terras (2000) had their subjects read sets of three related sentences in which the first established a general context, the second introduced a specific event, and the third contained a word that had to be integrated based on inferred information. For instance, in a story about a schoolteacher, the specific event involved writing a letter to a parent, and the target sentence mentioned "the pen." Given the specific "WRITING" context, subjects smoothly and quickly integrated "the pen" as they read the target sentence, " However, she was disturbed by a loud scream from the back of the class and the pen dropped on the floor." In other words, the subjects integrated the dominant or frequent role filler—*pen* for "WRITING"—rapidly and automatically. The same rapid bonding effect, early and automatic inference, was not found when role fillers that were less predictable or simply of lower frequency were used. Instead, integrating these references (e.g., *chalk* in the setting of writing on the blackboard) was a slower process and seemed to occur at the final integration stage rather than online when the word was encountered (see also Murray, Klin, & Myers, 1993).

Individual Differences Interestingly, there is now accumulating evidence that reference and inference processes depend significantly on individual characteristics of the reader, particularly on the reader's skill. For instance, Long and De Ley (2000) found that less skilled readers resolve ambiguous pronouns just as well as more skilled readers, but they do so only when they are integrating meanings together; the more skilled readers resolve the pronouns earlier, probably when they first encounter the pronoun. Several studies have also examined inferences as a function of the limited capacity of working memory (e.g., Fletcher & Bloom, 1988). One such study, by Singer, Andrusiak,

Reisdorf, and Black (1992), went one step further than this, explaining individual differences in bridging as a function of working memory capacity and vocabulary knowledge. The gist of this work is that the greater your working memory capacity and vocabulary size, the greater is the likelihood that information necessary for an inference will still be in working memory and hence can be used for building the bridge between concepts (see also Long, Oppy, & Seely, 1997; Miyake, Just, & Carpenter, 1994).

Enhancement and Suppression Enhancement and suppression effects, respectively higher and lower memory performance for ideas or characters in the discourse, have also been demonstrated. For example, Albrecht and O'Brien (1991) found that concepts rated as central to a passage are more interconnected in the memory representation and therefore are retrieved more rapidly than other, tangential concepts. Gernsbacher and Jescheniak (1995) found that the indefinite *this* (e.g., "There was *this* guy in my class last semester") highlights the referent concept (e.g., *guy*), making it more accessible, more central to the focus of the discourse, and less subject to suppression.

Suppression, on the other hand, can occur merely because a concept was negated. For instance, if you read "There was *no* bread in the house," the concept "BREAD" is suppressed (MacDonald & Just, 1989). Concepts also undergo suppression if they are simply dropped from mention or reference in the discourse, thereby slowing down responses to those words. And in Gernsbacher (1990), suppression was isolated as one of the important differences between good and poor readers. In that research, poor readers seemed to be less adept at suppressing irrelevant information. This would mean that ideas unrelated to the discourse focus would remain activated during comprehension. Using sentence 5 as an example, it's as if a less skilled reader maintains both the "dog" and "fighter" senses of the word *boxer* even after reading about the pet store. Long and De Ley (2000) found the same effect, that less skilled readers apparently maintained more inferred information in memory, by failing to suppress activated information that was irrelevant to the passage of text (see also Gernsbacher, 1993; Gernsbacher & Robertson, 1995). Poor readers also shift from building one substructure to another too frequently, according to Gernsbacher's research (e.g., 1990, Chapter 5), making the end product of comprehension less coherent.

■ Section Summary

- Reference and inference in language involve the notion of bridging, by which a speaker intends a certain meaning that the listener must infer. A variety of reference types exist, some requiring fairly complex bridges on the part of the listener for comprehension to succeed. The source of knowledge that permits speakers to include reference in their messages and listeners to infer the basis for those bridges is not just our knowledge of syntax and word meanings but the entirety of semantic memory and much top-down processing. Evidence also shows the capacity and operation of working memory to be important factors in understanding individual differences in reading comprehension.

Reading

For years, the standard methodology for studying reading had subjects read a passage of text, then take a memory test, such as a multiple choice or recall test. Such tasks certainly have face validity; they test people's memory for the text they have just read, because much of our reading is for the purpose of learning and remembering what we read. And as you know from standardized tests, the task is easily instrumented.

But this standard methodology suffers the same weaknesses we noted in the previous section in connection with traditional research on comprehension. It reveals almost none of the details of mental processing that we want to understand. In Figure 10-5 you saw a graph showing the hypothetical activation levels for concepts mentioned in a set of sentences. We would like to know *directly* how concepts vary in their activation levels across a passage of text because that would tell us a great deal about online comprehension. But a multiple choice test is far too blunt an instrument to give us such answers.

Gaze Duration Procedures

In contrast, at the end of Chapter 9, you saw a figure of eye fixation times, where those times went up when the ambiguity of the sentence became apparent (see Figure 9-12). *This* is the methodology we need, a research procedure that reveals mental processing at the microscopic level of eye gazes, levels of activation, and so on. And this is the methodology you'll read about in this section, describing what cognitive psychology knows about reading based on online reading tasks.

In addition to using online measures described in the previous section, reading research relies especially on the gaze duration or eye fixation method. The equipment for this method is called an eye tracker, a camera- and computer-based apparatus that records both eye movements and the exact stimuli that are fixated in successive eye fixations or gazes; one is depicted in Figure 10-6 (newer models of the apparatus resemble virtual reality helmets, with an attached video camera that films the visual scene and the subject's fixations). After appropriate calibration, the machine records the movements of the eyes and the exact duration of the eyes' gaze as they scan across lines of print. In a similar task, subjects are shown text on a computer screen in a moving window methodology: A word appears briefly at the appropriate physical location for the current eye fixation, and as the eyes shift to the next fixation point, the first word is concealed as the next one appears. In both of these tasks, the researcher knows which word is being processed on a moment-by-moment basis and *how long the eyes dwell on each word*, so **gaze duration** is the primary window through which we investigate what's going on when we read (see Rayner, 1998, for a thorough discussion of alternative measurements).

Two Assumptions Two central assumptions, common to all online research on reading, have been named the immediacy assumption and the eye-mind assumption by Just and Carpenter (1980, 1987, 1992). The **immediacy assumption** states that *readers try to interpret each content word of a text as that word is encountered in the passage.*

Figure 10-6

A student is reading from the computer-controlled display. The video camera on the left remotely registers the light reflections from the reader's eye. A computer uses this information to determine where the reader is fixating. *Source.* From Just and Carpenter (1987).

In other words, we don't take in some group of words, say in a phrase, before starting to process them. Instead, we begin interpreting and comprehending immediately. This is normally a good strategy for reading, even though it occasionally leads to mistakes that must be fixed. For example, consider the following sentence, from Just and Carpenter (1980):

(16) Although he spoke softly, yesterday's speaker could hear the little boy's question.

As you reach "hear the little boy's question," you realize that you've misinterpreted the *he* in the early part of the sentence; in the jargon of this research, you've been "garden pathed." You no doubt initially assigned *he* to the agent "SPEAKER". Then when you read *little boy*, you had to repair or recover from this mistake by *re*assigning *he* to the agent "BOY" (refer back to Figure 9-12, which shows the garden path effect on gaze durations). Note also that this is not a straightforward instance of direct pronoun reference because the pronoun *he* occurs before the antecedent is mentioned. In such circumstances, the general strategy for determining a referent, connecting the pronoun to the nearest available referent, yields a mistake. Note finally that the immediacy assumption explicitly contradicts the notion that each level of analysis in language must complete itself before the next level begins to operate. In other words, the immediacy assumption is an interactive processing assumption.

The second central assumption is the **eye–mind assumption.** Although this was formerly a controversial idea, it is now widely accepted that "there is a close link between eye movements and cognitive processes" (Reichle, Pollatsek, Fisher, & Rayner, 1998). Specifically, the eye–mind assumption states that *the eye remains fixated on a word as long as that word is being actively processed during reading;* in other words, the eyes fixate a word and reveal something very near a measurement of the mental time spent on that word. Generally, this time includes both a subject's initial fixation of a word and the additional time spent on the word when it is refixated, on the assumption that repeated fixations signal some difficulty in comprehension that requires extra time (see Rayner, 1998, and Rayner & Pollatsek, 1989, for reviews of the measurement difficulties in these situations). This is contrasted with the notion that information from several consecutive fixations is held in some sort of temporary buffer to be analyzed only after several fixations have been collected. If this were the case, there should be short gaze durations across several positions in a sentence, followed by a much longer one during which the semantic processing of the buffered information takes place. Yet the data we consider next explicitly disconfirm this possibility.

Basic Online Reading Effects

An early example of online reading research examined regressive eye movements, that is, movements back to a portion of text that had been read earlier. Just (1976) was specifically interested in such eye movements when the referents in the sentence could not be immediately determined: If an initial assignment of a character to a case role was wrong, then what happened during reading? Was there a regressive eye movement back to the correct referent? Subjects read sentences such as 17 and 18, and the camera apparatus monitored their eye movements.

(17) The tenant complained to his landlord about the leaky roof. The next day, he went to the attic to get his luggage.

(18) The tenant complained to his landlord about the leaky roof. The next day, he went to the attic to repair the damage.

Film of the subjects' eye movements provided spectacular evidence about comprehension during reading. In sentence 17, the blotch of light on the film that represented the subject's fixation point moved along until *luggage* was encountered, then bounced up immediately to the word *tenant.* In sentence 18, the blotch of light came to *repair the damage* and bounced up to *landlord.* These eye movements seemed to provide early confirmation of the eye–mind assumption and illustrated the underlying mental processes of finding antecedents and determining case roles.

More recent research provides a clear demonstration of the exquisite detail afforded by the more modern apparatus presented in Figure 10-7, taken from Just and Carpenter's (1987) important theory of reading (see also Just & Carpenter, 1980). In the figure, you see two sentences taken from a scientific passage that Just and Carpenter's college subjects

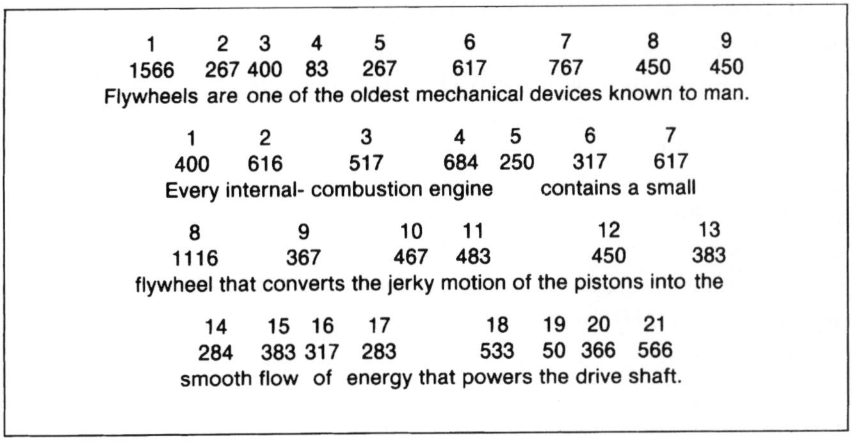

```
  1      2   3    4    5        6          7        8      9
1566   267 400   83  267      617        767      450    450
Flywheels are one of the oldest mechanical devices known to man.

  1      2        3      4    5      6        7
 400   616      517    684  250    317      617
Every internal- combustion engine     contains a small

  8      9        10    11            12          13
1116   367       467   483           450         383
flywheel that converts the jerky motion of the pistons into the

 14     15   16    17          18    19  20    21
284    383  317   283         533    50 366   566
smooth flow  of energy that powers the drive shaft.
```

Figure 10-7

Eye fixations of a college student reading a scientific passage. Gazes within each sentence are sequentially numbered above the fixated words with the durations (in msec) indicated below the sequence number. *Source.* From Just and Carpenter (1980).

were asked to read. Above the words in the sentence are two numbers. The top number indicates the order in which subjects fixated or gazed at the elements in the sentence; 1–9 in the first sentence and 1–21 in the second. The number below this is the gaze duration (measured in milliseconds), or how long this subject fixated each element in the sentences. So, as an example, the initial word in sentence 1, *Flywheels*, was fixated for 1566 msec, slightly over a second and a half. The next word, *are*, was fixated only 267 msec. The fourth word, *of*, wasn't fixated at all by this subject, so neither a gaze number nor time is presented there (this is exactly why the "FINISHED FILES" example in Chapter 2 worked: You didn't fixate the function word *of*; see Koriat & Greenberg, 1996).

A few words of explanation are in order before we turn to the theory of reading built on such results. Just and Carpenter's (1980) data were for scientific passages, read by college subjects who were asked to read naturally, without memorizing, and then be ready to recall each passage. The passages were representative of technical writing, in which a new concept, such as a flywheel, is introduced, defined, and then explained (indeed, subjects rated themselves as "entirely unfamiliar" with the topic before reading the passage). The average reading rate of Just and Carpenter's subjects was about 225 words per minute, somewhat slower than reading rates for simpler material, such as newspaper stories or novels.

A few general characteristics of the data afforded by this technique deserve preliminary mention as well. To begin with, note that every content word in Figure 10-7 was fixated by the subject (and by all the other subjects as well). According to Just and Carpenter, this is the norm for all kinds of text that have been studied. "There is a common misconception that readers do not fixate every word, but only some small proportion of the text. . . . However, the data . . . show that during ordinary reading, almost all content words are fixated" (pp. 329–330). In fact, their data indicate that about 85% of the content words in a passage are fixated. Short function words, however, like *the* or *of* often are not fixated; Rayner and Duffy (1988) estimate that function words are fixated only about 35% of the time. Readers also tend to skip some content words if the passage is very simple for them (say, a children's story given to an adult), if they are skimming or speed reading, or if a word is very predictable, based on other constraints in the sentence (Rayner & Well, 1996).

Another obvious feature of the gaze durations is their variability. Recall in Chapter 3 that the duration of a saccade was estimated at about 100 msec, followed by a fixation that lasts around 200–250 msec. These estimates come from situations in which the viewer is merely gazing out upon some scene, for instance. In the reading studies, however, subjects are reading for comprehension. Here, saccades are shorter than for scene perception; Rayner (1998) suggests that a typical saccade during reading lasts 30–50 msec. Although single fixations on words may be very brief, readers often make repeated fixations on the *same* word. In reading studies, these successive fixations often are summed together; alternatively, investigators report the first-pass fixation duration, the time spent fixating the word the first time, and sometimes total fixation duration as well (subjects are generally told not to reread or refixate earlier parts of a passage, so they dwell on a word until they've processed it completely). Irwin (1998), however, makes the case that mental processing continues during saccades, suggesting that we should add saccade time to gaze durations.

The notion of total fixation time is a critical part of Just and Carpenter's approach because the total gaze duration on words and larger segments of text provides the basic empirical ingredient of the model: "Unlike a listener, a reader can control the rate of input. . . . A reader can take in information at a pace that matches the internal comprehension processes. By examining where a reader pauses, it is possible to learn about the comprehension processes themselves" (Just & Carpenter, 1980, p. 329). Thus the differences in gaze duration for different words, and for different sections of the entire passage, gave Just and Carpenter a window on the process of comprehension.

The Just and Carpenter Model

A real strength of the online reading task is that it provides evidence at *two* levels of comprehension. First, the figure shows the durations of rather microscopic, word-level processes. These are crucial to an understanding of reading, of course, and a good deal of evidence at this microscopic level exists. For instance, several studies attest to the very early use of syntactic features of a sentence when we comprehend, not just major syntactic characteristics such as phrase boundaries but even characteristics such as subject–verb agreement (Pearlmutter, Garnsey, & Bock, 1999) and pronoun gender (McDonald & MacWhinney, 1995). Reichle et al. (1998) provide an impressive account of such word-level processes with their E-Z Reader model of eye movement control in reading.

In Just and Carpenter's work, however, gaze durations are also used to examine larger, macroscopic processes, such as comprehension time at the level of ideas and propositions. The word-by-word gaze durations presented in Figure 10-7 addressed the microscopic level and were analyzed by Just and Carpenter in terms of various word-level variables (e.g., length, frequency in the language, position in the sentence, whether the word was repeated or not). Just and Carpenter then combined gaze durations across the words in a clause, phrase, or sentence, adding together the gaze durations of the individual words. By this method, Just and Carpenter examined the overall time to process larger units of text.

Table 10-5 presents the "Flywheel" passage in a sector-by-sector fashion—roughly speaking, an idea unit. To the left of each line there is a category label; each sector was categorized as to its role in the overall paragraph structure. To the right are two columns of numbers—observed gaze durations for a group of subjects and estimated durations—based on the "READER" model's predictions. For example, the 1,921 msec observed for sector 1 is the sum of the separate gaze durations for that sector (averaged across subjects). Note also that different kinds of sectors take different amounts of time; for instance, definition sectors tend to have more difficult words in them and are a bit longer than other sector types, so they show longer gaze durations. Even a casual examination

Table 10-5 SECTOR-BY-SECTOR ANALYSIS OF "FLYWHEEL" PASSAGE

		Gaze Duration (msec)	
Category	**Sector**	**Observed**	**Estimated**
Topic	Flywheels are one of the oldest mechanical devices	1,921	1,999
Topic	known to man.	478	680
Expansion	Every internal-combustion engine contains a small flywheel	2,316	2,398
Expansion	that converts the jerky motion of the pistons into the smooth flow of energy	2,477	2,807
Expansion	that powers the drive shaft.	1,056	1,264
Cause	The greater the mass of a flywheel and the faster it spins,	2,143	2,304
Consequence	the more energy can be stored in it.	1,270	1,536
Subtopic	But its maximum spinning speed is limited by the strength of the material	2,400	2,553
Subtopic	it is made from.	615	780
Expansion	If it spins too fast for its mass,	1,414	1,502
Expansion	any flywheel will fly apart.	1,200	1,304
Definition	One type of flywheel consists of round sandwiches of fiberglass and rubber	2,746	3,064
Expansion	providing the maximum possible storage of energy	1,799	1,870
Expansion	when the wheel is confined in a small space	1,522	1,448
Detail	as in an automobile.	769	718
Definition	Another type, the "superflywheel," consists of a series of rimless spokes.	2,938	2,830
Expansion	This flywheel stores the maximum energy	1,416	1,596
Detail	when space is unlimited.	1,289	1,252

Source. Just and Carpenter (1980).

of the observed and predicted scores shows that the model does a commendably good job of predicting gaze durations.

Model Architecture and Processes Figure 10-8 illustrates the overall architecture and processes of the Just and Carpenter (1980, 1987, 1992) model. Note first that several elements of this model are already familiar to you. For instance, the model claims that working memory is the location where all sorts of knowledge—visual, lexical, syntactic, semantic, and so forth—are combined during comprehension. Long-term memory contains a wide variety of knowledge types, semantic or conceptual knowledge, and knowledge of discourse structure, essentially the kind of information that tells us how passages of text are structured. Additionally, scheme of domain information, which we've called scripts, as well as the episodic information a person has, is also included. Each of these types of knowledge can match the current contents of working memory and update or alter those contents. In simple terms, what you know combines with what you've already read and understood, and together these permit comprehension of what you are reading now.

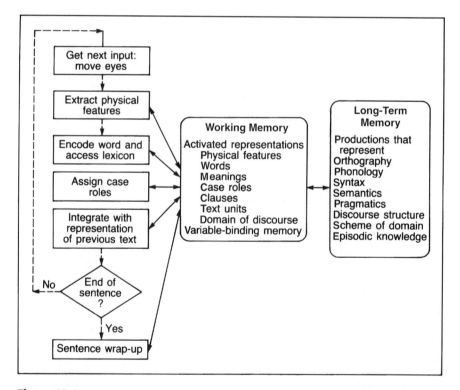

Figure 10-8

The Just and Carpenter (1980) model, showing the major structures and processes that operate during reading. Solid lines represent the pathways of information flow; the dashed line shows the typical sequence of processing.

Finally, in more lengthy passages such as the "Flywheel" text, two additional processes are observed. Sentence wrap-up is an integrative process that occurs at the end of a sentence. During sentence wrap-up, readers tie up any remaining loose ends; for instance, any remaining inconsistencies or uncertainties about reference are resolved here, and any final bridging inferences that may be necessary are drawn here. Note that sentence wrap-up occurs at the ends of sentences. Interclause integration seems to be a similar component, but one that operates on the separate clauses within a sentence.

An Overview Table 10-6 summarizes the local and global processing effects Just and Carpenter (1980) found. It also illustrates the claim that the cognitive approach, in the form of online examination of reading and comprehension, has made significant headway in understanding the complex processes of reading. Careful inspection of the table and the gaze duration values in Figure 10-7 and Table 10-5 shows several correspondences between textual characteristics and gaze durations. For instance, the word *flywheels*, at the beginning of the passage, commands a lengthy gaze for several reasons: It is at the beginning of a line, it is a rare word, and it is a topic word in the discourse structure. Note that the second occurrence of *flywheel* commands a shorter duration, partly because it is a repetition of a word held in working memory. In Table 10–5, contrast sector 9, "it is made from" with sector 18, "when space is unlimited." Although each has four words, sector 9 receives an observed gaze duration of only 615 msec, compared with the 1,289 msec on sector 18. Part of this difference results from the frequency of the words in sector 9 and the fact that this sector conveys less information. Sector 18, conversely, contains a word with four syllables, contains the last word in a sentence, and contains the last word in a paragraph.

Table 10-6 VARIABLES AND EFFECTS THAT INFLUENCE GAZE DURATIONS

Gaze Duration Affected by	Effect on Gaze Duration
Sweep of eyes to start new line	Increase
Number of syllables in word	Increase
Word frequency in English	Decrease
Beginning of line	Increase
Novel word	Increase
Repetition of infrequent word	Decrease
Topic or content word	Increase
Semantic-based expectation (if confirmed)	Decrease
Case role assignment	Varies by case role
Reassignment of case role	Increase
Other error recovery	Increase
Integration of information (after each word, after clauses, at the end of a sentence, a sector, and a paragraph)	Increase
Retrieval difficulty of scripted knowledge	Increase
Sentence wrap-up	Increase
Reference and inference processes	Increase

Source. Adapted from Just and Carpenter (1980, 1987).

As a final note here, Just and Carpenter's comments on top-down and bottom-up processing are worth considering. They note that some models of reading, especially those concerned with the initial encoding phase of reading, focused on bottom-up, or data-driven, processing; the kinds of visual features that are extracted from print, how those features are combined into patterns that then permit word encoding and recognition, and so on (but cf. Reichle et al., 1998). Other models focus primarily on top-down, conceptually driven processes, explaining how contextual effects influence reading comprehension. Just and Carpenter's model is between these extremes. That is, it includes the influences of context and a person's knowledge along with syntactic and semantic factors. But it also emphasizes the importance of the printed words themselves and suggests that no amount of top-down processing can substitute for comprehension derived from the text itself. As they put it, "top-down processes can influence the bottom-up ones, but the role is to participate in selecting interpretations rather than to dominate the bottom-up processes" (p. 353).

Summary

An in-depth description of the experiments that support the general relationships of Just and Carpenter's model is not possible here, if for no other reason than lack of space. Reading comprehension research has become one of the most active areas of investigation; an adequate review not only would be lengthy but would be out of date almost as soon as it was written. Suffice it to say that every level of language analysis has been examined in terms of reading comprehension effects, and the outlines provided by Reichle et al. (1998) at the word level and Just and Carpenter at more macroscopic levels seem flexible enough that most of the results can fit comfortably within them. Here is just a brief list of some recent work attesting to the importance of factors listed in Table 10-6:

- The effects of word frequency, syntactic structure, and context (Altmann, Garnham, & Dennis, 1992; Inhoff, 1984; Schilling, Rayner, & Chumbley, 1998)

- The effects of sentence context on word identification (Paul et al., 1992; Schustack, Ehrlich, & Rayner, 1987; Simpson, Casteel, Peterson, & Burgess, 1989), including ERP work showing how rapidly we resolve anaphoric references (van Berkum, Brown, & Hagoort, 1999)

- The effects of ambiguity (Frazier & Rayner, 1990; Rayner & Frazier, 1989) and figurative language (Frisson & Pickering, 1999)

- The effects of topic, plausibility, and thematic structure on reading (O'Brien & Myers, 1987; Pickering & Traxler, 1998; Speer & Clifton, 1998; Taraban & McClelland, 1988), especially the relatedness of successive paragraphs and the presence of an informative introductory paragraph (Lorch, Lorch, & Matthews, 1985)

- The effects of scripted knowledge on word recognition and comprehension (Sharkey & Mitchell, 1985)

- The effects of discourse structure on the understanding of reference (Malt, 1985; Murphy, 1985) and the resolution of ambiguity (Vu, Kellas, Metcalf, & Herman, 2000)

Additionally, recent work is demonstrating more and more that phonology plays an important role in reading comprehension, such as research showing that phonological information is activated as rapidly as semantic knowledge in silent reading (Lee, Rayner, & Pollatsek, 1999; Rayner, Pollatsek, & Binder, 1998), especially for readers of somewhat lower skill levels who rely more on print-to-sound-to-meaning processes than a direct print-to-meaning route (Jared, Levy, & Rayner, 1999).

When we examine these studies in detail, we find that each uses a somewhat different methodology, focuses on different aspects of reading, and examines different kinds of hypotheses. When viewed at arm's length, however, they all converge on the same overall position: Reading and reading comprehension are affected by linguistic effects in the text, to be sure, but they are also dramatically influenced by cognitive effects. These cognitive factors, including the structure of the mental lexicon, the nature of semantic and scripted knowledge, and the effects of expectations or top-down processes, exert a tremendous *interactive influence* on how we read.

The usual effect of such cognitive influences is to smooth and facilitate our reading. Words and ideas are more predictable in one context than in another, and the cognitive system capitalizes on its immense store of knowledge to develop and use an elaborate context. Embedding the new information into an existing contextual framework should, of course, lead to better comprehension and a stronger, more durable memory record of the information. Sentences such as 19 and 20,

(19) How many animals of each kind did Moses take onto the ark?

(20) What is the nationality of Thomas Edison, inventor of the telephone?

on the other hand, or the garden path sentences mentioned previously, show the less-than-desirable context and cognitive effects that occasionally crop up. Read sentences 19 and 20 again, if you didn't notice the semantic illusion (Erickson & Mattson, 1981; Reder & Kusbit, 1991). The reason we fall for the illusion, that we do not immediately notice what is wrong with the sentence, should be clear: It's merely another illustration of the power of conceptually driven processing. Just and Carpenter's remarks notwithstanding, semantic and contextual effects can exert a remarkably strong effect, even on the reading of simple statements.

■ Section Summary

- Tremendous progress has been made in understanding the mental processes of reading, largely by using the online method of recording the durations and locations of eye fixations during reading. Just and Carpenter's (1987) model of reading is built on this kind of data and makes predictions about gaze durations and comprehension based on a variety of local and global factors; for instance, word frequency and recency in the passage influence local processing, whereas the difficulty of retrieving semantic and scripted knowledge influences global processing factors. The technology that enables this kind of investigation promises to provide a wealth of information about reading and comprehension.

Spoken Language and Conversation

We turn now to the last major section of the chapter; production and comprehension of spoken language, especially the comprehension of conversation. There is important and interesting work on the production of spoken language, some of it covered in Chapter 9 (e.g., the articulation of phonemes), some covered only in full-length treatments of language (e.g., work on speech errors such as "slicely thinned"; see Whitney, 1998, for a thorough treatment). But we focus here on conversation, normal, everyday language interactions, such as an ordinary talk among friends. The issues we consider are not limited to just this kind of conversation, however. Many of them apply to all spoken language interactions: how professors lecture and students comprehend, how people converse on the telephone, how an interviewer and a job applicant talk, how we reason and argue with one another (Rips, 1998), and so on.

As important as an understanding of spoken language is, note that there is much less research on speech comprehension than there is about reading; although "language by ear" is far more common than "language by eye," it is very difficult to investigate spoken language comprehension with the same rigor as can be achieved for written language. In fact, only recently have online techniques been developed to investigate the moment-by-moment mental processes of speech comprehension. One especially promising technique is the auditory moving window method discussed in Ferreira, Henderson, Anes, Weeks, and McFarlane (1996), an auditory analog to the visual technique you just read about. In this method, recorded passages are coded into units—words or short phrases—then played to subjects one at a time. The subjects press a button to hear the successive units, and of course the computer records the timing of the button presses. It's then a straightforward (though painstaking) process of computing the elapsed time between button presses and thus the time spent comprehending the individual speech units.

On the other hand, much of what we've learned about reading and writing should apply to conversation and spoken language comprehension; it's the same comprehension system doing the understanding in both formats, after all. And indeed, results with the new auditory online methods are showing very similar results to those obtained with eye-gaze techniques. For example, Ferreira et al. (1996) examined the effects of word frequency and garden path sentences on auditory comprehension and found remarkably similar effects in auditory comprehension as are found in studies of reading. So it's a reasonable assumption that models you've read about already, such as Gernsbacher's (1990) structure building framework or Reichle et al.'s (1998) E-Z Reader model, are specifying mental mechanisms and processes that apply to speech comprehension as well. And

During a conversation, speakers develop a rhythm as each person takes successive turns speaking. Nonverbal interaction can occur during a turn, such as when a listener nods to indicate attention or agreement.

furthermore, much of the higher-level processing in a conversation occurs at a conscious level. Therefore, our intuitions might be more useful in these settings than in understanding the fast, automatic components of reading.

The Structure of Conversations

Let's examine two very general characteristics of conversations, the issue of turn taking and the issue of social roles, to get started on this topic and introduce some of the more cognitive effects we're especially interested in.

Taking Turns   Conversations are structured by a variety of cognitive and social variables and rules governing the what and how of our contributions. To begin with, we take turns. Typically, there is little overlap between participants' utterances. Generally, two people speak simultaneously only at the change of turns, when one speaker is finishing and the other is beginning. In fact, interchanges in conversation often come in an adjacency pair, a pair of turns that sets the stage for another part of the conversation. For instance, if Ann wants to ask Betty a question, there can be an adjacency pair of utterances in which Ann sets the stage for the actual question:

Ann: Oh there's one thing I wanted to ask you.

Betty: mhm

Ann: in the village, they've got some of those . . . rings. . . . Would you like one?" (From Svartik & Quirk, 1980, cited in Clark, 1994)

Clearly, the neutral "mhm" is both an indication of attention and a signal that Ann can go ahead and ask the question (Duncan, 1972).

CALVIN and HOBBES

The rules we follow for turn taking are straightforward (Sacks, Schegloff, & Jefferson, 1974). First, the current speaker is in charge of selecting the next speaker. This is often accomplished by directing a comment or question toward another participant ("What do you think about that, Fred?"). The second rule is that if the first rule isn't used, then any participant can become the current speaker. Third, if no one else takes the turn, the current speaker may continue to speak but is not obliged to.

Speakers use a variety of signals to indicate whether they are finished with their turn. For example, a long pause at the end of a sentence is a turn-yielding signal, as is a comment directed at another participant, a drop in the pitch or loudness of the utterance, and establishing direct eye contact with another participant; the latter is often merely a nonverbal way of selecting the next speaker. If the current speaker is not relinquishing the conversational turn, however, these signals are withheld. Other "failure to yield" signals include trailing off in midsentence without completing the grammatical clause or the thought, withholding such endings as "you know," or even looking away from other participants during a pause (Cook, 1977).

Social Roles and Settings The social roles of conversational partners, along with conversational setting, exert a strong influence on the contributions made by participants (Kemper & Thissen, 1981). Formal settings among strangers or mere acquaintances lead to more structured, rule-governed conversations than informal settings among friends (Blom & Gumperz, 1972). Conversations with a "superior"—for instance, your boss or a police officer—are more formal and rule-governed than conversations with peers (e.g., Brown & Ford, 1961; Edwards & Potter, 1993, and Holtgraves, 1994, discuss the social and interpersonal aspects of such situations).

Because of the status relationship between participants, a "superior" is given (or takes) more leeway in breaking the turn-taking rules. Gender may also be a factor here. Some reports indicate that men interrupt women far more often than the reverse (Zimmerman & West, 1975), although other studies have not found this effect, such as Beattie's (1981) analysis of interruptions in university tutorial classes (see Whitney, 1998, for a more complete discussion of these points).

Cognitive Conversational Characteristics

Conversations are also structured by cognitive factors. We focus on three: the conversational rules we follow, the issue of topic maintenance, and the online theories of conversational partners.

Conversational Rules Grice (1975; see also Norman & Rumelhart, 1975) suggested a set of four **conversational rules** or maxims, *rules that govern our conversational interactions with others,* all derived from the **cooperative principle,** the idea *that each participant in a conversation implicitly assumes that all speakers are following the rules and that each contribution to the conversation is a sincere, appropriate contribution.* In a very real sense, we enter into a contract or pact with our conversational partner, pledging in essence to abide by certain rules, and adopt certain conventions so as to make our conversations understandable (Brennan & Clark, 1996; Wilkes-Gibbs & Clark, 1992). This pact even extends to issues of syntax, where we choose syntactic structures that mention important, discourse focus information early in our sentences (Ferreira & Dell, 2000), all the way up to nonverbal gestures we use to amplify or disambiguate our speech (Goldin-Meadow, 1997; Kelly, Barr, Church, & Lynch, 1999). As Table 10-7 shows, the four maxims specify in more detail how to follow the cooperative principle. (Two additional rules have been added to the list, for purposes that will become clear in a moment.)

A simple example or two should help you understand the point behind these maxims. When a speaker violates or seems to violate one of the maxims, the listener assumes there is a reason for the violation. That is, the listener still assumes that the speaker was following the overarching cooperative principle so must have intended the remark as something else, maybe sarcasm, maybe a nonliteral meaning (Kumon-Nakamura, Glucksberg, & Brown, 1995). As an example, imagine studying in the library when your friend asks,

(21) Can I borrow a pencil?

Table 10-7 GRICE'S (1975) CONVERSATIONAL MAXIMS, WITH TWO ADDITIONAL RULES
The Cooperative Principle
Be sincere, reasonable, and appropriate • **Relevance:** Make your utterances relevant to the conversation (e.g., stick to the topic; don't state what others aren't interested in). • **Quantity:** Be as informative as required (e.g., don't overspecify; don't say more or less than you know; don't be too informative). • **Quality:** Say what is true (e.g., don't mislead; don't lie; don't exaggerate). • **Manner and tone:** Be clear (e.g., avoid obscurity and ambiguity; be brief; be polite; don't interrupt).
Two Additional Rules
• **Relations with conversational partner:** Infer and respond to partner's knowledge and beliefs (e.g., tailor contributions to partner's level; correct misunderstandings). • **Rule violations:** Signal or mark intentional violations of rules (e.g., use linguistic or pragmatic markers [stress, gestures]; use blatant violations; signal the reason for the violation).

Source. From Grice (1975); see also Norman and Rumelhart (1975).

This is a perfectly straightforward speech act, a simple request you could respond to directly. But if you had just lent a pencil to your friend, and then he said,

(22) Can I borrow a pencil with lead in it?

the question means something entirely different. Assuming that your friend was being cooperative, you now have to figure out why he broke the quantity maxim about over-specifying; because all pencils have lead in them, mentioning the lead is a violation of a rule. Your inference, furthermore, is that it was probably a deliberate violation, where the friend's authorized implication can be expressed as "The pencil you lent me doesn't have any lead in it, so would you please lend me one I *can* use?"

Topic Maintenance We also follow the conversational rules in terms of **topic maintenance,** *making our contributions relevant and to the topic and sticking to the topic.* Topic maintenance actually depends on two processes; comprehension of the speaker's remark, and then expansion, contributing something new to the topic.

Schank (1977; see also Litman & Allen, 1987) provides a provocative analysis of topic maintenance and topic shift, including a consideration of what is and is not a permissible response, called simply a move, after one speaker's turn is over. The basic idea here is that the listener comprehends the speaker's comment and stores it in memory as a proposition. As in reading, the listener must infer what the speaker's main point was, or what the discourse focus was in the speaker's remark. If the speaker, Ben, says,

(23) I bought a new car in Baltimore yesterday,

then Ed, his conversational partner, needs to infer Ben's main point and then expand on that in his reply. Thus, sentence (24) would be a legal move because it apparently responds to the speaker's authorized implication, whereas sentence (25#) is probably not a legal move (denoted by the # sign).

(24) Ed: Really? I thought you said you couldn't afford a car.

(25#) Ed: I bought a new shirt yesterday.

Sentence 24 intersects with two main elements in the proposition for sentence 23, "BUY" and "CAR," so it is probably an acceptable expansion for a conversational turn, according to Schank (1977). Sentence 25# intersects with "BUY," but the other common concept seems to be the time case role "YESTERDAY," an insufficient basis for most expansions. Thus, in general a participant's responsibility is to infer the speaker's focus and then expand on that in an appropriate way. That's the relevance maxim: Sticking to the topic means you have to infer it correctly. Ed seems to have failed to draw the correct inference.

On the other hand, maybe Ed *did* comprehend Ben's statement correctly. If so, then he has deliberately violated the relevance maxim in sentence 25#. But it's such a blatant violation that it suggests some other motive; Ed may be expressing disinterest in what Ben did or may be saying indirectly that he thinks Ben is bragging. And if Ed suspects Ben is telling a lie, then he makes his remark even more blatant, as in 26.

(26) Yeah, and I had lunch with the Queen of England.

Drawing by Mulligan © © The New Yorker Magazine, Inc.

"I want you to know that I'm not nearly the great human being everyone seems to think me to be."

Online Theories During Conversation A final cognitive point involves the theories we develop of our conversational partners. The most obvious one we construct can be called a **direct theory.** This is the theory or mental model of *what the conversational partner knows and is interested in, what the partner is like.* We tailor our speech so that we're not being too complex or too simplistic, so we're not talking about something of no interest to the listener. Some of the clearest examples of this involve adult–child speech, where a child's lesser vocabulary and knowledge prompt adults to modify and simplify their utterances in a remarkably large number of ways (DePaulo & Bonvillian, 1978; Snow, 1972; Snow & Ferguson, 1977). But this sensitivity to the partner's knowledge and interests is displayed to some degree in all conversations. I don't talk to a college class the way I would to a group of second graders, nor do I launch into a conversation with a bank teller about my research.

But there is another layer of theories during a conversation, an interpersonal level related to "face management," or public image (Holtgraves, 1994, 1998). Let's call this the **second-order theory** during conversation. This second-order theory is *an evaluation of the other participant's direct theory: what you think the other participant believes about you.*

Let's develop a full example of these two theories to illustrate their importance to conversation and comprehension. Imagine that you're registering for classes next semester and say to your friend Frank that you've decided to take Psychology of Personality. What would your reaction be if Frank responded to you with these statements?

(27) Why would you want to take that? It's just a bunch of experiments with rats, isn't it?

(28) Yeah, I'm taking Wilson's class next term too. John told me he's going to assign some books he thinks I'll really like.

(29) Maybe you shouldn't take Wilson's class next term. Don't you have to be pretty smart to do all that reading?

In 27, you assume that your friend has made the remark in all sincerity, that it was intended to mean just what it says. Because you know that research on laboratory

Table 10-8 EXAMPLES OF DIRECT AND SECOND-ORDER THEORIES
Setting: For all three conversations, Chris's first sentence and direct theory are the same.
Chris: "I think I'll take Personality with Dr. Wilson next term."
Chris's direct theory: Frank is interested in the courses I'm taking.
Conversation 1
Frank replies: "Personality? Ah, that's just a bunch of experiments with rats, isn't it?"
Chris's direct theory: Frank doesn't know much about Personality research.
Conversation 2
Frank replies: "Yeah, I am too. John told me he's going to assign some books he thinks I'll really like."
Chris's direct theory: Frank knows the professor on a first-name basis, and he's bragging about it by calling him John.
Chris's second-order theory: Frank thinks I'll be impressed that he calls the professor John.
Conversation 3
Frank replies: "Hmm, maybe you shouldn't take that class. Don't you have to be pretty smart to do all that reading?"
Chris's direct theory: Frank is a jerk, he just insulted me.
Chris's second-order theory: Frank thinks I'm not smart.

animals had little to do with the field of personality, you conclude that your friend knows a lot less about personality theory than you do. In other words, this becomes part of your direct theory, as shown in Table 10-8. For sentence 28, you probably interpret Frank's remark as boastful, intended to show that he's on a first-name basis with the professor. Indeed, Frank has authorized that inference by using a more familiar term of address than is customary for professors (for an analysis of usage of proper names, see Brown & Ford, 1961). You update both your direct theory of Frank and your second-order theory. You update your direct and second-order theories after sentence 29 too, of course, but the nature of the updates is rather different: You've been insulted by the implication in Frank's response, something like "he thinks I'm not smart enough to take the class."

Empirical Effects in Conversation

Let's conclude with some evidence about the conversational effects we've been discussing. One of the most commonly investigated aspects of conversation involves **indirect requests,** such as when *we ask someone to do something* ("Close the window"; "Tell me what time it is") *by an indirect and presumably more polite statement* ("It's cold in here"; "Excuse me, but do you have the correct time?")

One of the most impressive investigations of such indirect requests was reported by Clark (1979). The study involved telephone calls to some 950 merchants in the San Francisco area in which the caller asked a question that the merchant normally would be expected to deal with on the phone (e.g., "What time do you close?" "Do you take credit cards?" "How much does something cost?"). The caller would immediately write

PROVE IT

One of the best student demonstration projects I ever graded was a test of the politeness ethic in conversational requests. On five randomly selected days, the student sat next to a stranger on the bus, turned, and asked, "Excuse me, but do you have the correct time?" All five strangers answered her. On five other randomly selected days, she said to the stranger, "Tell me what time it is," not in an unpleasant tone, but merely in a direct fashion; none of the strangers answered. Devise other situations in which you violate the politeness ethic or other conversational rules and note people's reactions. If you do it properly you'll learn about the rules of conversation; but be careful so it doesn't turn into a demonstration project on aggression. Do the same thing again, but this time with a close friend or family member. You'll see how necessary some polite forms are with strangers and how inappropriate they are with people you know well.

down a verbatim record of the call immediately after hanging up. A typical conversational interaction was as follows:

(30) *Merchant: "Hello, Scoma's Restaurant."*

Caller: "Hello. Do you accept any credit cards?"

Merchant: "Yes we do; we even accept Carte Blanche."

Of course, the caller's question here was indirect: "Yes" isn't an acceptable answer to "Do you accept any credit cards?" because the authorized implication of the question was, "What credit cards do you take?" Merchants almost always responded to the authorized implication rather than merely to the literal question posed by the caller. Furthermore, they tailored their answers to be as informative as possible while not saying more than is necessary (obeying the second rule, on quantity), as in "We *only* accept Visa and MasterCard," or "We accept *all* major credit cards." Such responses are both informative and brief.

Such research has been extended recently to include not just indirect requests, but a variety of indirect statements and replies to questions. For instance, Holtgraves (1994) examined comprehension speed for indirect requests as a function of the status of the speaker, whether the speaker was of higher status than the listener (e.g., boss and employee) or whether both were of equal status (two employees). Participants read a short scenario (e.g., getting a conference room ready for a board of directors meeting), which concluded with one of two kinds of indirect statements. Conventional statements were normal indirect requests, such as "Could you go fill the water glasses?" Negative state remarks were even more indirect, merely stating a negative situation and only indirectly implying that the listener should do something (e.g., "The water glasses seem to be empty."). Subjects showed no effects of status when comprehending regular indirect requests; it didn't matter whether it was a peer or the boss who said "Could you go fill the water glasses?" But comprehension time increased significantly with negative state remarks made by peers. In other words, when the boss says "The water glasses seem to be empty," we comprehend the conventional indirect request easily. But when a peer says it, we need additional time to comprehend.

More recently, Holtgraves's (1998) work has focused on indirect replies, especially the notion of making a "face saving" reply. His subjects read a description of a situation, such as

(31) Nick and Paul are taking the same history class. Students in this class have to give a 20-minute presentation to the class on some topic.

They then read a sentence that gave positive (32) or negative (33) information about Nick's presentation or a sentence that was neutral (34):

(32) Nick gave his presentation and it was excellent. He decides to ask Paul what he thought of it: "What did you think of my presentation?"

(33) Nick gave his presentation and it was truly terrible. He decides to ask Paul what he thought of it: "What did you think of my presentation?"

(34) Nick gave his presentation and then decided to ask Paul what he thought of it: "What did you think of my presentation?"

If you were Paul and faced the prospect of telling Nick that his presentation was awful, wouldn't you look for some face-saving response? This is exactly how Holtgraves's subjects responded when they comprehended Paul's responses. In the excuse condition, Paul says,

(35) It's hard to give a good presentation,

in effect giving Nick a face-saving excuse for his poor performance. Another possible conversational move is to change the topic, to avoid embarrassing Nick, as in

(36) I hope I win the lottery tonight.

Holtgraves (1998) collected several measures of comprehension, including overall comprehension time for the critical sentences 35 or 36. The comprehension times, shown in Figure 10-9 (from Experiment 2), were very clear. When subjects had heard positive information—the talk was excellent—it took them a long time to comprehend either the excuse (35) or topic change (36) responses. But having heard negative information—the talk was terrible—was nearly the same as having heard nothing about the talk; subjects comprehended the excuse or topic change responses much more rapidly, and there was no major difference between no information and negative information. People clearly interpreted the violations of the relevance maxim as attempts to save face and avoid embarrassment. (The Nick and Paul scenario was an "opinion" setting, where Paul is asked to give his opinion. Holtgraves also tested "self-disclosure" scenarios, as when a little boy comes home with his report card and responds with an excuse or a topic change when his mother asks about his grades. The results from the two scenario types were largely the same, so the data in Figure 10-9 are averaged across these two conditions.)

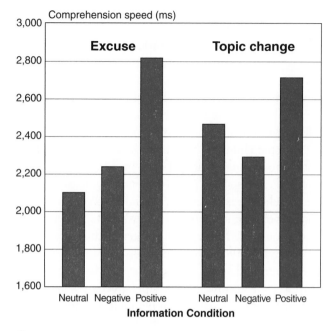

Figure 10-9

Comprehension times from Holtgraves's (1998) study. Participants read settings in which either negative information, positive information, or neutral information was offered about a character, followed by a conversational move in which the speaker made an excuse for the character or changed the topic. In both cases, it took longer to comprehend the remark when positive information about the character had just been encountered.

Egocentric speech One way to conceptualize Holtgraves's evidence on face-saving is in terms of the politeness ethic: Telling someone an unvarnished, difficult truth, or being so honest as to insult someone or hurt their feelings, usually is considered a violation of the politeness ethic (see the rule on manner and tone). On the other hand, when you abruptly change the conversational topic as a face-saving move of your own, a big part of your motive is to influence the other person's second-order theory, as if we think, "I gave a lousy presentation, but I'll make an excuse so he'll think more highly of me." We perhaps give ourselves more credit than is due when we claim that people routinely and easily tailor their conversation to manipulate others—not that it doesn't happen, of course, but that it isn't as simple cognitively as we've been implying.

Recent work by Keysar (1994; Keysar, Barr, & Horton, 1998) illustrates this cautionary note quite well. A general idea in theories of conversation and pragmatics is called the optimal design principle (Clark, 1992), the notion that speakers "design their utterances so that their addressees have sufficient information to understand them" (Keysar et al., 1998, p. 47). In other words, the principle says that we tailor our speech to optimize the listener's chances of full understanding, a seemingly noncontroversial idea clearly related to the relevance rule in Table 10-7, along with the rule on relationships with conversational partners (infer your partner's knowledge, interests, etc.). To test this idea, Keysar et al. had their subjects read about conversational settings in which one person happens to know something that the other one doesn't know and should therefore tailor his or her remarks to inform the other person. The simplest example, drawn from research on children's ability to take someone else's perspective, involves familiar Peanuts characters; Lucy has an old pair of red shoes and a new pair but merely asks Linus to bring her the "red shoes." Because the children knew that Lucy really wanted her new shoes, they were surprised when Linus brought the old pair. In other words, the children expected Linus to know about Lucy's unspoken preference merely because they knew about it. In other words, children's behavior is egocentric: Children seem able to take only their own perspective and cannot take another person's (Linus's) perspective.

Keysar's work demonstrated a surprising effect, with Keysar as surprised as anyone (Keysar, 1998; Keysar et al., 1998). Adults often do the same thing: They disregard the principle of optimal design and speak (and comprehend) as egocentrically as children. They either fail to appreciate another person's perspective or take that perspective into account only after their utterances have been planned. In the research, adults' explanations of conversational remarks, their comprehension times, even their eye movements showed evidence that their initial utterances were egocentric, taking into account only their own perspectives. Adjustments occurred later, almost as afterthoughts, and were particularly prone to errors. In comprehension studies, such adjustments took additional time for subjects to process. In Keysar et al.'s view, our first pass at an utterance is egocentric, taking into account just our own perspective, knowledge, and viewpoint. Then, time and mental resources permitting, we monitor or edit our speech plan and adjust it as needed. Importantly, we would expect this adjustment phase to be error prone, especially under time pressure or other constraints (for instance, working memory limitations), and to miss at least some of the egocentric utterances that are originally planned. The overall message, accordingly, is that our conversational speech is driven in part by our direct and second-order theories but may be more fundamentally driven by a self-centered, egocentric perspective.

■ Section Summary

- Conversations follow an extensive but largely implicit set of conversational rules. Some of these involve turn taking and social status and conventions, but many more govern the nature or topic of participants' contributions. Conversational topic shifts involve selecting some part of a participant's utterance to form the basis for a new contribution but then adding some new information. Schank's work on topic shift is a particularly important analysis of this process of topic shifting.
- Participants in a conversation develop theories of the other speakers, called direct theories, as well as theories of what the other speakers think of them, called second-order theories. When we engage in conversation, we not only tailor our contribu-

tions to these theories but also follow a set of conversational rules, the unspoken contract between conversational partners. When a rule is being violated intentionally, usually to make some other point (e.g., sarcasm), we mark our violation so that its apparent illegality as a conversational move is noticed and understood.

- Empirical work on conversational interaction often tests general notions about direct theories, the politeness rule, or indirect requests. Although we sometimes attempt to manipulate another person's direct theory of us, research also shows that the initially planned utterance usually is from a very egocentric perspective, whereas later adjustments may take the other person's perspective into account.

Key Terms

advantage of clause recency (p. 407)

advantage of first mention (p. 407)

anaphoric reference (p. 413)

antecedent (p. 413)

authorized (p. 416)

bridging (p. 415)

conversational rules (p. 433)

cooperative principle (p. 433)

direct theory (p. 435)

enhancement (p. 411)

gaze duration (p. 420)

eye–mind assumption (p. 422)

immediacy assumption (p. 420)

implication (p. 414)

indirect request (p. 436)

inference (p. 414)

online comprehension tasks (p. 404)

reference (p. 413)

second-order theory (p. 435)

situation model (p. 411)

suppression (p. 411)

topic maintenance (p. 434)

unauthorized (p. 416)

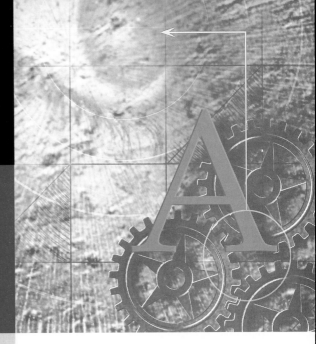

CHAPTER 11

Decisions, Judgments, and Reasoning

It does not trouble people much that their heads are full of incomplete, inconsistent, and uncertain information. With little trepidation they go about drawing rather doubtful conclusions from their tangled mass of knowledge, for the most part unaware of the tenuousness of their reasoning. The very tenuousness of the enterprise is bound up with the power it gives people to deal with a language and a world full of ambiguity and uncertainty. (Collins, Warnock, Aiello, & Miller, 1975, p. 383)

From the psychologist's point of view, thinking must not be confused with logic because human thinking frequently is not rigorous or correct, does not follow the path of step-by-step deduction—in short, is not usually "logical." (Newell & Simon, 1972, p. 876)

This chapter and Chapter 12, on problem solving, probably come closer to everyday conceptions of human thought than any of the material presented so far in this book. It's important that you appreciate the material you've already studied as a crucial part of cognitive psychology. As you read in the first chapter, simply because you are relatively unaware of mental processes doesn't mean that they aren't important to a complete understanding of cognition. Nonetheless, it's time to delve into the topics of decision making, reasoning, and problem solving, the slow and deliberate kinds of thinking that will round out our study of cognitive psychology.

A general thread that runs through much of the decision-making and reasoning research is that we are often overly influenced by the general world knowledge stored in our memories. The influence of stored information is pervasive; it affects how we perform in the classic forms of reasoning as well as less well-defined judgment and decision-making situations. A second thread is just as pervasive and just as important in decision making: Far more than is logical, we tend to search for evidence that confirms our decisions, beliefs, and hypotheses, and thus are much less skeptical than we ought to be.

We begin by examining two classic kinds of reasoning problems and then switch to a seemingly very simple kind of decision making and reasoning; mental comparisons between concepts or objects. We then proceed to the study of a somewhat different kind of situation; reasoning about the likelihood of events for which relevant information in memory is generally lacking or insufficient. The strategies people use to make these judgments are of particular interest because they reveal a variety of rules of thumb or short-cut methods on which people rely. These methods work well sometimes, but sometimes they lead to distortions and biases in reasoning. Overall, this research provides convincing examples of the uncertainty of human reasoning and the often surprising inaccuracies in our stored knowledge.

Formal Logic and Reasoning

At some point during their college careers, most students are exposed to the classic forms of reasoning, often in a course on logic. For our purposes, two of these forms, *syllogisms* and *conditional reasoning* problems, are important to understand. A general finding in the research on such reasoning tasks is that people are not particularly good at solving such problems correctly when the problems are presented in an abstract form. Our solutions often are better when the problems are presented in terms of concrete, real-world concepts. If we generate our own examples, however, the accuracy of our solutions depends on how critically or skeptically we generated the examples. In some situations, our general world knowledge almost prevents us from seeing the "pure" (i.e., logical) answer to logic problems.

Syllogisms

A **syllogism,** or categorical syllogism, is a *three-statement logical form, with the first two parts stating the premises or statements taken to be true and the third part stating a conclusion based on those premises.* The goal of syllogistic reasoning is to understand how different premises can be combined to yield logically true conclusions and to understand what combinations of premises lead to invalid or incorrect conclusions.

Often, syllogisms are presented in an abstract form, such as

(1a) All A are B.
   All B are C.
   Therefore, all A are C.

In this example, the two premises state a certain relation between the abstract elements *A*, *B*, and *C*, basically a class inclusion or subset–superset relation. "*All A are B*" says that the set *A* is a subset of the group *B*, that *A* is included in the set *B*. The third statement is the conclusion. By applying the rules of syllogistic reasoning, it can be determined that the conclusion "*All A are C*" is true in this example; that is, the conclusion follows logically from the premises. Inserting words into the syllogism will verify the truth of the conclusion: for instance,

(1b) All poodles are dogs.
   All dogs are animals.
   Therefore, all poodles are animals.

One difficulty or confusion that people have is illustrated by the following example:

(1c) All poodles are animals.
   All animals are wild.
   Therefore, all poodles are wild.

The difficulty here is that the conclusion is logically true; because the conclusion follows from the premises, the syllogism is valid. Of course, it's easy to think of counterexamples, situations in which the conclusion is not true in the real world of poodles; hardly any poodles are wild, after all (Feldman, 1992). Yet the rules of syllogistic reasoning are that the truth of the premises is *separate* from the validity of the syllogistic argument. What matters is that the conclusion does or does not follow from the premises. In the case of example (1c), the conclusion is valid even though the second premise is empirically false. Thus applying syllogistic reasoning to real-world problems is at least a two-step process. First, determine whether the syllogism itself is valid; second, if the syllogism is valid, determine the empirical truth of the premises.

Now consider another example:

(2a*) All A are B.
Some B are C.
Therefore, some A are C.

(In formal logic, *some* means "at least one and possibly all.") Try inserting words into this example to see whether the conclusion is correct. For example,

(2b*) All polar bears are animals.
Some animals are white.
Therefore, some polar bears are white.

Despite the fact that words can be substituted that lead to a correct statement of fact, this second syllogism is *false*. Because the two premises do *not* invariably lead to a correct conclusion, the entire form of the syllogism is invalid (the reason for the asterisk). The incorrectness of the conclusion in (2a) stems from the qualifier *some*. Although the conclusion may be empirically true when you use one or another concrete example, this isn't necessarily the case for *all* examples. Thus the second conclusion is false, as shown by the following:

(2c*) All polar bears are animals.
Some animals are brown.
Therefore, some polar bears are brown.

As shown in Figure 11-1, a Venn diagram illustration often can help in determining whether a syllogism is true. For instance, in the first illustration, the "All–All" form shows that it is necessarily true that "All *A* are *C*." The circles, which represent the class of things known as *A*, *B*, and *C*, are nested such that *A* is a subset of *B*, and *B* is a subset of *C*. There is simply no other way to represent the premises in Venn diagrams except by concentric circles (when *A* and *B* are identical, their boundaries overlap completely, and the diagram merely shows one circle labeled both *A* and *B*).

In the second entry in the figure, the *incorrectness* of syllogism 2 is illustrated by the first Venn diagram. In that illustration, a portion of *B* that does not contain *A* is exactly the portion that overlaps with *C*. Thus it isn't necessarily true that some *A* are *C*. The second Venn diagram for this problem, however, illustrates the "Some polar bears are white" conclusion, one that is true of the real world even though the syllogism is not

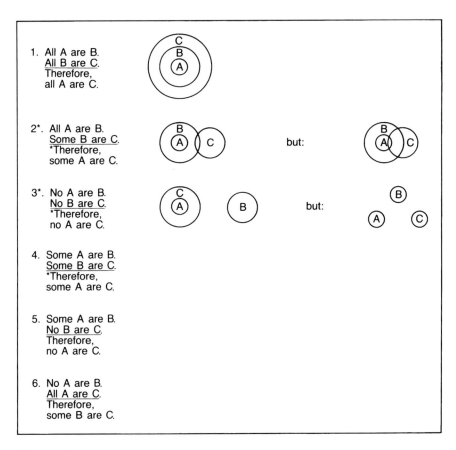

Figure 11-1

Venn diagram illustrations for three categorical syllogisms. If a diagram can be constructed that shows the conclusion doesn't hold for all cases, then the conclusion is false. The first diagram in (2*) shows why (2*) is incorrect because it is not necessarily true that some A are C. The second diagram in (2*) shows that an arrangement can be found that seems to support the argument. Likewise, the first diagram in (3*) shows why (3*) is incorrect because it is not necessarily true that no A are C. The second diagram in (3*) shows an arrangement that does seem to support the conclusion.

true. (The third syllogism is similar to the second; that is, it's false, but the second Venn diagram seems to show that it's true.)

In general, people's performance on syllogisms improves when they are shown how to use Venn diagrams or how to generate specific examples (Helsabeck, 1975). This procedure will only work, however, if you try to find ways to show the syllogism to be false. That is, it is all too easy to come up with examples or Venn diagrams that mistakenly confirm an incorrect conclusion. Adopting a skeptical attitude about the conclusion and trying to diagram the situation to show how the conclusion is false are more likely to be helpful strategies. As an exercise, try generating Venn diagrams for the final three syllogisms in the figure. As you work, bear in mind that the best strategy is to search for negative evidence. In other words, try to diagram the problem so that the syllogism is shown to be false (see work by Chater & Oaksford, 1999, on a probability-based rather than logic-based explanation of such reasoning).

Conditional Reasoning

Conditional reasoning is a second important kind of logical reasoning to understand. Conditional reasoning problems always contain two major parts: a *conditional clause* or statement that expresses some relationship, followed by some *evidence* pertaining to the conditional clause. **Conditional reasoning** involves a *logical determination of whether the evidence supports, refutes, or is irrelevant to the stated relationship.*

In conditional reasoning, you are given two statements. The first statement, the conditional, actually consists of two subclauses, which follow an *if–then* format. Respectively, the *if* clause and the *then* clause are known as the **antecedent** and the **consequent** of the conditional clause (for clarity, we'll drop the word *clause* and simply refer to "the *if*" or "the antecedent," and "the *then*" or "the consequent"). The *if* states the possible cause, and the *then* states the effect of that possible cause. After the *if–then*, you are given a second statement, some evidence about the truth or falsity of one of the propositions in the *if–then* relationship. The goal of such reasoning is to take the evidence and decide what follows from the evidence and the *if–then* statement. In other words, is the conditional *if–then* statement true or false given this observed evidence, or is the evidence irrelevant to the *if–then?*

The most general form of the conditional statement is

If P, then Q.

The conditional statement is then followed by the evidence, any one of the following four possibilities:

P (that is, P is true)
not P (that is, P is not true)
Q (that is, Q is true)
not Q (that is, Q is not true)

When combined with the conditional, there are four possibilities:

If P, then Q.	If P, then Q.	If P, then Q.	If P, then Q.
P.	Not P.	Q.	Not Q.
Therefore Q.	No conclusion.	No conclusion.	Therefore not P.

According to the conditional *if–then* statement, if some antecedent condition P is true, then its consequence (the *consequent*) Q is true. If there is evidence showing that P is indeed true, it follows logically that Q must be true. As a simple example of such conditional reasoning, consider the following example (adapted from Matlin, 1983):

If I am a freshman, then I must register for next semester's classes today.

Table 11-1 **CONDITIONAL REASONING**		
Form	**Name**	**Example**
If *p*, then *q*. Evidence: *p*. Therefore, *q*.	*Modus ponens:* affirming the antecedent (valid inference)	If I am a freshman, I have to register today. Evidence: I am a freshman. Therefore, I have to register today.
If *p*, then *q*. Evidence: not *p*. *Therefore, not *q*.	Denying the antecedent (invalid inference)	If I am a freshman, I have to register today. Evidence: I am not a freshman. *Therefore, I do not have to register today.
If *p*, then *q*. Evidence: *q*. *Therefore, *p*.	Affirming the consequent (invalid inference)	If I am a freshman, I have to register today. Evidence: I have to register today. *Therefore, I am a freshman.
If *p*, then *q*. Evidence: not *q*. Therefore, not *p*.	*Modus tollens:* denying the consequent (valid inference)	If I am a freshman, I have to register today. Evidence: I do not have to register today. Therefore, I am not a freshman.

When given the evidence that *P* is true, "I am a freshman," then the consequent *Q* must be true, "I do have to register today." Likewise, on evidence that *Q* is not true, "I do not have to register today," it must therefore be that *P* is not true, "*I am not a freshman.*"

In a conditional reasoning problem, one may use the evidence to affirm or to deny a proposition in the *if–then* statement; the affirming or denying can be applied to either the *if* or the *then*. This yields four possibilities, which are called *affirming the antecedent*, *denying the antecedent*, *affirming the consequent*, and *denying the consequent*. All four of these possibilities are illustrated in Table 11-1.

Valid Arguments As the table shows, only two of these four possibilities lead to a true conclusion according to the rules of logic. In the first possibility, you may affirm the antecedent; this is the same as saying that the evidence shows that *p* is true. Affirming the antecedent, also known as the *modus ponens*, then permits the conclusion that the consequent is also true. In the other valid form of conditional reasoning, you may deny the consequent, a method also known as the *modus tollens*. This means that the evidence *not q* is true (in other words, that *q* is not true). The valid conclusion here is that *p* is not true. Because of the evidence *not q*, we conclude *not p*.

Invalid Arguments Whereas both of these arguments lead to a correct conclusion, the other two possibilities are not valid. That is, denying the antecedent does not permit the conclusion that the consequent is false; likewise, affirming the consequent does not permit the conclusion that the antecedent is true. Let's continue with the college registration example, where the conditional statement is "If I am a freshman, then I must register today." If we deny the antecedent by offering the evidence "I am not a freshman," this does not lead to the conclusion that "I do not have to register today." It could

Safety	If you are sitting in an exit row and you can not read this card or can not see well enough to follow these instructions, please tell a crew member.

安全
安全
안전

Sicherheit
Sécurité
Seguridad

非常口の隣にご着席で、英語がおわかりにならない方は、乗務員にお申し出ください。

您若坐在走道位子並且不懂英文,請告知本機服務員。

출구복 줄에 앉으시고 영어를 못읽어드시면 승무원에게 밀씀하십시오.

Wenn sie neben einem ausgang sitzen und sie verstehen kein Englisch, bitte verständigen sie die flugzeugbesatzung.

Si vous êtes assis dans une rangée de sièges à côté d'une sortie, et vous ne comprenez pas la langue anglaise, veuillez le dire à un membre de l'équipage.

Si usted se encuentra sentado/a en una fila de asientos a la par de una salida u usted no entiende el idioma inglés, favor de avisarle a un tripulante.

be that two groups of students must register today; all freshmen and all sophomores in the first half of the alphabet. Thus just because you're not a freshman doesn't necessarily mean you don't have to register today. Likewise, if we affirm the consequent, we assert that "I must register today." This does not permit the conclusion that "I'm a freshman," however; you might be a sophomore in the first half of the alphabet.

Evidence on Conditional Reasoning Generally, the research shows that people are good at inferring the truth of the consequent given evidence that the antecedent is true (affirming the antecedent, the *modus ponens*). When given the conditional *if p, then q* and the evidence that *p* is true, people usually infer correctly that *q* is true. For instance, Rips and Marcus (1977) found that 100% of their sample drew this correct conclusion. Much more difficult, apparently, is denying the consequent (the *modus tollens*), in which the evidence *not q* leads to the valid conclusion *therefore, not p*. Only 57% of Rips and Marcus's subjects drew this conclusion correctly (in a simpler version of the problem, 77% concluded correctly that *p* could never be true given the evidence *not q*). Wason and Johnson-Laird (1972) found similar results in their investigation of conditional reasoning, in which problems were stated in either concrete or abstract form (see Table 11-2 for examples of each kind of problem and the conclusions that can be drawn).

People's errors in conditional reasoning seem to fall into three broad categories, involving the form of the reasoning problem, the search for evidence, and memory-related phenomena.

Table 11-2 CONCRETE AND ABSTRACT CONDITIONAL REASONING PROBLEMS
Concrete
Rembrandt's work is known to every artist. Everyone who knows Rembrandt's work appreciates its beauty. John does not know Rembrandt's work. Is it true, therefore, that John is not an artist? Is it true, therefore, that John does not appreciate the beauty of Rembrandt's work?   *Conditional A:*   If a person is an artist, then that person knows Rembrandt's work.   <u>Evidence: John does not know Rembrandt's work.</u>   Correct conclusion: John is not an artist.   The evidence here is *not q,* denying the consequent. Therefore, we conclude correctly *not p.*   *Conditional B:*   If one knows Rembrandt's work, then one appreciates its beauty.   <u>Evidence: John does not know Rembrandt's work.</u>   Incorrect conclusion: John does not appreciate its beauty.   The evidence here is *not p,* denying the antecedent. Therefore we cannot conclude *not q.*
Abstract
If the object is square, then it is blue.   1. Evidence: The object is square.   Is the object blue? *Yes: affirming the antecedent.*   2. Evidence: The object is not square.   Is the object blue? *No conclusion possible: denying the antecedent.*   3. Evidence: The object is blue.   Is the object square? *No conclusion possible: affirming the consequent.*   4. Evidence: The object is not blue.   Is the object square? *No: denying the consequent.*

Source: Wason and Johnson-Laird (1972).

Form Errors First, people sometimes draw incorrect conclusions simply by using one of the two invalid forms, denying the antecedent and affirming the consequent. Another form error is more subtle error. People have a tendency to reverse the propositions in the *if* and *then.* They then proceed to evaluate the given evidence against the now-reversed conditional. This kind of error is an *illicit conversion.* As an example, with a conditional of *If p, then q* and evidence *q,* people tend to switch the conditional to **If q, then p.* They then decide that the evidence *q* implies that *p* is true. Clearly, this is incorrect because the order of *p* and *q* in the conditional is meaningful. The *if* often specifies some possible cause, and the *then* specifies a possible effect. Obviously, we cannot draw correct cause–effect conclusions if we reverse the roles of the cause (*p*) for some outcome and the result (*q*) of some cause.

Search Errors The second kind of error involves the search for evidence. People often don't search for evidence but instead rely on a first impression or on the first example—the first mental model—that comes to mind (Evans, Handley, Harper, & Johnson-Laird, 1999). Another flaw in the search is called *searching for positive evidence,* also called the **confirmation bias.** Despite the rules of logic, we often seek only the information that confirms a conclusion, information that is consistent with a conclusion we have already drawn.

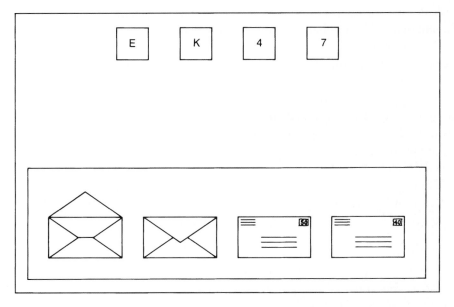

Figure 11-2

At the top of the illustration are the four cards in the Wason card problem. Which card or cards would you turn over to obtain conclusive evidence about the following rule: A card with a vowel on it will have an even number on the other side? At the bottom of the illustration are four envelopes. Which envelopes would you turn over to detect postal cheaters, under the rule that an unsealed envelope can be stamped with the less expensive stamp?

As a demonstration, consider the now-classic study of conditional reasoning (reported in Wason & Johnson-Laird, 1972) illustrated at the top of Figure 11-2, the "Wason card trick" problem. Four cards are visible to you, as shown in the figure, and each card has a letter on one side and a number on the other. The task is to pick the card or cards you would turn over to gather conclusive evidence on the following rule:

If a card has a vowel on one side, then it has an even number on the other side.

Give this statement some thought and decide how you'd test that rule before you continue reading.

Of the subjects Wason tested on this problem, 33% turned over only the E card, a correct choice conforming to the *modus ponens* method of affirming the antecedent. A thorough test of the rule's validity, however, requires that another card be turned over (in other words, the rule might be rephrased "Only if a card has a vowel on one side will it have an even number on the other side"). Only 4% of the subjects turned over the correct combination to check on this possibility, the E card (*modus ponens*) and the 7 card (the *modus tollens*). That is, turning over the 7, which would serve as negative evidence (*not Q*), was rarely considered by the subjects. Instead, they much preferred turning over the E and the 4 card: 46% of the subjects did this. Note two points. First, turning over the 4 is an instance of the invalid process of affirming the consequent (in other words, the rule doesn't say anything about what will be on the other side of a consonant; it could be an odd or an even number). Second, turning over the E represents a search for positive evidence about the rule, the (tentative) "yes" conclusion that *P* is true. Our general tendency is either to stop the search after turning over the E (positive evidence) or to continue searching for additional positive evidence (turning over the 4).

In a different situation, however, Johnson-Laird, Legrenzi, and Legrenzi (1972) found that 21 of 24 subjects made both of the correct choices. The difference between the two studies had to do with the concreteness of the situation. In the Johnson-Laird et al. study, subjects were trying to find cheaters on the postal regulations, where unsealed envelopes could be mailed with a less expensive stamp than sealed envelopes.

Think about this situation. What *if–then* rule is being tested? Because either a sealed or an unsealed envelope could be mailed with a more expensive stamp, the rule must be:

If the envelope is sealed, then it must carry the expensive stamp.

When asked to detect cheaters, subjects not only turned over the sealed envelope (*modus ponens*) but also the envelope stamped with the less expensive stamp, that is, the *modus tollens* choice corresponding to the 7 card. Because the subjects were not postal workers, it seems clear that it was the concreteness of the situation that oriented the subjects toward the skeptical attitude mentioned earlier. Their skepticism led them to search actively for negative evidence; in the process, they demonstrated logical conditional reasoning.

There is an unmistakable similarity here to the stages of concrete and formal operations in Piaget's theory of cognitive development, in which children around 12 years of age begin to reason formally, that is, abstractly (see Piaget, 1967, or Flavell, 1963). Interestingly, the present evidence suggests that adults often fail to demonstrate formal or abstract reasoning processes, even though they can reason correctly in more concrete situations.

Memory-Related Errors The third category of errors involves limitations in memory. A major proponent of this type of explanation is Johnson-Laird, who proposes that we perform reasoning tasks not by some formal logic but by constructing semantic-based **mental models,** *mental representations of meanings of the terms in reasoning problems* (Johnson-Laird, Byrne, & Schaeken, 1992). It's difficult to flesh out a set of semantic meanings in conditional reasoning problems of the "If *P* then *Q*" variety, but because of our semantic knowledge, it's far easier in problems such as

If it was foggy, then the match was canceled.
It was foggy.
Therefore, the match was canceled.

Furthermore, if additional terms appear in the problem, additional mental models must be derived, two additional ones in the following case:

If it was foggy, then the match was canceled.
The match was not canceled.
Therefore, it was not foggy.

When additional models are necessary, the load on working memory mounts and can begin to interfere with the reasoning process. And finally, as noted earlier, Evans et al. (1999) point out that if a conclusion matches the first mental model derived from the problem, it is particularly easy to accept the conclusion, leading to fallacies or errors in reasoning.

Hypothesis Testing

Part of the importance of conditional reasoning derives from its connection to scientific hypothesis testing. Consider a typical experimental hypothesis:

If theory A is true, then data resembling X should be obtained in the experiment.

If data resembling *X* are indeed obtained, there is a strong tendency to conclude that theory *A* must be true. That is, if the evidence is that data resembling *X* were obtained, this affirms the consequent. We then feel as if this evidence lets us conclude that *P* is true, that theory *A* is correct. What's wrong with this? It's a simple error of affirming the consequent, and concluding mistakenly that this is evidence that the antecedent is true. Note how seductive this error is. Of course, it might be true that theory *A* is correct. But it's also possible that theory *A* is incorrect and that some other (correct) theory would also predict data *X*.

Because of the illogic of affirming the consequent and because we want to test hypotheses, our experiments test a *different* hypothesis than "Theory *A* is correct." As you learned (or will learn) in statistics, we test the *null* hypothesis in hopes that our evidence will be inconsistent with the predicted null outcome. Note the form of such a test:

If the null hypothesis is true (if P), then there will be no effect of the variable (then Q).

If we obtain evidence that there *is* an effect of the variable, that is, that the consequent is not true, we can conclude that the antecedent is not true; we conclude that the null hypothesis is false, in other words. This is the essence of hypothesis testing, to conclude that the *if* portion of the null hypothesis is false based on an outcome that denies the consequent of the null hypothesis. Although subjects make a variety of errors in such situations, especially when the *if–then* relationship becomes more complex (Cummins, Lubart, Alksnis, & Rist, 1991), the typical mistake is simply to search for positive, confirming evidence (Klayman & Ha, 1989).

■ Section Summary

- Human reasoning is not especially logical, as shown in formal syllogistic and conditional reasoning problems. In reasoning tasks using syllogisms, conditional reasoning *if–then* problems, and hypothesis testing, people often fail to search for negative evidence. Instead, they often look for positive evidence for a conclusion, called confirmation bias, and are often influenced, both positively and negatively, by semantic knowledge. When a more skeptical attitude is adopted, and when the reasoning involves more concrete concepts, reasoning accuracy tends to improve.

Decisions

How do we make decisions? How do we choose among several alternatives, say, on a multiple choice test, or decide which of several options is the best under some set of circumstances? What role does the information stored in memory play in decision making, and how certain are the decisions we make based on that information?

In a sense, we've been studying decision making all along in this book, although the decisions often were fairly simple, for example, deciding "yes" or "no" in semantic or lexical decision tasks. Although performance in such tasks usually is interpreted in terms of search and retrieval processes, the Collins and Loftus (1975) model of semantic memory proposes a decision-based explanation for performance differences. Imagine that each semantic node that is activated during a search is evaluated in a decision mechanism. If so, then each node might be thought to contribute evidence for or against a decision in almost a democratic, voting-like process. That is, some retrieved connections are very positive evidence for a decision; if the statement is "A robin has feet," then the *isa* pathways to "BIRD" and "ANIMAL" would be persuasive evidence for a "yes" decision. Alternatively, for a sentence like "A bat is a bird," both positive and negative evidence would accumulate, until eventually some criterion is reached for a "no" decision.

This is a useful notion, one we encounter several times in this chapter. At base, decision making can be viewed as a search for evidence, where the ultimate decision depends on some criterion or rule for evaluating the evidence. A search may turn up either positive or negative evidence or may uncover both positive and negative evidence. How we make decisions as a function of such evidence, and how the evidence itself is evaluated, is at the heart of the decision-making and reasoning process.

Let's turn to a very simple setting, in which we compare two objects or symbols, to see how the information stored in memory can influence comparison processes. We'll then turn to more complex decision-making and reasoning situations, again looking for the influence of stored knowledge and the evaluation of that information.

Decisions About Physical Differences

One of the very earliest areas of research in psychology was the area of **psychophysics;** indeed, a great deal of research on psychophysics was conducted well before psychology per se came into existence (Fechner, 1860). The topic of interest in psychophysics was the *psycho*logical experience of physical stimulation, that is, *how perceptual experience differs from the physical stimulation being perceived.* In particular, research on psychophysics investigated the relationships between the physical dimensions of stimuli and the subjective, psychological experience of perceiving those stimuli.

In general, what was discovered by these early researchers was that the subjective experience of magnitude, regardless of the particular dimension involved (brightness, loudness, etc.), was not identical to the physical magnitude of the display. Instead, there is a psychological dimension of magnitude that forms the basis of our perceptions. The psychological dimension is different from the physical dimension such that our perceptual experience is not a direct and perfect function of the physical stimulus.

For instance, the perceived brightness of a light is not a direct function of the light's physical brightness. Instead, perceived brightness depends on several factors, such as the absolute level of brightness, the brightness of the background, and the duration of the stimulus. Likewise, the amount by which brightness must be changed in order to perceive the change depends on more than just the amount of physical change in brightness. Perceived change depends critically on the initial level of the light's brightness. A dim light needs only a small boost in brightness for subjects to detect a difference, whereas a very bright light needs a much larger boost for the change to be noticed. *The amount of change needed for people to detect the change* is called a **jnd,** a *just noticeable difference* (as in Weber's law; see Haber & Hershenson, 1973, for example). The point is that the size of the jnd increases as the physical stimulus becomes more intense. If only one jnd separates two dim lights, the same physical difference in brightness between two bright lights may not be detectable. Our perceptual mechanism is affected by the psychological dimension of brightness, a different dimension than physical brightness. Thus psychological processing of a stimulus does not accurately mirror the physical stimulus properties. Instead, distortions and alterations of the stimulus are introduced during perception, and these distortions and alterations can be attributed to the human perceiver.

Of particular relevance to our discussion is a phenomenon called the **distance** or **discriminability effect:** *The greater the distance or difference between the two stimuli being compared, the faster the decision that they differ* (Woodworth & Schlosberg, 1954). In other words, it's easier to discriminate between two physical stimuli that are very different (a finger snap versus a gunshot) than between two stimuli that are very similar (shots from two different guns). This is not at all a new finding in psychology;

Decisions about size differences are psychophysical judgments, which are speeded up when stimuli differ by a great amount.

Moyer and Bayer (1976) cite four separate sources for this effect that were published before 1940.

Decisions About Symbolic Differences

More recently, investigators have found that a variety of similar effects are obtained in tasks involving **symbolic comparisons,** that is, comparisons not between two physical objects or stimuli but between two symbols, two objects represented by written or spoken symbols. The connection with the earlier work is that the distance effect still holds for mental comparisons of symbols. But because the effect is now based on symbolic rather than physical differences, the effect is called the **symbolic distance effect.** Just as in psychophysical judgments, the source of the symbolic distance effect is the person making the mental comparison and forming the judgment. The big difference here is that semantic and other long-term memory knowledge, rather than perceptual information, is influencing the decision-making process.

Consider the stimuli in panels A and B of Figure 11-3. Which dot is higher? Despite the simple nature of this decision, it is true that it takes some amount of time to make the decision. To begin with, the time to decide which dot is higher depends on the separation of the dots; the greater the separation, the faster the decision. This is the simple physical distance effect again: Two stimuli can be discriminated more quickly when they differ more (Moyer & Bayer, 1976).

Now consider the bottom two illustrations. For panel C in Figure 11-3, which balloon is higher? For panel D, which yo-yo is lower? It is probably not obvious to you at a conscious level, but when subjects are asked "Which balloon is higher?" their judgments are affected not only by the discriminability of the two heights but also by the semantic dimension needed for the judgments (Banks, Clark, & Lucy, 1975). In other words, the semantic knowledge that balloons are held at the bottom by strings, float up in the air, and are therefore oriented in terms of highness was a significant influence on the subjects' decision times; describing the illustrations as balloons led subjects to treat the pictures symbolically rather than as mere physically different stimuli. When the same pictured display was accompanied by the question "Which balloon is lower?" judgments were much slower. And as you would expect, the situation was reversed when subjects judged stimuli such as those in panel D, the yo-yos. "Which yo-yo is lower?" yielded faster decisions than "Which yo-yo is higher?" because semantic knowledge about yo-yos is that they hang down from their strings.

The name for this second effect is the **semantic congruity effect** (Banks, 1977; Banks et al., 1975). It states that the subject's *decision is faster when the dimension being judged matches or is congruent with the implied semantic dimension* in the figure. In other words, the implied dimension in the balloon illustration is height because balloons float up. When asked to judge "how high" some "high" object is, the judgment is speeded up because "height" is semantically congruent with "high." Likewise, "lowness" is implied in the yo-yo display, so judging which of two "low things" is lower is also a congruent decision. Figure 11-4 displays the general form of the symbolic distance effect and the semantic congruity effect (Banks, 1977).

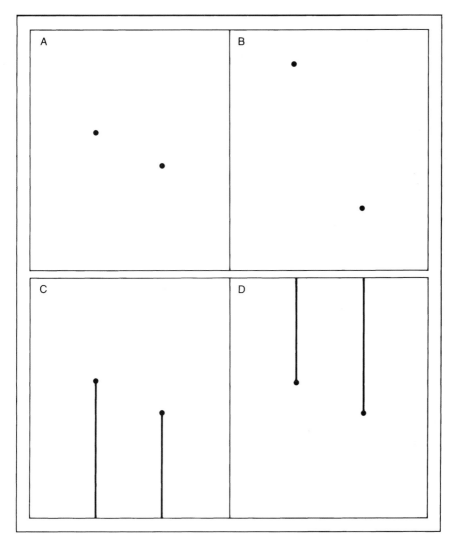

Figure 11-3

Stimuli used by Banks et al. (1975) in a study of physical and symbolic comparisons. In the top two panels, subjects were asked which dot is higher or lower. In the bottom two panels, subjects were asked which balloon is higher/lower and which yo-yo is higher/lower.

Number Magnitude Some of the clearest research supporting these idealized curves comes from Banks's work on judgments of numerical magnitude. In this research, subjects are shown a pair of digits, say, 1 and 2 or 7 and 8. In one condition, the instructions are to pick the smaller of the two values; in another, subjects are asked to pick the larger value. Of course, in all conditions, the RT to make the judgments is the dependent variable of major interest.

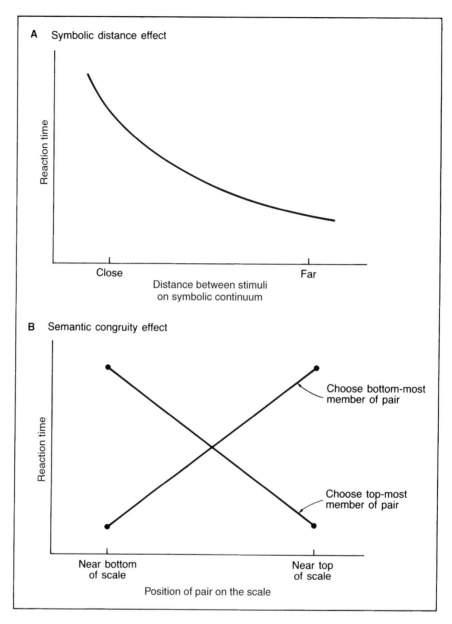

Figure 11-4

Idealized curves: **A,** the symbolic distance effect; **B,** the semantic congruity effect. *Source.* Banks (1977).

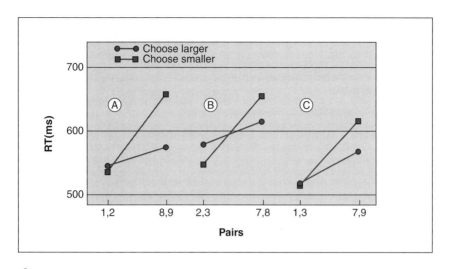

Figure 11-5

At performance on number comparisons. *Source.* Banks et al. (1976), Figure 1.

Can you predict what the results of such comparisons are, based on the distance and congruity effects? First, the larger the difference between the digits, the faster the judgments are made. In other words, picking the smaller of the pair 1 and 3 will be faster than picking the smaller of 2 and 3 because 1 and 3 differ from each other more than 2 and 3 do. This is the symbolic distance effect, similar to the physical distance effect but now based purely on the symbolic meanings of the digits and the magnitudes to which they refer; panels B and C in Figure 11-5 show this clearly. Second, judgment time is affected by semantic congruity. Picking the smaller of two small digits is faster than picking the larger of two small digits, and the difference is more pronounced when picking the larger instead of the smaller of two large digits; for instance, the 8 and 9 pair in Figure 11-5. When the instructions ask for a judgment of smallness, symbols referring to small quantities are faster; when the instructions ask for a judgment of largeness, symbols referring to large quantities are faster to judge. This is the semantic congruity effect.

A variety of fascinating conclusions are supported by results such as these. First, when people make mental comparisons and judge magnitudes of purely symbolic quantities, there is a pronounced semantic distance effect. Just as in psychophysics, the psychological difference is not the same as the physical difference; the psychological differences between digits do not perfectly mirror the actual numerical differences between digits. Banks's research (Banks, Fujii, & Kayra-Stuart, 1976) suggests strongly that our mental representation of number and numerical magnitude is a nonlinear one, one in which the psychological distances between larger numbers are *compressed*, relative to the distances between smaller numbers. Thus just as two bright lights are perceived as being more similar than two dim lights, two large numbers are psychologically closer together than two small numbers; 1 and 2 are more different psychologically than 8 and 9 are. Psychological distance between mental symbols is a strong determinant of performance.

Second, when we are asked to judge magnitudes, the dimension of judgment must match the implied semantic dimension for the comparison to be made quickly. A mismatch between the psychological dimension and the one specified by instructions (e.g., "choose the larger one" when the two things are small) slows down the comparison, even when the same quantities are being compared (see also Marschark & Paivio, 1979; Shoben, Sailor, & Wang, 1989).

At a more global level, the research also attests to another important idea: The particular *form* of a concept's representation in memory exerts an influence on the judgments we make. This is not a new idea, of course; after all, the network distances between concepts in semantic memory were said to be responsible for RT differences in semantic memory research. What is new, however, is the generality of this effect. We are asking subjects to compare two concepts stored in memory on some dimension of magnitude. By timing their judgments, we can come to understand how those concepts are represented in memory. This kind of task, timed mental comparisons, can be applied widely to all sorts of symbolic concepts, even cases where the underlying magnitude dimension is arbitrary and learned only by trial and error (Tzelgov, Yehene, Kotler, & Alon, 2000).

Imagery Which is larger, a squirrel or a rabbit? Which is smaller, a mouse or a dog? Several investigators, notably Moyer (1973), have documented the symbolic distance and semantic congruity effects when people make judgments of this sort. What is fascinating is that the judgments are being made on the basis of the visual image of the object. That is, the evidence suggests that when people make these larger/smaller judgments about real-world objects, they retrieve mental images of the objects, then mentally scan the images to determine which one is larger or smaller. Moyer had his subjects estimate the absolute sizes of animals and then make timed comparisons between different pairs. His results showed that RT decreased as the differences in size between the animals increased—the symbolic distance effect, of course. Furthermore, the relationship between image size and RT was logarithmic; in other words, the size differences are smaller at the larger end of the scale than at the smaller end, exactly what Banks (1977) found about the mental number line.

A final important aspect of these results relates to the mental imagery basis for the judgments. As Moyer (1973) and others (Kosslyn & Pomerantz, 1977) argue, results such as these imply strongly that the semantic information being retrieved from memory is imaginal. That is, the retrieved information is in the form of visual images that have been stored in long-term memory, not simply verbal-based propositions (see also Anderson, 1983).

Semantic Orderings Consider some results by Holyoak and Walker (1976). These investigators had subjects make comparisons of pairs of concepts along the semantic orderings of time, quality, and temperature; for example, compare "minute versus hour," "average versus poor," "cool versus cold." The instructions given to subjects said either to choose the longer, better, or warmer or the shorter, worse, or colder of the two concepts in the pair. Just as was found in the numerical judgment task, subjects' performance demonstrated both the symbolic distance and the semantic congruity effects. Judgments were faster when the pair of terms differed a great deal (e.g., perfect versus poor) than when they differed by less (perfect versus excellent). And judgments were faster if the dimension of judgment was congruent with the stimulus values; for example, choosing the longer of "century versus decade" was easier than choosing the shorter of those two. And in a study by Friedman (1978), the same kind of symbolic distance and semantic congruity effects were found when the concepts being compared had no physical or quantitative dimension at all; for example, choose the better or worse of pairs such as "lose versus peace" or "hate versus pressure."

The important extension that these results provide is that the distance and congruity effects were found to influence decisions even when the underlying representation of the compared concepts was not quantitative. The strong implication here is that more abstract orderings must be mentally represented in a very similar fashion to number and other quantity-based orderings because they all "behave" in a similar way. Our mental representations of such semantic terms, and in particular the way those terms are ordered, influence our judgments in very much the same way as more quantitative representations do. The nature of the mental representation, furthermore, can introduce distortions that are analogous to those found in perceptual tasks. We make simple comparisons and decisions based on our stored knowledge. The form of that knowledge can distort our judgments to a surprising degree.

Decisions About Geographical Distances

Perhaps not surprisingly, people's judgments of geographical distance seem to follow the same principles (Baum & Jonides, 1979; Holyoak & Mah, 1982). The point in this research is to have subjects make distance or location comparisons, then examine those comparisons to determine what the subjects' mental maps are like. In one such study, Holyoak and Mah (1982) tested subjects at the University of Michigan, asking them to rate the distances between American cities on a 1 to 9 scale. When no particular geographical reference point was given—the neutral condition—subjects based their judgments on their own local viewpoint. As Figure 11-6 shows, they overestimated distances for nearby Midwestern cities; they rated Kansas City, a fairly nearby city, as much further away than it really is, but Denver and Salt Lake City, more distant cities from Ann Arbor, as much closer together. Thus Holyoak and Mah demonstrated the familiar symbolic distance effect: The further away the cities were, the closer together they were in the mental representation. They also confirmed a certain egocentrism in adult thought; in a sense, the distorted "New Yorker's view of the world" can be transplanted anywhere.

In a thorough investigation of people's reasoning about geography, Friedman and Brown (2000) asked subjects to estimate the latitude of 34 North American cities (from Edmonton to Miami) and 34 European and North African cities (from Oslo to Cairo). People's estimates fit what Friedman and Brown called a *plausible-reasoning process*, where

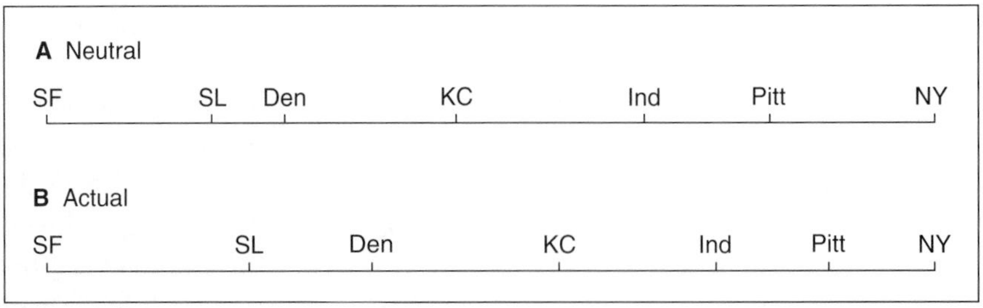

Figure 11-6

Results of Holyoak and Mah's (1982) study of the relative locations of cities along an east–west line. Estimates in the neutral perspective were made from the subjects' current location, Ann Arbor, Michigan, roughly halfway between Indianapolis and Pittsburgh on the east–west line. Subjects overestimated the distances to Denver, Kansas City, and Indianapolis, as shown by the actual distances at the bottom.

knowledge from a variety of sources is factored into a decision. In particular, people may have some specific knowledge of the location of certain cities. For others they may only know the city's general region but do know something about the region's location. Thus, among other things, the Friedman and Brown studies replicated evidence of the so-called Chicago–Rome illusion, the illusion that Chicago is much further north than Rome (in fact, they have the same latitude). People maintain the illusion because they view Chicago as being in "northern North America," whereas Rome is viewed as southern European or Mediterranean; of course, all of this is based on the misconception that North America and Europe are aligned in latitude (they aren't) and that "northern" and "southern" refer to approximately the same latitudes in both (they don't). Just as found in reasoning based on magnitude, imagery, and semantic ordering, reasoning about geography is also influenced by conceptual knowledge, by information stored in memory and retrieved to help solve the reasoning problem, however faulty or incomplete that knowledge is.

■ Section Summary

• Deciding which of two physical stimuli is louder, brighter, and so on is a psychophysical judgment. These decisions are speeded up when the two stimuli differ by a great amount. When symbolic stimuli are compared, the same effect is obtained, called the symbolic distance effect. Additionally, judgments are speeded up when the evaluated dimension (e.g., choose the larger) matches the stimuli being compared (e.g., two "large" digits); this is called the semantic congruity effect. Both of these results are obtained in simple comparisons of numbers and in comparisons of qualities such as "hot/cold." In all symbolic and reasoning situations, including those about geographical location, our mental representation and knowledge influence our judgments.

Decisions and Reasoning Under Uncertainty

Some of the decisions we've been discussing, such as judging which of two numbers is smaller, are rapid and fairly automatic. We are not consciously aware of the differences in time necessary to make the digit judgments, nor can we introspect accurately on the basis of those decisions. Typically we are aware only of the outcome of those automatic processes: We know consciously that we responded "7" to the question "Which is larger, 4 or 7?" If asked to indicate why we responded that way, however, we tend to give intellectualized answers that probably have little if anything to do with the actual mental basis for the decision we made (Ericsson & Simon, 1993). Furthermore, we are unaware of the exact nature of the mental representation that leads us to the judgment; to be blunt, nobody has conscious awareness of the compressed mental number line, although the research indicates that this is how numerical magnitude is mentally represented from young children up through adults (Banks, 1977; Duncan & McFarland, 1980).

In contrast to such relatively automatic decision making, the bulk of the cognitive research on decisions involves very deliberate and slow reasoning and decision-making situations. In fact, in many ways the research on such decisions is very similar to the area of problem solving, in which there is a clear connotation of slow, deliberate processing. One aspect of this similarity relates to familiarity: The domains of reasoning and problem solving we investigate usually are not well known or understood by the subject, or they involve material that is not highly familiar to most people. Another similarity involves the notion of uncertainty: There is often no certain answer to the problems, or at least no good way of deciding whether a particular type of solution is the correct approach.

And finally, the major conclusions of this kind of research are similar to the conclusions you'll read about in Chapter 12, on problem solving. People make decisions and base their reasoning on a variety of strategies, some good and some not so good. This is also a characteristic of much problem solving. Because of these similarities, investigations of such strategies often are impossible to categorize clearly as reasoning on the one hand or problem solving on the other. Thus, to an extent, choosing whether to put a topic in a chapter on reasoning or in a chapter on problem solving is arbitrary and suggests a neater division than is truly possible.

Algorithms and Heuristics

By far the most influential work done in this area of decision making has been that of Tversky and Kahneman (1973, 1974, 1980; Kahneman & Tversky, 1972, 1973; Kahneman, Slovic, & Tversky, 1982; Shafir & Tversky, 1992). It is quite rare that research in cognitive psychology influences other fields as well, yet Tversky and Kahneman's work has had an impact in such diverse areas as law, medicine, and business. Indeed, any situation involving human reasoning and decision making probably would be an appropriate area to study within the framework these authors have provided.

A basic distinction is necessary at the outset to understand the nature of this important research. In many reasoning and problem-solving settings, two general approaches

A rich source of evidence about human reasoning is gambling.

can be taken to achieve a problem solution or reason out an appropriate answer—an algorithmic approach and a heuristic approach.

An **algorithm** is a *specific rule or solution procedure, often detailed and complex, that is guaranteed to furnish the correct answer if it is followed correctly.* We are familiar with algorithms largely through our schoolwork in arithmetic and mathematics. For example, we all learned an algorithmic approach to complex multiplication, a set of rules for applying operations in certain orders to arrive at the correct answer. If the rules are applied correctly, the algorithm provides the correct answer.

In the contrasting approach, the solution method involves what is known as a **heuristic.** A heuristic is an informal guideline rather than a formal, specified rule. It's a "seat of the pants" *strategy or approach that works under some circumstances,* for some of the time, but *is not guaranteed to yield the correct answer.* (The word *heuristic* comes from the Greek stem meaning "to invent or discover." The same word stem leads to the word *eureka*, the classic exclamation, supposedly uttered by Archimedes in his bathtub, meaning roughly "Aha, I've found it!")

The Eight-Letter Problem As an example, consider the following question: How many four- and five-letter words can be formed from the set of letters *A, B, M, N, O, R, S,* and *T?* There is a perfectly appropriate and accurate algorithm that will provide the answer to this question: Take all possible four- and five-letter combinations, write them down, then check each combination against a dictionary to see whether it is a word (for reasons to become clear later on, spend a moment right now simply estimating the total number of four- and five-letter combinations that are possible, regardless of whether the combination spells a word). Such a procedure is likely to be similar to the way we might

"This CD player costs less than players selling for twice as much."

Drawing by Weber © 19889, The New Yorker Magazine, Inc.

program a computer to solve the problem: Follow a very systematic and orderly procedure that is guaranteed to yield the result, however long it takes to get there.

A heuristic approach to this problem, in stark contrast, seems very human; it is not particularly systematic or orderly, it relies fairly heavily on educated guessing, and it is especially prone to distortions, inaccuracies, and, in the present example, omissions. One heuristic for this problem might be "Assume that most of the words start with a consonant." Another might be to attempt to find words beginning with familiar spelling patterns such as *st* and *sm* (e.g., *star*, *smart*). Note that neither of these heuristics will generate all the candidate words. For instance, if you rely on the first heuristic, you'll miss such words as *abort*. The second heuristic will steer you away from unusual spelling combinations such as the *oa* in *boat* and *moat*. And neither heuristic reminds you to form plurals, such as *boats* and *bars*. Indeed, these characteristics are the very hallmarks of the heuristic approach: It will work part of the time or for part of the answer, but it is very unlikely to furnish the complete, accurate answer.

Table 11-3 shows the correct algorithmic approach for the first part of this problem, the formula that specifies the number of possible combinations. It also illustrates an important point, one reason why people rely so heavily on heuristic rather than algorithmic approaches. The algorithm here, with a total of eight letters to be arranged, will generate 8,400 four- and five-letter combinations. This is a staggering number of

---

Table 11-3 COMPUTING THE NUMBER OF COMBINATIONS

Let's use the example of the eight letters *A, B, M, N, O, R, S,* and *T.* The first part of the question involves computing the number of different four-letter combinations possible among these eight letters, then the number of different five-letter combinations, then adding these two together. The second part, scanning the resulting list of combinations to see which are words, has a different solution, so we'll focus here on just the first part.

The rule for computing combinations is as follows. Let *N* be the number of elements that can be combined, here the eight letters. Let *r* be the number of elements that should appear in the combinations; here we are interested first in four-element combinations, then five-element combinations. The rule for computing the number of combinations is

$$N!/(N - r)!$$

where the symbol "!" means factorial (e.g., 4!, is $4 \times 3 \times 2 \times 1$). Thus for the four-letter combinations, we have 8!(8 − 4)! which reduces to 8!/4!, or 40,320/24 = 1,680 letter combinations of length four. Likewise, for the five-letter combinations, we have 8!/(8 − 5)!, which reduces to 8!/3!, or 40,320/6 = 6,720 letter combinations of length five. Thus for the total number of four- and five-letter combinations, we have 1,680 + 6,720 = 8,400 unique combinations.

Compare these values to the following: In a demonstration study, subjects estimated the total number of four- and five-letter combinations to be 300, well short of 8,400.

---

combinations, far more than people can realistically be expected to generate on their own (this is another reason we use computers to do such algorithmic work: They don't get bored by such repetitive tasks as taking all combinations). It's almost as if people realize at the outset that the algorithmic approach is too lengthy for either a mental or pencil-and-paper solution, so they opt instead for the passable heuristic approach. It won't supply all the answers, but it'll be good enough (see satisficing in Chapter 12).

As an exercise, see how many four- and five-letter words you can generate from the list of letters, trying to keep track of the different heuristics you used. Having done this, work the problem again, this time writing the letters down on scraps of paper that can be rearranged on your desk. Most people are surprised at how many more words are immediately apparent when they can physically manipulate the letters in front of them. Clearly, using scraps of paper is a better heuristic than trying to rearrange the letters mentally, which entails maintaining in memory all the combinations you've tried.

Heuristic Reasoning and Judgments

Kahneman and Tversky's research has focused extensively on a set of reasoning heuristics and biases that appear to characterize much of people's everyday reasoning about uncertain events; this area is now called behavioral decision research (Medin & Bazerman, 1999). That is, their interest has been in how people predict the likelihood of future events, how people categorize events or occurrences, and how various biases and errors in such judgments can be accounted for by an understanding of the reasoning process.

In some of the situations they have studied, an appropriate algorithm can be applied to arrive at the correct answer. Many of these kinds of situations involve probabilistic reasoning, the sort of judgments and likelihood estimations students often are asked to make in the probability chapter of an undergraduate statistics book. Knowledge of the algorithms doesn't necessarily mean that the person understands them, can use them spontaneously, or can recognize all the situations when they should be applied, of course. Indeed, Kahneman and Tversky found that a sample of graduate students in psychology, all of whom had been exposed to the relevant statistical algorithms, did well on very simple problems but still relied on a heuristic rather than an algorithm when given more complex situations. On the other hand, several studies have shown more positive effects—good transfer and improved reasoning—when some relevant training is given (Agnoli, 1991; Agnoli & Krantz, 1989; Fong & Nisbett, 1991; Lehman, Lempert, & Nisbett, 1988). (Incidentally, reading Tversky and Kahneman's work, such as the 1973 article, often is very helpful to students as they *study* probability in a statistics class. See Nisbett, Krantz, Jepson, and Kunda, 1983, on statistical heuristics that people use in everyday reasoning).

Other situations that have been studied involve peoples' estimates of likelihood when precise probabilities cannot be assigned or have not been supplied, although elements of statistical and probabilistic reasoning are still appropriate to a correct reasoning solution, or in situations contrasting verbal and numerical descriptions (for instance, "rain is likely" vs. "there's a 70% chance of rain;" Windschitl & Weber, 1999). And finally, some of the settings that have been studied involve very uncertain or even impossible situations, such as asking people to predict the outcome of some hypothetical event. For instance, how would the outcome of World War II have changed if Germany had developed the atomic bomb before the United States?

We begin with the most heavily researched of Kahneman and Tversky's heuristics, the representativeness and availability heuristics, then devote some attention to other kinds of judgment processes. As you read, try to develop your own examples of reasoning situations that are similar to the stated examples. You'll be surprised at how often we use such heuristics in everyday decision making and reasoning, even though we may feel that we seldom if ever use probability in the real world.

The Representativeness Heuristic

If you toss a coin six times in a row, which of the following two outcomes is more likely: HHHTTT or HHTHTT? Most of us would agree, and quite rapidly at that, that the second alternative, the one with the alternations between heads and tails, is a more likely outcome than the run of three heads followed by three tails. But if you stop and think about it for a moment, you'll realize that each of these alternatives is *exactly* as likely as the other because each is just one of the possible ways six coin tosses can occur (the total number of distinct outcomes is 2^6, or 64 distinct sequences of heads and tails).

Part of what fools us is that we think of the alternating pattern HHTHTT as a representative of a whole class of outcomes, the class where most of the outcomes are random-looking alternations between heads and tails. This is incorrect, of course, because the problem asked about the likelihood of exactly the two given sequences, not the general class of sequences with alternations. But the mistake we make is an important indicator of how we often reason in similar situations (see the coin toss explanation in the Appendix at the end of this chapter).

According to Kahneman and Tversky (1972), when we judge the likelihood or probability of uncertain events, we do so on the basis of the event's representativeness. The **representativeness heuristic** is a judgment rule in which *an estimate of the probability of an event is determined by one of two features: how similar the event is to the population of events it came from or whether the event seems similar to the process that produced it.* In other words, we judge whether event *A* belongs to class *B* based on the extent to which *A* is representative of *B*, the degree to which it resembles *B*, or the degree to which it resembles the kind of process that *B* is known to be.

Random Processes In our coin toss example, we all know that getting heads or tails is a chance or random process. Given that tossing coins is random, we judge the sequence HHTHTT as much more likely or probable than HHHTTT because the alternating sequence HHTHTT resembles the outcome of a random process more than HHHTTT. The thinking here, illogical but nonetheless understandable, is that a random process ought to look random; it ought to generate a random-looking outcome. Accordingly, the sequence of three heads then three tails looks nonrandom and thus seems to be much less likely. Likewise, because the likelihood for six tosses is three heads and three tails (in the long run), almost any sequence with three of each will appear more representative than sequences with more of one outcome than the other. (See Pollatsek, Konold, Well, & Lima, 1984, for evidence on people's beliefs about random sampling processes; see Gilovich, Vallone, & Tversky, 1985, on people's, including coaches', beliefs about "shooting streaks" in basketball.)

Representativeness of the Parent Population Consider a situation more like Kahneman and Tversky's first criterion, where the event is similar in essential characteristics to its parent population (i.e., to the population of events from which the event of interest is drawn). These authors' example of this situation goes as follows:

> In a certain town there are two hospitals. In one, about 45 babies are born each day, in the other only about 15. As you know, about 50% of all babies are boys, although on any day, of course, this percentage may be higher or lower. Across one year, the hospitals recorded the number of days on which 60% or more of the babies were male. Which hospital do you think had more such days? (After Kahneman & Tversky, 1972, p. 443. Decide on your own answer before reading further.)

The majority of Kahneman and Tversky's subjects claimed that the number of days with 60% or more male babies would be about the same for the two hospitals; 28 of the 50 subjects drew this conclusion. Twelve of the 50 subjects said the larger hospital would have more such days, and only 10 subjects said the smaller hospital would have more days with 60% or more male babies. Another group of subjects was tested with a slightly different question, which asked about days on which "less than 60%" of the babies were male. These results were largely comparable. Thus with either question, most subjects believed that both hospitals would have about the same number of days on which 60% or more (or fewer) of the babies would be male.

Let's explain this. Consider the conclusion that subjects drew, that both the small and large hospital have about the same number of "extreme" days. People know that there will be variations around the expected percentage of 50% and that 60% is somewhat extreme. Because events that are "somewhat extreme" occasionally happen, a small and a large hospital both having 60% or more male babies is viewed as representative of a larger population, that being the population of all hospitals having a few days on which 60% or more of the babies are male. Note that there is an implicit and incorrect assumption here that "extreme" means the same thing for the two hospitals.

In fact, the correct answer here is that the smaller hospital probably will have more days on which 60% or more of the babies are male. The reason for this is an elementary notion in statistics and sampling. Extreme or unlikely outcomes are more likely to be seen as the sample size gets smaller. That is, with fewer events, the likelihood is greater that the events will vary from the expected proportion. Thus, in reality, it is more likely that the small hospital will have more extreme days, days on which 60% or more babies are male, than the large hospital. The reason is that the 60% proportion is being computed on an average of 15 births instead of 45. Another way of saying this is that, given the fifty–fifty odds, 60% is not as extreme an occurrence out of 15 opportunities as it is out of 45 opportunities; 60% or more male babies is not as extreme for the small hospital as it is for the large one (see the Appendix).

On statistical grounds, this is precisely the same reasoning as the fact that all heads is a more likely outcome for two coin tosses than it is for six coin tosses. All heads for two coin tosses has a probability of .25, whereas all heads for six coin tosses has a probability of .0156. The Appendix explains the algorithmic, statistical basis for both the six-flip coin toss and the hospital examples; Table 11-4 summarizes the representativeness heuristic and several of the biases that stem from its use.

This particular bias in the representativeness heuristic is called insensitivity to sample size. It means that when people reason about such events, they fail to take into account the size of the sample or group on which the event is based. They seem to believe that both small and large samples should be equally similar to the population they were drawn from. Another way of expressing this insensitivity is that people believe in the law of small numbers. Now the law of large numbers—that a large sample is more representative of its population—is true. But people erroneously believe that the law of small numbers is true as well. People incorrectly assume that a small sample is just as representative of its parent population as a large sample (see also Bar-Hillel, 1980), but it isn't, of course.

Stereotypes Another bias, also resulting from the representativeness heuristic, is of particular importance because it probably affects our everyday reasoning about other people more than the statistical or probabilistic situations (Table 11-4 provides additional examples and explanations of the representativeness effects and biases). Kahneman and Tversky (1973) reported some fascinating evidence on estimations of likelihood based on

---

Table 11-4 BIASES IN THE REPRESENTATIVENESS HEURISTIC

Ignoring base rates (ignoring prior odds) (Adapted from Johnson & Finke, 1985)
Questions:
(a) Why are more graduate students first-born than second-born children?
(b) Why do more hotel fires start on the first ten floors than the second ten floors?
(c) In baseball, are more runners thrown out by pitchers on first base or on second base?
The bias: In all three questions, people tend to ignore base rates. To answer the questions correctly, we should consider:
(a) How many first-born versus second-born people are there?
(b) How many hotels even *have* a second ten floors?
(c) How many runners on first base versus second base are there?

Base rates and stereotypes
Question:
Frank is a meek and quiet person whose only hobby is playing chess. He was near the top of his college class and majored in philosophy. Is Frank a librarian or a businessman?
The bias: The personality description seems to match a librarian stereotype, whether the stereotype is true or not. Second, we fail to consider base rates, that is, the relative frequencies of the two professions. In other words, there are far more businessmen than librarians, a base rate that tends to be ignored because of the stereotype "match."

Gambler's fallacy
Question:
You've watched a (fair) coin toss come up heads five times in a row. If you bet $10 on the next toss, would you choose heads or tails?
The bias: The gambler's fallacy is that the next toss is more likely to be tails, because "it's time for tails to show up." Of course, the five previous tosses have no bearing at all on the sixth toss, assuming a fair coin. The bias is related to the law of small numbers, in particular, that we expect randomness even on the "local" or short-run outcomes. Thus getting tails after five heads seems more representative of the random process that produces the outcomes, so we mistakenly prefer to bet $10 on tails.

---

personality descriptions. They read various personality descriptions to subjects, then had them estimate the likelihood or probability that the described person was a member of one or another profession. To a surprising degree, people's estimations can be influenced by the similarity of a description to a widely held **stereotype.**

Consider first the situation: 100 people are in a room, 70 of them lawyers, 30 of them engineers. Given this situation, answer the following question:

1. A person named Bill was randomly selected from this roomful of 100 people. What is the likelihood that Bill is a lawyer?

Simple probability tells us that the chances of selecting a lawyer are .70, given the situation described. People generally reason correctly in such situations, according to Kahneman and Tversky, that is, in a "bare bones" situation. The technical term for these "bare bones," the 70:30 proportion, is *prior odds*, or simply *base rates*. Before any other information, the probability of sampling a lawyer is .70, and the probability of sampling an engineer is .30.

Consider two slightly different situations. There are still the same 70 lawyers and 30 engineers. But now, you are given a description of two randomly selected people and are asked "What is the likelihood that this person is an engineer?" (adapted from Kahneman & Tversky, 1973, pp. 241–242):

2. "Dick is a 30-year-old man. He is married with no children. A man of high ability and high motivation, he promises to be quite successful in his field. He is well liked by his colleagues."

3. "Jack is a 45-year-old man. He is married and has four children. He is generally conservative, careful, and ambitious. He shows no interest in political and social issues and spends most of his free time on his many hobbies, which include home carpentry, sailing, and mathematical puzzles."

Kahneman and Tversky's subjects did *not* judge the probabilities for these two descriptions to be the same as the prior odds, that is, .70 for lawyers, .30 for engineers. Instead, they assumed that the personality descriptions contained relevant information and adjusted their estimates accordingly. In particular, for descriptions 2 and 3, subjects responded that the probability was close to .50, that is, about a fifty–fifty chance that Dick and Jack were engineers.

Note that description 3 was intended to resemble the stereotype many people have of engineers. It mentions such factors as "careful" and "mathematical puzzles," which presumably are representative of engineers—at least they are representative of our stereotypes of engineers. Here, subjects essentially ignored the prior odds and based their judgments on the description itself. The same thing happened with description 2, even though it was intentionally written to be uninformative with regard to Dick's profession.

It's illogical but probably understandable that description 3 led to distorted estimates. People viewed the personality description as representative of the engineering profession, so they adjusted their estimates upward from the .30 level. The stereotype may be wrong, or at least biased or inaccurate in some details, but people still based their judgments on the description and stereotype more than on the prior odds. Of course, the appropriate strategy is to weight the new evidence, taking into account its predictive accuracy along with the prior odds (there's an algorithm for this too, but it requires knowledge of the predictive accuracy of the new evidence). Instead, people tend to view *any such evidence* as a basis for accurate prediction, particularly if it seems strong (Griffin & Tversky, 1992), and in the process they lose sight of prior odds (see also Fischhoff & Bar-Hillel, 1984).

But it's hardly understandable at all that subjects would accept description 2 as even remotely relevant. And yet this is what they do, even when the evidence is intentionally neutral. In fact, Fischhoff and Bar-Hillel (1984) found that very few of their subjects regarded intentionally neutral descriptions as truly neutral. Instead, they categorized the personality descriptions as belonging to one of the two professions, despite the description's neutrality, and were surprisingly confident in their categorizations as well. It may be, in such situations, that subjects believe that the evidence is *meant* to be taken as relevant (e.g., see the "be relevant" conversational rule in Chapter 10). Apparently, as Kahneman and Tversky put it, "people respond differently when given no specific evidence and when given worthless evidence. When no specific evidence is given, the prior probabilities are properly utilized; when worthless specific evidence is given, prior probabilities are ignored" (1973, p. 242).

The Usefulness of the Representativeness Heuristic We've focused on the biases and errors that crop up when people rely on the representativeness heuristic. Basically, people tend to ignore the relevant information available in a situation and base their reasoning instead on how much an outcome resembles or seems representative of the population or process being considered. On the other hand, heuristics were defined as strategies that sometimes *do* provide a correct answer. In other words, heuristics are not invariably misleading; if they were, then we presumably would never use them. As Nisbett and Ross (1980) point out, heuristics are generally useful but lead to errors when they are overapplied or misapplied or when they substitute for use of a more complex but appropriate strategy.

What is useful about the representativeness heuristic is that it often provides a very good basis for judging likelihoods of general classes of outcomes. Imagine that the original six coin toss example is changed slightly. Instead of being asked which of these two outcomes is more likely, imagine being asked which of these two *kinds* of outcomes is more likely. In such a rewording, it is now obvious that the specific sequences are of less interest than the general classes they represent, one being an alternating pattern in the fifty–fifty situation, and one being a pair of straight runs with lengths of three. Of course, the kind of pattern represented by HHTHTT is much more likely than the kind represented by HHHTTT (see the Appendix). Thus if you had bet money on the coin and then saw a sequence like HHHTTT, you'd be much more suspicious that the coin was rigged than if you saw a sequence like HHTHTT.

Likewise, we have to imagine that professional stereotypes have at least some relationship to the people who engage in that profession, even though we would admit that the stereotype is only a loose description, that it isn't necessary that each person in that profession have this or that characteristic, and that stereotypes are often related to deplorable practices such as discrimination. For example, it is not surprising that one stereotype about engineers is that they are more interested in quantitative topics than "the average person." After all, much of engineering involves highly quantitative information. Hearing that some person, either a lawyer or engineer, *enjoys* mathematical puzzles matches an engineering stereotype and therefore seems representative of the kind of person in that profession. Such stereotyping affects all sorts of processes, from priming due to gender-based stereotypes (Banaji & Hardin, 1996) through impression formation tasks (Hoffman, Lau, & Johnson, 1986).

The Availability Heuristic

What proportion of all medical doctors are women? What proportion of U.S. households own a microwave oven, a color TV, or a VCR? How much safer are you in a commercial airliner than in a private car, or vice versa? Questions such as these ask you to estimate the frequency or probability of real-world events, even though you are unlikely to have the evidence or knowledge stored in memory. Each of the questions is answerable in the sense that the precise answer is a matter of public record (although it may not be easy to obtain). And yet because we do not know the precise answer, we must estimate the answer based on the shreds of information we have in memory. How do we perform this estimation?

The simplest basis for making these estimates is to try to recall relevant information or examples from memory. The frequency with which events occur is a kind of information that is coded in memory (Hasher & Zacks, 1984), perhaps automatically. So when we attempt to retrieve examples of the events from memory, their frequency, as coded in memory, is an important factor. If the retrieval of examples is easy, we infer that the event must be fairly frequent or common. If retrieval is difficult, then we estimate that the event must not be frequent. Interestingly, frequency of encountering information also has an effect on your eventual judgments about the information: If it's repeated often enough, even a false statement becomes "truer" (Brown & Nix, 1996).

Frequency is closely related to the second important heuristic that Tversky and Kahneman (1973) discuss, the **availability heuristic.** In this heuristic, we evaluate "the frequency of classes or the probability of events . . . by the ease with which relevant instances come to mind" (p. 207). "Ease of retrieval" is what the term *availability* means here (note that this is not what it meant in the encoding specificity context of Chapter 6). In short, when people have to make estimates of likelihood or frequency, their *estimates are influenced by the ease with which relevant examples can be remembered.*

The Usefulness of the Availability Heuristic The availability heuristic often provides a very good strategy for responding. That is, the ease of remembering examples is reasonably well correlated with objective frequency; in general, frequent events are indeed more easily remembered than infrequent events, simply because events of all sorts are noticed and then coded in memory as they occur (Brown & Siegler, 1992). But as Kahneman and Tversky (1996) point out, our judgments about frequency can be biased too.

Biases Within the Availability Heuristic Although the availability heuristic often is a reliable way of making estimates (indeed, it is often the *only* way we have of making estimates in many situations), some distortions and biases may stem from it. Any factor that leads to storage of information or events in memory can influence our reasoning here because our judgments are based on what we can remember easily. If reasonably accurate and undistorted information is in memory, then the availability heuristic probably does a reasonable job. But if memory contains information that is inaccurate, incomplete, or influenced by factors other than objective frequency, there may be biases and distortions in our reasoning.

In particular, any factor besides frequency that calls attention to the event may make the event more memorable, make it stand out more in memory. In the terms we used in Chapter 6, such events may be more accessible for retrieval. This will bias our estimates because the ease of retrieval would be influenced not simply by frequency but also by those other memorability factors. Some of these biases can result from personal preferences, dislikes, or other idiosyncratic factors. As a simple example, if your friend's Volvo needs repeated trips to the mechanic, you may develop a biased view of how unreliable Volvos are. If your only source of knowledge is the friend's opinion, the availability heuristic has biased your judgment.

More generally, our biases result from other kinds of knowledge stored in memory. These other factors, sometimes obvious and sometimes subtle, also influence how easily we can remember examples and thus introduce errors in our estimates.

General World Knowledge As an illustration of the availability heuristic, estimate the ratio of the number of Chevrolet cars sold to the number of Cadillacs sold. According to the availability heuristic, you base your estimate on whatever frequency-based knowledge you may have in memory. If you have no personal reason to notice one kind of car more than another, your estimate may be a reasonably fair guess about the relative frequency of different makes of cars. Apart from personal biases, however, your general world knowledge tells you that Cadillacs are expensive, whereas Chevrolets are less expensive. Given such economic factors, you might estimate that fewer Cadillacs are sold than Chevrolets.

Alternatively, the cost factor might cause you to adjust your initial guess upward, in a sense correcting your frequency estimate by the additional information that Cadillacs may be less common than your initial guess because of their cost; this is called the anchoring and adjusting heuristic (Carlson, 1990). Most people estimate that Chevrolets are about 10 or 15 times more numerous than Cadillacs. According to recent General Motors data, however, the ratio is almost exactly 5:1 for all models of Chevrolets versus all models of Cadillacs. Subjects almost uniformly report that the cost factor led them to their high estimates; most are surprised at the actual ratio. (Here's another surprise, especially for city dwellers; the GM truck division sells almost exactly the same number of vehicles per year as the car division, a 1:1 ratio.)

Familiarity Biases Another example, studied directly by Tversky and Kahneman, shows very clearly how the bias in availability is related to ease of recall. The authors constructed lists of names, 39 names per list, with 19 women's and 20 men's names per list. One group of subjects heard the lists and then had to recall as many names as they could remember. Another group heard the lists, then estimated whether the list contained more names of men or women. In two of the four lists that were tested, the women's names were famous (e.g., Elizabeth Taylor) and the men's names were not; in the other two lists, the men's names were famous (e.g., Richard Nixon) and the women's names were not. In the recall groups, subjects remembered an average of 12 of the 19 famous names but only 8 of the 20 less famous names. This shows that familiar or famous names were more easily recalled.

The important connection between ease of recall and estimation bias came from the groups that had to estimate the proportion of male versus female names. Here too, the fame of the names influenced the judgments. Subjects who heard the "famous female" lists estimated that there had been more women's names, and those who heard the "famous male" lists said there had been more men's names. Thus in this study, there was clear evidence, first, that the famous names were more easily recalled and second, that this greater availability for recall influenced the estimates of frequency. So the **familiarity bias** is just that, *judging events as more frequent or important just because they are more familiar in memory.*

Salience and Vividness Biases   Examples of the availability heuristic in the everyday world are not difficult to imagine. For instance, consider people's feelings about traveling by airplane. Many people do not know that, statistically, one is far safer traveling by commercial airliner than traveling by private car; the National Transportation Safety Board and National Highway Transportation Safety Council statistics state that air travel is many times safer, based on normalized passenger-miles traveled. People who have no particularly relevant information stored in memory, that is, those whose only information comes from casual attention to news media and the like, presumably would judge that one is much safer when traveling by car than by airliner.

This bias can be attributed to the factor of **salience** or **vividness.** The news accounts of an airline accident are far more vivid, and given far more attention, than accounts of passenger car accidents. And even though airplane crashes are rare, the number of victims involved often is dramatic enough that the event makes a much stronger impression than is objectively called for. But when you estimate air versus car safety factors, of course, the vividness of the recalled information tends to bias your judgment. For those who know intellectually that air travel is safer, we might look for other evidence of the bias; for instance, people are surely more nervous when traveling in an airliner, on the average, than when traveling in a private car.

The Simulation Heuristic

The final heuristic to be discussed is called the **simulation heuristic.** In this heuristic, we are asked to make some prediction of future events or we are asked to imagine some different outcome of an event or action. The use of the term *simulation* here comes from computer simulation. In a computer simulation, certain starting values are entered, and the simulation then proceeds to forecast or predict some set of outcomes based on the processes written into the program. In similar fashion, the simulation heuristic involves *a mental construction or imagining of outcomes, a forecasting of how some event will turn out or how it might have turned out under another set of circumstances.*

The ease with which these plausible scenarios or outcomes can be imagined is the basis for the simulation heuristic. To the extent that a hypothetical sequence of events can easily be imagined, the events are available in the sense of Tversky and Kahneman's term. Alternatively, if it is difficult to construct a plausible scenario, the hypothetical event or outcome would be viewed as unlikely or possibly would not be constructed or imagined at all. In short, the ease of construction or ease of imagining the outcomes is the operative factor in the simulation heuristic.

An example of this heuristic was given earlier, when you were asked to imagine possible outcomes if Germany had developed the atomic bomb before the United States. Given the role the atomic bomb played in ending World War II, people presumably would give far more weight to this in answering the question than if they were asked about the development of some other device, say a long-range bomber or submarine.

On the other hand, imagining an outcome different from the actual one may be difficult, especially in less dramatic examples. This should also affect the way the simulation heuristic guides our thinking.

Consider an example discussed by Kahneman and Tversky (1982, p. 203):

> Mr. Crane and Mr. Tees were scheduled to leave the airport on different flights, at the same time. They traveled from town in the same limousine, were caught in a traffic jam, and arrived at the airport 30 minutes after the scheduled departure time of their flights. Mr. Crane is told that his flight left on time. Mr. Tees is told that his flight was delayed, and just left five minutes ago. Who is more upset, Mr. Crane or Mr. Tees?

As you would expect, almost everyone decides that Mr. Tees is more upset; in Kahneman and Tversky's study, 96% of the subjects made this judgment. The unusual aspect of this, as the authors note, is that from an objective standpoint, Mr. Crane and Mr. Tees are in identical positions: Both missed their planes, and because of the traffic jam, both *expected* to miss their planes. Kahneman and Tversky continue by explaining that the only reason Mr. Tees might be more upset is that it was more "possible," in some sense, for him to have caught his flight. That is, people can imagine a variety of scenarios in which the limousine could have arrived at the airport a mere 5 minutes earlier than it did; for example, the traffic jam could have cleared or the driver could have taken an alternate route. All these scenarios involve the simulation heuristic, in which the initial values (e.g., traffic jam, departure time) are entered into the subject's mental simulation of "getting to the airport as quickly as possible." Because it's easier to imagine an outcome in which the limousine arrives a few minutes earlier than it is to imagine one in which it arrives a half-hour earlier, we feel that the traveler who "nearly caught his flight" will be more upset.

The Undoing Heuristic A much more complete example of the simulation heuristic, including the data reported by Kahneman and Tversky (1982), is contained in Table 11-5. This example illustrates a particular version of the simulation heuristic, the undoing of some outcome by changes in the events that led up to it. This is also called **counterfactual reasoning,** *when a line of reasoning deliberately contradicts the facts in a "what if" kind of way* (e.g., "what would have happened if Germany had developed the bomb first?"; see Mandel & Lehman, 1996; Roese, 1997, 1999; Spellman & Mandel, 1999). This is essentially the process of judging that some event "nearly happened," "could have occurred," "might have happened if only," and so on. Read the story now and decide how you would complete the "If only" phrase before continuing.

Kahneman and Tversky characterize the changes people make in the sequence of events, that is, possible changes that lead to different outcomes, as belonging to one of three types. **Downhill changes** are those that remove a surprising or otherwise unusual event from a story or scenario, thereby making the story more coherent or "typical." In

Table 11-5 STORIES FOR THE SIMULATION HEURISTIC

Route Version

1. Mr. Jones was 47 years old, the father of three, and a successful banking executive. His wife has been ill at home for several months.

2a. On the day of the accident, Mr. Jones left his office at the regular time. He sometimes left early to take care of home chores at his wife's request, but this was not necessary on that day. Mr. Jones did not drive home by his regular route. The day was exceptionally clear and Mr. Jones told his friends at the office that he would drive along the shore to enjoy the view.

3. The accident occurred at a major intersection. The light turned amber as Mr. Jones approached. Witnesses noted that he braked hard to stop at the crossing, although he could easily have gone through. His family recognized this as a common occurrence in Mr. Jones's driving. As he began to cross after the light changed, a light truck charged into the intersection at top speed and rammed Mr. Jones' car from the left. Mr. Jones was killed instantly.

4a. It was later ascertained that the truck was driven by a teenage boy, who was under the influence of drugs.

5. As commonly happens in such situations, the Jones family and their friends often thought and often said, "If only . . . ," during the days that followed the accident. How did they continue this thought? Please write one or more likely completions.

Time Version

(substitute 2b)

2b. On the day of the accident, Mr. Jones left the office earlier than usual to attend to some household chores at his wife's request. He drove home along his regular route. Mr. Jones occasionally chose to drive along the shore, to enjoy the view on exceptionally clear days, but that day was just average.

"Boy" Focus Version

(substitute 4b)

4b. It was later ascertained that the truck was driven by a teenage boy named Tom Searler. Tom's father had just found him at home under the influence of drugs. This was a common occurrence, as Tom used drugs heavily. There had been a quarrel, during which Tom grabbed the keys that were lying on the living room table and drove off blindly. He was severely injured in the accident.

Number of Subjects Responding to the "If Only" Stem in the Five Different Response Categories

Response Category	Story Version	
"If Only" Completion Focuses On:	Route Version	Time Version
Route	33	8
Time	2	16
Crossing	14	19
Boy	13	18
Other	3	1
	65 respondents	62 respondents

Source. Kahneman and Tversky (1982).

the sample story, the majority of subjects who heard the "route" version of the story made a downhill change by suggesting, for instance, that "if he had taken his usual route rather than a different one, the accident could have been avoided."

An **uphill change** is one that brings some new and unlikely event into the story, one that might change the outcome but would be unusual or unanticipated in such a scenario; this is the category labeled "Other" in Table 11-5. An uphill change might have been something like "Shortly after he left work, Mr. Jones had a flat tire that delayed him, and thus he avoided the accident."

Horizontal changes, finally, are those in which one detail or event in the story is replaced by another of comparable likelihood. Such a change in this story could have Mr. Jones arriving at the intersection 2 or 3 seconds earlier or later than he did. Given the realities of driving, such a difference would be easy to imagine, presumably, although the focus of the story apparently led the subjects to think about other possible events instead.

Kahneman and Tversky's results for this story suggested that people confine themselves largely to downhill changes when they "undo" or imagine alternate outcomes. Uphill changes were rarely introduced by the subjects, and horizontal changes were, in the authors' term, "nonexistent." Note the biases operating here. A downhill change "normalizes" the story by substituting a regular for an unusual event or detail. We seem to have a bias to make such downhill changes, for two apparent reasons. First, downhill changes can be more easily imagined—there's ease of retrieval again. Second, downhill changes seem more plausible; it's more plausible that Mr. Jones left on time than it is that he left early and then had a flat tire. (The metaphor for "downhill" and "uphill" is cross-country skiing, where skiing downhill is far easier than skiing uphill.)

Uphill changes, in which an unusual event is introduced, might objectively be just as likely as any detail in the original story and could just as easily alter the outcome of the story. And yet people apparently do not make uphill changes very frequently. The bias is that unusual or atypical events are difficult to imagine or construct. Therefore, they are not usually generated by the mental simulation; it's as if the simulation goes for the default, typical values. Finally, it's rather odd that a simple substitution of one detail for another is never made. Mr. Jones could have left work 3 seconds earlier or later, the truck could have been going slower, and so on.

Strangest of all, subjects seldom focused on the actual cause of the accident, the teenage boy. That is, they seldom altered anything concerning the boy's behavior, even though it was his actions, not Mr. Jones's, that caused the accident. Kahneman and Tversky speculate that this tendency is caused by a focus rule: We tend to maintain properties of the main object or focus of the story unless a different focus is provided. In support of this speculation, the alternate version of the story shown at the bottom of the table ("Boy focus") was substituted, in which the boy becomes the principal focus. In this version, subjects were much more likely to complete the "if only" sentences by removing the cause of the accident, the boy himself. In the original version, only 28% of the subjects mentioned the boy in their constructed versions, but 68% mentioned him in the revised focus version.

Hindsight Note, finally, that the simulation heuristic provides a compelling explanation of the **hindsight bias** or effect, *the after-the-fact judgment that some event was very likely to happen or was very predictable, even though it wasn't predicted to happen beforehand:* the "I knew it all along" effect. In thinking about the now-completed event, the scenario under which that event could have happened is very easy to imagine; after all, that scenario just happened. The connection between the initial situation and the final outcome is very available after the fact, and this availability makes other possible connections seem less plausible than they otherwise would seem. In terms of the simulation heuristic, the hindsight effect may be nothing more than a bias in which otherwise plausible outcomes are now less easy to imagine than the outcome that actually happened (for recent evidence on hindsight bias, see Hell, Gigerenzer, Gauggel, Mall, & Muller, 1988, and Hoch & Loewenstein, 1989). And the hindsight effect even extends to memory. People routinely "remember" their original position or judgment to be more consistent with their final decision than it really was (Erdfelder & Buchner, 1998; Holyoak & Simon, 1999).

Applications of the Simulation Heuristic In many ways, it seems that the simulation heuristic may come closer to what people mean by such terms as thinking and considering than anything else we've covered so far. That is, it is easy to recognize less dramatic examples of undoing and other kinds of forecasting or simulating in our everyday thinking and the influence of factors such as salience and hindsight bias. For example:

If I stop for a cup of coffee, I might miss my bus.
If I hadn't been so busy yesterday, I would have remembered to cash a check.
In looking back, I guess I could have predicted that waiting until senior year to take statistics was a bad idea.

Presumably, such thinking often is the reason we decide to do one thing versus another; we think through the possible outcomes of different actions, then base our decision on the most favorable of the forecasted outcomes. Thus the mental simulation process, taking certain input conditions then forecasting possible outcomes, could be an important way to understand general cognitive processes related to planning.

A general warning is important to bear in mind here, based on studies of how people generate possible outcomes of future events. Hoch (1984) asked one group of subjects to think of favorable outcomes when predicting some future event and asked another group to think of unfavorable outcomes. Subjects who first generated favorable outcomes were then less able to imagine unfavorable outcomes when they were asked to consider the "other side of the question." Initial predictions also influenced the estimates of how likely one or the other outcome might be; subjects who began by generating favorable outcomes were much more "certain" that a favorable outcome would actually happen. On the other hand, if subjects generate reasons that some outcome might *not* happen, their confidence in their predictions tends to be much more realistic (Hoch, 1985). The warning should be clear. Overly optimistic predictions at the outset bias our ability to imagine negative outcomes and inflate our view of the likelihood of a positive outcome. ("Hey, what could go wrong if I wait until next week to start my term paper?")

■ Section Summary

- Algorithms are systematic rules and procedures that generate correct answers to problems, whereas heuristics are quick, informal rules that are often useful but are not guaranteed to yield the correct solution. Three important heuristics have been investigated in circumstances when people reason about uncertain events.
- The representativeness heuristic guides people to judge outcomes as likely if they seem representative of the type of event being evaluated; for instance, a random-looking sequence of coin tosses is judged more representative of coin toss outcomes almost regardless of the true probabilities involved. Included among the reasoning effects predicted by this heuristic are various stereotyping results.
- In the availability heuristic, people judge the likelihood of events by how easily they can remember examples or instances. These judgments therefore can be biased by any other factor, such as salience or vividness, that affects the storing of examples in memory.
- In the simulation heuristic, people forecast or predict how some outcome could have been different. These forecasts are influenced by how easily the alternative outcomes can be imagined. Interestingly, when people complete "if only" statements, the changes they include tend to normalize the original situation by removing an unusual event and substituting a more common one. Such normalizations can be affected by the *focus* of the situation.

Limitations in Reasoning

Answer this question:

If each of 10 people at a business meeting shakes hands (once) with each other person, then how many handshakes are exchanged?

A central fact in investigations of decision making and reasoning bears repeating here. We use heuristics in decision making and reasoning because of limitations. There are limitations in our knowledge, both of relevant facts and also relevant algorithms. You had to estimate the latitudes of Chicago and Rome because you (probably) didn't know them; you simply didn't have those facts stored in memory. Likewise, you probably estimated the number of handshakes in the preceding question, probably because you don't know the relevant algorithm (which, by the way, is easy; if N is the number of people, then the number of handshakes is $N \times (N-1)/2$; for 10 people, that's 45 handshakes; $10 \times 9/2$). And there are also limitations in the reasoner that are important, sometimes as ordinary as unwillingness to make the effort needed but sometimes more central than that.

Limited Domain Knowledge

Everyday examples of how limited knowledge affects decision making and reasoning are abundant. Kempton (1986), for example, looked at reasoning based on analogies, particularly how we develop analogies based on known events and situations to reason

Drawing by Weber © 1972 The New Yorker Magazine, Inc.

"Oh, just put me down as undecided."

about unknown or poorly understood domains. Focusing on a mechanical device, Kempton investigated people's understanding of home heating, particularly their understanding of a furnace thermostat. The results indicated that some people's (incorrect) understanding is that a thermostat works in an analogous fashion to a water faucet: Turn it up higher to get a faster flow of heat. Likewise, many people's behavior suggests that they believe that the call button on an elevator works like a doorbell: If the elevator doesn't arrive reasonably soon, press the button again (there can also be an element of superstitious belief here too, or possibly quasimagical thinking, as when someone blows on a pair of dice before throwing them; see Shafir & Tversky, 1992).

It should be obvious that our mental models—our cognitive representations of the reasoning or decision-making situation—can vary from true and complete knowledge (expertise, in other words) all the way down to no knowledge or information at all, ignorance. (People's awareness that they do not know something is actually quite interesting itself; see Gentner & Collins, 1981, and Glucksberg & McCloskey, 1981.) The most interesting situation to study is when knowledge is incomplete or inaccurate. Indeed, the fact that we are so concerned with how people estimate under uncertainty, and with their errors in reasoning, implies that complete and certain knowledge usually is not available to people. This focus on errors in the reasoning and decision literature is reminiscent of the Piagetian tradition of analyzing children's errors in logical thought problems. It also represents the general tendency in cognitive psychology to study accuracy or inaccuracy in performance as a way of understanding mental processing.

A Mental Model of the Physical World: McCloskey's Naive Physics Some of the most intriguing (and entertaining) research on mental models and reasoning has been

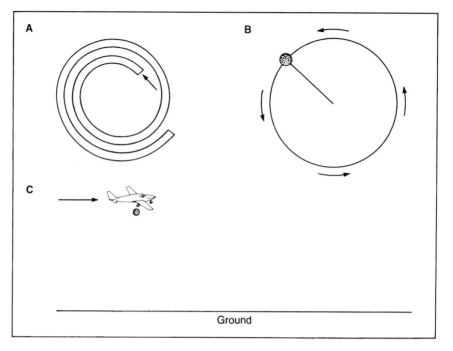

Figure 11-7

Stimuli used by McCloskey. **A,** Imagine that the curved tube is on a table top, and a ball or marble is tossed in (see arrow). Draw the path of the ball when it exits the tube. For **B,** Imagine that the ball is being twirled around and that the string breaks. Draw the path the ball will take once the string breaks. **C,** Imagine an airplane is traveling at a constant speed and a ball is dropped from the airplane. Draw the path of the ball is it falls to the ground.

reported by McCloskey and his colleagues. McCloskey has investigated *people's conceptions of the physical world, in particular, their understanding of the principles of motion,* called **naive physics.** Figure 11-7 presents several of the problems McCloskey has studied. The remaining section will be more meaningful to you if you spend a few moments working through the problems before reading further.

By asking subjects to complete such diagrams and then explain their answers, McCloskey (1983) has provided a very convincing example of the misconceptions or faulty mental models people often have. For instance, in one of his studies (McCloskey, Caramazza, & Green, 1980; see also Freyd & Jones, 1994), 51% of the subjects believed that a marble would follow a curved path after leaving the tube depicted in Figure 11-7A. Likewise, some 30% responded that the ball in Figure 11-7B would continue on a curved path after the string broke, often adding that this curved path eventually would straighten out. In the airplane question (Figure 11-7C), only 40% gave the correct answer; the most common incorrect answer (36% of the subjects) was that the ball would fall straight down. Figure 11-8 shows both the correct and incorrect answers people gave to these problems, along with the percentage of people who gave the answers.

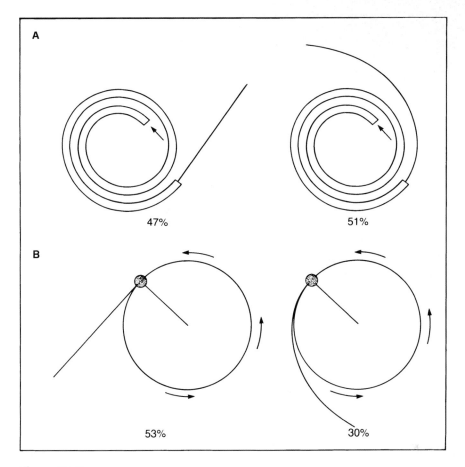

Figure 11-8

Stimuli and subjects' responses to McCloskey's Problems in Figure 11-7, with the percentages of subjects making that response.

One compelling aspect of McCloskey's results involves the domain of knowledge that was being tested, the motion of physical objects. This is not a rarefied, unusual kind of knowledge that is foreign to people. As McCloskey notes, we have countless opportunities in our everyday experience to witness the behavior of objects in motion and to derive an understanding of the principles of motion from that experience. Anyone who has ever thrown a ball has had such opportunities. And yet the mental model we derive from that experience is flawed, although there is some evidence that the cognitive model we develop is rather different from the perceptual–motor model that actually governs throwing a ball (Krist, Fieberg, & Wilkening, 1993; Schwartz & Black, 1999).

A second compelling aspect to the research concerns the nature of the mental model itself. As analyzed by McCloskey, people's erroneous understanding of bodies in motion is amazingly similar to the so-called impetus theory of motion, which states that

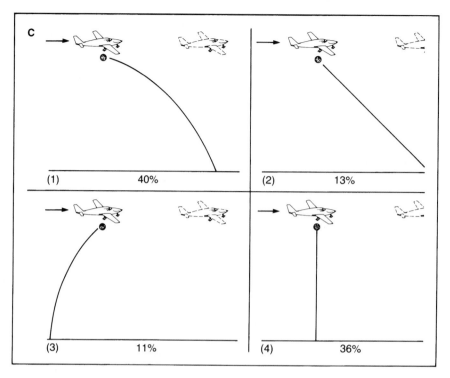

Figure 11-8

(Continued)

setting an object in motion puts some impetus or "movement force" into the object, with the impetus slowly dissipating across time (but see Cooke & Breedin, 1994, and Hubbard, 1996, on the notion of impetus). For instance, in the tube problem in Figure 11-7A, one subject said: "The momentum from the curve [of the tube] gives it [the ball] the arc. . . . The force that the ball picks up from the curve eventually dissipates and it will follow a normal straight line" (McCloskey, 1983, p. 309).

The punchline here is that the impetus theory was the accepted explanation of motion during the 13th and 14th centuries, a view that was finally abandoned by physics when Newton's laws of gravity and motion were advanced some 300 years ago. The correct mental model, basically, is that a body in motion continues in a straight line unless some other force, such as gravity, is applied. If some other force is applied, then that force combines with the continuing straight line movement. Thus when the ball leaves the tube, or when the string breaks, the ball moves in a straight line; no "curved force" continues to act on it because no such thing as "impetus" has been given to it. Likewise, the horizontal movement of the ball dropped from the airplane continues until the ball hits the ground. This movement is augmented by a downward movement caused by gravity; the ball accelerates vertically as it continues its previous horizontal motion. (If you demonstrated a naive belief in impetus, you might take some consolation in the fact

PROVE IT

Naive Physics

Having people complete the diagrams on the naive physics beliefs is an almost fail-safe project. Be sure you interview your subjects on their reasons for drawing the pathways they drew (be sure you understand the correct pathways before you try explaining the principles behind them). And come up with some new diagrams or problems to test other aspects of people's intuitive understanding of motion and gravity.

It would be interesting to know how other groups of subjects respond. For example, in Donley and Ashcraft's (1992) article, the professors in the physics de-partment performed essentially perfectly, whereas professors in other departments were no more accurate than students in the undergraduate physics sequence. It's not clear whether children would perform less accurately than adults; after all, adults do pretty badly. On the other hand, perhaps children will report more interesting reasons for their beliefs. Some adults complete the cliff-and-ball problem below with a "straight out, then straight down" pathway, a pathway called the Road Runner effect, from the cartoon character. It would be interesting to know whether children (or adults) appeal to that in justifying their answers.

Ground

The ball is rolling toward a cliff. Draw the path of the ball as it goes over the edge.

Ground

If the two balls are dropped at the same time, do they hit the ground at the same time or at different times?

that, across recorded history, people have believed in impetus theory longer than they have in Newton's laws.)

Only a little research addresses the nature of our experience and the kind of information we derive from it. In some of the naive physics problems, especially the plane problem, an optical illusion seems partly responsible for the "straight down belief" (McCloskey, 1983). Beyond that, some inattentiveness on the reasoner's part, or perhaps difficulty in profiting from real-world feedback, may also account for some of the inaccuracy. To be sure, some of the difficulties we experience involve the difficulty of the problems themselves (Proffitt, Kaiser, & Whelan, 1990). For example, Medin and Edelson (1988) found that, depending on the structure and complexity of the problem, subjects may use base rate information appropriately, may use it inappropriately, or may ignore it entirely. We do know that instruction and training influence reasoning. Taking a physics class improves your knowledge of the rules of motion, but it doesn't completely eliminate the misbeliefs (Donley & Ashcraft, 1992). Likewise, instruction in statistics, probability, and hypothesis testing improves your ability to reason accurately in those domains (Agnoli & Krantz, 1989; Fong & Nisbett, 1991; Lehman et al., 1988). In short, acquiring a fuller knowledge of the domain is an important part of making more accurate decisions.

Limitations in Processing Resources

Likewise, several studies attest to the role of processing resources in adequate decision making and problem solving. Cherniak (1984; see also Tversky & Kahneman, 1983) has studied the prototypicality heuristic, a strategy in which we generate examples to reason out an answer rather than follow the correct, logical procedures of deductive reasoning. The heuristic is useful in the sense that it reduces subjects' errors when they are working under time constraints. But it depends on a limitation, possibly of working memory, possibly of time in which to perform the task, or possibly in the subjects' willingness to do the slow, effortful work of following the algorithmic procedure. As an example, what is the answer to the following?

$$8 \times 7 \times 6 \times 5 \times 4 \times 3 \times 2 \times 1$$

Be honest—even though you know how to multiply, you didn't really multiply out all those values, did you? You probably estimated; you used a heuristic. One way we know this is by comparing your estimate to a different problem,

$$1 \times 2 \times 3 \times 4 \times 5 \times 6 \times 7 \times 8$$

In Tversky and Kahneman's (1983) data, people's estimates for the first problem averaged 2,250, but for the second problem, estimates averaged 512. Heuristic processing was clearly involved, because the estimates depended on whether the arithmetically identical sequences began with a large or small number and because both estimates were wildly inaccurate: The correct answer to 8! is 40,320.

Although it's tempting to say the limitation was in your lack of willingness to solve the problem (a nice way of saying laziness), note that a full solution would take considerable working memory resources if you attempted to solve the problem mentally. Even if you were only approximating in your calculations, a sequence of problem solving and keeping track steps would tax working memory. Surely such a limited system as working memory would interfere with this type of processing.

An intriguing recent study demonstrates an entirely compatible result, that limited working memory resources compromise the ability to reason and make decisions in difficult situations. The study, by Waltz et al. (1999), tested normal participants, six patients with brain damage in the prefrontal cortex, and five with damage to the anterior temporal lobes. Subjects were given two reasoning tasks. In the first, subjects read transitive inference problems such as "Beth is taller than Tina. Tina is taller than Amy," where anywhere from two to four propositions were included (the "Beth" example has two propositions), and then had to arrange the sentences in order of height (so the

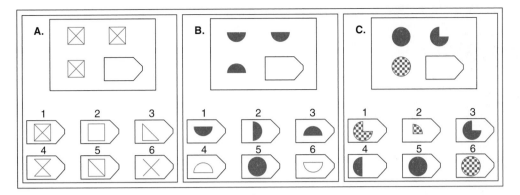

Figure 11-9

Examples of reasoning problems taken from the Raven Standard Progressive Matrices test. The task asks subjects to pick the one correct choice out of six possibilities at the bottom to complete the pattern at the top. **A,** Level 0 problem (nonrelational). **B,** Level 1 problem (one-relation problem). **C,** Level 2 problem (two-relation problem). Correct answers are choice 1 in A, choice 3 in B, and choice 1 in C. *Source.* Figure 2 from Waltz et al. (1999).

"Beth" sentence would be at the top). Problems presented in this order were at Level 1 complexity, and performance was contrasted with Level 2 complexity, in which the propositions were in scrambled order (e.g., for a four-proposition problem, "Beth is taller than Tina. Sally is taller than Laura. Tina is taller than Joyce. Laura is taller than Beth."). The critical difference between conditions was that level 1 problems, because they were in correct transitive order, never required more than one relation ("Beth is taller than Tina") to be held in mind at one time, whereas the level 2 sentences required simultaneous consideration and integration of two relations (and that happened two to four times per trial, depending on how many propositions were shown).

In the other half of the experiment, subjects solved a set of matrix problems from the Raven's Standard Progressive Matrices test (Raven, 1941). Figure 11-9 illustrates three such problems. The problem in Figure 11-9A was a "nonrelational" level 0 problem; the correct answer merely involved finding the matching pattern among the six choices at the bottom. Figure 11-9B shows a one-relation, level 1 problem (technically, the relation is "reflect the pattern across the *x*-axis," that is, flip the pattern from bottom to top; the answer is choice 3), and Figure 11-9C, a two-relation, level 2 problem (the two relations are from solid to checked, and remove the upper-right quarter; the correct answer is choice 1).

Waltz et al.'s results for transitive inference are shown in the left half of Figure 11-10. Normal control subjects (dashed line) showed only a modest decline in the level 2 condition and did only slightly better than the patients with temporal lobe damage (the dotted line). But patients with frontal lobe damage (solid line) dropped from more than 80% correct on level 1 problems to around 20% correct on level 2 problems, seemingly unable to consider and integrate multiple propositions at the same time. And in the right half of the results, it's clear that the frontal lobe patients

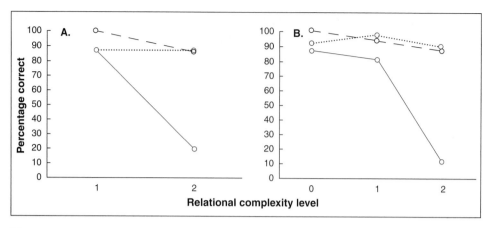

Figure 11-10

Percentage correct in the transitive inference (A) and Raven's Matrices (B) problems, as a function of relational complexity (levels 0, 1, and 2), for normal subjects (dashed lines), temporal lobe patients (dotted lines), and prefrontal lobe patients (solid lines).

were unable to maintain two relational changes at the same time, their performance dropping from about 80% down to around 10% at level 2. The temporal lobe patients were again very close in performance to the normal controls. Despite this very poor performance by the prefrontal patients, their accuracy on memory tests (for instance, "Which of these names did you read about, Amy or Susan?") was very high, about 96% correct, actually about 10% higher than the normal control subjects. Here, consistent with material in Chapter 6, it was the temporal lobe patients whose declarative memory for the tasks was poor; their name recognition performance was at 56%, not appreciably different from chance. Thus declarative memory for the tasks was damaged selectively for the temporal lobe patients, but reasoning performance was selectively damaged for the prefrontal patients.

The results are very compatible with the notion that frontal lobe regions are especially important for reasoning, and in particular for maintaining relational information in working memory while the reasoning task is being performed. The connection between the dorsolateral prefrontal cortex (DLPFC) and executive control in working memory was discussed in Chapter 5. The Waltz et al. results extend that research: "In other words, relational integration may be the 'work' done by working memory. We thus view our results as being consistent with the idea that the DLPFC, which was severely damaged in all our prefrontal patients, is critical for working memory" (1999, p. 123).

■ Section Summary

• In everyday reasoning, we rely on mental models of the device or event to make our judgments. These mental models sometimes are quite inaccurate. In the best-known research, people's mental models of physical motion lead them to incorrect predictions (e.g., the trajectory of a ball dropped from an airplane). Ongoing research is focused on the kinds of limitations that lead to incorrect reasoning and decision making, including limited domain knowledge and limitations in working memory processes.

Key Terms

algorithm (p. 464)
antecedent (p. 447)
availability heuristic (p. 473)
conditional reasoning (p. 447)
confirmation bias (p. 450)
consequent (p. 447)
counterfactual reasoning (p. 476)
distance or discriminability effect (p. 455)

downhill change (p. 476)
familiarity bias (p. 475)
heuristic (p. 464)
hindsight bias (p. 479)
horizontal change (p. 478)
jnd (p. 455)
mental models (p. 452)
naive physics (p. 482)
psychophysics (p. 454)
representativeness heuristic (p. 468)
salience or vividness (p. 475)

semantic congruity effect (p. 456)
simulation heuristic (p. 475)
stereotypes (p. 470)
syllogisms (p. 444)
symbolic comparisons (p. 456)
symbolic distance effect (p. 456)
uphill change (p. 478)

Appendix: Algorithms for Coin Tosses and Hospital Births

Coin Tosses

To begin with the obvious, the probability of a head on one coin toss is .50. Flipping a coin twice and keeping track of the possible sequences yields a .25 probability for each of the four possibilities HH, HT, TH, TT. In general, when the simple event has a probability of .50, the number of possibilities for a sequence of n events is 2 raised to the nth power. Thus the number of distinct sequences for six coin tosses is 2^6, a total of 64 possibilities.

Two of the 64 possibilities are pure sequences, HHHHHH and TTTTTT. Two more are double sequences, HHHTTT and TTTHHH. All the remaining 60 possibilities involve either or both of the following characteristics; more of one outcome (e.g., heads) than the other and at least one alternation between the two outcomes at a position *other than* halfway through the sequence. Thus the probability of a pure sequence is 2/64, as is the probability of a double sequence. Getting any one of the other 60 possibilities has a likelihood of 1/64. But getting a "random-like" outcome, that is, any outcome other than straight or double, has a probability of 60/64.

Hospital Births

Many statistics texts contain tables of the binomial distribution, the best way to understand the hospital births example. Because most of these tables go up only to a sample size of 20, we'll use a revised hospital example, comparing hospitals with three versus

Table 11-A BINOMIAL PROBABILITIES FOR EXACT NUMBER OF RELEVANT OUTCOMES, WHERE THE SIMPLE PROBABILITY OF THE OUTCOME IS .50

$N = 3$		$N = 9$		$N = 15$		$N = 45$	
Exact Number of Relevant Outcomes:							
0	.1250	0	.0020	9	.1527	27	.0488
1	.3750	1	.0176	10	.0916	28	.0314
2	.3750	2	.0703	11	.0417	29	.0184
3	.1250	3	.1641	12	.0139	30	.0098
		4	.2461	13	.0032	31	.0047
		5	.2461	14	.0005	32	.0021
		6	.1641	15	.0000	33	.0008
		7	.0703	etc.		34	.0003
		8	.0176	.		35	.0001
		9	.0020	.		36	.0000
						.	
						.	

nine births per day (note that the 1:3 ratio is the same as the original example, 15:45). The probabilities for the original example are more extreme than these, but they'll be in the same direction.

Just like with coin tosses, we are dealing with an event whose basic probability is .50, the likelihood that a newborn infant is male (ignoring the fact that male births are actually slightly more common than 50%). What is the probability that, in three births, all three will be boys? According to the binomial tables (Table 11-A), this probability is .1250. This is the probability that on any randomly selected day, the three-birth hospital will have all boys, $p = .1250$. Across the 365 days in a year, we expect an average of 45.625 such days (365 × .1250).

The temptation now is to consider the likelihood of exactly three boys in the nine-birth hospital. But this is not the relevant comparison. The relevant comparison to the all-boys probability in the three-birth hospital would be all-boys in the nine-birth hospital. This puts the comparison on the same footing as the original problem, 60% as the "extreme" cutoff.

The probability of exactly nine boys out of nine births is .0020, two chances in a thousand. For a whole year, we expect only 0.73 such days (365 × .0020). Now it should be clearer. The criterion of "extreme," all boys, is much more likely in the smaller sample than in the larger one, $p = .1250$ versus .0020. Multiplied out, the prediction is 45 days for the small hospital and .70 days for the large one.

By extension, and using the appropriate binomial values, the 15-birth hospital should have about 111 days per year with 60% or more boys, contrasted with 42 such days per year for the 45-birth hospital.

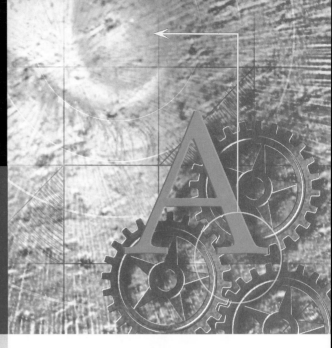

CHAPTER 12

Problem Solving

It seems that all cognitive activities are fundamentally problem solving in nature. The basic argument . . . is that human cognition is always purposeful, directed to achieving goals and to removing obstacles to those goals. (Anderson, 1985, pp. 199–200)

The Newell and Simon approach to problem-solving did not produce a flurry of related experiments by other cognitive psychologists, and problem solving never became a central research area in information-processing cognition. . . . Newell and Simon's conceptual work, however, formed a cornerstone of the information-processing approach. (Lachman et al., 1979, p. 99)

My favorite example of "problem solving in action" is the following true story. When I was a graduate student, I attended a departmental colloquium at which a candidate for a faculty position was to present his research. As he started his talk, he realized that his first slide was projected too low on the screen. A flurry of activity around the projector ensued, one professor asking out loud, "Does anyone have a book or something?" Someone volunteered a book, the professor tried it, but it was too thick; the slide image was now too high. "No, this one's too big. Anyone got a thinner one?" he continued. After several more seconds of hurried searching for something thinner, another professor finally exclaimed, "Well, for Pete's sake, I don't believe this!" He marched over to the projector, grabbed the book, opened it halfway, and then put it under the projector. He looked around the lecture hall and shook his head, saying, "I can't believe it. A roomful of Ph.D.s, and no one knows how to open a book!"

This chapter examines the slow and deliberate cognitive processing called problem solving. Just as in the area of decision making and reasoning, problem solving studies a person who is confronted with a difficult, time-consuming task: A problem has been presented to the person, the solution to the problem is not immediately obvious, and the person often is uncertain what to do next. We are interested in all aspects of the person's activities, from initial understanding of the problem, the steps that lead to a final solution, and, in some cases, the way a person decides that a problem has finally been solved. Our interest in these questions needs no further justification or explanation than this: We confront countless problems in our daily lives, problems that are important for us to figure out and solve. We rely on our wits in these situations. We attempt to solve the problem by mentally analyzing the situation, devising a plan of action, then carrying out that plan. Therefore, the mental processing involved in problem solving is, by definition, part of cognitive psychology.

Let's start with a simple "recreational" problem (Anderson, 1993). It will take you a minute or two at most to solve the problem, even if you lose patience with brain teasers very quickly; VanLehn's (1989) 9-year-old subject seemed to understand it completely in about 20 seconds and solved it out loud in about 2 minutes.

> Three men want to cross a river. They find a boat, but it is a very small boat. It will only hold 200 pounds. The men are named Large, Medium, and Small. Large weighs 200 pounds, Medium weighs 120 pounds, and Small weighs 80 pounds. How can they all get across? They might have to make several trips in the boat. (VanLehn, 1989, p. 532)

Why should we be interested in such recreational problems? The answer is very straightforward. As is typical of all scientific disciplines, cognitive science studies the simple before the complex, searches simpler settings to find basic principles that generalize to more difficult settings. After all, not all the everyday problems we confront are tremendously complex; figuring out how to prop up a slide projector is not of earth-shaking significance (well, it probably was to the fellow interviewing for the job). In either case, the reasoning is that we can often see large-scale issues and important processes more clearly when they are embedded in simple situations. Indeed, one aspect of problem solving you'll read about, functional fixedness, provides an exact account of why a roomful of Ph.D.s didn't think about opening the book to make it thinner. Needless to say, functional fixedness was discovered with a simple, recreational problem.

The Status of the Problem-Solving Area

Some view problem solving as an odd topic in cognitive psychology. In Bruner's view, problem solving was an obviously important goal to be pursued by psychology, one of the many that had been excluded by the behaviorist tradition. Because the overriding concern during the birth of cognitive psychology in the 1950s was to reintroduce the significant mental activities that had been ignored by behaviorism, Bruner's remarks about problem solving fell on receptive ears.

And yet, in the view of Lachman et al., the early research in problem solving, exemplified by Newell and Simon's work on chess, cryptarithmetic problems, and logic theorems, did not spawn the same kind of research tradition in cognitive psychology as, say, Tulving's work on retrieval cues or Collins and Quillian's work on semantic memory. A major reason—possibly *the* reason—for this was methodological. That is, Newell and Simon (1972) pointed out that studying significant problem solving requires us to examine a lengthy sample of behavior, often up to 20 or 30 min of activity. This means that the typical measures of RT and accuracy are irrelevant to experiments on problem solving. Instead, the major kind of data in problem solving is the **verbal protocol,** the *transcription and analysis of the subjects' verbalizations as they solve the problem.*

Without a doubt, the use of verbal protocols influenced many researchers' opinions about problem solving, especially given the similarities between verbal protocols and the discredited method of introspectionism. In fact, the status of verbal reports as data is still a topic of some debate; see Ericsson and Simon (1980, 1993) and Russo, Johnson, and Stephens (1989) for contrasting views. This aspect of problem-solving research, along with issues of experimental design, control of variables, and so on, placed problem solving outside the strict information-processing tradition of stage models, flowcharts, and the like. The irony here, of course, is that Newell and Simon's conceptual approach—that humans can be conceived of as processors of information—was the very foundation of the information-processing approach. (See Lachman et al., 1979, Chapter 4, for a full account of these influences.)

There are still lingering signs of the division between the information processors and the problem solvers in contemporary cognitive psychology, to be sure. But in most respects, the division has either broken down or become irrelevant. Each group has made discoveries that have been important for the other tradition. For instance, the notion of heuristics, originally derived from problem solving, is applicable and important to a thorough understanding of reasoning, as you read in Chapter 11. Likewise, theories of language comprehension are critical to an understanding of some important problem-solving activities (Kintsch & Greeno, 1985). Thus problem solving deserves as prominent a place in mainstream cognitive psychology as any topic you've studied so far.

Let's begin with a description of the classic problem-solving research of the Gestalt psychologists during the period 1920–1950. As you read in Chapter 1, the Gestalt movement coexisted with behaviorism early in this century but never achieved the central status that behaviorism did. In retrospect, however, it was an important influence on cognitive psychology, particularly with respect to problem solving.

Possibly more than in any material you've read so far, it's important for you to spend time working through the examples and problems. Hints usually accompany the problems, and the solutions to all problems are presented in the text or, for numbered problems, at the end of the chapter. Many of the insights of the problem-solving literature pertain to conscious, strategic activities you'll discover on your own as you work through the sample problems. Furthermore, simply by working the examples you'll probably improve your own problem-solving skills; to paraphrase Bruner (1973), no one ever gets better at problem solving without solving problems.

Gestalt Psychology and Problem Solving

Gestalt is a German word that translates very poorly into English: The one-word translations "whole" or "field" fail miserably at indicating what the term actually means. Roughly speaking, a **Gestalt** is a *whole pattern, a form, or a configuration*. It is a cohesive grouping, a perspective from which the entire field can be seen. A variety of translations have been used at one point or another (*holism* is probably the best of them; note, however, that holistic psychology, whatever that is, is certainly not the same as Gestalt psychology). No single translation of the word ever caught on, however, which prompted Boring (1950) to remark that Gestalt psychology "suffered from its name." Consequently, we use the German term *Gestalt* itself, rather than some inadequate translation. Figure 12-1 shows several patterns that demonstrate various Gestalt principles (e.g., closure, good continuation). They demonstrated (to the Gestalters, anyway) that

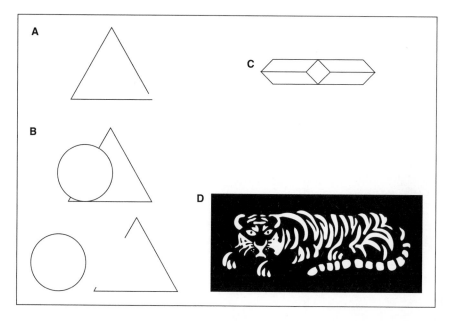

Figure 12-1

Several figures that illustrate various Gestalt principles of perception. **A,** We perceive the figure as a triangle, despite the missing segment. **B,** We tend to "see" a triangle partially blocked by a sphere; as the second version shows, the two parts can be separated to show how the lines may not continue. **C,** We generally do not see a two-dimensional pattern; instead, we tend to see an optical illusion, a three-dimensional figure that switches orientation. **D,** We "see" a complete pattern because the Gestalt principle of closure. (Part D from Matlin, 1983.)

humans tend to perceive and therefore deal with integrated, cohesive wholes. As Boring (1950) describes it, "The most concise way to characterize *Gestalt* psychology is to say that it deals with *wholes*. . . . In perceiving a melody you get the melodic form, not a string of notes, a unitary whole that is something more than the total list of its parts or even the serial pattern of them. That is the way experience comes to man, put up in significant structured forms, *Gestalten*" (p. 588). Thus it was the Gestalt psychology movement that advanced the notion that "the whole is different from or greater than the sum of its individual parts."

Early Gestalt Research

The connection between the term *Gestalt* and interest in problem solving is best explained by anecdote (see Boring, 1950, pp. 595–597). In 1913, Wolfgang Kohler, a German psychologist, went to the Spanish island of Tenerife to study "the psychology of anthropoid apes" (Boring, 1950, p. 596). Trapped there by the outbreak of World War I, Kohler experimented with visual discrimination among several animal species. In the course of this research, he began to apply Gestalt principles to animal perception. His

Grande builds a three-box structure to reach the bananas, while Sultan watches from the ground. *Insight,* sometimes referred to as an "Ah-ha" experience, was the term Kohler used for the sudden perception of useful relations among objects during problem solving.

ultimate conclusion was that animals do not perceive individual elements in a stimulus, but that they perceive relations among stimuli. Furthermore, "Kohler also observed that the perception of relations is a mark of intelligence, and he called the sudden perception of useful or proper relations *insight*" (Boring, 1950, p. 596).

Still stranded on the island, Kohler continued to examine "insight learning." He presented problems to his subjects and searched for evidence of genuine problem solving in their behavior. By far the most famous of his subjects was a chimpanzee named Sultan (Kohler, 1927). In a simple demonstration, Sultan was able to use a long pole to reach through the bars of his cage and get a bunch of bananas. Kohler made the situation more difficult by giving Sultan two shorter poles, neither of which was long enough to reach the bananas. After failing to get the bananas and sulking in his cage for a while, Sultan (as the story goes) suddenly went over to the poles and put one inside the end of the other, thus creating one pole that was long enough to reach the bananas.

Kohler found this to be an apt demonstration of insight, a sudden solution to a problem by means of an insightful discovery. In another situation, Sultan discovered how to stand on a box to reach a banana that was otherwise too high to reach. In yet another, he discovered how to get a banana that was just out of reach through the cage bars: He walked *away* from the banana, out a distant door, and around the cage. All these problem solutions seemed to illustrate Sultan's perception of relations and the importance of insight in problem solving.

Difficulties in Problem Solving

Other Gestalt psychologists, most notably Duncker and Luchins, pursued the research tradition with human subjects. Two major contributions of this later work are generally acknowledged, essentially the two sides of the problem-solving coin. One involved a set of negative effects related to rigidity or difficulty in problem solving, the other insight and creativity during problem solving.

Functional Fixedness Two articles on functional fixedness, one by Maier (1931) and one by Duncker (1945), identify and define this particular difficulty that arises during problem solving. **Functional fixedness** is *a tendency to use objects and concepts in the problem environment in only their customary and usual way.* Maier (1931), for instance, had subjects work on the two-string problem. Two strings are suspended from the ceiling, and the goal is to tie them together. The problem is that the strings are too far apart for a person merely to hold one, reach the other, then tie them together. Available to the subject are several other objects, including a chair, some paper, and a pair of pliers. Even standing on the chair does not get the subject close enough to the two strings.

In Maier's results, only 39% of the subjects came up with the correct solution during a 10-minute period. The solution (if you haven't tried solving the problem, do so now) involves using an object in the room in a novel fashion. The correct solution is to tie the pliers to one string, swing it like a pendulum, then catch it while holding the other string. Thus the functional fixedness in this situation was failing to conceive of the pliers in any but their customary function; subjects were fixed on the normal use for pliers and failed to appreciate how they could be used as a weight for a pendulum.

A similar demonstration is illustrated in Figure 12-2, the candle problem from Duncker (1945). The task is to find a way to mount the candle on a door or wall, using just the objects illustrated. Can you solve the problem? If you haven't come up with a solution after a minute or two, here's a hint: Can you think of another use for a box besides using it as a container? In other words, the notion of functional fixedness is that we generally think only of the customary uses for objects, whereas successful problem solving often involves finding novel uses for objects. By conceiving of the box as a platform or means of support, you can then solve the problem (empty the box, thumbtack it to the door or wall, then mount the candle in it).

It's probably not surprising that problem solvers experience functional fixedness. After all, we comprehend the problem situation by means of our general world knowledge, along with whatever procedural knowledge we have that might be relevant to the situation. When you find "PLIERS" in semantic memory, surely the most accessible properties involve the normal use for pliers. Far down on your list would be characteristics related

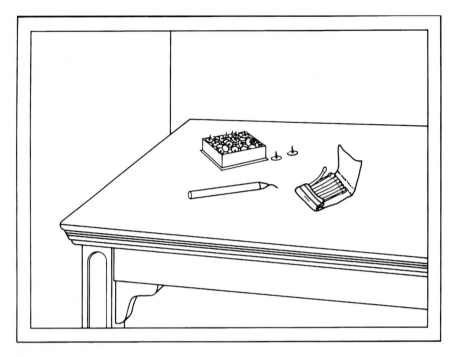

Figure 12-2

The candle problem used by Duncker. Using only the pictured objects, figure out how to mount the candle to the wall.

to the weight of the pliers or aspects of their shape that would enable you to tie a string to them. Likewise, "BOX" probably is stored in semantic memory in terms of "container" meanings—that a box can hold things, that you put things into a box—and not in terms of "platform or support" meanings (see Greenspan, 1986, for evidence on retrieval of central and peripheral properties). Simply from the standpoint of routine retrieval from memory, then, we can understand why people often experience functional fixedness.

Negative Set A related difficulty in problem solving is called **negative set** (or simply *set effects*). This refers to *a bias or tendency to solve problems in one particular way, using a single specific approach, even when a different approach might be more productive*. The term *set* is a rough translation of the original German term *Einstellung*, which means something like "approach" or "orientation"; the (awful) phrase "mind set" probably is the closest expression we have to the term in English.

The classic demonstration of set effects comes from the water jug problems, studied by Luchins (1942). In these problems, you are given three jugs, each of a different capacity, and are asked to measure out a desired quantity of water using just the three jugs. As a simple illustration, consider the first problem in Table 12-1. You need to measure out 28 cups of water and can use containers that hold 5, 40, and 18 cups (jugs A, B, and C). The solution is to fill A twice, then fill C once, each time pouring the contents

Table 12-1 WATERJUG PROBLEMS

Problem	Capacity of Jug A	Capacity of Jug B	Capacity of Jug C	Desired Quantity
1	5 cups	40 cups	18 cups	28 cups
2	21 cups	127 cups	3 cups	100 cups

Luchins's Water Jug Problems

Problem	Capacity of Jug A	Capacity of Jug B	Capacity of Jug C	Desired Quantity
1	21	127	3	100
2	14	163	25	99
3	18	43	10	5
4	9	42	6	21
5	20	59	4	31
6	23	49	3	20
7	15	39	3	18
8	28	76	3	25
9	18	48	4	22
10	14	36	8	6

Note. All volumes are in cups.

into a destination jug. This approach is an addition solution because you add the quantities together. For the second problem, a subtraction solution is appropriate, fill B (127), subtract jug C from it twice (−3, −3), then subtract jug A (−21), yielding 100.

Luchins's (1942) demonstration of negative set involved sequencing the problems so that subjects developed a particular set or approach for measuring out the quantities. The second group of problems in Table 12-1 illustrates such a sequence. Go ahead and work the problems now before you read any further.

If you were like most subjects, your experience on problems 1 through 7 led you to develop a particular approach or set: specifically, B − 2C − A: Fill jug B, subtract C from it twice, then subtract A from it to yield the necessary amount (subtracting A can be done before subtracting 2C, of course). Subjects with such a set or *Einstellung* generally failed to notice the far simpler solution possible for problems 6 and 10, simply A − C. That is, about 80% of the subjects who saw all 10 problems used the lengthy B − 2C − A method for these problems. Compare this with the control subjects, who saw only problems 6 through 10: Only 1% of these subjects used the longer method. Clearly, the control subjects had not developed a set for using the lengthy method, so they were much more able to find the simpler solution.

Consider problem 8 now. Only 5% of Luchins's control subjects failed to solve problem 8. This was a remarkable result because 64% of the "negative set" subjects, those who saw all 10 problems, failed to solve it correctly. These subjects had such an orientation toward the method they had already developed that they were surprisingly unable to generate a method that would work on problem 8 (B − 2C − A does not work on this problem). Greeno's (1978) description here is very useful: By repeatedly solving the first seven problems with the same formula, subjects learned an integrated

Table 12-2 SAMPLE NEGATIVE SET PROBLEMS
Buddhist Monk
One morning, exactly at sunrise, a Buddhist monk began to climb a tall mountain. The narrow path, no more than a foot or two wide, spiraled around the mountain to a glittering temple at the summit. The monk ascended the path at varying rates of speed, stopping many times along the way to rest and to eat the dried fruit he carried with him. He reached the temple shortly before sunset. After several days of fasting and meditation, he began his journey back along the same path, starting at sunrise and again walking at variable speeds with many pauses along the way. His average descending speed was, of course, greater than his average climbing speed. Show that there is a spot along the path that the monk will occupy on both trips at precisely the same time of day.
Drinking Glasses
Six drinking glasses are lined up in a row. The first three are full of water, the last three are empty. By handling and moving only one glass, change the arrangement so that no full glass is next to another full one, and no empty glass is next to another empty one.
Six Pennies
Show how to move only two pennies in the left diagram to yield the pattern at the right.

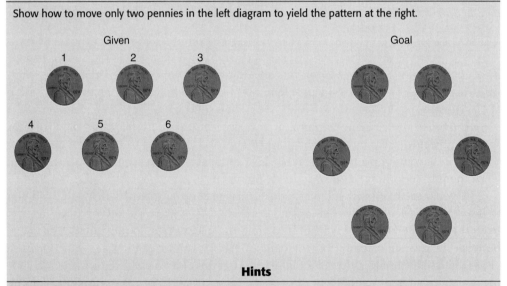

Given

1   2   3

4   5   6

Goal

Hints
Buddhist monk. Although the problem seems to ask for a quantitative solution, think of a way of representing the problem using visual imagery. *Drinking glasses.* How else can you handle a glass of water besides moving it to another location? *Six pennies.* From a different perspective, some of the pennies might already be in position.

algorithm. This algorithm was strong enough to bias their later solution attempts and prevent them from seeing the simple solution, $28 - 3 = 25$.

Several problems that often yield such negative set effects are presented in Table 12-2; hints to help overcome negative set, if you experience it, are at the bottom of the table. These problems lack the precision of Luchins's demonstration, of course: We cannot point to the exact equation or method that is the negative set in these problems but only to the general approach or incorrect representation people often adopt. On the other hand, the problems are useful in that they seem to resemble real-world problems much more closely than the rather arbitrary water jugs do.

As the slide projector problem in the introduction suggests, functional fixedness and negative set probably are very common everyday occurrences. Possibly because we eventually find an adequate solution to our everyday problems despite the negative set or without overcoming our functional fixedness (e.g., eventually locating a thinner book), we are less aware of these set and functional fixedness difficulties in our problem-solving behavior. The classic demonstrations however, illustrate dramatically how rigid such behavior can be, and how barriers to successful problem solving can arise.

■ Section Summary

- Newell and Simon's insights on the role of computer simulation in an understanding of human information processing were central to the development of cognitive psychology in the late 1950s. Their research methods were different from those developed in verbal learning, so the area of problem solving has only recently become a mainstream topic within cognitive psychology.
- The early Gestalt psychologists studied problem solving and discovered two major barriers to successful performance: functional fixedness and negative set.

Insight and Analogy

Insight

On the more positive side of problem solving are the topics of insight and problem solving by analogy. **Insight** usually is thought of as *a deep, useful understanding of the nature of something, especially a difficult problem.* We often include in this idea that the insight occurs suddenly—the "aha!" reaction—possibly because a novel approach to the problem has been taken or a novel interpretation of the problem has been made (Sternberg, 1996). Puzzle over the insight problems in Table 12-3 for a moment to see whether you have a sudden "Aha" experience when you realize how to solve the problems.

Sometimes, the necessary insight for solving a problem comes from an analogy: An already-solved problem is similar to a current one, so the old solution can be adapted to the new situation. The standard historical example of this is the story of Archimedes, the Greek scientist who had to determine whether the king's crown was solid gold or some silver had been mixed with the gold. Archimedes knew the weights of both gold and silver per unit of volume but could not imagine how to measure the volume of the crown. As the anecdote goes, he stepped into his bath one day, and noticed how the water level rose as he sank into the water. He then realized the solution to his problem. The volume of the crown could be determined by immersing it in water and measuring how much water it displaced. Excited by his insight, he then jumped from the bath and ran naked through the streets, shouting "Eureka! I have found it!" (Etymologically, the

Table 12-3 INSIGHT PROBLEMS

Chain Links

A woman has four pieces of chain. Each piece is made up of three links. She wants to join the pieces into a single closed ring of chain. To open a link costs 2 cents and to close a link costs 3 cents. She has only 15 cents. How does she do it?

Four Trees

A landscape gardener is given instructions to plant four special trees so that each one is exactly the same distance from each of the others. How would you arrange the trees?

Prisoner's Escape

A prisoner was attempting to escape from a tower. He found in his cell a rope which was half long enough to permit him to reach the ground safely. He divided the rope in half and tied the two parts together and escaped. How could he have done this?

Bronze Coin

A stranger approached a museum curator and offered him an ancient bronze coin. The coin had an authentic appearance and was marked with the date 544 B.C. The curator had happily made acquisitions from suspicious sources before, but this time he promptly called the police and had the stranger arrested. Why?

Nine Dots

Connect the nine dots with four connected straight lines without lifting your pencil from the page as you draw.

Bowling Pins

The ten bowling pins below are pointing toward the top of the page. Move any three of them to make the arrangement point down toward the bottom of the page.

Table 12-3 (Continued)

Hints

Chain links. You don't have to open a link on each piece of chain.
Four trees. We don't always plant trees on flat lawns.
Prisoner's escape. Is there only one way to divide a rope in half?
Bronze coin. Imagine that you lived in 544 B.C. What did it say on your coins?
Nine dots. How long a line does the problem permit you to draw?
Bowling pins. Pins 1, 2, 3, and 5 form a diamond at the top of the drawing. Consider where the diamond might be for the arrangement that points down.

Source. Adapted from Metcalfe (1986); Metcalfe and Wiebe (1987).

"I heard von Schleflin yell 'Eureka,' and then kerblam!"

Drawing by Stevenson © 1974 The New Yorker Magazine, Inc.

words *eureka* and *heuristic* come from the same Greek words, *heureka*, meaning "I have found it," and *heuriskein*, meaning "to find.")

Metcalfe and Wiebe (1987; also Metcalfe, 1986) studied how people solved such problems and compared that with how they solved algebra and other routine problems. They found two especially interesting results. First, people were rather accurate in predicting whether they'd be successful in solving routine problems but not accurate at all in predicting success with the insight problems. Second, solutions to the insight problems seemed to come suddenly, almost without warning. This second result is shown in Figure 12-3. That is, as they worked through the problems, the

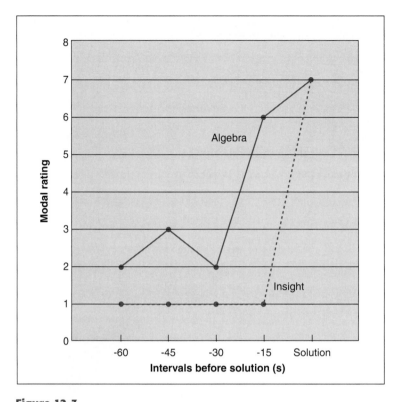

Figure 12-3

Modal (most frequent) warmth rating in the four time periods leading up to a problem solution. *Source.* Data from Metcalfe and Wiebe (1987).

participants were interrupted and asked to indicate how "warm" they were, that is, how close they felt to finding the solution. For routine algebra problems, the "warmth" ratings grew steadily as the participants worked through the problems, reflecting their feeling of getting closer and closer to the solution. But there was little or no such increase for the insight problems even a mere 15 s before the solution was found.

Although these results lend a degree of support to the notion that insight arrives suddenly, some people remain unconvinced that true insight really exists or that it is critical to problem solving. Some have noted that classic insight problems can often be thought of in simpler terms, say overcoming functional fixedness or negative set (as in prisoner's escape and nine-dot), taking a different perspective (bronze coin), and the like (Smith, 1995). In some circumstances, *insight* may simply mean that we've drawn a critical inference that leads to a solution; for example, there's more than one way to divide a rope in half (Wickelgren, 1974). Weisberg (1995) reports that some people solve so-called insight problems like those in the table without any of the sudden restructuring or understanding that supposedly accompanies insight.

Other evidence, however, suggests that verbalization during problem solving can interfere with insight, can disrupt "nonreportable processes that are critical to achieving insight solutions" (Schooler, Ohlsson, & Brooks, 1993, p. 166). Furthermore, being unable to report the restructuring that accompanies insight, or the actual insight itself, may be more common in insight situations than we realize. For instance, Siegler and Stern (1998; see also Siegler, 2000) recently reported a study of second graders solving arithmetic problems then reporting verbally on their solutions. There was the regular computational, non-insightful way to solve the problems, which the second graders followed, but also a shortcut way that represented an insight (e.g., for a problem like $18 + 24 - 24$, simply state 18). Almost 90% of the sample discovered the insight for solving such problems, as shown by the dramatic decrease in their solution times from around 12 s for the computational method to a mean of 2.7 s with the shortcut. But they were unaware of their discovery when questioned about how they solved the problems. Within another five trials, however, 80% of the children's verbal reports indicated that they had become aware of their discovery. Siegler suggests that, at least for children, insights can "arise first at an unconscious level, and only later become conscious" (2000, p. 79). Although the results did not speak directly to adult's insights, consider Siegler's thought-provoking conclusion: "Having a thought, or even an insight, is not the same as being aware of having that thought or insight. Learning how consciousness is related to insight remains one of the basic challenges in understanding human psychology, just as it was in the days of Archimedes" (2000, p. 82; see Nelson, 1996, for a thoughtful article on consciousness and metacognition).

Analogy

In general, an **analogy** is a *relationship between two similar situations, problems, or concepts.* Understanding an analogy means putting the two situations into some kind of alignment or relationship so that the similarities and differences can be seen (Gentner & Markman, 1997). Take a simple example, the analogy "MERCHANT : SELL :: CUSTOMER : _____." Here, you must figure out or induce the structure (Greeno, 1978) for the first pair of terms and then project or *map* that structure onto the second part of the analogy. Because "SELL" is the critical activity of "MERCHANT," the critical activity relationship is then mapped onto "CUSTOMER," and retrieval from memory yields "BUY."

Several authors argue strongly that analogies provide excellent, widely applicable methods for solving problems. That is, if you're confronted with a difficult problem, a useful heuristic is to find a similar or related situation and build an analogy from it to the current problem. According to these authors, such reasoning and problem solving may help us understand a huge variety of situations, such as how students should be taught in school, how people adopt professional role models, and how we empathize with others (Holyoak & Thagard, 1997; Kolodner, 1997). And it's long been held that important scientific ideas, breakthroughs, and explanations have often depended on finding analogies, for instance that neurotransmitters fit into the receptor sites of a neuron much the way a key fits into a lock (see Gentner & Markman, 1997, for a compelling description of reasoning by analogy in Kepler's discovery of the laws of planetary motion).

Table 12-4 THE PARADE PROBLEM

A small country was controlled by a dictator. The dictator ruled the country from a strong fortress. The fortress was situated in the middle of the country, surrounded by farms and villages. Many roads radiated outward from the fortress like spokes on a wheel. To celebrate the anniversary of his rise to power, the dictator ordered his general to conduct a full-scale military parade. On the morning of the anniversary, the general's troops were gathered at the head of one of the roads leading to the fortress, ready to march. However, a lieutenant brought the general a disturbing report. The dictator was demanding that this parade had to be more impressive than any previous parade. He wanted his army to be seen and heard at the same time in every region of the country. Furthermore, the dictator was threatening that if the parade was not sufficiently impressive he was going to strip the general of his medals and reduce him to the rank of private. But it seemed impossible to have a parade that could be seen throughout the whole country.

The Solution

The general, however, knew just what to do. He divided his army up into small groups and dispatched each group to the head of a different road. When all was ready he gave the signal, and each group marched down a different road. Each group continued down its road to the fortress, so that the entire army finally arrived together at the fortress at the same time. In this way, the general was able to have the parade seen and heard through the entire country at once, and thus please the dictator.

Analogy Problems To gain some feeling for analogies, read the parade story at the top of Table 12-4, a story used by Gick and Holyoak (1980) in an important study of problem solving. Try to solve the problem now, before reading the solution at the bottom of the table.

Gick and Holyoak had their participants read either the parade problem, a somewhat different army fortress story, or no story at all. They then asked them to read and solve a second problem, the classic Duncker (1945) radiation problem, shown in Table 12-5 (which you should read and try to solve now).

The radiation problem is interesting to study for a variety of reasons, including the fact that it is rather ill defined and thus comparable to many problems in the real world. Duncker's participants produced two general approaches that led to dead ends: Trying to avoid contact between the ray and nearby tissue and trying to change the sensitivity of surrounding tissue to the effects of the ray. But the third approach, reducing the intensity of the rays, was more productive, especially if an analogy from some other, better understood situation was available.

Gick and Holyoak (1980) used this problem to study problem solving by analogy. In fact, we've just simulated one of their experiments here by having you read the parade story first and then the radiation problem. In case you didn't notice, there are strong similarities between the problems, suggesting that the parade story can be used to develop an analogy for the radiation problem.

Gick and Holyoak found that only 49% of the participants who first solved the parade problem realized it could be used as an analogy for the radiation problem. A different initial story, in which armies are attacking a fortress, provided a stronger hint about the radiation problem. Fully 76% of these participants used the attack analogy in solving the radiation problem. In contrast, only 8% of the control group, which merely

Table 12-5   RADIATION AND ATTACK DISPERSION PROBLEMS

Radiation Problem

Suppose you are a doctor faced with a patient who has a malignant tumor in his stomach. It is impossible to operate on the patient, but unless the tumor is destroyed the patient will die. There is a kind of ray that can be used to destroy the tumor. If the rays reach the tumor all at once at a sufficiently high intensity, the tumor will be destroyed. Unfortunately, at this intensity the healthy tissue that the rays pass through on the way to the tumor will also be destroyed. At lower intensities the rays are harmless to healthy tissue, but they will not affect the tumor either. What type of procedure might be used to destroy the tumor with the rays without destroying the healthy tissue?

Attack Dispersion Story

A small country was controlled by a dictator. The dictator ruled the country from a strong fortress. The fortress was situated in the middle of the country, surrounded by farms and villages. Many roads radiated outward from the fortress like spokes on a wheel. A general arose who raised a large army and vowed to capture the fortress and free the country of the dictator. The general knew that if his entire army could attack the fortress at once it could be captured. The general's troops were gathered at the head of one of the roads leading to the fortress, ready to attack. However, a spy brought the general a disturbing report. The ruthless dictator had planted mines on each of the roads. The mines were set so that small bodies of men could pass over them safely because the dictator needed to be able to move troops and workers to and from the fortress. However, any large force would detonate the mines. Not only would this blow up the road and render it impassable, but the dictator would then destroy many villages in retaliation. It therefore seemed impossible to mount a full-scale direct attack on the fortress.

Solution to the Radiation Problem

The ray can be divided into several low-intensity rays, no one of which will destroy the healthy tissue. If these several rays are positioned at different locations around the body and focused on the tumor, their effect will combine, thus being strong enough to destroy the tumor.

Solution to the Attack Dispersion Story

The general, however, knew just what to do. He divided his army up into small groups and dispatched each group to the head of a different road. When all was ready he gave the signal, and each group marched down a different road. Each group continued down its road to the fortress, so that the entire army finally arrived together at the fortress at the same time. In this way, the general was able to capture the fortress and thus overthrow the dictator.

---

attempted to solve the radiation problem, came up with the dispersion solution (i.e., multiple pathways) described at the bottom of Table 12-5.

When Gick and Holyoak provided a strong hint to their subjects, telling them that the attack solution might be helpful as they worked on the radiation problem, 92% of them used the analogy to solve the radiation problem, and most found it "very helpful." In dramatic contrast, only 20% of the people in the no-hint group produced the dispersion solution, even though they too had read the attack dispersion story. In short, only 20% spontaneously noticed and used the analogous relationship between the problems. Table 12-6 summarizes Gick and Holyoak's results.

Multiconstraint Theory   Holyoak and Thagard (1997) proposed an overall theory of analogical reasoning and problem solving, based on such results. The theory, called the multiconstraint theory, predicts how people use analogies in problem solving and what

Table 12-6 SUMMARY OF GICK AND HOLYOAK'S (1980) RESULTS

Study 1 (Experiment II originally; after Gick & Holyoak, Table 10)

Subjects in groups A and B are given a general hint that their solution to one of the earlier stories may be useful in solving the radiation problem.

Group	Order of Stories	Percentage of Subjects Who Used the Analogy on the Radiation Problem
Group A	Parade, radiation	49%
Group B	Attack dispersion, radiation	76%
Group C	No story, radiation	8%

Study 2 (Experiment IV originally)

Subjects in group A are given the general hint (as above). Subjects in group B are given no hint whatsoever.

Group	Order of Stories	Percentage of Subjects Who Used the Analogy on the Radiation Problem
Group A (hint)	Attack dispersion, radiation	92%
Group B (no hint)	Attack dispersion, radiation	20%

factors govern the analogies people construct. In particular, the theory says that people are constrained by three factors when they try to use or develop analogies.

The first factor is problem similarity. There must be a reasonable degree of similarity between the already-understood situation, the *source* domain, and the current problem being solved, the *target* domain. In the parade story, for example, the fortress and troops can be seen as similar to the tumor and the rays. Similarity between source and target has been shown to be important in several other studies. For instance, Novick (1988) found that novices focus especially on similarities, even when they are only superficial and thus end up interfering with performance.

The second factor is problem structure. People must establish a parallel structure between the source and target problems so they can map elements from the source to comparable elements in the target. Figuring out these one-to-one correspondences or mappings is especially important in Holyoak and Thagard's view because it corresponds to working out the exact relationships that the analogy depends on. In the parade–radiation analogy, you have to map troops on to rays so that the important relationship of different converging roads can serve as the basis for the solution. The most prominent mappings from parade to radiation are shown in Figure 12-4. In a clever investigation of this, Spellman and Holyoak (1992) analyzed analogical mapping in people's reasoning about the 1991 Persian Gulf War (i.e., "If Saddam is Hitler then who is George Bush?").

Third is the purpose of the analogy. The problem solver's goals, and the goal stated in the problem, are an important constraint in solving by analogy. This is deeper than merely the general purpose of trying to solve the problem, of course. Notice that the goals in the attack and radiation stories match, whereas the goals do not match for

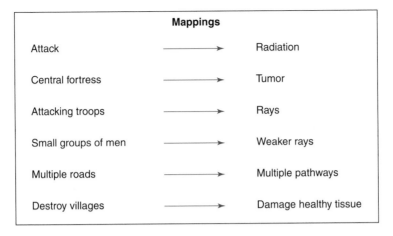

Figure 12-4

Prominent mappings between the attack and radiation problems.

parade and radiation (parade involves sending troops *out* from the central fortress, for display purposes, but radiation involves sending rays *in* toward the tumor). This mismatch may have been responsible for the low use of parade as a source for the analogy to radiation. Likewise, Spellman and Holyoak (1996) report a study in which college students drew analogies between two soap opera plots. When different purposes or goals were given in the instructions, the students developed different analogies; that is, their problem solving by analogy was sensitive to purposes and overall goals.

Neurocognition in Analogy and Insight

Some very recent, exciting work has been reported on the cognitive neuropsychology of analogical reasoning and insight. In an impressive report, Wharton et al. (2000) identified brain regions that seem particularly associated with the mapping process in analogical reasoning. In their study, subjects saw a source picture of geometric shapes, followed by a target picture. They had to judge whether the target picture was an analog pattern—whether it had the same system of relations as the source picture. In the control condition, they judged whether the target was literally the same as the source. See Figure 12-5 for sample stimuli. In the top stimulus, the correct target preserves both the spatial relations in the source (a shape in all four quadrants) and the object relations (the patterned figures on the main diagonal are the same shape, and the shapes on the minor diagonal are different). Reaction times to analogy trials were in the 1,400- to 1,500-msec range and approximately 900–1,000 msec in the literal condition; accuracy was at or above 90% in both kinds of trials.

But the stunning result came from positron emission tomography (PET) scan images taken during the trials. In particular, Wharton et al. found significant activation in the medial frontal cortex, left prefrontal cortex, and left inferior parietal cortex; these

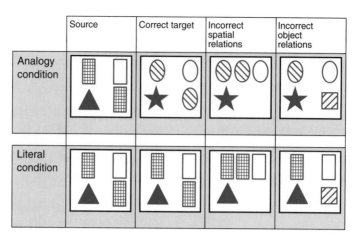

Figure 12-5

A depiction of analogy condition and literal condition trials. The first column shows the source stimuli, the second shows the correct choice, and the third and fourth show incorrect choices for the stated reasons. *Source.* Wharton et al. (2000), Figure 2, p. 179.

patterns are shown in the final picture on the color plate page. The coronal and transverse views show the smallish medial region of the frontal lobe and the widespread left hemisphere activation very clearly. And the sagittal view shows the large involvement of the parietal region especially clearly. (The coronal view is a vertical slice, as if from ear to ear, viewed from the front; transverse is a view looking down from the top; sagittal is a side view, with the front of the brain shown on the left.)

In contrast, Bowden and Beeman (1998) found a significant role for *right* hemisphere processing in solving insight problems. Subjects were given three words on a trial, such as *pie, luck,* and *belly,* and had to think of a fourth word that combines with each of the three initial words to yield a familiar word pair. After 15 s, they saw a target word and simply had to name it out loud. When the target word was unrelated to the three words seen before (e.g., "school"), there was only the typical effect, that targets presented to the right visual field–left hemisphere of the brain were named faster than those presented to the left visual field–right hemisphere. But when the target was the word that solved the insight problem (*pot*, in this case), there was a significant semantic priming effect. As shown in Figure 12-6, naming time was significantly shorter for the solution words than for the unrelated words. And the priming effect—the drop-off from "unrelated" to "solution"—was greater for targets presented to the right hemisphere than to the left. In other words, semantic priming in the right hemisphere was more prominent than in the left hemisphere for these problems: Subjects were faster to name *pot* when it was presented to the right hemisphere, presumably because it had been primed by the initial three words. As the authors noted, this seems to be very similar to the right hemisphere's role in language comprehension that you read about in Chapter

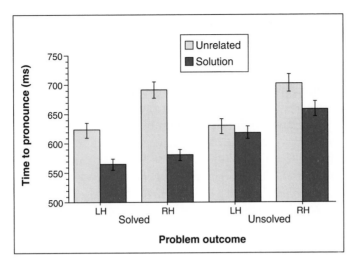

Figure 12-6

Mean naming time (time to pronounce) the target word for solved and unsolved trials. Bars labeled LH refer to target words presented to the right visual field, left hemisphere of the brain; RH means left visual field, right hemisphere. The figure shows priming effects for solution words, especially in the right hemisphere. *Source.* Bowden and Beeman (1998).

10, especially the part having to do with drawing inferences (Bowden, Beeman, & Gernsbacher, 1995).

■ Section Summary

- Insight is a deep understanding of a situation or problem, often thought to occur suddenly and without warning. Although there is some debate on the nature of insight, recent work suggests that insights may be discovered and used unconsciously and only later be available to consciousness for verbal reporting.
- Reasoning by analogy is a complex kind of problem solving in which relationships in one situation are mapped onto another to solve a problem. People are better at developing analogies if given a useful source problem and an explicit hint that the problem might be used in solving a target problem. Holyoak and Thagard's multi-constraint theory of analogical problem solving claims that we work under three constraints as we develop analogies: constraints related to the similarity of the source and target domains, the structure of the problems, and our purposes or goals in developing the analogies.
- Some new evidence suggests a particularly important role for the left frontal and parietal lobes in solving problems by analogy and a right hemisphere role in insight problems involving semantic priming.

Basics of Problem Solving

What the Gestalt psychologists lacked, as many critics pointed out, was a careful and scientifically precise way to define their concepts and explanatory variables. Their fundamental assumption, concerning the futility of studying a phenomenon by reducing it to components, also made their research difficult to accept at face value. For instance, a subject might spend a long time on the radiation problem, musing over different possibilities, trying different plans, and then finally arrive at a useful solution. And yet the Gestalt preference was to consider the final solution but not break the lengthy solution process into components. From our modern perspective, this preference was ill-advised. If you tried three plans to solve a problem, found each of them deficient, then finally found a fourth that worked, wouldn't we learn a lot about your problem-solving processes by analyzing the unworkable as well as the workable plans? In fact, Gick and McGarry (1992) have gone one step beyond that, showing that initial solution failures on one problem can often improve your solutions on a second problem, showing that people can "learn from their mistakes."

For these reasons, modern cognitive psychology adopted a more reductionistic approach to the study of problem solving. For instance, Newell and Simon's analysis of a cryptarithmetic problem (1972, Chapter 6) consists of a microscopic analysis and interpretation of every statement made by a single subject as he solved a problem, all 2,186 words and 20 or so minutes of problem-solving activity. When we compare the influence of Newell and Simon's work with the much more modest and general influence of Gestalt psychology, we must conclude that the modern approach is better suited to the task of investigating human problem solving.

We cycle back here to an elementary question to profit from the greater degree of precision offered by modern cognitive psychology's examination of problem solving. The question, simply enough, is, "What is a problem?"

In Newell and Simon's (1972) thumbnail description, "A person is confronted with a *problem* when he wants something and does not know immediately what series of actions he can perform to get it" (p. 72). The "something" in this definition can be renamed for more general use as a **goal,** *the desired end-point or solution of the problem-solving activity.* Problem solving consists of goal-directed activity, moving from some initial configuration or state through a series of intermediate steps until finally the overall goal has been reached: an adequate or correct solution. The difficulty is in determining which intermediate states are indeed on a correct pathway ("Will step A get me to step B or not?") and in devising operations or moves that achieve those intermediate states ("How do I get to step B from here?").

Characteristics of Problem Solving

Let's start by listing several characteristics that define what is and what is not a genuine instance of problem solving. Anderson (1980, 1985), for example, lists the following:

- *Goal directedness.* The overall behavior or activity we're examining is directed toward achieving some goal or purpose. By such a characteristic, we would exclude daydreaming, for instance; it's mental, but it's not goal directed. Alternatively, if you've locked your keys in your car, both physical and mental activity are going on. The goal-directed nature of those activities, your repeated attempts to get into the locked car, make this an instance of true problem solving.

• *Sequence of operations.* An activity must involve a sequence of operations or steps to qualify as problem solving. In other words, a simple retrieval from memory, say, remembering that 2×3 is 6, is not a serious instance of problem solving because it does not entail a slow, discernible sequence of separate operations or stages. Doing a long division problem or solving the locked car problem, on the other hand, definitely involves a sequence of mental operations, so these are instances of problem solving.

• *Cognitive operations.* Solving the problem—achieving a solution to the overall goal—involves the application of various cognitive operations. Various operators can be applied to different problems, where each operator is a distinct cognitive act in the sequence, a permissible step or move in the problem space. For long division, retrieving an answer would be an operator, as would be subtracting or multiplying two numbers at some other stage in problem solution. Often, the cognitive operations have some behavioral counterpart, some physical act that completes the mental operation, such as writing down a number during long division.

• *Subgoal decomposition.* As implied by the third characteristic, each step in the sequence of operations is itself a kind of goal, a **subgoal.** A subgoal is *an intermediate goal along the route to eventual solution of the problem.* Subgoals represent the decomposition, or breaking apart, of the overall goal into separate components. In many instances, subgoals themselves must be further decomposed into smaller subgoals. Thus solving a problem involves breaking the overall goal into subgoals, then pursuing the subgoals, and *their* subgoals, one after another until the final solution is achieved. This yields a hierarchical or nested structure to the problem-solving attempt.

An intuitive illustration of such a nested solution structure is presented in Figure 12-7, a possible solution route to the locked car problem. Note that during the solution, the first two plans led to barriers or blocks, thus requiring that another plan be devised (much like the radiation problem). The problem solver finally decided on another plan, breaking a window to get into the locked car. This decision is followed by a sequence of related acts; the search for some heavy object that will break a window, the decision as to which window to break, and so forth. Each of these decisions is a subgoal nested within the larger subgoal of breaking into the car, itself a subgoal in the overall solution structure.

A Vocabulary of Problem Solving

These four characteristics define what qualifies as an instance of problem solving. Many important ideas beyond just these characteristics are embedded in these four points, however. Let's reexamine some of these points, looking now toward an expanded vocabulary

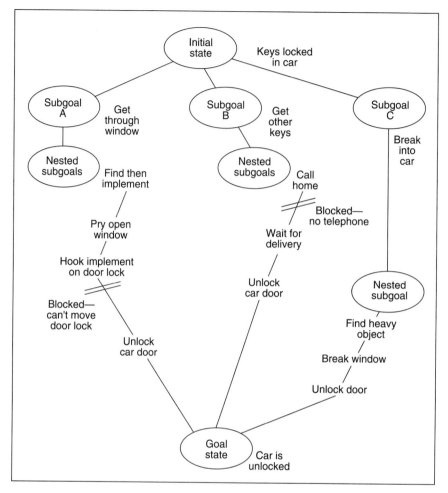

Figure 12-7

A representation of part of the problem space for getting into a locked car. Note the barriers encountered under plans A and B.

of problem solving, a set of terms we will use to describe and understand how people solve problems.

The Problem Space The term *problem space* is critical in analyzing problem solving. Anderson (1985) defines it as simply the various states or conditions that are possible in the problem. More concretely, the **problem space** includes *the initial, intermediate, and goal states of the problem. It also includes the problem solver's knowledge at each of these steps,* both knowledge that is currently being applied and knowledge that could be retrieved from memory and applied. Any external devices, objects, or resources that are available can also be included in the description of the problem space. Thus a difficult arithmetic

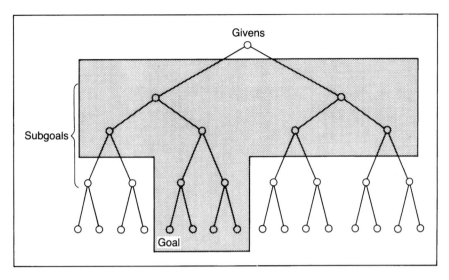

Figure 12-8

A general diagram of a problem space, with various branches of the space illustrated. Often a hint or an inference can prune the search tree, restricting the search to just one portion; this idea is represented by the shaded area of the figure. Note that in most problems, the problem space tree is much larger, so the beneficial effect of pruning is far greater. *Source:* Adapted from Wickelgren (1974).

problem that must be completed mentally has a somewhat different problem space than the same problem as completed with pencil and paper.

To illustrate, VanLehn (1989) describes a 60-year-old man's initial error in the "three men and a rowboat" problem. The man focused only on the arithmetic of the problem and said essentially "400 pounds of people, 200 pounds per trip, it'll take two trips of the boat." When he was reminded that the rowboat couldn't row itself back to the original side, he adopted a completely different problem space.

In some problem contexts, we can speak of problem solving as a search of the problem space or, metaphorically, a search of the solution tree, in which each branch and twig represents a possible pathway from the initial state of the problem. For problems that are "wide open," that is, those that have many possibilities that must be checked, there may be no alternative but to start searching the problem space, node by node, until some barrier or block is reached. As often as not, there is information in the problem that permits us to restrict the search space, that is, information that reduces the relevant search space to a manageable size. Metaphorically, this information permits us to prune the search tree.

A general depiction of this situation is in Figure 12-8. The initial state of the problem is the top node, and the goal state is some terminal node at the bottom. For "wide open" problems, each branch may need to be searched until a dead end is encountered. For other problems, information may be inferred that permits a restriction in the branches that are searched (the shaded area of the figure). Clearly, if the search space can be restricted, if the solution tree can be pruned of its dead-end branches, then problem-solving efficiency is increased.

The Operators Operators are *the set of legal operations or moves that can be performed during problem solution.* The term *legal* means permissible in the rules of the problem. For example, an illegal operator in the six-penny problem of Table 12-2 would be to move more than two pennies. In "three men and a rowboat," an illegal operator is having the men swim across the river or loading the boat with too heavy a load.

For transformation problems (Greeno, 1978), applying an operator transforms the problem into a new or revised state from which further work can be done. In general, applying a legal transformation operator moves you from one node to the next along some connecting pathway in the search space. For instance, in solving algebraic equations, one transformation operator is "move the unknowns to the left." Thus for the equation $2X + 7 = X + 10$, applying the operator would move the single X to the left of the equal sign by subtracting X from both sides of the equation.

Often, constraints within the problem prevent us from applying certain operators. In a vague way, the destruction of healthy tissue was such a constraint in the radiation problem. That constraint prevented the simple solution of applying the ray directly, where direct application would be a simple operator. In algebra, by contrast, constraints are imposed by the rules of algebra; for example, you can't subtract X from one side of the equation without subtracting it from the other side too.

The Goal The goal is the ultimate destination, goal state, or solution to the problem. For recreational problems in particular, the goal is nearly always stated explicitly in the problem. Given that recreational problems usually present *an explicit and complete specification of the initial and goal states,* we can describe such problems as **well-defined problems.** Solutions to such problems involve progressing through the legal intermediate states, by means of known operators, until the goal is reached. In contrast, in **ill-defined problems,** *the states, operators, or both may be only vaguely specified.* For instance, the Buddhist monk problem in Table 12-2 states a vague goal ("Show that there is a spot . . ."). Likewise, problems with more real-world character often are distressingly vague in their specification of the goal ("write a term paper that will earn you an A," "write a computer program that does X in as economical and elegant a fashion as possible," and so on).

An Example: DONALD + GERALD Let's consider a well-known recreational problem now, to pin down some of these terms and ideas. The problem is a cryptarithmetic problem, in which letters of the alphabet are substituted for the digits in an addition problem. Your task is to reverse the substitutions, to figure out which digits go with which letters to yield a correct addition problem. The obvious restriction is that the digits and letters must be in one-to-one correspondence (only one digit per letter and vice versa). Plan on spending 15 minutes or so on the problem, about the average amount of time it takes people on their first attempt. Make notes on paper as you work so you can go back later to retrace and analyze your attempt to solve the problem. (Incidentally, this is the cryptarithmetic problem Newell and Simon's single subject worked on.)

$$DONALD \qquad (Hint: D = 5)$$
$$+ GERALD$$
$$\overline{ROBERT}$$

Now that you've worked on the problem and have found (or come close to) the solution, we can use the insights you developed to fill in our definitions of terms. To begin with, the initial state of the problem consists of the statement of the problem, including the rules, restrictions, and hint you are given. These, along with your own knowledge of arithmetic (and pencil and paper), are your problem-solving tools for this problem. Each conceivable assignment of letters to digits makes up the entire problem space, and each substitution operator you might apply constitutes a branch or pathway on the search tree (a substitution operator here is an operator that substitutes a digit for a letter). Like the shaded area of Figure 12-8, the hint D = 5 prunes the search tree by a tremendous amount. Without the hint, you can only start working on the problem by trying some arbitrary assignments, then working through until an error shows up, then returning to an earlier node and reassigning the letters to different digits. (Even without the hint, however, there is only one solution to this problem.)

You no doubt started working on the problem by replacing the Ds in the 1s column with 5s, then immediately replacing the T with a 0. You also probably wrote a 1 above the 10s column, for the carry operation from 5 + 5. A quick scan of the problem revealed one more D that could be rewritten. Note that the position you were in at this point, with three Ds and a T converted to digits, is a distinct step in the solution, an intermediate state in the problem, a node in the problem space. Furthermore, each substitution you made reflected the application of an operator, a cognitive operation that transforms the problem to a different intermediate state.

As you continued to work the problem, you were forced to infer information as a way of making progress. For instance, in working on the 10s column, L + L + the carried 1, you can infer that R is an odd number because any number added to itself and augmented by 1 yields an odd number. Likewise, you can infer from the D + G column that R must be in the range 5 to 9 and that 5 + G can't produce a carried 1. Putting these together, R must be a large odd number, and G must be 4 or less. Each of these separate inferences, each mental conclusion you draw, is also an instance of a cognitive operation, a simple mental process or operator that composes a step in the problem-solving sequence. Each of these, furthermore, accomplishes some progress toward the immediate subgoal, find out about L.

Greeno (1978) calls this process a constructive search. Rather than blindly assigning digits and trying them out, people usually draw inferences from the other columns and use those to limit the possible values the letters can take. This approach is typical in arrangement problems, the third of Greeno's (1978) categories, in which some combination of the given components must be found that satisfies the constraints in the problem. In other kinds of arrangement problems, say, anagrams, a constructive search heuristic would be to look for spelling patterns and form candidate words from those familiar units. The opposite approach, sometimes known as generate and test, merely uses some scheme to generate all possible arrangements, then tests those one by one to determine whether the problem solution has been found (recall the algorithmic solution to the eight-letter example in Chapter 11).

A related aspect of problem solving here (it can be postponed, but your solution will be more organized if it's done now) is quite general and almost constitutes good advice rather than an essential feature of subjects' performance. Some mechanism or system for keeping track of the information you know about the letters is needed, if only to prevent you from forgetting inferences you've already drawn. Indeed, such an external memory aid can go a long way toward making your problem solving more efficient. In some instances, it may even help you generalize from one problem variant to another (as in the next example, the Tower of Hanoi problem). Table 12-7 presents a compressed verbal protocol of the solution to the DONALD problem, which you might want to compare with your own solution pathway. The table also shows intermediate steps and a notational system for keeping track of known values. Table 12-8 presents more cryptarithmetic problems that you might want to solve.

■ Section Summary

- We are solving a problem when our behavior is goal directed and involves a sequence of cognitive steps or stages. The sequence involves separate cognitive operations, where each goal or subgoal can be decomposed into separate, smaller subgoals. The overall problem, including our knowledge, is called the problem space, within which we apply operators, draw inferences, and conduct a constructive search for moves that bring us closer to the goal.

Professor Herbert A. Simon

Table 12-7

Intermediate

State	Known Values	Reasons and Statements from Protocol
1 5ONAL5 <u>GE RAL5</u> ROBERØ	0123456789 T D R is odd	Because D is 5, then T = 0, and carry a 1 to the next column. So the first column is 5 + something = odd because L + L + 1 = R will make R odd
	G is less than 5 R is odd and greater than 5	R must be bigger than 5 because less than 5 would yield a two-digit sum in the D × G column and there would be an extra column in the answer. G is less than 5.
1 1 5ONAL5 <u>G9RA15</u> ROB9 RØ	0123456789 T D E G is less than 5 R is odd, greater than 5	O + E is next. If E were 0, it would be fine, but T is already 0. So this column must have a carry brought to it. This means that E must be 9, so that the 0 + 9 + the carried 1 = 0.
1 11 5ONAL5 <u>G9RAL5</u> ROB9RØ		If E = 9, then A + A must have a carry brought to it, so then the A + A + the carried 1 = 9. 4 would work for A and so would 9, but 9 is already taken.
1 11 5ON4L5 <u>G9R4L5</u> ROB9RØ	0123456789 T AD E R is odd, greater than 5 G is less than 5 L is greater than 5	So A has to be 4. So L + L + the carried 1 has to produce a carry, so L is greater than 5. 5 and 9 are taken.
1 11 5ON4L5 <u>G97 4L5</u> 7OB97Ø	0123456789 T AD R E G is less than 5, L is greater than 5	So the odd R must be 7. Because L + L yields a carry, L isn't 3.
11 11 5ON485 <u>G97 485</u> 7OB97Ø	0123456789 T AD RLE N is greater than or equal to 3 G is less than 5	L must be 8 because 8 + 8 + 1 = 17. That only leaves O, N, G, and B. Because O + 9 needs a carry, N + 7 has to yield a carry. So N has to be at least 3.
11 11 5ON485 <u>197 485</u> 7OB97Ø	0123456789 TG AD RLE N is greater than or equal to 3	So G looks like 1. That leaves O, N, and B, for 2, 3, and 6. N can't be 3 because B can't be the 0 in 3 + 7 = 10. And it can't be 2 because 2 + 7 = 9 and the 9 is taken.
11 11 506485 <u>197485</u> 7O397Ø	0123456789 TGBADNRLE	That leaves N to be 6, so that makes B = 3.
11 11 526485 <u>197485</u> 723970	0123456789 TGOBADNRLE	So O has to be 2. Check the addition.

A sample solution of the DONALD problem, showing intermediate states, known values, and an edited protocol. (Zero is drawn with the slash, Ø, to distinguish it from the letter O.)

Table 12-8 ADDITIONAL CRYPTARITHMETIC PROBLEMS		

6.   CROSS
+   ROADS
    DANGER
Hint: R = 6
	7. L ETS
	+ WAVE
	    LATER
		8. SEND
		+ MORE
		    MONEY

Means–End Analysis: A Fundamental Heuristic

Several heuristics for problem solving have been discovered and investigated in problem-solving research. You've already read about the analogy approach, and the final section of the chapter describes and illustrates several others. But in terms of overall significance, as well as importance to the field of research, no other heuristic comes close to the heuristic known as means–end analysis. This heuristic formed the basis for Newell and Simon's groundbreaking work (1972), including their very first presentation of the information-processing framework in 1956 (on the "day cognitive psychology was born"; see footnote 2 in Chapter 1). Because it shaped the entire area and the theories devised to account for problem solving, it deserves special attention here.

The Basics of Means–End Analysis

Means–end analysis is the best known of the heuristics of problem solving. In this approach, *the problem is solved by repeatedly determining the difference between the current state and the goal or subgoal state, then finding and applying an operator that reduces this difference.* Means–end analysis nearly always implies the use of subgoals because achieving the goal state usually involves the intermediate steps of achieving several subgoals along the way.

The basic notions of a means–end analysis can be summarized in a sequence of five steps.

1. Set up a goal or subgoal.

2. Look for a difference between the current state and the goal or subgoal state.

3. Look for an operator that will reduce or eliminate this difference. One such operator is the setting of a new subgoal.

4. Apply the operator.

5. Apply steps 2–4 repeatedly until all subgoals and the final goal are achieved.

At an intuitive level, means–end analysis and subgoals are very familiar to us and represent "normal" problem solving. If you have to write a term paper for class, you break the overall goal down into a series of subgoals: select a topic, find relevant material, read and understand the material, and so forth. Each of these may contain its own subgoals: If you can't type or word process the paper yourself, an added subgoal is to arrange for someone to do this by the deadline, arrange to deliver the paper, then pick up the final copy.

Table 12-9 THE MISSIONARY–CANNIBAL PROBLEM

Three missionaries and three cannibals are on one side of a river and need to cross to the other side. The only means of crossing is a boat, and the boat can hold only two people at a time. Devise a set of moves that will transport all six people across the river, bearing in mind the following constraint: The number of cannibals can never exceed the number of missionaries in any location, for the obvious reason. Remember that someone will have to row the boat back across each time.

Hint: At one point in your solution, you will have to send more people back to the original side than you just sent over to the destination.

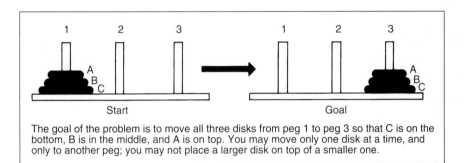

The goal of the problem is to move all three disks from peg 1 to peg 3 so that C is on the bottom, B is in the middle, and A is on top. You may move only one disk at a time, and only to another peg; you may not place a larger disk on top of a smaller one.

Figure 12-9

The Tower of Hanoi problem.

Means–End Analysis and the Tower of Hanoi

The most thoroughly investigated recreational problems are the missionary–cannibals problem in Table 12-9 (it's also known as the Hobbits–Orcs problem) and the Tower of Hanoi problem in Figure 12-9. These famous problems show very clearly the strengths and limitations of the means–end approach.

Work on the Tower of Hanoi problem very carefully, using the three-disk version in the figure. Try to keep track of your solution so you'll understand how it demonstrates the usefulness of a means–end analysis. So that you'll be familiar with the problem and be able to reflect on your solution, work it several times again after you've solved it. See whether you can become very skilled at solving the three-disk problem by remembering your solution and being able to generate it repeatedly. (By the way, an excellent heuristic for this problem is to solve it physically; draw the pegs on a piece of paper, and move three coins of different sizes around to find the solution.)

Having done that, consider your solution in terms of subgoals and means–end analysis. Your goal, as stated in the problem, is to move the ABC stack of disks from peg 1 to peg 3. Applying the means–end analysis, your first step sets up this goal. The second step in the analysis reveals a difficulty: There is a difference between your current state and the goal, simply the difference between the starting and ending configurations. You then look for a method or operator that will reduce this difference, and then apply

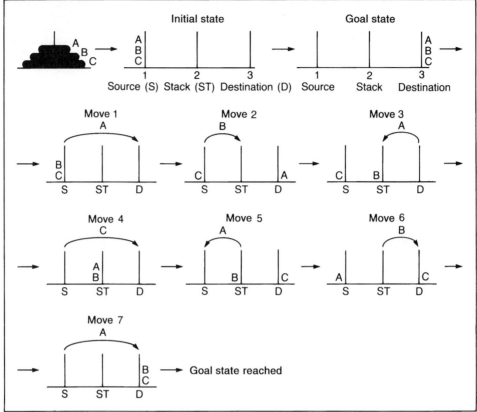

Figure 12-10

The seven-step solution for the Tower of Hanoi problem. Note that the pegs have been renamed as "Source," "Stack," and "Destination." Moving the three disks takes seven moves. Consider these seven moves as one unit, called "moving a pyramid of three disks."

that operator. As you no doubt learned from your solution, your first major subgoal is "Clear off disk C." This entails getting B off of C, which entails another subgoal, getting A off of B.

The next step involves a simple operator that satisfies the most immediate subgoal, "Move A to 3," which permits satisfying the next subgoal, "getting B off of C." So the next operator is "move B to 2"; it can't go on top of A (rule violation) and it can't stay on top of C because that prevents achieving a subgoal. Now peg 3 can be cleared by moving A to 2. This allows the major subgoal to be accomplished, putting C on 3.

From here, it's easy to see the final route to solution: "unpack" A from 2, putting it temporarily on 1, move B to 3, then move A to 3. The seven moves that solve the problem are shown in Figure 12-10.

The Four-Disk Version After you've worked the problem several times, solving it again becomes easy. You come to see how each disk must move to get C on 3, then B, and finally A. Spend some time now on the same problem but use four disks instead of three. Don't work on this larger version blindly, however. Think of it as a variation on the three-disk problem, where parts of the new solution are "old." As a hint, try renaming the pegs as the source peg, the stack peg, and the destination peg. Furthermore, think of the seven moves not as seven discrete steps but as a single chunk, "moving a pyramid of 3 disks," which should help you see the relationships between the problems more clearly (Simon, 1975). According to Catrambone (1996), almost any label attached to a sequence of moves probably will help you remember the sequence better.

What did you discover as you solved the four-disk problem? Most people eventually come to the realization that the four-disk problem has two distinct three-disk problems embedded in it, separated by the bridging move of D to 3. That is, to free D so it can move to peg 3 you must first move the top three disks out of the way, moving a "pyramid of 3 disks," getting D to peg 3 on the eighth move. Then the ABC pyramid has to move again to get them on top of D—another seven moves. Moving the disks entails the same order of moves as in the simpler problem, although the pegs take on different functions: For the four-disk problem, peg 2 serves as the destination for the first half of the solution, then as the source for the last half. The entire scheme of 15 moves is illustrated in Figure 12-11. Because the three-disk solution is embedded in the four-disk problem—and likewise, the four-disk solution is embedded in the five-disk problem—this is known as a recursive problem, where *recursive* simply means that simpler components are embedded in the more difficult versions. (According to legend, a group of Buddhist monks is working on the 64-disk version of the Tower of Hanoi problem, and when they solve it the world will come to an end. This implies a "conspiracy of silence" on our part because by recursive extension, "the 64-disk problem is really just the 63-disk version with an extra disk at the bottom, and the 63-disk problem is really just the 62-disk problem, etc.").

General Problem Solver

Means–end analysis was an early focus of modern research on problem solving, largely because of early work by Newell, Shaw, and Simon (1958; Ernst & Newell, 1969; Newell & Simon, 1972). Their computer simulation was called general problem solver **(GPS).** This program was the first genuine computer simulation of problem-solving behavior. It was a general-purpose, problem-solving program, not limited to just one kind of problem but widely applicable to a large class of problems in which means–end analysis was appropriate. Newell and Simon ran their simulation on various logical proofs, on the missionary–cannibal problem, on the Tower of Hanoi, and on many other problems to demonstrate its generality. (Notice the critical analogy here. Newell and Simon drew an analogy between the way computer programs solved problems and the way humans do: Human mental processes are of a symbolic nature, so the computer's manipulation of symbols is a fruitful analogy to those processes. This was a stunningly provocative and useful analogy for the science of cognition.)

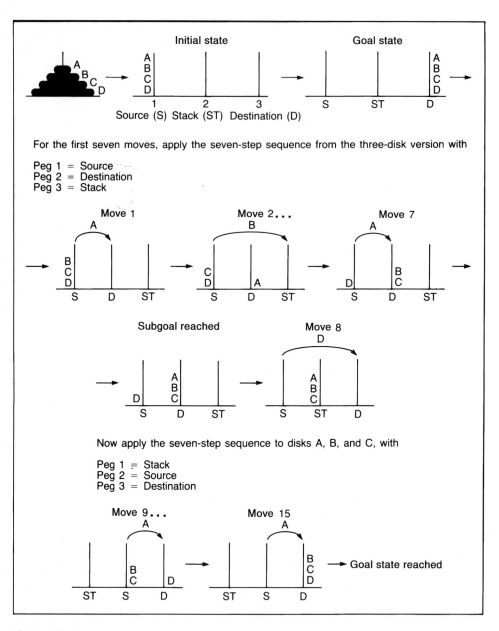

Figure 12-11

The four-disk Tower of Hanoi problem, with solution. The variation from the three-disk version is that the pegs must switch roles. In the beginning, the subgoal is to move a pyramid of three disks so that D can move to peg 3. After that, the subgoal again is to move a three-disk pyramid. In both the first and second halves, the pegs must switch roles for the problem to be solved.

PROVE IT

The problems you've been solving throughout the chapter can be used without change to demonstrate the principles of problem solving. Here are some interesting contrasts and effects you might want to test.

Compare either the time or number of moves subjects make in learning and mastering the Tower of Hanoi problem when the pegs are labeled *1, 2,* and *3*

and when they are labeled *source, stack,* and *destination.* Try drawing the pegs in a triangular pattern rather than in a left-to-right display to see whether that makes the "stack" peg idea more salient. Compare how long it takes to master the problem when your subjects learn to do it by moving three coins around on paper and when they keep track of their moves mentally.

Production Systems An important characteristic of GPS was its formulation as a production system model, essentially the first such model proposed in psychology. A **production** is a pair of statements, called either a *condition–action pair or an if–then pair.* In such a scheme, if the production's conditions are satisfied, the action part of the pair takes place. In the GPS application to the Tower of Hanoi, three sample productions might be as follows:

1. IF the destination peg is clear and the largest disk is free, THEN move the largest disk to the destination peg.

2. IF the largest disk is not free, THEN set up a subgoal to free it.

3. IF a subgoal to free the largest disk is set up and a smaller disk is on it, THEN move the smaller disk to the stack peg.

Such an analysis suggests a very "planful" solution on the part of GPS: Setting up a goal and then subgoals that will achieve the goal sounds exactly like what we would call planning. And indeed, such planning characterizes both people's and GPS's solutions to problems, not just the Tower of Hanoi, but all kinds of transformation problems. GPS had what amounted to a planning mechanism, a mechanism that abstracted the essential features of situations and goals, then devised a plan that would produce a problem-solving sequence of moves. Provided with such a mechanism and the particular representational system necessary to encode the problem and the legal operators, GPS yielded an output that resembles the solution pathways taken by human problem solvers.

Limitations of GPS Later investigators working with the general principles of GPS found some instances when the model did not do a particularly good job of characterizing or simulating human problem solving. Consider now the missionary–cannibal problem in Table 12-9; the solution pathway is presented in Figure 12-12. The problem is especially difficult, most people find, at step 6, where the only legal move is to return one missionary and one cannibal back to the original side of the river. Having just

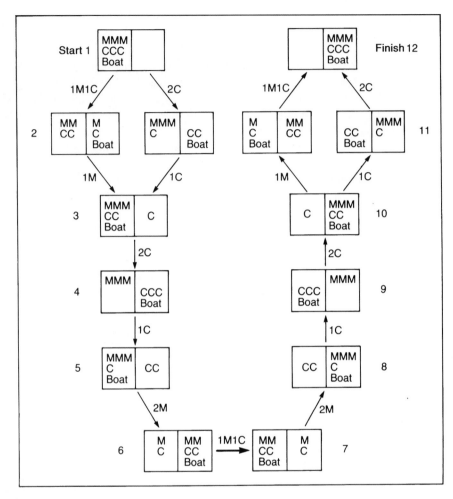

Figure 12-12

An illustration of the steps needed to solve the missionary–cannibal problem. The left half of each box is the "start side" of the river, and the right half is the "destination side." The numbers and letters next to the arrows represent who is traveling on the boat. *Source.* Glass and Holyoak (1986).

brought two missionaries over, this return trip seems to be moving away from the overall goal. That is, returning one missionary and one cannibal seems to be incorrect because it appears to increase the distance to the goal: It's the only return trip that moves two characters back to the original side. Despite the fact that this is the only available move (other than returning the same two missionaries who just came over), people have difficulty in selecting this move (Thomas, 1974).

GPS did not have this difficulty because sending one missionary and one cannibal back was consistent with its immediate subgoal. On the other hand, at step 10, GPS is trying to fulfill its subgoal of getting the last cannibal to the destination side and seemingly can't let go of this subgoal. People, however, realize that this subgoal should be abandoned: Anyone can row back over to bring the last cannibal across and in the process finish the problem (Greeno, 1974). GPS was simply too rigid in its application of the means–end heuristic, however: It tried to bring the last cannibal across and then send the boat back again.

Beyond GPS Newell and Simon's GPS model, and models based on it, often provided a very good description of human problem-solving performance (Atwood & Polson, 1976) and provided a precise set of predictions against which new experimental results could be compared (Greeno, 1974). Despite some limitations (Hayes & Simon, 1974), the model demonstrated the importance of means-end analysis for an understanding of human problem solving.

Atomic Components of Thought

More recently, Anderson (1983, 1990) has proposed a general model called ACT* (pronounced "act-star"); *ACT* stands for *adaptive control of thought;* a more recent version of the model, ACT-R (Anderson & Lebiere, 1998) decodes the acronym as *atomic components of thought.* Although the model covers the entire array of cognitive processes we've been discussing throughout this book, we'll limit our consideration to just the domain of problem solving.

The Structure of ACT As shown in Figure 12-13, ACT has three major components: declarative memory, production memory, and working memory.

Declarative memory is essentially what you studied in Chapters 6 and 7; long-term memory, whether episodic or semantic. In Anderson's scheme, declarative memory consists of interrelated nodes representing information, a memory network accessed by means of spreading activation. This is essentially what you learned about the structure and processes in semantic long-term memory.

Production memory in this model is the stored collection of *if–then* pairs that run the system, that accomplish all the various cognitive acts involved in problem solving (and everything else). For instance, for simple addition there is an *if–then* production in production memory that states

IF the goal is to add two numbers, THEN retrieve their sum from declarative memory.

When a goal is set that matches the *if,* the *then* part of the pair—the *action* part—is executed, causing a retrieval from declarative memory.

Notice, finally, that this matching process occurs in working memory. That is, when a goal is set, it is registered in working memory, as is the outcome of an *if–then* pair when it's executed. Thus, working memory is the "keeping track" mechanism in ACT. As shown in Figure 12-13, it is also the cognitive component that receives information from the outside world and governs the output of responses or performances.

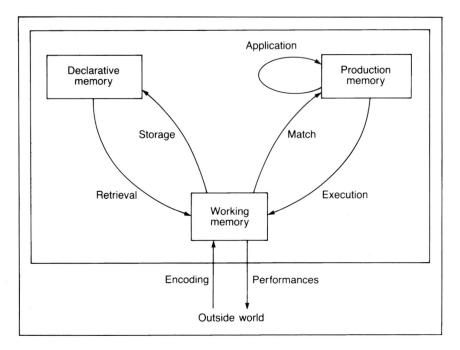

Figure 12-13

The architecture of Anderson's (1983) ACT* model, showing the major components and the processes that occur within the system.

How does the system know what to do next? Essentially, there is a scan through working memory to see what the current state or condition of the system is (e.g., A, B, and C). This scan is then compared to the *ifs* stored in production memory. If one of those productions matches the current contents of working memory (if *A* and *B* and *C*, then do *X*), that production acts. This satisfies the *if–then* condition (*X* happens), updates the contents of working memory, and moves the system one step closer to solving the problem.

Of the three components, production memory is the least familiar to you but the most important component of the ACT architecture. In many ways, production memory is related to **procedural knowledge** (Anderson, 1976, 1982), which means *knowledge of how to do things*, such as knowledge of how to ride a bicycle, how to drive a car, how to add and subtract. Thus, production memory is the long-term memory store for procedures, for procedural knowledge, for "knowing how."

An important distinction between procedural and declarative knowledge involves verbalization. You can easily verbalize your declarative knowledge but usually cannot verbalize the contents of production memory, the procedures you know; your declarative knowledge is explicit, but your production memory is implicit. Thus, you can verbalize the meanings of words you know (declarative) but usually cannot state the rules you follow for forming sentences (production or procedural).

Empirical Support for ACT The empirical tests of ACT principles have, for the most part, been supportive of the model and the general approach. This is especially the case for the domain of problem solving. As Anderson (1993) notes, ACT assumes a means–end approach to problem solving. By adopting this approach, presumably a great deal of human problem-solving performance—including the errors people make—can be understood.

In fact, this is exactly the approach being taken in the development of computer-based tutors. For example, Anderson (1992; also Anderson, Boyle, Corbett, & Lewis, 1990) reports on tutoring programs, derived from the ACT framework, that are being used to help students in high school mathematics. As the student interacts with the tutor, the tutor tries to interpret the student's problem-solving attempt by consulting its stored productions. In a sense, the computerized tutor asks itself "which rules of mathematics does this student still not understand?" Based on this analysis of rules yet to be mastered, the tutor selects new problems for the student to work on.

By tailoring the questions it asks in this fashion, the program tutors the student who is learning mathematics. Early results of this work are impressive: "Typical evaluations have students performing approximately one standard deviation better than control classrooms (if given [the] same amount of time on task) or taking one half to one third the time to reach the same achievement levels as control students" (Anderson, 1993, p. 42). Impressive evidence indeed.

■ Section Summary

- The best-known heuristic for problem solving is means–end analysis, in which the problem solver cycles between determining the difference between the current and goal states and applying legal operators to reduce that difference. The importance of sub-goals is revealed most clearly in problems such as the Tower of Hanoi.
- Newell and Simon's general problem solver (GPS) was the earliest cognitive theory of problem solving, implemented as a computer simulation. Studying GPS and comparing its performance with human problem solving showed the importance of means–end analysis to human problem solving. A more recent theory of problem solving, ACT, embeds problem solving within a cognitive system that includes working memory, long-term memory, and production memory. Several applications of ACT to topics in classroom education have yielded impressive evidence in support of the model and the production system approach it's based on.

Improving Your Problem Solving

Sprinkled liberally through this chapter have been hints and suggestions about how to improve your problem solving. Some of these were based on empirical research and some on intuitions that various people have had about the problem-solving process. Let's close this chapter by pulling these hints and suggestions together and offering a few new ones. Table 12-10 provides a convenient list of these suggestions.

Table 12-10 SUGGESTIONS FOR IMPROVING PROBLEM SOLVING
Increase your domain knowledge.
Automate some components of the problem-solving solution.
Follow a systematic plan.
Draw inferences.
Develop subgoals.
Work backward.
Search for contradictions.
Search for relations between problems.
Find a different problem representation.
If all else fails, try practice.

Increase Your Domain Knowledge

In thinking about what makes problems difficult, Simon suggests that the likeliest factor is the person's **domain knowledge,** what you know about the topic. Not surprisingly, a person who has only limited knowledge or familiarity with a topic is far less able to solve problems efficiently in that domain (but see Wiley, 1998, on some of the disadvantages of extensive domain knowledge). In contrast, extensive domain knowledge leads to expertise, a fascinating topic in its own right (see Ericsson & Charness, 1994, and Medin, Lynch, Coley, & Atran, 1997, for example, as well as several of the Suggested Readings for this chapter).

Much of the research supporting this generalization comes from Simon's work on the game of chess (Chase & Simon, 1973; Gobet & Simon, 1996; see also Reeves & Weisberg, 1993). In several studies of chess masters, an important but not surprising result was obtained: Chess masters need only a glimpse of the arrangement of chess pieces to remember or reconstruct the arrangement, far beyond what novices or players of moderate skill can do. This advantage holds, however, only when the pieces are in legal locations (i.e., sensible within the context of a real game of chess). When the locations of the pieces are random, then there is no advantage for the skilled players.

Automate Some Components of the Problem-Solving Solution

A second connection also exists between the question "What makes problems difficult?" and the topics you've already studied. Kotovsky, Hayes, and Simon (1985) tested adult subjects on various forms of the Tower of Hanoi problem and also on problem isomorphs, problems with the same form but different details. Their results showed that a heavy working memory load was a serious impediment to successful problem solving: If the person had to hold three or four nested subgoals in working memory all at once, performance deteriorated.

Thus, a solution to this memory load problem, they suggested, was to automate the rules that govern moves in the problems, just as you were supposed to master and automate the seven-step sequence in the Tower of Hanoi. Doing this frees working memory to be used for higher-level subgoals (Carlson, Khoo, Yaure, & Schneider,

Table 12-11 TWO TRAINS AND FIFTEEN PENNIES PROBLEMS
Two Trains
Two train stations are 50 miles apart. At 2 P.M. one Saturday afternoon, the trains start toward each other, one from each station. Just as the trains pull out of the stations, a bird springs into the air in front of the first train and flies ahead to the front of the second train. When the bird reaches the second train it turns back and flies toward the first train. The bird continues to do this until the trains meet.   If both trains travel at the rate of 25 miles per hour and the bird flies at 100 miles per hour, how many miles will the bird fly before the trains meet?
Fifteen Pennies
Fifteen pennies are placed on a table in front of two players. Players must remove at least one but not more than five pennies on their turns. The players alternate turns of removing pennies until the last penny is removed. The player who removes the last penny from the table is the winner. Is there a method of play that will guarantee victory?
Hints
Fifteen pennies. What do you want to force your opponent to do to leave you with the winning move? What will the table look like when your opponent makes that move?

Source. Two trains problem from Posner (1973, pp. 150–151).

1990). This is the same reasoning you encountered early in the book, where automatic processing uses few if any of the limited conscious resources of working memory.

Follow a Systematic Plan

Especially in long, multistep problems, it's important to follow a systematic plan (Bransford & Stein, 1993; Polya, 1957). The plan will help you keep track of what you've done or tried and also keep you focused on the overall goal or subgoals you're working on. For example, on DONALD + GERALD, you need to devise a way to keep track of which digits you've used, which letters remain, and what you know about them. If nothing else, developing and following a systematic plan will help you avoid redoing what you've already done.

Draw Inferences

Wickelgren's (1974) advice is to draw inferences from the givens, the terms, and the expressions in a problem before working on the problem itself. If you do this appropriately, it can often save you from wasting time on blind alleys, as in the two trains problem in Table 12-11. It can also help you abandon a misleading representation of the problem and find one that's more suitable to solving the problem (Simon, 1995). Here's a hint: Don't think about how far the bird is flying; think of how far the trains will travel and how long that will take.

Beware of unwarranted inferences, the kinds of restrictions we place on ourselves that may lead to dead ends. For instance, for the nine dot problem in Table 12-3, an unwarranted inference is that you must stay within the boundaries of the nine dots.

Drawing a diagram to represent a problem helps to improve problem-solving abilities.

Develop Subgoals

Wickelgren also recommends a subgoal heuristic for problem solving, that is, breaking a large problem into separate subgoals. This is the heart of the means–end approach, which we discussed extensively. There is a slightly different slant to the subgoal approach, however, that bears mention here. Sometimes in our real-world problem solving, there is only a vaguely specified goal and, as often as not, even more vaguely specified subgoals. How do you know when you've achieved a subgoal, say when the subgoal is "find enough articles on a particular topic to write a term paper that will earn an A"?

Simon's (1979) term ***satisficing*** is important to bear in mind here; satisficing is *a heuristic for finding a solution to a goal or subgoal that is satisfactory although not necessarily the best possible solution.* At least for some problems, the term paper problem included, an initial satisfactory solution to subgoals may give you additional insight for further refinement of your solution. For instance, as you begin to write your rough draft, you realize there are gaps in your information. Your originally satisfactory solution to the subgoal of finding references turned out to be insufficient, so you can recycle back to that subgoal to improve your solution. You might only discover this deficiency by going ahead and working on that next subgoal, the rough draft.

Work Backward

Another heuristic Wickelgren discussed was working backward, in which a well-specified goal may permit a tracing of the solution pathway in reverse order, thus working back to the givens. The fifteen pennies problem in Table 12-11 is an illus-

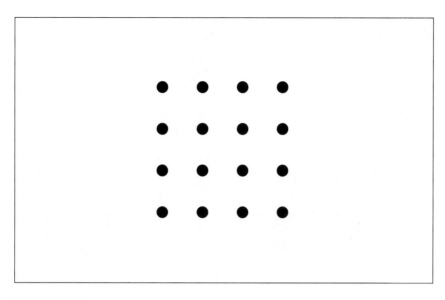

Figure 12-14

Without lifting your pencil, join all 16 dots with six straight lines.

tration, a problem that can be solved only by working backward. Many math and algebra proofs can also be worked backward or in a combination of forward and backward methods.

Search for Contradictions

In problems that ask "Is it possible to?" or "Is there a way that?", you should search for contradictions in the givens or goal state. Wickelgren uses the following illustration: Is there an integer x that satisfies the equation $x^2 + 1 = 0$? A simple algebraic operation, subtracting 1 from both sides, yields $x^2 = -1$, which contradicts the known property that any squared number is positive. This heuristic can also be helpful in multiple-choice exams. That is, maybe some of the alternatives contradict some idea or fact in the question or some fact you learned in the course. Either will enable you to rule those out choices out immediately.

Search for Relations Among Problems

In searching for relations among problems, you actively consider how the current problem may resemble one you've already solved or one you already know about. The four- and more-disk Tower of Hanoi problems are clear examples of this, as are situations in which you search for an analogy (Bassok & Holyoak, 1989; Ross, 1987). Don't become impatient, by the way. Bowden (1985) found that people often found and used information from related problems, but only if sufficient time was allowed for them to do so. Try it on the problem in Figure 12-14.

Becoming an effective problem solver requires practice to strengthen certain knowledge, as these chess players exhibit.

Find a Different Problem Representation

Another heuristic involves the more general issue of the problem representation, or how you choose to represent and think about the problem you're working on. Often, when you get stuck on a problem, it is useful to go back to the beginning and reformulate or reconceptualize the problem in some way. For instance, as you discovered in the Buddhist monk problem, a quantitative representation of the situation is unproductive. Return to the beginning and try to think of other ways to conceptualize the situation, such as a visual imagery approach, especially a mental movie that includes action. In the Buddhist monk problem, superimposing two such mental movies permits you to see him walking up and down at the same time, thus yielding the solution.

For other kinds of problems, try a numerical representation, including working the problem out with some examples, or a physical representation, using objects, scratch paper, and so forth. Simon (1995) makes a compelling point that one representation of a problem may highlight a particular feature of a problem while masking or obscuring a different, possibly important feature. According to Ahlum-Heath and DiVesta (1986), verbalizing your thinking also helps in the initial stages of problem solving (but see Schooler et al., 1993).

Earlier, it was suggested that you might master the Tower of Hanoi problem more easily if you took three coins of different sizes and moved them around on three pegs you drew on a sheet of paper. This is more than just good advice. Recall from Chapter 6 where you read about patient H.M., who suffers profound anterograde amnesia. H.M. seems unable to form new explicit long-term memories but apparently is quite normal when implicit learning is tested. The major result you read about was the mirror tracing study: H.M. showed normal learning curves on this task, despite not remembering the task from day to day. Interestingly, H.M. has also been tested on the Tower of Hanoi task, and he learns this task as well as anyone (although he has no explicit memory of ever solving the problem before). The important ingredient here seems to be the motoric aspect of the tower problem: Learning a set of motor responses, even a complex sequence, relies heavily on implicit memory. Thus, working the Tower of Hanoi manually by moving real disks or coins around should enable you to learn how to solve the problem from both an explicit and an implicit basis.

If All Else Fails, Try Practice

Finally, for problems we encounter in classroom settings, from algebra or physics problems up through such vague problems as writing a term paper and studying effectively for an exam, a final heuristic should help your problem solving. It's a well-known effect in psychology; even Ebbinghaus recommended it. If you want to be good at problem solving, *practice* problem solving. Practice within a particular knowledge domain strengthens that knowledge, pushes the problem-solving components closer to an automatic basis, and gives you a deeper understanding of the domain. Although it isn't flashy, practice is without doubt a major component of skilled problem solving and of gaining expertise in any area (Ericsson & Charness, 1994). In Ericsson and Charness's (1994) review, people routinely believe that stunning talent and amazing accomplishments result from inherited, genetic, or "interior" explanations, when in fact the explanation usually is dedicated, regular, long-term practice.

■ Section Summary

• The set of 10 recommendations for improving your problem solving includes increasing your knowledge of the domain, automaticity of components in problem solving, and developing and following a plan. Several special-purpose heuristics are also listed, including the mundane yet important advice about practice.

Key Terms

ACT (p. 527)	insight (p. 501)	production (p. 525)
analogy (p. 505)	means–end analysis (p. 520)	satisficing (p. 532)
domain knowledge (p. 530)	negative set (p. 498)	subgoal (p. 513)
functional fixedness (p. 497)	operator (p. 516)	verbal protocol (p. 493)
Gestalt (p. 494)	problem space (p. 514)	well-defined problems
goal (p. 512)	procedural knowledge	(p. 516)
GPS (p. 523)	(p. 528)	
ill-defined problems (p. 516)		

Answers to Chapter 12 Problems

Three Men and a Rowboat Medium and Small row themselves across the river, then either one of them rows back to the start side. Large rows himself across to the destination side. The man who stayed on the destination side now rows back to the start side, and both of the lighter men row to the destination.

Buddhist Monk Rather than thinking in terms of one monk, let a different monk walk down from the top on the same day as the other walks up. Looking at it this way, isn't it obvious that the two will meet during their journey? Thus, his walking on separate days is irrelevant to the goal, "Show that there is a spot. . . ."

Six Glasses Numbering the glasses from left to right, pour the contents of glass 2 into glass 5.

Six Pennies Coins 1, 2, 4, and 6 are already in place, so move coins 3 and 5.

Chains and Links Open all three links on one chain; that's 6 cents. Put one opened link at the end of each other piece, then join the pieces by looping a closed link into an opened one. Closing the three links costs 9 cents, for a total of 15 cents.

Cryptarithmetic

$Cross + Roads$	7. $Lets + Wave$	8. $Send + More$
96,233	1,567	9,567
+ 62,513	+ 9,085	+ 1,085
158,746	10,652	10,652

Four Trees Dead-end approaches try to arrange the trees on a flat, two-dimensional lawn. Instead, think in three dimensions. Put three trees around the base of a hill and the fourth one at the top of the hill. The arrangement is that of an equilateral, three-sided pyramid.

Prisoner's Escape Divide the rope in half by cutting with the length rather than across the length, similar to unbraiding the rope. Tie the two thinner pieces together and lower yourself to the ground.

Bronze Coin In 544 B.C., no one knew what might happen 544 years later, so coins could not have had B.C. stamped on them. The dealer is a crook.

Nine Dots

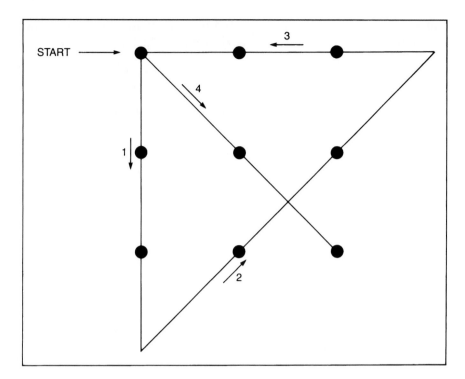

Ten Bowling Pins

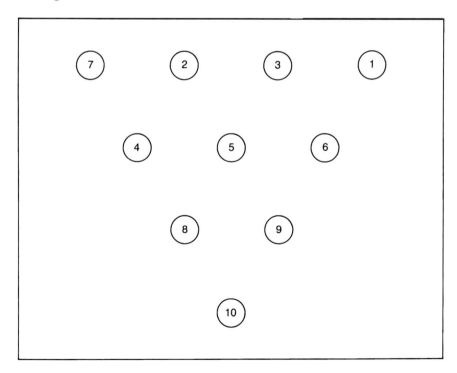

Two Trains The trains are 50 miles apart and travel at 25 miles per hour. The trains will meet halfway between the cities in exactly 1 hour. The bird flies at 100 miles per hour, so it will fly 100 miles.

Fifteen Pennies On your last move you must remove the final penny or pennies. There must be from one to five pennies on the table for you to be the winner. By working backward from this goal, on your next-to-last turn, you must force your opponent to leave you at least one penny on the table. So leave your opponent six pennies when you finish your next-to-last turn. To guarantee victory, make sure that your opponent leaves you from one to five pennies, so remove only as many pennies as you must to leave your opponent with six pennies on the table.

Sixteen Dots

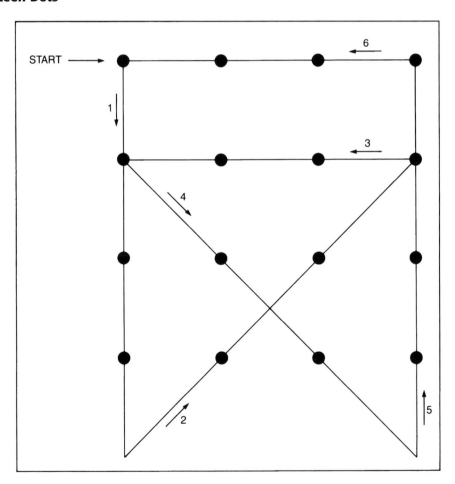

Glossary

Accessibility The degree to which information can be retrieved from memory. A memory is said to be accessible if it is retrievable; memories that are not currently retrievable are said to have become inaccessible (Ch. 6).

Acoustic–articulatory code The form of mental representation using sound- (acoustic) or pronunciation-related (articulatory) information (e.g., as distinct from the visual code) (Ch. 5).

ACT Anderson's (e.g., 1983) model of human cognitive processes. The acronym stands for *adaptive control of thought* and, in the more recent version, *atomic components of thought*. ACT is a computer-based production system model composed of declarative, production, and working memory components (Ch. 12).

Actor See **Agent**.

Advantage of clause recency The speed-up of RT to information in the most recently processed clause (Ch. 10).

Advantage of first mention The speed-up of RT to information mentioned first in the sentence (Ch. 10).

Agent (also **Actor**) In the case grammar approach, the person who performs some action in a sentence is the agent, such as Bill in "Bill hit the ball with the bat." See also **Case grammar** (Ch. 8).

Agnosia A disruption in the ability to recognize objects (Ch. 3).

Agraphia A disruption in the ability to write, caused by a brain disorder or injury (Ch. 9).

Alexia A disruption in the ability to read or recognize printed letters or words, caused by a brain disorder or injury (Ch. 9).

Algorithm A specific rule or solution procedure that is certain to yield the correct answer if followed correctly (contrast with **Heuristic**) (Ch. 11).

Ambiguous Having more than one meaning, said both of words (e.g., "bank") and sentences (e.g., "They are eating apples") (Chs. 7, 9).

Amnesia Memory loss caused by brain damage or injury. Retrograde amnesia is loss of memory for information before the damage, anterograde amnesia is loss of memory for information after the damage (Ch. 6).

Analogy A relationship between two similar systems, problems, and so on; a heuristic in which a problem is solved by finding an analogy to a similar problem (Ch. 12).

Anaphoric reference The act of using a pronoun or possessive (or synonym) to refer back to a previously mentioned concept (Ch. 10).

Anomia A disruption of word finding or retrieval, caused by a brain disorder or injury (Chs. 7, 9).

Anomic aphasia See **Anomia**.

Antecedent (in conditional reasoning) The *if* clause in standard conditional reasoning (*if–then*) tasks. In the statement "If it rains, then the picnic will be canceled," the antecedent is "If it rains" (Ch. 11).

Antecedent (in language) The concept to which a later word refers; for example, *he* refers to the antecedent *Bill* in "Bill said he was tired" (Ch. 10).

Aphasia A loss of some or all of previously intact language skills, caused by brain disorder or damage (Ch. 9).

Apperceptive agnosia A form of agnosia in which individual features cannot be integrated into a whole percept or pattern; a basic disruption in perceiving patterns. (Ch. 3).

Arbitrariness One of Hockett's (1960) linguistic universals, that the connections between linguistic units (sounds, words) and the concepts or meanings referred to by those units are entirely arbitrary; for example, it is arbitrary that we refer to a table by the linguistic unit *table* (Ch. 9).

Arguments In a proposition, the arguments are the ordered concepts that specify the meaning of the proposition. The arguments of the relation "HIT" in the sentence "Bill hit the ball yesterday" are "BILL" as the agent, "BALL" as the object, and "YESTERDAY" as the time. See also **Case grammar** (Ch. 8).

Articulatory (phonological) loop In Baddeley and Hitch's (1974) working memory system, the articulatory loop is the component responsible for recycling verbal material via rehearsal (Ch. 5).

Association A general term referring to a connection or link between two elements. In classic behaviorism, an association was formed between a stimulus and a response. In various models of long-term memory, associations are the links or pathways between concept nodes, such as the *isa* pathway between "ROBIN" and "BIRD" (Ch. 7).

Associative agnosia A form of agnosia in which the individual can combine perceived features into a whole pattern but cannot associate the pattern with meaning, cannot link the perceived whole with stored knowledge about its identity (Ch. 3).

Attend The verb form of *attention*, meaning "to pay attention to" (Chs. 3, 4).

Attention The mental energy or resource necessary for completing mental processes, believed to be limited in quantity and under the control of some executive control mechanism (Chs. 3, 4).

Audition The sense of hearing (Ch. 3).

Auditory sensory memory (also **Echoic memory**) The sensory memory system that encodes incoming auditory information and holds it briefly for further mental processing (Chs. 3, 4).

Authorized Intended or correct. An implication of a speaker's statement is said to be authorized if the speaker intended the implication to be drawn; if the listener draws the intended inference, the inference is said to be authorized (contrast with **Unauthorized**) (Ch. 10).

Autobiographical memory Memories of specific, personally experienced real-world information, such as of one's activities upon learning of the *Challenger* space shuttle disaster; the study of those memories (Ch. 8).

Automatic, Automaticity Occurring without conscious awareness or intention and consuming little if any of the available mental resources (Ch. 4).

Available (in memory research)   Present in the memory system. Information is said to be available if it is currently stored in memory (contrast with **Accessibility**) (Ch. 6).

Availability heuristic   A decision-making heuristic in which we judge the frequency or probability of some event on the basis of how easily examples or instances can be recalled or remembered; thus the basis of this heuristic is ease of retrieval (Ch. 11).

Axon   The long, extended portion of a neuron (Ch. 2).

Axon terminals   The branchlike ending of the axon in the neuron, containing neurotransmitters (Ch. 2).

Backward masking   See **Masking.**

Behaviorism   The movement or school of psychology in which the organism's observable behavior was the primary topic of interest, and the learning of new stimulus–response associations, whether by classical conditioning or by reinforcement principles, was deemed the most important kind of behavior to study (Ch. 1).

Beliefs   The fifth level of analysis of language, according to Miller, in which the listener's attitudes and beliefs about the speaker influence what is comprehended and remembered (Ch. 10).

Benefits   See **Facilitation.**

Bottom-up processing   See **Data-driven processing.**

Bridging   Clark's (1977) term for the mental processes of reference, implication, and inference during language comprehension. Metaphorically, a bridge must be drawn from *he* back to *Gary* to comprehend the sentence "Gary pretended he wasn't interested" (Ch. 10).

Broca's aphasia   A form of aphasia characterized by severe difficulties in producing spoken speech; that is, the speech is hesitant, effortful, and distorted phonemically (contrast with **Wernicke's aphasia**). The aphasia is caused by damage in Broca's area, a region of the cortex next to a major motor control center (Ch. 9).

Brown-Peterson Task   A short-term memory task showing forgetting caused by proactive interference (Ch. 5).

Case grammar   An approach in psycholinguistics in which the meaning of a sentence is determined by analyzing the semantic roles or cases played by different words, such as which word names the overall *relationship* and which names the *agent* or *patient* of the action. Other cases include *time, location, and manner* (Chs. 9, 10).

Case roles (also **Semantic case**)   The various semantic roles or functions of different words in a sentence; see also **Case grammar** (Chs. 9, 10).

Categorical perception   The perception of similar language sounds as being the same phoneme, despite the minor physical differences among them; for example, the classification of the initial sounds of *cool* and *keep* as both being the /k/ (hard c) phoneme, even though these initial sounds differ physically (Ch. 9).

Category-specific deficit   A disruption in which a person loses access to one semantic category of words or concepts while not losing others (Ch. 7).

Central executive   In Baddeley's working memory system, the mechanism responsible for assessing the attentional needs of the different subsystems and furnishing attentional resources to those subsystems. Any executive or monitoring component of the memory system that is responsible for sequencing activities, keeping track of processes already completed, and diverting attention from one activity to another can be called an executive controller (Ch. 5).

Cerebral cortex   See **Neocortex.**

Cerebral hemispheres (left and right)   The two major structures in the neocortex. In most people, the left cerebral hemisphere is especially responsible for language and other symbolic processing, and the right for nonverbal, perceptual processing (Ch. 2).

Cerebral lateralization   The principle that different functions or actions within the brain tend to be localized in one or the other hemisphere. For instance, motor control of the left side of the body is lateralized in the right hemisphere of the brain (Ch. 2).

Channel capacity   An early analogy for the limited capacity of the human information-processing system (Ch. 2).

Characteristic feature   In the Smith et al. (1974) model of semantic memory, characteristic features are the features and properties of a concept that are common but are not essential to the meaning of the concept; for example, "eats worms" may be characteristic of "BIRD," but the feature is not essential to the central meaning of the concept (contrast with **Defining feature**) (Ch. 7).

Chunk   A unit or grouping of information held in short-term memory (Ch. 5).

Clustering   The grouping together of related items during recall (e.g., recalling the words *apple, pear, banana, orange* together in a cluster, regardless of their order of presentation); see also **Organization** (Ch. 6).

Coarticulation   The simultaneous or overlapping articulation of two or more of the phonemes in a word (Ch. 9).

Cognition   The collection of mental processes and activities used in perceiving, remembering, thinking, and understanding, and the act of using those processes (Ch. 1).

Cognitive economy   The principle, now largely discredited, that information is not stored redundantly in semantic memory if it can be inferred from already-stored information; under the principle, "WINGS" would be stored only with "BIRD" rather than being stored repeatedly for "ROBIN," "SPARROW," "EAGLE," and so on (Ch. 7).

Cognitive science   A new term designating the study of cognition from the multiple standpoints of psychology, linguistics, computer science, and neuroscience (Chs. 1, 2).

Competence   In linguistics, the internalized knowledge of language and its rules that fully fluent speakers of a language possess, uncontaminated by flaws in performance (contrast with **Performance**) (Ch. 9).

Conceptual knowledge   The fourth level of analysis of language in Miller's scheme, roughly equivalent to semantic memory (Ch. 10).

Conceptually driven processing (also **Top-down processing**)   Mental processing is said to be conceptually driven when it is guided and assisted by the knowledge already stored in memory (contrast with **Data-driven processing**) (Chs. 2, 3).

Conditional reasoning   The form of reasoning in which the logical consequences of an *if–then* statement and some evidence are determined; for example, given "If it rains, then the picnic will be canceled," the phrase "It is raining" determines whether the picnic is canceled (Ch. 11).

Conduction aphasia A disruption of language in which the person is unable to repeat what has just been heard (Ch. 9).

Confirmation bias In reasoning, the tendency to search for evidence that confirms a conclusion (Ch. 11).

Connectionist (also **Connectionism, Neural net modeling, PDP modeling**) The terms refer to a recent development in cognitive theory, based on the notions that the several levels of knowledge necessary for performance can be represented as massive, interconnected networks; that performance consists of a high level of parallel processing among the several levels of knowledge; and that the basic building block of these interconnected networks is the simple connection between nodes stored in memory. For instance, perception of spoken speech involves several levels of knowledge, including knowledge of phonology, lexical information, syntax, and semantics. Processing at each level continually interacts with and influences processing at the other levels, in parallel. The connections in connectionist modeling are the network pathways both within and among the levels of knowledge (Chs. 2, 3, 7).

Conscious attention Awareness; a slower attentional mechanism especially influenced by top-down processing (Ch. 4).

Conscious processing Mental processing that is intentional, involves conscious awareness, and consumes mental resources (contrast with **Automatic, Automaticity**) (Ch. 4).

Consequent In conditional reasoning, the consequent is the *then* statement; in "If it rains, then the picnic will be canceled," the consequent is "then the picnic will be canceled" (Ch. 11).

Content accuracy Accuracy in recall, recognition, and so on, based on the content or meaning of the stimulus rather than on the literal or verbatim stimulus that was presented (contrast with **Technical accuracy**) (Ch. 8).

Context The surrounding situation and its effect on cognition, including the concepts and ideas activated during comprehension (Ch. 3).

Contralaterality The principle that control of one side of the body is localized in the opposite-side cerebral hemisphere. The fact that the left hand, for instance, is largely under the control of the right cerebral hemisphere illustrates the principle of contralaterality (Ch. 2).

Controlled attention The deliberate, voluntary allocation of mental effort or concentration (ch. 4).

Conversational rules The rules, largely tacit, that govern our participation in and contributions to conversations (Ch. 10).

Cooperative principle The most basic conversational postulate, stating that participants cooperate by sharing information in an honest fashion (Ch. 10).

Corpus callosum The fiber of neurons that connects the left and right cerebral hemispheres (Ch. 2).

Costs See **Inhibition.**

Counterfactual reasoning A line of reasoning that deliberately contradicts the facts in a "what-if" kind of way; in the simulation heuristic, the changing of details or events in a story to alter the (unfortunate or undesirable) outcome; also **Undoing** (Ch. 11).

Data-driven processing (also **Bottom-up processing**) When mental processing of a stimulus is guided largely or exclusively by the features and elements in the pattern itself, this processing is described as being data-driven (contrast with **Conceptually driven processing**) (Chs. 2, 3).

Decay Simple loss of information across time, presumably caused by a fading process, especially in sensory memory; also, an older theory of forgetting from long-term memory (Chs. 3, 5, 6).

Declarative long-term memory (also **Declarative knowledge**) The portion of long-term memory in which facts and information are stored (contrast with **Procedural LTM** or **Procedural knowledge**) (Ch. 8).

Declarative memory Long-term memory knowledge that can be retrieved and then reflected on consciously; see also explicit memory (Ch. 6).

Deep structure In linguistics and psycholinguistics, the deep structure of a sentence is the meaning of the sentence; a deep structure is presumably the most basic and abstract level of representation of a sentence or idea (contrast with **Surface structure**) (Ch. 9).

Default value The common or ordinary value of some variable. In script theory, default value refers to an aspect of a story or scene that conforms to the typical or ordinary state of affairs; for instance, "MENU" is the default value that fills the slot in a script in which customers find out what can be ordered in a restaurant (Ch. 8).

Defining feature In Smith et al.'s (1974) theory of semantic memory, a defining feature is a property or feature of a concept that is essential to the meaning of that concept; for instance, bearing live young is a defining feature of the concept "MAMMAL" (contrast with **Characteristic feature**) (Ch. 7).

Dendrites The branching, input structures of the neuron (Ch. 2).

Depth of processing See **Levels of processing.**

Direct theory In conversation, a direct theory is a person's appraisal of or informal theory about the other participant in the conversation, including information about that other person's knowledge, sophistication, and personal motives (contrast with **Second-order theory**) (Ch. 10).

Displacement One of Hockett's (1960) linguistic universals, referring to the fact that language permits us to talk about times other than the immediate present; language thus permits us to displace ourselves in time, by talking about the past, future, and so on (Ch. 9).

Dissociations Patterns of abilities and performance, especially among brain-damaged patients, revealing that one cognitive process can be disrupted while another remains intact. In a double dissociation, two patients show opposite patterns of disruption and preserved function, further evidence that the cognitive processes are functionally and anatomically separate (Ch. 2).

Distance effect (also **Discriminability effect**) An effect, seen particularly in reaction time, in which two distant or highly discriminable stimuli are more easily judged than two nearby or less discriminable stimuli; for instance, judgments are faster to "poor versus excellent" than to "good versus excellent" (Ch. 11).

Domain knowledge A general term referring to one's knowledge of a specific domain or topic, especially in problem solving (Ch. 12).

Downhill change In the simulation heuristic, a downhill change is an unusual or unexpected aspect of a story or situation that is changed to be more normal or customary. If a story character left work early and then was involved in a car accident, a likely downhill change would be to normalize the unusual characteristic and substitute a more customary aspect, such as leaving work on time (Ch. 11).

Dual coding hypothesis According to Paivio (1971), concrete words can be encoded into memory twice, once as verbal symbols and once as image-based symbols, thus increasing the likelihood that they will be recalled or remembered (Ch. 6).

Dual task or dual message procedure A method in which two tasks are performed simultaneously, such that the attentional and processing demands of one or both tasks can be assessed and then varied. Dual task methodology is commonly used in studies of attention and attention-dependent mental processing (Ch. 4).

Dysfluencies Errors, flaws, and irregularities in spoken speech (Ch. 9).

Echoic memory See **Auditory sensory memory.**

Ecological validity The hotly debated principle that research must resemble the situations and task demands that are characteristic of the real world rather than rely on artificial laboratory settings and tasks so that results will generalize to the real world, that is, will have ecological validity (Chs. 2, 3).

Elaborative rehearsal (also **Type II rehearsal**) In the levels of processing framework, elaborative rehearsal involves any rehearsal activity that processes a stimulus into the deeper, more meaningful levels of memory; any rehearsal that involves meaning, images, and other complex information from long-term memory (contrast with **maintenance rehearsal**) (Ch. 6).

Encoding To input or take into memory, to convert to a usable mental form, to store into memory. We are said to encode auditory information into sensory memory; if that information is transferred to short-term memory, then it is said to have been encoded into STM (Ch. 2).

Encoding specificity Tulving's hypothesis that the specific nature of an item's encoding, including all related information that was encoded along with it, determines how effectively the item can be retrieved; encode *bulb* along with the target *light* and it will be a better retrieval cue than, say, *heavy* (Ch. 6).

Enhancement In Gernsbacher's theory, the boosting of concepts' levels of activation during comprehension (Ch. 10).

Episodic memory Tulving's term for the portion of long-term memory in which personally experienced information is stored; one's autobiographical long-term memory (contrast with **Semantic memory**) (Ch. 6).

Erasure The masking or loss of information caused by subsequent presentation of another stimulus; usually in sensory memory (see also **Masking**) (Ch. 3).

Event-related potentials (ERPs) Minute changes in electrical potentials in the brain, measured by EEG recording devices and related specifically to the presentation of a particular stimulus; the research technique used for determining neural correlates of cognitive activity (Chs. 2, 7).

Executive control See **Central executive.**

Explicit memory Long-term memory retrieval or performance that entails deliberate recollection or awareness (Ch. 6).

Explicit processing Involving conscious processing, conscious awareness that a task is being performed, and usually conscious awareness of the outcome of that performance (Ch. 4).

Eye-gaze duration See **Gaze duration.**

Eye–mind assumption The assumption that the eye normally remains fixated on a word as long as that word is being actively processed during reading (Ch. 10).

Eyewitness memory Study of memory for personally experienced episodes with an emphasis on the accuracy or inaccuracy of the report as it relates to misinformation encountered since the original event (Ch. 8).

Facilitation (also **Benefits**) Any positive or advantageous effect on processing, usually because of prior presentation of related information; in RT research, a speedup of RT due to related information (Chs. 4, 7).

False alarm (also **False positive**) An error in a recognition task in which a response of "yes" is made to a new stimulus; any "yes" response in recognition when a "no" response is correct (Ch. 8).

False memory Memory for something that didn't happen (Ch. 8).

Familiarity bias In reasoning, the bias in the availability heuristic in which personal familiarity influences estimates of frequency, probability, and so on (Ch. 11).

Feature detection (also **Feature analysis**) A theoretical approach, most commonly in pattern recognition, in which stimuli (patterns) are identified by breaking them up into their constituent features (Ch. 3).

Feature list See **Semantic features.**

Filtering Especially in auditory perception, unwanted, unattended messages are filtered or screened out so that only the attended message is encoded into the central processing mechanism (e.g., Broadbent's filter theory) (Ch. 4).

Fixation In visual perception, the pause during which the eye is almost stationary and is taking in visual information; also, the visual point on which the eyes focus during the fixation pause (see also **Gaze duration**) (Chs. 3, 10).

Flashbulb memories Memories of specific, emotionally salient events, reported subjectively to be as detailed and accurate as a photograph but now considered possibly to be no different from any other highly accurate memory (Ch. 8).

Flexibility of symbols The characteristic that enables the meaning of a language symbol to be changed and enables new symbols to be added to the language (Ch. 9).

Focal attention Neisser's (1967) term for mental attention directed toward, for example, the contents of visual sensory memory and therefore responsible for transferring that information into short-term memory (Ch. 3).

Forgetting Colloquially, losing information previously stored in memory. More technically, the term usually implies that the stored information is no longer in memory, that it is no longer available in the memory system (Ch. 6).

Fovea The highly sensitive region of the retina responsible for precise, focused vision, composed largely of cones (Ch. 3).

Frames In script theory, the slots or events in a stored script. In the restaurant script, for instance, there are frames for "How the customer gets the food" and "Who prepares the food" (Ch. 8).

Free recall The memory task in which the list items may be recalled in any order, regardless of their order of presentation (contrast with **Serial recall**) (Ch. 5).

Functional fixedness In problem solving, an inability to think of or consider any but the customary uses for objects and tools (Ch. 12).

Functional MRI A use of MRI technology that provides online evidence about dynamic (functional) processes in the brain (Ch. 2).

Functionalism The movement in psychology, closely associated with James, in which the functions of various mental and physical capacities were studied (contrast with **Structuralism**) (Ch. 1).

Fuzzy boundaries A characteristic of natural categories in which the boundary of category membership is indistinct or fuzzy. For example, is "CHICKEN" a member of the "BIRD" or "FARM ANIMAL" category? (Ch. 7).

Garden path sentence A sentence in which an early word or phrase tends to be misinterpreted and thus must be reinterpreted after the mistake is noticed; for example, "After the musician played the piano was moved off the stage" (Ch. 9).

Gaze duration How long the eyes fixate on a specific word during reading, the principal measure of online comprehension during reading (Ch. 10).

Generativity See **Productivity.**

Geons In Biederman's recognition by components model, the basic primitives, the simple three-dimensional geometric forms in the human recognition system (Ch. 3).

Gestalt A German term adopted into psychological terminology referring to an entire pattern, form, or configuration. The term always carries the connotation that decomposing a pattern into its components in some way loses the essential wholeness of the cohesive pattern (Ch. 12).

Gist General meaning, especially of a passage of text or prose (Ch. 8).

Goal In problem solving, the end-point or solution to the problem, the ending state toward which the problem-solving attempt is directed (Ch. 12).

GPS (general problem solver) The first serious computer-based model of problem solving, by Newell, Shaw, and Simon (1958) (Ch. 12).

Grammar In linguistics and psycholinguistics, a set of rules for forming the words or sentences in a language; optimally, the complete set of rules that characterizes a language, such that the rules generate only acceptable or legal sentences and do not generate any sentences that are unacceptable (Ch. 9).

Habituation A gradual reduction of the orienting response back to baseline (Ch. 4).

Headers In script theory, the key phrases or words that activate a script; for example, *hungry* or *waitress* for the "Restaurant" script (Ch. 8).

Hemineglect (or hemi-inattention) A disorder of attention in which half of the perceptual world, often the left, is neglected to some degree, or cannot be attended to (Ch. 4).

Hemispheric specialization The principle that each cerebral hemisphere has specialized functions and abilities (Ch. 2).

Heuristic An informal, "rule of thumb" method for solving problems, not necessarily guaranteed to solve the problem correctly but usually much faster or more tractable than the correct algorithm (Ch. 11).

Hindsight bias In reasoning, the bias or attitude that some completed event was very likely to have had just that outcome (Ch. 11).

Hippocampus An internal brain structure, just internal to the temporal lobes, strongly implicated in the storing of new information into long-term memory (Ch. 2).

Horizontal change In the simulation heuristic, substituting one detail in a story or situation for another, where both are at the same level of generality or "commonness"; for example, changing "left work early" to "had a flat tire," both details being somewhat out of the ordinary (Ch. 11).

Icon The contents of iconic (visual sensory) memory; the brief-duration visual image or record of a visual stimulus held in visual sensory memory (Ch. 3).

Iconic memory See **Visual sensory memory.**

Ill-defined problem A problem in which the initial, intermediate, or final goal states are poorly or vaguely defined or a problem in which the legal operators (moves) are not well specified (Ch. 12).

Immediacy assumption The assumption that readers try to interpret each content word of a text as that word is encountered during reading (Ch. 10).

Implication An unstated connection or conclusion that was nonetheless intended by a speaker (Ch. 10).

Implicit memory Long-term memory performance affected by prior experience with no necessary awareness of the influence (Chs. 6, 7, 8).

Implicit processing Processing in which there is no necessary involvement of conscious awareness (Ch. 4).

Indirect request A question or statement that is not intended to be taken literally but instead is a polite way of expressing the intended meaning; for example, "Do you have the time?" is an indirect way of asking "What time is it?" (Ch. 10).

Inference Drawing a conclusion based on some statement, as in conversation or reading (Ch. 10).

Inferred or intended topic The idea inferred by the listener or intended by the speaker to be the conversational topic (Ch. 10).

Information-processing approach Broadly defined, the approach that describes cognition as the coordinated operation of active mental processes within a multicomponent memory system. As it was originally used, the term referred to mental processing as a sequence of mental operations, each operation taking in information, manipulating or changing it in some fashion, then forwarding the result to the next stage for further processing. Today the term is taken to refer more generally to the fact that humans encode and process information (Ch. 2).

Inheritance The principle that members of a category possess or inherit the properties of the category itself (Ch. 7).

Inhibition (also **Costs**) Any negative or disadvantageous effect on processing, usually because of prior presentation of some specific kind of information; in RT research, a slowing of RT caused by the prior information (Chs. 4, 7).

Input attention The basic processes of getting sensory information into the cognitive system (Ch. 4).

Insight or illumination Said to be an essential step in creativity and problem solving, though little if any research supports this notion empirically (Ch. 12).

Interference An explanation for "forgetting" of some target information in which related or recent information competes with or causes the loss of the target information (Chs. 3, 6).

Internal structure Natural categories are said to have internal structure, that is, to display members that differ in their degree of typicality or "goodness," as distinct from all-or-none membership in artificial categories (Ch. 7).

Intersection In network models, the connecting pathway between two concepts, the location where activation from two separate nodes meets (Ch. 7).

Introspection The largely abandoned method of investigation in which subjects look inward and describe their mental processes and thoughts; historically, the method of investigation promoted by Wundt and Titchener (Ch. 1).

Isa In network models of semantic memory, the superordinate pathway or link; for instance, an *isa* pathway connects "ROBIN" and "BIRD," as in "Robin *isa* Bird" (Ch. 7).

jnd (just noticeable difference) In psychophysics, the amount by which two stimuli must differ so that the difference can be perceived (Ch. 11).

Lag In studies of mental processing, the number of intervening trials between a prime and a target (Ch. 7).

Language A shared symbolic system for communication (Ch. 9).

Lesion Any damage to brain tissue, regardless of cause (e.g., from an accident, stroke, or surgery) (Ch. 2).

Levels of processing (also **Depth of processing**) Craik and Lockhart's (1972) alternative to the standard three-component memory model. Information subjected only to maintenance rehearsal is not being processed more deeply into the meaning-based levels of the memory system and therefore tends not to be recalled or recognized as accurately as information subjected to elaborative rehearsal (Ch. 6).

Lexical ambiguity The term refers to the fact that a word (such as *bank*) may have more than one meaning (Ch. 7).

Lexical decision task A simple yes/no task in which subjects are timed as they decide whether the letter string being presented is a word; sometimes called simply the word/nonword task (Chs. 2, 7).

Lexical memory The mental lexicon or dictionary where our word knowledge (as distinct from conceptual knowledge) is stored (Ch. 7).

Lexicon See **Mental lexicon.**

Linguistic intuitions One's subjective judgments that a sentence is or is not "acceptable" or "correct"; the basis for most theorizing in linguistics (Ch. 9).

Linguistic relativity hypothesis The hypothesis, credited to Whorf, that one's language determines—or at least influences strongly—what one can think about (Ch. 9).

Linguistic universals Features and characteristics that are universally true of all human languages (see also **Displacement, Productivity**) (Ch. 9).

Linguistics The discipline that studies language as a formal system (Ch. 9).

Location The semantic case or argument in a proposition specifying the place or location of some event (Ch. 8).

Long-term memory (LTM) The portion of the memory system responsible for holding information for more than a period of seconds or minutes; virtually permanent storage of information (Ch. 2).

LTM See **Long-term memory.**

Maintenance rehearsal (also **Type I rehearsal**) In the levels of processing approach, rehearsal that merely repeats, recycles, or refreshes information at a particular level via repetition, without processing it to deeper, more meaningful levels of storage (Ch. 6).

Mapping In Gernsbacher's theory, drawing the connections between words and their meanings to the overall meaning of the sentence; in general, the process of determining the connections between two sets of elements (Ch. 10).

Masking An effect, often in perception experiments, in which a mask or pattern is presented very shortly after a stimulus and disrupts or even prevents the perception of the earlier stimulus (see also **Erasure**) (Ch. 3).

Means–end analysis A major heuristic in problem solving, assessing the distance between the current and the goal states, then applying some operator that reduces that distance (Ch. 12).

Memory The mental processes of acquiring and retaining information for later retrieval; the mental storage system that enables these processes (Ch. 1).

Memory impairment A specific interpretation of early eyewitness memory results in which a subsequent piece of information replaces a memory formed earlier, thus impairing memory of the original information (Ch. 8).

Mental lexicon The mental dictionary of long-term memory, that is, the portion of long-term memory in which words and word meanings are stored (Ch. 9).

Mental model The mental representation of a situation or physical device; for example, a person's mental model of the physical motion of bodies or a person's mental model of a thermostat (Ch. 11).

Mental rotation Mental manipulation of a visual short-term memory code that reorients the imaged object in space (Ch. 5).

Metacognition Awareness and monitoring of one's own cognitive state or condition; knowledge about one's own cognitive processes and memory system (Ch. 6).

Metamemory Knowledge about one's own memory system and its functioning (Ch. 6).

Metatheory A general theoretical framework consisting of the assumptions made by practitioners of a science that guide the research activities of those practitioners (Ch. 2).

Method of loci A classic mnemonic device in which the to-be-remembered items are mentally placed, one by one, into a set of prememorized locations, with retrieval consisting of a mental walk through the locations (Ch. 6).

Misinformation acceptance The tendency to accept information presented after some critical event as being true of the original event itself; for example, accepting, then reporting, that a Yield sign had appeared in an earlier description of a traffic accident (Ch. 8).

Misinformation effect Incorrectly claiming to remember information that was not part of some original experience (Ch. 8).

Mnemonic device Any mental device or strategy that provides a useful rehearsal strategy for storing and remembering difficult material; see **Method of loci,** for instance (Ch. 6).

Modality effect In sensory memory research, the advantage in recall of the last few items in a list when those items have been presented orally rather than visually (Ch. 3).

Morpheme Smallest unit of meaning in language (Ch. 9).

MRI (Magnetic resonance imaging) A medical scanning technology that reveals anatomical structure, especially of the brain; see also **Functional MRI** (Ch. 2).

Naive physics The study of people's misconceptions about the motion of physical objects, such as a ball rolling off a cliff (Ch. 11).

Naming The characteristic that human languages have names or labels for all the objects and concepts encountered by the speakers of the language (e.g., as opposed to most animal communication systems (Ch. 9).

Natural categories In research on categorization (see especially Rosch, 1975, 1978) in semantic memory, the groupings or clusters of objects and concepts that occur naturally in the world; that is, groups of objects that resemble one another and share common features and uses, as distinct from artificial categories such as *mammal*, which rely on a technical definition for category membership (Ch. 7).

Negative set In problem solving, a tendency to become accustomed to a single approach or way of thinking about a problem, making it difficult to recognize or generate alternative approaches (Ch. 12).

Neocortex (also **Cerebral cortex**) The top layer of the brain, newest (*neo-*) in terms of the evolution of the species, divided into left and right hemispheres; the locus of most higher-level mental processes (Ch. 2).

Network A structure for information stored in long-term semantic memory, assumed by several popular models of mental processing. In most network models, concepts are represented as nodes that are interconnected by means of links or pathways; activation is presumed to spread from concept to concept along these connecting pathways (Ch. 7).

Neural net modeling See **Connectionist.**

Neurocognition The neurological basis of cognition and the study of the combination of neurological and cognitive factors (Ch. 2).

Neuron A specialized cell that conducts neural information through the nervous system, the basic building block of the nervous system (Ch. 2).

Neurotransmitter The chemical substance released into the synapse between two neurons, responsible for activating or inhibiting the next neuron in sequence (Ch. 2).

Node Especially in network models, a point or location in the long-term memory representation of knowledge; a concept or its representation in memory (Ch. 7).

Nondeclarative memory See implicit memory (Ch. 6).

Object See **Patient.**

On-line comprehension tasks Tasks in which measurements of performance are obtained as comprehension takes place; *online* means happening and being measured right now (Ch. 10).

Operator In problem solving, a legal move or operation that can occur during solution of a problem; the set of legal moves within some problem space (e.g., in algebra, one operator is "multiply both sides by the same number") (Ch. 12).

Organization Especially in studies of episodic long-term memory, the tendency to recall related words together, or the tendency to impose some form of grouping or clustering on information being stored in/retrieved from memory; related to chunking or grouping in short-term memory (Ch. 6).

Orienting reflex (or Orienting response) The reflexive redirection of attention that orients you toward the unexpected stimulus (Ch. 4).

Paired-associate learning (PA learning) A task in which pairs of items, respectively the stimulus and response terms, are to be learned, so that upon presentation of a stimulus, the response term can be recalled; a favorite learning task during the verbal learning period of human experimental psychology (Ch. 6).

Pandemonium Selfridge's early model of letter identification (Ch. 3).

Parallel distributed processing(PDP) See **Connectionist.**

Parallel processing Any mental processing in which more than one process or operation occurs simultaneously (Ch. 2).

Parse To divide or separate the words in a sentence into logical or meaningful groupings (Ch. 9).

Partial report condition An experimental condition in Sperling's (1960) research in which only a randomly selected portion of the entire stimulus display was to be reported (contrast with **Whole report condition**) (Ch. 3).

Pathway In network representations in long-term memory, the connecting link between two concepts or nodes (Ch. 7).

Patient The object or recipient that receives the action in a sentence; one of the semantic cases in a case grammar approach (see also **Case grammar**) (Ch. 8).

PDP modeling See **Connectionist.**

Peg word mnemonic The mnemonic device in which a pre-memorized set of peg word connections is used to remember some new information; the peg words typically used are "One is a bun, Two is a shoe," and so on (Ch. 6).

Perception The process of interpreting and understanding sensory information; the act of sensing and then interpreting that information (Ch. 3).

Performance Any observable behavior; in the context of linguistics, any behavior related to language (e.g., speech), influenced not only by linguistic factors but also by factors related to lapses in attention, memory, and so on (contrast with **Competence**) (Ch. 9).

Pertinence The momentary importance of information, whether caused by permanent or transitory factors, especially in Norman's theory of selective attention (Ch. 4).

Phoneme A sound or set of sounds judged to be the same by speakers of a language (e.g., the initial sound in the words *cool* and *keep* for speakers of English). Note that because of categorical perception, we tend to judge some physically different sounds as the same and other different sounds as different, that is, belonging to a different phoneme category (Chs. 3, 9).

Phonemic competence   One's basic knowledge of the phonology of the language (Ch. 9).

Phonology   The study of the sounds of language, including how they are produced and how they are perceived (Ch. 9).

Phrase structure   The underlying structure of a sentence in terms of the groupings of words into meaningful phrases, such as "[The young man] [ran quickly]" (Ch. 9).

PI   See **Proactive interference.**

Pragmatics   The aspects of language that are "above and beyond" the words, so-called extralinguistic factors. For instance, part of our pragmatic knowledge of language rules includes the knowledge that the sentence "Do you happen to know what time it is?" is actually an indirect request rather than a sentence to be taken literally.

Primacy effect   In a recall task, the elevation of recall at the early positions of the list (contrast with **Recency effect**) (Chs. 5, 6).

Prime   The first stimulus in a prime–target pair, intended to exert some influence on the second stimulus (see also **Priming**) (Ch. 7).

Priming   Mental activation of a concept by some means, or the spread of that activation from one concept to another; also, the activation of some target information by action of a previously presented prime; sometimes loosely synonymous with the notion of accessing information in memory (Chs. 4, 7).

Proactive interference (PI)   Interference or difficulty, especially during recall, because of some previous activity, often the stimuli learned on some earlier list; any interference in which material presented at one time interferes with material presented later (Chs. 5, 6).

Problem of invariance   In psycholinguistics, the problem that spoken sounds are not invariant, that they change depending on what sounds precede and follow in the word (Chs. 3, 9).

Problem space   The initial, intermediate, and goal states in a problem, along with the problem solver's knowledge and any external resources that can be used to solve the problem (Ch. 12).

Procedural knowledge   Knowledge of how to do something; the part of Anderson's (1983) ACT* model dealing with knowledge of processes and procedures (e.g., how to add, how to ride a bicycle) (Ch. 12).

Procedural LTM   See **Procedural knowledge.**

Process model   A stage model designed to explain the several mental steps involved in performance of some task, usually implying that the stages occur sequentially and that they operate independently of one another (Chs. 2, 5).

Processing fluency   The ease with which something is processed or comes to mind (Ch. 8).

Production, production system   A production is a simple *if–then* rule in models of memory processing, stating the conditions (*if*) necessary for some action (*then*) to be taken, whether that action is a physical response or a mental step or operation. A production system is a large-scale model of some kind of performance or mental activity based on productions (see especially **ACT**) (Ch. 12).

Productivity (also **Generativity**)   One of Hockett's (1960) linguistic universals, referring to the rule-based nature of language, such that an infinite number of sentences can be generated or produced by applying the rules of the language (Ch. 9).

Property statements   Simple statements in which the relationship being expressed is "*X* has the property or feature *Y*" (e.g., "A robin has wings") (Ch. 7).

Proposition   A simple semantic relation between two concepts; a basic unit of meaning, expressing a simple relationship or idea; the representation of the meaning of an entire sentence, including all the relationships among all the words (Chs. 7, 8).

Prosopagnosia   Disruption in the ability to recognize faces (Ch. 3).

Prototype   The typical or average member of a category; the central or most representative member of a category. Note that a prototype may not exist for some categories, in which case the category's prototype would be some "average-like" combination of the various members (Ch. 7).

Psycholinguistics   The study of language from the perspective of psychology; the study of language behavior and processes (Ch. 9).

Psychophysics   The study of the relationship between physical stimuli and the perceived characteristics of those stimuli; the study of how perceptual experience differs from the physical stimulation that is being perceived (Ch. 11).

Reaction time (RT)   The elapsed time, usually measured in milliseconds, between some stimulus event and the subject's response to that event; a particularly common measure of performance in cognitive psychology (Chs. 1, 7).

Recall   See **Free recall** and **Serial recall.**

Recency effect   In recall performance, the elevated recall of the last few items in a list, presumably because the items are stored in and retrieved from short-term memory (contrast with **Primacy effect**) (Ch. 5).

Recipient   See **Patient.**

Recoding   Mentally transforming or translating a stimulus into another code or format; grouping items into larger units, as when recoding a written word into an acoustic–articulatory code (Ch. 5).

Recognition task   Any yes/no task in which subjects are asked to judge whether they have seen the stimulus before; more generally, any task asking for a simple yes/no (alternatively, true/false, same/different) response, often including a reaction time measurement (Ch. 6).

Reconstructive memory   The tendency in recall or recognition to include ideas or elements that were inferred or related to the original stimulus but were not part of the original stimulus itself (Ch. 8).

Reductionism   The scientific approach in which a complex event or behavior is broken down into its constituents; the individual constituents are then studied individually (Ch. 1).

Reference   In language, the allusion to or indirect mention of an element from elsewhere in the sentence or passage, as by using a pronoun or synonym (Ch. 10).

Rehearsal   The mental repetition or practicing of some to-be-learned material (Ch. 6).

Rehearsal buffer   The component of short-term memory that holds information currently being rehearsed (Ch. 5).

Relation   In case grammar, the central idea or relationship being asserted in a sentence or phrase. For instance, in "Bill hit the ball with the bat," the central relation is "HIT" (see also **Case grammar**) (Chs. 8, 10).

Relearning task An experimental task in which some material is learned, set aside for a period of time, and then relearned to the same criterion in hopes that the relearning will take less time or effort to achieve the same level of accuracy; the task used by Ebbinghaus in his research on memory (Ch. 6).

Release from proactive interference (Release from PI) The sudden reduction in proactive interference when the material to be learned is changed in some fashion, such as improved recall on a list of plant names after several trials involving animal names. The initial decline was caused by proactive interference, and the improvement on the last trial is caused by release from PI (Ch. 5).

Repetition priming A priming effect caused by the exact repetition of a stimulus; often used in implicit memory tests (Chs. 6, 10).

Representation A general term referring to the way information is stored in memory. The term always carries the connotation that we are interested in the format or organization of the information as it is stored (is the information stored in a semantic representation? a sound-based representation?) (Ch. 2).

Representation of knowledge See **Representation**.

Representativeness heuristic A reasoning heuristic in which we judge the likelihood of some event by deciding how representative that event seems to be of the larger group or population from which it was drawn (Ch. 11).

Repression Intentional forgetting of painful or traumatic experiences, especially in Freudian theory (Ch. 8).

Retina The layer of the eye covered with the rods and cones that initiate the process of visual sensation and perception (Ch. 3).

Retrieval Accessing information stored in memory, whether or not that access involves conscious awareness (Chs. 1, 2).

Retrieval cue Any cue, hint, or piece of information used to prompt retrieval of some target information (Ch. 6).

Retroactive interference The interference from a recent event or experience that influences memory for an earlier event, such as trying to recall the items from list 1 but instead recalling the items from list 2 (Ch. 5).

Rewrite rules In a phrase structure grammar, the rules that specify the individual components of a phrase; for example, a noun phrase is rewritten as a determiner, an adjective, and a noun, NP → det + (adj) + N (Ch. 9).

RI See **Retroactive interference**.

RT See **Reaction time**.

Saccade The voluntary sweeping of the eyes from one fixation point to another (Chs. 3, 9).

Salience, Vividness Sources of bias in the availability heuristic in which a particularly notable or vivid memory influences judgments about the frequency or likelihood of such events (Ch. 11).

Satisficing Finding an acceptable or satisfactory solution to a problem, even though the solution may not be optimal (Ch. 12).

Savings score In a relearning task, the score showing how much was saved on second learning compared with original learning. For instance, if original learning took 10 trials and relearning took only 6 trials, then savings would be 40% (10 − 6)/10 (Ch. 6).

Schema (plural, **Schemata**) In Bartlett's (1932, p. 201) words, "an active organization of past reactions or past experiences"; a knowledge structure in memory (Ch. 8).

Script Schank's term for a schema, a long-term memory representation of some complex event such as going to a restaurant (Ch. 8).

Second-order theory In conversation, the informal theory we develop that expresses our knowledge of what the other participant knows about us, summarized by the phrase "what he/she thinks I know" (contrast with **Direct theory**) (Ch. 10).

Selecting See **Filtering** (Ch. 4).

Selective attention The ability to attend to one source of information while ignoring or excluding other ongoing messages. (Ch. 4).

Semantic case (also **Case roles**) In a case grammar approach, the particular case played by a word or concept is said to be that word's semantic case (see also **Case grammar**) (Chs. 8, 9).

Semantic congruity effect In the mental comparison task, reaction time is speeded or judgments are made easier when the basis for a judgment is congruent or similar to the stimuli being compared; for instance, a congruent condition would be "choose the smaller of *second* or *minute*," and an incongruent condition would be "choose the smaller of *decade* or *century*" (Ch. 11).

Semantic distance effect See **Semantic relatedness effect**.

Semantic features (also **Feature list**) Properties or characteristics stored in the mental representation of some concept, presumed by some theories to be accessed and evaluated in the process of making semantic judgments (Ch. 7).

Semantic integration The tendency to store related pieces of information into an integrated, unified representation (Ch. 8).

Semanticity One of Hockett's (1960) linguistic universals, expressing the fact that the elements of language convey meaning (Ch. 9).

Semantic memory The long-term memory component in which general world knowledge, including knowledge of language, is stored (contrast with **Episodic memory**) (Chs. 6, 7).

Semantic relatedness effect In semantic memory tasks, reaction time is speeded up or judgments are made easier when the concepts are closer together in semantic distance, when they are more closely related. Note that the effect is reversed when the comparison is false; that is, RT is longer for the comparison "A whale is a fish" than for "A whale is a bird" (Ch. 7).

Semantics The study of meaning (Ch. 9).

Sensation The reception of physical stimulation and encoding of it into the nervous system (Ch. 3).

Sensory memory The initial mental storage system for sensory stimuli. There are presumably as many modalities of sensory memory as there are kinds of stimulation that we can sense (Chs. 2, 3).

Sentence verification task A task in which subjects must respond *true* or *false* to simple sentences (Ch. 7).

Sequential stages of processing An assumption in most process models that the separate stages of processing occur in a fixed sequence, with no overlap of the stages (Ch. 2).

Serial exhaustive search A search process in which all possible elements are searched one by one before the decision is made, even if the target is found early in the search process (Ch. 5).

Serial position curve The display of accuracy in recall across the original positions in the to-be-learned list, often found to have a bowed shape, indicating lower recall in the middle of the list than in the initial or final positions (Chs. 5, 6).

Serial processing   Mental processing in which only one process or operation occurs at a time (Ch. 2).

Serial recall   A recall task in which subjects must recall the list items in their original order of presentation (contrast with **Free recall**) (Ch. 5).

Shadowing task   A task in which subjects hear a spoken message and must repeat the message out loud in a very short time; often used as one of the two tasks in a dual task method (Ch. 4).

Short-term memory (STM)   The component of the human memory system that holds information for up to 20 s; the memory component where current and recently attended information is held; sometimes loosely equated with attention and consciousness (Ch. 2).

Simulation heuristic   A reasoning heuristic in which we predict a future event or imagine a different outcome to completed events; a forecasting of how some event will turn out or how it might have turned out under another set of circumstances (Ch. 11).

Situation model   A memory representation of a real-world situation, for example of a situation described in a passage of text (Ch. 10).

SOA   See **stimulus onset asynchrony.**

Source memory   Memory of the exact source of information (Ch. 8).

Source misattribution   Inability to distinguish whether an original event or a later event was the true source of information (Ch. 8).

Span of apprehension (also **Span of attention**)   The number of simple elements (e.g., digits, letters) that can be heard and immediately reported in their correct order; a standard short-term memory task, common on standardized intelligence tests (Ch. 3).

Split brain   Refers to patients in whom the corpus callosum has been severed surgically and the resultant changes in their performance because of the surgery or, more generally, to research showing various specializations of the two cerebral hemispheres (Ch. 2).

Spotlight attention   A rapid attentional mechanism operating in parallel and automatically across the visual field, especially for detecting simple visual features (Ch. 4).

Spreading activation   The commonly assumed theoretical process by which long-term memory knowledge is accessed and retrieved. Some form of mental excitation or activation is believed to be passed or spread along the pathways that connect concepts in a memory network. When a concept has been activated, it has been retrieved or accessed within the memory representation. The process is loosely analogous to the spread of neural excitation in the brain (Ch. 7).

Stereotypes   In reasoning, bias in judgments related to the typical characteristics of a profession, type of person, and so on (Ch. 11).

Sternberg task   The short-term memory scanning task devised by Saul Sternberg (Ch. 5).

Stimulus onset asynchrony (SOA)   In priming studies, the interval of time separating the prime and the target, usually a few hundred milliseconds (Ch. 7).

STM   See **Short-term memory.**

Structuralism   The approach, most closely identified with Wundt and Titchener, in which the structure of the conscious mind—that is, the sensations, images, and feelings that are the elements of consciousness—was studied; the first major school of psychological thought, beginning with Wundt in the late 1800s (contrast with **Functionalism**) (Ch. 1).

Structure building   The process of comprehension in Gernsbacher's theory, of building a mental representation of the meaning of sentences (Ch. 10).

Subgoal   In problem solving, an intermediate goal that must be achieved to reach a final goal (Ch. 12).

Subjective organization   The grouping or organizing of items that are to be learned according to some scheme or basis devised by the subject (Ch. 6).

Suppression   In Gernsbacher's theory, the active process of reducing the activation level of concepts no longer relevant to the meaning of a sentence (Ch. 10).

Surface structure   In linguistics and psycholinguistics, the actual form of a sentence, whether written or spoken (contrast with **Deep structure**); the literal string of words or sounds present in a sentence (Ch. 9).

Syllogism (also **Categorical syllogism**)   A classic reasoning form composed of two premises and one conclusion in which the logical truth of the conclusion must be derived from the premises (Ch. 11).

Symbolic comparison   Mental comparisons of symbols, such as digits, usually in a "choose smaller/larger" task (Ch. 11).

Symbolic distance effect   The result, in symbolic comparison tasks, in which two relatively different stimuli (e.g., 1 and 8) are judged more rapidly than two relatively similar stimuli (e.g., 1 and 2) because of greater symbolic distance between 1 and 8 (Ch. 11).

Synapse   The junction of two neurons; the small gap between the terminal buttons of one neuron and the dendrites of another; as a verb, to form a junction with another neuron (Ch. 2).

Syntax   The arrangement of words as elements in a sentence to show their relationship to one another; grammatical structure; the rules governing the order of words in a sentence (Ch. 9).

Tabula rasa   Latin term meaning "blank slate." The term refers to a standard assumption of behaviorists that learning and experience write a record on the "blank slate"; in other words, the assumption that learning, as opposed to innate factors, is the most important factor in determining behavior (Ch. 1).

Tachistoscope (also **T-scope**)   An apparatus designed to present visual stimuli in a controlled position for a short period of time, usually milliseconds; today, visual stimuli often are presented via computer in tachistoscopic fashion (Ch. 3).

Target   The second part of a prime–target stimulus (see **Priming**); any concept or material that is designated as being of special interest (Ch. 7).

Technical accuracy   Accuracy in recall or recognition that is scored according to verbatim criteria (contrast with **Content accuracy**) (Ch. 8).

Template   A model or pattern. In theories of pattern recognition, a template is the pattern stored in memory against which incoming stimuli are compared to recognize the incoming patterns (Ch. 3).

Thematic effects A reconstructive memory influence on recall or recognition when the person's knowledge of the theme influences performance (see also **Content accuracy, Reconstructive memory**) (Ch. 8).

Tip-of-the-tongue (TOT) effect Momentary retrieval failure, with the sense of being on the verge of retrieving the target concept (Chs. 6, 10).

Top-down processing See **Conceptually driven processing**.

Topic maintenance Making conversational contributions relevant to the topic, sticking to the topic (Ch. 10).

Transformational grammar Chomsky's theory of the structure of language, a combination of a phrase structure grammar and a set of transformational rules (Ch. 9).

Transformational rules In Chomsky's transformational grammar, the syntactic rules that transform an idea (a deep structure sentence) into its surface structure; for instance, rules that form a passive sentence or a negative sentence (Ch. 9).

Type I/II rehearsal See **Maintenance rehearsal** and **Elaborative rehearsal**.

Typicality In semantic categories, the degree to which items are viewed as typical, central members of a category; the central tendency of a category (Ch. 7).

Typicality effect In semantic memory research, the result that typical members of a category tend to be judged more rapidly than atypical members (Ch. 7).

Unauthorized Not intended, especially said of inferences drawn during a conversation (contrast with **Authorized**) (Ch. 10).

Unconscious processing Mental processing outside of awareness (Ch. 2).

Undoing See **Counterfactual reasoning**.

Unit See **Chunk**.

Uphill change In the simulation heuristic, a change in a story or setting that brings a new and unlikely event into the story, an event that might change the outcome but is unusual or unanticipated in such a scenario (Ch. 11).

Verbal learning The branch of human experimental psychology, largely replaced by cognitive psychology in the late 1950s and early 1960s, investigating the learning and retention of "verbal,"

that is, language-based, stimuli; influenced directly by Ebbinghaus's methods and interests (Ch. 1).

Verbal protocol In studies of problem solving, a word-for-word transcription of what the subject said aloud during the problem-solving attempt (Chs. 2, 12).

Visual imagery The mental representation of visual information; the skill or ability to remember visual information (Ch. 6).

Visual persistence The perceptual phenomenon in which a visual stimulus still seems to be present even after its termination, usually a few hundred milliseconds to a few seconds (Ch. 3).

Visual sensory memory (also **Iconic memory**) The short-duration memory system specialized for holding visual information, lasting no more than about 250–500 ms (Ch. 3).

Visuospatial sketchpad The visual and perceptual component of Baddeley's working memory model (Ch. 5).

von Restorff effect In a recall task, the elevated accuracy for an item that was noticeably different during list presentation, for instance, because it was written in a different color of ink (Ch. 8).

Well-defined problem A problem in which the initial and final states and the legal operators are clearly specified (Ch. 12).

Wernicke's aphasia One of two common forms of aphasia in which the language disorder is characterized by a serious disruption of comprehension and the use of invented words as well as semantically inappropriate substitutions (contrast with **Broca's aphasia**). The aphasia is caused by damage in the region of the neocortex called Wernicke's area (Ch. 9).

Whole report condition Especially in Sperling's (1960) research, the condition in which the entire visual display was to be reported (contrast with **Partial report condition**) (Ch. 3).

Whorf's linguistic relativity hypothesis See **Linguistic relativity hypothesis**.

Word frequency effect Finding that frequent words in the language are processed more rapidly than infrequent words (Ch. 2).

Working memory The component, similar to short-term memory, in Baddeley and Hitch's (1974) theory in which verbal rehearsal and other conscious processing takes place; also, the component that contains the executive controller in charge of devoting conscious processing resources to the various other components in the memory system (Ch. 5).

References

Abbot, V., Black, J. B., & Smith, E. E. (1985). The representation of scripts in memory. *Journal of Memory and Language, 24*, 179–199.

Abelson, R. P. (1981). Psychological status of the script concept. *American Psychologist, 36*, 715–729.

Agnoli, F. (1991). Development of judgmental heuristics and logical reasoning: Training counteracts the representativeness heuristic. *Cognitive Development, 6*, 195–217.

Agnoli, F., & Krantz, D. H. (1989). Suppressing natural heuristics by formal instruction: The case of the conjunction fallacy. *Cognitive Psychology, 21*, 515–550.

Ahlum-Heath, M. E., & DiVesta, F. J. (1986). The effect of conscious controlled verbalization of a cognitive strategy on transfer in problem solving. *Memory & Cognition, 14*, 281–285.

Ainsworth-Darnell, K., Shulman, H. G., & Boland, J. E. (1998). Dissociating brain responses to syntactic and semantic anomalies: Evidence from event-related potentials. *Journal of Memory and Language, 38*, 112–130.

Albrecht, J. E. & O'Brien, E. J. (1991). Effects of centrality on retrieval of text-based concepts. *Journal of Experimental Psychology: Learning, Memory, and Cognition, 17*, 932–939.

Allen, P. A., & Madden, D. J. (1990). Evidence for a parallel input serial analysis (PISA) model of word processing. *Journal of Experimental Psychology: Human Perception and Performance, 16*, 48–64.

Allport, A. (1989). Visual attention. In M. I. Posner (Ed.), *Foundations of cognitive science* (pp. 631–682). Cambridge, MA: Bradford.

Altmann, G. T. M., Garnham, A., & Dennis, Y. (1992). Avoiding the garden path: Eye movements in context. *Journal of Memory and Language, 31*, 685–712.

American Heritage College Dictionary (3rd ed.). (1997). Boston: Houghton Mifflin.

Anderson, J. R. (1976). *Language, memory, and thought.* Hillsdale, NJ: Erlbaum.

Anderson, J. R. (1980). *Cognitive psychology and its implications.* San Francisco: Freeman.

Anderson, J. R. (1982). Acquisition of cognitive skill. *Psychological Review, 89*, 369–406.

Anderson, J. R. (1983). *The architecture of cognition.* Cambridge, MA: Harvard University Press.

Anderson, J. R. (1985). *Cognitive psychology and its implications* (2nd ed.). New York: Freeman.

Anderson, J. R. (1990). *The adaptive character of thought.* Hillsdale, NJ: Erlbaum.

Anderson, J. R. (1992). Intelligent tutoring and high school mathematics. In *Proceedings of the Second International Conference on Intelligent Tutoring Systems* (pp. 1–10). Montreal: Springer-Verlag.

Anderson, J. R. (1993). Problem solving and learning. *American Psychologist, 48*, 35–44.

Anderson, J. R. (1996). Implicit memory and metacognition: Why is the glass half full? In L. M. Reder (Ed.), *Implicit memory and metacognition* (pp. 123–136). Hillsdale, NJ: Erlbaum.

Anderson, J. R., & Bower, G. H. (1973). *Human associative memory.* Washington, DC: Winston & Sons.

Anderson, J. R., Boyle, C. F., Corbett, A., & Lewis, M. W. (1990). Cognitive modelling and intelligent tutoring. *Artificial Intelligence, 42*, 7–49.

Anderson, J. R., & Lebiere, C. (1998). *The atomic components of thought.* Hillsdale, NJ: Erlbaum.

Anderson, J. R., & Schooler, L. J. (1991). Reflections of the environment in memory. *Psychological Science, 2*, 396–408.

Antrobus, J. (1991). Dreaming: Cognitive processes during cortical activation and high afferent thresholds. *Psychological Review, 98*, 96–121.

Arrigo, J. M., & Pezdek, K. (1997). Lessons from the study of psychogenic amnesia. *Current Directions in Psychological Science, 6*, 148–152.

Ashcraft, M. H. (1976). Priming and property dominance effects in semantic memory. *Memory & Cognition, 4*, 490–500.

Ashcraft, M. H. (1978a). Property dominance and typicality effects in property statement verification. *Journal of Verbal Learning and Verbal Behavior, 17*, 155–164.

Ashcraft, M. H. (1978b). Property norms for typical and atypical items from 17 categories: A description and discussion. *Memory & Cognition, 6*, 227–232.

Ashcraft, M. H. (1993). A personal case history of transient anomia. *Brain and Language, 44*, 47–57.

Ashcraft, M. H. (1995). Cognitive psychology and simple arithmetic: A review and summary of new directions. *Mathematical Cognition, 1*, 3–34.

Ashcraft, M. H., & Christy, K. S. (1995). The frequency of arithmetic facts in elementary texts: Addition and multiplication in grades 1–6. *Journal for Research in Mathematics Education, 26*, 396–421.

Ashcraft, M. H., Kellas, G., & Needham, S. (1975). Rehearsal and retrieval processes in free recall of categorized lists. *Memory & Cognition, 3*, 506–512.

Atkinson, R. C., & Shiffrin, R. M. (1968). Human memory: A proposed system and its control processes. In W. K. Spence & J. T. Spence (Eds.), *The psychology of learning and motivation: Advances in research and theory* (Vol. 2, pp. 89–195). New York: Academic Press.

Atkinson, R. C., & Shiffrin, R. M. (1971). The control of short-term memory. *Scientific American, 225*, 82–90.

Atwood, M. E., & Polson, P. (1976). A process model for water jug problems. *Cognitive Psychology, 8*, 191–216.

Averbach, E., & Coriell, A. S. (1961). Short-term memory in vision. *Bell System Technical Journal, 40*, 309–328. (Reprinted in Coltheart, M. (1973). *Readings in cognitive psychology.* Toronto: Holt, Rinehart & Winston of Canada)

Averbach, E., & Sperling, G. (1961). Short term storage and information in vision. In C. Cherry (Ed.), *Information theory* (pp. 196–211). London: Butterworth.

Ayers, M. S., & Reder, L. M. (1998). A theoretical review of the misinformation effect: Predictions from an activation-based memory model. *Psychonomic Bulletin & Review, 5*, 1–21.

Baddeley, A. (1992a). Is working memory working? The Fifteenth Bartlett Lecture. *Quarterly Journal of Experimental Psychology, 44A*, 1–31.

Baddeley, A. (1992b). Working memory. *Science, 255*, 556–559.

Baddeley, A. (1999, November). *The episodic buffer: A new component of working memory?* Paper presented at the meetings of the Psychonomic Society, Los Angeles.

Baddeley, A., & Wilson, B. (1988). Comprehension and working memory: A single case neuropsychological study. *Journal of Memory and Language, 27*, 479–498.

Baddeley, A. D. (1976). *The psychology of memory.* New York: Basic Books.

Baddeley, A. D. (1978). The trouble with levels: A reexamination of Craik and Lockhart's framework for memory research. *Psychological Review, 85*, 139–152.

Baddeley, A. D. (1986). *Working memory.* Oxford, England: Oxford University Press.

Baddeley, A. D., & Hitch, G. (1974). Working memory. In G. H. Bower (Ed.), *The psychology of learning and motivation* (Vol. 8, pp. 47–89). New York: Academic Press.

Baddeley, A. D., & Lieberman, K. (1980). Spatial working memory. In R. Nickerson (Ed.), *Attention and performance VIII.* Hillsdale, NJ: Erlbaum.

Baddeley, A. D., Thomson, N., & Buchanan, M. (1975). Word length and the structure of short-term memory. *Journal of Verbal Learning and Verbal Behavior, 14*, 575–589.

Bahrick, H. P. (1983). The cognitive map of a city: 50 years of learning and memory. In G. H. Bower (Ed.), *The psychology of learning and motivation: Advances in research and theory* (Vol. 17, pp. 125–163). New York: Academic Press.

Bahrick, H. P. (1984). Semantic memory content in permastore: Fifty years of memory for Spanish learned in school. *Journal of Experimental Psychology: General, 113*, 1–29.

Bahrick, H. P., Bahrick, L. E., Bahrick, A. S., & Bahrick, P. E. (1993). Maintenance of foreign language vocabulary and the spacing effect. *Psychological Science, 4*, 316–321.

Bahrick, H. P., Bahrick, P. C., & Wittlinger, R. P. (1975). Fifty years of memories for names and faces: A cross-sectional approach. *Journal of Experimental Psychology: General, 104*, 54–75.

Bahrick, H. P., & Hall, L. K. (1991). Lifetime maintenance of high school mathematics content. *Journal of Experimental Psychology: General, 120*, 20–33.

Bahrick, H. P., Hall, L. K., & Berger, S. A. (1996). Accuracy and distortion in memory for high school grades. *Psychological Science, 7*, 265–271.

Balota, D. A., & Paul, S. T. (1996). Summation of activation: Evidence from multiple primes that converge and diverge within semantic memory. *Journal of Experimental Psychology: Learning, Memory, and Cognition, 22*, 827–845.

Banaji, M. R., & Crowder, R. G. (1989). The bankruptcy of everyday memory. *American Psychologist, 44*, 1185–1193.

Banaji, M. R., & Hardin, C. D. (1996). Automatic stereotyping. *Psychological Science, 7*, 136–141.

Banich, M. T. (1997). *Neuropsychology: The neural bases of mental function.* Boston: Houghton Mifflin.

Banks, W. P. (1977). Encoding and processing of symbolic information in comparative judgments. In G. H. Bower (Ed.), *The psychology of learning and motivation* (Vol. 11, pp. 101–159). New York: Academic Press.

Banks, W. P., Clark, H. H., & Lucy, P. (1975). The locus of the semantic congruity effect in comparative judgments. *Journal of Experimental Psychology: Human Perception and Performance, 1*, 35–47.

Banks, W. P., Fujii, M., & Kayra-Stuart, F. (1976). Semantic congruity effects in comparative judgments of magnitude of digits. *Journal of Experimental Psychology: Human Perception and Performance, 2*, 435–447.

Bar-Hillel, M. (1980). What features make samples seem representative? *Journal of Experimental Psychology: Human Perception and Performance, 6*, 578–589.

Barshi, I., & Healy, A. F. (1993). Checklist procedures and the cost of automaticity. *Memory & Cognition, 21*, 496–505.

Bartlett, F. C. (1932). *Remembering: A study in experimental and social psychology.* London: Cambridge University Press.

Bassok, M., & Holyoak, K. H. (1989). Interdomain transfer between isomorphic topics in algebra and physics. *Journal of Experimental Psychology: Learning, Memory, and Cognition, 15*, 153–166.

Bates, E., Masling, M., & Kintsch, W. (1978). Recognition memory for aspects of dialogue. *Journal of Experimental Psychology: Human Learning and Memory, 4*, 187–197.

Battig, W. F., & Montague, W. E. (1969). Category norms for verbal items in 56 categories: A replication and extension of the Connecticut category norms. *Journal of Experimental Psychology Monograph, 80* (3, Pt. 2), 1–46.

Baum, D. R., & Jonides, J. (1979). Cognitive maps: Analysis of comparative judgments of distance. *Memory & Cognition, 7*, 462–468.

Beattie, G. (1983). *Talk: An analysis of speech and nonverbal behaviour in conversation.* Milton Keynes, England: Open University Press.

Belli, R. F. (1989). Influences of misleading postevent information: Misinformation interference and acceptance. *Journal of Experimental Psychology: General, 118*, 72–85.

Belli, R. F., Lindsay, D. S., Gales, M. S., & McCarthy, T. T. (1994). Memory impairment and source misattribution in postevent misinformation experiments with short retention intervals. *Memory & Cognition, 22*, 40–54.

Benjamin, L. T., Jr., Durkin, M., Link, M., Vestal, M., & Acord, J. (1992). Wundt's American doctoral students. *American Psychologist, 47*, 123–131.

Benson, D. J., & Geschwind, N. (1969). The alexias. In P. Vincken & G. W. Bruyn (Eds.), *Handbook of clinical neurology* (Vol. 4, pp. 112–140). Amsterdam: North-Holland.

Besner, D., & Stolz, J. A. (1999). What kind of attention modulates the Stroop effect? *Psychonomic Bulletin & Review, 6,* 99–104.

Bestgen, Y., & Vonk, W. (2000). Temporal adverbials as segmentation markers in discourse comprehension. *Journal of Memory and Language, 42,* 74–87.

Biederman, I. (1987). Recognition by components: A theory of human image understanding. *Psychological Review, 94,* 115–147.

Biederman, I. (1990). Higher-level vision. In E. N. Osherson, S. M. Kosslyn, & J. M. Hollerbach (Eds.), *An invitation to cognitive science* (Vol. 2, pp. 41–72). Cambridge, MA: MIT Press.

Biederman, I., & Blickle, T. (1985). *The perception of objects with deleted contours.* Unpublished manuscript, State University of New York, Buffalo.

Biederman, I., Glass, A. L., & Stacy, E. W. (1973). Searching for objects in real world scenes. *Journal of Experimental Psychology, 97,* 22–27.

Birch, S. L., & Garnsey, S. M. (1995). The effect of focus on memory for words in sentences. *Journal of Memory and Language, 34,* 232–267.

Birch, S. L., & Rayner, K. (1997). Linguistic focus affects eye movements during reading. *Memory & Cognition, 25,* 653–660.

Bisiach, E., & Luzzatti, C. (1978). Unilateral neglect of representational space. *Cortex, 14,* 129–133.

Blakemore, C. (1977). *Mechanics of the mind.* Cambridge, England: Cambridge University Press.

Blom, J. P., & Gumperz, J. J. (1972). Social meaning in linguistic structure: Code-switching in Norway. In J. J. Gumperz & D. Hymes (Eds.), *Directions in sociolinguistics: The ethnography of communication* (pp. 407–434). New York: Holt.

Bloom, F. E., & Lazerson, A. (1988). *Brain, mind, and behavior.* New York: W. H. Freeman.

Bock, J. K. (1982). Toward a cognitive psychology of syntax: Information processing contributions to sentence formulation. *Psychological Review, 89,* 1–47.

Bock, J. K. (1986). Meaning, sound, and syntax: Lexical priming in sentence production. *Journal of Experimental Psychology: Learning, Memory, and Cognition, 12,* 575–586.

Bock, K. (1996). Language production: Methods and methodologies. *Psychonomic Bulletin & Review, 3,* 395–421.

Bock, K., & Griffin, Z. M. (2000). The persistence of structural priming: Transient activation or implicit learning? *Journal of Experimental Psychology: General, 129,* 177–192.

Bock, K., & Miller, C. A. (1991). Broken agreement. *Cognitive Psychology, 23,* 45–93.

Bonebakker, A. E., Bonke, B., Klein, J., Wolters, G., Stijnen, T., Passchier, J., & Merikle, P. M. (1996). Information processing during general anesthesia: Evidence for unconscious memory. *Memory & Cognition, 24,* 766–776.

Boring, E. G. (1929). *A history of experimental psychology.* New York: Century.

Boring, E. G. (1950). *A history of experimental psychology* (2nd ed.). New York: Appleton-Century-Crofts.

Bourne, L. E., Jr., & Bunderson, C. V. (1963). Effects of delay of informative feedback and length of postfeedback interval on concept identification. *Journal of Experimental Psychology, 65,* 1–5.

Bousfield, W. A. (1953). The occurrence of clustering in the recall of randomly arranged associates. *Journal of General Psychology, 49,* 229–240.

Bousfield, W. A., & Sedgewick, C. H. W. (1944). An analysis of sequences of restricted associative responses. *Journal of General Psychology, 30,* 149–165.

Bowden, E. M. (1985). Accessing relevant information during problem solving: Time constraints on search in the problem space. *Memory & Cognition, 13,* 280–286.

Bowden, E. M., & Beeman, M. J. (1998). Getting the right idea: Semantic activation in the right hemisphere may help solve insight problems. *Psychological Science, 9,* 435–440.

Bowden, E. M., Beeman, M., & Gernsbacher, M. A. (1995, March). *Two hemispheres are better than one: Drawing coherence inferences during story comprehension.* Paper presented at the annual meeting of the Cognitive Neuroscience Society, San Francisco.

Bower, G. H. (1970). Analysis of a mnemonic device. *American Scientist, 58,* 496–510.

Bower, G. H., Black, J. B., & Turner, T. J. (1979). Scripts in memory for text. *Cognitive Psychology, 11,* 177–220.

Bower, G. H., Clark, M. C., Lesgold, A. M., & Winzenz, D. (1969). Hierarchical retrieval schemes in recall of categorical word lists. *Journal of Verbal Learning and Verbal Behavior, 8,* 323–343.

Brainerd, C. J., & Reyna, V. F. (1998). When things that were never experienced are easier to "remember" than things that were. *Psychological Science, 9,* 484–489.

Branigan, H. P., Pickering, M. J., & Cleland, A. A. (1999). Syntactic priming in written production: Evidence for rapid decay. *Psychonomic Bulletin & Review, 6,* 635–640.

Bransford, J. D. (1979). *Human cognition: Learning, understanding and remembering.* Belmont, CA: Wadsworth.

Bransford, J. D., & Franks, J. J. (1971). The abstraction of linguistic ideas. *Cognitive Psychology, 2,* 331–350.

Bransford, J. D., & Franks, J. J. (1972). The abstraction of linguistic ideas: A review. *Cognition: International Journal of Cognitive Psychology, 1,* 211–249.

Bransford, J. D., & Johnson, M. K. (1972). Contextual prerequisites for understanding: Some investigations of comprehension and recall. *Journal of Verbal Learning and Verbal Behavior, 11,* 717–726.

Bransford, J. D., & Stein, B. S. (1984). *The ideal problem solver.* New York: Freeman.

Bransford, J. D., & Stein, B. S. (1993). *The ideal problem solver* (2nd ed.). New York: Freeman.

Breedin, S. D., & Saffran, E. M. (1999). Sentence processing in the face of semantic loss: A case study. *Journal of Experimental Psychology: General, 128,* 547–562.

Bremner, J. D., Shobe, K. K., & Kihlstrom, J. F. (2000). False memories in women with self-reported childhood sexual abuse: An empirical study. *Psychological Science, 11,* 333–337.

Brennan, S. E., & Clark, H. H. (1996). Conceptual pacts and lexical choice in conversation. *Journal of Experimental Psychology: Learning, Memory, and Cognition, 22,* 1482–1493.

Bresnan, J. (1978). A realistic transformational grammar. In J. Bresnan, M. Halle, & G. Miller (Eds.), *Linguistic theory and psychological reality* (pp. 1–59). Cambridge, MA: MIT Press.

Bresnan, J., & Kaplan, R. M. (1982). Introduction: Grammars as mental representations of language. In J. Bresnan (Ed.), *The mental representation of grammatical relations* (pp. xvii–iii). Cambridge, MA: MIT Press.

Brewer, W. F., & Hay, A. E. (1984). Reconstructive recall of linguistic style. *Journal of Verbal Learning and Verbal Behavior, 23,* 237–249.

Bridgeman, B. (1988). *The biology of behavior and mind.* New York: Wiley.

Bridgman, P. W. (1927). *The logic of modern physics.* New York: Macmillan.

Broadbent, D. E. (1952). Speaking and listening simultaneously. *Journal of Experimental Psychology, 43,* 267–273.

Broadbent, D. E. (1958). *Perception and communication.* London: Pergamon.

Brooks, J. O. III, & Watkins, M. J. (1990). Further evidence of the intricacy of memory span. *Journal of Experimental Psychology: Learning, Memory, and Cognition, 16,* 1134–1141.

Brooks, L. R. (1968). Spatial and verbal components of the act of recall. *Canadian Journal of Experimental Psychology, 22,* 349–368.

Brown, A. L. (1975). The development of memory: Knowing, knowing about knowing, and knowing how to know. In H. W. Reese (Ed.), *Advances in child development and behavior* (Vol. 10, pp. 104–152). New York: Academic Press.

Brown, A. S., Neblett, D. R., Jones, T. C., & Mitchell, D. B. (1991). Transfer of processing in repetition priming: Some inappropriate findings. *Journal of Experimental Psychology: Learning, Memory, and Cognition, 17,* 514–525.

Brown, A. S., & Nix, L. A. (1996). Turning lies into truths: Referential validation of falsehoods. *Journal of Experimental Psychology: Learning, Memory, and Cognition, 22,* 1088–1100.

Brown, J. A. (1958). Some tests of the decay theory of immediate memory. *Quarterly Journal of Experimental Psychology, 10,* 12–21.

Brown, N. R., & Siegler, R. S. (1992). The role of availability in the estimation of national populations. *Memory & Cognition, 20,* 406–412.

Brown, N. R., & Siegler, R. S. (1993). Metrics and mappings: A framework for understanding real-world quantitative estimation. *Psychological Review, 100,* 511–534.

Brown, R., & Ford, M. (1961). Address in American English. *Journal of Abnormal and Social Psychology, 62,* 375–385.

Brown, R., & Kulik, J. (1977). Flashbulb memories. *Cognition, 5,* 73–99.

Brown, R., & McNeill, D. (1966). The "tip-of-the-tongue" phenomenon. *Journal of Verbal Learning and Verbal Behavior, 5,* 325–337.

Bruner, J. S. (1973). *Beyond the information given: Studies in the psychology of knowing* (J. Anglin, Ed.). New York: Norton.

Bruner, J. S., Goodnow, J. J., & Austin, G. A. (1956). *A study of thinking.* New York: Wiley.

Bryden, M. P. (1982). *Laterality: Functional asymmetry in the intact human brain.* New York: Academic Press.

Buchner, A., & Wippich, W. (2000). On the reliability of implicit and explicit memory measures. *Cognitive Psychology, 40,* 227–259.

Bundesen, C. (1990). A theory of visual attention. *Psychological Review, 97,* 523–547.

Burke, D. M., MacKay, D. G., Worthley, J. S., & Wade, E. (1991). On the tip of the tongue: What causes word finding failures in young and older adults? *Journal of Memory and Language, 30,* 542–579.

Burns, D. J. (1996). The bizarre imagery effect and intention to learn. *Psychonomic Bulletin & Review, 3,* 254–257.

Busey, T. A., Tunnicliff, J., Loftus, G. R., & Loftus, E. F. (2000). Accounts of the confidence–accuracy relation in recognition memory. *Psychonomic Bulletin & Review, 7,* 26–48.

Campbell, J. I. D., & Graham, D. J. (1985). Mental multiplication skill: Structure, process, and acquisition. *Canadian Journal of Psychology, 39,* 338–366.

Caramazza, A. (1986). On drawing inferences about the structure of normal cognitive systems from the analysis of patterns of impaired performance: The case for single-patient studies. *Brain and Cognition, 5,* 41–66.

Caramazza, A., & McCloskey, M. (1988). The case for single-patient studies. *Cognitive Neuropsychology, 5,* 517–528.

Carlson, B. W. (1990). Anchoring and adjustment in judgments under risk. *Journal of Experimental Psychology: Learning, Memory, and Cognition, 16,* 665–676.

Carlson, R. A., Khoo, B. H., Yaure, R. G., & Schneider, W. (1990). Acquisition of a problem-solving skill: Levels of organization and use of working memory. *Journal of Experimental Psychology: General, 119,* 193–214.

Carr, T. H., & Dagenbach, D. (1986). Now you see it, now you don't: Relations between semantic activation and awareness. *Brain and Brain Sciences, 9,* 26–27.

Carr, T. H., McCauley, C., Sperber, R. D., & Parmalee, C. M. (1982). Words, pictures, and priming: On semantic activation, conscious identification, and the automaticity of information processing. *Journal of Experimental Psychology: Human Perception and Performance, 8,* 757–777.

Carreiras, M., Gernsbacher, M. A., & Villa, V. (1995). The advantage of first mention in Spanish. *Psychonomic Bulletin & Review, 2,* 124–129.

Carroll, D. W. (1986). *Psychology of language.* Pacific Grove, CA: Brooks/Cole.

Casey, P. J. (1992). A reexamination of the roles of typicality and category dominance in verifying category membership. *Journal of Experimental Psychology: Learning, Memory, and Cognition, 18,* 823–834.

Catrambone, R. (1996). Generalizing solution procedures learned from examples. *Journal of Experimental Psychology: Learning, Memory, and Cognition, 22,* 1020–1031.

Cave, K. R., & Bichot, N. P. (1999). Visuospatial attention: Beyond a spotlight model. *Psychonomic Bulletin & Review, 6,* 204–223.

Cave, K. R., & Kosslyn, S. M. (1989). Varieties of size-specific visual selection. *Journal of Experimental Psychology: General, 118,* 148–164.

Chang, T. M. (1986). Semantic memory: Facts and models. *Psychological Bulletin, 99,* 199–220.

Chase, W. G., & Ericsson, K. A. (1982). Skill and working memory. In G. H. Bower (Ed.), *The psychology of learning and motivation* (Vol. 16, pp. 1–58). New York: Academic Press.

Chase, W. G., & Simon, H. A. (1973). Perception in chess. *Cognitive Psychology, 4,* 55–81.

Chater, N., & Oaksford, M. (1999). The probability heuristics model of syllogistic reasoning. *Cognitive Psychology, 38,* 191–258.

Cherniak, C. (1984). Prototypicality and deductive reasoning. *Journal of Verbal Learning and Verbal Behavior, 23,* 625–642.

Cherry, E. C. (1953). Some experiments on the recognition of speech, with one and with two ears. *Journal of the Acoustical Society of America, 25,* 975–979.

Cherry, E. C., & Taylor, W. K. (1954). Some further experiments on the recognition of speech with one and two ears. *Journal of the Acoustical Society of America, 26,* 554–559.

Chomsky, N. (1957). *Syntactic structures.* The Hague: Mouton.

Chomsky, N. (1959). A review of Skinner's *Verbal behavior. Language, 35,* 26–58.

Chomsky, N. (1965). *Aspects of a theory of syntax.* Cambridge, MA: Harvard University Press.

Christianson, S. (1989). Flashbulb memories: Special, but not so special. *Memory & Cognition, 17,* 435–443.

Clapp, F. L. (1924). *The number combinations: Their relative difficulty and frequency of their appearance in textbooks.* Research Bulletin No. 1. Madison, WI: Bureau of Educational Research.

Clark, H. H. (1977). Bridging. In P. N. Johnson-Laird & P. C. Wason (Eds.), *Thinking: Readings in cognitive science* (pp. 411–420). Cambridge: Cambridge University Press.

Clark, H. H. (1979). Responding to indirect speech acts. *Cognitive Psychology, 11,* 430–477.

Clark, H. H. (1992). *Arenas of language use.* Chicago: University of Chicago Press.

Clark, H. H. (1994). Discourse in production. In M. A. Gernsbacher (Ed.), *Handbook of psycholinguistics* (pp. 985–1021). San Diego: Academic Press.

Clark, H. H., & Wasow, T. (1998). Repeating words in spontaneous speech. *Cognitive Psychology, 37,* 201–242.

Coghill, G. E. (1929). *Anatomy and the problem of behavior.* Cambridge, MA: Cambridge University Press. (Reprinted 1963, New York: Hafner.)

Collins, A., Warnock, E. H., Aiello, N., & Miller, M. L. (1975). Reasoning from incomplete knowledge. In D. Bobrow & A. Collins (Eds.), *Representation and understanding: Studies in cognitive science* (pp. 383–415). New York: Academic Press.

Collins, A. M., & Loftus, E. F. (1975). A spreading-activation theory of semantic processing. *Psychological Review, 82,* 407–428.

Collins, A. M., & Quillian, M. R. (1969). Retrieval time from semantic memory. *Journal of Verbal Learning and Verbal Behavior, 8,* 240–247.

Collins, A. M., & Quillian, M. R. (1970). Does category size affect categorization time? *Journal of Verbal Learning and Verbal Behavior, 9,* 432–438.

Collins, A. M., & Quillian, M. R. (1972). How to make a language user. In E. Tulving & W. Donaldson (Eds.), *Organization of memory* (pp. 309–351). New York: Academic Press.

Coltheart, M. (1973). *Readings in cognitive psychology.* Toronto: Holt, Rinehart & Winston of Canada.

Coltheart, M. (1983). Ecological necessity of iconic memory. *The Behavioral and Brain Sciences, 6,* 17–18.

Conrad, C. (1972). Cognitive economy in semantic memory. *Journal of Experimental Psychology, 92,* 149–154.

Conrad, R. (1964). Acoustic confusions in immediate memory. *British Journal of Psychology, 55,* 75–84.

Conway, A. R. A., Cowan, N., & Bunting, M. F. (in press). The cocktail party phenomenon revisited: The importance of working memory capacity. *Psychonomic Bulletin & Review.*

Conway, M. A. (1991). In defense of everyday memory. *American Psychologist, 46,* 19–26.

Conway, M. A., Anderson, S. J., Larsen, S. F., Donnelly, C. M., McDaniel, M. A., McClelland, A. G. R., Rawles, R. E., & Logie, R. H. (1994). The formation of flashbulb memories. *Memory & Cognition, 22,* 326–343.

Conway, M. A., Cohen, G., & Stanhope, N. (1991). On the very long-term retention of knowledge acquired through formal education: Twelve years of cognitive psychology. *Journal of Experimental Psychology: General, 120,* 395–409.

Conway, M. A., & Pleydell-Pearce, C. W. (2000). The construction of autobiographical memories in the self-memory system. *Psychological Review, 107,* 261–288.

Cook, M. (1977). Gaze and mutual gaze in social encounters. *American Scientist, 65,* 328–333.

Cooke, N. J., & Breedin, S. D. (1994). Constructing naive theories of motion on the fly. *Memory & Cognition, 22,* 474–493.

Cooper, E. H., & Pantle, A. J. (1967). The total-time hypothesis in verbal learning. *Psychological Bulletin, 68,* 221–234.

Cooper, L. A., & Shepard, R. N. (1973). Chronometric studies of the rotation of mental images. In W. G. Chase (Ed.), *Visual information processing* (pp. 75–176). New York: Academic Press.

Corballis, M. C. (1989). Laterality and human evolution. *Psychological Review, 96,* 492–505.

Coren, S., & Ward, L. M. (1989). *Sensation and perception* (3rd ed.). Ft. Worth, TX: Harcourt.

Coughlan, A. K., & Warrington, E. K. (1978). Word comprehension and word retrieval in patients with localised cerebral lesions. *Brain, 101,* 163–185.

Cowan, N. (1995). *Attention and memory: An integrated framework.* New York: Oxford University Press.

Cowan, N., & Stadler, M. A. (1996). Estimating unconscious processes: Implications of a general class of models. *Journal of Experimental Psychology: General, 125,* 195–200.

Cowan, N., Wood, N. L., Wood, P. K., Keller, T. A., Nugent, L. D., & Keller, C. V. (1998). Two separate verbal processing rates contributing to short-term memory span. *Journal of Experimental Psychology: General, 127,* 141–160.

Craik, F. I. M., & Lockhart, R. S. (1972). Levels of processing: A framework for memory research. *Journal of Verbal Learning and Verbal Behavior, 11,* 671–684.

Craik, F. I. M., & Tulving, E. (1975). Depth of processing and the retention of words in episodic memory. *Journal of Experimental Psychology, 104,* 268–294.

Craik, F. I. M., & Watkins, M. J. (1973). The role of rehearsal in short-term memory. *Journal of Verbal Learning and Verbal Behavior, 12,* 599–607.

Crick, F. H. C., & Asanuma, C. (1986). Certain aspects of the anatomy and physiology of the cerebral cortex. In D. E. Rumelhart, J. L. McClelland, & PDP Research Group (Eds.), *Parallel distributed processing* (Vol. 2, pp. 333–371). Cambridge, MA: MIT Press.

Crowder, R. G. (1970). The role of one's own voice in immediate memory. *Cognitive Psychology, 1,* 157–178.

Crowder, R. G. (1972). Visual and auditory memory. In J. F. Kavanaugh & I. G. Mattingly (Eds.), *Language by ear and by eye: The relationships between speech and reading* (pp. 251–276). Cambridge, MA: MIT Press.

Crowder, R. G., & Morton, J. (1969). Precategorical acoustic storage (PAS). *Perception and Psychophysics, 5,* 365–373.

Cummins, D. D., Lubart, T., Alksnis, O., & Rist, R. (1991). Conditional reasoning and causation. *Memory & Cognition, 19,* 274–282.

Damasio, H., & Damasio, A. R. (1997). The lesion method in behavioral neurology and neuropsychology. In T. E. Feinberg & M. J. Farah (Eds.), *Behavioral neurology and neuropsychology* (pp. 69–82). New York: McGraw-Hill.

Daneman, M., & Carpenter, P. A. (1980). Individual differences in working memory and reading. *Journal of Verbal Learning and Verbal Behavior, 19,* 450–466.

Daneman, M., & Merikle, P. M. (1996). Working memory and language comprehension: A meta-analysis. *Psychonomic Bulletin & Review, 3,* 422–433.

Danziger, S., Kingstone, A., & Rafal, R. D. (1998). Orienting to extinguished signals in hemispatial neglect. *Psychological Science, 9,* 119–123.

Darwin, C. J., Turvey, M. T., & Crowder, R. G. (1972). An auditory analogue of the Sperling partial report procedure: Evidence for brief auditory storage. *Cognitive Psychology, 3,* 255–267.

Deese, J. (1959). On the prediction of occurrence of particular verbal intrusions in immediate recall. *Journal of Experimental Psychology, 58,* 17–22.

Dell, G. S. (1986). A spreading-activation theory of retrieval in sentence production. *Psychological Review, 93,* 283–321.

Dell, G. S., & Newman, J. E. (1980). Detecting phonemes in fluent speech. *Journal of Verbal Learning and Verbal Behavior, 20,* 611–629.

Dempster, F. N. (1985). Proactive interference in sentence recall: Topic-similarity effects and individual differences. *Memory & Cognition, 13,* 81–89.

DePaulo, B. M., & Bonvillian, J. D. (1978). The effect on language development of the special characteristics of speech addressed to children. *Journal of Psycholinguistic Research, 7,* 189–211.

Descartes, R. (1972). *Treatise on man* (T. S. Hall, Trans.). Cambridge, MA: Harvard University Press. (Original work published 1637)

Deutsch, G., Bourbon, T., Papanicolaou, A. C., & Eisenberg, H. M. (1988). Visuospatial tasks compared via activation of regional cerebral blood flow. *Neuropsychologia, 26,* 445–452.

Deutsch, J. A., & Deutsch, D. (1963). Attention: Some theoretical considerations. *Psychological Review, 70,* 80–90.

De Vega, M. (1995). Backward updating of mental models during continuous reading of narratives. *Journal of Experimental Psychology: Learning, Memory, and Cognition, 21,* 373–385.

Dillon, R. F., & Reid, L. S. (1969). Short-term memory as a function of information processing during the retention interval. *Journal of Experimental Psychology, 81,* 261–269.

Donchin, E. (1981). Surprise! . . . Surprise? *Psychophysiology, 18,* 493–513.

Donders, F. C. (1969). Over de snelheid van psychische processen [Speed of Mental Processes]. Onderzoekingen gedann in het Psysiologish Laboratorium der Utrechtsche Hoogeschool (W. G. Koster, Trans.). In W. G. Koster (Ed.), Attention and performance II. *Acta Psychologica, 30,* 412–431. (Original work published 1868)

Donley, R. D., & Ashcraft, M. H. (1992). The methodology of testing naive beliefs in the physics classroom. *Memory & Cognition, 20,* 381–391.

Dooling, D., & Lachman, R. (1971). Effects of comprehension on retention of prose. *Journal of Experimental Psychology, 88,* 216–222.

Dooling, D. J., & Christiaansen, R. E. (1977). Episodic and semantic aspects of memory for prose. *Journal of Experimental Psychology: Human Learning and Memory, 3,* 428–436.

Dosher, B. A., & Ma, J-J. (1998). Output loss or rehearsal loop? Output-time versus pronunciation-time limits in immediate recall for forgetting-matched materials. *Journal of Experimental Psychology: Learning, Memory, and Cognition, 24,* 316–335.

Drachman, D. A. (1978). Central cholinergic system and memory. In M. A. Lipton, A. D. Mascio, & K. F. Killam (Eds.), *Psychopharmacology: A generation of process.* New York: Raven.

Dunbar, K., & MacLeod, C. M. (1984). A horse race of a different color: Stroop interference patterns with transformed words. *Journal of Experimental Psychology: Human Perception and Performance, 10,* 622–639.

Duncan, E. M., & McFarland, C. E., Jr. (1980). Isolating the effects of symbolic distance and semantic congruity in comparative judgments: An additive-factors analysis. *Memory & Cognition, 8,* 612–622.

Duncan, J., Bundesen, C., Olson, A., Humphreys, G., Chavda, S., & Shibuya, H. (1999). Systematic analysis of deficits in visual attention. *Journal of Experimental Psychology: General, 128,* 450–478.

Duncan, J., & Humphreys, G. W. (1989). Visual search and stimulus similarity. *Psychological Review, 96,* 433–458.

Duncan, J., & Humphreys, G. W. (1992). Beyond the search surface: Visual search and attentional engagement. *Journal of Experimental Psychology: Human Perception and Performance, 18,* 578–588.

Duncan, S. (1972). Some signals and rules for taking speaking turns in conversations. *Journal of Personality and Social Psychology, 23,* 283–292.

Duncker, K. (1945). On problem solving. *Psychological Monographs, 58* (Whole no. 270).

Ebbinghaus, H. (1885/1913). *Memory: A contribution to experimental psychology* (H. A. Ruger & C. E. Bussenius, Trans.). New York: Columbia University, Teacher's College. (Reprinted 1964, New York: Dover).

Ebbinghaus, H. (1908). *Abriss der Psychologie [Survey of Psychology].* Leipzig: Veit & Comp. (Also cited as 1910)

Eberhard, K. M. (1999). The accessibility of conceptual number to the processes of subject–verb agreement in English. *Journal of Memory and Language, 41,* 560–578.

Eddy, D. M. (1982). Probabilistic reasoning in clinical medicine: Problems and opportunities. In D. Kahneman, P. Slovic, & A. Tversky (Eds.), *Judgment under uncertainty: Heuristics and biases* (pp. 249–267). Cambridge, England: Cambridge University Press.

Edridge-Green, F. W. (1900). *Memory and its cultivation.* New York: Appleton & Co.

Edwards, D., & Potter, J. (1993). Language and causation: A discursive action model of description and attribution. *Psychological Review, 100,* 23–41.

Egan, P., Carterette, E. C., & Thwing, E. J. (1954). Some factors affecting multichannel listening. *Journal of the Acoustic Society of America, 26,* 774–782.

Eimas, P. D. (1975). Speech perception in early infancy. In L. B. Cohen & P. Salapatek (Eds.), *Infant perception: From sensation to cognition: Vol. II. Perception of space, speech, and sound* (pp. 193–231). New York: Academic Press.

Einstein, G. O., & McDaniel, M. A. (1987). Distinctiveness and the mnemonic benefits of bizarre imagery. In M. A. McDaniel & M. Pressley (Eds.), *Imagery and related mnemonic processes: Theories, individual differences and applications* (pp. 78–102). New York: Springer-Verlag.

Ellis, H. D. (1983). The role of the right hemisphere in face perception. In A. W. Young (Ed.), *Functions of the right cerebral hemisphere* (pp. 33–64). New York: Academic Press.

Ellis, N. C., & Hennelly, R. A. (1980). A bilingual word-length effect: Implications for intelligence testing and the relative ease of mental calculation in Welsh and English. *British Journal of Psychology, 71,* 43–52.

Engle, R. W. (2000). (in press.) What is working memory capacity? In H. L. Roediger, J. S. Nairne, I. Neath, & A. M. Suprenant (Eds.), *The nature of remembering: Essays in honor of Robert G. Crowder.*

Erdelyi, M. H., & Goldberg, B. (1979). Let's not sweep repression under the rug: Toward a cognitive psychology of repression. In J. F. Kihlstrom & F. J. Evans (Eds.), *Functional disorders of memory* (pp. 355–402). Hillsdale, NJ: Erlbaum.

Erdfelder, E., & Buchner, A. (1998). Decomposing the hindsight bias: A multinomial processing tree model for separating recollection and reconstruction in hindsight. *Journal of Experimental Psychology: Learning, Memory, and Cognition, 24,* 387–414.

Erickson, T. D., & Mattson, M. E. (1981). From words to meanings: A semantic illusion. *Journal of Verbal Learning and Verbal Behavior, 20,* 540–551.

Ericsson, K. A., & Charness, N. (1994). Expert performance: Its structure and acquisition. *American Psychologist, 49,* 725–747.

Ericsson, K. A., & Kintsch, W. (1995). Long-term working memory. *Psychological Review, 102,* 211–245.

Ericsson, K. A., & Simon, H. A. (1980). Verbal reports as data. *Psychological Review, 87,* 215–251.

Ericsson, K. A., & Simon, H. A. (1993). *Protocol analysis: Verbal reports as data* (Rev. ed.). Cambridge, MA: MIT Press.

Eriksen, C. W., & Johnson, H. J. (1964). Storage and decay characteristics of nonattended auditory stimuli. *Journal of Experimental Psychology, 68,* 28–36.

Ernst, G. W., & Newell, A. (1969). *GPS: A case study in generality and problem solving.* New York: Academic Press.

Evans, J. St. B. T., Handley, S. J., Harper, C. N. J., & Johnson-Laird, P. H. (1999). Reasoning about necessity and possibility: A test of the mental model theory of deduction. *Journal of Experimental Psychology: Learning, Memory, and Cognition, 25,* 1495–1513.

Eysenck, M. W. (1982). *Attention and arousal: Cognition and performance.* Heidelberg: Springer-Verlag.

Farah, M. J., & McClelland, J. L. (1991). A computational model of semantic memory impairment: Modality specificity and emergent category specificity. *Journal of Experimental Psychology: General, 120,* 339–357.

Fechner, G. (1860). *Elements of psychophysics* (English ed. of Vol. 1; H. E. Adler, Trans., D. H. Howes & E. G. Boring, Eds.). New York: Holt, Rinehart & Winston, 1966.

Feinberg, T. E., & Farah, M. J. (1997). The development of modern behavioral neurology and neuropsychology. In T. E. Feinberg & M. J. Farah (Eds.), *Behavioral neurology and neuropsychology* (pp. 3–24). New York: McGraw-Hill.

Feldman, D. (1992). *When did wild poodles roam the earth? An Imponderables™ book.* New York: HarperCollins.

Ferreira, F. (1994). Choice of passive voice is affected by verb type and animacy. *Journal of Memory and Language, 33,* 715–736.

Ferreira, F., Henderson, J. M., Anes, M. D., Weeks, P. A., Jr., McFarlane, D. K. (1996). Effects of lexical frequency and syntactic complexity in spoken-language comprehension: Evidence from the auditory moving-window technique. *Journal of Experimental Psychology: Learning, Memory, and Cognition, 22,* 324–335.

Ferreira, V. S. (1996). Is it better to give than to donate? Syntactic flexibility in language production. *Journal of Memory and Language, 35,* 724–755.

Ferreira, V. S., & Dell, G. S. (2000). Effect of ambiguity and lexical availability on syntactic and lexical production. *Cognitive Psychology, 40,* 296–340.

Fillenbaum, S. (1974). Pragmatic normalization: Further results for some conjunctive and disjunctive sentences. *Journal of Experimental Psychology, 102,* 574–578.

Fillmore, C. J. (1968). Toward a modern theory of case. In D. A. Reibel & S. A. Schane (Eds.), *Modern studies in English* (pp. 361–375). Englewood Cliffs, NJ: Prentice Hall.

Finke, R. A., & Freyd, J. J. (1985). Transformations of visual memory induced by implied motions of pattern elements. *Journal of Experimental Psychology: Learning, Memory, and Cognition, 11,* 780–794.

Fischhoff, B., & Bar-Hillel, M. (1984). Diagnosticity and the base-rate effect. *Memory & Cognition, 12,* 402–410.

Flavell, J. H. (1963). *The developmental psychology of Jean Piaget.* New York: Van Nostrand.

Flavell, J. H., & Wellman, H. M. (1977). Metamemory. In R. V. Kail & J. W. Hagen (Eds.), *Perspectives on the development of memory and cognition.* Hillsdale, NJ: Erlbaum.

Fletcher, C. R., & Bloom, C. P. (1988). Causal reasoning in the comprehension of simple narrative texts. *Journal of Memory and Language, 27,* 235–244.

Fodor, J. A. (1983). *The modularity of mind.* Cambridge, MA: MIT Press.

Fodor, J. A., & Garrett, M. (1966). Some reflections on competence and performance. In J. Lyons & R. J. Wales (Eds.), *Psycholinguistic papers* (pp. 135–154). Edinburgh: Edinburgh University Press.

Fong, G. T., & Nisbett, R. E. (1991). Immediate and delayed transfer of training effects in statistical reasoning. *Journal of Experimental Psychology: General, 120,* 34–45.

Forgus, R. H., & Melamed, L. E. (1976). *Perception: A cognitive-stage approach.* New York: McGraw-Hill.

Foss, D. J., & Hakes, D. T. (1978). *Psycholinguistics: An introduction to the psychology of language.* Englewood Cliffs, NJ: Prentice Hall.

Frazier, L., & Rayner, K. (1982). Making and correcting errors during sentence comprehension: Eye movements in the analysis of structurally ambiguous sentences. *Cognitive Psychology, 14,* 178–210.

Frazier, L., & Rayner, K. (1990). Taking on semantic commitments: Processing multiple meanings vs. multiple senses. *Journal of Memory and Language, 29,* 181–200.

Frederiksen, C. H. (1975). Acquisition of semantic information from discourse: Effects of repeated exposures. *Journal of Verbal Learning and Verbal Behavior, 14,* 158–169.

Freedman, J. L., & Loftus, E. F. (1971). Retrieval of words from long-term memory. *Journal of Verbal Learning and Verbal Behavior, 10,* 107–115.

Freud, S. (1953). Three essays on the theory of sexuality. In J. Strachey (Ed.), *The standard edition of the complete psychological works of Sigmund Freud* (Vol. 7, pp. 135–423). London: Hogarth. (Original work published 1905)

Freyd, J. J., & Jones, K. T. (1994). Representational momentum for a spiral path. *Journal of Experimental Psychology: Learning, Memory, and Cognition, 20,* 968–976.

Friederici, A. D., Hahne, A., & Mecklinger, A. (1996). Temporal structure of syntactic parsing: Early and late event-related brain potential effects. *Journal of Experimental Psychology: Learning, Memory, and Cognition, 22,* 1219–1248.

Friedman, A. (1978). Memorial comparisons without the "mind's eye." *Journal of Verbal Learning and Verbal Behavior, 17,* 427–444.

Friedman, A., & Brown, N. R. (2000). Reasoning about geography. *Journal of Experimental Psychology: General, 129,* 193–219.

Friedman, A., & Polson, M. C. (1981). Hemispheres as independent resource systems: Limited-capacity processing and cerebral specialization. *Journal of Experimental Psychology: Human Perception and Performance, 7,* 1031–1058.

Friedrich, F. J., Henik, A., & Tzelgov, J. (1991). Automatic processes in lexical access and spreading activation. *Journal of Experimental Psychology: Human Perception and Performance, 17,* 792–806.

Frisson, S., & Pickering, M. J. (1999). The processing of metonymy: Evidence from eye movements. *Journal of Experimental Psychology: Learning, Memory, and Cognition, 25,* 1366–1383.

Fromkin, V. A. (1971). The non-anomalous nature of anomalous utterances. *Language, 47,* 27–52.

Fromkin, V. A. (1973). *Speech errors as linguistic evidence.* The Hague: Mouton.

Fromkin, V. A., & Rodman, R. (1974). *An introduction to language.* New York: Holt, Rinehart & Winston.

Galanter, E. (1962). Contemporary psychophysics. In R. Brown, E. Galanter, E. H. Hess, & G. Mandler (Eds.), *New directions in psychology* (Vol. 1, pp. 87–156). New York: Holt, Rinehart & Winston.

Garcia, J., McGowan, B. K., & Green, K. F. (1972). Constraints on conditioning. In M. E. P. Seligman & J. L. Hager (Eds.), *Biological boundaries of learning.* New York: Appleton-Century-Crofts.

Gardner, H. (1985). *The mind's new science: A history of the cognitive revolution.* New York: Basic Books.

Garrett, M. F. (1975). The analysis of sentence production. In G. H. Bower (Ed.), *The psychology of learning and memory* (Vol. 9, pp. 133–177). New York: Academic Press.

Garrod, S., & Terras, M. (2000). The contribution of lexical and situational knowledge to resolving discourse roles: Bonding and resolution. *Journal of Memory and Language, 42,* 526–544.

Garry, M., Manning, C. G., Loftus, E. F., & Sherman, S. J. (1996). Imagination inflation: Imagining a childhood event inflates confidence that it occurred. *Psychonomic Bulletin & Review, 3,* 208–214.

Gazzaniga, M. S. (1995). Principles of human brain organization derived from split-brain studies. *Neuron, 14,* 217–228.

Gazzaniga, M. S., Ivry, R. B., & Mangun, G. R. (1998). *Cognitive neuroscience: The biology of the mind.* New York: W.W. Norton.

Gazzaniga, M. S., & Sperry, R. W. (1967). Language after section of the cerebral commissures. *Brain, 90,* 131–148.

Geary, D. C. (1992). Evolution of human cognition: Potential relationship to the ontogenetic development of behavior and cognition. *Evolution and Cognition, 1,* 93–100.

Geary, D. C. (1994). *Children's mathematical development: Research and practical applications.* Washington, D. C.: American Psychological Association.

Gentner, D. (1975). Evidence for the psychological reality of semantic components: The verbs of possession. In D. A. Norman & D. E. Rumelhart (Eds.), *Explorations in cognition* (pp. 211–246). San Francisco: Freeman.

Gentner, D., & Collins, A. (1981). Studies of inference from lack of knowledge. *Memory & Cognition, 9,* 434–443.

Gentner, D., & Markman, A. B. (1997). Structure mapping in analogy and similarity. *American Psychologist, 52,* 45–56.

Gernsbacher, M. A. (1985). Surface information loss in comprehension. *Cognitive Psychology, 17,* 324–363.

Gernsbacher, M. A. (1990). *Language comprehension as structure building.* Hillsdale, NJ: Erlbaum.

Gernsbacher, M. A. (1991). Cognitive processes and mechanisms in language comprehension: The structure building framework. In G. H. Bower (Ed.), *The psychology of learning and motivation* (Vol. 27, pp. 217–263). New York: Academic Press.

Gernsbacher, M. A. (1993). Less skilled readers have less efficient suppression mechanisms. *Psychological Science, 4,* 294–298.

Gernsbacher, M. A. (1997). Two decades of structure building. *Discourse Processes, 23,* 265–304.

Gernsbacher, M. A., & Hargreaves, D. (1988). Accessing sentence participants: The advantage of first mention. *Journal of Memory and Language, 27,* 699–717.

Gernsbacher, M. A., Hargreaves, D., & Beeman, M. (1989). Building and accessing clausal representations: The advantage of first mention versus the advantage of clause recency. *Journal of Memory and Language, 28,* 735–755.

Gernsbacher, M. A., & Jescheniak, J. D. (1995). Cataphoric devices in spoken discourse. *Cognitive Psychology, 29,* 24–58.

Gernsbacher, M. A., & Robertson, D. A. (1999, November). *Imaging higher-level cognition: Insights from discourse processing.* Paper presented at the meeting of the Psychonomic Society, Los Angeles.

Gernsbacher, M. A., & Robertson, R. R. W. (1995). Reading skill and suppression revisited. *Psychological Science, 6,* 165–169.

Gernsbacher, M. A., & Shroyer, S. (1989). The cataphoric use of the indefinite *this* in spoken narratives. *Memory & Cognition, 17,* 536–540.

Geschwind, N. (1967). The varieties of naming errors. *Cortex, 3,* 97–112.

Geschwind, N. (1970). The organisation of language and the brain. *Science, 170,* 940–944.

Gibbs, R. W., Jr., & Nayak, N. P. (1991). Why idioms mean what they do. *Journal of Experimental Psychology: General, 120,* 93–95.

Gibson, E. J. (1965). Learning to read. *Science, 148,* 1066–1072.

Gick, M. L., & Holyoak, K. J. (1980). Analogical problem solving. *Cognitive Psychology, 12,* 306–355.

Gick, M. L., & McGarry, S. J. (1992). Learning from mistakes: Inducing analogous solution failures to a source problem produces later successes in analogical transfer. *Journal of Experimental Psychology: Learning, Memory, and Cognition, 18,* 623–639.

Gilovich, T., Vallone, R., & Tversky, A. (1985). The hot hand in basketball: On the misperception of random sequences. *Cognitive Psychology, 17,* 295–314.

Glanzer, M. (1972). Storage mechanisms in recall. In G. H. Bower & J. T. Spence (Eds.), *The psychology of learning and motivation* (Vol. 5, pp. 129–193). New York: Academic Press.

Glanzer, M., & Cunitz, A. R. (1966). Two storage mechanisms in free recall. *Journal of Verbal Learning and Verbal Behavior, 5,* 351–360.

Glanzer, M., Fischler, B., & Dorfman, D. (1984). Short-term storage in reading. *Journal of Verbal Learning and Verbal Behavior, 23,* 467–486.

Glass, A. L., & Holyoak, K. J. (1975). Alternative conceptions of semantic memory. *Cognition, 3,* 313–339.

Glass, A. L., & Holyoak, K. J. (1986). *Cognition* (2nd ed.). New York: Random House.

Glass, A. L., Holyoak, K., & O'Dell, C. (1974). Production frequency and the verification of quantified statements. *Journal of Verbal Learning and Verbal Behavior, 13,* 237–254.

Glaze, J. A. (1928). The association value of nonsense syllables. *Journal of Genetic Psychology, 35,* 255–269.

Glenberg, A., & Adams, F. (1978). Type I rehearsal and recognition. *Journal of Verbal Learning and Verbal Behavior, 17,* 455–464.

Glenberg, A. M., Schroeder, J. L., & Robertson, D. A. (1998). Averting the gaze disengages the environment and facilitates remembering. *Memory & Cognition, 26,* 651–658.

Glenberg, A., Smith, S. M., & Green, C. (1977). Type I rehearsal: Maintenance and more. *Journal of Verbal Learning and Verbal Behavior, 11,* 403–416.

Glucksberg, S., & Danks, J. H. (1975). *Experimental psycholinguistics: An introduction.* Hillsdale, NJ: Erlbaum.

Glucksberg, S., & Keysar, B. (1990). Understanding metaphorical comparisons: Beyond similarity. *Psychological Review, 97,* 3–18.

Glucksberg, S., & McCloskey, M. (1981). Decisions about ignorance: Knowing that you don't know. *Journal of Experimental Psychology: Human Learning and Memory, 7,* 311–325.

Gobet, F., & Simon, H. A. (1996). Recall of random and distorted chess positions: Implications for the theory of expertise. *Memory & Cognition, 24,* 493–503.

Goldin-Meadow, S. (1997). When gestures and words speak differently. *Psychological Science, 6,* 138–143.

Goodglass, H., Kaplan, E., Weintraub, S., & Ackerman, N. (1976). The "tip-of-the-tongue" phenomenon in aphasia. *Cortex, 12,* 145–153.

Gordon, B., Hart, J., Jr., Boatman, D., & Lesser, R. P. (1997). Cortical stimulation (interference) during behavior. In T. E. Feinberg & M. J. Farah (Eds.), *Behavioral neurology and neuropsychology* (pp. 667–672). New York: McGraw-Hill.

Graesser, A. C. (1981). *Prose comprehension beyond the word.* New York: Springer-Verlag.

Graesser, A. C., & Nakamura, G. V. (1982). The impact of a schema on comprehension and memory. In G. H. Bower (Ed.), *The psychology of learning and motivation* (pp. 59–109). New York: Academic Press.

Graf, P., & Schacter, D. L. (1987). Selective effects of interference on implicit and explicit memory for new associations. *Journal of Experimental Psychology: Learning, Memory, and Cognition, 13,* 45–53.

Greenberg, J. H. (1978). Generalizations about numeral systems. In J. H. Greenberg (Ed.), *Universals of human language: Vol. 3.*

Word structure (pp. 249–295). Stanford, CA: Stanford University Press.

Greene, R. L. (1986). Effects of intentionality and strategy on memory for frequency. *Journal of Experimental Psychology: Learning, Memory, and Cognition, 12,* 489–495.

Greene, R. L., & Crowder, R. G. (1984). Modality and suffix effects in the absence of auditory stimulation. *Journal of Verbal Learning and Verbal Behavior, 23,* 371–382.

Greene, R. L., & Crowder, R. G. (1986). Recency effects in delayed recall of mouthed stimuli. *Memory & Cognition, 14,* 355–360.

Greeno, J. G. (1974). Hobbits and orcs: Acquisition of a sequential concept. *Cognitive Psychology, 6,* 270–292.

Greeno, J. G. (1978). Natures of problem-solving abilities. In W. K. Estes (Ed.), *Handbook of learning and cognitive processes: Vol. 5. Human information processing* (pp. 239–270). Hillsdale, NJ: Erlbaum.

Greenspan, S. L. (1986). Semantic flexibility and referential specificity of concrete nouns. *Journal of Memory and Language, 25,* 539–557.

Grice, H. P. (1975). Logic and conversation. In P. Cole & J. L. Morgan (Eds.), *Syntax and semantics: Vol. 3. Speech acts* (pp. 41–58). New York: Seminar Press.

Griffin, D., & Tversky, A. (1992). The weighing of evidence and the determinants of confidence. *Cognitive Psychology, 24,* 411–435.

Gross, D., Fischer, U., & Miller, G. A. (1989). The organization of adjectival meanings. *Journal of Memory and Language, 28,* 92–106.

Haber, R. N. (1983). The impending demise of the icon: A critique of the concept of iconic storage in visual information processing. *Behavioral and Brain Sciences, 6,* 1–54 (includes commentaries).

Haber, R. N., & Hershenson, M. (1973). *The psychology of visual perception.* New York: Holt, Rinehart & Winston.

Hall, J. F. (1971). *Verbal learning and retention.* Philadelphia: Lippincott.

Hampton, J. A. (1984). The verification of category and property statements. *Memory & Cognition, 12,* 345–354.

Hanson, C., & Hirst, W. (1988). Frequency encoding of token and type information. *Journal of Experimental Psychology: Learning, Memory, and Cognition, 14,* 289–297.

Harlow, H. F. (1953). Mice, monkeys, men and motives. *Psychological Review, 60,* 23–60.

Hasher, L., Stoltzfus, E. R., Zacks, R. T., & Rypma, B. (1991). Age and inhibition. *Journal of Experimental Psychology: Learning, Memory, and Cognition, 17,* 163–169.

Hasher, L., & Zacks, R. T. (1984). Automatic processing of fundamental information: The case of frequency of occurrence. *American Psychologist, 39,* 1372–1388.

Haviland, S. E., & Clark, H. H. (1974). What's new? Acquiring new information as a process in comprehension. *Journal of Verbal Learning and Verbal Behavior, 13,* 512–521.

Hayes, J. R., & Simon, H. A. (1974). Understanding written problem instructions. In L. W. Gregg (Ed.), *Knowledge and cognition* (pp. 167–200). Hillsdale, NJ: Erlbaum.

Hebb, D. O. (1961). Distinctive features of learning in the higher animal. In J. Dalafresnaye (Ed.), *Brain mechanisms and learning.* London: Oxford University Press.

Hell, W., Gigerenzer, G., Gauggel, S., Mall, M., & Muller, M. (1988). Hindsight bias: An interaction of automatic and motivational factors? *Memory & Cognition, 16,* 533–538.

Hellyer, S. (1962). Frequency of stimulus presentation and short-term decrement in recall. *Journal of Experimental Psychology, 64,* 650.

Helsabeck, F., Jr. (1975). Syllogistic reasoning: Generation of counterexamples. *Journal of Educational Psychology, 67,* 102–108.

Hildreth, E. C., & Ullman, S. (1989). The computational study of vision. In M. I. Posner (Ed.), *Foundations of cognitive science* (pp. 581–630). Cambridge, MA: Bradford.

Hilgard, E. R. (1964). Introduction to Ebbinghaus, 1885, *Memory: A contribution to experimental psychology* (pp. vii–x). New York: Dover.

Hintzman, D. L. (1978). *The psychology of learning and memory.* San Francisco: Freeman.

Hirshman, E., & Durante, R. (1992). Prime identification and semantic priming. *Journal of Experimental Psychology: Learning, Memory, and Cognition, 18,* 255–265.

Hirshman, E., Whelley, M. M., & Palij, M. (1989). An investigation of paradoxical memory effects. *Journal of Memory and Language, 28,* 594–609.

Hirst, W., & Kalmar, D. (1987). Characterizing attentional resources. *Journal of Experimental Psychology: General, 116,* 68–81.

Hoch, S. J. (1984). Availability and interference in predictive judgment. *Journal of Experimental Psychology: Learning, Memory, and Cognition, 10,* 649–662.

Hoch, S. J. (1985). Counterfactual reasoning and accuracy in predicting personal events. *Journal of Experimental Psychology: Learning, Memory, and Cognition, 11,* 719–731.

Hoch, S. J., & Loewenstein, G. F. (1989). Outcome feedback: Hindsight *and* information. *Journal of Experimental Psychology: Learning, Memory, and Cognition, 15,* 605–619.

Hockett, C. F. (1960a). Logical considerations in the study of animal communication. In W. E. Lanyon & W. N. Tavolga (Eds.), *Animal sounds and communication* (pp. 392–430). Washington, DC: American Institute of Biological Sciences.

Hockett, C. F. (1960b). The origin of speech. *Scientific American, 203,* 89–96.

Hockett, C. F. (1966). The problem of universals in language. In J. H. Greenberg (Ed.), *Universals of language* (2nd ed., pp. 1–29). Cambridge, MA: MIT Press.

Hoffman, C., Lau, I., & Johnson, D. R. (1986). The linguistic relativity of person cognition: An English–Chinese comparison. *Journal of Personality and Social Psychology, 51,* 1097–1105.

Hoffman, R. R., Bringmann, W., Bamberg, M., & Klein, R. (1987). Some historical observations on Ebbinghaus. In D. S. Gorfein & R. R. Hoffman (Eds.), *Memory and learning: The Ebbinghaus Centennial Conference* (pp. 57–75). Hillsdale, NJ: Erlbaum.

Holcomb, P. J. (1993). Semantic priming and stimulus degradation: Implications for the role of the N400 in language processing. *Psychophysiology, 30,* 47–61.

Holcomb, P. J., Kounios, J., Anderson, J. E., & West, W. C. (1999). Dual-coding, context availability, and concreteness effects in sentence comprehension: An electrophysiological investigation. *Journal of Experimental Psychology: Learning, Memory, and Cognition, 25,* 721–742.

Hollan, J. D. (1975). Features and semantic memory: Set-theoretic or network model? *Psychological Review, 82,* 154–155.

Holtgraves, T. (1994). Communication in context: Effects of speaker status on the comprehension of indirect requests. *Journal of Experimental Psychology: Learning, Memory, and Cognition, 20,* 1205–1218.

Holtgraves, T. (1998). Interpreting indirect replies. *Cognitive Psychology, 37,* 1–27.

Holyoak, K. J., & Mah, W. A. (1982). Cognitive reference points in judgments of symbolic magnitude. *Cognitive Psychology, 14,* 328–352.

Holyoak, K. J., & Simon, D. (1999). Bidirectional reasoning in decision making by constraint satisfaction. *Journal of Experimental Psychology: General, 128,* 3–31.

Holyoak, K. J., & Thagard, P. (1997). The analogical mind. *American Psychologist, 52,* 35–44.

Holyoak, K. J., & Walker, J. H. (1976). Subjective magnitude information in semantic orderings. *Journal of Verbal Learning and Verbal Behavior, 15,* 287–299.

Hothersall, D. (1984). *History of psychology.* New York: Random House.

Howard, D. V. (1983). *Cognitive psychology: Memory, language, and thought.* New York: Macmillan.

Hubbard, T. L. (1996). Representational momentum, centripetal force, and curvilinear impetus. *Journal of Experimental Psychology: Learning, Memory, and Cognition, 22,* 1049–1060.

Hubel, D. H., & Wiesel, T. N. (1962). Receptive fields, binocular interaction, and functional architecture in the cat's visual cortex. *Journal of Physiology, 160,* 106–154.

Huitema, J. S., Dopkins, S., Klin, C. M., & Myers, J. L. (1993). Connecting goals and actions during reading. *Journal of Experimental Psychology: Learning, Memory, and Cognition, 19,* 1053–1060.

Hull, C. L. (1943). *Principles of behavior.* New York: Appleton-Century-Crofts.

Hunt, E., & Agnoli, F. (1991). The Whorfian hypothesis: A cognitive psychology perspective. *Psychological Review, 98,* 377–389.

Hyman, I. E., Jr., & Pentland, J. (1996). The role of mental imagery in the creation of false childhood memories. *Journal of Memory and Language, 35,* 101–117.

Hyman, I. E., Jr., & Rubin, D. C. (1990). Memorabeatlia: A naturalistic study of long-term memory. *Memory & Cognition, 18,* 205–214.

Inhoff, A. W. (1984). Two stages of word processing during eye fixations in the reading of prose. *Journal of Verbal Learning and Verbal Behavior, 23,* 612–624.

Irwin, D. E. (1991). Information integration across saccadic eye movements. *Cognitive Psychology, 23,* 420–456.

Irwin, D. E. (1992). Memory for position and identity across eye movements. *Journal of Experimental Psychology: Learning, Memory, and Cognition, 18,* 307–317.

Irwin, D. E. (1998). Lexical processing during saccadic eye movements. *Cognitive Psychology, 36,* 1–27.

Irwin, D. E., & Carlson-Radvansky, L. A. (1996). Cognitive suppression during saccadic eye movements. *Psychological Science, 7,* 83–88.

Iversen, L. L. (1979). The chemistry of the brain. In *The brain: A Scientific American book* (pp. 70–83). San Francisco: Freeman.

Jackendoff, R. S. (1992). *Languages of the mind: Essays on mental representation.* Cambridge, MA: MIT Press.

Jacoby, L. L. (1991). A process dissociation framework: Separating automatic from intentional uses of memory. *Journal of Memory and Language, 30,* 513–541.

Jacoby, L. L., & Dallas, M. (1981). On the relationship between autobiographical memory and perceptual learning. *Journal of Experimental Psychology: General, 110,* 306–340.

Jacoby, L. L., Toth, J. P., & Yonelinas, A. P. (1993). Separating conscious and unconscious influences of memory: Measuring recollection. *Journal of Experimental Psychology: General, 122,* 139–154.

Jacoby, L. L., Woloshyn, V., & Kelley, C. (1989). Becoming famous without being recognized: Unconscious influences of memory produced by dividing attention. *Journal of Experimental Psychology: General, 118,* 115–125.

James, W. (1890). *The principles of psychology.* New York: Dover.

Jared, D., Levy, B. A., & Rayner, K. (1999). The role of phonology in the activation of word meanings during readings: Evidence from proofreading and eye movements. *Journal of Experimental Psychology: General, 128,* 219–264.

Jarvella, R. J. (1970). Effects of syntax on running memory span for connected discourse. *Psychonomic Science, 19,* 235–236.

Jarvella, R. J. (1971). Syntactic processing of connected speech. *Journal of Verbal Learning and Verbal Behavior, 10,* 409–416.

Jenkins, J. G., & Dallenbach, K. M. (1924). Obliviscence during sleep and waking. *American Journal of Psychology, 35,* 605–612.

Jenkins, J. J. (1974). Remember that old theory of memory? Well forget it! *American Psychologist, 29,* 785–795.

Johnson, J. T., & Finke, R. A. (1985). The base-rate fallacy in the context of sequential categories. *Memory & Cognition, 13,* 63–73.

Johnson, N. F. (1970). The role of chunking and organization in the process of recall. In G. H. Bower (Ed.), *The psychology of learning and motivation* (Vol. 4, pp. 172–247). New York: Academic Press.

Johnson-Laird, P. N. (1983). *Mental models: Towards a cognitive science of language, inference and consciousness.* Cambridge, MA: Harvard University Press.

Johnson-Laird, P. N., Byrne, R. M. J., & Schaeken, W. (1992). Propositional reasoning by model. *Psychological Review, 99,* 418–439.

Johnson-Laird, P. N., Legrenzi, P., & Legrenzi, M. S. (1972). Reasoning and a sense of reality. *British Journal of Psychology, 63,* 395–400.

Johnston, J. C., McCann, R. S., & Remington, R. W. (1995). Chronometric evidence for two types of attention. *Psychological Science, 6,* 365–369.

Johnston, W. A., & Heinz, S. P. (1978). Flexibility and capacity demands of attention. *Journal of Experimental Psychology: General, 107,* 420–435.

Jones, G. V. (1989). Back to Woodworth: Role of interlopers in the tip-of-the-tongue phenomenon. *Memory & Cognition, 17,* 69–76.

Jonides, J., & Jones, C. M. (1992). Direct coding for frequency of occurrence. *Journal of Experimental Psychology: Learning, Memory, and Cognition, 18,* 368–378.

Jonides, J., Smith, E. E., Koeppe, R. A., Awh, E., Minoshima, S., & Mintun, M. (1993). Spatial working memory in humans as revealed by PET. *Nature, 363,* 623–625.

Jusczyk, P. W., Smith, L. B., & Murphy, C. (1981). The perceptual classification of speech. *Perception and Psychophysics, 1,* 10–23.

Just, M. A. (1976, May). *Research strategies in prose comprehension.* Paper presented at the meetings of the Midwestern Psychological Association, Chicago.

Just, M. A., & Carpenter, P. A. (1980). A theory of reading: From eye fixations to comprehension. *Psychological Review, 87,* 329–354.

Just, M. A., & Carpenter, P. A. (1987). *The psychology of reading and language comprehension.* Boston: Allyn & Bacon.

Just, M. A., & Carpenter, P. A. (1992). A capacity theory of comprehension. *Psychological Review, 99,* 122–149.

Kahneman, D. (1968). Method, findings and theory in studies of visual masking. *Psychological Bulletin, 70,* 404–426.

Kahneman, D. (1973). *Attention and effort.* Englewood Cliffs, NJ: Prentice Hall.

Kahneman, D., Slovic, P., & Tversky, A. (Eds.). (1982). *Judgment under uncertainty: Heuristics and biases.* Cambridge: Cambridge University Press.

Kahneman, D., & Tversky, A. (1972). Subjective probability: A judgment of representativeness. *Cognitive Psychology, 3,* 430–454.

Kahneman, D., & Tversky, A. (1973). On the psychology of prediction. *Psychological Review, 80,* 237–251.

Kahneman, D., & Tversky, A. (1982). The simulation heuristic. In D. Kahneman, P. Slovic, & A. Tversky (Eds.), *Judgment under uncertainty: Heuristics and biases* (pp. 201–208). Cambridge, England: Cambridge University Press.

Kahneman, D., & Tversky, A. (1996). On the reality of cognitive illusions. *Psychological Review, 103,* 582–591.

Kane, M. J., Bleckley, M. K., Conway, A. R. A., & Engle, R. W. (in press). A controlled-attention view of working-memory capacity. *Journal of Experimental Psychology: General, 129.*

Kane, M. J., & Engle, R. W. (2000). Working memory capacity, proactive interference, and divided attention: Limits on long-term memory retrieval. *Journal of Experimental Psychology: Learning, Memory, and Cognition, 26,*. 336–358.

Kanwisher, N., & Driver, J. (1992). Objects, attributes, and visual attention: *Which, what, and where. Psychological Science, 1,* 26–31.

Karni, A., Tanne, D., Rubenstein, B. S., Akenasy, J. J. M., & Sagi, D. (1994). Dependence on REM sleep of overnight performance of a perceptual skill. *Science, 265,* 679–682.

Kay, J., & Ellis, A. (1987). A cognitive neuropsychological case study of anomia: Implications for psychological models of word retrieval. *Brain, 110,* 613–629.

Kazdin, A. E. (2000). (Ed.). *Encyclopedia of psychology.* Washington, D.C.: American Psychological Association and Oxford University Press.

Keil, F. C. (1991). On being more than the sum of the parts: The conceptual coherence of cognitive science. *Psychological Science, 2,* 283–293.

Kelley, C. M., & Jacoby, L. L. (1996). Memory attributions: Remembering, knowing, and feeling of knowing. In L. M. Reder (Ed.), *Implicit memory and metacognition* (pp. 287–308). Hillsdale, NJ: Erlbaum.

Kelley, C. M., & Lindsay, D. S. (1993). Remembering mistaken for knowing: Ease of retrieval as a basis for confidence in answers to general knowledge questions. *Journal of Memory and Language, 32,* 1–24.

Kelly, S. D., Barr, D. J., Church, R. B., & Lynch, K. (1999). Offering a hand to pragmatic understanding: The role of speech and gesture in comprehension and memory. *Journal of Memory and Language, 40,* 577–592.

Kempen, G., & Hoehkamp, E. (1987). An incremental procedural grammar for sentence formulation. *Cognitive Science, 11,* 201–258.

Kemper, S., & Thissen, D. (1981). Memory for the dimensions of requests. *Journal of Verbal Learning and Verbal Behavior, 20,* 552–563.

Kempton, W. (1986). Two theories of home heat control. *Cognitive Science, 10,* 75–90.

Keppel, G., & Underwood, B. J. (1962). Proactive inhibition in short-term retention of single items. *Journal of Verbal Learning and Verbal Behavior, 1,* 153–161.

Kertesz, A. (1982). Two case studies: Broca's and Wernicke's aphasia. In M. A. Arbib, D. Caplan, & J. C. Marshall (Eds.), *Neural models of language processes* (pp. 25–44). New York: Academic Press.

Kesner, R. P. (1998). Neural mediation of memory for time: Role of the hippocampus and medial prefrontal cortex. *Psychonomic Bulletin & Review, 5,* 585–596.

Keysar, B. (1994). The illusory transparency of intention: Linguistic perspective taking in text. *Cognitive Psychology, 26,* 165–208.

Keysar, B. (1998). Language users as problem solvers: Just what ambiguity problem do they solve? In S. R. Fussell & R. J. Kreuz (Eds.), *Social and cognitive psychological approaches to interpersonal communication* (pp. 175–200). Hillsdale, NJ: Erlbaum.

Keysar, B., Barr, D. J., & Horton, W. S. (1998). The egocentric basis of language use: Insights from a processing approach. *Current Directions in Psychological Science, 7,* 46–50.

Kinsbourne, M., & Cook, J. (1971). Generalized and lateralized effects of concurrent verbalization on a unimanual skill. *Quarterly Journal of Experimental Psychology, 23,* 341–345.

Kintsch, W. (1970). *Learning, memory, and conceptual processes.* New York: Wiley.

Kintsch, W. (1974). *The representation of meaning in memory.* Hillsdale, NJ: Erlbaum.

Kintsch, W. (1977). *Memory and cognition* (2nd ed.). New York: Wiley.

Kintsch, W. (1985). Reflections on Ebbinghaus. *Journal of Experimental Psychology: Learning, Memory, and Cognition, 11,* 461–463.

Kintsch, W., & Bates, E. (1977). Recognition memory for statements from a classroom lecture. *Journal of Experimental Psychology: Human Learning and Memory, 3,* 150–159.

Kintsch, W., & Greeno, J. G. (1985). Understanding and solving word arithmetic problems. *Psychological Review, 92,* 109–129.

Kirk, E. P., & Ashcraft, M. H. (2001). Telling stories: The perils and promise of using verbal reports to study math strategies. *Journal of Experimental Psychology: Learning, Memory, and Cognition, 27,* 157–175.

Klatzky, R. L. (1980). *Human memory: Structures and processes* (2nd ed.). San Francisco: Freeman.

Klayman, J., & Ha, Y.-W. (1989). Hypothesis testing in rule discovery: Strategy, structure, and content. *Journal of Experimental Psychology: Learning, Memory, and Cognition, 15,* 596–604.

Klin, C. M. (1995). Causal inferences in reading: From immediate activation to long-term memory. *Journal of Experimental Psychology: Learning, Memory, and Cognition, 21,* 1483–1494.

Kohler, W. (1927). *The mentality of apes.* New York: Harcourt, Brace.

Kolb, B., & Whishaw, I. Q. (1996). Fundamentals of human neuropsychology (4th ed.). New York: Freeman.

Kolers, P. A., & Roediger, H. L. III (1984). Procedures of mind. *Journal of Verbal Learning and Verbal Behavior, 23,* 425–449.

Kolodner, J. L. (1997). Educational implications of analogy: A view from case-based reasoning. *American Psychologist, 52,* 57–66.

Koriat, A., & Greenberg, S. N. (1996). The enhancement effect in letter detection: Further evidence for the structural model of reading. *Journal of Experimental Psychology: Learning, Memory, and Cognition, 22,* 1184–1195.

Kosslyn, S. M. (1978). Imagery and internal representation. In E. Rosch & B. B. Lloyd (Eds.), *Cognition and categorization* (pp. 217–257). Hillsdale, NJ: Erlbaum.

Kosslyn, S. M. (1981). The medium and the message in mental imagery: A theory. *Psychological Review, 88,* 46–66.

Kosslyn, S. M., & Pomerantz, J. P. (1977). Imagery, propositions, and the form of internal representations. *Cognitive Psychology, 9,* 52–76.

Kotovsky, K., Hayes, J. R., & Simon, H. A. (1985). Why are some problems hard? Evidence from Tower of Hanoi. *Cognitive Psychology, 17,* 248–294.

Kounios, J. (1996). On the continuity of thought and the representation of knowledge: Electrophysiological and behavioral time-course measures reveal levels of structure in semantic memory. *Psychonomic Bulletin & Review, 3,* 265–286.

Kounios, J., & Holcomb, P. J. (1992). Structure and process in semantic memory: Evidence from event-related brain potentials and reaction times. *Journal of Experimental Psychology: General, 121,* 459–479.

Kounios, J., & Holcomb, P. J. (1994). Concreteness effects in semantic processing: ERP evidence supporting dual-coding theory. *Journal of Experimental Psychology: Learning, Memory, and Cognition, 20,* 804–823.

Kounios, J., Kotz, S. A., & Holcomb, P. J. (2000). On the locus of the semantic satiation effect: Evidence from event-related brain potentials. *Memory & Cognition, 28,* 1366–1377.

Krauss, R. M., Morrel-Samuels, P., & Colosante, C. (1991). Do conversational hand gestures communicate? *Journal of Personality and Social Psychology, 61,* 743–754.

Krist, H., Fieberg, E. L., & Wilkening, F. (1993). Intuitive physics in action and judgment: The development of knowledge about projectile motion. *Journal of Experimental Psychology: Learning, Memory, and Cognition, 19,* 952–966.

Kroll, N. E. A., Schepeler, E. M., & Angin, K. T. (1986). Bizarre imagery: The misremembered mnemonic. *Journal of Experimental Psychology: Learning, Memory, and Cognition, 12,* 42–53.

Kucera, H., & Francis, W. N. (1967). *Computational analysis of present day American English.* Providence, RI: Brown University Press.

Kuhn, T. S. (1962). *The structure of scientific revolutions.* Chicago: University of Chicago Press.

Kumon-Nakamura, S., Glucksberg, S., & Brown, M. (1995). How about another piece of pie: The allusional pretense theory of discourse irony. *Journal of Experimental Psychology: General, 124,* 3–21.

Lachman, R., Lachman, J. L., & Butterfield, E. C. (1979). *Cognitive psychology and information processing: An introduction.* Hillsdale, NJ: Erlbaum.

Lashley, K. D. (1950). In search of the engram. *Symposia for the Society for Experimental Biology, 4,* 454–482.

Leahey, T. H. (1992a). *A history of psychology: Main currents in psychological thought* (3rd ed.). Englewood Cliffs, NJ: Prentice Hall.

Leahey, T. H. (1992b). The mythical revolutions of American psychology. *American Psychologist, 47,* 308–318.

Leahey, T. H. (2000). *A history of psychology: Main currents in psychological thought* (3rd ed.). Englewood Cliffs, NJ: Prentice Hall.

Lee, H-W., Rayner, K., & Pollatsek, A. (1999). The time course of phonological, semantic, and orthographic coding in reading: Evidence from the fast-priming technique. *Psychonomic Bulletin & Review, 6,* 624–634.

LeFevre, J., Bisanz, J., Daley, K. E., Buffone, L., Greenham, S. L., & Sadesky, G. S. (1996). Multiple routes to solution of single-digit multiplication problems. *Journal of Experimental Psychology: General, 125,* 284–306.

Lehman, D. R., Lempert, R. O., & Nisbett, R. E. (1988). The effects of graduate training on reasoning. *American Psychologist, 43,* 431–442.

Leonesio, R. J., & Nelson, T. O. (1990). Do different metamemory judgments tap the same underlying aspects of memory?

Journal of Experimental Psychology: Learning, Memory, and Cognition, 16, 464–470.

Levine, M. W., & Schefner, J. M. (1981). *Fundamentals of sensation and perception.* London: Addison-Wesley.

Lewis, J. L. (1970). Semantic processing of unattended messages using dichotic listening. *Journal of Experimental Psychology, 85,* 225–228.

Lewontin, R. C. (1990). The evolution of cognition. In D. N. Osherson & E. E. Smith (Eds.), *Thinking: An invitation to cognitive science* (Vol. 3, pp. 229–246). Cambridge, MA: MIT Press.

Liberman, A. M. (1957). Some results of research on speech perception. *Journal of the Acoustical Society of America, 29,* 117–123.

Liberman, A. M. (1970). The grammars of speech and language. *Cognitive Psychology, 1,* 301–323.

Liberman, A. M., Harris, K. S., Hoffman, H. S., & Griffith, B. C. (1957). The discrimination of speech sounds within and across phoneme boundaries. *Journal of Experimental Psychology, 54,* 358–368.

Libkuman, T. M., Nichols-Whitehead, P., Griffith, J., & Thomas, R. (1999). Source of arousal and memory for detail. *Memory & Cognition, 27,* 166–190.

Lindsay, P. H., & Norman, D. A. (1977). *Human information processing: An introduction to psychology.* New York: Academic Press.

Lindsley, J. R. (1975). Producing simple utterances: How far ahead do we plan? *Cognitive Psychology, 7,* 1–19.

Linton, M. (1975). Memory for real-world events. In D. A. Norman & D. E. Rumelhart (Eds.), *Explorations in cognition* (pp. 376–404). San Francisco: Freeman.

Linton, M. (1978). Real world memory after six years: An in vivo study of very long term memory. In M. M. Gruneberg, P. E. Morris, & R. N. Sykes (Eds.), *Practical aspects of memory* (pp. 69–76). Orlando: Academic Press.

Litman, D. J., & Allen, J. F. (1987). A plan recognition model for subdialogues in conversation. *Cognitive Science, 11,* 163–200.

Loftus, E. F. (1980). *Memory.* Reading, MA: Addison-Wesley.

Loftus, E. F. (1991a). Made in memory: Distortions in recollection after misleading information. In G. H. Bower (Ed.), *The psychology of learning and motivation* (Vol. 27, pp. 187–215). New York: Academic Press.

Loftus, E. F. (1991b). Resolving legal questions with psychological data. *American Psychologist, 46,* 1046–1048.

Loftus, E. F. (1993). The reality of repressed memories. *American Psychologist, 48,* 518–537.

Loftus, E. F., & Coan, D. (1994). The construction of childhood memories. In D. Peters (Ed.), *The child witness in context: Cognitive, social, and legal perspectives.* New York: Kluwer.

Loftus, E. F., Donders, K., Hoffman, H. G., & Schooler, J. W. (1989). Creating new memories that are quickly accessed and confidently held. *Memory & Cognition, 17,* 607–616.

Loftus, E. F., & Hoffman, H. G. (1989). Misinformation and memory: The creation of new memories. *Journal of Experimental Psychology: General, 118,* 100–104.

Loftus, E. F., & Ketcham, K. (1991). *Witness for the defense.* New York: St. Martin's Press.

Loftus, E. F., & Palmer, J. C. (1974). Reconstruction of automobile destruction: An example of the interaction between language and memory. *Journal of Verbal Learning and Verbal Behavior, 13,* 585–589.

Loftus, G. R. (1983). The continuing persistence of the icon. *Behavioral and Brain Sciences, 6,* 28.

Loftus, G. R., & Hanna, A. M. (1989). The phenomenology of spatial integration: Data and models. *Cognitive Psychology, 21,* 363–397.

Loftus, G. R., & Irwin, D. E. (1998). On the relations among different measures of visible and informational persistence. *Cognitive Psychology, 35,* 135–199.

Loftus, G. R., & Loftus, E. F. (1974). The influence of one memory retrieval on a subsequent memory retrieval. *Memory & Cognition, 2,* 467–471.

Loftus, G. R., & Loftus, E. F. (1976). *Human memory: The processing of information.* Hillsdale, NJ: Erlbaum.

Logan, G. D. (1988). Toward an instance theory of automatization. *Psychological Review, 95,* 492–527.

Logan, G. D. (1990). Repetition priming and automaticity: Common underlying mechanisms? *Cognitive Psychology, 22,* 1–35.

Logan, G. D., & Etherton, J. L. (1994). What is learned during automatization? The role of attention in constructing an instance. *Journal of Experimental Psychology: Learning, Memory, and Cognition, 20,* 1022–1050.

Logan, G. D., & Klapp, S. T. (1991). Automatizing alphabet arithmetic: I. Is extended practice necessary to produce automaticity? *Journal of Experimental Psychology: Learning, Memory, and Cognition, 17,* 179–195.

Logie, R. H., Zucco, G., & Baddeley, A. D. (1990). Interference with visual short-term memory. *Acta Psychologica, 75,* 55–74.

Long, D. L., & De Ley, L. (2000). Implicit causality and discourse focus: The interaction of text and reader characteristics in pronoun resolution. *Journal of Memory and Language, 42,* 545–570.

Long, D. L., Golding, J., Graesser, A. C., & Clark, L. F. (1990). Inference generation during story comprehension: A comparison of goals, events, and states. In A. C. Graesser & G. H. Bower (Eds.), *The psychology of learning and motivation* (Vol. 25). New York: Academic Press.

Long, D. L., Golding, J. M., & Graesser, A. C. (1992). A test of the on-line status of goal-related inferences. *Journal of Memory and Language, 31,* 634–647.

Long, D. L., Oppy, B. J., & Seely, M. R. (1997). Individual differences in readers' sentence- and text-level representations. *Journal of Memory and Language, 36,* 129–145.

Lorch, R. F., Jr., Lorch, E. P., & Matthews, P. D. (1985). On-line processing of the topic structure of a text. *Journal of Memory and Language, 24,* 350–362.

Luchins, A. S. (1942). Mechanization in problem solving. *Psychological Monographs, 54* (Whole no. 248).

MacDonald, M. C., & Just, M. A. (1989). Changes in activation levels with negation. *Journal of Experimental Psychology: Learning, Memory, and Cognition, 15,* 633–642.

MacDonald, M. C., Just, M. A., & Carpenter, P. A. (1992). Working memory constraints on the processing of syntactic ambiguity. *Cognitive Psychology, 24,* 56–98.

MacLeod, C. M. (1988). Forgotten but not gone: Savings for pictures and words in long-term memory. *Journal of Experimental Psychology: Learning, Memory, and Cognition, 14,* 195–212.

MacLeod, C. M. (1991). Half a century of research on the Stroop effect: An integrative review. *Psychological Bulletin, 109,* 163–203.

MacLeod, C. (1992). The Stroop task: The "gold standard" of attentional measures. *Journal of Experimental Psychology: General, 121,* 12–14.

Madigan, S., & O'Hara, R. (1992). Short-term memory at the turn of the century: Mary Whiton Calkins's memory research. *American Psychologist, 47,* 170–174.

Maier, N. R. F. (1931). Reasoning in humans: II. The solution of a problem and its appearance in consciousness. *Journal of Comparative Psychology, 12,* 181–194.

Maki, R. H. (1989). Recognition of added and deleted details in scripts. *Memory & Cognition, 17,* 274–282.

Malt, B. C. (1985). The role of discourse structure in understanding anaphora. *Journal of Memory and Language, 24,* 271–289.

Malt, B. C. (1990). Features and beliefs in the mental representation of categories. *Journal of Memory and Language, 29,* 289–315.

Mandel, D. R., & Lehman, D. R. (1996). Counterfactual thinking and ascriptions of cause and preventability. *Journal of Personality and Social Psychology, 71,* 450–463.

Mandler, G. (1967). Organization and memory. In K. W. Spence & J. T. Spence (Eds.), *The psychology of learning and motivation* (Vol. 1, pp. 327–372). New York: Academic Press.

Mandler, G. (1972). Organization and recognition. In E. Tulving & W. Donaldson (Eds.), *Organization of memory* (pp. 139–166). New York: Academic Press.

Mandler, G. (1984). *Mind and body: Psychology of emotion and stress.* New York: Norton.

Mandler, G. (1985). From association to structure. *Journal of Experimental Psychology: Learning, Memory, and Cognition, 11,* 464–468.

Mandler, J. M., & Mandler, G. (1969). The diaspora of experimental psychology: The gestaltists and others. In D. Fleming & B. Bailyn (Eds.), *The intellectual migration: Europe and America, 1930–1960* (pp. 371–419). Cambridge, MA: Harvard University Press.

Marcel, A. J. (1980). Conscious and preconscious recognition of polysemous words: Locating the selective effects of prior verbal context. In R. S. Nickerson (Ed.), *Attention and performance VIII* (pp. 435–457). Hillsdale, NJ: Erlbaum.

Marcel, A. J. (1983). Conscious and unconscious perception: Experiments on visual masking and word recognition. *Cognitive Psychology, 15,* 197–237.

Marian, V., & Neisser, U. (2000). Language-dependent recall of autobiographical memories. *Journal of Experimental Psychology: General, 129,* 361–368.

Marler, P. (1967). Animal communication signals. *Science, 35,* 63–78.

Marschark, M., & Cornoldi, C. (1990). Imagery and verbal memory. In C. Cornoldi & M. McDaniel (Eds.), *Imagery and cognition* (pp. 133–182). New York: Springer-Verlag.

Marschark, M., & Paivio, A. (1979). Semantic congruity and lexical marking in symbolic comparisons: An expectancy hypothesis. *Memory & Cognition, 7,* 175–184.

Marschark, M., Yuille, J. C. Richman, C. L., & Hunt, R. R. (1987). The role of imagery in memory: On shared and distinctive information. *Psychological Bulletin, 102,* 28–41.

Marshall, J. C., & Halligan, P. W. (1994). Left in the dark: The neglect of theory. *Neuropsychological Rehabilitation, 4,* 161–167.

Marslen-Wilson, W. D., & Welsh, A. (1978). Processing interactions and lexical access during word recognition in continuous speech. *Cognitive Psychology, 10,* 29–63.

Martin, E., & Noreen, D. L. (1974). Serial learning: Identification of subjective subsequences. *Cognitive Psychology, 6,* 421–435.

Martindale, C. (1991). *Cognitive psychology: A neural-network approach.* Pacific Grove, CA: Brooks/Cole.

Massaro, D. W. (1988). Some criticisms of connectionist models of human performance. *Journal of Memory and Language, 27,* 213–234.

Masson, M. E. J. (1984). Memory for the surface structure of sentences: Remembering with and without awareness. *Journal of Verbal Learning and Verbal Behavior, 23,* 579–592.

Masson, M. E. J. (1995). A distributed memory model of semantic priming. *Journal of Experimental Psychology: Learning, Memory, and Cognition, 21,* 3–23.

Matlin, M. (1983). *Cognition.* New York: Holt.

Maunsell, J. H. R., & Newsome, W. T. (1987). Visual processing in monkey extrastriate cortex. *Annual Review of Neuroscience, 10,* 363–401.

Maylor, E. A. (1996). Does prospective memory decline with age? In M. Brandimonte, G. O. Einstein, M.A. McDaniel (Eds.), *Prospective memory: Theory and applications* (pp. 173–198). Mabway, NJ: Erlbaum.

Maylor, E. A. (1997). Proper name retrieval in old age: Converging evidence against disproportionate impairment. *Aging, Neuropsychology, and Cognition, 4,* 211–226.

Mazzoni, G., & Cornoldi, C. (1993). Strategies in study time allocation: Why is study time sometimes not effective? *Journal of Experimental Psychology: General, 122,* 47–60.

McCandliss, B. D., Posner, M. I., & Givon, T. (1997). Brain plasticity in learning visual words. *Cognitive Psychology, 33,* 88–110.

McCarthy, R. A., & Warrington, E. K. (1984). A two route model of speech production: Evidence from aphasia. *Brain, 107,* 463–485.

McCarthy, R. A., & Warrington, E. K. (1990). *Cognitive neuropsychology: A clinical introduction.* San Diego: Academic Press.

McClelland, J. L. (1979). On the time relations of mental processes: An examination of systems of processes in cascade. *Psychological Review, 86,* 287–330.

McClelland, J. L., & Elman, J. L. (1986). The TRACE model of speech perception. *Cognitive Psychology, 18,* 1–86.

McClelland, J. L., & Rumelhart, D. E. (1981). An interactive activation model of context effects in letter perception: Part 1. An account of basic findings. *Psychological Review, 88,* 375–407.

McClelland, J. L., Rumelhart, D. E., & Hinton, G. E. (1986). The appeal of parallel distributed processing. In D. E. Rumelhart, J. L. McClelland, & PDP Research Group (Eds.), *Parallel distributed processing* (Vol. 1, pp. 3–44). Cambridge, MA: MIT Press.

McCloskey, M. (1983). Naive theories of motion. In D. Gentner & A. L. Stevens (Eds.), *Mental models* (pp. 299–324). Hillsdale, NJ: Erlbaum.

McCloskey, M. (1991). Networks and theories: The place of connectionism in cognitive science. *Psychological Science, 2,* 387–395.

McCloskey, M. (1992). Cognitive mechanisms in numerical processing: Evidence from acquired dyscalculia. *Cognition, 44,* 107–157.

McCloskey, M., Caramazza, A., & Green, B. (1980). Curvilinear motion in the absence of external forces: Naive beliefs about the motion of objects. *Science, 210,* 1139–1141.

McCloskey, M., Wible, C. G., & Cohen, N. J. (1988). Is there a special flashbulb-memory mechanism? *Journal of Experimental Psychology: General, 117,* 171–181.

McCloskey, M., & Zaragoza, M. (1985). Misleading postevent information and memory for events: Arguments and evidence against memory impairment hypotheses. *Journal of Experimental Psychology: General, 114,* 1–16.

McDaniel, M. A., & Einstein, G. O. (1986). Bizarre imagery as an effective memory aid: The importance of distinctiveness. *Journal of Experimental Psychology: Learning, Memory, and Cognition, 12,* 54–65.

McDonald, J. L., & MacWhinney, B. (1995). The time course of anaphor resolution: Effects of implicit verb causality and gender. *Journal of Memory and Language, 34,* 543–566.

McGeoch, J. A. (1932). Forgetting and the law of disuse. *Psychological Review, 39,* 352–370.

McKoon, G., & Ratcliff, R. (1986). Inferences about predictable events. *Journal of Experimental Psychology: Learning, Memory, and Cognition, 12,* 82–91.

McKoon, G., & Ratcliff, R. (1989). Inferences about contextually defined categories. *Journal of Experimental Psychology: Learning, Memory, and Cognition, 15,* 1134–1146.

McKoon, G., & Ratcliff, R. (1992). Inference during reading. *Psychological Review, 99,* 440–466.

McKoon, G., Ratcliff, R., Ward, G., & Sproat, R. (1993). Syntactic prominence effects on discourse processes. *Journal of Memory and Language, 32,* 593–607.

McNamara, T. P. (1992). Priming and constraints it places on theories of memory and retrieval. *Psychological Review, 99,* 650–662.

McNamara, T. P., & Diwadkar, V. A. (1996). The context of memory retrieval. *Journal of Memory and Language, 35,* 877–892.

McRae, K., & Boisvert, S. (1998). Automatic semantic similarity priming. *Journal of Experimental Psychology: Learning, Memory, and Cognition, 24,* 558–572.

McRae, K., de Sa, V. R., & Seidenberg, M. S. (1997). On the nature and scope of featural representations of word meaning. *Journal of Experimental Psychology: General, 126,* 99–130.

Medin, D. L., & Bazerman, M. H. (1999). Broadening behavioral decision research: Multiple levels of cognitive processing. *Psychonomic Bulletin & Review, 6,* 533–546.

Medin, D. L., & Edelson, S. M. (1988). Problem structure and the use of base-rate information from experience. *Journal of Experimental Psychology: General, 117,* 68–85.

Medin, D. L., Goldstone, R. L., & Gentner, D. (1993). Respects for similarity. *Psychological Review, 100,* 254–278.

Medin, D. L., Lynch, E. B., Coley, J. D., & Atran, S. (1997). Categorization and reasoning among tree experts: Do all roads lead to Rome? *Cognitive Psychology, 32,* 49–96.

Mehler, J., Morton, J., & Jusczyk, P. W. (1984). On reducing language to biology. *Cognitive Neuropsychology, 1,* 83–116.

Melton, A. W. (1963). Implications of short-term memory for a general theory of memory. *Journal of Verbal Learning and Verbal Behavior, 2,* 1–21.

Merikle, P. M. (1982). Unconscious perception revisited. *Perception & Psychophysics, 31,* 298–301.

Metcalfe, J. (1986). Feeling of knowing in memory and problem solving. *Journal of Experimental Psychology: Learning, Memory, and Cognition, 12,* 288–294.

Metcalfe, J., & Wiebe, D. (1987). Intuition in insight and noninsight problem solving. *Memory & Cognition, 15,* 238–246.

Meyer, A. S., & Bock, K. (1992). The tip-of-the-tongue phenomenon: Blocking or partial activation? *Memory & Cognition, 20,* 715–726.

Meyer, D. E., & Schvaneveldt, R. W. (1971). Facilitation in recognizing pairs of words: Evidence of a dependence between retrieval operations. *Journal of Experimental Psychology, 90,* 227–234.

Meyer, D. E., Schvaneveldt, R. W., & Ruddy, M. G. (1975). Loci of contextual effects on visual word-recognition. In P. M. A. Rabbitt & S. Dornic (Eds.), *Attention and performance* (Vol. 5, pp. 98–118). London: Academic Press.

Micco, A., & Masson, M. E. J. (1991). Implicit memory for new associations: An interactive process approach. *Journal of Experimental Psychology: Learning, Memory, and Cognition, 17,* 1105–1123.

Miller, G. A. (1956). The magical number seven, plus or minus two: Some limits on our capacity for processing information. *Psychological Review, 63,* 81–97.

Miller, G. A. (1973). Psychology and communication. In G. A. Miller (Ed.), *Communication, language, and meaning: Psychological perspectives* (pp. 3–12). New York: Basic Books.

Miller, G. A. (1977). Practical and lexical knowledge. In P. N. Johnson-Laird & P. C. Wason (Eds.), *Thinking: Readings in cognitive science* (pp. 400–410). Cambridge: Cambridge University Press.

Miller, G. A., Galanter, E., & Pribram, K. H. (1960). *Plans and the structure of behavior.* New York: Henry Holt.

Miller, G. A., & Isard, S. (1963). Some perceptual consequences of linguistic rules. *Journal of Verbal Learning and Verbal Behavior, 2*, 217–228.

Millis, K. K., & Graesser, A. C. (1994). The time-course of constructing knowledge-based inferences for scientific texts. *Journal of Memory and Language, 33*, 583–599.

Millis, K. K., & Just, M. A. (1994). The influence of connectives on sentence comprehension. *Journal of Memory and Language, 33*, 128–147.

Milner, B., Corkin, S., & Teuber, H. L. (1968). Further analysis of the hippocampal amnesic syndrome: 14-year follow up study of H.M. *Neuropsychologia, 6*, 215–234.

Mitchell, D. C., & Holmes, V. M. (1985). The role of specific information about the verb in parsing sentences with local structural ambiguity. *Journal of Memory and Language, 24*, 542–559.

Mitchell, K. J., & Zaragoza, M. S. (1996). Repeated exposure to suggestion and false memory: The role of contextual variability. *Journal of Memory and Language, 35*, 246–260.

Miyake, A., Friedman, N. P., Emerson, M. J., Witzki, A. H., Howerter, A., & Wager, T. D. (2000). The unity and diversity of executive functions and their contributions to complex "frontal lobe" tasks: A latent variable analysis. *Cognitive Psychology, 41*, 49–100.

Miyake, A., Just, M. A., & Carpenter, P. A. (1994). Working memory constraints on the resolution of lexical ambiguity: Maintaining multiple interpretations in neutral contexts. *Journal of Memory and Language, 33*, 175–202.

Miyake, A., & Shah, P. (Eds.). (1999). *Models of working memory: Mechanisms of active maintenance and executive control.* New York: Cambridge University Press.

Mook, D. G. (1983). In defense of external invalidity. *American Psychologist, 38*, 379–387.

Moray, N. (1959). Attention in dichotic listening: Affective cues and the influence of instructions. *Quarterly Journal of Experimental Psychology, 11*, 56–60.

Moray, N., Bates, A., & Barnett, T. (1965). Experiments on the four-eared man. *Journal of the Acoustical Society of America, 38*, 196–201.

Morris, C. D., Bransford, J. D., & Franks, J. J. (1977). Levels of processing versus transfer appropriate processing. *Journal of Verbal Learning and Verbal Behavior, 16*, 519–533.

Morris, R. K., & Folk, J. R. (1998). Focus as a contextual priming mechanism in reading. *Memory & Cognition, 26*, 1313–1322.

Morton, J. (1979). Facilitation in word recognition: Experiments causing change in the logogen models. In P. A. Kolers, M. E. Wrolstad, & H. Bouma, (Eds.), *Processing of visible language* (Vol. 1, pp. 259–268). New York: Plenum.

Moscovitch, M. (1979). Information processing and the cerebral hemispheres. In M. S. Gazzaniga (Ed.), *Handbook of behavioral neurobiology: Vol. 2. Neuropsychology* (pp. 379–446). New York: Plenum.

Moyer, R. S. (1973). Comparing objects in memory: Evidence suggesting an internal psychophysics. *Perception and Psychophysics, 13*, 180–184.

Moyer, R. S., & Bayer, R. H. (1976). Mental comparison and the symbolic distance effect. *Cognitive Psychology, 8*, 228–246.

Murdock, B. B., Jr. (1962). The serial position effect of free recall. *Journal of Experimental Psychology, 64*, 482–488.

Murphy, G. L. (1985). Processes of understanding anaphora. *Journal of Memory and Language, 24*, 290–303.

Murphy, G. L., & Medin, D. L. (1985). The role of theories in conceptual coherence. *Psychological Review, 92*, 289–316.

Murray, J. D., Klin, C. M., & Myers, J. L. (1993). Forward inferences in narrative text. *Journal of Memory and Language, 32*, 464–473.

Nadel, L., & Jacobs, W. J. (1998). Traumatic memory is special. *Current Directions in Psychological Science, 7*, 154–156.

Nairne, J. S. (1983). Associative processing during rote rehearsal. *Journal of Experimental Psychology: Learning, Memory, and Cognition, 9*, 3–20.

Nakamura, G. V., Graesser, A. C., Zimmerman, J. A., & Riha, J. (1985). Script processing in a natural situation. *Memory & Cognition, 13*, 140–144.

Navon, D. (1984). Resources: A theoretical soup stone? *Psychological Review, 91*, 216–234.

Neely, J. H. (1976). Semantic priming and retrieval from lexical memory: Evidence for facilitatory and inhibitory processes. *Memory & Cognition, 4*, 648–654.

Neely, J. H. (1977). Semantic priming and retrieval from lexical memory: Roles of inhibitionless spreading activation and limited-capacity attention. *Journal of Experimental Psychology: General, 106*, 226–254.

Neely, J. H., Keefe, D. E. & Ross, K. L. (1989). Semantic priming in the lexical decision task: Roles of prospective prime-generated expectancies and retrospective semantic matching. *Journal of Experimental Psychology: Learning, Memory, and Cognition, 15*, 1003–1019.

Neisser, U. (1964). Visual search. *Scientific American, 210*, 94–102.

Neisser, U. (1967). *Cognitive psychology.* New York: Appleton-Century-Crofts.

Neisser, U. (1976). *Cognition and reality.* San Francisco: Freeman.

Neisser, U. (1978). Memory: What are the important questions? In M. M. Gruneberg, P. E. Morris, & R. N. Sykes (Eds.), *Practical aspects of memory* (pp. 3–24). London: Academic Press.

Neisser, U. (1981). John Dean's memory: A case study. *Cognition, 9*, 1–22.

Neisser, U. (1982). *Memory observed: Remembering in natural contexts.* San Francisco: Freeman.

Neisser, U. (1988). New vistas in the study of memory. In U. Neisser & E. Winograd (Eds.), *Remembering reconsidered: Ecological and traditional approaches to the study of memory* (pp. 1–10). Cambridge: Cambridge University Press.

Neisser, U. (1991). A case of misplaced nostalgia. *American Psychologist, 46*, 34–36.

Neisser, U., Novick, R., & Lazar, R. (1963). Searching for ten targets simultaneously. *Perceptual and Motor Skills, 17*, 955–961.

Nelson, D. L., McKinney, V. M., Gee, N. R., & Janczura, G. A. (1998). Interpreting the influence of implicitly activated memories on recall and recognition. *Psychological Review, 105,* 299–324.

Nelson, T. O. (1978). Savings and forgetting from long-term memory. *Journal of Verbal Learning and Verbal Behavior, 10,* 568–576.

Nelson, T. O. (1985). Ebbinghaus's contribution to the measurement of retention: Savings during relearning. *Journal of Experimental Psychology: Learning, Memory, and Cognition, 11,* 472–479.

Nelson, T. O. (1988). Predictive accuracy of the feeling of knowing across different criterion tasks and across different subject populations and individuals. In M. Gruneberg, P. Morris, & R. Sykes (Eds.), *Practical aspects of memory: Current research and issues* (Vol. 1, pp. 190–196). New York: Wiley.

Nelson, T. O. (1993). Judgments of learning and the allocation of study time. *Journal of Experimental Psychology: General, 122,* 269–273.

Nelson, T. O. (1996). Consciousness and metacognition. *American Psychologist, 51,* 102–116.

Nelson, T. O., McSpadden, M., Fromme, K., & Marlatt, G. A. (1986). Effects of alcohol intoxication on metamemory and on retrieval from long-term memory. *Journal of Experimental Psychology: General, 115,* 247–254.

Newell, A., Shaw, J. C., & Simon, H. A. (1958). Elements of a theory of human problem solving. *Psychological Review, 65,* 151–166.

Newell, A., & Simon, H. A. (1972). *Human problem solving.* Englewood Cliffs, NJ: Prentice Hall.

Newport, E. L., & Bellugi, W. (1978). Linguistic expression of category levels in a visual–gestural language: A flower is a flower is a flower. In E. Rosch & B. B. Lloyd (Eds.), *Cognition and categorization* (pp. 49–71). Hillsdale, NJ: Erlbaum.

Nickerson, R. S., & Adams, M. J. (1979). Long-term memory for a common object. *Cognitive Psychology, 11,* 287–307.

Nisbett, R. E., Krantz, D. H., Jepson, C., & Kunda, Z. (1983). The use of statistical heuristics in everyday inductive reasoning. *Psychological Review, 90,* 339–363.

Nisbett, R., & Ross, L. (1980). *Human inference: Strategies and shortcomings of social judgment.* Englewood Cliffs, NJ: Prentice Hall.

Noordman, L. G. M., Vonk, W., & Kempff, H. J. (1992). Causal inferences during the reading of expository texts. *Journal of Memory and Language, 31,* 573–590.

Norman, D. A. (1968). Toward a theory of memory and attention. *Psychological Review, 75,* 522–536.

Norman, D. A. (1986). Reflections on cognition and parallel distributed processing. In J. L. McClelland, D. E. Rumelhart, & PDP Research Group (Eds.), *Parallel distributed processing: Explorations in the microstructure of cognition: Vol. 2. Psychological and biological models* (pp. 531–546). Cambridge, MA: MIT Press.

Norman, D. A., & Rumelhart, D. E. (Eds.). (1975). *Explorations in cognition.* San Francisco: Freeman.

Norris, D., McQueen, J. M., Cutler, A., & Butterfield, S. (1997). The possible-word constraint in the segmentation of continuous speech. *Cognitive Psychology, 34,* 191–243.

Novick, L. R. (1988). Analogical transfer, problem similarity, and expertise. *Journal of Experimental Psychology: Learning, Memory, and Cognition, 14,* 510–520.

O'Brien, E. J., & Albrecht, J. E. (1991). The role of context in accessing antecedents in text. *Journal of Experimental Psychology: Learning, Memory, and Cognition, 17,* 94–102.

O'Brien, E. J., Albrecht, J. E., Hakala, C. M., & Rizzella, M. L. (1995). Activation and suppression of antecedents during reinstatement. *Journal of Experimental Psychology: Learning, Memory, and Cognition, 21,* 626–634.

O'Brien, E. J., & Myers, J. L. (1987). The role of causal connections in the retrieval of text. *Memory & Cognition, 15,* 419–427.

O'Brien, E. J., Plewes, P. S., & Albrecht, J. E. (1990). Antecedent retrieval processes. *Journal of Experimental Psychology: Learning, Memory, and Cognition, 16,* 241–249.

O'Brien, E. J., Shank, D. M., Myers, J. L., & Rayner, K. (1988). Elaborative inferences during reading: Do they occur online? *Journal of Experimental Psychology: Learning, Memory, and Cognition, 14,* 410–420.

Ofshe, R. J. (1992). Inadvertent hypnosis during interrogation: False confession due to dissociative state, misidentified multiple personality, and the satanic cult hypothesis. *International Journal of Clinical and Experimental Hypnosis, 40,* 125–156.

Ojemann, G. A. (1982). Models of the brain organization for higher integrative functions derived with electrical stimulation techniques. *Human Neurobiology, 1,* 243–250.

Ojemann, G. A., & Creutzfeldt, O. D. (1987). Language in humans and animals: Contribution of brain stimulation and recording. In *Handbook of physiology: The nervous system* (Vol. 5). Bethesda: American Physiological Society.

O'Seaghdha, P. G. (1989). The dependence of lexical relatedness effects on syntactic connectedness. *Journal of Experimental Psychology: Learning, Memory, and Cognition, 15,* 73–87.

O'Seaghdha, P. G. (1997). Conjoint and dissociable effects of syntactic and semantic context. *Journal of Experimental Psychology: Learning, Memory, and Cognition, 23,* 807–828.

Osterhout, L., & Holcomb, P. J. (1992). Event-related brain potentials elicited by syntactic anomaly. *Journal of Memory and Language, 31,* 785–806.

Paivio, A. (1971). *Imagery and verbal processes.* New York: Holt.

Paivio, A. (1990). *Mental representations: A dual coding approach.* New York: Oxford University Press.

Palermo, D. S. (1978). *Psychology of language.* Glenview, IL: Scott, Foresman.

Palmer, S. E. (1975). The effects of contextual scenes on the identification of objects. *Memory & Cognition, 3,* 519–526.

Palmeri, T. J., & Flanery, M. A. (1999). Learning about categories in the absence of training: Profound amnesia and the relationship between perceptual categorization and recognition memory. *Psychological Science, 10,* 526–530.

Pashler, H. (1992). Attentional limitations in doing two tasks at the same time. *Current Directions in Psychological Science, 1,* 44–48.

Pashler, H. (1994). Dual-task interference in simple tasks: Data and theory. *Psychological Bulletin, 116,* 220–244.

Paul, S. T., Kellas, G., Martin, M., & Clark, M. B. (1992). Influence of contextual features on the activation of ambiguous word meanings. *Journal of Experimental Psychology: Learning, Memory, and Cognition, 18,* 703–717.

Payne, D. G., Toglia, M. P., & Anastasi, J. S. (1994). Recognition performance level and the magnitude of the misinformation effect in eyewitness memory. *Psychonomic Bulletin & Review, 1,* 376–382.

Pearlmutter, N. J., Garnsey, S. M., & Bock, K. (1999). Agreement processes in sentence comprehension. *Journal of Memory and Language, 41,* 427–456.

Penfield, W. (1958). *The excitable cortex in conscious man.* Liverpool, UK: Liverpool University Press.

Penfield, W., & Jasper, H. H. (1954). *Epilepsy and the functional anatomy of the human brain.* Boston: Little, Brown.

Penfield, W., & Milner, B. (1958). Memory deficit produced by bilateral lesions in the hippocampal zone. *Archives of Neurology and Psychiatry, 79,* 475–497.

Pennington, B. F. (1997). Attention deficit hyperactivity disorder. In T. E. Feinberg & M. J. Farah (Eds.), *Behavioral neurology and neuropsychology* (pp. 803–808). New York: McGraw-Hill.

Peterson, L. R., & Peterson, M. J. (1959). Short-term retention of individual items. *Journal of Experimental Psychology, 58,* 193–198.

Peterson, L. R., Peterson, M. J., & Miller, A. (1961). Short-term retention and meaningfulness. *Canadian Journal of Psychology, 15,* 143–147.

Pezdek, K., Whetstone, T., Reynolds, K., Askari, N., & Dougherty, T. (1989). Memory for real-world scenes: The role of consistency with schema expectation. *Journal of Experimental Psychology: Learning, Memory, and Cognition, 15,* 587–595.

Piaget, J. (1967). *Six psychological studies* (A. Tenzer, Trans.). New York: Random House.

Pickering, M. J., & Traxler, M. J. (1998). Plausibility and recovery from garden paths: An eye-tracking study. *Journal of Experimental Psychology: Learning, Memory, and Cognition, 24,* 940–961.

Piercey, C. D., & Joordens, S. (2000). Turning an advantage into a disadvantage: Ambiguity effects in lexical decision versus reading tasks. *Memory & Cognition, 28,* 657–666.

Pinker, S. (1994). *The language instinct: How the mind creates language.* New York: William Morrow & Cog.

Pitt, M. A., & Samuel, A. G. (1995). Lexical and sublexical feedback in auditory word recognition. *Cognitive Psychology, 29,* 149–188.

Pollack, I., & Pickett, J. M. (1964). Intelligibility of excerpts from fluent speech: Auditory vs. structural context. *Journal of Verbal Learning and Verbal Behavior, 3,* 79–84.

Pollatsek, A., Konold, C. E., Well, A. D., & Lima, S. D. (1984). Beliefs underlying random sampling. *Memory & Cognition, 12,* 395–401.

Polya, G. (1957). *How to solve it.* Garden City, NY: Doubleday/Anchor.

Posner, M. I. (1973). *Cognition: An introduction.* Glenview, IL: Scott, Foresman.

Posner, M. I. (1978). *Chronometric explorations of mind.* Hillsdale, NJ: Erlbaum.

Posner, M. I. (1997). Introduction: Neuroimaging of cognitive processes. *Cognitive Psychology, 33,* 2–4.

Posner, M. I., & Cohen, Y. (1984). Components of visual orienting. In H. Bouma & D. G. Bouwhuis (Eds.), *Attention and performance X* (pp. 531–556). Hillsdale, NJ: Erlbaum.

Posner, M. I., & Keele, S. W. (1967). Decay of visual information from a single letter. *Science, 158,* 137–139.

Posner, M. I., Kiesner, J. Thomas-Thrapp, L., McCandliss, B., Carr, T. H., & Rothbart, M. K. (1992, November). *Brain changes in the acquisition of literacy.* Paper presented at the meetings of the Psychonomic Society, St. Louis.

Posner, M. I., Nissen, M. J., & Ogden, W. C. (1978). Attended and unattended processing modes: The role of set for spatial location. In H. L. Pick & I. J. Saltzman (Eds.), *Modes of perceiving and processing information* (pp. 137–157). Hillsdale, NJ: Erlbaum.

Posner, M. I., & Synder, C. R. R. (1975). Facilitation and inhibition in the processing of signals. In P. M. A. Rabbitt & S. Dornic (Eds.), *Attention and performance V* (pp. 669–682). New York: Academic Press.

Posner, M. I., Snyder, C. R. R., & Davidson, B. J. (1980). Attention and the detection of signals. *Journal of Experimental Psychology: General, 109,* 160–174.

Postman, L., & Underwood, B. J. (1973). Critical issues in interference theory. *Memory & Cognition, 1,* 19–40.

Price, R. H. (1987). *Principles of psychology.* Glenview, IL: Scott, Foresman.

Pritchard, R. M. (1961). Stabilized images on the retina. *Scientific American, 204,* 72–78.

Proffitt, D. R., Kaiser, M. K., & Whelan, S. M. (1990). Understanding wheel dynamics. *Cognitive Psychology, 22,* 342–373.

Provins, K. A. (1997). Handedness and speech: A critical reappraisal of the role of genetic and environmental factors in the cerebral lateralization of function. *Psychological Review, 104,* 554–571.

Pylyshyn, Z. W. (1984). *Computation and cognition: Toward a foundation for cognitive science.* Cambridge, MA: Bradford.

Pylyshyn, Z. W. (1989). Computing in cognitive science. In M. I. Posner (Ed.), *Foundations of cognitive science* (pp. 49–91). Cambridge, MA: Bradford.

Quillian, M. R. (1968). Semantic memory. In M. Minsky (Ed.), *Semantic information processing* (pp. 216–270). Cambridge, MA: MIT Press.

Quillian, M. R. (1969). The teachable language comprehender: A simulation program and theory of language. *Communications of the ACM, 12,* 459–476.

Radvansky, G. A. (1998). The organization of information retrieved from situation models. *Psychonomic Bulletin & Review, 5,* 283–289.

Radvansky, G. A., Spieler, D. H., & Zacks, R. T. (1993). Mental model organization. *Journal of Experimental Psychology: Learning, Memory, and Cognition, 19,* 95–114.

Radvansky, G. A., Wyer, R. S., Jr., Curiel, J. M., & Lutz, M. F. (1997). Situation models and abstract ownership relations. *Journal of Experimental Psychology: Learning, Memory, and Cognition, 23,* 1233–1246.

Radvansky, G. A., & Zacks, R. T. (1991). Mental models and the fan effect. *Journal of Experimental Psychology: Learning, Memory, and Cognition, 17,* 940–953.

Rafal, R. D. (1997). Hemispatial neglect: Cognitive neuropsychological aspects. In T. E. Feinberg & M. J. Farah (Eds.), *Behavioral neurology and neuropsychology* (pp. 319–336). New York: McGraw-Hill.

Rapp, B., & Goldrick, M. (2000). Discreteness and interactivity in spoken word production. *Psychological Review, 107,* 460–499.

Ratcliff, G., & Newcombe, F. (1982). Object recognition: Some deductions from the clinical evidence. In A. W. Ellis (Ed.), *Normality and pathology in cognitive functions* (p. 162). London: Academic Press.

Ratcliff, R., & McKoon, G. (1978). Priming in item recognition: Evidence for the propositional structure of sentences. *Journal of Verbal Learning and Verbal Behavior, 17,* 403–418.

Ratcliff, R., & McKoon, G. (1988). A retrieval theory of priming in memory. *Psychological Review, 95,* 385–408.

Raven, J. C. (1941). Standardization of progressive matrices, 1938. *British Journal of Medical Psychology, 19,* 137–150.

Rayner, K. (1998). Eye movements in reading and information processing: 20 years of research. Psychological Bulletin, 124, 372–422.

Rayner, K., Carlson, M., & Frazier, L. (1983). The interaction of syntax and semantics during sentence processing: Eye movements in the analysis of semantically biased sentences. *Journal of Verbal Learning and Verbal Behavior, 22,* 358–374.

Rayner, K., & Duffy, S. A. (1988). On-line comprehension processes and eye movements in reading. In M. Daneman, G. E. MacKinnon, & T. G. Waller (Eds.), *Reading research: Advances in theory and practice* (pp. 13–66). New York: Academic Press.

Rayner, K., & Frazier, L. (1989). Selection mechanisms in reading lexically ambiguous words. *Journal of Experimental Psychology: Learning, Memory, and Cognition, 15,* 779–790.

Rayner, K., Garrod, S., & Perfetti, C. A. (1992). Discourse influences during parsing are delayed. *Cognition, 45,* 109–139.

Rayner, K., Inhoff, A. W., Morrison, P. E., Slowiaczek, M. L., & Bertera, J. H. (1981). Masking of foveal and parafoveal vision during eye fixations in reading. *Journal of Experimental Psychology: Human Perception and Performance, 7,* 167–179.

Rayner, K., & Pollatsek, A. (1989). *The psychology of reading.* Hillsdale, NJ: Erlbaum.

Rayner, K., Pollatsek, A., & Binder, K. S. (1998). Phonological codes and eye movements in reading. *Journal of Experimental Psychology: Learning, Memory, and Cognition, 24,* 476–497.

Rayner, K., & Well, A. D. (1996). Effects of contextual constraint on eye movements in reading: A further examination. *Psychonomic Bulletin & Review, 3,* 504–509.

Reason, J. (1990). *Human error.* New York: Cambridge University Press.

Reder, L. M., & Kusbit, G. W. (1991). Locus of the Moses illusion: Imperfect encoding, retrieval, or match? *Journal of Memory and Language, 30,* 385–406.

Reder, L. M., & Schunn, C. D. (1996). Metacognition does not imply awareness: Strategy choice is governed by implicit learning and memory. In L. M. Reder (Ed.), *Implicit memory and metacognition* (pp. 45–78). Mahwah, NJ: Erlbaum.

Reed, S. K. (1992). *Cognition: Theory and applications* (3rd ed.). Pacific Grove, CA: Brooks/Cole.

Reeves, L. M., & Weisberg, R. W. (1993). Abstract versus concrete information as the basis for transfer in problem solving: Comment on Fong and Nisbett (1991). *Journal of Experimental Psychology: General, 122,* 125–128.

Reichle, E. D., Carpenter, P. A., & Just, M. A. (2000). The neural bases of strategy and skill in sentence–picture verification. *Cognitive Psychology, 40,* 261–295.

Reichle, E. D., Pollatsek, A., Fisher, D. L., & Rayner, K. (1998). Toward a model of eye movement control in reading. *Psychological Review, 105,* 125–157.

Reisberg, D. (1997). *Cognition: Exploring the science of the mind.* New York: Norton.

Reiser, B. J., Black, J. B., & Abelson, R. P. (1985). Knowledge structures in the organization and retrieval of autobiographical memories. *Cognitive Psychology, 17,* 89–137.

Richardson, J. T. E. (1985). Integration versus decomposition in the retention of complex ideas. *Memory & Cognition, 13,* 112–127.

Riley, K. P. (1989). Psychological interventions in Alzheimer's disease. In G. C. Gilmore, P. J. Whitehouse, & M. R. Wykle (Eds.), *Memory, aging and dementia.* New York: Springer.

Rinck, M., & Bower, G. H. (1995). Anaphora resolution and the focus of attention in situation models. *Journal of Memory and Language, 34,* 110–131.

Rips, L. J. (1975). Inductive judgments about natural categories. *Journal of Verbal Learning and Verbal Behavior, 14,* 665–681.

Rips, L. J. (1989). Similarity, typicality, and categorization. In S. Vosniadou & A. Ortony (Eds.), *Similarity and analogical reasoning* (pp. 21–59). Cambridge: Cambridge University Press.

Rips, L. J. (1998). Reasoning and conversation. *Psychological Review, 105,* 411–441.

Rips, L. J., & Collins, A. (1993). Categories and resemblance. *Journal of Experimental Psychology: General, 122,* 468–486.

Rips, L. J., & Marcus, S. L. (1977). Supposition and the analysis of conditional sentences. In M. A. Just & P. A. Carpenter (Eds.), *Cognitive processes in comprehension* (pp. 185–220). Hillsdale, NJ: Erlbaum.

Rips, L. J., Shoben, E. J., & Smith, E. E. (1973). Semantic distance and the verification of semantic relations. *Journal of Verbal Learning and Verbal Behavior, 12,* 1–20.

Robertson, D. A., & Gernsbacher, M. A. (November, 1999). *fMRI evidence of the general cognitive processes underlying discourse comprehension.* Paper presented at the meetings of the Psychonomic Society, Los Angeles.

Robertson, D. A., Gernsbacher, M. A., Guidotti, S. J., Robertson, R. R. W., Irwin, W., Mock, B. J., & Campana, M. E. (2000). Functional neuroanatomy of the cognitive process of mapping during discourse comprehension. *Psychological Science, 11*, 255–260.

Roediger, H. L., III. (1990). Implicit memory: Retention without remembering. *American Psychologist, 45*, 1043–1056.

Roediger, H. L., III. (1996). Memory illusions. *Journal of Memory and Language, 35*, 76–100.

Roediger, H. L., III, Jacoby, D., & McDermott, K. B. (1996). Misinformation effects in recall: Creating false memories through repeated retrieval. *Journal of Memory and Language, 35*, 300–318.

Roediger, H. L., III, & McDermott, K. B. (1995). Creating false memories: Remembering words not presented in lists. *Journal of Experimental Psychology: Learning, Memory, and Cognition, 21*, 803–814.

Roediger, H. L., III, Stadler, M. L., Weldon, M. S., & Riegler, G. L. (1992). Direct comparison of two implicit memory tests: Word fragment and word stem completion. *Journal of Experimental Psychology: Learning, Memory, and Cognition, 18*, 1251–1269.

Roese, N. J. (1997). Counterfactual thinking. *Psychological Bulletin, 121*, 133–148.

Roese, N. (1999). Counterfactual thinking and decision making. *Psychonomic Bulletin & Review, 6*, 570–578.

Rosch, E. H. (1973). On the internal structure of perceptual and semantic categories. In T. E. Moore (Ed.), *Cognitive development and the acquisition of language* (pp. 111–144). New York: Academic Press.

Rosch, E. H. (1975). Cognitive representations of semantic categories. *Journal of Experimental Psychology: General, 104*, 192–233.

Rosch, E. H. (1978). Principles of categorization. In E. H. Rosch & B. B. Lloyd (Eds.), *Cognition and categorization* (pp. 27–48). Hillsdale, NJ: Erlbaum.

Rosch, E. H., & Mervis, C. B. (1975). Family resemblances: Studies in the internal structure of categories. *Cognitive Psychology, 7*, 573–605.

Rosch Heider, E. (1972). Universals in color naming and memory. *Journal of Experimental Psychology, 93*, 10–21.

Rosen, V. M., & Engle, R. W. (1997). The role of working memory capacity in retrieval. *Journal of Experimental Psychology: General, 126*, 211–227.

Rosler, F., Pechmann, T., Streb, J., Roder, B., & Hennighausen, E. (1998). Parsing of sentences in a language with varying word order: Word-by-word variations of processing demands are revealed by event-related brain potentials. *Journal of Memory and Language, 38*, 150–176.

Ross, B. H. (1987). This is like that: The use of earlier problems and the separation of similarity effects. *Journal of Experimental Psychology: Learning, Memory, and Cognition, 13*, 629–640.

Ross, B. H., & Murphy, G. L. (1999). Food for thought: Cross-classification and category organization in a complex real-world domain. *Cognitive Psychology, 38*, 495–553.

Ross, J., & Lawrence, K. A. (1968). Some observations on memory artifice. *Psychonomic Science, 13*, 107–108.

Rubin, D. C. (Ed.). (1996). *Remembering our past: Studies in autobiographical memory.* Cambridge, England: Cambridge University Press.

Rubin, D. C., Rahhal, T. A., & Poon, L. W. (1998). Things learned in early adulthood are remembered best. *Memory & Cognition, 26*, 3–19.

Rugg, M. D., & Coles, M. G. H. (Eds.). (1995). *Electrophysiology of mind: Event-related brain potential and cognition.* New York: Oxford University Press.

Rumelhart, D. E. (1989). The architecture of mind: A connectionist approach. In M. I. Posner (Ed.), *Foundations of cognitive science* (pp. 133–159). Cambridge, MA: MIT Press.

Rumelhart, D. E., Lindsay, P. H., & Norman, D. A. (1972). A process model for long-term memory. In E. Tulving & W. Donaldson (Eds.), *Organization of memory* (pp. 197–246). New York: Academic Press.

Rumelhart, D. E., & McClelland, J. L. (1986). *Parallel distributed processing: Explorations in the microstructure of cognition: Vol. 1. Foundations.* Cambridge, MA: Bradford.

Rundus, D. (1971). Analysis of rehearsal processes in free recall. *Journal of Experimental Psychology, 89*, 63–77.

Rundus, D., & Atkinson, R. C. (1970). Rehearsal processes in free recall: A procedure for direct observation. *Journal of Verbal Learning and Verbal Behavior, 9*, 99–105.

Russo, J. E., Johnson, E. J., & Stephens, D. L. (1989). The validity of verbal protocols. *Memory & Cognition, 17*, 759–769.

Sachs, J. S. (1967). Recognition memory for syntactic and semantic aspects of connected discourse. *Perception & Psychophysics, 2*, 437–442.

Sacks, H., Schegloff, E. A., & Jefferson, G. (1974). A simplest systematics for the organization of turntaking for conversation. *Language, 50*, 696–735.

Sacks, O. (1970). *The man who mistook his wife for a hat.* New York: Harper & Row.

Sakitt, B. (1975). Locus of short-term visual storage. *Science, 190*, 395–403.

Salame, P., & Baddeley, A. D. (1982). Disruption of short-term memory by unattended speech: Implications for the structure of working memory. *Journal of Verbal Learning and Verbal Behavior, 21*, 150–164.

Salthouse, T. A. (1984). Effects of age and skill in typing. *Journal of Experimental Psychology: General, 113*, 345–371.

Samuel, A. G. (1996). Does lexical information influence the perceptual restoration of phonemes? *Journal of Experimental Psychology: General, 125*, 28–51.

Samuel, D. (1999). *Memory: How we use it, lose it and can improve it.* New York: New York University Press.

Sarter, M., Berntson, G. G., & Cacioppo, J. T. (1996). Brain imaging and cognitive neuroscience: Toward strong inference in attributing function to structure. *American Psychologist, 51*, 13–21.

Sattler, J. M. (1982). *Assessment of children's intellectual and special abilities* (2nd ed.). Boston: Allyn & Bacon.

Schab, F. R. (1990). Odors and the remembrance of things past. *Journal of Experimental Psychology: Learning, Memory, and Cognition, 16*, 648–655.

Schacter, D. L. (1987). Implicit memory: History and current status. *Journal of Experimental Psychology: Learning, Memory, and Cognition, 13*, 501–518.

Schacter, D. (1989). Memory. In M. I. Posner (Ed.). *Foundations of cognitive science* (pp. 683–725). Cambridge, MA: MIT Press.

Schacter, D. L. (1996). *Searching for memory.* New York: Basic Books.

Schacter, D. L. (1999). The seven sins of memory: Insights from psychology and cognitive neuroscience. *American Psychologist, 54,* 182–203.

Schank, R. C. (1972). Conceptual dependency: A theory of natural language understanding. *Cognitive Psychology, 3,* 552–631.

Schank, R. C. (1977). Rules and topics in conversation. *Cognitive Science, 1,* 421–441.

Schank, R. C., & Abelson, R. P. (1977). *Scripts, plans, goals and understanding.* Hillsdale, NJ: Erlbaum.

Schilling, H. E. H., Rayner, K., & Chumbley, J. I. (1998). Comparing naming, lexical decision, and eye fixation times: Word frequency effects and individual differences. *Memory & Cognition, 26,* 1270–1281.

Schmidt, S. R. (1985). Encoding and retrieval processes in the memory for conceptually distinctive events. *Journal of Experimental Psychology: Learning, Memory, and Cognition, 11,* 565–578.

Schneider, W., & Shiffrin. R. M. (1977). Controlled and automatic human information processing: I. Detection, search, and attention. *Psychological Review, 84,* 1–66.

Schnorr, J. A., & Atkinson, R. C. (1969). Repetition versus imagery instructions in the short- and long-term retention of paired associates. *Psychonomic Science, 15,* 183–184.

Schooler, J. W., Ohlsson, S., & Brooks, K. (1993). Thoughts beyond words: When language overshadows insight. *Journal of Experimental Psychology: General, 122,* 166–183.

Schooler, L. J., & Anderson, J. R. (1997). The role of process in the rational analysis of memory. *Cognitive Psychology, 32,* 219–250.

Schrauf, R. W., & Rubin, D. C. (2000). Internal languages of retrieval: The bilingual encoding of memories for the personal past. *Memory & Cognition, 28,* 616–623.

Schulkind, M. D., Hennis, L. K., & Rubin, D. C. (1999). Music, emotion, and autobiographical memory: They're playing your song. *Memory & Cognition, 27,* 948–955.

Schustack, M. W., Ehrlich, S. F., & Rayner, K. (1987). Local and global sources of contextual facilitation in reading. *Journal of Memory and Language, 26,* 322–340.

Schwartz, D. L., & Black, T. (1999). Inferences through imagined actions: Knowing by simulated doing. *Journal of Experimental Psychology: Learning, Memory, and Cognition, 25,* 116–136.

Sehulster, J. R. (1989). Content and temporal structure of autobiographical knowledge: Remembering twenty-five seasons at the Metropolitan Opera. *Memory & Cognition, 17,* 590–606.

Seidenberg, M. S. (1993). Connectionist models and cognitive theory. *Psychological Science, 4,* 228–235.

Seidenberg, M. S., & McClelland, J. L. (1989). A distributed, developmental model of word recognition and naming. *Psychological Review, 96,* 523–568.

Seifert, C. M., Robertson, S. P., & Black, J. B. (1985). Types of inferences generated during reading. *Journal of Memory and Language, 24,* 405–422.

Selfridge, O. G. (1959). Pandemonium: A paradigm for learning. In *The mechanisation of thought processes.* London: H. M. Stationery Office.

Seron, X. (1982). Introduction: Toward a cognitive neuropsychology. *International Journal of Psychology, 17,* 149–156.

Shafir, E., & Tversky, A. (1992). Thinking through uncertainty: Nonconsequential reasoning and choice. *Cognitive Psychology, 24,* 449–474.

Shah, P., & Miyake, A. (1996). The separability of working memory resources for spatial thinking and language processing: An individual differences approach. *Journal of Experimental Psychology: General, 125,* 4–27.

Shallice, T., & Warrington, E. K. (1970). Independent functioning of the verbal memory stores: A neuropsychological study. *Quarterly Journal of Experimental Psychology, 22,* 261–273.

Shand, M. A. (1982). Sign-based short-term coding of American Sign Language signs and printed English words by congenitally deaf signers. *Cognitive Psychology, 14,* 1–12.

Sharkey, N. E., & Mitchell, D. C. (1985). Word recognition in a functional context: The use of scripts in reading. *Journal of Memory and Language, 24,* 253–270.

Shaw, J. S., III. (1996). Increases in eyewitness confidence resulting from postevent questioning. *Journal of Experimental Psychology: Applied, 2,* 126–146.

Shaw, J. S., III, Bjork, R. A., & Handal, A. (1995). Retrieval-induced forgetting in an eyewitness-memory paradigm. *Psychonomic Bulletin & Review, 2,* 249–253.

Shelton, J. R., & Caramazza, A. (1999). Deficits in lexical and semantic processing: Implications for models of normal language. *Psychonomic Bulletin & Review, 6,* 5–27.

Shepard, R. N., & Cooper, L. A. (1992). Representation of colors in the blind, color-blind, and normally sighted. *Psychological Science, 3,* 97–104.

Shepard, R. N., & Metzler, J. (1971). Mental rotation of three-dimensional objects. *Science, 153,* 652–654.

Shiffrin, R. M., & Schneider, W. (1977). Controlled and automatic human information processing: II. Perceptual learning, automatic attending, and a general theory. *Psychological Review, 84,* 127–190.

Shoben, E. J., Sailor, K. M., & Wang, M.-Y. (1989). The role of expectancy in comparative judgments. *Memory & Cognition, 17,* 18–26.

Siegler, R. S. (2000). Unconscious insights. *Current Directions in Psychological Science, 9,* 79–83.

Siegler, R. S., & Stern, E. (1998). A microgenetic analysis of conscious and unconscious strategy discoveries. *Journal of Experimental Psychology: General, 127,* 377–397.

Simon, H. A. (1975). The functional equivalence of problem solving skills. *Cognitive Psychology, 7,* 268–288.

Simon, H. A. (1979). *Models of thought.* New Haven: Yale University Press.

Simon, H. A. (1992). What is an "explanation" of behavior? *Psychological Science, 3,* 150–161.

Simon, H. A. (1995, May). *Thinking in words, pictures, equations, numbers: How do we do it and what does it matter?*

Invited address presented at the meeting of the Midwestern Psychological Association, Chicago.

Simpson, G. B. (1981). Meaning dominance and semantic context in the processing of lexical ambiguity. *Journal of Verbal Learning and Verbal Behavior, 20,* 120–136.

Simpson, G. B. (1984). Lexical ambiguity and its role in models of word recognition. *Psychological Bulletin, 96,* 316–340.

Simpson, G. B. (May, 2000). *Lexical and phonological information in visual word recognition: How much control?* Invited presentation, Midwestern Psychological Association, Chicago.

Simpson, G. B., Casteel, M. A., Peterson, R. R., & Burgess, C. (1989). Lexical and sentence context effects in word recognition. *Journal of Experimental Psychology: Learning, Memory, and Cognition, 15,* 88–97.

Singer, M. (1990). *Psychology of language: An introduction to sentence and discourse processes.* Hillsdale, NJ: Erlbaum.

Singer, M., Andrusiak, P., Reisdorf, P., & Black, N. L. (1992). Individual differences in bridging inference processes. *Memory & Cognition, 20,* 539–548.

Singer, M., Graesser, A. C., & Trabasso, T. (1994). Minimal or global inference during reading. *Journal of Memory and Language, 33,* 421–441.

Sitaran, N., Weingartner, H., Caine, E. D., & Gillin, J. C. (1978). Choline: Selective enhancement of serial learning and encoding of low imagery words in man. *Life Sciences, 22,* 1555–1560.

Skinner, B. F. (1957). *Verbal behavior.* New York: Appleton-Century-Crofts.

Skinner, B. F. (1984). The shame of American education. *American Psychologist, 39,* 947–954.

Skinner, B. F. (1990). Can psychology be a science of mind? *American Psychologist, 45,* 1206–1210.

Slamecka, N. J. (1966). Differentiation versus unlearning of verbal associations. *Journal of Experimental Psychology, 71,* 822–828.

Slamecka, N. J. (1985). Ebbinghaus: Some associations. *Journal of Experimental Psychology: Learning, Memory, and Cognition, 11,* 414–435.

Smith, D. A., & Graesser, A. C. (1981). Memory for actions in scripted activities as a function of typicality, retention interval, and retrieval task. *Memory & Cognition, 9,* 550–559.

Smith, E. E. (1978). Theories of semantic memory. In W. K. Estes (Ed.), *Handbook of learning and cognitive processes* (Vol. 6, pp. 1–56). Hillsdale, NJ: Erlbaum.

Smith, E. E. (2000). Neural bases of human working memory. *Current Directions in Psychological Science, 9,* 45–49.

Smith, E. E., & Jonides, J. (1999). Storage and executive processes in the frontal lobes. *Science, 283,* 1657–1661.

Smith, E. E., Rips, L. J., & Shoben, E. J. (1974a). Semantic memory and psychological semantics. In G. H. Bower (Ed.), *The psychology of learning and motivation* (Vol. 8, pp. 1–45). New York: Academic Press.

Smith, E. E., Shoben, E. J., & Rips, L. J. (1974b). Structure and process in semantic memory: A featural model for semantic decisions. *Psychological Review, 81,* 214–241.

Smith, J. D., & Minda, J. P. (2000). Thirty categorization results in search of a model. *Journal of Experimental Psychology: Learning, Memory, and Cognition, 26,* 3–27.

Smith, M. C., Besner, D., & Miyoshi, H. (1994). New limits to automaticity: Context modulates semantic priming. *Journal of Experimental Psychology: Learning, Memory, and Cognition, 20,* 104–115.

Smith, S. M. (1995). Getting into and out of mental ruts: A theory of fixation, incubation, and insight. In R. J. Sternberg & J. E. Davidson (Eds.), *The nature of insight* (pp. 229–251). Cambridge, MA: MIT Press.

Smith, S. M., & Rothkopf, E. Z. (1984). Contextual enrichment and distribution of practice in the classroom. *Cognition and Instruction, 1,* 341–358.

Snow, C. (1972). Mother's speech to children learning language. *Child Development, 43,* 549–565.

Snow, C., & Ferguson, C. (Eds.). (1977). *Talking to children: Language input and acquisition.* Cambridge, England: Cambridge University Press.

Solso, R. L. (1998). *Cognitive Psychology* (5th ed.). Boston: Allyn & Bacon.

Son, L. K., & Metcalfe, J. (2000). Metacognitive and control strategies in study-time allocation. *Journal of Experimental Psychology: Learning, Memory, and Cognition, 26,* 204–221.

Speer, S. R., & Clifton, C., Jr. (1998). Plausibility and argument structure in sentence comprehension. *Memory & Cognition, 26,* 965–978.

Spelke, E., Hirst, W., & Neisser, U. (1976). Skills of divided attention. *Cognition, 4,* 215–230.

Spellman, B. A., & Holyoak, K. J. (1992). If Saddam is Hitler then who is George Bush? Analogical mapping between systems of social roles. *Journal of Personality and Social Psychology, 62,* 913–933.

Spellman, B. A., & Holyoak, K. J. (1996). Pragmatics in analogical mapping. *Cognitive Psychology, 31,* 307–346.

Spellman, B. A., & Mandel, D. R. (1999). When possibility informs reality: Counterfactual thinking as a cue to causality. *Current Directions in Psychological Science, 8,* 120–123.

Sperling, G. (1960). The information available in brief visual presentations. *Psychological Monographs, 74* (Whole No. 48).

Sperling, G. (1963). A model for visual memory tasks. *Human Factors, 5,* 9–31.

Sperry, R. W. (1964). The great cerebral commissure. *Scientific American, 210,* 42–52.

Spieth, W., Curtis, J. F., & Webster, J. C. (1954). Responding to one of two simultaneous messages. *Journal of the Acoustical Society of America, 26,* 391–396.

Squire, L. R. (1986). Mechanisms of memory. *Science, 232* (4578), 1612–1619.

Squire, L. R. (1987). *Memory and brain.* New York: Oxford University Press.

Squire, L. R. (1992). Memory and the hippocampus: A synthesis from findings with rats, monkeys, and humans. *Psychological Review, 99,* 195–231.

Squire, L. R. (1993). The organization of declarative and nondeclarative memory. In T. Ono, L. R. Squire, M. E. Raichle,

D. I. Perrett, & M. Fukuda (Eds.), Brain mechanisms of perception and memory: From neuron to behavior (pp. 219–227). New York: Oxford University Press.

Stazyk, E. H., Ashcraft, M. H., & Hamann, M. S. (1982). A network approach to simple multiplication. *Journal of Experimental Psychology: Learning, Memory, and Cognition, 17,* 355–376.

Sternberg, R. J. (1996). *Cognitive psychology.* Fort Worth, TX: Harcourt Brace.

Sternberg, S. (1966). High-speed scanning in human memory. *Science, 153,* 652–654.

Sternberg, S. (1969). The discovery of processing stages: Extensions of Donder's method. In W. G. Koster (Ed.), Attention and performance II. *Acta Psychologica, 30,* 276–315.

Sternberg, S. (1975). Memory scanning: New findings and current controversies. *Quarterly Journal of Experimental Psychology, 27,* 1–32.

Stroop, J. R. (1935). Studies of interference in serial verbal reactions. *Journal of Experimental Psychology, 18,* 643–662.

Sulin, R. A., & Dooling, D. J. (1974). Intrusion of a thematic idea in retention of prose. *Journal of Experimental Psychology, 103,* 255–262.

Svartvik, J., & Quirk, R. (Eds.). (1980). *A corpus of English conversation.* Lund: CWK Gleerup.

Talland, G. A. (1967). Short-term memory with interpolated activity. *Journal of Verbal Learning and Verbal Behavior, 6,* 144–150.

Taraban, R., & McClelland, J. L. (1988). Constituent attachment and thematic role assignment in sentence processing: Influences of content-based expectations. *Journal of Memory and Language, 27,* 597–632.

Thapar, A., & Greene, R. L. (1994). Effects of level of processing on implicit and explicit tasks. *Journal of Experimental Psychology: Learning, Memory, and Cognition, 20,* 671–679.

Theeuwes, J., Kramer, A. F., Hahn, S., & Irwin, D. E. (1998). Our eyes do not always go where we want them to go: Capture of the eyes by new objects. *Psychological Science, 9,* 379–385.

Thiede, K. W. (1999). The importance of monitoring and self-regulation during multitrial learning. *Psychonomic Bulletin & Review, 6,* 662–667.

Thomas, J. C., Jr. (1974). An analysis of behavior in the hobbits–orcs problem. *Cognitive Psychology, 6,* 257–269.

Thomas, M. H., & Wang, A. Y. (1996). Learning by the keyword mnemonic: Looking for long-term benefits. *Journal of Experimental Psychology: Applied, 2,* 330–342.

Thompson, R. F. (1986). The neurobiology of learning and memory. *Science, 233,* 941–947.

Thompson-Schill, S. L., Kurtz, K. J., & Gabrieli, J. D. E. (1998). Effects of semantic and associative relatedness on automatic priming. *Journal of Memory and Language, 38,* 440–458.

Thomson, D. M., & Tulving, E. (1970). Associative encoding and retrieval: Weak and strong cues. *Journal of Experimental Psychology, 86,* 255–262.

Thorndike, E. L. (1914). *The psychology of learning.* New York: Teachers College.

Titchener, E. B. (1919). *A text-book of psychology.* New York: Macmillan.

Toga, A. W., & Mazziotta, J. C. (Eds.). (1996). *Brain mapping: The methods.* New York: Academic Press.

Tolman, E. C. (1948). Cognitive maps in rats and men. *Psychological Review, 55,* 189–208.

Tourangeau, R., & Rips, L. (1991). Interpreting and evaluating metaphors. *Journal of Memory and Language, 30,* 452–472.

Treisman, A. M. (1960). Contextual cues in selective listening. *Quarterly Journal of Experimental Psychology, 12,* 242–248.

Treisman, A. M. (1964). Monitoring and storage of irrelevant messages in selective attention. *Journal of Verbal Learning and Verbal Behavior, 3,* 449–459.

Treisman, A. M. (1965). The effects of redundancy and familiarity on translating and repeating back a foreign and a native language. *British Journal of Psychology, 56,* 369–379.

Treisman, A. (1982). Perceptual grouping and attention in visual search for features and for objects. *Journal of Experimental Psychology: Human Perception and Performance, 8,* 194–214.

Treisman, A. (1988). Features and objects: The Fourteenth Bartlett Memorial Lecture. *Quarterly Journal of Experimental Psychology, 40A,* 201–237.

Treisman, A. (1991). Search, similarity, and integration of features between and within dimensions. *Journal of Experimental Psychology: Human Perception and Performance, 17,* 652–676.

Treisman, A. (1992). Spreading suppression or feature integration? A reply to Duncan and Humphreys (1992). *Journal of Experimental Psychology: Human Perception and Performance, 18,* 589–593.

Treisman, A., & Gelade, G. (1980). A feature integration theory of attention. *Cognitive Psychology, 12,* 97–136.

Treisman, A. M., Russell, R., & Green, J. (1975). Brief visual storage of shape and movement. In P. M. A. Rabbitt & S. Dornic (Eds.), *Attention and performance* (Vol. 5, pp. 699–721). New York: Academic Press.

Trigg, G. L., & Lerner, R. J. (Eds.). (1981). *Encyclopedia of physics.* Reading, MA: Addison-Wesley.

Tulving, E. (1962). Subjective organization in free recall of "unrelated" words. *Psychological Review, 69,* 344–354.

Tulving, E. (1972). Episodic and semantic memory. In E. Tulving & W. Donaldson (Eds.), *Organization of memory* (pp. 381–403). New York: Academic Press.

Tulving, E. (1983). *Elements of episodic memory.* Oxford, England: Clarendon.

Tulving, E. (1985). How many memory systems are there? *American Psychologist, 40,* 385–398.

Tulving, E. (1989). Remembering and knowing the past. *American Scientist, 77,* 361–367.

Tulving, E. (1991). Memory research is not a zero-sum game. *American Psychologist, 46,* 41–42.

Tulving, E. (1993). What is episodic memory? *Current Directions in Psychological Science, 2,* 67–70.

Tulving, E., & Pearlstone, Z. (1966). Availability versus accessibility of information in memory for words. *Journal of Verbal Learning and Verbal Behavior, 5,* 381–391.

Tulving, E., & Thompson, D. M. (1973). Encoding specificity and retrieval processes in episodic memory. *Psychological Review, 80,* 352–373.

Tversky, A. (1977). Features of similarity. *Psychological Review, 84,* 327–352.

Tversky, A., & Kahneman, D. (1973). Availability: A heuristic for judging frequency and probability. *Cognitive Psychology, 5,* 207–232.

Tversky, A., & Kahneman, D. (1974). Judgment under uncertainty: Heuristics and biases. *Science, 185,* 1124–1131.

Tversky, A., & Kahneman, D. (1980). Causal schemas in judgments under uncertainty. In M. Fishbein (Ed.), *Progress in social psychology* (Vol. 1, pp. 49–72). Hillsdale, NJ: Erlbaum.

Tversky, A., & Kahneman, D. (1983). Extensional versus intuitive reasoning: The conjunction fallacy in probability judgment. *Psychological Review, 90,* 293–315.

Tyler, L. K., Voice, J. K., & Moss, H. E. (2000). The interaction of meaning and sound in spoken word recognition. *Psychonomic Bulletin & Review, 7,* 320–326.

Tzelgov, J., Yehene, V., Kotler, L., & Alon, A. (2000). Automatic comparisons of artificial digits never compared: Learning linear ordering relations. *Journal of Experimental Psychology: Learning, Memory, and Cognition, 26,* 103–120.

Underwood, B. J. (1957). Interference and forgetting. *Psychological Review, 64,* 49–60.

Underwood, B. J., Keppel, G., & Schulz, R. W. (1962). Studies of distributed practice: XXII. Some conditions which enhance retention. *Journal of Experimental Psychology, 64,* 112–129.

Underwood, B. J., & Postman, L. (1960). Extraexperimental sources of interference in forgetting. *Psychological Review, 67,* 73–95.

Underwood, B. J., & Schulz, R. W. (1960). *Meaningfulness and verbal learning.* Philadelphia: Lippincott.

Utta, W. R. (1983). Don't exterminate perceptual fruit flies! *Behavioral and Brain Sciences, 6,* 39–40.

Vallar, G., & Baddeley, A. D. (1984). Fractionation of working memory: Neuropsychological evidence for a phonological short-term store. *Journal of Verbal Learning and Verbal Behavior, 23,* 151–161.

Van Berkum, J. J. A., Brown, C. M., & Hagoort, P. (1999). Early referential context effects in sentence processing: Evidence from event-related brain potentials. *Journal of Memory and Language, 41,* 147–182.

Van Dijk, T. A., & Kintsch, W. (1983). *Strategies in discourse comprehension.* New York: Academic Press.

VanLehn, K. (1989). Problem solving and cognitive skill acquisition. In M. I. Posner (Ed.), *Foundations of cognitive science* (pp. 527–579). Cambridge, MA: MIT Press.

Vecera, S. P., Behrmann, M., & McGoldrick, J. (2000). Selective attention to the parts of an object. *Psychonomic Bulletin & Review, 7,* 301–308.

Vu, H., Kellas, G., Metcalf, K., & Herman, R. (2000). The influence of global discourse on lexical ambiguity resolution. *Memory & Cognition, 28,* 236–252.

Wagenaar, W. A. (1986). My memory: A study of autobiographical memory over six years. *Cognitive Psychology, 18,* 225–252.

Waltz, J. A., Knowlton, B. J., Holyoak, K. J., Boone, K. B., Mishkin, F. S., Santos, M. M., Thomas, C. R., & Miller, B. L. (1999). A system for relational reasoning in human prefrontal cortex. *Psychological Science, 10,* 119–125.

Warren, R. M., & Warren, R. P. (1970). Auditory illusions and confusions. *Scientific American, 223,* 30–36.

Warrington, E. K., & James, M. (1988). Visual apperceptive agnosia: A clinico-anatomical study of three cases. *Cortex, 24,* 13–32.

Warrington, E. K., & McCarthy, R. (1983). Category specific access dysphasia. *Brain, 106,* 859–878.

Warrington, E. K., & Shallice, T. (1969). The selective impairment of auditory verbal short-term memory. *Brain, 92,* 885–896.

Warrington, E. K., & Shallice, T. (1984). Category specific semantic impairments. *Brain, 107,* 829–854.

Warrington, E. K., & Weiskrantz, L. (1970). The amnesic syndrome: Consolidation or retrieval? *Nature, 228,* 628–630.

Wason, P. C., & Johnson-Laird, P. N. (1972). *Psychology of reasoning: Structure and content.* Cambridge, MA: Harvard University Press.

Wasow, T. (1989). Grammatical theory. In M. I. Posner (Ed.), *Foundations of cognitive science* (pp. 161–205). Cambridge, MA: MIT Press.

Watkins, M. H., Peynircioglu, Z. F., & Brems, D. J. (1984). Pictorial rehearsal. *Memory & Cognition, 12,* 553–557.

Watkins, M. J., & Tulving, E. (1975). Episodic memory: When recognition fails. *Journal of Experimental Psychology: General, 104,* 5–29.

Watkins, O. C., & Watkins, M. J. (1980). The modality effect and echoic persistence. *Journal of Experimental Psychology: General, 109,* 251–278.

Watson, J. B. (1913). Psychology as the behaviorist sees it. *Psychological Review, 20,* 158–177.

Watson, J. B. (1924). *Behaviorism.* New York: Norton.

Watson, R. I. (1968). *The great psychologists from Aristotle to Freud.* New York: Lippincott.

Waugh, N. C., & Norman, D. A. (1965). Primary memory. *Psychological Review, 72,* 89–104.

Weaver, C. A. III. (1993). Do you need a "flash" to form a flashbulb memory? *Journal of Experimental Psychology: General, 122,* 39–46.

Webster's New World Dictionary of the American Language. (1980). 2nd college edition. Cleveland: William Collins.

Weisberg, R. (1995). Prolegomena to theories of insight in problem solving: A taxonomy of problems. In R. J. Sternberg & J. E. Davidson (Eds.), *The nature of insight* (pp. 157–196). Cambridge, MA: MIT Press.

Wenger, M. J., & Payne, D. G. (1995). On the acquisition of mnemonic skill: Application of skilled memory theory. *Journal of Experimental Psychology: Applied, 1,* 194–215.

Werner, H. (1935). Studies on contour. *American Journal of Psychology, 47,* 40–64.

West, R. F., & Stanovich, K. E. (1986). Robust effects of syntactic structure on visual word processing. *Memory & Cognition, 14,* 104–112.

Whaley, C. P. (1978). Word–nonword classification time. *Journal of Verbal Learning and Verbal Behavior, 17,* 143–154.

Wharton, C. M., Grafman, J., Flitman, S. S., Hansen, E. K., Brauner, J., Marks, A., & Honda, M. (2000). Toward neuroanatomical models of analogy: A positron emission tomography study of analogical mapping. *Cognitive Psychology, 40,* 173–197.

Wheeler, M. A., & Roediger, H. L., III. (1992). Disparate effects of repeated testing: Reconciling Ballard's (1913) and Bartlett's (1932) results. *Psychological Science, 3,* 240–245.

Wheeler, M. A., Stuss, D. T., & Tulving, E. (1997). Toward a theory of episodic memory: The frontal lobes and autonoetic consciousness. *Psychological Bulletin, 121,* 331–354.

Whitney, P. (1998). *The psychology of language.* Boston: Houghton Mifflin.

Whitney, P., Ritchie, B. G., & Crane, R. S. (1992). The effect of foregrounding on readers' use of predictive inferences. *Memory & Cognition, 20,* 424–432.

Whorf, B. L. (1956). Science and linguistics. In J. B. Carroll (Ed.), *Language, thought, and reality: Selected writings of Benjamin Lee Whorf* (pp. 207–219). Cambridge, MA: MIT Press.

Wickelgren, W. A. (1965). Acoustic similarity and retroactive interference in short-term memory. *Journal of Verbal Learning and Verbal Behavior, 4,* 53–61.

Wickelgren, W. A. (1974). *How to solve problems.* San Francisco: Freeman.

Wickens, C. D. (1984). *Engineering psychology and human performance.* Columbus, OH: Charles E. Merrill.

Wickens, D. D. (1972). Characteristics of word encoding. In A. W. Melton & E. Martin (Eds.), *Coding processes in human memory* (pp. 191–215). New York: Winston.

Wickens, D. D., Born, D. G., & Allen, C. K. (1963). Proactive inhibition and item similarity in short-term memory. *Journal of Verbal Learning and Verbal Behavior, 2,* 440–445.

Wiley, J. (1998). Expertise as mental set: The effects of domain knowledge in creative problem solving. *Memory & Cognition, 26,* 716–730.

Wilkes-Gibbs, D., & Clark, H. H. (1992). Coordinating beliefs in conversation. *Journal of Memory and Language, 31,* 183–194.

Windschitl, P. D., & Weber, E. U. (1999). The interpretation of "likely" depends on the context, but "70%" is 70%—right? The influence of associative processes on perceived certainty. *Journal of Experimental Psychology: Learning, Memory, and Cognition, 25,* 1514–1533.

Wingfield, A., Goodglass, H., & Lindfield, K. C. (1997). Separating speed from automaticity in a patient with focal brain atrophy. *Psychological Science, 8,* 247–249.

Winograd, E., & Killinger, W. A., Jr. (1983). Relating age at encoding in early childhood to adult recall: Development of flashbulb memories. *Journal of Experimental Psychology: General, 112,* 413–422.

Wixted, J. T. (1991). Conditions and consequences of maintenance rehearsal. *Journal of Experimental Psychology: Learning, Memory, and Cognition, 17,* 963–973.

Wixted, J. T., & Ebbesen, E. B. (1991). On the form of forgetting. *Psychological Science, 2,* 409–415.

Wood, F., Taylor, B., Penney, R., & Stump, B. (1980). Regional cerebral blood flow response to recognition memory versus semantic classification tasks. *Brain and Language, 9,* 113–122.

Wood, N. L., & Cowan, N. (1995a). The cocktail party phenomenon revisited: Attention and memory in the classic selective listening procedure of Cherry (1953). *Journal of Experimental Psychology: General, 124,* 243–262.

Wood, N., & Cowan, N. (1995b). The cocktail party phenomenon revisited: How frequent are attention shifts to one's name in an irrelevant auditory channel? *Journal of Experimental Psychology: Learning, Memory, and Cognition, 21,* 255–260.

Woodworth, R. S., & Schlosberg, H. (1954). *Experimental psychology* (Rev. ed.). New York: Holt, Rinehart & Winston.

Yamauchi, T., & Markman, A. B. (2000). Inference using categories. *Journal of Experimental Psychology: Learning, Memory, and Cognition, 26,* 776–795.

Yates, F. A. (1966). *The art of memory.* Chicago: University of Chicago Press.

Yuille, J. C., & Paivio, A. (1967). Latency of imaginal and verbal mediators as a function of stimulus and response concreteness-imagery. *Journal of Experimental Psychology, 75,* 540–544.

Zaragoza, M. S., & Koshmider, J. W., III. (1989). Misled subjects may know more than their performance implies. *Journal of Experimental Psychology: Learning, Memory, and Cognition, 15,* 246–255.

Zaragoza, M. S., & Lane, S. M. (1994). Source misattributions and the suggestibility of eyewitness memory. *Journal of Experimental Psychology: Learning, Memory, and Cognition, 20,* 934–945.

Zaragoza, M. S., McCloskey, M., & Jamis, M. (1987). Misleading postevent information and recall of the original event: Further evidence against the memory impairment hypothesis. *Journal of Experimental Psychology: Learning, Memory, and Cognition, 13,* 36–44.

Zbrodoff, N. J., & Logan, G. D. (1986). On the autonomy of mental processes: A case study of arithmetic. *Journal of Experimental Psychology: General, 115,* 118–130.

Zimmerman, D. H., & West, C. (1975). Sex roles, interruptions, and silences in conversation. In B. Thorne & N. Henley (Eds.), *Language and sex: Differences and dominance* (pp. 105–129). Rowley, MA: Newbury House.

Zola-Morgan, S., Squire, L., & Amalral, D. G. (1986). Human amnesia and the medial temporal region: Enduring memory impairment following a bilateral lesion limited to field CA1 of the hippocampus. *Journal of Neuroscience, 6,* 2950–2967.

Zwaan, R. A. (1996). Processing narrative time shifts. *Journal of Experimental Psychology: Learning, Memory, and Cognition, 22,* 1196–1207.

Zwaan, R. A. (1999). Situation models: The mental leap into imagined world. *Current Directions in Psychological Science, 8,* 15–17.

Zwaan, R. A., & Radvansky, G. A. (1998). Situation models in language comprehension and memory. *Psychological Bulletin, 123,* 162–185.

Credits

Photos and Cartoons:

p. 15: The Bettmann Archive. **p. 17:** The Bettmann Archive. **p. 18:** By permission of the Houghton Library, Harvard University. **p. 23:** © Fritz/Monkmeyer. **p. 24:** THE FAR SIDE copyright 1985, 1986 & 1991 FAR-WORKS, INC. Distributed by UNIVERSAL PRESS SYNDICATE. Reprinted with permission. All rights reserved. **p. 27:** Donna Coveney/The MIT Museum. **p. 61:** Sidney Harris. **p. 65:** From The Excitable Cortex in Conscious Man, by Wilder Penfield. Liverpool University Press, 1958. Reprinted by permission. **p. 69:** Sidney Harris. **p. 79:** Sovfoto. **p. 81:** Tom Ives. **p. 82:** Estate of Sybil Shelton/Peter Arnold. **p. 94:** Fine Arts Museums of San Francisco, Achenbach Foundation for Graphic Arts, Bruno and Sadie Adriani Collection, 1971.28.103.7. **p. 97:** © 1997 Paul Silverman/Fundamental Photographs. **p. 98:** © 1997 Paul Silverman/Fundamental Photographs. **p. 133:** © Bill Bachmann/Photo Researchers. **p. 134:** Jean-Claude LeJeune. **p. 139:** ZIGGY copyright ZIGGY AND FRIENDS, INC. Distributed by UNIVERSAL PRESS SYNDICATE. Reprinted with permission. All rights reserved. **p. 148:** UPI/Corbis-Bettman. **p. 151:** Mark Antman/The Image Works. **p. 163:** Tony Freeman/ PhotoEdit. **p. 190:** Akos Szilvasi/Stock Boston. **p. 215:** Kagan/Monkmeyer. **p. 236:** © Walt Disney Productions Inc., Photofest. **p. 239:** Drawing by W. Miller. © 1973 The New Yorker Magazine, Inc. **p. 262:** George Horton/Photo Researchers. **p. 266:** AP/Wide World. **p. 332:** Shostal. **p. 337:** © 1993 Barbara Rios/Photo Researchers. **p. 340:** Spencer Grant/The Picture Cube. **p. 342:** Photofest. **p. 345:** Michael Evans/The White House. **p. 349:** Michael Newman/PhotoEdit. **p. 353:** CALVIN & HOBBES copyright Watterson. Distributed by UNIVERSAL PRESS SYNDICATE. Reprinted with permission. All rights reserved. **p. 356:** THE FAR SIDE copyright 1985, 1986 & 1991 FARWORKS, INC. Distributed by UNIVERSAL PRESS SYNDICATE. Reprinted with permission. All rights reserved. **p. 359:** Sidney Harris. **p. 377:** With the permission of Bob Thaves. **p. 400:** With permission of Bob Thaves. **p. 404:** Scott, Foresman, and Company. **p. 421:** Sybil Shelton/Peter Arnold, Inc. **p. 431:** Elle Schuster. **p. 432:** CALVIN & HOBBES copyright Watterson. Distributed by UNIVERSAL PRESS SYNDICATE. Reprinted with permission. All rights reserved. **p. 435:** Drawing by Mulligan. **p. 449:** Scott, Foresman, and Company. **p. 455:** Pictor/DPI/Uniphoto. **p. 464:** John Niebauer/PhotoEdit. **p. 465:** Drawing by Weber, © 1989 The New Yorker Magazine, Inc. **p. 481:** Drawing by Weber. © 1989 The New Yorker Magazine, Inc. **p. 496:** Plate IV from Kohler, "The Mentality of Apes," 1925. Reprinted in 1973 by Routledge & Kegal Paul Ltd. **p. 503:** Drawing by Stevenson, © 1974 The New Yorker Magazine, Inc. **p. 518:** UPI/Corbin-Bettmann. **p. 532:** Myron Davis/Life Magazine/Time Warner Inc. **p. 534:** Joel Gordon.

Figures:

p. 10: Definition of "cognition." Copyright © 2000 by Houghton Mifflin Company. Reproduced by permission from *The American Heritage College Dictionary*, 3/e. **p. 13:** Figure from Event-related brain potentials elicited by syntactic anomaly by L. Osterhout and P.J. Holcomb, *Journal of Memory and Language*, vol. 31, 790. Copyright © 1992 by Academic Press. Reproduced by permission of the publisher. **p. 38:** From Mental Multiplication Skill: Structure, process, and acquisition by Jamie I.D. Campbell and David Jeffrey Graham, *Canadian Journal of Psychology*, vol. 39, 2. Copyright © 1985 by the Canadian Psychological Association. Reprinted with permission. **p. 40:** From Two storage mechanisms in free recall by M. Glanzer and A.R. Cunitz, *Journal of Verbal Learning and Verbal Behavior*, vol. 5, 354–358. Copyright © 1966 by Academic Press. Reproduced by permission of the publisher. **p. 43:** From The control of short-term memory by R.C. Atkinson and R.M. Shiffrin, *Scientific American*, 225, 82–90. Copyright © 1971. **p. 66:** Reprinted with permission from "Introduction and Overview," by E. D. Bigler, R. A. Yeo, and F. Turkheimer, in *Neuropsychological Function and Brain Imaging* (p. 10), edited by E. D. Bigler, R. A. Yeo, and E. Turkheimer, 1989, New York, Plenum Press. **p. 71:** From An interactive activation model of context effects in letter perception: Part I. An account of basic findings by J.L. McClelland and D.E. Rumelhart, *Psychological Review*, 88, 380. Copyright © 1981 by the American Psychological Association. Reprinted with permission. **p. 85:** From Short term storage of information in vision by E. Averbach and G. Sperling, C. Cherry (ed.), *Information Theory* (pp. 196–211). London: Butterworth. Copyright © 1960. Reprinted by permission. **p. 92:** From Pandemonium: A paradigm for learning by O.G. Selfridge, in Teddington Symposium, *Mechanization of Thought Processes*, p. 517. Copyright © 1959 National Physical Laboratory, Teddington, England. **p. 95:** Figure from *Sensation and Perception*, 3/e by Stanley Coren and Lawrence Ward. Copyright © 1989 by Harcourt, Inc. Reproduced by permission of the publisher.

p. 96: From Visual search by Ulric Neisser. Copyright © 1964 by *Scientific American, Inc.* All rights reserved. **p. 102:** From The appeal of parallel distributed processing by J.L. McClelland and D. Rumelhart, *Parallel Distributed Processing*, vol. 1, 23. Copyright © 1986 by MIT Press. Reproduced by permission. **p. 103:** From Higher-level vision by I. Biederman. E.N. Osherson, S.M. Kosslyn, and J.M. Hollerbach (eds.), *An Invitation to Cognitive Science, 2*, 41–72. Copyright © 1990 by MIT Press, Cambridge, Massachussetts. Reprinted with permission. **pp. 104 and 105:** From The perception of objects with deleted contours by I. Biederman, *Psychological Review, 94*, 115–147. Copyright © 1987 by the American Psychological Association. Reprinted by permission. **p. 107:** *Neuropsychology: The Neural Bases of Mental Function*, by Maria T. Banich. Copyright © 1997 by Houghton Mifflin Company. Adapted with permission. **p. 110:** From *Principles of Psychology*, by R.H. Price. Copyright © 1987 by Scott, Foresman, and Company. Reprinted by permission. **p. 113:** Figure from An auditory analogue of the Sperling partial report procedure: Evidence for brief auditory storage by C.J. Darwin et al., *Cognitive Psychology*, vol. 3, 259. Copyright © 1972 by Academic Press. Reproduced by permission of the publisher. **p. 115:** Figure from The role of one's own voice in immediate memory by R.C. Crowder, *Cognitive Psychology*, vol. 1, pp. 166. Copyright © 1970 by Academic Press. Reproduced by permission of the publisher. **p. 128:** From Attention and the detection of signals by Posner, Synder, & Davidson, *Journal of Experimental Psychology: General, 109*, 160–174. Copyright © 1980 by the American Psychological Association. Reprinted with permission. **p. 131:** Figure from A feature integration theory of attention by A. Treisman and G. Gelade, *Cognitive Psychology*, vol. 12, 104. Copyright © 1980 by Academic Press. Reproduced by permission of the publisher. **p. 132:** From *Cognitive Psychology*, 5/e by Robert L. Solso. Copyright © 1998 by Allyn & Bacon. Reprinted by permission. **p. 137:** From Selective attention in man by A.M. Treisman, *British Medical Bulletin*, vol. 20, pp.12–16. Copyright © 1964. Reprinted by permission. **p. 138:** Figure adapted from *Human Information Processing: An Introduction to Psychology*, 2/e by Peter H. Lindsay and Donald A. Norman. Copyright © 1977 by Harcourt, Inc. Reprinted by permission of the publisher. **p. 140:** From Toward a theory of memory and attention by D.A. Norman, *Psychological Review, 75*, 522–536. Copyright © 1968 by the American Psychological Association. Adapted with permission. **pp. 141 and 142:** From Flexibility and capacity demands of attention by W.A. Johnston and S.P. Heinz, *Journal of Experimental Psychology, 107*, 69–76. Copyright © 1978 by the American Psychological Association. Reprinted by permission. **p. 153:** From Checklist procedures and the cost of automaticity by I. Barshi and A.F. Healy, *Memory and Cognition, 21*, 496–505. Copyright © 1993 by the Psychonomic Society. Reprinted by permission. **p. 156:** From *Brain, Mind, and Behavior* by Floyd E. Bloom and Arlyne Lazerson, **p. 300.** Copyright © 1985, 1988, 2000 by Educational Broadcasting Corporation. Used with the permission of Worth Publishers. **p. 157:** From Left in the dark: The neglect of theory by J.C. Marshall and P.W. Halligan, *Neuropsychological Rehabilitation, 4*, 161–167. Copyright © 1994. Reprinted by permission of ITPS, England. **p. 166:** From short-term retention of individual items by L.R. Peterson and M.J. Peterson, *Journal of Experimental Psychology, 58*, 193–198. Copyright © 1959. **p. 167:** From Primary memory by N.C. Waugh and D.A. Norman, *Psychological Review, 72*, 91. Copyright © 1965 by the American Psychological Association. Adapted with permission. **p. 169:** Figure from Proactive inhibition and item similarity in short-term memory by Wickens, et al., *Journal of Verbal Learning and Verbal Behavior, 2*, 442. Copyright © 1963 by Academic Press. Reprinted with permission. **p. 170:** From The serial position effects in free recall by B.J. Murdock, *Journal of Experimental Psychology, 64*, 486. **p. 170:** Figure from Two storage mechanisms in free recall by M. Glanzer and A.R. Cunitz, *Journal of Verbal Learning and Verbal Behavior*, vol. 5, 354, 358. Copyright © 1966 by Academic Press. Reproduced by permission of the publisher. **p. 177:** From Memory Scanning by S. Sternberg, *American Scientist*, vol. 57, 1969. Adapted by permission of *American Scientist*, Journal of Sigma Xi, the Scientific Research Society. **p. 182:** From *Recall Accuracy in a Release from PI Experiment*, by Wickens. Reprinted by permission of Hemisphere Publishing Corp., Washington, D.C. **p. 184:** From Mental rotation of three-dimensional objects by R.N. Shepard, *Science, 171*, 702. Copyright © 1971 by American Association for the Advancement of Science. Reprinted with permission. **p. 192:** Figure from Working memory by A.D. Baddeley and G. Hitch, in Gordon H Bower (ed.), *The Psychology of Learning and Motivation*, vol. 8. Copyright © 1974 by Academic Press. Reproduced by permission of the publisher. **p. 195:** From Storage and executive processes in the frontal lobes by E.E. Smith and J. Jonides, *Science, 283*, 1657–1661. Copyright © 1999 by the American Association for the Advancement of Science. Reprinted with permission. **p. 196:** From Neural bases of human working memory by E.E. Smith, *Current Directions in Psychological Science, 9*, 45–49. Copyright © 2000. Reprinted by permission of Blackwell Publishers. **p. 199:** Figure from Individual differences in working memory and reading by M. Daneman and P.A. Carpenter, *Journal of Verbal Learning and Verbal Behavior*, vol. 19, 450–466. Copyright © 1980 by Academic Press. Reproduced by permission of the publisher. **p. 200:** From The role of working memory capacity in retrieval by V.M. Rosen and R.W. Engle, *Journal of Experimental Psychology: General, 126*, 211–227. Copyright © 1997 by the American Psychological Association. Reprinted with permission. **p. 205:** From The medial temporal lobe memory system by Squire and Zola-Margan,

Copyright © 1983 by Allyn and Bacon. Reprinted by permission. **p. 498:** From Verbal behavior and problem solving by S. Glucksberg and R.W. Weisberg, *Journal of Experimental Psychology*, 71, 659–664. Copyright © 1966 by the American Psychological Association. Reprinted with permission. **p. 510:** Figure from Toward neuroanatomical models of analogy: A positron emission tomography study of analogical mapping by C.M. Wharton, J. Grafman, S.S. Flitman, E.K. Hansen, J. Brauner, A. Marks, and M. Honda, *Cognitive Psychology*, vol. 40, 173–197. Copyright © 2000 by Academic Press. Reproduced by permission of the publisher. **p. 511:** From Getting the right idea: Semantic activation in the right hemisphere may help solve insight problems by E.M. Bowden and M.J. Beeman, *Psychological Science*, 9, 435–440. Copyright © 1998. Reprinted by permission of Blackwell Publishers. **p. 515:** From *How To Solve Problems*, by Wayne Wickelgran. Copyright © 1974 by W.H. Freeman and Company. Used with permission. **p. 526:** From *Cognition*, by A.L. Glass and K.J. Holyoak. Copyright © 1986 by McGraw Hill, Inc. Reprinted by permission of the authors. **p. 528:** From *The Architecture of Cognition*, by J.R. Anderson. Copyright © 1983 by The President and Fellow of Harvard College, Harvard University Press, Cambridge, Massachussetts. Reprinted by permission of the author.

Tables:

p. 62: Adaptation of Table 9.6, p. 205 from *Fundamentals of Human Neuropsychology*, 4/e by Brian Kolb and Ian Q. Whishaw. Copyright © 1980, 1985, 1990, and 1996 by W.H. Freeman and Company. Used with the permission of Worth Publishers. **p. 220:** Table from The role of rehearsal in short-term memory by Craik and Watkins, *Journal of Verbal Learning and Verbal Behavior*, vol. 12, 600, 601. Copyright © 1973 by Academic Press. Reproduced by permission of the publisher. **p. 225:** Table from Hierarchical retrieval schemes in recall of categorized word lists by G.H. Bower, et al., *Journal of Verbal Learning and Verbal Behavior*, vol. 8, **p. 326.** Copyright © 1969 by Academic Press. Reproduced by permission of the publisher. **p. 283:** From Semantic priming and retrieval from Lexical memory: Roles of inhibitionless spreading activation and limited-capacity attention by J.H. Neely, *Journal of Experimental Psychology: General*, 106, 226–254. Copyright © 1977 by the American Psychological Association. Reprinted with permission. **p. 237 and 238:** From *The Ideal Problem Solver*, 2/e by John D. Bransford and Barry Stein, pp. 142–143. Copyright © 1984, 1993 by W.H. Freeman and Company. Used with permission. **p. 281:** From Facilitation in recognizing pairs of words: Evidence of a dependence between retrieval operations by D.E. Meyer and R.W. Schvanevldt, *Journal of Experimental Psychology*, 90, 229. Copyright © 1971 by the American Psychological Association. Adapted with permission. **p. 299:** From *Remembering: A Study in Experimental and Social Psychology*, 1/e by F.C. Bartlett. Copyright © 1967 by Cambridge University Press. Reprinted with the permission of Cambridge University Press. **p. 304 and 305:** From Remember that old theory of memory? Well, forget it! By J.J. Jenkins, *American Psychologist*, 29, 791. Copyright © 1974 by the American Psychological Association. Adapted with permission. **p. 319:** From Recognition memory for syntactic and semantic aspects of connected discourse by J.S. Sachs, *Perception and Psychophysics*, 437–442. Reprinted by permission of the Psychonomic Society, Inc. **p. 321:** Table from Priming in item recognition: Evidence for the propositional structure of sentences by R. Ratcliff and G. McKoon, *Journal of Verbal Learning and Verbal Behavior*, vol. 17, 414. Copyright © 1978 by Academic Press. Reproduced by permission of the publisher. **p. 327:** From *Human Memory and Cognition: Learning, Understanding and Remembering*, by John D. Bransford. Copyright © 1979 by Wadsworth, Inc. Reprinted by permission of Brooks/Cole Publishing Company, Pacific Grove, California, 93950. **p. 351:** Copyright © 1960 by the American Institute of Biological Sciences. Reprinted by permission. **p. 361:** From *Experimental Psycholinguistics: An Introduction*, by S. Glucksberg and J.H. Danks. Copyright © 1975 by Lawrence Erlbaum Associates, Inc. Reprinted by permission. **p. 381:** From *Psychology of Language*, by David W. Carroll. Copyright © 1986 by Wadsworth, Inc. Reprinted by permission of Brooks/Cole Publishing Company, Pacific Grove, California, 93950. **p. 390:** Table from *Cognitive Neuropsychology: A Clinical Introduction*, by R.A. McCarthy and E.K. Warrington. Copyright © 1990 by Academic Press. Reproduced by permission of the publisher. **p. 392:** Table from Neural models of language processes by Kertesz, in M.A. Arbib, et al. (eds.), *Neural Models of Language Processes*, 25–44. Copyright © 1982 by Academic Press. Reproduced by permission of the publisher. **p. 415:** From Types of reference and implication by H.H. Clark, in Johnson-Laird and Wason (eds.), *Thinking: Readings in Cognitive Science*, 414–419. Copyright © 1977 by Cambridge University Press. Reprinted with the permission of Cambridge University Press. **p. 425 and 427:** From A theory of reading: From eye fixations to comprehension by M.A. Just and P.A. Carpenter, *Psychological Review*, 87, 348. Copyright © 1980 by the American Psychological Association. Reprinted by permission. **p. 433:** From Reflections on cognition and parallel distributed processing, in J.L. McClelland and D.E. Rumelhard (eds.), *Psychological Review*, vol.2, pp. 531–546. Copyright © 1975 by the American Psychological Association. Reprinted by permission. **p. 448:** Reprinted from *Cognitive Psychology: Memory, Language, and Thought*, 2/e by Darlene V. Howard. Copyright © 1993 by Macmillan

Name Index

Subject Index

A

Accessibility, 235, 539
Accuracy, 307–309
Accuracy measures, 37, 39–40
Acoustic–articulatory code, 181, 539
ACT, 527–529, 539
Active information processors, 31–32
Actor. *See* Agent
ACT-R, 527, 539
Adaptive components of thought (ACT), 527–529, 539
Advantage of clause recency, 407, 539
Advantage of first mention, 407, 539
Agent, 313, 539. *See also* Case grammar
Agnosia, 106–109, 539
Agraphia, 394, 539
Alertness, 123–125
Alexia, 394, 539
Algorithms
  coin tosses, 489
  defined, 539
  heuristics and, 463–466
  hospital births, 489–490
Ambiguous, 287, 375, 539
American Sign Language (ASL), 183–185
Amnesia, 239–248, 539
Analogies
  defined, 539
  information-processing approach, 41–42
  problem solving, 505–511
Analysis, of language, 357
Anaphoric reference, 413, 539
Animal communication systems, 355–356
Anomia, 292, 393–394, 539
Anomic aphasia. *See* Anomia
Anomic aphasia, 539
Antecedent, 413, 447, 539
Anterograde amnesia, 240, 242–245
Aphasia, 390–395, 539
Apperceptive agnosia, 107–108, 539
Arbitrariness, 352, 539
Arguments, 313
  defined, 539
  invalid, 448–449
  valid, 448
  See also Case grammar
Arousal, 123–125
Articulatory loop, 188, 539–540
Association, 540
Associative agnosia, 108, 540
Atomic components of thought (ACT-R), 527, 539

B

Backward masking, 87, 546
Behaviorism, 19–21
  defined, 540
  dissatisfaction with, 21–28
Beliefs, 540
Benefits, 127, 277, 543
Biases
  in availability heuristic, 473–474
  familiarity, 474–475
  hindsight, 479
  salience and vividness, 475
Bottleneck, in short-term memory, 162–170
Bottom-up processing. *See* Data-driven processing
Brain
  anatomy, 58–61
  connectionism and, 291–295
  language and, 390–397
  See also Neocortex; Neurocognition
Bridging, 415–416, 540
Broca's aphasia, 391, 540
Brown-Peterson task, 165–166, 168, 169, 540

Attend, 540
Attention, 120
  basics of, 121–123
  controlled/voluntary, 133–143
  defined, 540
  hemineglect, 154–158
  input, 123–133
  as mental resource, 144–153
  multiple meanings of, 120–121
Attenuation theory, 137–139
Audition, 110, 540
Auditory feature detection, 116
Auditory pattern recognition, 116–117
Auditory perception, 109–111
Auditory sensory memory, 111–115, 540
Authorized, 416, 540
Autobiographical memories, 339–346
Automatic processing/automaticity, 144–149
  defined, 540
  disadvantages of, 151–152
  priming and, 282–285
  problem solving, 530–531
  syntax, 379
  synthesis for, 149, 151
Availability heuristic, 473–475, 540
Available, 235, 540
Axon, 540
Axon terminals, 540

C

Case grammar, 311, 383–384, 389, 540
Case roles, 383, 540
Categorical perception, 363, 366–370, 540
Categorization, 270–276
Category retrieval, 267
Category-specific deficit, 292, 541
Central executive, 188, 541
Cerebral cortex. *See* Neocortex
Cerebral hemispheres, 541
Cerebral lateralization, 61, 63–64, 541
Channel capacity, 41, 541
Characteristic features, 256, 541
Chunks, 163, 224–225, 541
Classification, 270–276
Clustering, 541. *See also* Organization
Coarticulation, 368, 541
Cocktail party effect, 134–136
Cognition
  defined, 9–12, 541
  thinking about, 4–9
  See also Neurocognition
Cognitive economy, 260–261, 541
Cognitive operations, 513
Cognitive psychology, 2–3
  history of, 12–28
  information processing and, 29–32
  memory and cognition, 9–12
  thinking, 4–9
Cognitive science, 3
  agnosia and, 108–109
  defined, 541
  standard theory, 50–53
Coin tosses, algorithms for, 489
Communications systems, of animals, 355–356. *See also* Language
Competence, 358, 541
Components. *See* Recognition by components
Comprehension. *See* Language comprehension
Computer analogy, 41–42
Concept formation, 272
Conceptual knowledge, 399–401, 541
Conceptually driven processing, 52
  auditory pattern recognition, 116–117
  conscious processing, 147
  defined, 541
  written language pattern recognition, 94–98
Conditional reasoning, 447–453, 539, 541
Conduction aphasia, 393, 541